Migration and Religion
Volume I

The International Library of Studies on Migration

Series Editor: Professor Robin Cohen
Emeritus Professor of Development Studies and former Director,
International Migration Institute, University of Oxford, UK

Future titles will include:
Migration and Social Policy
Jenny Phillimore

Wherever possible, the articles in these volumes have been reproduced as originally published using facsimile reproduction, inclusive of footnotes and pagination to facilitate ease of reference.

For a list of all Edward Elgar published titles visit our website at
www.e-elgar.com

Migration and Religion
Volume I

Edited by

James A. Beckford

Professor Emeritus,
University of Warwick, UK

THE INTERNATIONAL LIBRARY OF STUDIES ON MIGRATION

An Elgar Research Collection
Cheltenham, UK • Northampton, MA, USA

Published by
Edward Elgar Publishing Limited
The Lypiatts
15 Lansdown Road
Cheltenham
Glos GL50 2JA
UK

Edward Elgar Publishing, Inc.
William Pratt House
9 Dewey Court
Northampton
Massachusetts 01060
USA

A catalogue record for this book is available from the British Library

Library of Congress Control Number: 2015943170

MIX
Paper from
responsible sources
FSC   FSC® C013056
www.fsc.org

ISBN 978 1 78347 257 4 (2 volume set)

Printed and bound in Great Britain by TJ International Ltd, Padstow

Contents

Acknowledgements

The editor and publishers wish to thank the authors and the following publishers who have kindly given permission for the use of copyright material.

Blackwell Publishing Ltd for articles: Peggy Levitt (2003), '"You Know, Abraham Was Really the First Immigrant": Religion and Transnational Migration', *International Migration Review*, **37** (3), Fall, 847–73; Carolyn Chen (2006), 'From Filial Piety to Religious Piety: Evangelical Christianity Reconstructing Taiwanese Immigrant Families in the United States', *International Migration Review*, **40** (3), Fall, 573–602; Nancy Foner and Richard Alba (2008), 'Immigrant Religion in the U.S. and Western Europe: Bridge or Barrier to Inclusion?', *International Migration Review*, **42** (2), Summer, 360–92; Catharina P. Williams (2008), 'Female Transnational Migration, Religion and Subjectivity: The Case of Indonesian Domestic Workers', *Asia Pacific Viewpoint*, **49** (3), December, 344–53; Phillip Connor (2009), 'International Migration and Religious Participation: The Mediating Impact of Individual and Contextual Effects', *Sociological Forum*, **24** (4), December, 779–803; Valerie A. Lewis and Ridhi Kashyap (2013), 'Piety in a Secular Society: Migration, Religiosity, and Islam in Britain', *International Migration*, **51** (3), June, 57–66; Margarita A. Mooney (2013), 'Religion as a Context of Reception: The Case of Haitian Immigrants in Miami, Montreal and Paris', *International Migration*, **51** (3), June, 99–112.

BYU Studies (http://byustidies.byu.edu), Fred. E. Woods and Nicholas J. Evans for article: Fred. E. Woods and Nicholas J. Evans (2002), 'Latter-day Saint Scandinavian Migration through Hull, England, 1852–1894', *BYU Studies*, **41** (4), 75–102.

Japanese Journal of Religious Studies for article: Frank Usarski (2008), '"The Last Missionary to Leave the Temple Should Turn Off the Light": Sociological Remarks on the Decline of Japanese "Immigrant" Buddhism in Brazil', *Japanese Journal of Religious Studies*, **35** (1), 39–59.

New England Quarterly Inc. and MIT Press Journals for article: Virginia DeJohn Anderson (1985), 'Migrants and Motives: Religion and the Settlement of New England, 1630–1640', *New England Quarterly*, **58** (3), September, 339–83.

Oxford University Press via the Copyright Clearance Center's RightsLink Service for articles: Celia McMichael (2002), '"Everywhere is Allah's Place": Islam and the Everyday Life of Somali Women in Melbourne, Australia', *Journal of Refugee Studies*, **15** (2), 171–88; Dianna J. Shandy (2002), 'Nuer Christians in America', *Journal of Refugee Studies*, **15** (2), 213–21; Pyong Gap Min and Dae Young Kim (2005), 'Intergenerational Transmission of Religion and Culture: Korean Protestants in the U.S.', *Sociology of Religion*, **66** (3), Autumn, 263–82; Marwa

Shoeb, Harvey M. Weinstein and Jodi Halpern (2007), 'Living in Religious Time and Space: Iraqi Refugees in Dearborn, Michigan', *Journal of Refugee Studies*, **20** (3), 441–60; Elena Fiddian-Qasmiyeh and Yousif M. Qasmiyeh (2010), 'Muslim Asylum-Seekers and Refugees: Negotiating Identity, Politics and Religion in the UK', *Journal of Refugee Studies*, **23** (3), 294–314.

Religion and Gender and Jeanne Rey for article: Jeanne Rey (2013), 'Mermaids and Spirit Spouses: Rituals as Technologies of Gender in Transnational African Pentecostal Spaces', *Religion and Gender*, **3** (1), 60–75.

Springer Science and Business Media B.V. for article: Miki Talebi and Michel Desjardins (2012), 'The Immigration Experience of Iranian Baha'is in Saskatchewan: The Reconstruction of Their Existence, Faith, and Religious Experience', *Journal of Religion and Health*, **51** (2), June, 293–309.

Taylor and Francis Ltd (www.taylorandfrancis.com) for articles: Alicia Re Cruz (1998), 'Migrant Women Crossing Borders: The Role of Gender and Religion in Internal and External Mexican Migration', *Journal of Borderlands Studies*, **XIII** (2), Fall, 83–97; Barbara Dietz (2003), 'Jewish Immigrants from the Former Soviet Union in Germany: History, Politics and Social Integration', *East European Jewish Affairs*, **33** (2), Winter, 7–19; John R. Bowen (2004), 'Beyond Migration: Islam as a Transnational Public Space', *Journal of Ethnic and Migration Studies*, **30** (5), September, 879–94; Gamze Avci (2005), 'Religion, Trans-nationalism and Turks in Europe', *Turkish Studies*, **6** (2), June, 201–13; Clara Saraiva (2008), 'Transnational Migrants and Transnational Spirits: An African Religion in Lisbon', *Journal of Ethnic and Migration Studies*, **34** (2), March, 253–69; Manuel A. Vásquez (2009), 'The Global Portability of Pneumatic Christianity: Comparing African and Latin American Pentecostalisms', *African Studies*, **68** (2), August, 273–86; Nicole Immig (2009), 'The "New" Muslim Minorities in Greece: Between Emigration and Political Participation, 1881–1886', *Journal of Muslim Minority Affairs*, **29** (4), December, 511–22; Phillip Connor (2010), 'Contexts of Immigrant Receptivity and Immigrant Religious Outcomes: The Case of Muslims in Western Europe', *Ethnic and Racial Studies*, **33** (3), March, 376–403; Luann Good Gingrich and Kerry Preibisch (2010), 'Migration as Preservation and Loss: The Paradox of Transnational Living for Low German Mennonite Women', *Journal of Ethnic and Migration Studies*, **36** (9), November, 1499–518; Ilana Redstone Akresh (2011), 'Immigrants' Religious Participation in the United States', *Ethnic and Racial Studies*, **34** (4), April, 643–61; Susana Trovão (2012), 'Religion and Civic Participation among the Children of Immigrants: Insights from the Postcolonial Portuguese Context', *Journal of Ethnic and Migration Studies*, **38** (5), May, 851–68; Mieke Maliepaard and Marcel Lubbers (2013), 'Parental Religious Transmission after Migration: The Case of Dutch Muslims', *Journal of Ethnic and Migration Studies*, **39** (3), 425–42.

University of Chicago Press for article: Paul Christopher Johnson (2002), 'Migrating Bodies, Circulating Signs: Brazilian Candomblé, the Garifuna of the Caribbean, and the Category of Indigenous Religions', *History of Religions*, **41** (4), May, 301–27.

Every effort has been made to trace all the copyright holders but if any have been inadvertently overlooked the publishers will be pleased to make the necessary arrangement at the first opportunity.

In addition the publishers wish to thank the Library of Indiana University at Bloomington, USA, for their assistance in obtaining these articles.

Introduction

James A. Beckford

Religion and Migration Research

Today's flows of human beings across territories, oceans and airspace have ancient historical precedents. And, while the scale and forms of migration have undergone massive changes over millennia, it remains a phenomenon that is intricately bound up with religions. In some cases migration has religious motivations and causes. In many more cases it has implications not only for how migrants and their descendants practise religion but also for the societies in which they settle. It would be an exaggeration to claim that religion was *invariably* an important aspect of migration – except in cases such as migration in response to religious persecution or migration in pursuit of religious objectives – but there can be no doubt that the religious dimensions of migration and settlement in new locations can be significant. Indeed, international flows of migrants are contributing to the redistribution of 'world religions' across regions of the globe (Pew Research Center 2015: 12–13). The early twenty-first century has therefore witnessed a growth of sensitivity among social scientists, politicians, religious authorities and policymakers to the importance of religion's multi-stranded interweaving with migration. This is reflected in the proliferation of publications and other research activities which focus on this topic. They all indicate that basic concepts and theoretical ideas about religion and migration are not only interesting in themselves but also imbricated with broader concerns about, for example, gender, globalisation, transnational networks, securitisation, virtual communication, multiculturalism, mobilities, processes of exclusion, human rights and secularism.

Some of the earliest studies of religion and immigration to the US highlighted the assimilation of immigrants into American institutions and ways of life through identification and affiliation with religions (Handlin 1951; Herberg 1955; Hammond 1963). In Europe, the focus was more on political questions about integration and exclusion, especially of the growing number of Muslim immigrants from North Africa, the Middle East and South Asia (Abramson 1979; Bastenier and Dassetto 1979; Mol 1979). But it was only towards the end of the twentieth century that the frequency and volume of research relating to other parts of the world began to accelerate. Since 2000, the following overviews of research on religion and migration have all appeared: Ebaugh and Chafetz 2000; Haddad, Smith and Esposito 2003; Alfonso et al. 2004; Leonard et al. 2005; Cadge and Ecklund 2007; Alba et al. 2009; Bramadat and Koenig 2009; Kaya 2009; Mutema 2010; Bonifacio and Angeles 2010; Garnett and Harris 2013; Pew Research Center 2012, 2013; Connor 2014; DeMarinis 2014; Gallo 2014; Kivisto 2014; Quero and Shoji 2014; Vilaça et al. 2014; Pace 2014. In addition, religion and migration has been the focus of special issues in academic journals as diverse as: *Journal of Refugee Studies* (15 [2] 2002; 24 [3] 2011); *American Behavioral Scientist* (49 [11] 2006); *African Studies* (68 [2] 2009); *Ethnic and Racial Studies* (33 [3] 2010); *International Migration* (51 [3] 2013); *Religion and Gender* (3 [1] 2013); and *Global Networks* (14 [3] 2014). Meanwhile, the number of websites, databases, research projects, conferences, seminars, university modules and research centres active in promoting the study of interactions between religion and migration has also grown steadily since 2000.

This collection of published articles interprets the concepts of religion and migration broadly in order capture the complexity and richness of relations between them. Admittedly, the term 'religion' is hotly contested, but it refers here to the wide range of emotions, actions, relationships, organisations, artefacts, roles, values, symbols and beliefs that are associated with faith in powers, beings and levels of reality transcending the purely human. Partial overlaps with terms such as 'spirituality' and 'faith' are inevitable but not necessarily problematic for a broad overview of religion and immigration. The 'fuzziness' of the conceptual boundaries may actually be an advantage (Beckford 2003; Voas 2009). The meaning of 'migration' is no less debatable, but its reference here is to changes in human residence that involve crossing regional, national or international boundaries. It is no exaggeration to characterise the current era as an 'age of migration' (Castles, de Haas and Miller 2014) in view of the continuing strength of migratory flows and their growing salience in public debates both in 'origin' societies and in 'receiving' societies. Migration is both a reversible process and an outcome that can vary from temporary to permanent, from voluntary to forced, and from individual to collective on a massive scale. It can also be associated with the formation of diasporas, with asylum-seeking, with internally displaced persons and with refugees. In this context it does not include nomadism, transhumance or pilgrimage. Nor, it should be added, has much research been conducted on religion's relevance to the circulation of migrants between the world's most stable and prosperous democracies.

Examining migration with a particular focus on religion has now become essential for a variety of reasons that will be explained at length in the selected articles. In a nutshell these reasons have to do with the effect of transnational and global forces on the capacity of religious ideas, networks and organisations to influence the lives and the life chances of growing numbers of people around the world. Taking full advantage of new electronic media of communication, information technology and mobilisation, it is now possible for religious agents, movements and organisations to extend their influence over both migrant and settled populations in ways that were virtually inconceivable before the twenty-first century (Hojsgaard and Warburg 2005; Cowan 2007). At the same time, of course, critical and hostile responses to the global reach of even relatively modest religious activities have also intensified, especially in places where claims to religious freedom clash with doctrines of secularism and various forms of opposition to particular – or all – religions. In short, globalisation has boosted processes of religious outreach and, in doing so, has also aggravated controversies and conflicts which can be particularly acute in relation to migrants even long after resettlement (Juergensmeyer 2003; Robertson 2003). Nevertheless, religion has also helped to control, regulate or even deter migration in some places.

In addition, the lived religion of migrants is shaped not only by their life before and after migration but also by the contexts in which they settle and the translocal social networks in which they participate (Connor, Chapter 15, Volume I). Migration may provide opportunities for developing new or hybrid religious beliefs, identities, practices and ways of integrating into society. Change in the gendering of religious identities and practices is especially controversial for migrants to Western liberal democracies. But adapting to new circumstances after migration can also give rise to tensions and divisions within previously solidary religious collectivities.

This means that the balance between continuity and change in migrants' engagement with religion is dynamic. Generational differences in migrants' engagement with religion are striking although not necessarily correlated in any simple way with changes in their socio-economic circumstances.

Another aspect of the nexus between religion and migration is the extent to which critical thinking about migration is a focus for theological and pastoral authorities within religious institutions (Hagan 2013). The sacred wisdom of most faith traditions contains reflections on the experience of being a 'stranger in a strange land' and on religious obligations to be hospitable to travellers and migrants. In addition, theologians and philosophers of religion have written extensively about migration; and religious organisations have established institutions and agencies for the welfare of migrants, refugees and asylum seekers. For example, groups of Christians have been particularly active in offering sanctuary to undocumented migrants crossing the border from Mexico to the US. And numerous Muslim associations provide humanitarian assistance to displaced populations in, for example, Africa, the Middle East and South East Asia (Benthall and Bellion-Jourdan 2009).

The fact that informal social networks and social movements as well as formal organisations claiming to represent the interests of migrants as members of particular religions are now active in the public spheres of many societies is another reason to regard religion and migration as an important focus of research. The translocal and transnational reach of some of these overlapping groupings makes them all the more significant (Allievi and Nielsen 2003; Davis and Robinson 2012; Cherry and Ebaugh 2014). Some of them are affiliates or branches of would-be global organisations claiming to represent entire faith traditions. In addition to providing support and resources for migrants long after initial settlement, these groupings help to shape public opinion and to influence policymakers and legislators in relation to such potentially contentious issues as education, family law, health, welfare services, ritual slaughter of animals and disposal of the dead. The changing landscape of urban areas is also testimony to the increasing number of religious buildings and monuments erected by migrants as symbols of their presence and as investments in the material, social and cultural fabric of the societies where their descendants are expected to continue practising their faith (Knott 2005). Controversies surrounding the religious buildings erected by immigrants are often intense in the public sphere even in countries as peaceful as Switzerland (Baumann 2009b). The proliferation of print and digital media, broadcasting channels, films, websites and social networking services designed specifically for migrant members of particular religions is further evidence of their institutional consolidation and their potential to exercise influence in wider public spheres (Lövheim and Axner 2011; Pype 2013).

The settlement of migrants who are identified (or self-identified) as minorities on the basis of their ethnicity, 'race', religion or nationality commonly gives rise to political debates about the merits and scale of immigration and to policy-oriented discussions about their entitlements (Berkley Center 2008; Brubaker 2013). Their rights to residence, work opportunities, housing, health and welfare programmes, education and citizenship are high on the political agenda of many countries. Philosophical doctrines of pluralism, secularism and multiculturalism are often employed to interpret, criticise or justify a wide range of public responses to immigration. In recent decades, however, questions about the religious aspects of migrants' ways of life have also come to dominate many of these political, policy-oriented and philosophical debates (Modood 1998; Jayaweera and Choudhury 2008; Bader 2009; Bramadat and Koenig 2009;

Kymlicka 2009; European Union 2011). Controversies are especially intense around claims that the practice of some forms of religion can be detrimental to the status of women, incompatible with Western ideas of citizenship, resistant to the ideals of universal education, and so on. Indeed, some migrants distance themselves from their religious backgrounds for these reasons, although relatively little research has been conducted on these contentious issues.

In spite of these controversies, the settlement of immigrants from a wide variety of faith backgrounds is viewed positively in many quarters for the diversity that they bring to religious, cultural, political, civic and social life. The willingness of migrants to engage in inter-faith and ecumenical activities is also an important part of the argument that religions of all kinds can make positive contributions to the vitality of civil society. Their contributions may also be welcomed for boosting cosmopolitanism and enriching some social movement campaigns.

Structure of the Volumes

The two main criteria guiding the selection of articles in these two volumes are significance and inclusiveness. The aim is to capture the most telling accounts in the English language of the variety and complexity of ways in which religions and migration are interwoven in different regions of the world and across transnational space. This means placing migration in many different contexts and adopting various levels of analysis ranging from the individual to the global; looking at the topic from the perspectives of a variety of academic disciplines and research methods; examining a wide variety of religions and forms of migration; exploring contexts of reception and integration strategies in many different countries as well as considering policy implications; taking account of intersections with gender, history, ethnicity, economics and generations; being sensitive to cultural, spatial, material and theological registers of experience; and paying attention to tensions and controversies no less than to positive outcomes. In addition, numerous articles also rehearse arguments about the most appropriate research methods and ethical stances to adopt in studies of phenomena as sensitive and subtle as religion and migration. As the articles are reprinted in their original format, their lists of bibliographical references provide indispensable information about the historical development of research in this field as well as pointers to the gaps to be filled in the future.

This set of two volumes is divided into 14 parts. The focus of each part is on a particular dimension of the intertwining of religion with migration, but there is also overlap and dialogue in some cases between articles in different parts. The division between parts is merely intended to mark out the major areas in which researchers have concentrated their efforts to understand the complex and ever changing relationships between religion and migration.

Volume I, Part I establishes some of the conceptual, theoretical and methodological ideas that are at the centre of most research on religion and migration. Part II examines some historical perspectives. Part III focuses on transnational and global dimensions. Part IV explores gender relations. Part V surveys the contexts of immigrants' reception. Part VI investigates change and continuity in religious identification and practice.

Volume II, Part I looks at integration strategies. Part II considers religion as resource. Part III reviews policies and welfare services. Part IV investigates economics and work. Part V reviews the role of religious organisations and professionals. Part VI takes stock of spatial and cultural dimensions. Part VII broaches some theological questions and Part VIII inspects some controversies.

Volume I Part I: Overviews of Migration and Religion

The two articles in **Volume I Part I** set the scene for understanding the complex intertwining of religion and migration by highlighting the methodological challenges and opportunities that accompany any attempt to investigate it empirically. Theoretical developments in thinking about religion in relation to migration have been relatively few in number and have tended to cluster around notions of the global, the 'glocal', the transnational and ethnicity (Lehmann 2002; Casanova and Zolberg 2003; Levitt et al. 2003; Grillo 2004; Beyer 2006, 2012, 2013; Kong 2010; Sherkat 2012; Abascal and Centeno 2013; Brubaker 2013; Pace 2014). But new ways of conceptualising the topic in specific contexts have been more numerous (Yang and Ebaugh 2001; Bowen, Chapter 8, Volume I; Solari 2006; Jayaweera and Choudhury 2008; Vásquez 2008). **Phillip Connor's** article (Chapter 1, Volume I) deploys many of the basic concepts and empirical measures that inform research on religion and migration in the US. In the context of a discussion about continuity or change in levels of immigrants' involvement in religious activities, he stresses the importance of taking both individual-level and contextual factors into account within, ideally, a longitudinal time frame. Using data from the New Immigrant Survey, 2003–2004, he tested various hypotheses and found that – subject to many qualifications – immigration at the aggregate level to the US was accompanied by 'declining religiosity', albeit less drastically for Christians than for people identified with other religions. Interpretation of these results and of subsequent studies continues to be central to much research on religion and migration – particularly in the US – although, as the articles in these two volumes attest, pre- and post-migration levels of identification with religions are far from being the only interesting item on the agenda. Indeed, **Peggy Levitt's** article (Chapter 2, Volume I) explores what can be learned from studying religion and migration at a transnational level of analysis where there is much more at stake than the pre- and post-immigration comparison or the integration of immigrants into American society. Building up a map of the levels and components of the 'transnational religious field', Levitt draws particular attention to three aspects of migrants' 'everyday religious lives across borders', namely, their religious organisations; their use of transnational religion to create new sources of belonging; and their involvement in transnational civic engagement. Studying the 'lived practice' of migrant religion in this way entails being methodological and epistemological; ideally, it would also tease out the tangled relations between religion, ethnicity, economics and politics.

   Many of the articles selected for these two volumes criticise and expand the conceptual apparatuses assembled by Connor and Levitt. In the process, they also add further concepts and problematics to the study of religion and migration, beginning with the advantages to be gained from placing them in historical perspectives.

Volume I Part II: Historical Perspectives

Major historical examples of the nexus between religion and migration include the movement of Indo-Aryan peoples from the Black Sea region into the Indus Valley over a period lasting several centuries beginning about 1700 BCE, the exodus of Hebrew tribes from ancient Egypt into Canaan around 1230 BCE, the migration of the Prophet Mohammed's followers from Mecca to Medina in 622 CE, the dispersion of various Anabaptist communities in the sixteenth and seventeenth centuries CE from the Netherlands and Central Europe to Russia and the Americas, the trek that many thousands of converts to the Church of Jesus Christ of Latter-day Saints made to the US from all over the world beginning in the mid-nineteenth century CE, and the flight of millions of Hindus, Muslims and Sikhs from the violence that marked the partition of India in 1947. The balance between the pull of religious ideals and the push of persecution is different in each case. And the outcomes were equally variable in terms of the immigrants' reception and their impact on their new societies (Eickelman and Piscatori 1990; Dolan 1998; Badillo 2001; Levitt, Chapter 2, Volume I; Hirschman 2004; Jensz 2010; Gorman 2011; Breathnach 2013; Moberg 2013). The four articles in **Volume I Part II** underline the importance of placing continuity and change in the religion of international migrants firmly in their historical contexts. Taking examples of migration among Christians, Jews and Muslims at different periods of history, each author identifies the variety of motives for migration and the diversity of contexts to which the migrants sought to adapt their religious lives. Drawing on a wealth of detail about the reasons for the hazardous 'Great Migration' of relatively prosperous colonists from England to New England between 1630 and 1640, **Virginia DeJohn Anderson** (Chapter 3, Volume I) argues that religious motives outweighed purely economic and political considerations. In contrast, the central argument of **Nicole Immig's** article (Chapter 4, Volume I) is that social and economic reasons predominated over religious considerations among the Muslims who emigrated from Thessaly in Greece to territories under Ottoman Governance in the 1880s (see also Antoniou 2005). Similarly, **Barbara Dietz's** article (Chapter 5, Volume I) signals the low salience of religious motives among the many Jews who migrated from the Former Soviet Union to Germany after the collapse of the USSR and German reunification. Consequently, integration into Jewish communities in Germany has not been easy for the immigrants, especially as many of them were ambivalent towards, or ignorant about, the religious and cultural practices of Judaism. But the arrival of relatively young newcomers has helped to turn Germany into the only country in Europe with an expanding Jewish population. And the article by **Fred E. Woods** and **Nicholas J. Evans** (Chapter 6, Volume I) demonstrates the importance of well-established trade routes, shipping companies and transport infrastructures in enabling British and Scandinavian converts to the Church of Jesus Christ of Latter-day Saints in the second half of the nineteenth-century to translate their religious motives into practical schemes for emigration to the US.

Volume I Part III: Transnational and Global Dimensions

Studies of migration in the twentieth century tended to explain the reasons for migration mainly in terms of economic hardship, displacement as a result of armed conflicts, and persecution on the basis of nationality, ethnicity or 'race'. These factors continue to be important, of course, but research conducted from the middle of the century onwards has increasingly acknowledged that the significance of religion for processes of migration and settlement also required closer scrutiny. The four articles in **Volume I Part III** provide insights into various ways in which relations between religion and migration are affected by – and take advantage of – factors which include the end of European colonialist regimes, the global spread of capitalism, the collapse of the Soviet Union, the continuing attractions of the US and Western Europe for immigrants from all over the world, the rapid – but uneven – growth of prosperity in countries such as China, India and Brazil, and the violent disturbances affecting whole regions of Central Africa, East Africa, North Africa and the Middle East. All these factors have implications for religions, migrants and their societies of origin and destination alike (Robbins 2004; McAuliffe 2007; Plüss 2009; Ebaugh 2010; Connor and Tucker 2011; Levitt 2013; Wong and Levitt 2014). Many of them have ratcheted up the inducements, the pressures and the opportunities to migrate. Indeed, religious ideas, identities and interests are at stake to varying degrees in all these developments and are right at the heart of some of them.

As **Gamze Avci's** article (Chapter 7, Volume I) reveals, religion is a matter of considerable importance to migrant Turkish workers in the Netherlands, but the major organisations that claim to represent them have differing and changing orientations both in Turkey and abroad. *Millî Görüş*, for example, has a strong identification with Islam and a measure of independence from the Turkish state, whereas *Diyanet* has a closer relationship with the Turkish state and a more distant relationship with Islamic organisations. In an increasingly transnational world the development of these two organisations in the Netherlands is inseparable from political and religious developments in Turkey – as well as from changes in Dutch politics. In a more radical vein, the necessity to see the nexus between religion and migration as merely one aspect of a much more extensive 'transnational public space' is argued in **John R. Bowen's** article (Chapter 8, Volume I) on Muslims in France. For him, transnational Islam involves a 'global public space of normative reference and debate' which is in tension with political pressure in France, in particular, towards 'national assimilation' into citizenship. To some extent, then, transnationalism helps to place migration and diasporas in a broader context by showing that they are subject to discussion in Islamic universalist terms that cut across all national boundaries and are therefore 'beyond migration'. The case of Mennonite women who speak Low German illustrates a different aspect of the transnational social spaces occupied by some international migrants, according to the article by **Luann Good Gingrich** and **Kerry Preibisch** (Chapter 9, Volume I). Migration to Canada from long-established Mennonite colonies in Mexico in response to economic pressures places them in a gendered double-bind in which the material advantages of life in Canada expose them to disruptions of family, religious and cultural life. Resisting assimilation into their 'home' *and* their 'host' countries, these Mennonite women are doubly isolated. The paradox is that the opportunities that they gain from migration in terms of access to work, citizenship, health care and personal freedom leave them with 'the day-to-day reality of having no choice in every act of choosing'. Further paradoxes are brought to light in **Paul Christopher Johnson's** article (Chapter 10, Volume I) about the ways in which the categories of 'the global' and 'the indigenous' penetrate each other, especially in Brazilian spirit possession religions such as Candomblé and the Honduran ancestor religion of the Garifuna. These religions are simultaneously globalised and indigenised as a result of emigration from their 'home' territories and return migration from the US. In this way, the dislocations of migration disturb taken-for-granted relations between religions and territories, thereby reimagining traditions.

Volume I Part IV: Gender Relations

The articles in **Volume I Part IV** highlight the varied implications of religion for women's experiences of migration in different settings. The gendering of migration is a well-established topic in academic and non-academic writings (Willis and Yeoh 2000), but the intersection between religion, gender and migration is now proving to be an important field for research and policy debate (Re Cruz, Chapter 12, Volume I; Ebaugh and Chafetz 2000; De Voe 2002; Werbner 2002; Chen 2005; Lorentzen and Mira 2005; Bendixsen 2010; Blanchet 2010; Bonifacio and Angeles 2010; Good Gingrich and Preibisch, Chapter 9, Volume I; Olagoke 2010; Furseth 2011; Troeva and Mancheva 2011; Dhar 2012; Jackson 2013; De Araújo Silva and Rodrigues 2013; Wong 2013a). Beginning with the everyday life of Somali Muslim women living in Melbourne, Australia, the article by **Celia McMichael** (Chapter 11, Volume I) identifies a wide range of practices and social interactions, articulated with Islam, that help them to respond constructively to the challenges of displacement and resettlement. The women draw on 'the shared framework of expression and ideology' of Islam to sustain their emotional well-being and resilience. But, although Islam provides a sense of continuity amid the disruptions experienced by Somali women migrants to Australia, **Alicia Re Cruz's** article (Chapter 12, Volume I) shows that the situation is different for many of the migrant women who crossed borders within Mexico and between Mexico and the US in the 1980s and 1990s. Female Mayan migrants from economically threatened rural communities on the Yucatán Peninsula to the tourist city of Cancún, no less than the Mexican women who migrated across the border to Texas, entered labour markets, participated in local politics and exercised more power in their households. This was paralleled by their active involvement in a variety of Protestant churches where women were also able to exercise authority and power. In other words, religion was articulated more with transformation than with continuity in the lives of these Mexican women migrants – in sharp contrast to McMichael's account of Islam's articulation with continuity in the lives of Somali women in Australia.

Yet another pattern becomes apparent in **Catharina P. Williams'** article (Chapter 13, Volume I) about the uses that women from poor areas of Eastern Indonesia make of Catholicism in order to negotiate the hazards and the opportunities presented by transnational migration. The women claimed that it was their religious faith which empowered them to make the initial decision to migrate, to survive the process of migrating and to make a new life as domestic workers on arrival in a new country. Their subjectivity shifted from that of 'protected daughters' to that of 'autonomous single women working and negotiating life in metropolitan households' without abandoning their Catholic identity. Finally, **Jeanne Rey's** article (Chapter 14, Volume I) about the predominantly Pentecostal churches that have flourished primarily among Congolese and Ghanaian immigrants in the Swiss region around Geneva since the 1980s underlines their capacity to construct notions of gendered sexuality and social relationships which remain rooted in African cosmologies, albeit relabelled as 'evil spirits' in Pentecostalism. The churches function as 'transnational spaces' in which ritual practices of deliverance or exorcism tend to objectify participants as relatively passive victims of these spirits. In particular, 'spirit spouses' and 'mermaid spirits' are depicted as jealous and possessive entities which seek to disrupt or delay marriages by deploying the 'seductive power of women' or the vulnerability of men to seduction in a Swiss context where African ideas of masculinity and femininity might seem to be under threat. In this way, immigrants negotiate gender relationships through Pentecostal rituals.

Volume I Part V: Contexts of Reception

The focus of articles in **Volume I Part V** is on the social, political, economic and religious contexts in which migrants choose to continue, to change or to abandon their identification with religion (Sabar 2004; Mooney, Chapter 18, Volume I; Pasura 2013; Cadge et al. 2013; Sarat 2013; Martikainen 2014). These contexts have important consequences for how, and to what extent, religion features in the lives of migrants in different locations and networks, taking due account of variables such as sex, age, socio-economic status, educational level and length of residence in the country of destination. For example, **Phillip Connor's** article (Chapter 15, Volume I) examines statistical evidence about the practice of Islam among Muslim immigrants to Western Europe. 'Immigrant contexts of reception' take many forms but include state policies, portrayals in the media and public opinion. The findings from the *European Social Survey* between 2002 and 2006 show that Muslim immigrants are likely to maintain higher levels of religious practice than the mean level for their host societies in Western Europe if the reception that they receive is relatively unwelcoming. The article by **Elena Fiddian-Qasmiyeh** and **Yousif M. Qasmiyeh** (Chapter 16, Volume I) casts further light on the notion of 'contexts of reception' – this time in relation to Muslim asylum seekers and refugees from the Middle East. They find themselves heavily impacted by the UK's battery of anti-terrorism measures and political concerns about global insecurity in such a way that they are increasingly identified in the public imagination by their Muslim and gendered identity rather than by their search for asylum or refuge. In this way, interactions with elements of British society in various public and private settings help to shape their self-presentation and self-identification – including experiences of racist treatment at the hands of British Muslims. The alienation that Muslim asylum seekers and refugees report has its roots not only in their experiences of a type of migration journey but also in their British context of reception which 'incriminates and forcibly categorizes them as a threat to national security' for being Muslims.

Another aspect of arguments about contexts of reception is offered in the article by **Nancy Foner** and **Richard Alba** (Chapter 17, Volume I) which compares the US with Western Europe in terms of the degree to which religion is able to facilitate the inclusion of Muslim migrants in their new societies. They argue that the key determinants of whether the practice of Islam serves as a 'bridge' or a 'barrier' to inclusion are the migrants' religious background; the religiosity of the 'native population'; and relations between the state and religious groups. As a result, the US is distinctive for the 'bridging role' that Islam and other religions play among immigrants, whereas countries in Western Europe tend to regard Islam as a problematic barrier to integration. The contrast remains stark despite recent changes on both sides of the Atlantic, thus reinforcing the importance of understanding differences in the contexts in which migrants and their religions are received. This general point is reinforced by **Margarita A. Mooney's** article (Chapter 18, Volume I) which examines the patterns of incorporation of migrants from Haïti into three jurisdictions with widely differing relations between religions and the state, namely, the US, Québec and France. On the basis of ethnographic fieldwork and interviews with government officials, Catholic leaders and Haïtian community activists in the cities of Miami, Montreal and Paris she identified the different ways in which each context of reception influenced migrants' chances of political and social 'incorporation' at the three levels of church–state relations, Haïtian mediating institutions and individual pathways. **Dianna J. Shandy's** article (Chapter 19, Volume I) documents the extent to which Christian organisations shape the reception that Nuer and other refugees fleeing from religious, ethnic, political and economic conflicts in southern Sudan have received in the US. Christian identities are implicated in Sudan's conflicts but are also instrumental in overcoming ethnic or tribal divisions and attracting international support for refugees. Their integration into American society is sponsored, managed and monitored mainly by Christian faith-based agencies and volunteers working in partnership with agencies of the federal government (Eby et al., Chapter 10, Volume II). Nevertheless, not all refugees show loyalty to the denominations or congregations that provided support to them, possibly because some American Christians undervalue the credentials of Sudanese pastors and ministers or show reluctance to welcome Sudanese lay people into their congregations.

Volume I Part VI: Religious Identification and Practice

The articles in **Volume I Part VI** build on the understanding of contexts of reception by examining their interactions with migrants' religious beliefs, identifications and practices. Here, the emphasis is on the immense variety of pressures and opportunities to adapt religion to new contexts either by maintaining pre-migration ways of being religious or by developing new, revised and hybrid forms of religion in response to new circumstances (Buenaventura 1996; Day and Içduygu 1998; Edelstein 2002; Casanova and Zolberg 2003; Cadge and Ecklund 2006; Chen, Chapter 21, Volume I; Vujcich 2007; Nissimi 2009; Baumann 2009a; Massey and Higgins, Chapter 6, Volume II; Gogonas 2012). Generational continuities and changes have an important bearing on these adaptations, some of which may also influence non-migrants in the destination societies (Men 2002; Min and Kim, Chapter 24, Volume I; Burnley 2010; Fleischmann and Phalet 2012; Maliepaard et al. 2012; Scourfield et al. 2012; Maliepaard and Lubbers, Chapter 23, Volume I). Indeed, Read's (2015: 46) conclusion of her study of Arab Muslim communities in the US is particularly interesting for insisting on the need to avoid 'overstating the positive integration of these groups' and to remain attentive to 'emerging signs of discontent among second-generation Arab and Muslim youth'.

In quantitative terms, **Ilana Redstone Akresh's** (Chapter 20, Volume I) analysis of data from the 2003 New Immigrant Survey demonstrates a tendency among immigrants to the US 'towards greater religious attendance with increased time in the US and no evidence of a decline'. **Carolyn Chen's** article (Chapter 21, Volume I) explains that Taiwanese Christian immigrants to the US come under pressure to adapt their Confucian traditions to new evangelical models of religious discipleship, democratic relationships between children and parents, and greater autonomy for children. In this way, Taiwanese congregations selectively mediate cultural assimilation to American evangelical culture. By contrast, the article by **Valerie A. Lewis** and **Ridhi Kashyap** (Chapter 22, Volume I), which analyses data from the England and Wales Citizenship Survey for 2008–2009, indicates that levels of religiosity are higher among foreign-born people than native Britons and that Muslims report higher levels of religiosity, regardless of where they were born, than other first generation immigrants. The level of religiosity does not decline among second generation Muslim immigrants and is not significantly affected by levels of educational attainment. Congruent findings are reported in **Mieke Maliepaard** and **Marcel Lubbers'** article (Chapter 23, Volume I) about the inter-generational transmission of religion among Muslims in the Netherlands. The relationship between Muslim parents' and their children's levels of participation in religious activities is positive and is not affected by high levels of educational attainment. Nevertheless, Muslims from Turkish backgrounds display higher levels than those from Moroccan backgrounds. The picture painted by **Pyong Gap Min** and **Dae Young Kim's** article (Chapter 24, Volume I) on the inter-generational transmission of religion and culture among Korean immigrants in the US is different in one important respect. The transmission of religion through participation in Korean Protestant congregations is highly successful, but transmission of other aspects of Korean culture, including language, is weak. This is attributed to the fact that 1.5- and second-generation Korean American Protestants experience strong tensions between traditional Korean values and Christian values. In this sense, religion does not mediate integration into American culture in the way that Taiwanese congregations appear to, according to Carolyn Chen's article.

Transnational migrants not only transmit religion and culture to their children but they also adapt some of their beliefs and rituals to their new societies. For example, **Clara Saraiva's** article (Chapter 25, Volume I) emphasises the intensity with which people, goods and ideas about the spirit world continue to circulate between Pepel migrants from Guinea-Bissau to Lisbon in Portugal and their places of origin in Africa. In particular, they adjust their beliefs and rituals about fostering good relations between the living and the dead in order to take account of the transnational religious networks in which they live. Similarly, the article by **Marwa Shoeb**, **Harvey M. Weinstein** and **Jodi Halpern** (Chapter 26, Volume I) about the mental health of the mostly Shi'a Iraqi refugees living in Dearborn, Michigan underlines the importance of their Muslim faith not only for helping them to cope with their memories of traumatic events but also for reconstructing notions of an 'alternative home' that transcends space, time, religious and ethnic differences. Another group that has endured forced migration is the community of Iranian Baha'is living in Saskatchewan. As the article by **Miki Talebi** and **Michel Desjardins** (Chapter 27, Volume I) makes clear, the Baha'is who made successful adaptations to their new life on the Canadian prairies found ways of allowing aspects of Iranian and Canadian cultures to coexist while privatising their religious faith.

But, according to the article by **Susana Trovão** (Chapter 28, Volume I) an entirely different strategy has been adopted by some of the young adult children of Christian migrants to Portugal from Cape Verde, São Tomé and of Muslim migrants from Indo-Mozambican origin. Instead of privatising their faith they choose to articulate it with civic activism as a central point of reference in their self-identity, which is structured by gender as well as ethnicity and religion. In turn, this 'religious-civic mobilisation' draws some of them into inter-ethnic and inter-faith networks at various levels, including the national and international. **Manuel A. Vásquez's** article (Chapter 29, Volume I) also shows how the participation of poor migrants in Pentecostal churches in various countries can offer them an 'authentic belonging' by helping them to package their sense of self and of their hopes for the future in a 'portable' format that 'circulates globally with great ease'. The key is its 'pneumatic materialism' or the belief that individual salvation, which entails a personal relationship with God, is also operative through health and wealth in this world – particularly through combating evil or disruptive spirits (see also Rey, Chapter 14, Volume I). Vásquez calls this 'the dialectic between the materialisation of the spirit and the spiritualisation of the material'. Nevertheless, not all forms of religion or spirituality are equally portable. Indeed, as **Frank Usarski's** article (Chapter 30, Volume I) shows, the main currents of Buddhism that Japanese immigrants began to transplant to Brazil early in the twentieth century have largely failed to retain the loyalty of successive generations of their descendants who were born and raised in Brazil or to attract converts outside the Japanese ethnic category. The tension between pressures to transmit a Buddhist cultural heritage to descendants of the original immigrants from Japan and pressures to integrate into Brazilian society has led to a steady decline in the number of participants in Buddhist groups and activities. It is also a factor in the growing number of conversions of the younger cohorts of Japanese Brazilians to Catholicism, the increasing numbers of inter-ethnic marriages and the declining number of Japanese Buddhist priests in Brazil. The triple link between traditional currents of Japanese Buddhism, the Japanese language and Japanese ethnicity accounts for the weakening of this particular 'migrant religion'.

Volume II Part I: Integration Strategies

Volume II Part I is about the varied strategies and practices that migrants adopt for finding ways of integrating into their societies of destination. This involves much more than simply being 'accepted' by their 'hosts'. At the very least these strategies include a wide range of activities aimed at obtaining access to safe and secure housing, food and clothing, health care, employment, education for children, status as an asylum seeker, refugee or migrant, and civil rights (Rex 1992; Reitz et al. 2009; De Castro 2010; Nielsen 2010; Fleischmann and Phalet 2012). Other strategies aim at becoming active in politics at local or national level, joining voluntary associations, participating in sports, learning or mastering the local language(s), entering friendship networks, taking part in cultural activities, finding an *entrée* to local media outlets, and so on (Lövheim and Axner 2011; Pype 2013). Religion can have a bearing on all the different ways in which migrants seek social integration, some of which may bring migrants into tension and conflict with other people and institutions (Kastoryano 2004; Kaya 2009). The public policies that create opportunities for, and place constraints on, migrants' strategies for integration will be considered in Volume II Part III.

The chapter by **Sebnem Koser Akcapar** (Chapter 1, Volume II) casts light on what is probably an unusual strategy for social integration. It concerns the extraordinary practice that some Iranian Shi'a Muslims have deployed for making their way as asylum seekers into Turkey as a transit country by converting to Christianity either before or after leaving Iran. Participation in Catholic or Protestant churches and transnational agencies provides access to many forms of spiritual and practical assistance which are used to enhance their chances of eventually reaching Western countries as refugees – as well as new self-identification as former Muslims. Regardless of the motivation for conversion, it opens up social networks which confer many kinds of advantages – not the least of which is that the international legal principle of *non-refoulement* prevents Iranian converts to Christianity from being deported from Turkey back to Iran because 'apostasy' is a capital offence there. A more conventional path to integration in conjunction with Islam is reported by **Susana Molins Lliteras** (Chapter 2, Volume II) in her article on Senegalese migrants who are not the only people in Cape Town to find a way into South African society through networks associated with a distinctively Senegalese expression of Islam. The Niassene branch of the Tijaniyya *tariqa* or multi-purpose spiritual brotherhood expanded rapidly after 1994 among Tijani migrants, but it has also had a significant impact on other ethnic and 'racial' groups in South Africa. In effect, the brotherhood's activities have boosted the integration of Tijanis into South African society while also connecting them with a wider transnational network of African Muslims from a variety of national and ethnic backgrounds. The activities combine worship, spiritual nurture, economic support and education, from which women are not excluded. The *tariqa* has experienced internal tensions at times, but it unquestionably functions as a 'vehicle for integration into South African society' and into transnational religious and ethnic networks at the same time. In a slightly ironic sense of 'integration', **Marc Sommers'** article (Chapter 3, Volume II) on young male Burundi illegal refugees in Dar es Salaam in the 1990s makes the important point that their participation in Pentecostal church networks helps to escape from rural settlements and to hide them from state authorities as well as to give them access to spiritual support, useful information and practical assistance. In this sense, their integration was effective but irregular and parallel to official schemes for confining refugees to camps outside Tanzanian cities. The evidence of Burundi refugees in Dar es Salaam is confirmation that there is a strong link, as Manuel A. Vásquez (Chapter 29, Volume I) has argued, between Pentecostalism and mobility: Pentecostalism offered a far more 'portable' integration strategy in Burundi and Tanzania than did Catholicism. And this argument has been developed further by **Manuel A. Vásquez** and **Kim Knott** in their article (Chapter 4, Volume II) about the strategies of migrant minorities in Kuala Lumpur, Johannesburg and London for drawing on religious resources to 'carve out spaces of livelihood' within the limits imposed by public authorities. This can involve creating spaces and times for intense prayer among migrants to Johannesburg, which links the local praying community into wider transnational networks; it can also involve creating sacred places and buildings which 'embed' the religious identities and practices of the Hindu and Chinese minorities in Kuala Lumpur as well as the Muslim majority; and it can involve tension between various religious migrant minorities, as in parts of London, over the scale of their ambitions for place making to reflect their self-image as actors on a global stage. Place making links 'physical migrations with spiritual journeys'.

Volume II Part II: Religion as Resource

It is widely taken for granted that religion can serve as a resource for migrants, but researchers have given relatively little attention to questions about the nature of the resource or the ways in which it is used at different stages of the migration process (but see Hagan and Ebaugh 2003; Hirschman 2004; Connor 2011, 2012; Skirbekk et al. 2012; Mellor and Gilliat-Ray 2015; Kivisto 2014). The articles in **Volume II Part II** offer various answers to these questions, acknowledging that it is also important to examine the extent to which the resources that can be mediated through religions are actually beneficial for migrants, their kinship networks, their local communities and their societies of origin and destination. The sheer diversity of the resources potentially associated with religions becomes immediately clear from **James R. Cochrane's** article (Chapter 5, Volume II) about the 'religious health assets' that are widespread – but not always well articulated with public health structures – among migrant and refugee communities in South African cities. These assets form a 'type of endogenous resource' that can be activated through kin, local communities and special associations that offer religious or spiritual healing practices to individuals and their environment. Examining the case of the severely deprived area of Imizamo Yethu in the Hout Bay valley on the outskirts of Cape Town where official attempts to improve public health and the environment have largely failed, Cochrane argues that religion can make a positive contribution through infusing the daily life of migrants and refugees – experiencing dislocation, ill health and deprivation – with 'questions of meaning, trust, agency and purpose'. This may mean going beyond the biomedical models of disease and treatment in the direction of a more holistic conception of health and well-being so that 'the religious beliefs, rituals and practices that represent vital cultural capital' can be mobilised 'alongside any biomedical strategies' (see also Chinouya and O'Keefe 2005). Nevertheless, Cochrane recognises that religion's capacity to be divisive and exclusive must also be taken into account when assessing the potential of religious health assets to work in partnership with public authorities. His proposals for more extensive research on religion as a resource in health care in Africa would also do well to take account of other potential drawbacks, including the fact that religious groups can be selective, thereby possibly putting non-participants at a disadvantage if public authorities enter into partnerships with religious organisations. Similar reservations are at least implicit in the article by **Douglas S. Massey** and **Monica Espinoza Higgins** (Chapter 6, Volume II) which, in addition to finding that the latest waves of legal immigrants in the US tend to be less Christian than previous waves, suggests that migration actually disrupts the identification of many immigrants with religions, thereby 'alienating' them from religious practice rather than 'theologising' them in the sense of turning them towards religion. One implication is that religion may not serve as an important resource for as many migrants as some of the research literature suggests. This reasoning runs counter to much scholarship on religion and migration in the US, but Massey and Higgins argue that this may be because qualitative researchers have tended to study congregations or other organised groups, thereby focusing too narrowly on people who are already religiously committed. Analysis of data from the first wave of the New Immigrant Survey in the US showed, by contrast, that 'the most common and immediate response to international migration is a decline, not an increase, in the level of religious participation'. This calls into question the 'theologising hypothesis', suggesting instead an 'alienating hypothesis' which indicates the disruptive effect of migration to the US on religious practice, at least in the period immediately following arrival. Connor (2014: 34) believes that the two hypotheses are mutually compatible, however, in the case of migrants whose experience of migration is particularly difficult.

Another article which nuances some of the more far-reaching claims often made about the use that migrants make of religion as a resource is **Damaris Seleina Parsitau's** account of the role played by four faith-based organisations (FBOs) in bravely assisting internally displaced persons (IDPs) in Nakuru and Nairobi in Kenya (Chapter 7, Volume II). Without downplaying either the vital humanitarian assistance, prayer and trauma counselling provided by the FBOs, she makes four main points. First, the FBOs were themselves the target of violence and intimidation. Second, the FBOs were widely accused of 'negative ethnicity' in the sense of allegedly failing to rise about tribalism or to function as neutral arbiters. Third, the work of FBOs did not differ significantly from that of various non-religious agencies. And fourth, the IDPs – especially women – drew on their own personal resources of religious faith and spiritual capital for support in the face of extensive sexual and gender-based violence and post-conflict trauma. The conclusion is that 'more than relying on FBOs and clergy, IDPs largely relied on their own individual faith and spirituality'.

A sharply different and usually overlooked angle on the resources that religion can supply to migrants is explored in **Peter van der Veer's** article (Chapter 8, Volume II) on transnational Hindu and Muslim movements that originated from India. While accepting that movements such as the Vishva Hindu Parishad and the Tablighi Jama'at are often depicted as forces for conservative and traditionalist views with questionable loyalty to the nation states to which many of their followers have migrated, he argues that the Hindu movement adapts its highly political objectives and tactics to different national contexts and that the Muslim movement is deliberately a-political. But both of them are also active in 'ideological work' that keeps transforming their discourses in 'positive and creative moments' which, in turn, generate more than merely 'religious enclaves' or 'safe havens of the self'. Instead, van der Veer claims that they creatively develop new religious understandings of the predicaments facing migrants and that they 'engage global issues in an innovative manner'. In other words, they can be considered as an ideological resource that evolves partly in response to the changing circumstances in which Hindu and Muslim migrants find themselves.

Volume II Part III: *Policies and Services*

Research on religion and migration has understandably tended to focus on either migrants or the religious organisations and groups that offer spiritual, moral or practical assistance to them. Concern with inter-generational patterns of change and continuity in religious identities and affiliations also looms large. But the wider picture needs to take account of the contextual factors that shape every stage of migration processes and their outcomes. As the contributions to Volume I Part V indicated, the contexts of reception exert powerful effects on the religious lives of migrants; and these contexts are, in turn, shaped by a wide range of public policies and services. The articles in **Volume II Part III** examine aspects of the broadly political and policy-oriented debates that bear on the provision of facilities and services with consequences for migrants, many – but not all – of whom identify themselves with religions (Ebaugh and Pipes 2001; Nawyn 2006; Bramadat and Koenig 2009; Joppke 2009; Knoll 2009; Karyotis and Patrikios 2010; Ives et al. 2010; Martikainen 2014). There is widespread agreement on the value of taking the religion and spirituality of migrants into account in resettlement policies and programmes, but opinions are divided on precisely how to do this without aggravating ethical and political dilemmas (Werbner 2005; Zetter et al. 2006; Vellenga 2008; Hattam and Yescas 2010; Rose 2012; Boubeker 2013; Gallo and Sai 2013). This division of opinion is clear in relation to policies and practices regulating the provision of pastoral care and chaplains in institutions such as the military, hospitals and prisons (Beckford and Gilliat 1998; Beckford et al. 2005; Bertossi 2007; Bowen 2009; Gilliat-Ray et al. 2013).

Paul Bramadat's article (Chapter 9, Volume II) brings to the fore the dilemmas and challenges that arise when religiously affiliated agencies offer assistance to migrants, especially refugees, in the Canadian province of British Columbia, which has a distinguished record of hospitality towards immigrants. Faith-based agencies which are, or are associated with, a recognised 'Sponsorship Agreement Holder' – an organisation with a formal arrangement to work with the government department Citizenship and Immigration Canada (CIC) – are authorised to work with CIC in supporting privately sponsored refugees and would-be refugees. The private sponsorship system requires sponsors to demonstrate their ability to pay for and to provide a range of services and goods which might cost as much as $35,000 CAN for a family of five for one year. Questions arise, therefore, about the capacity of the agencies to meet these demanding obligations at a time when mainstream Christian denominations continue to decline and when many agencies depended on a small and dwindling pool of volunteers. Another challenge facing the agencies is the difficulty of working with an increasingly risk-averse government bureaucracy and the 'securitisation' of refugee policies. Bramadat's discussion is particularly interesting when it turns to 'the ideological environment' in which the agencies' volunteers have to work with public officials who may feel themselves constrained by norms of secularity and who give the impression of a 'studied indifference toward the core religious sensibilities' of the agencies. The 'evidence of the deep entrenchment of secularist logic' was so strong that Bramadat interpreted it as a tacit agreement on the part of volunteers and officials alike to remain virtually silent about religion despite the fact that Canada has never had a sharp separation between religions and the state (see also Ager and Ager 2011 on secularism and humanitarianism). Taking the example of Church World Service (CWS) in the US, the article by **Jessica Eby et al.** (Chapter 10, Volume II) makes no allusions to anything akin to Bramadat's concerns about the environment of secularism and silence about religion which affects the work of faith-based agencies in British Columbia. Instead, it attributes the success of refugee resettlement in the US precisely to the active engagement of the many local communities of faith that work in partnership with public authorities such as the Bureau of Population, Refugees and Migration – principles of church–state separation notwithstanding – to accomplish 70 per cent of the resettlement caseload in accordance with the Refugee Act of 1980. Partnership with secular resettlement agencies to co-sponsor refugees is also common, as is advocacy for social justice and increased public funding for the resettlement of refugees. In short, the public–private partnership model increases opportunities for local faith communities and for faith-based organisations at all levels of American society to produce 'the largest resettled refugee population in the world'.

In contrast to the articles on faith-based initiatives for the resettlement of refugees in Canada and the US, the article by **Elżbieta M. Goździak** (Chapter 11, Volume II) on the resettlement of Albanians fleeing Kosavar in 1999 highlights the difficulties that arose when Western service providers tended to distance themselves from the religious or spiritual aspects of the suffering experienced by the refugees and forced migrants. Her argument is that policy debates and programme strategies at the international and national levels took virtually no account of religion, despite the fact that faith-based agencies were prominent in relief efforts. Her first-hand account of the processing of the Kosovars sent to Fort Dix in the US emphasises the tension between the Muslim Kosovars' tendency to frame their problems in religious terms and the unwillingness of the Western mental health professions who worked in Operation Provide Refuge to accept religion's relevance to an adequate psychotherapeutic response to the Kosovars' suffering and trauma. But as a reminder of how difficult it can be to translate policy into practice successfully if humanitarian aid and religious proselytising are combined, **Alexander Horstmann's** article (Chapter 12, Volume II) illustrates some of the ethical dilemmas facing the providers of assistance to Karen refugees and displaced persons in the Burma–Thailand borderland. He argues that some faith-based and secular humanitarian agencies have been drawn into 'the nationalist project' of the Christian Baptist Karen with the result that preference has been shown to them rather than to other religious or ethnic groups such as animists, the Buddhist Shan or Indian Muslims. The value of the aid provided by many Christian agencies is not in doubt, but the 'centrality of Christian networks' to the well-being of Karen refugees has major implications for the political and military future of the region. Other serious problems that arise in situations of conflict where humanitarian aid may be provided by ethnic and faith communities that are central to the conflict are analysed in **Nkwachukwu Orji's** article (Chapter 13, Volume II) about the city of Jos in north-central Nigeria. This was the site of virulent sectarian violence that was aggravated by ethnic and political divisions in the first decade of the current century. The Christian and Muslim communities that were badly affected were both 'protagonists' in the conflict and 'providers of relief' to hundreds of thousands of displaced persons. In fact, the faith-based agencies at various levels from the local to the international dominated relief operations in Jos, benefiting from the availability of volunteers, funds from faith groups and strong support from co-religionists. But faith-based agencies were also hampered by the difficulty of reaching out to displaced persons from other faiths and by their tendency to regard relief materials as belonging to a particular religious group rather than to everyone in an affected locality. A more universalistic approach is encouraged by international aid agencies associated with, for example, the Catholic and Mennonite churches; and attempts are made to initiate inter-faith partnership in relief operations. But the author's conclusion is that the faith-specific approach may be 'invaluable'.

At a higher level of generality, **Matthias Koenig's** article (Chapter 14, Volume II) underlines the importance of understanding how the place occupied by religion in different national frameworks of politics and collective identity (or 'institutional logics') contributes towards their differential ways of incorporating Muslim migrants and settlers. Comparison between the UK, France and Germany reveals a wide range of policies for the governance of religious diversity. More importantly, however, some convergences are also evident not only in public policy responses to the growing presence of Muslims in Europe and their claims for recognition but also in the responses of Muslims themselves to these policies. In particular, the articulation has grown stronger in all three countries between discourses of human rights and Muslim claims for public recognition. In turn, the formulation of Muslim claims for recognition increasingly draws on 'transnational repertoires of contestation', thereby helping to secure religion of many kinds as a 'legitimate category of identity' in the public sphere. The consequences of these developments for the continuing arrival of Muslim migrants in the UK, France and Germany at a time of heightened concern with violent extremism could be substantial. For very different reasons, the case of Israel is interesting because the notion of institutionally incorporating new immigrants has long included a state policy that promotes the conversion of non-Jews to Judaism. **Michal Kravel-Tovi's** article (Chapter 15, Volume II) analyses this policy as a 'national mission' which has significant implications for the more than 300,000 non-Jewish people who have migrated to Israel from the Former Soviet Union after 1990. In this sense, religion is subject to population policy, and conversion is promoted and managed through an extensive apparatus of institutions funded directly or indirectly by the state under the general supervision of the Conversion Administration and the Prime Minister's Office – and in the context of tense dynamics between the state, ultra-Orthodox Haredi and Orthodox–Zionist interests. In this way, political power is deployed to shape the Israeli population by subjecting non-Jewish immigrants to a policy of religious conversion. The policy is gendered in so far as women are regarded as the primary agents for controlling reproduction and conforming to Israel's 'pro-natalist fertility policy'. Nevertheless, the statistical outcomes of the policy appear to be modest in view of the state's investment of money and effort.

The well-known historical mutations of Australia's immigration policies – from assimilation to integration to multiculturalism – are not unique among liberal democracies, but the article by **Jeremy Northcote**, **Peter Hancock** and **Suzy Casimiro** (Chapter 16, Volume II) suggests that 'the growing fear of cultural difference based on religious affiliation' has led to questions about the efficacy of the current policy and of the extensive services that it has ensured for refugee settlers since the 1990s. Rejecting the idea that Muslim women refugees in particular are disadvantaged either because of factors unique to their Muslim background or because of factors specific to the 'structural and cultural conditions' of Australia, they used data from focus group discussions with first generation women refugees from Iraqi, Sudanese and Afghan backgrounds to devise a model that captured the complex interactions between many different factors. The model of 'the isolation cycle' indicates how the factors work in concert to reinforce the isolation and marginalisation from the wider Australian community reported by female Muslim refugees. The question arises of how far the current policies and arrangements for the settlement of refugees, which emerged from previous patterns of settlement from Europe and Southeast Asia, need to be adapted to the needs of refugees from significantly different backgrounds. In raising this question, the authors are all too aware of the risk that they run of being considered in support of negative stereotypes of Muslim immigrants and refugees, but their response is that no single factor or group can be held responsible for the level of isolation that settlement policies need to address.

Volume II Part IV: Economics and Work

No aspect of migration has attracted more interest from researchers and policymakers than the broadly economic circumstances in which decisions to migrate are taken and attempts are made to secure well-being in societies of destination. Questions about physical security, housing, income, language competence, remittances and employment usually take priority, especially as they intersect with factors such as gender, nationality, 'race' and ethnicity (Barot 2002; Galush 2002; Smith Kelly and Solomon, Chapter 20, Volume II; Stambouli and Soltane 2010; Cohen 2011; Norman 2011; Sherkat 2012). But, as the articles in **Volume II Part IV** show, religion can also have an important bearing on the economic and material dimensions of migration – both for origin societies and receiving societies (Alba et al. 2009; Connor 2011; Voas and Fleischmann 2012; Wong 2013b). The phrase 'religion as resource' often refers to the spiritual, psychological and social benefits that many migrants derive from participation in religious activities and groups. But it is clear that religion can also be associated with material resources – and can entail material 'investments' of time and money. Indeed, the distinction between the economic and the spiritual or religious is debatable (Vásquez 2011).

Reinforcing and refining many of the points made in Volume 1 Part V about the need to understand the impact of their contexts of reception on migrants' chances of achieving integration into their new societies, the article by **Phillip Connor** and **Matthias Koenig** (Chapter 17, Volume II) examines the effect of religious affiliation and participation on the occupational attainments of first and second generation immigrants to Canada, the US and countries of Western Europe. Rejecting the rigid idea that religion is either a 'bridge' or a 'barrier' to integration (Foner and Alba, Chapter 17, Volume I), they use general survey data to show that variations in the configuration of religion in each site account for the differential attainments of immigrants from different religious backgrounds. These variations include, most importantly, the degree to which 'religious boundary configurations' are sharp and the degree to which the religious 'market' is pluralistic and voluntaristic. The findings show that in contexts where boundaries between religious groups are sharp (Western Europe and Canada), the impact of religious affiliation on the occupational attainment of immigrants from religious minorities may seem to be somewhat negative – but only among the first generation and only in certain circumstances. But in the more pluralistic context of the US there tends to be a clearly positive association between involvement in religion and occupational attainment, especially among second generation immigrants – albeit only if they are members of religious majorities.

The case of undocumented Latina women from South America working in Israel illustrates many of the dilemmas facing women from relatively poor countries who undertake international migration in the search for employment but find that their jobs do not correspond to their levels of skill and that they are forced to live on the margins of Israeli society. Those who migrate in order to secure a better future for their children (who remain in the country of origin) paradoxically experience the emotional stress of not being able to fulfil what they regard as their maternal roles. The article by **Rebecca Raijman**, **Silvina Schammah-Gesser** and **Adriana Kemp** (Chapter 18, Volume II) not only examines the dilemmas that arise from downward occupational mobility, illegal status and disruption of family life but also raises questions about gendered coping strategies. Religious organisations are the most accessible social space available to Latina women in Israel. In both Catholic and Evangelical Protestant churches, it is women who fill the congregations and assume leadership positions in religious and communal associations. Churches function as 'surrogate families' and 'a form of self-help'. Women experience the Evangelical churches, in particular, as places of safety and well-being as a result of the churches' theologically inspired imposition of strict discipline and lifestyle norms (see also Raijman and Kemp 2004). For undocumented workers in Israel, then, Evangelical churches are not only 'protected spaces', especially if the police are reluctant to enter them, but also arenas for a limited form of public visibility. And as Gemma Tulud Cruz (2010: 32) reports about Filipina domestic workers in Hong Kong, they develop 'faith-informed strategies for survival'.

The interpenetration of religion and economic activity is particularly strong among Somali refugees in Johannesburg. **Samadia Sadouni's** article (Chapter 19, Volume II) about the 'diasporic culture of solidarity' that has developed among these immigrants to South Africa, via various East African countries, since the mid-1990s emphasises the importance of the clan-based networks of kinship, credit and religion that they strengthened on their migratory journeys. These networks have helped to facilitate successful economic integration primarily in the Mayfair district of Johannesburg, notably through the agency of faith-based organisations such as the Somali Islamic Resource Centre. It fosters a 'pan-Somali identity' that to some extent transcends South Africa's racial categories and the clan divisions endemic to Somalia; and it offers a degree of security and protection in the face of xenophobia and violence. Indeed, a form of 'imagined pan-Somalianism' is activated through the local Islamic community and the transnational trading links that at least its more prosperous members can exploit.

The remittances that migrants send back to their societies of origin amount to an important economic resource (Cohen 2011), and the article by **Claudia Smith Kelly** and **Blen Solomon** (Chapter 20, Volume II) shows that religion can have an important influence on this activity. Logistic regression analyses of data from the Pilot for the New Immigrant Survey, showed that twentieth century legal immigrants to the US are more likely to send remittances if they identify themselves with a religion. Among those reporting a religious identity, Protestants and members of certain other religions are more likely than Catholics to send remittances. Perhaps surprisingly, levels of attendance at religious services are positively, but not significantly, related to the propensity to send remittances.

Volume II Part V: Religious Organisations and Professionals

The focus of most research on religion and migration has been on migrants, their contexts of reception and the benefits that flow from participation in faith communities, but relatively little attention has been given to the religious organisations with which many, but not all, migrants associate (Warner and Wittner 1998; Yang and Ebaugh 2001; Oxford 2010; Trzebiatowska 2010). The contributions to **Volume II Part V** help to fill this gap by examining how the work of religious organisations, their professional staff and volunteers mediates the involvement of migrants with religions (Menjivar 2003; Wanner 2004; Anoniou 2005; Hagan, Chapter 31, Volume II; Bruce 2006; Solari 2006; Kotin et al. 2011; Nteta and Wallsten 2012). In many cases, these organisations function within transnational networks that extend well beyond the migrants' societies of origin and destination. Their ideologies also convey awareness of, or aspirations towards, truly global outreach.

   Michael Baffoe's article (Chapter 21, Volume II) demonstrates the complex structure of Christian churches mostly founded and frequented by West Africans who migrated to Canada and became active in a variety of churches in Montreal, Toronto and Winnipeg, most of which are associated with the 'African initiated' Pentecostal or Charismatic churches which developed in Africa independently of the churches created by missionaries in the colonial period. Participation in these churches responds to a wide range of personal and social needs and interests and is often structured by ethnicity, culture and language. The role that these churches can play in validating the ethnic and religious identity of African migrants to Europe has long been understood (Adogame 2003), and their appeal in Canada is no less strong or complex. The organisational structure of the churches tends to combine a lack of clear structures with leadership by 'strong and powerful' leaders, many of whom also founded the churches. Management is in the hands of 'small circles of trusted followers' of the pastors, and this has aggravated tensions and a propensity to breakaway factions in a recurring pattern of division and multiplication. The spectacularly high rates of growth in West African churches are due more to divisiveness than to population growth. Grievances about the allegedly lavish or flashy lifestyle of the leaders are at the root of many divisions, thereby ironically reproducing the complaints previously made about 'colonial masters'.

   The role of religious organisations is not confined to providing support and security for migrants and their families. **Denis Kim's** article (Chapter 22, Volume II) draws attention to the importance of Christian faith-based organisations in political activism and legal advocacy for changes in immigration policy and the enhancement of migrants' rights. Faith-based NGOs were critical to the success of campaigns leading to the liberalisation of migration policy in the Republic of Korea in 2007 in three ways. They outnumbered non-religious NGOs and were sufficiently numerous to make a difference; their leaders, especially Protestant pastors and laywomen from various churches, were active in advocacy coalitions; activist clergy, many of whom had participated in movements for democratisation in the 1970s and 1980s, were able to guide the direction that advocacy took; and both Protestant and Catholic churches drew on their transnational networks for guidance and support. Christianity's doctrinal orientation towards universalism and charity – notably in the form of Korea's characteristically progressive *minjung* theology – provided the ideological impetus towards overcoming nationalist resistance to the liberalisation of immigration controls. Nevertheless, critics point to the hierarchical structure of the NGOs, to the lack of democratic decision-making, to the risk of making immigrants dependent on the NGOs' services, and to the activist clergy's authoritarian style of management – all of which may also be characteristic of non-religious organisations in Korea.

In a similar vein, **Margarita Mooney's** article (Chapter 23, Volume II) comparing the work of the Catholic Bishops Conferences in the US and France analyses the ways in which they have constituted migration as a topic on the political agenda in two countries with contrasting configurations of religion, the state and public life (see also Gunn 2004; Zoller 2006). For Mooney, this represents the Church's 'reassertion of its prophetic voice in society' about the need for a humane approach to salient issues affecting undocumented migrants, refugees and family reunification. But, although the Catholic Church is a 'supranational' organisation with one billion members, its operations at the level of each national state and diocese are to some extent moulded by contextual laws and opportunities for religious voices to be heard in public spheres. In the US, the Church has long been a direct provider of various practical and spiritual services to immigrants in keeping with the country's traditions of voluntarism in civil society, whereas this is a much smaller part of official Catholic activities in France where it tends to act as an intermediary with the agencies of the state which dominate the provision of services to immigrants. This difference in the opportunity structures helps to explain the different forms and degrees of visibility that the engagement of Bishops Conferences in the US and France has taken in public debates about immigration. The prophetic voice is common, but the modes and opportunities for its expression are different.

The case of Austria raises a further consideration about the indirect effects of minority religious immigration on religious organisations. According to the article by **Julia Mourão Permoser**, **Sieglinde Rosenberger** and **Kristina Stoeckl** (Chapter 24, Volume II), the increasingly politicised debates about the integration of immigrants in Austrian society have boosted the visibility of their representative religious organisations. More importantly, however, these debates have also induced agencies of the state to engage in more broadly based negotiations with religious minority organisations, thereby giving them the opportunity to serve as 'political entrepreneurs' in a context which combines religious diversity with the integration of immigrants. Muslims and Orthodox Christians, who are the religious 'denominations' with the highest percentage of immigrant members in Austria, are in the process of becoming the government's chosen 'representatives of immigrants'. In turn, these developments have created some tensions within minority religions as well as between them and other religious and political actors, especially because the state appears to regard all immigrants as 'primarily religious persons'.

The character of the contribution that religious professionals may or may not make to the well-being of immigrants is one of the issues discussed in **Albert Kraler's** article (Chapter 25, Volume II) about the special immigration rules governing the issue of visas and work permits to Imams seeking to work in Europe or Canada. This is a rarely visited corner of immigration policy, but it has great significance for the members of any migrant faith community who are dependent on the services of ministers of religion (or at least leaders) from their country of origin. It is also related to the broader field of government management of religious and ethnic diversity. Analysing the policies of nine European countries that make special exceptions to their immigration controls in favour of 'third-country nationals carrying out religious work', Kraler found that in three countries special rules for ministers of religion were dependent on official recognition of faith communities; in six other countries, third-country nationals are exempt from the requirement to obtain a work permit. Other rules specified a minimum size for a qualifying faith community and the necessity for applicants to have specific qualifications or experience. Additional restrictions may be imposed on the length of the permit, the ability to change employment and access to citizenship. The salience of these rules and requirements has increased as a consequence of concerns not only about the integration of Muslims into European societies but also about the perceived threats of violent extremism and Islamist radicalisation. Questions about the granting of special exemptions to Imams are nested in efforts to establish training institutions for Muslim clerics 'in country', to weaken the dependency of mosques on foreign funding, to enhance the training of teachers about Islam in schools, and to set up centralised agencies to represent Muslims in dialogue with the state.

Continuing with the topic of transnational clergy mobility, **Maïté Maskens'** article (Chapter 26, Volume II) analyses the narratives about religion and migration recounted by men who migrated to Brussels from sub-Saharan Africa and Latin America and became Pentecostal pastors. Their narratives imply a 'double process of mobility and religion' in the sense that their accounts of migration acknowledge that miraculous 'divine agency' empowered them, unlike other migrants, to become missionaries but that their 'enacted destiny' was also shaped, in turn, by their experiences of living in their new social context. Depicting their experiences as 'God's immigration' they distinguish themselves from other immigrants to Belgium and do not regard themselves as in any way dependent on Belgian society. In this way, Pentecostalism has a transformative effect on interpretations of migration at the level of individual pastors and their sermons, reflecting a distinctive mode of societal insertion.

Volume II Part VI: Space and Culture

The spatial dimension of immigrants' religious practices has been a prominent feature of anthropological research (Coleman 2000; Meyer 2004; Robbins 2004; Knott 2005; Vertovec 2007a; Bava 2011) and geographical research (Gale and Naylor 2002; Gale 2005, 2013; Kong 2010; Dwyer et al. 2013). The articles in **Volume II Part VI** show that, when the spatial is combined with studies of the built form of immigrants' worship places and their activities designed to claim areas of the public sphere for their own purposes (for example, cemeteries), some highly significant aspects of religion and migration come clearly into focus (Burkhalter 2001; McLoughlin 2005; Jonker 2005; Abdullah 2009; Baumann 2009a, 2009b; Ehrkamp and Nagel 2012). In this way, the cultural meanings of immigrants' religious practices can be interpreted in relation to their spatial contexts as well as to policy-oriented discussions about planning (Pype 2013).

Indeed, the crossings of spatial and cultural boundaries are at the centre of **John Eade's** article (Chapter 27, Volume II) about the sometimes politically sensitive processes whereby Anglican, Methodist and Catholic churches have sought to make or re-make homes for themselves in London at a time of immigration on a global scale. It shows that religious diversity is a feature of Christianity and is not just about the variety of world religions. It also emphasises the growing importance of London's suburbs and inner boroughs as spaces where religious and ethnic diversity are interwoven among immigrants and other residents (Dwyer et al. 2013). The gentrification of certain inner boroughs, in particular, has entailed religious growth – and not only among immigrants – rather than secularisation. Adaptive strategies have enabled some churches to respond positively and with theological or liturgical creativity to high rates of geographical mobility among a wide variety of 'natives' and immigrants, including those from Eastern Europe in the twenty-first century. Immigrants' religion has had a major impact on the theological orientations, styles of worship and social outreach of many churches which had previously seemed at risk of failing or closing. This change has, of course, been accompanied by tensions and disputes in some congregations.

Another striking feature of recent religious change in London's inner boroughs is the sight and sound of immigrants and diaspora dwellers giving public performances of rituals and music testifying to their minority faiths. **David Garbin's** article (Chapter 28, Volume II) takes the example of members of the 'Church of Jesus Christ on Earth by His special envoy Simon Kimbangu' (or Kimbanuists) whose marching brass band participates in London's New Year's Day Parade. Their charismatic and 'prophetist' church, which had been founded by Simon Kimbangu in 1921 in the former Belgian colony of Congo, survived persecution under both colonial and post-colonial powers to achieve recognition by the World Council of Churches (Martin 1975; Garbin 2014). Garbin's argument is that the Kimbanguists' brass band embodies and expresses not just their church's theology but also the 'poetics of diasporic belonging' by asserting their place simultaneously in a global (but divided) Congolese network, in the local setting of London and in the succession of migrant generations of Kimbanguists. These performances of faith 'sanctify' localities which might be considered evil and take a religious message, in visible and aural forms, to an often *blasé* public. But, as **Amber Gemmeke's** article (Chapter 29, Volume II) demonstrates, there are other ways for migrants to publicise their activities these days, especially as the Internet assumes ever greater importance for transnational religious movements, including those offering ostensibly traditional or timeless wisdom and services. Comparing the work of Senegalese *marabouts* (the imams, teachers, healers, diviners and leaders of Sufi Islamic brotherhoods in parts of North and West Africa) in their home country and in the Netherlands, she highlights the growing public presence of *marabouts* advertising their spiritual services through websites, email lists as well as print and broadcast media and, in the process, reconfiguring some of the underlying ideas and symbols. Echoing Meyer's analysis of Ghanaian Pentecostalism (Meyer 2006), however, her findings uncover extensive scepticism about the *marabouts'* use of new media in both Senegal and the Netherlands, albeit for different reasons. Misgivings in Senegal (where *marabouts* are 'everywhere') centre on allegations of 'aggressive entrepreneurialism' in disregard of Sufi ideals of modesty and honesty, whereas Dutch scepticism centres on notions of an exotic 'African otherness' that is supposedly incompatible with Western rationality and health care. In short, *maraboutic* practices are refracted by local media environments and public discourses both in their home territories and in countries where migrants have exported them.

Nowhere more than in France have public discourses about the growing presence of Muslim immigrants and their descendants been so outspoken and polarised in the twenty-first century. This was not the result of a gradual evolution in relations between France and Muslims, according to **Marcel Maussen's** article (Chapter 30, Volume II), which argues that these relations had passed through three overlapping phases in the twentieth century: colonial-style control; 'immigrant worker' segregated status; and a regime of equality for 'Islam of France'. The changing character of discussion about the construction of mosques in France reflected these different regimes and the emergence this century of anxiety that Muslims might retreat into small or local organisations that would be free from the state's tutelage – and therefore a threat to the Republic's official self-description as unitary, indivisible and secular. Discussions about the construction of mosques provide an important key to understanding how the integration of Muslims in France and other European countries has become such a sensitive issue (Cesari 2005).

Volume II Part VII: Theological Interpretations

Researchers, journalists, politicians, religious leaders and policymakers repeatedly insist that the interweaving of religion and migration needs to be taken seriously at a time when transnational and global flows of people, goods and ideas are accelerating. The notion of 'superdiversity' captures the mutual interactions that take place among the increasingly diverse populations and cultures of 'global cities' (Vertovec 2007b). Admittedly, much of the heightened interest in religion is driven by anxieties about the spread of religiously inflected extremism, radicalisation and violence. These anxieties are aggravated in Western countries by fears about 'home grown' terrorists who may be second or third generation immigrants and/or converts to religions imported from other parts of the world. There is now also concern about the international mobility of 'radicalised' Muslims into and out of conflict zones in the Middle East and parts of Africa. Yet, relatively little attention has been given to theological reflections on the experience of migration. The articles in **Volume II Part VII** illustrate some of the ways in which theology, in the sense of methodical analysis of the truths claimed in the name of religions, can therefore be a relevant dimension of research on religion and migration – not necessarily because it somehow trumps the insights of social scientific investigation but because it reflects continuity and change in interpretations of religion's engagement with migration *sub specie aeternitatis* or from the viewpoint of putatively eternal truth (Karagiannis and Glick Schiller 2006; Ekué 2009; Groody 2009; Gerloff 2010; Hollenbach 2011; Asamoah-Gyadu 2012; Tan 2012).

Jacqueline Hagan's article (Chapter 31, Volume II) explores the variety of theological justifications that religious leaders articulate in Latin America for the pastoral care and advocacy for social justice that they undertake in support of migrants at the beginning of, and in the course of, their often harrowing and hazardous journeys towards the US (Groody 2009; Hagan 2013; Sarat 2013). The 'social theology' deployed by Catholic leaders, which roots the causes of migration in injustices such as poverty and religious intolerance, promotes 'the right to migrate' in keeping with ideas of human dignity through strategies of solidarity, advocacy and hospitality. The theological response of mainly liberal Protestant clergy is similar, but others from churches in the Pentecostal, Southern Baptist, Evangelical and Fundamentalist traditions are less supportive of migration and more insistent on the need for individuals to keep their families intact at home and to give priority to their relationship with the divine. In addition, inter-faith projects for the welfare of migrants have long been active along the US's southern border trying to reduce the number of deaths among would-be migrants and to provide sanctuary in imitation of various biblical models (Golden and McConnell 1986; Hagan 2013).

Moving beyond the differences and tensions that exist among Christian theological ideas about migration, **Caroline Jeannerat's** article (Chapter 32, Volume II) examines the 'theological landscape' of the numerous Pentecostal churches with global outreach that cater specifically for Nigerian immigrants in Johannesburg. Although they share interests in faith healing, glossolalia and deliverance from witchcraft and evil spirits these churches develop their own specialised ministries, which are at odds with the 'prosperity gospel' preached by many other Charismatic and Pentecostal churches originating in West Africa (Meyer 1998;

Gifford 2004) and which appeal to distinctive sub-groups of Nigerians. The Zoe Ministries Church in Hillbrow, for example, demands the full engagement of members, including the free use of bodily postures and movements as conduits of communication with the divine – contrary to mainstream Protestantism's insistence on the need for tight control over the body. The physicality of prayers associated with deliverance from evil and witchcraft is another prominent feature of Pentecostal theology and practice which is attractive to Nigerian immigrants because it does not simply reject 'traditional' ideas about the sources of evil: instead, it acknowledges their existence and offers regular spiritual practices to counteract their ongoing impact. Tensions and conflicts with jealous relatives or ancestors, who are portrayed as resentful of the opportunities enjoyed by migrants, are often treated as the sources of evil, curses and trickery. Following Vásquez (Chapter 29, Volume I), the conclusion is that 'Pentecostalism allows members to deal with the tensions of a globalised capital economy that imposes systems of exclusion and lack in third world areas' (Jeannerat, Chapter 32, Volume II: 265).

Gemma Tulud Cruz's article (Chapter 33, Volume II) switches the focus to the millions of Filipina women 'overseas contract workers' and their strategies for combating the compounded discriminations and oppressions based on gender and 'race' or ethnicity that they encounter in their global search for work – in some cases at the hands of their more affluent fellow migrant Filipinos in places such as Hong Kong (Tulud Cruz 2010). Most of them remain practising Catholics, drawing on currents of their Church's theology to support their resistance to marginalisation by means of regular street demonstrations, public gatherings and 'creative' uses of language games in which their sense of 'home' can be re-conceived and conserved. Attendance at Sunday Mass is 'non-negotiable' for the Filipinas in Hong Kong, even if it means making their own 'churches' in parks, gyms and auditoriums. Their experience of migrant religion is more about community and 'collective liberation' than about the individual salvation purveyed in Pentecostal churches (see also Tulud Cruz 2014).

Volume II Part VIII: Controversies

Although theological resources are widely deployed in support of migrants' strategies for refracting, resisting and reinterpreting some of the most damaging aspects of their experiences, controversies continue to beset the nexus between religion and migration (Amiraux and Simon 2006). **Volume II Part VIII** examines some of the controversies that have attracted adverse publicity in Western countries with religious minorities from migrant backgrounds. They range from allegations of fraud (Van Eck Duymaer Van Twist 2014) to the maltreatment of animals in the slaughtering process (Haupt 2007) to uncertainties about disposal of the dead (Gardner 2002), to the use of conspicuous symbols of religious identity in public spaces (Arribas 2009; Edmunds 2012) and to the appointment of chaplains representing minority faiths in publicly funded institutions (Beckford 2012, 2013).

The list of controversies surrounding religion and migration is lengthy and changing, but particularly sensitive issues often arise in connection with the demands made by some religious minorities for the right to slaughter animals for food or for sacrifice in ways which are opposed by people who find the ritual practices offensive or objectionable for various reasons. In fact, **Florence Bergeaud-Blackler's** article (Chapter 34, Volume II) traces the changing nature of objections to Jewish (*shehita*) and Islamic (*dhabiha*) ritual slaughter in a variety of European countries. Anti-semitism lay behind much of the opposition to the Jewish practice of *shehita* in the first half of the twentieth century, but it was not until later in the century that the Islamic practice of *dhabiha* was also found objectionable. Opposition came mainly from animal welfare and rights movements and veterinarians' organisations, but both the Council of Europe and the EU permit these practices as specific exemptions from the regulations that normally require the pre-stunning of animals prior to slaughter. However, countries vary widely in their willingness to grant such an exemption; and legal challenges have been frequent and contentious. More importantly, the stakes have changed to some degree as concerns about animal welfare and rights have been bundled up in controversies about the safety and traceability of food in the context of the BSE problem and consumers' increasingly forceful assertion of their right to choose their food on the basis of reliable knowledge about its provenance and how it was slaughtered. Two unexpected developments have occurred in the controversies. First, theological-cum-legal divisions about aspects of Islamic ritual slaughter have appeared among Muslims. Second, the defenders and the opponents of ritual slaughter seem to have reached agreement that the traceability of food is essential regardless of method of slaughter. In short, controversies that originated with Jewish and Muslim migrations to Europe have evolved into much wider controversies about public health, food security, consumer rights and derogations from European laws.

Another example of a controversy which had its origins in the immigration of religious minorities into the Montréal region of Québec but which has expanded to cover other issues is that of disputes about the planning and siting of new mosques. The article by **Annick Germain** and **Julie Elizabeth Gagnon** (Chapter 35, Volume II) brings to light tensions between Canada's commitment to the ideal of multiculturalism at the federal level and the reluctance of some local administration officials to make urban planning decisions that reflect the same normative orientation. Research on the fate of sixteen planning applications submitted by ethno-religious minorities for places of worship showed that municipal authorities had become less accommodating since the 1960s. Indeed, the City Council placed a moratorium on issuing new permits in 1999 amid controversies about the zoning of land for industrial use, property taxes, residents' quality of life, and the problem of incomplete projects. Particularly controversial issues arose in connection with a proposal from Hassidic Jews to create an *eruv* – a symbolically defined private area for religious purposes – and to build a new synagogue in a residential sector. Thus, plans for the construction of places of worship for ethno-religious minorities gave rise to heated controversies at local level in Montréal and to reconsideration of policies at national level.

Italy is another country where plans for the construction of mosques, beginning late in the twentieth century, also generated intense controversies at local and national level, but **Chantal Saint-Blancat** and **Ottavia Schmidt di Friedberg's** article (Chapter 36, Volume II) draws attention to three additional features of a protracted and notorious Italian case, which centred on the small town of Lodi in the northern region of Lombardy (see also Triandafyllidou 2006; Saint-Blancat 2014). First, the disputes about a local administration's willingness to sell a piece of communal land as the site for an Islamic centre quickly became mapped on to pre-existing tensions and ambiguities in Italian politics. Second, the Lodi case proved to be a template for many subsequent controversies about mosque building plans elsewhere in the country in which politicians and religious leaders exploited the case for their own purposes. And, third, the role of the media – especially in conjunction with the right-wing political movement of *Lega Nord* – significantly aggravated the controversy not only by bridging the local and national levels of disputes but also by situating events in Lodi in the much wider context of 'international anti-Islamic sentiment'. The Lodi case illustrates a more general point about the capacity of controversies concerning religion and migration to attract and refract all manner of other social, political and ethical problems.

Conclusion

The interweaving of religion and migration is complex, subtle and changing. Understanding it requires analysis at different levels of society, at different points in time, in different locations, in different theological frameworks and in conjunction with variables such as ethnicity, gender, nationality, age, generation, and socio-economic status. Moreover, the positive outcomes that are widely attributed to religion's involvement with migratory flows must be fully acknowledged – but also kept in a proportionate perspective. They need to be balanced by an awareness that religions can be implicated in reinforcing negative stereotypes, motivating social exclusion or perpetuating beliefs and practices that could be deemed to undermine the human rights and human dignity of migrants, asylum seekers and refugees. The scale of religion's association with migration also needs to be kept in mind when so many investigations of the topic are based on local ethnographic and congregational studies which are unable to gauge its significance in comparison with expressions of religion having little or no connection with migration.

Improvements in the methods of studying religion and migration in the future will need to take account of changing patterns of both religion and migration. The topic is likely to become more interesting if the proportion of migrants and people in the contexts of reception who describe themselves as non-religious or 'spiritual-but-not-religious' continues to increase while the identification of others with religion continues to intensify at the same time. Immigrants in some societies may find themselves caught up in a process of polarisation along lines of religion/non-religion.

Another likely development in relations between religion and migration is the growing importance of the Internet and of transnational social media in simultaneously facilitating the circulation of migrants and in helping to sustain their separate religious and ethnic identities in their societies of destination. The fact that immigrants can choose to live their religious lives at least partly in 'transnational spaces' adds further interest to long-running public debates in liberal democracies about religious freedom, multiculturalism, secularism, human rights and equalities. In this way, it is possible for the religious ideas and practices of migrants to shape public debates and policymaking in their destination societies – and, in some cases, in their societies of origin as well. In short, the lived religious experiences of migrants are undoubtedly important, but there is also much more at stake in terms of their wider implications for politics, law, public policy, ethics, economics, gender relations, social cohesion, and demography. The articles in this collection are a guide to the range and complexity of these implications.

Acknowledgements

I am grateful for all the encouragement, kindness and assistance that I have received from Professor Robin Cohen, Ruth Atherton and Dr Araceli Suzara.

References

Abascal, Maria and Miguel A. Centeno 2013. 'A holistic approach to language, religion, and ethnicity'. *Studies in Ethnicity and Nationalism* 13(1): 101–4.

Abdullah, Zain 2009. 'African "soul brothers" in the 'hood: immigration, Islam, and the black encounter'. *Anthropological Quarterly* 82(1): 37–62.

Abramson, Harold J. 1979. 'Migrants and cultural diversity: on ethnicity and religion in society'. *Social Compass* 26(1): 5–29.

Adogame, Afe 2003. 'Betwixt identity and security: African new religious movements and the politics of religious networking in Europe'. *Nova Religio* 7(2): 24–41.

Ager, Alastair and Joey Ager 2011. 'Faith and the discourse of secular humanitarianism'. *Journal of Refugee Studies* 24: 440–55.

Alba, R., A.J. Raboteau and J. DeWind (eds) 2009. *Immigration and Religion in America: Comparative and Historical Perspectives.* New York: New York University Press.

Alfonso, Carolin, Waltraud Kokot and Khachig Tölölyan (eds) 2004. *Diaspora, Identity and Religion: New Directions in Theory and Research.* London: Routledge.

Allievi, Stefano and Jørgen Nielsen (eds) 2003. *Muslim Networks and Transnational Communities in and across Europe.* Leiden: Brill.

Amiraux, Valérie and Patrick Simon 2006. 'There are no minorities here. Cultures of scholarship and public debate on immigrants and integration in France'. *International Journal of Comparative Sociology* 47(3–4): 191–215.

Antoniou, Dimitris 2005. 'Western Thracian Muslims in Athens. From economic migration to religious organization'. *Balkanologie. Revue d'Etudes Pluridisciplinaires* 9(1–2): 79–101.

Arribas, Santiago Cañamares 2009. 'Religious symbols in Spain: a legal perspective'. *Ecclesiastical Law Journal* 11(2): 181–93.

Asamoah-Gyadu, J.K. 2012. '"To the ends of the earth": mission, migration and the impact of African-led Pentecostal churches in the European diaspora'. *Mission Studies: Journal of the International Association for Mission Studies* 29(1): 23–44.

Bader, Veit 2009. 'The governance of religious diversity: theory, research, and practice', in Bramadat, P. and Koenig, M. (eds), *International Migration and the Governance of Religious Diversity* (pp. 43–72). Kingston, ON: School of Policy Studies, Queen's University.

Badillo, David A. 2001. 'Religion and transnational migration in Chicago: the case of the Potosinos'. *Journal of the Illinois State Historical Society* 94(4): 420–40.

Barot, Rohit 2002. 'Religion, migration and wealth creation in the Swaminarayan movement', in Fahy Bryceson, D. and Vuorela, U. (eds), *The Transnational Family: New European Frontiers and Global Networks* (pp. 197–216). Oxford: Berg.

Bastenier, Albert and Felice Dassetto 1979. 'Hypothèses pour une analyse des stratégies religieuses au sein du monde migratoire en Europe', *Social Compass* 26(1): 145–70.

Baumann, Martin 2009a. 'Templeisation: continuity and change of Hindu traditions in diaspora', *Journal of Religion in Europe* 2(2): 149–79.

Baumann, Martin 2009b. 'Temples, cupolas, minarets: public space as contested terrain in contemporary Switzerland'. *Religio* 17(2): 141–53.

Bava, Sophi 2011. 'Migration–religion studies in France: evolving toward a religious anthropology of the movement'. *Annual Review of Anthropology* 40: 493–507.

Beckford, James A. 2003. *Social Theory and Religion.* Cambridge: Cambridge University Press.

Beckford, James A. 2012. 'Public responses to religious diversity in Britain and France', in Beaman, L.G. (ed.), *Reasonable Accommodation. Managing Religious Diversity* (pp.109–38). Vancouver: UBC Press.

Beckford, James A. 2013. 'Religious diversity in prisons: chaplaincy and contention'. *Studies in Religion/ Sciences Religieuses* 42: 190–205.

Beckford, James A. and Sophie Gilliat 1998. *Religion in Prison: Equal Rites in a Multi-Faith Society.* Cambridge: Cambridge University Press.

Beckford, James A., Danièle Joly and Farhad Khosrokhavar 2005. *Muslims in Prison: Challenge and Change in Britain and France.* Basingstoke: Palgrave Macmillan.

Bendixsen, Synnove 2010. 'Islam as a new urban ministry? Young female Muslims creating a religious youth culture in Berlin', in Bonafacio, G.T. and Angelese, V.S.M. (eds), *Religion, Gender, and Migration* (pp. 95–114). Plymouth: Lexington Books.

Benthall, Jonathan and Jérôme Bellion-Jourdan 2009. *The Charitable Crescent: Politics of Aid in the Muslim World.* London: I.B. Tauris.

Berkley Center for Religion, Peace and World Affairs 2008. *Religion, Migration and Foreign Policy.* Georgetown: Berkley Center for Religion, Peace and World Affairs.

Bertossi, Christophe 2007. 'Ethnicity, Islam and allegiances in the French military', in Bertossi, C. (ed.), *European Anti-Discrimination and the Politics of Citizenship: France and Britain* (pp. 193–216). Basingstoke: Palgrave Macmillan.

Beyer, Peter 2006. *Religion in a Global Society.* London: Routledge.

Beyer, Peter 2012. 'Religion and immigration in a changing Canada: the reasonable accommodation of "reasonable accommodation"?', in Beaman, L.G. (ed.), *Reasonable Accommodation. Managing Religious Diversity* (pp. 13–31). Vancouver: UBC Press.

Beyer, Peter 2013. 'Religion in the contemporary globalised world: construction, migration, challenge, diversity', in Hefner, R.W., Hutchinson, J., Mels, S. and Timmerman, C. (eds), *Religions in Movement* (pp. 159–79). New York: Routledge.

Blanchet, Thérèse 2010. 'Migration to the bars of Bombay: women, village religion and sustainability'. *Women's Studies International Forum* 33(4): 345–53.

Bonifacio, Glenda Tibe and Vivienne S.M. Angeles (eds) 2010. *Gender, Religion, and Migration: Pathways of Integration.* Plymouth: Lexington.

Boubeker, Ahmed 2013. 'The outskirts of politics: the struggles of the descendants of postcolonial immigration in France'. *French Cultural Studies* 24(2): 184–95.

Bowen, John 2009. 'Recognising Islam in France after 9/11'. *Journal of Ethnic and Migration Studies* 35(3): 439–52.

Bramadat, Paul and Matthias Koenig (eds) 2009. *International Migration and the Governance of Religious Diversity.* Montreal and Kingston: McGill-Queen's University Press.

Breathnach, Ciara 2013. 'Irish Catholic identity in 1870s Otago, New Zealand'. *Immigrants and Minorities* 31(1): 1–26.

Brubaker, Rogers 2013. 'Language, religion and the politics of difference'. *Nations and Nationalism* 19(1): 1–20.

Bruce, Tricia 2006. 'Contested accommodation on the meso level: discursive adaptation within Catholic charities' immigration and refugee service'. *American Behavioral Scientist* 49(11): 1489–508.

Buenaventura, Steffi San 1996. 'Filipino folk spirituality and immigration: from mutual aid to religion'. *Amerasia Journal* 22(1): 1.

Burkhalter, Sarah 2001. 'Négociations autour du cimetière musulman en Suisse: un exemple de recomposition religieuse en situation d'immigration'. *Archives de Sciences Sociales des Religions* 113.

Burnley, Ian 2010. 'Submergence, persistence and identity: generations of German origin in the Barossa and Adelaide Hills, South Australia'. *Geographical Research* 48(4): 427–39.

Cadge, Wendy and Elaine H. Ecklund 2006. 'Religious service attendance among immigrants: evidence from the New Immigrant Survey – Pilot'. *American Behavioral Scientist* 49(11): 1574–95.

Cadge, Wendy and Elaine H. Ecklund 2007. 'Immigration and religion'. *Annual Review of Sociology* 33: 359–79.

Cadge, Wendy, Peggy Levitt, Bernadette Nadya Jaworsky and Casey Clevenger 2013. 'Religious dimensions of contexts of reception: comparing two New England cities'. *International Migration* 51(3): 84–98.

Casanova, José and Aristide Zolberg 2003. *Religion and Immigrant Incorporation in New York.* New York: International Center for Immigration, Ethnicity and Citizenship.

Castles, Stephen, Hein de Haas and Mark J. Miller 2014. *The Age of Migration: International Population Movements on the Modern World* (5th edition). Basingstoke: Palgrave Macmillan.

Cesari, Jocelyne 2005. 'Mosque conflicts in European cities: introduction'. *Journal of Ethnic and Migration Studies* 31(6): 1015–24.

Chen, Carolyn 2005. 'A self of one's own: Taiwanese immigrant women and religious conversion'. *Gender & Society* 19(3): 336–57.

Cherry, Stephen M. and Helen Rose Ebaugh (eds) 2014. *Global Religious Movements across Borders*. Farnham: Ashgate.

Chinouya, Martha and Eileen O'Keefe. 2005. 'God will look after us: Africans, HIV and religion in Milton Keynes'. *Diversity in Health and Social Care* 2(3): 177–86.

Cohen, Jeffrey H. 2011. 'Migration, remittances, and household strategies'. *Annual Review of Anthropology* 40: 103–14.

Coleman, Simon 2000. *The Globalisation of Charismatic Christianity. Spreading the Gospel of Prosperity*. Cambridge: Cambridge University Press.

Connor, Phillip 2011. 'Religion as resource: religion and immigrant economic incorporation'. *Social Science Research* 40(5): 1350–61.

Connor, Phillip 2012. 'International migration and religious selection'. *Journal for the Scientific Study of Religion* 51(1): 184–94.

Connor, Phillip 2014. *Immigrant Faith: Patterns of Immigrant Religion in the United States, Canada, and Western Europe*. New York: New York University Press.

Connor, Phillip and Catherine Tucker 2011. 'Religion and migration around the globe: introducing the global religion and migration database'. *International Migration Review* 45(4): 985–1000.

Cowan, Douglas E. 2007. 'Religion on the Internet', in Beckford, J.A. and Demerath III, N.J. (eds), *The SAGE Handbook of the Sociology of Religion* (pp. 357–76). London: Sage.

Davis, Nancy J. and Robert V. Robinson 2012. *Claiming Society for God: Religious Movements and Social Welfare*. Bloomington, IN: Indiana University Press.

Day, Lincoln H. and Ahmet Icduygu 1998. 'International migration, religious observance, and attitudes in Turkey', *Journal for the Scientific Study of Religion* 37(4): 596–607.

De Araújo Silva, Marcos and Donizete Rodrigues 2013. 'Religion, migration and gender strategies: Brazilian (Catholic and Evangelical) missionaries in Barcelona', *Religion and Gender* 3(1): 42–59.

De Castro, Cristina Maria 2010. 'Muslim women in Brazil: notes on religion and integration', in Bonifacio, G.T. and Angeles, V.S.M. (eds), *Religion, Gender, and Migration* (pp. 167–81). Plymouth: Lexington Books.

De Voe, Pamela A. 2002. 'Symbolic action: religion's role in the changing environment of young Somali women', *Journal of Refugee Studies* 15(2): 234–46.

DeMarinis, Valerie 2014. 'Migration and religion', in Leeming, D.A. (ed.), *Encyclopedia of Psychology and Religion* (pp. 1109–12). New York: Springer.

Dhar, Ruby 2012. 'Women and international migration: a cross-cultural analysis', *Social Change* 42(1): 93–102.

Dolan, Jay P. 1998. 'The immigrants and their gods: a new perspective in American religious history', in Butler, J. and Stout, H.S. (eds), *Religion in American History: A Reader* (pp. 146–56). New York: Oxford University Press.

Dwyer, Claire, David Gilbert and Bindi Shah 2013. 'Faith and suburbia: secularisation, modernity and the changing geographies of religion in London's suburbs'. *Transactions of the Institute of British Geographers* 38: 403–19.

Ebaugh, Helen Rose 2010. 'Transnationality and religion in immigrant congregations: the global impact'. *Nordic Journal of Religion and Society* 23(2): 105–19.

Ebaugh, Helen Rose and Janet S. Chafetz 2000. *Religion and the New Immigrants: Continuities and Adaptations in Immigrant Congregations*. Walnut Creek, CA: AltaMira Press.

Ebaugh, Helen Rose and Paula Pipes 2001. 'Immigrant congregations as social service providers: are they safety nets for welfare reform', in Nesbitt, P.D. (ed.), *Religion and Social Policy* (pp. 95–110). Walnut Creek, CA: AltaMira Press.

Edelstein, Monika D. 2002. 'Lost tribes and coffee ceremonies: *Zar* spirit possession and the ethno-religious identity of Ethiopian Jews in Israel'. *Journal of Refugee Studies* 15(2): 153–70.

Edmunds, June 2012. 'The limits of post-national citizenship: European Muslims, human rights and the hijab'. *Journal of Ethnic and Migration Studies* 35: 1181–99.

Ehrkamp, Patricia and Caroline Nagel 2012. 'Immigration, places of worship and the politics of citizenship in the US South'. *Transactions of the Institute of British Geographers* 37(4): 624–38.

Eickelman, Dale and James Piscatori (eds) 1990. *Muslim Travellers: Pilgrimage, Migration, and the Religious Imagination*. London: Routledge.

Ekué, Amélé Adamavi-Aho 2009. 'Migrant Christians: believing wanderers between cultures and nations'. *Ecumenical Review* 61(4): 387–99.

European Union, Directorate-General for Research and Innovation 2011. 'Pluralism and religious diversity, social cohesion and integration in Europe Insights from European research'. Brussels: EU, Directorate-General for Research and Innovation, Socio-Economic Sciences and Humanities.

Fleischmann, Fenella and Karen Phalet 2012. 'Integration and religiosity among the Turkish second generation in Europe: a comparative analysis across four capital cities'. *Ethnic and Racial Studies* 35(2): 320–41.

Furseth, Inger 2011. 'The hijab: boundary work and identity negotiations among immigrant Muslim women in the Los Angeles area'. *Review of Religious Research* 52(4): 365–85.

Gale, R. 2005. 'Representing the city: mosques and the planning process in Birmingham'. *Journal of Ethnic and Migration Studies*, 31: 1161–79.

Gale, R. 2013. 'Religious residential segregation and internal migration: the British Muslim case'. *Environment and Planning A* 45: 872–91.

Gale, Richard and Simon Naylor 2002. 'Religion, planning and the city: the spatial politics of ethnic minority expression in British cities and towns'. *Ethnicities* 2: 387–409.

Gallo, Ester (ed.) 2014. *Migration and Religion in Europe: Comparative Perspectives on South Asian Experiences*. Farnham: Ashgate.

Gallo, Ester and Silvia Sai 2013. 'Should we talk about religion? Migrant associations, local politics and representations of religious diversity: the case of Sikh communities in central Italy', in Blanes, R. and Mapril, J. (eds), *Sites of Politics and Religious Diversity in Southern Europe: The Best of All Gods* (pp. 279–308). Leiden: Brill.

Galush, William J. 2002. 'Journeys of spirit and space: religion and economics in migration'. *Polish American Studies* 59(2): 5–16.

Garbin, David 2014. 'Regrounding the sacred: transnational religion, place making and the politics of diaspora among the Congolese in London and Atlanta'. *Global Networks* 14: 363–82.

Gardner, Katy 2002. 'Death of a migrant: transnational death rituals and gender among British Sylhetis'. *Global Networks* 2: 191–204.

Garnett, Jane and Alana Harris (eds) 2013. *Rescripting Religion in the City. Migration and Religious Identity in the Modern Metropolis*. Farnham: Ashgate.

Gerloff, Roswith. 2010. 'The African diaspora and the shaping of Christianity in Africa: perspectives on religion, migration, identity and collaboration'. *Missionalia: Southern African Journal of Mission Studies* 38(2): 307–20.

Gifford, Paul 2004. *Ghana's New Christianity. Pentecostalism in a Globalising African Economy*. London: Hurst & Company.

Gilliat-Ray, Sophie, Mansur Ali and Stephen Pattison 2013. *Understanding Muslim Chaplaincy*. Farnham: Ashgate.

Gogonas, Nikos 2012. 'Religion as a core value in language maintenance: Arabic speakers in Greece'. *International Migration* 50(2): 113–29.

Golden, Renny and Michael McConnell 1986. *Sanctuary: The New Underground Railroad*. New York: Orbis.

Gorman, Robert F. 2011. 'Classical diasporas of the third kind: the hidden history of Christian dispersion'. *Journal of Refugee Studies* 24(4): 635–54.

Grillo, Ralph 2004. 'Islam and transnationalism'. *Journal of Ethnic and Migration Studies* 30(5): 861–78.

Groody, Daniel G. 2009. Crossing the divide: foundations of a theology of migration and refugees. *Theological Studies* 70: 638–67.

Gunn, T. Jeremy 2004. 'Under God but not the scarf: the founding myths of religious freedom in the United States and laïcité in France'. *Journal of Church and State* 46: 7–24.

Haddad, Yvonne Y., Jane I. Smith and John L. Esposito (eds) 2003. *Religion and Immigration: Christian, Jewish, and Muslim Experiences in the United States*. Walnut Creek, CA: AltaMira Press.

Hagan, Jacqueline M. 2013. 'Crossing borders: transnational sanctuary, social justice, and the Church', in Bender, C., Cadge, W., Levitt, P. and Smilde, D. (eds), *Religion on the Edge. De-Centering and Re-Centering the Sociology of Religion* (pp. 263–83). New York: Oxford University Press.

Hagan, Jacqueline M. and Helen Rose Ebaugh 2003. 'Calling upon the sacred: migrants' use of religion in the migration process'. *International Migration Review* 37: 1145–62.

Hammond, Phillip E. 1963. 'The migrating sect: an illustration from early Norwegian immigration'. *Social Forces* 41: 275–83.

Handlin, Oscar 1951. *The Uprooted: The Epic Story of the Great Migrations that Made the American People*. Boston: Little, Brown and Company.

Hattam, Victoria and Carlos Yescas 2010. 'From immigration and race to sex and faith: reimagining the politics of opposition'. *Social Research* 77(1): 133–62.

Haupt, Claudia E. 2007. 'Free exercise of religion and animal protection: a comparative perspective on ritual slaughter'. *George Washington International Law Review* 39: 839–86.

Herberg, Will 1955. *Protestant, Catholic, Jew: An Essay in American Religious Sociology*. Garden City, NY: Doubleday & Co.

Hirschman, Charles 2004. 'The role of religion in the origins and adaptation of immigrant groups in the United States'. *International Migration Review* 38(3): 1206–33.

Højsgaard, Morten T. and Margit Warburg (eds) 2005. *Religion and Cyberspace*. London: Routledge.

Hollenbach, David 2011. 'Migration as a challenge for theological ethics'. *Political Theology* 12(6): 807–12.

Ives, Nicole, Jill Witmer Sinha and Ram Cnaan 2010. 'Who is welcoming the stranger? Exploring faith-based service provision to refugees in Philadelphia'. *Journal of Religion and Spirituality in Social Work* 29(1): 71–89.

Jackson, Vivienne 2013. '"This is not the Holy Land": gendered Filipino migrants in Israel and the intersectional diversity of religious belonging', *Religion and Gender* 3(1): 6–21.

Jayaweera, Hiranthi and Tufyal Choudhury 2008. *Immigration, Faith and Cohesion. Evidence from Local Areas with Significant Muslim Populations*. York: Joseph Rowntree Foundation.

Jeannerat, Caroline 2009. 'Of lizards, misfortune and deliverance: Pentecostal soteriology in the life of a migrant', *African Studies* 68(2): 251–71.

Jensz, Felicity 2010. 'Religious migration and political upheaval: German Moravians at Bethel in South Australia, 1851–1907'. *Australian Journal of Politics and History* 56(3): 351–65.

Jonker, Gerdien 2005. 'Mosques and the public space: conflict and cooperation in Bradford.' *Journal of Ethnic and Migration Studies* 31(6): 1067–81.

Joppke, Christian 2009. 'Limits of integration policy: Britain and her Muslims'. *Journal of Ethnic and Migration Studies* 35(3): 453–72.

Juergensmeyer, Mark (ed.) 2003. *Global Religions. An Introduction*. New York: Oxford University Press.

Karagiannis, Evangelos and Nina Glick Schiller 2006. 'Contesting claims to the land: Pentecostalism as a challenge to migration theory and policy'. *Sociologus* 56(2): 137–71.

Karyotis, Georgios and Stratos Patrikios 2010. 'Religion, securitization and anti-immigration attitudes: the case of Greece'. *Journal of Peace Research* 47(1): 43–57.

Kastoryano, Riva 2004. 'Religion and incorporation: Islam in France and Germany'. *International Migration Review* 38(3): 1234–55.

Kaya, Ayhan 2009. *Islam, Migration and Integration: The Age of Securitization*. Basingstoke: Palgrave Macmillan.

Kivisto, Peter 2014. *Religion and Immigration: Migrant Faiths in North America and Western Europe*. Cambridge: Polity Press.

Knoll, Benjamin R. 2009. '"And who is my neighbor?" Religion and immigration policy attitudes', *Journal for the Scientific Study of Religion* 48(2): 313–31.

Knott, Kim 2005. *The Location of Religion: A Spatial Analysis*. London: Equinox.

Kong, Lily 2010. 'Global shifts, theoretical shifts: changing geographies of religion'. *Progress in Human Geography* 34: 755–76.

Kotin, Stephanie, Grace R. Dyrness and Clara Irazábal 2011. 'Immigration and integration'. *Progress in Development Studies* 11(4): 263–84.

Kymlicka, Will 2009. 'The governance of religious diversity: the old and the new', in Paul Bramadat, P. and Koenig, M. (eds), *International Migration and the Governance of Religious Diversity* (pp. 323–34). Kingston, Ontario: School of Policy Studies, Queen's University.

Lehmann, David 2002. 'Religion and globalization', in Woodhead, L., Fletcher, P., Kawanami, H. and Smith, D. (eds), *Religions in the Modern World* (pp. 299–315). London: Routledge.

Leonard, Karen I., Alex Stepick, Manuel A. Vásquez and Jennifer Holdaway (eds) 2005. *Immigrant Faiths: Transforming Religious Life in America*. Walnut Creek, CA: AltaMira Press.

Levitt, Peggy 2013. 'Religion on the move: mapping global cultural production and consumption', in Bender, C., Cadge, W., Levitt, P. and Smilde, D. (eds), *Religion on the Edge. De-Centering and Re-Centering the Sociology of Religion* (pp. 159–75). New York: Oxford University Press.

Levitt, Peggy, Josh DeWind and Steven Vertovec 2003. 'International perspectives on transnational migration'. *International Migration Review* 37(3): 565–75.

Lorentzen, Lois Ann and Rosalina Mira 2005. 'El milagro está en casa: gender and private/public empowerment in a migrant Pentecostal church'. *Latin American Perspectives* 32(1): 57–71.

Lövheim, Mia and Marta Axner 2011. 'Halal-TV: negotiating the place of religion in Swedish public discourse', *Nordic Journal of Religion and Society* 24(1): 57–74.

Maliepaard, Mieke, Marcel Lubbers and Mérove Gijsberts 2012. 'Generational differences in ethnic and religious attachment and their interrelation: a study among Muslim minorities in the Netherlands'. *Journal of Ethnic and Migration Studies* 33(3): 451–72.

Martikainen, Tuomas 2014. 'Immigrant religions and the context of reception in advanced industrial societies', in Vilaça, H., Pace, E., Furseth, I. and Pettersson, P. (eds), *The Changing Soul of Europe* (pp. 47–65). Farnham: Ashgate.

Martin, Marie-Louise 1975. *Kimbangu: An African Prophet and His Church*. Oxford: Blackwell.

McAuliffe, Cameron 2007. 'A home far away? Religious identity and transnational relations in the Iranian diaspora'. *Global Networks* 7(3): 307–27.

McLoughlin, Sean 2005. 'Mosques and the public space: conflict and cooperation in Bradford'. *Journal of Ethnic and Migration Studies* 31(6): 1045–66.

Mellor, Jody and Sophie Gilliat-Ray 2015. 'The early history of migration and settlement of Yemenis in Cardiff, 1939–1970: religion and ethnicity as social capital'. *Ethnic and Racial Studies* 38(1): 176–91.

Men, Chean Rithy 2002. 'The changing religious beliefs and ritual practices among Cambodians in diaspora'. *Journal of Refugee Studies* 15(2): 222–33.

Menjívar, Cecilia 2003. 'Religion and immigration in comparative perspective: Catholic and Evangelical Salvadorans in San Francisco, Washington, D.C., and Phoenix'. *Sociology of Religion* 64(1): 21–45.

Meyer, Birgit 1998. 'The power of money: politics, occult forces, and Pentecostalism in Ghana'. *African Studies Review* 41: 15–37.

Meyer, Birgit 2004. 'Christianity in Africa: from African independent to Pentecostal-charismatic churches'. *Annual Review of Anthropology* 33: 447–74.

Meyer, Birgit 2006. 'Religious revelation, secrecy and the limits of visual representation'. *Anthropological Theory* 6: 431–53.

Moberg Robinson, Emily 2013. 'Sacred memory: the covenanter use of history in Scotland and America'. *Journal of Transatlantic Studies* 11(2): 135–57.

Modood, Tariq 1998. 'Anti-essentialism, multiculturalism and the "recognition" of religious groups'. *Journal of Political Philosophy* 6(4): 356–77.

Mol, Hans 1979. 'Theory and data on the religious behaviour of migrants'. *Social Compass* 26(1): 31–39.

Mutema, Gaudencia 2010. 'Religion and African migration: a survey'. *Religion Compass* 4(5): 271–86.

Nawyn, Stephanie J. 2006. 'Faith, ethnicity, and culture in refugee resettlement'. *American Behavioral Scientist* 49(11): 1509–27.

Nielsen, Helene Pristed 2010. 'Islam: a dead end for integration of female immigrants in Denmark?' in Bonifacio, G.T. and Angeles, V.S.M. (eds), *Religion, Gender, and Migration* (pp. 133–46). Plymouth: Lexington Books.

Nissimi, Hilda 2009. 'Individual redemption and family commitment: the influence of mass immigration to Israel on the Crypto-Jewish women of Mashhad'. *Nashim: A Journal of Jewish Women's Studies & Gender Issues* 18: 39–70.

Norman, Jon 2011. 'The fluidity of human capital: theorizing the relationship between religion and immigration'. *Method and Theory in the Study of Religion* 23(1): 48–63.

Nteta, Tatishe M. and K.J. Wallsten 2012. 'Preaching to the choir? Religious leaders and American opinion on immigration reform'. *Social Science Quarterly* 93(4): 891–910.

Olagoke, Abolade Ezekiel 2010. 'Ethno-religious power: Yoruba immigrant women in the United States', in Bonifacio, G.T. and Angeles, V.S.M. (eds), *Gender, Religion, and Migration* (pp. 217–35). Plymouth: Lexington Books.

Oxford, Connie 2010. 'No greater law: illegal immigration and faith-based activism' in Bonifacio, G.T. and Angeles, V.S.M. (eds), *Gender, Religion, and Migration* (pp. 275–89). Plymouth: Lexington Books.

Pace, Enzo 2014. 'Religion in motion: migration, religion and social theory', in Vilaça, H., Pace, E., Furseth, I. and Pettersson, P. (eds), *The Changing Soul of Europe. Religions and Migrations in Northern and Southern Europe* (pp. 9–23). Farnham: Ashgate.

Pasura, Dominic 2013. 'Modes of incorporation and transnational Zimbabwean migration to Britain', *Ethnic and Racial Studies* 36(1): 199–218.

Pew Research Center. 2012. *Faith on the Move. The Religious Affiliation of International Migrants*. Princeton, NJ: Pew Research Center.

Pew Research Center. 2013. *The Religious Affiliation of U.S. Immigrants: Majority Christian, Rising Share of Other Faiths*. Princeton, NJ: Pew Research Center.

Pew Research Center. 2015. *The Future of World Religions: Population Growth Projections, 2010–2050. Why Muslims are Rising Fastest and the Unaffiliated are Shrinking as a Share of the World's Population*. Washington, DC: Pew Research Center.

Plüss, Caroline 2009. 'Migration and the globalization of religion', in Clarke, P.B. (ed.), *The Oxford Handbook of the Sociology of Religion* (pp. 491–506). Oxford: Oxford University Press.

Pype, Katrien 2013. 'Religion, migration and media aesthetics: notes on the circulation and reception of Nigerian films in Kinshasha', in Krings, M. and Okome, O. (eds), *Global Nollywood: The Transnational Dimensions of an African Video Film Industry* (pp. 199–222). Bloomington, IN: Indiana University Press.

Quero, Hugo Córdova and Rafael Shoji (eds) 2014. *Transnational Faiths. Latin-American Immigrants and their Religions in Japan*. Farnham: Ashgate.

Raijman, Rebecca and Adriana Kemp 2004. 'Consuming the Holy Spirit in the Holy Land: evangelical churches, labor migration and the Jewish state', in Carmeli, Y.S. and Applbaum, K. (eds), *Consumption and Market Society in Israel* (pp. 163–84). Oxford: Berg.

Read, Jen'nan Ghazal 2015. 'Gender, religious identity, and civic engagement among Arab Muslims in the United States', *Sociology of Religion* 76(1): 30–48.

Reitz, Jeffrey G., Rupa Banerjee, Mai Phan and Jordan Thompson 2009. 'Race, religion, and the social integration of new immigrant minorities in Canada', *International Migration Review* 43(4): 695–726.

Rex, John 1992. 'The integration of Muslim immigrants in Britain'. *Innovation* 5(3): 91–107.

Robbins, Joel 2004. 'The globalization of Pentecostal and charismatic Christianity'. *Annual Review of Anthropology* 33: 117–43.

Robertson, Roland 2003. 'Antiglobal religion' in Juergensmeyer, M. (ed.), *Global Religions: An Introduction* (pp. 110–23). New York: Oxford University Press.

Rose, Ananda 2012. *Showdown in the Sonoran Desert: Religion, Law, and the Immigration Controversy*. New York: Oxford University Press.

Sabar, Galia 2004. 'African Christianity in the Jewish state: adaptation, accommodation and legitimization of migrant workers' churches, 1990–2003'. *Journal of Religion in Africa* 34(4): 407–37.

Saint-Blancat, Chantal 2014. 'Italy', in Cesari, J. (ed.), *The Oxford Handbook of European Islam* (pp. 265–310). Oxford: Oxford University Press.

Sarat, Leah 2013. *Fire in the Canyon: Religion, Migration, and the American Dream*. New York: New York University Press.

Scourfield, Jonathan, Chris Taylor, Graham Moore and Sophie Gilliat-Ray 2012. 'The intergenerational transmission of Islam in England and Wales: evidence from the citizenship survey'. *Sociology* 46(1): 91–108.

Sherkat, Darren 2012. 'Immigration, religion and economics', in Macleary, R. (ed.), *Oxford Handbook of the Economics of Religion* (pp. 151–67). Oxford: Oxford University Press.

Skirbekk, Vegard, Éric Caron Malenfant, Stuart Basten and Marcin Stonawski 2012. 'The religious composition of the Chinese diaspora, focusing on Canada'. *Journal for the Scientific Study of Religion* 51(1): 173–83.

Solari, Cinzia 2006. 'Transnational politics and settlement practices: Post-Soviet immigrant churches in Rome', *American Behavioral Scientist* 49(11): 1528–53.

Stambouli, Jamel and Sonia Ben Soltane 2010. 'Muslim immigrants in France: religious markets and new mechanisms of integration', in Bonifacio, G.T. and Angeles, V.S.M. (eds), *Religion, Gender, and Migration* (pp. 147–66). Plymouth: Lexington Books.

Tan, Jonathan Y. 2012. 'Migration in Asia and its missiological implications: insights from the migration theology of the Federation of Asians Bishops' Conferences (FABC)', *Mission Studies: Journal of the International Association for Mission Studies* 29(1): 45–61.

Triandafyllidou, Anna 2006. 'Religious diversity and multiculturalism in Southern Europe: the Italian mosque debate', in Modood, T., Triandafyllidou, A. and Zapata-Barrero, R. (eds), *Multiculturalism, Muslims and Citizenship* (pp. 117–42). London: Routledge.

Troeva, Evgenia and Mila Mancheva 2011. 'Migration, religion and gender: female Muslim immigrants in Bulgaria', in Hajdinjak, M. (eds), *Migrations, Gender and Intercultural Interactions in Bulgaria* (pp. 155–92). Sofia: International Center for Minority Studies and Intercultural Relations.

Trzebiatowska, Marta 2010. 'The advent of the 'easyJet priest': dilemmas of Polish Catholic integration in the UK', *Sociology* 44(6): 1055–72.

Tulud Cruz, Gemma 2010. 'It cuts both ways: religion and Filipina domestic workers in Hong Kong', in Bonifacio, G.T. and Angeles, V.S.M. (eds), *Gender, Religion, and Migration* (pp. 17–36). Lanham, MD: Lexington Books.

Tulud Cruz, Gemma 2014. *Toward a Theology of Migration: Social Justice and Religious Experience.* New York: Palgrave Macmillan.

Van Eck Duymaer Van Twist, Amanda (ed.) 2014. *Minority Religions and Fraud.* Farnham: Ashgate.

Vásquez, Manuel A. 2008. 'Studying religion in motion: a networks approach'. *Method and Theory in the Study of Religion* 20(2): 151–84.

Vásquez, Manuel A. 2011. *More Than Belief: A Materialist Theory of Religion.* New York: Oxford University Press.

Vellenga, Sipco J. 2008. '"Huntington" in Holland: the public debate on Muslim immigrants in the Netherlands'. *Nordic Journal of Religion and Society* 21(1): 21–41.

Vertovec, Steven 2007a. 'Introduction: new directions in the anthropology of migration and multiculturalism', *Ethnic and Racial Studies* 30: 961–78.

Vertovec, Steven 2007b. 'Super-diversity and its implications'. *Ethnic and Racial Studies* 30: 1024–54.

Vilaça, Helena, Enzo Pace, Inger Furseth and Per Pettersson (eds) 2014. *The Changing Soul of Europe: Religions and Migrations in Northern and Southern Europe.* Farnham: Ashgate.

Voas, David 2009. 'The rise and fall of fuzzy fidelity in Europe', *European Sociological Review* 25(2): 155–68.

Voas, David and Fenella Fleischmann 2012. 'Islam moves West: religious change in the first and second generations'. *Annual Review of Sociology* 38: 525–45.

Vujcich, Daniel 2007. 'Faith, flight and foreign policy: effects of war and migration on Western Australian Bosnian Muslims', *Australian Journal of Social Issues* 42(1): 71–86.

Wanner, Catherine 2004. 'Missionaries of faith and culture: evangelical encounters in Ukraine'. *Slavic Review* 63(4): 732–55.

Warner, R. Stephen and Judith Wittner (eds) 1998. *Gatherings in Diaspora: Religious Communities and the New Immigration.* Philadelphia, PA: Temple University Press.

Werbner, Pnina 2002. 'The place which is diaspora: citizenship, religion and gender in the making of chaordic transnationalism'. *Journal of Ethnic and Migration Studies* 28(1): 119–33.

Werbner, Pnina 2005. 'Pakistani migration and diaspora religious politics in a global age', in Ember, M., Ember, C.R. and Skoggard, I. (eds), *Encyclopedia of Diasporas* (pp. 475–84). New York: Springer.

Willis, Katie and Brenda Yeoh (eds) 2000. *Gender and Migration.* Cheltenham, UK and Northampton, MA: Edward Elgar Publishing.

Wong, Diana and Peggy Levitt 2014. 'Travelling faiths and migrant religions: the case of circulating models of *da'wa* among the Tablighi Jamaat and Foguangshan in Malaysia', *Global Networks* 14(3): 348–62.

Wong, Sam 2013a. 'Gendering religious capital. A case study of female mainland Chinese migrants in Hong Kong', in Reilly, N. and Scriver, S. (eds), *Religion, Gender, and the Public Sphere* (pp. 45–57). New York: Routledge.

Wong, Sam 2013b. 'Using religious capital to alleviate poverty? A case study of cross-border migration in South-China'. *International Development Policy: Religion and Development* 4: 174–91.

Yang, Fenggang and Helen Rose Ebaugh 2001. 'Transformations in new immigrant religions and their global implications'. *American Sociological Review* 66(2): 269–88.

Zetter, Roger, David Griffiths, Nando Sigona, Don Flynn, Tauhid Pasha and Rhian Beynon 2006. *Immigration, Social Cohesion and Social Capital*. York: Joseph Rowntree Foundation.

Zoller, Elisabeth 2006. 'Laïcité in the United States or the separation of church and state in a pluralist society'. *Indiana Journal of Global Legal Studies* 13: 561–94.

Part I
Overviews of Migration and Religion

[1]

■ Sociological Forum

Sociological Forum, Vol. 24, No. 4, December 2009 (© 2009)
DOI: 10.1111/j.1573-7861.2009.01136.x

International Migration and Religious Participation: The Mediating Impact of Individual and Contextual Effects[1]

Phillip Connor[2]

Supported by previous empirical work, theory from sociology of religion and migration provide testable hypotheses in predicting changes in immigrant religious participation surrounding the migratory event. Due to data constraints, however, these hypotheses have escaped broad-based analysis. Using the New Immigrant Survey (NIS), religious participation from pre- to postmigration time periods is found to decrease among recent immigrants to the United States. Individual-level characteristics (i.e., gender, familial conditions, employment) do not substantially explain this decline; alternatively, contextual-level factors (i.e., religious pluralism and religious concentration) partially mediate this drop in immigrant religiosity.

KEY WORDS: cross-sectional time series; immigrant religion context; immigration; New Immigrant Survey; religion.

INTRODUCTION

The act of migration is described as a "theologizing" experience (Smith, 1978). In fact, many ethnographic studies demonstrate that migrants use spiritual terms to portray their migratory experiences (Chen, 2008; Hagan, 2006; Hagan and Ebaugh, 2003). Some note that the resettlement period also involves an increase in religious consciousness (Kurien, 2002; Warner, 1998). Additionally, religion serves as a prominent vehicle for the migrant's incorporation into U.S. society (Chen, 2008; Handlin, 1973; Herberg, 1960; Kurien, 1998). But is migration a spiritual pilgrimage, or is it a disruptive event that decreases religious participation? How do individual- and contextual-level characteristics mediate any rise or decline in religious behavior?

[1] Thanks are expressed to Douglas Massey and Monica Higgins for their assistance in accessing the restricted data files for the New Immigrant Survey as well as their helpful comments. I also thank Robert Wuthnow, Elaine Howard Ecklund, Hana Shepherd, the editor of this journal, and three anonymous reviewers for their comments on earlier versions of this article. This article represents a revised version of an earlier draft presented to the Society for the Scientific Study of Religion Meetings in Tampa, Florida in 2007. I also gratefully acknowledge the support of Princeton University's Center for the Study of Religion in funding this research.
[2] Department of Sociology, 119 Wallace Hall, Princeton University, Princeton, New Jersey 08544. E-mail: pconnor@princeton.edu.

Immigrant religiosity has become an important issue to both religion and migration scholars (Ebaugh and Chafetz, 2000; Edgell and Docka, 2007; Hirschman, 2004; Massey and Higgins, 2007; Portes and Rumbaut, 2006; Warner, 1998), resulting in numerous comparative and qualitative studies (e.g., Cadge, 2005; Chen, 2008; Ebaugh and Chafetz, 2000; Min and Kim, 2002; Warner and Wittner, 1998). Despite the growing amount of research on immigrant religion using survey data (Alanezi, 2005; Cadge and Ecklund, 2006; Connor, 2008; Connor and Burgos, 2007; Massey and Higgins, 2007; van Tubergen, 2006), little research has investigated changes in immigrant religious life surrounding the migratory event at a national level. This is mostly due to a lack of national immigrant cohort data (Ebaugh, 2003), a significant limitation to immigrant religion research (Cadge and Ecklund, 2007). In light of the growing religious diversity in the United States (Fischer and Hout, 2006) and the challenges this diversity presents to U.S. society (Wuthnow, 2005), the study of immigrant religious adaptation is timely and important to both academia and the public.

RELIGIOUS PARTICIPATION AND MIGRATION: RISE OR DECLINE?

Religion among immigrants is particularly important in the associational style of religiosity found in the United States (Warner, 1998). Hirschman (2004) identifies three Rs for understanding the motives of immigrant involvement in a religious community—refuge, respect, and resources. As Portes and Rumbaut (2006) point out in their newly added section on immigrant religion in *Immigrant America*, refuge and respect correlate well to Durkheim's theory of anomie. Involvement in a religious community provides both sanctuary and self-esteem for the immigrant, especially when the congregation is ethnically or linguistically similar to the immigrant's religious community in his or her country of origin. Furthermore, Hirschman's final R—resources—coincides with Weber's elaboration of the latent economic consequences associated with religion. A litany of qualitative studies enumerate the economic and social benefits associated with involvement in a religious community (Dolan, 1972; George, 1998; Min, 1992; Zhou *et al.*, 2002) Furthermore, immigrant religious activity facilitates the immigrant's transnational ties to his or her country of origin (Levitt, 2003; McAlister, 1998).

Yet, the question remains as to whether this supposed rise in spiritual consciousness actually translates into increased public religious participation. Contrary to the more prevalent position in the literature that immigrant religiosity increases following migration, other empirical studies tell a different story. Finke and Stark (2005) suggest that migrants to the American frontier during the eighteenth and nineteenth centuries were not religiously active. Like the Latino migrants of today, frontier migrants maintained transient lifestyles and worked long hours, leaving them little time to participate in religious activities. Wuthnow and Christiano (1979) study the religious participation of similar internal migrants within the United States in the twentieth century and find they are less likely to be involved in a local religious center with each additional migration. Massey and Higgins (2007) find that U.S. immigrants reduce their religious participation after they receive their permanent residency status.[3] Additional research from Quebec confirms that immigrant religious participation declines after the migratory event (Connor, 2008).

One challenge in addressing the rise versus decline debate is the appropriate sampling frame. The increased religiosity hypothesis has been demonstrated using data at the congregational level; therefore, conclusions are selectively drawn from those already involved in religious activities. Moreover, some of the studies indicating a decline in immigrant religiosity use data from earlier time periods. Conclusions may not capture how more recent immigrant waves to the United States are religiously adapting to the new society. This is especially true given the greater religious diversity now in the United States compared to the nineteenth and twentieth centuries. Finally, the literature refers to many different immigrant populations (e.g., documented, undocumented, refugees, temporary workers). Therefore, this article builds on previous work by using a random, nationally representative sample of newly arrived immigrants to the United States.

MEDIATING FACTORS: INFLUENTIAL OR INSIGNIFICANT?

A number of factors, both contextual and individual, are posited to mediate the effect of migration on religious participation. Reflecting on religious context, Stark and Bainbridge (1996) propose a number of hypotheses, the most debated and tested of which is that increasing levels of religious pluralism (an increasing number of religious groups in a given geographic space) contributes to increasing religious participation. Although the statistical evidence for the religious pluralism hypothesis has been questioned extensively (Montgomery, 2003; Voas *et al.*, 2002), as well as the historical support criticized (Bruce, 1999) and the theoretical project as a whole probed (Neitz and Mueser, 1997), the hypothesis still merits additional exploration among subpopulations before it can be summarily dismissed (Voas *et al.*, 2002). Given that immigration researchers find religious competition, a byproduct of religious pluralism, is associated with aggressive recruitment techniques among immigrant congregations (Chen, 2008; Ebaugh and Chafetz, 2000), Stark and Bainbridge's religious pluralism hypothesis especially warrants testing.

Other theoretical work directly contradicts Stark and Bainbridge's religious pluralism hypothesis and suggests that higher levels of religious pluralism are associated with *lower* levels of religious participation. Berger (1967) argues for a demand-side approach to religion and concludes that a greater diversity of

---

[3] Massey and Higgins (2007) analyze the complete NIS sample, which includes both new arrivals and individuals who adjusted their immigrant status while living in the United States. This article limits its analysis to those respondents who received their permanent residency outside of the United States.

religious products available to the religious consumer actually decreases religious participation. Religion in a pluralistic society becomes more of an individual matter, releasing religion from the function of social integration. Furthermore, the plurality of religions causes the individual to question the notion of the sacred; subsequently, commitment to religious groups declines. Given the greater religious pluralism most immigrants face upon arrival in the United States, it is plausible that immigrants withdraw from religious involvement out of confusion or concern over selecting an incorrect religious group.

In addition to religious pluralism, the impact of religious concentration or religious market share is also a critical element that shapes immigrant religious behavior. Minority groups such as Hindus and Muslims report being more religious after settling in the United States (Yang and Ebaugh, 2001). Ebaugh and Chafetz (2000) conclude that immigrants of religious minorities generally expend more effort and commitment to maintain their religious identity as compared to those in their countries of origin. For example, Kurien (2002) finds that Hindus in the United States, a spatially scattered, minority religion in most U.S. jurisdictions, describe themselves as being "better Hindus" than if they were living in India.

A greater market share for the individual migrant's religious group can also be associated with higher levels of public religious participation. Drawing from their work on ethnic enclaves, Portes and Rumbaut (2006) build a widely used typology for explaining the economic and linguistic outcomes of immigrants upon resettlement. For example, immigrants residing in an ethnic enclave tend to be more monolingual than bilingual. Additionally, immigrants within ethnic enclaves generally confine their economic activity (employment, consumption) to the enclave. Since religion and ethnicity are so intertwined for immigrant populations (Smith, 1978), these immigrant enclaves can also serve as ethnoreligious enclaves. Here the religious concentration of a particular religious group is of critical importance. Similar to the monolingual outcomes among immigrants residing in ethnic enclaves, we would expect that a higher proportion of co-religionists in a given region would also create higher social expectations for active religious participation. This is contrary to the earlier proposed hypothesis whereby spatially scattered, religious minorities have a higher level of religiosity.

Beyond religious contextual factors, studies also indicate a number of individual-level factors that mediate the rise or decline of immigrant religious participation upon resettlement in the new society. For example, immigrant males are found to have a higher likelihood of immigrant religious participation than females (van Tubergen, 2006). Many studies find that males exercise leadership and authority in a local congregation where such opportunities are not as available in the secular world, leading to a high level of congregational commitment (Abusharaf, 1998; Chen, 2008; George, 1998; Min, 1992). Conversely, using evidence from the eighteenth and nineteenth centuries, Finke and Stark (2005) argue that immigrants are often single, young, laboring men with no children or spouse who have little time for religious activity.

Having a spouse and, more importantly, children in the home often leads to cultural and religious reproduction within the family. Beyond cultural reproduction, many immigrant families also wish to transfer particular moral values to their children, and religion often becomes the medium for this transfer. For these reasons, it is at this stage of an immigrant's lifecourse that an immigrant family's religious participation will often increase (Kurien, 2002; Saran, 1985; Williams, 1988).

The employment status of the immigrant also affects religious participation. Alanezi (2005) proposes a social capital explanation for increased religious involvement whereby immigrants socially tied to a community's religious organization have increased chances for employment and business within the ethnic enclave economy. Immigrants often share information for adjustment to the new society, especially educational and job opportunities, within their religious congregations (Zhou *et al.*, 2002). The quintessential example of this can be found in Christian Korean-American communities where religious organizations provide information about job opportunities as well as financial capital for business startups (Min, 1992). Therefore, potential information about employment within a religious organization leads to higher religious affiliation for the reasons of social capital and, when employment is found, immigrants often feel indebted to the religious organization, solidifying their commitment to the congregation (Chen, 2008). However, both Killian (2001) and Finke and Stark (2005) argue that long workdays in combination with cultural stress make religious participation difficult. Survey data (Cadge and Ecklund, 2006; Massey and Higgins, 2007; van Tubergen, 2006) supports this alternative employment hypothesis as a reason for a decreasing immigrant religiosity.

Although evidence for the impact of individual-level characteristics (gender, familial conditions, and employment) on immigrant religious participation exists, it is slight and lacks empirical consensus for the direction of these hypotheses. As demonstrated by Connor (2008) for the province of Quebec, these individual-level factors have little explanatory power in mediating the change in religious participation. Previous empirical testing of the mediating impact of religious contextual factors such as religious pluralism and religious concentration do provide significant effects (Alanezi, 2005; van Tubergen, 2006). However, these earlier studies are limited to cross-sectional data. More reliable hypothesis testing requires a longitudinal data set among an immigrant cohort where contextual-level variables can be tested alongside individual-level characteristics. Additionally, reliable measures of immigrant religious participation both prior and following migration are necessary. The newly released New Immigrant Survey (NIS) conducted by principal investigators Jasso *et al.* (in press) provides for these data requirements.[4]

[4] This research uses data from the New Immigrant Survey, a research project designed by G. Jasso, D. Massey, M. Rosenzweig, and J. Smith, and funded by NIH HD33843, NSF, USCIS, ASPE & Pew. Restricted Use Data, Version (1 or 2), May 2007. Retrieved August 2007. Persons interested in obtaining NIS Restricted Use Data should see http://nis.princeton.edu/data/data_restricted.html for further information.

DATA AND METHODS

Data

The NIS sampled immigrants receiving their permanent residency to the United States during 2003 to 2004 using a stratified random sample according to immigrant visa category (Jasso *et al.*, in press). In all, 12,500 adults aged 18 years and older were selected with 8,573 adult respondents interviewed, representing a 68.6% response rate. Respondents were asked questions on a variety of topics, including income, housing, employment, health, and social activities. Interviews were conducted in 19 different languages, with English and Spanish being the language of choice among 46% and 26% of respondents, respectively. The NIS provides the researcher with a unique data source, capable of providing generalizable results to immigrants entering the country as legal permanent residents.

To ensure analysis is performed on newly arrived immigrants, the sample is limited to those immigrants receiving their permanent residency while living outside the United States. This selected subsample represents 3,848 cases. Additionally, the subsample was reduced by 275 cases (approximately 7% of the available cases after deletion of immigrant visa adjusters and nonresponse to the religious module) due to missing data for dependent or independent variables (the data are missing at random). In all, this results in a final respondent count of 3,573. Although this is a sizeable reduction in the number of respondents, the research question of religious contextual mediation effects justifies the selection of immigrants who have not been privy to contextual factors in the United States for any extended period prior to migration. The subsample of new arrivals limits the potential selection of geographic residence within the United States for religious reasons, which could reverse the causal direction of the contextual level factors.

As with any data, the NIS does have drawbacks. For those immigrants who received their permanent residency while residing outside the United States, interviews were conducted approximately 6 months after their arrival in the United States. This short time period is a limitation to the interpretation of the findings as it can take several months or years for immigrants to settle into their religious patterns; however, as Connor (2008) finds in Quebec, the first year after migration sets a definite trajectory for immigrant religiosity in subsequent years. Moreover, the key question of concern is the impact of the migratory event on immigrant religious participation as either a disruptive or spiritual experience evidenced by changes in public religious behavior. The intent is not to evaluate religious change throughout the resettlement process. Based on the previously cited literature, immigrants are presumed to alter their habits of participation soon after migration; therefore, the short time period from migration to interview should not substantially alter the interpretation of results. To verify this presumption, a separate analysis for the complete sample of NIS respondents (new and adjusting immigrants) is provided in Table A in the Appendix. Although this additional analysis is subject to the religious selectivity problem mentioned earlier, a similar pattern of results between the subsample of newly arrived immigrants and the complete sample points to the consistency of the results.

Respondents were not interviewed prior to their migration, but they were asked to reflect retrospectively on their circumstances in their country of origin, which provides the necessary data for two time periods—premigration (t_1) and postmigration (t_2). However, as demonstrated by Presser and Stinson (1998), self-reporting of religious participation is often biased in an upward direction. This can be particularly true among immigrants nostalgically recalling religious participation in their country of origin. However, social desirability bias and direct comparisons by the respondent between pre- and postmigration religious participation levels are unlikely because of the differences in question wording for the two time periods. For the premigration time period, the religious participation question was, "Before coming to the United States to live, how often did you attend religious services in your country of last foreign residence?" with an ordinal list of 11 frequency categories ranging from "Never" to "More than once a day." For the postmigration time period, the question was: "Since becoming a permanent resident, how many times have you attended religious services?" Although different from the previous categorical response, it is expected that this postmigration count measure for religious frequency minimizes potential bias.

Telescoping of previous religious behavior (compressing time whereby the frequency of religious participation is greater than in reality) can bias estimates upward (Smith, 1998). As a cross-check, adjusted means for monthly or more religious participation in the NIS by religious-national groupings were compared to adjusted means of religious participation of the same religious-national group within the World Values Survey (WVS), adjusting for the NIS sample means by education, age, gender, employed full time, income, and spouse in the residence. Although the WVS sample does not represent the would-be immigrant population to the United States, simple comparisons of these adjusted means do not indicate any systematic upward biasing of estimates within the NIS.[5] Despite

---

[5] The countries of previous residence with the highest frequency of respondents by major religious group in the NIS were determined. Each religious-national group's adjusted mean for monthly religious participation in the NIS was compared to the mean for the same religious group in that country's most recent World Values Survey (WVS), adjusting for the mean values of gender, education, employed full time, income, and spouse in the residence found in the NIS immigrant sample. Among Catholics in Mexico and the Philippines, the two largest nationalities affiliated with Catholicism in the NIS, adjusted religious participation of monthly or more is 80% and 87%, respectively, in the WVS. The adjusted proportion of monthly religious participation of immigrant Catholics in the NIS from Mexico is 96% and 89% among Catholics from the Philippines, indicating a potential upward bias in NIS estimates for Mexican Catholics. However, the story changes when looking at Protestants in the Philippines and Nigeria, the two largest nationalities affiliated with Protestantism in the NIS. The adjusted proportion of the WVS sample with religious participation of monthly or more is 96% and 98%, respectively, much higher than the adjusted means found in the NIS sample of 82% and 84%. These results do not confirm the expected upward bias due to telescoping. A similar theme of inconsistency among adjusted means by religious-national grouping exists for the remaining religious groups; therefore, it cannot be stated that consistent upwardly biased estimates for premigration religious participation are systematic.

these data limitations, the NIS data represent the best, contemporary U.S. data for an immigrant cohort.

Contextual mediating variables (i.e., religious pluralism, religious concentration) within the United States require religious census data derived from a local geographic unit of analysis. Since the U.S. Census Bureau does not collect religious affiliation data, the closest stand-in is the Religious Congregations and Membership Study 2000 (RCMS). This dataset is an amalgamation of data from various denominational and religious bodies in the United States who voluntarily provide church and membership statistics to the Glenmary Research Center for compilation. The varying denominations and religious groups were classified and coded to match the world religions categorized in the NIS data structure for religious affiliation. For the purposes of this study, the units of analysis selected from the RCMS data is the county level.[6]

The selection of an appropriate data set for the application of religious contextual variables by the immigrant's country of origin is more challenging. The most exhaustive data set for religious affiliation by country is the World Christian Database (WCD) (Johnson and Barrett, 2007). Given the potential bias of information collected for Christian missionary purposes, the reliability of these data is questionable, yet the database contains the most complete data for calculating religious pluralism and concentration by country. A recent study analyzing the reliability of WCD data in comparison to similar data sources finds it is the most complete data source available for cross-national religious composition statistics. The WCD also correlates highly with other international religious composition data sets of its kind (Hsu *et al.*, 2008). Religious group categories were again coded to match the religious categorization found in the NIS.[7]

---

[6] The NIS religious affiliation categories include: Catholic, Orthodox Christian, Protestant, Muslim, Jewish, Buddhist, Hindu, other religion, and no religion. "Other religion" refers to religious groups that do not fit into existing religious categories in the survey. This can represent a variety of quasi-Christian groups and other world religions such as Bahai, Zoroastrianism, and Sikhism. The coding of the RCMS data follows the recommended categories provided by RCMS editors, yet still places religious groups and denominations within the same broad religion categories found in the NIS. When membership counts were not available for a particular religious group within the RCMS data, the national number of adherents for the religious group were drawn from the American Religious Identification Survey (ARIS) 2001 and divided by the number of congregations for that particular religion across the nation from RCMS data. This way, an average number of members for each religious category by county is available for analysis. To compensate for missing denominational and religion data, each county's level of religiously affiliated persons was corrected using Finke and Scheitle's adjusted adherence rates by state (Finke and Scheitle, 2005). This accounts for the underrepresentation of African-American congregations and other ethnic groups. Also corrected was the Jewish membership estimate as this was originally based on a population count for Jewish heritage rather than religious adherence (Finke and Scheitle, 2005).

[7] Although the geographic levels of U.S. counties for the postmigration time period do not match the same geographic level of country for the premigration time period, it is expected that immigrants will respond to the local conditions of religious context within the United States compared to the country as a whole. Furthermore, data at an administrative level equivalent to U.S. county are simply unavailable for all migrant countries of origin.

Dependent Variable

As already mentioned, immigrant religious participation in the NIS exists for both the respondent's country of origin prior to migration and since receiving his or her permanent residency.[8] Religious participation prior to migration as expressed by attendance at a church, temple, or mosque was an ordinal variable ranging from none to more than once a day. This variable was recoded to monthly or more. To calculate an average monthly level of participation, the postmigration count was divided by the number of months since the respondent received permanent residency status in the United States. Any count of one or more was coded as 1 while anything less than one occasion per month was coded as 0.[9]

Independent Variable

The key independent variable of importance to this study is the change in immigrant religious participation following the migratory event; therefore, a dummy variable for the postmigration time period is included in each model.

Mediating Variables Religious pluralism is conventionally measured by the Herfindahl index (H). It is calculated by subtracting the summation of the squared proportion of each religious group from 1 or $H_j = 1 - \sum P^2_{ij}$ (Finke and Stark, 1988), where P is the proportion of a particular religion, and i is each individual religion represented for each j geographic location. Eight religious categories were used in the analysis: Catholic, Christian Orthodox, Protestant, Jewish, Buddhist, Hindu, Muslim, and other religious groups. A value approaching 0 indicates a religious monopoly or low religious pluralism while a value approaching 1 indicates many religious groups of equal size or high religious pluralism. In this article, the religious affiliation categories used for the religious pluralism measure mirror those found in the NIS.[10]

---

[8] Other measures of religiosity within the NIS include membership in a local religious center and religious items in the home. Although these variables could serve as indicators for immigrant religiosity, immigrant participation as indicated by religious service attendance is the best variable for comparison purposes to previous studies. Additionally, it is the only variable available within the dataset for both the pre- and postmigration time periods.

[9] Although the Christian experience would advocate for active religious participation as a weekly event, non-Christian religions may not distinguish such frequent attendance as being active religious participation; therefore, this analysis uses a more conservative estimate for religious participation. A weekly, dichotomous dependent variable was tested, providing similar results to those found using the monthly cutpoint. As an alternative metric, an imputed count model was tested using Poisson regression, again revealing similar results. The binary, monthly dependent variable was selected since it involves the least amount of data manipulation for reconciling the differences between the pre- and postmigration measures.

[10] The proportion of the population unclaimed by no religious group is not included in the calculation of the religious pluralism index. Therefore, the denominator is the sum of all religious groups rather than the actual population for the given geographic area.

Immigrant respondents in the NIS were then matched by their country of origin and U.S. county of residence to the appropriate level of religious pluralism for pre- and postmigration time periods, respectively.[11]

Religious concentration for country of origin and U.S. county of residence is derived from the same contextual datasets (i.e., RCMS, WCD) for the identical eight religious categories. Respondents are matched to their respective religious affiliation as indicated in the NIS to the proportion (0 to 1) of the population that also adheres to that same world religion. Therefore, a value of religious concentration approaching 0 indicates a low religious concentration within the particular geographic area (U.S. county or country of origin). A value of religious concentration approaching 1 indicates a high proportion of co-religionists. As with the religious pluralism measure, this religious concentration measure is attached to the respondent by his or her county of U.S. residence for the postmigration time period and the respondent's country of origin for the premigration time period.[12]

Individual-level variables hypothesized to impact immigrant religious participation include the dichotomous variables of gender, spouse in the home, children in the home, and employed full time.[13] Additionally, age and education levels at the time of interview are included as control variables for each regression model.[14] Although there is no substantial evidence in the literature for the impact of immigrant category (independent, refugee, and family classes) on immigrant religious participation, it is intuitive to believe that social embeddedness (Ellison, 1995) may impact immigrant religious participation among those in the family class more than those in the independent categories. Finally, since different religions have alternative

---

[11] Geocoding of NIS respondents was performed by matching the particular zipcode for their permanent residency address to the appropriate U.S. county where that zipcode exists. Zipcode for the location of the interview is available and correlates highly with the permanent residency address. The decision to use the permanent residency address over the interview address is due to more cases being available for the former than the latter.

[12] There are a total of 142 unique countries of origin and 295 unique U.S. counties of settlement.

[13] Data for children and spouse in the residence for the premigration time period are imputed since specific variables for these considerations are not available in the NIS. Therefore, it is assumed that a married respondent resided with his or her spouse prior to migration. Similarly, a respondent with a child under 18 years old was assumed to be in the respondent's residence prior to migration. Employed full time (employed 35+ hours a week, 48+ weeks a year) was included as a dichotomous variable in order to take into account combined employment levels for both a weekly and yearly basis. Models using employment hours per week provide the same directional results.

[14] Although age and education could be employed as explanatory variables for religious participation, qualitative evidence for the impact of these demographic predictors on immigrant populations in particular is not extensive. Income is not included in these models as education and income reflect similar aspects for the individual.

expectations for degrees of religious participation, religious affiliation is also taken into account.[15]

Methods of Analysis Following descriptive statistics, logistic cross-sectional time series regression is employed to test the change in immigrant religious participation following migration. Since many of the effects are time variant and the regression analysis uses a dichotomous dependent variable, it is prudent to use random-effects models (Frees, 2004). Random-effects modeling permits the testing of characteristics that are fixed (i.e., gender, familial situation, employment) as well as the dummy postmigration variable.

In testing the key question of change in religious participation from pre- to postmigration time periods, a negative coefficient for the postmigration dummy indicates a lower likelihood of monthly religious participation following migration. A positive coefficient indicates an increase in the likelihood of monthly religious participation. In assessing any impact of mediating variables on this change during pre- to postmigration time periods, the postmigration coefficient will change in magnitude as each mediating variable is introduced.

For testing the explanatory power of each set of hypotheses, likelihood-ratio tests using nested models is preferable, but not possible when applying weights to the sample; therefore, changes in the Bayesian information criteria (BIC) and the Akaike information criteria (AIC) are employed in comparing one regression model with another. Although the ambition of this article is to determine the impact of the migratory event on religious behavior regardless of religious affiliation, predicted probabilities for monthly religious participation by time period and religious affiliation are nonetheless presented.

RESULTS

In reviewing descriptive statistics (Table I), the most pertinent item to note is the decline of monthly religious participation among respondents from 64% during the premigration time period to 42% in the postmigration time period. This initial statistic seems to support the decreasing religious participation hypothesis. On another note and not surprisingly, the religious affiliation distribution of immigrants does not correlate with current religious affiliations in

---

[15] Intuitively, it would be advisable to remove respondents declaring no religion from the sample; however, about 4% (20 cases) of respondents declaring no religion are monthly participants of a religion organization in the premigration time period. This group grows to 5% (25 cases) in the postmigration time period. As seen in ethnographic work (Chen, 2008; Yang, 1999), conversions from irreligious or nonreligious immigrants at time of entry do occur during and following the migratory event. Subsequently, dismissing this subsample of respondents would limit the generalizability of results to religiously affiliated immigrants, overlooking the potentiality of religious behavior among those claiming no religious affiliation. Although no religious affiliation is not an organized movement in the United States, this cannot be assumed for other immigrant source countries where atheism is prevalent (former USSR, China); therefore, the change in religious concentration for no religion is of importance to these immigrants.

Table I. Descriptive Statistics[a]

Variable	Description	Premigration			Postmigration		
		Mean/Prop.	SD	Min/Max	Mean/Prop.	SD	Min/Max
Dependent Variable							
Religious participation	0 = less than monthly 1 = monthly or more	.64		0/1	.42		0/1
Religious affiliation	Religious affiliation at migration						
Catholic (reference)		.36					
Christian Orthodox		.09					
Protestant		.14					
Muslim		.10					
Jewish		.01					
Buddhist		.06					
Hindu		.07					
No religion (reference)		.14					
Other religion		.03					
Demographic predictors							
Age	Age at migration (years)	41.10	15.10	18/95	41.10	15.10	18/95
Education	Schooling at migration (years)	11.82	4.88	0/36	11.82	4.88	0/36
Immigrant visa category							
Family (reference)	Spouse, parent, child	.58			.58		
Independent	Employment, business	.06			.06		
Other	Diversity, refugee, legalization	.35			.35		

Table I. (*Continued*)

Variable	Description	Premigration			Postmigration		
		Mean/Prop.	SD	Min/Max	Mean/Prop.	SD	Min/Max
Mediating Test Variables							
Gender	0 = female 1 = male	.43	.50	0/1			
Spouse	0 = spouse not in residence 1 = spouse in residence	.66	.47	0/1	.60	.49	0/1
Children	0 = child(ren) (18 years and younger) not in residence 1 = child(ren) in residence	.40	.49	0/1	.33	.47	0/1
Employment	0 = not employed full time (35+ hours/week, 48+ weeks/year) 1 = employed full time	.23	.42	0/1	.17	.37	0/1
Religious pluralism	RP—country of origin (pre), U.S. county of residence (post)	.40	.18	.01/.79	.60	.07	.14/.74
Religious concentration	RC—country of origin (pre), U.S. county of residence (post)	.53	.34	.00/.99	.20	.19	.00/.73

[a]Sample restricted to permanent residency visa nonadjusters (i.e., immigrants not already living in the United States).
N = 3,573.
Sources: NIS Wave 1 (2003-2004), WCD (2007), RCMS (2000).

Table II. Logistic Regression Coefficients Predicting Monthly or Greater Religious Participation—Cross-Sectional Time Series[a]

	Model 1	Model 2	Model 3	Model 4	Model 5	Model 6	Model 7	Model 8	Model 9
Religious Affiliation									
Catholic (ref category)	—	—	—	—	—	—	—	—	—
Christian Orthodox	-.770***	-.771***	-.778***	-.758***	-.768***	-.713***	-.636***	-.642***	-.647***
Protestant	.009	.017	.017	.022	.021	.031	.092	-.088	-.080
Muslim	-2.267***	-2.311***	-2.318***	-2.335***	-2.343***	-2.359***	-2.270***	-2.319***	-2.353***
Jewish	-2.280***	-2.300***	-2.293***	-2.293***	-2.287***	-2.233***	-2.184***	-2.175***	-2.168***
Buddhist	-3.342***	-3.342***	-3.335***	-3.357***	-3.363***	-3.301***	-3.228***	-3.224***	-3.264***
Hindu	-.875***	-.887***	-.884***	-.902***	-.913***	-.860***	-.796***	-.812***	-.853***
No religion	-5.433***	-5.407***	-5.413***	-5.400***	-5.409***	-5.352***	-5.312***	-5.303***	-5.312***
Other religion	.433	.415	.498	.397	.389	.441	.577†	.539†	.503†
Demographic Predictors									
Age	-.015	-.016	-.014	-.010	-.008	-.016	-.015	-.015	-.007
Age-squared	.000	.000	.000	.000	.000	.000	.000	.000	.000
Education	-.011	-.008	-.008	-.003	-.003	-.007	-.007	-.007	-.002
Family immigrant (ref category)	—	—	—	—	—	—	—	—	—
Independent immigrant	.281†	.295†	.306†	.415*	.427*	.312†	.309†	.317†	.447*
Other immigrant	.008	.046	.061	.061	.080	.060	.048	.058	.093
Micro-Level Test Variables									
Gender		-.232**	-.234**	-.177*	-.179*	-.231**	-.231**	-.231**	-.179*
Spouse			.040		.053				.062
Children			-.075		-.081				-.086
Employment				-.492***	-.494***				-.487***
Contextual-Level Test Variables									
Religious pluralism						-.731*		-.529†	-.521†

Table II. (*Continued*)

	Model 1	Model 2	Model 3	Model 4	Model 5	Model 6	Model 7	Model 8	Model 9
Religious concentration							.407*	.265†	.247
Time Period									
Postmigration (reference = premigration)	-1.778***	-1.781***	-1.784***	-1.813***	-1.812***	-1.635***	-1.623***	-1.574***	-1.618†
Intercept	2.455***	2.513***	2.480***	2.406**	2.373***	2.752***	2.197***	2.645***	2.351***
df	16	17	19	18	20	18	18	19	22
BIC	6489.422	6492.764	6510.031	6481.380	6498.478	6495.984	6496.668	6503.239	6509.515
AIC	6379.433	6375.901	6379.419	6357.643	6360.992	6372.246	6372.930	6372.627	6358.280

†p < .10; *p < .05; **p < .01; ***p < .001, one-tailed.
aSample restricted to permanent residency visa nonadjusters (i.e., immigrants not already living in the United States).
N = 3,573.
Sources: NIS Wave 1 (2003–2004), WCD (2007), RCMS (2000).

U.S. society. Although a majority of immigrants profess affiliation with a Christian religion (59%), a sizeable minority of immigrants arriving to the United States represent non-Christian religions (e.g., 10% Muslim, 6% Buddhist, 7% Hindu) that are not as equally represented across the U.S. landscape.

Descriptive statistics also indicate a change in various individual-level factors hypothesized to explain variation in immigrant religious participation. Representing the familial and economic interruption many immigrants realize, means for spouse and children in the home and employed full time decline for the pooled sample from pre- to postmigration time periods. Additionally, high standard deviations for age and child/spouse in the home indicate that this sample represents a wide, demographic diversity of immigrants. Contextual-level variable means also change during the two time periods, with mean religious pluralism increasing substantially from pre- to postmigration time periods (.40 to .60). This indicates both the pluralistic nature of the U.S. host society, but also the more religiously monopolistic context of origin for many immigrants. In contrast, the drop in mean religious concentration from pre- to postmigration time periods (.53 to .20) further demonstrates the presence of religious monopolies abroad.

Moving onto more explanatory analysis, Table II presents logistic regression coefficients using cross-sectional time series in testing the mediating impact of individual-level and contextual-level factors on immigrant religious participation. In terms of change in immigrant religious participation from the pre- and postmigration time periods, negative time period coefficients for all models indicate a general decline in immigrant religious participation from country of origin to host society. In Model 1, where only control variables are included, the odds of monthly religious participation in the postmigration time period over the premigration time period declines by 83% ($1 - \exp\{-1.788\} = 0.831$).

Individual-level variables are consistent throughout all models, and when grouped remain generally the same as when tested separately. Agreeing with Finke and Stark's (2005) analysis of immigrant religiosity, being male predicts a lower probability of monthly religious participation ($b = -0.179$; Model 5 of Table II); however, family considerations (i.e., spouse, children in the residence) have no significant impact on immigrant religious participation. Having full-time employment status also lowers the probability of monthly religious participation ($b = -0.494$; Model 5). By looking at model fit (BIC) for Models 2 through 5, full-time employment makes the most substantial change to the model (Δ BIC from Model 1 to Model 4 $= -8.475$). Actually, the insertion of full-time employment into the model provides the best model fit compared to the inclusion of any other mediating variable. This finding agrees with the increasing employment hypothesis in that full-time employment provides less time for extra-curricular activities like religious participation. However, this improvement in the model fit only recognizes the fact that immigrant religious participation is negatively affected by full-time employment status more generally, regardless of time period. As evidenced by the lack of change in the coefficient for the postmigration time period when

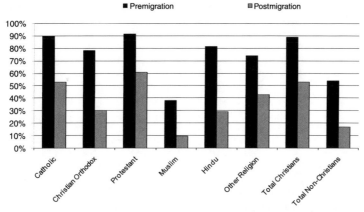

Sources: NIS (2003-2004), WCD (2007), RCMS (2000).

Fig. 1. Predicted probabilities for monthly or greater religious participation among immigrants to the United States in 2003 by migration time period and religious affiliation.

employment is included in the model, full-time employment does not operate as an important mediating variable in the decline of immigrant religious participation from pre- to postmigration time periods.

Testing religious contextual variables provides a more precise understanding of the postmigration decline in religious participation. Not only does model fit improve in Models 6 through 9 of Table II compared to Model 1, but each contextual variable on its own presents interesting results. As Model 6 indicates, increasing levels of religious pluralism over the two time periods are associated with a lower likelihood of monthly religious participation (b = −0.731). Since the majority of immigrants are moving from a less pluralistic society than the United States, these results seem to agree with the hypothesis proposed by Berger and other secular religionists that increased levels of religious pluralism are associated with lower levels of immigrant religious participation. Likewise, increasing levels of religious concentration are associated with a higher likelihood of monthly religious participation (b = 0.407; Model 7). This result supports the ethnoreligious enclave argument that a larger proportion of co-religionists in a region yields a higher level of religious participation. This result continues to remain constant when religious pluralism and individual-level factors are reintroduced, albeit the religious context coefficients are reduced and become statistically less significant. This is invariably due to the high correlation between these two contextual factors (r = 0.61).

Religious context operates as a better mediating factor than individual-level factors in explaining the decline of religious participation. Whereas the inclusion of individual-level characteristics into the model hardly alters the postmigration coefficient, the inclusion of religious pluralism and religious concentration does reduce the absolute value of the postmigration coefficient by a beta change of 0.207 (−1.781 minus −1.574, from Model 1 to Model 8 of Table II). Although this change in the postmigration coefficient is not a dramatic reduction, it is still substantial and indicates a partial mediating effect for religious context on immigrant religious participation following migration.

It could be expected that any change in immigrant religious participation from pre- to postmigration time periods would differ by religious group. Figure 1 displays predicted probabilities for monthly religious participation by religious group with a statistically significant change from the pre- to post-migration periods. (see Appendix Table B for actual coefficients of postmigration and mediating variables). Looking at Christian groups, Catholics and Protestants seem to share similar levels of decline in predicted probability of monthly immigrant religious participation, around 90% predicted probability at premigration down to 50–60% in the postmigration time period. Christian Orthodox also has a similar decline in predicted probability of monthly religious participation; however, the decrease is more pronounced for Christian Orthodox as compared to Catholics and Protestants.

Reviewing non-Christian groups, a more nuanced pattern emerges. Muslims and Hindus also have a declining probability of monthly religious participation in the postmigration over the premigration time period; however, the decline is steeper when compared to Christian groups. Predicted Muslim religious participation in the postmigration time period drops to less than a third of the premigration period (40% pre to 10% post), while the Hindu participation drops to half. This dramatic decline is further defined when Protestants, Catholics, and Christian Orthodox are combined and compared to all other religious groups. The predicted probability for the total Christian group lowers by 38 percentage points or a little less than half that in the premigration time period. Comparatively, total non-Christian groups decline by a similar margin in terms of percentage points (36 percentage points) but this represents an almost three-fold reduction compared to their premigration levels.

DISCUSSION

In light of previous empirical work and the results of this article, the question arises: Are we any further along the path of understanding the impact of migration on religiosity, particularly religious participation? As is customary in any research that seeks to confirm or discount hypotheses, this article creates more questions than answers. However, while standing on the shoulders of previous research, the results in this article have contributed to our knowledge of immigrant religious adaptation in four major streams.

First, the issue of rise versus decline in immigrant religious participation surrounding the migratory event has now become more nuanced than originally conceived. On the aggregate, there is a definite pattern of declining religiosity surrounding the migratory event. Based on these data, migration is a disruptive event for immigrant religious participation, not a spiritual one that results in increased public religious attendance. However, the decreasing trend of active religious participation among Christians is generally less dramatic than it is for non-Christian groups. This difference in magnitude should not come as a complete surprise. Ralston (1998), in her qualitative work, finds that lack of access to religious products and services (i.e., centers of worship, clergy, etc.) dampens religious participation among immigrants. The more dramatic decline in religious participation for non-Christian groups could simply reflect a lack of access to their preferred congregations compared to the situation of Protestant and Catholic groups, who typically have a more extensive selection list of congregations from which to choose.

Second, the statistical analysis in this article downplays the impact of individual-level characteristics on immigrant religious participation. In general, previous studies have found no or little effect for these considerations on immigrant religious participation (Cadge and Ecklund, 2006; Connor, 2008; Massey and Higgins, 2007; van Tubergen, 2006). This article does find statistically significant results for gender and employment. For instance, being male generally predicts a lower probability in monthly religious participation, as does full-time employment. However, neither of these factors greatly mediates the decline of immigrant religious participation from the pre- to postmigration time periods; subsequently, the individual-level factors tested in this article cannot be posited to explain this drop in religious participation following migration.

Third, in understanding changes in immigrant religiosity from pre- to postmigration time periods, contextual-level factors cannot be ignored. As this analysis demonstrates, a key component in understanding variation in immigrant religious participation is the mediating influence of religious context. Religious context partially mediates changes in immigrant religious participation surrounding the migratory event. The results indicate that religious pluralism on the aggregate has a negative impact on monthly religious participation. It must also be reiterated that the index of religious pluralism employed in this article is not based on a denominational division of religious affiliation; it is based on world religion categories. Therefore, this form of religious pluralism is more global compared to most studies that test for the impact of religious pluralism as denominational competition within Christian groups. This could infer that immigrants may begin to reevaluate their religious commitment once exposed to the multitude of world religions present in their communities. However, it could be argued that this depth of religious reflection is unlikely to occur within the first few months after entry into the United States. A more pragmatic explanation might be that immigrants, now faced with such a plethora of Christian and non-Christian religious options, delay or decline religious participation due to a lack of certainty in selecting the correct religious group. Again, these possible explanations are purely speculative and require further research in the field plus additional analysis at further waves of the NIS. Religious concentration hypothesis testing demonstrates a significant positive impact on monthly religious participation for the pre- and postmigration time periods. In other words, a greater concentration of the immigrant's religious group predicts a higher likelihood of monthly or more religious participation. This should also be expected given the fact that this analysis measures the impact of religious concentration for both U.S. county of residence and country of origin.

Lastly, since both model fit and hypothesis testing indicate that the religious context of origin and settlement mediates the drop in immigrant religious participation following migration, the study of context at neighborhood, regional, and national levels requires further exploration. This concurs with Cadge and Ecklund (2007) recommendations in their overview of immigrant religiosity where they suggest further research regarding immigrant exit and receiving contexts. Due to data constraints, this study could examine religious context only by country of origin and U.S. county of settlement; however, future research in other nations using lower levels of geography will enhance our understanding of immigrant religious adaptation. Furthermore, future immigrant religion research focusing on contextual measures, such as the host society's level of religiosity or other nonreligious variables (e.g., ethnic, economic, and linguistic considerations), may provide a more thorough explanation for the decline in immigrant religious participation surrounding the migratory event.

It is true that immigrant religious adaptation patterns can take years to develop and stabilize. For this reason, additional replication of this article's analysis at further waves of the NIS and other immigrant panel data is still required. Additional data beyond the 6-month interviews will more adequately reveal the social mechanisms at play in the decline of immigrant religious participation after the migratory event. Now that hard evidence exists for a decline in immigrant religious participation, the inductive-deductive cycle of research and theoretical development continues. This continued work of immigrant religion researchers worldwide will uncover more patterns of immigrant religious behavior, social phenomena that will surely vary at a minimum as affected by context, religious affiliation, and time.

REFERENCES

Abusharaf, Rogaia Mustafa. 1998. "Structural Adaptations in an Immigrant Muslim Congregation in New York," In R. S. Warner and J. G. Wittner (eds.), *Gatherings in Diaspora: Religious Communities and the New Immigration.* Philadelphia, PA: Temple University Press.

Alanezi, Fawaz. 2005. "Theoretical Explanations for Variations in Religious Participation Among U.S. Immigrants: The Impact of Nativity, Ethnic Community, Family Structure, and Religious Markets," Unpublished Ph.D. Dissertation, Department of Sociology, Southern Illinois University, Carbondale, IL.

Berger, Peter. 1967. *The Sacred Canopy: Elements of a Sociological Theory of Religion.* New York: Anchor Books.

Bruce, Steve. 1999. *Choice and Religion: A Critique of Rational Choice Theory.* Oxford: Oxford University Press.

Cadge, Wendy. 2005. *Heartwood: The First Generation of Theravada Buddhism in America.* Chicago, IL: Chicago University Press.

Cadge, Wendy, and Elaine Howard Ecklund. 2006. "Religious Service Attendance Among Immigrants: Evidence from the New Immigrant Survey—Pilot," *American Behavioral Scientist* 49: 1574–1595.

Cadge, Wendy, and Elaine Howard Ecklund. 2007. "Immigration and Religion," *Annual Review of Sociology* 33: 359–379.

Chen, Carolyn. 2008. *Getting Saved in America: Taiwanese Immigration and Religious Experience.* Princeton, NJ: Princeton University Press.

Connor, Phillip. 2008. "Increase or Decrease? The Impact of the International Migratory Event on Immigrant Religious Participation," *Journal for the Scientific Study of Religion* 47: 243–257.

Connor, Phillip, and Givoani Burgos. 2007. "Contextualizing Immigrant Religious Participation: A Test of Religious Heterogeneity and Religious Proportionality," Paper presented at the American Sociological Association, New York, August.

Dolan, Jay P. 1972. "Immigrants in the City: New York's Irish and German Catholics," *Church History* 41: 354–368.

Ebaugh, Helen Rose. 2003. "Religion and the New Immigrants," In Michele Dillon (ed.), *Handbook of the Sociology of Religion.* Cambridge: Cambridge University Press.

Ebaugh, Helen Rose, and Janet Chafetz (eds.). 2000. *Religion and the New Immigrants: Continuities and Adaptations in Immigrant Congregations.* Walnut Creek, CA: AltaMira Press.

Edgell, Penny, and Danielle Docka. 2007. "Beyond the Nuclear Family? Familialism and Gender Ideology in Diverse Religious Communities," *Sociological Forum* 22: 1: 25–50.

Ellison, Christopher G. 1995. "Rational Choice Explanations of Individual Religious Behavior: Notes on the Problem of Social Embeddedness," *Journal for the Scientific Study of Religion* 34: 89–97.

Finke, Roger, and Christopher P. Scheitle. 2005. "Accounting for the Uncounted: Computing Correctives for the 2000 RCMS Data," *Review of Religious Research* 47: 5–22.

Finke, Roger, and Rodney Stark. 1988. "Religious Economies and Sacred Canopies: Religious Mobilization in American Cities," *American Sociological Review* 53: 41–49.

Finke, Roger, and Rodney Stark. 2005. *The Churching of America, 1776–2005: Winners and Losers in our Religious Economy.* New Brunswick, NJ: Rutgers University Press.

Fischer, Claude S., and Michael Hout. 2006. *Century of Difference: How the Country Changed During the Twentieth Century.* New York: Russell Sage Foundation.

Frees, Edward W. 2004. *Longitudinal and Panel Data: Analysis and Applications in the Social Sciences.* New York: Cambridge University Press.

George, Sheba. 1998. "Caroling with the Keralites: The Negotiation of Gendered Space in an Indian Immigrant Church," In R. S. Warner and J. G. Wittner (eds.), *Gatherings in Diaspora: Religious Communities and the New Immigrants:* Philadelphia, PA: Temple University Press.

Hagan, Jacqueline. 2006. "Making Theological Sense of the Migration Journey from Latin America: Catholic, Protestant and Interfaith Perspectives," *American Behavioral Scientist* 49: 1554–1573.

Hagan, Jacqueline, and Helen Rose Ebaugh. 2003. "Calling Upon the Sacred: Migrants' Use of Religion in the Migration Process," *International Migration Review* 37: 1145–1153.

Handlin, Oscar. 1973. *The Uprooted: The Epic Story of the Great Migrations that Made the American People.* Boston, MA: Little Brown.

Herberg, Will. 1960. *Protestant-Catholic-Jew.* Garden City, NY: Anchor Books.

Hirschman, Charles. 2004. "The Role of Religion in the Origins and Adaptation of Immigrant Groups in the United States," *International Migration Review* 28: 1206–1234.

Hsu, Becky, Amy Reynolds, Conrad Hackett, and James Gibbons. 2008. "Estimating the Religious Composition of All Nations: An Empirical Assessment of the World Christian Database," *Journal for the Scientific Study of Religion* 47: 678–693.

Jasso, G., D. Massey, M. Rosenzweig, and J. Smith. In press. "The U.S. New Immigrant Survey: Overview and Preliminary Results Based on the New-Immigrant Cohorts of 1996 and 2003," In Beverley Morgan and Ben Nicholson (eds.), *Longitudinal Surveys and Cross-Cultural Survey Design.* UK Immigration Research and Statistics Service.

Johnson, Todd, and David Barrett. 2007. *World Christian Database.* Brill Online Publishing (http://www.worldchristiandatabase.org).

Killian, Caitlin. 2001. *Cultural Choices and Identity Negotiation of Muslim Maghredbin Women in France.* Atlanta, GA: Emory University, Sociology Department.

Kurien, Prema. 1998. "Becoming American by Becoming Hindu: Indian Americans Take Their Place at the Multi-Cultural Table," In R. S. Warner and J. G. Wittner (eds.), *Gatherings in Diaspora: Religious Communities and the New Immigration.* Philadelphia, PA: Temple University Press.

Kurien, Prema. 2002. "We are Better Hindus Here," In Pyong Gap Min and Jung Ha Kim (eds.), *Religion in Asian America: Building Faith Communities.* Walnut Creek, CA: AltaMira Press.

Levitt, Peggy. 2003. "'You Know, Abraham Was Really the First Immigrant': Religion and Transnational Migration," *International Migration Review* 37: 847–873.

Massey, Douglas S., and Monica Espinosa Higgins. 2007. "What Role Does Religion Play in the Migration Process? And Vice Versa?: Evidence from the New Immigrant Survey," Paper presented at the Population Association of America, New York, March.

McAlister, Elizabeth. 1998. "The Madonna of 115th Street Revisited: Voudou and Haitian Catholicism in the Age of Transnationalism," In R. S. Warner and J. G. Wittner (eds.), *Gatherings in Diaspora: Religious Communities and the New Immigration*. Philadelphia, PA: Temple University Press.

Min, Pyong Gap. 1992. "The Structure and Social Functions of Korean Immigrant Churches in the United States," *International Migration Review* 26: 1370–1394.

Min, Pyong Gap, and Jung Ha Kim (eds.). 2002. *Religion in Asian America: Building Faith Communities*. Walnut Creek, CA: AltaMira Press.

Montgomery, James D. 2003. "A Formalization and Test of the Religious Economies Model," *American Sociological Review* 68: 782–809.

Neitz, Mary Jo, and P. R. Mueser. 1997. "Economic Man and the Sociology of Religion: A Critique of the Rational Choice Approach," In Lawrence A. Young (ed.), *Rational Choice Theory and Religion*. New York: Routledge.

Portes, Alejandro, and Ruben G. Rumbaut. 2006. *Immigrant America: A Portrait*. Berkeley, CA: University California Press.

Presser, Stanley, and Linda Stinson. 1998. "Data Collection Mode and Social Desirability Bias in Self-Reported Religious Attendance," *American Sociological Review* 63: 137–145.

Ralston, Helen. 1998. "Identity Reconstruction and Empowerment of South Asian Immigrant Women in Canada, Australia, and New Zealand," In M. Cousineau (ed.), *Religion in a Changing World: Comparative Studies in Sociology*. Westport, CT: Praeger.

Saran, Parmatma. 1985. *The Asian Indian Experience in the United States*. Cambridge, MA: Schenkman.

Smith, Timothy L. 1978. "Religion and Ethnicity in America," *American Historical Review* 83: 1115–1185.

Smith, Tom W. 1998. "A Review of Church Attendance Measures," *American Sociological Review* 63: 131–136.

Stark, Rodney, and William S. Bainbridge. 1996. *A Theory of Religion*. New York: Peter Lang Publishing.

van Tubergen, Frank. 2006. "Religious Affiliation and Attendance Among Immigrants in Eight Western Countries: Individual and Contextual Effects," *Journal for the Scientific Study of Religion* 45: 1–22.

Voas, David, Alasdair Crockett, and Daniel V. A. Olsen. 2002. "Religious Pluralism and Participation: Why Previous Research is Wrong," *American Sociological Review* 67: 212–231.

Warner, R. Stephen. 1998. "Religion and Migration in the United States," *Social Compass* 45: 123–134.

Warner, R. Steven, and Judith G. Wittner (eds.). 1998. *Gatherings in Diaspora: Religious Communities and the New Immigration*. Philadelphia, PA: Temple University Press.

Williams, Raymond Brady. 1988. *Religions of Immigrants from India and Pakistan: New Threads in the American Tapestry*. Cambridge: Cambridge University Press.

Wuthnow, Robert. 2005. *America and the Challenges of Religious Diversity*. Princeton, NJ: Princeton University Press.

Wuthow, Robert, and Kevin Christiano. 1979. "The Effects of Residential Migration on Church Attendance in the United States," In Robert Wuthnow (ed.), *The Religious Dimension: New Directions in Quantitative Research*: New York: Academic Press.

Yang, Fenggang. 1999. *Chinese Christians in America: Conversion, Assimilation, and Adhesive Identities*. University Park, PA: Penn State Press.

Yang, Fenggang, and Helen Rose Ebaugh. 2001. "Religion and Ethnicity Among New Immigrants: The Impact of Majority/Minority Status in Home and Host Countries," *Journal for the Scientific Study of Religion* 40: 367–378.

Zhou, Min, Carl L. Bankston III, and Rebecca Y. Kim. 2002. "Rebuilding Spiritual Lives in the New Land: Religious Practices Among Southeast Asian Refugees in the United States," In Pyong Gap Min and Jung Ha Kim (eds.), *Religion in Asian America: Building Faith Communities*. Walnut Creek, CA: AltaMira Press.

APPENDIX

Table A.   Logistic Regression Coefficients Predicting Monthly or Greater Religious Participation—Cross-Sectional Time Series—Full Sample

	Model 1	Model 2	Model 3	Model 4	Model 5	Model 6	Model 7	Model 8	Model 9
Religious Affiliation									
Catholic (ref category)	—	—	—	—	—	—	—	—	—
Christian Orthodox	-.214***	-.214***	-.213***	-.214***	-.213***	-.159**	.178**	.178**	.179**
Protestant	-.290***	-.290***	-.290***	-.290***	-.289***	-.233***	.034	.037	.037
Muslim	-.095	-.095	-.093	-.098	-.096	-.126*	.097	.086	.086
Jewish	-.481***	-.481***	-.484***	-.478***	-.481***	-.433**	-.114	-.114	-.114
Buddhist	-.334***	-.334***	-.331***	-.335***	-.333***	-.295***	-.008	-.009	-.008
Hindu	.010	.010	.009	.009	.007	.027	.225***	.223***	.219***
No religion	-.459***	-.459***	-.457***	-.459***	-.457***	-.410***	-.289***	-.284***	-.282***
Other religion	-.258**	-.258**	-.258**	-.261**	-.261**	-.232*	-.215*	-.208*	-.206*
Demographic Predictors									
Age	-.013*	-.013*	-.014*	-.012*	-.013*	-.012*	-.012*	-.012*	-.012*
Age-squared	.000	.000	.000†	.000	.000†	.000†	.000†	.000†	.000†
Education	-.016***	-.016***	-.016***	-.052***	-.015***	-.014***	-.015***	-.015***	-.014***
Family immigrant (ref category)	—	—	—	—	—	—	—	—	—
Independent immigrant	-.168***	-.168***	-.169***	-.164***	-.165***	-.153***	-.144***	-.142**	-.139***
Refugee immigrant	-.345***	-.345***	-.346***	-.340***	-.340***	-.305***	-.254***	-.249***	-.244***
Other immigrant	.155***	.153***	.154***	.150***	.153***	.165***	.157	.160***	.159***
Years in U.S.	.001	.001	.001	.001	.001	.000	.001	.000	.000
Individual-Level Test Variables									
Gender		.004	.005	.013	.013	.004	.007	.008	.015
Spouse			.005		.007				.004
Children			.021		.020				.021
Employment				-.048	-.047				-.044
Contextual-Level Test Variables									
Religious pluralism						-.765***	1.048***	-.150	-.144
Religious concentration								1.021***	1.021***
Time Period									
Postmigration (ref = premigration)	-.368***	-.368***	-.368***	-.362***	-.360***	-.214***	-.040	-.019	-.012
Intercept	1.244***	1.242***	1.249***	1.224***	1.231***	1.484***	.487**	.555***	.542***

(continued overleaf)

Table A. *(Continued)*

	Model 1	Model 2	Model 3	Model 4	Model 5	Model 6	Model 7	Model 8	Model 9
df	18	18	18	18	18	18	18	18	18
BIC	18405.96	18415.47	18434.17	18423.69	18442.39	18395.62	18244.53	18253.06	18280.19
AIC	18270.40	18272.38	18276.02	18273.06	18276.71	18244.99	18093.90	18094.91	18099.44

†p < .10; *p < .05; **p < .01; ***p < .001, one-tailed.
N = 6,892.
Sources: NIS Wave 1 (2003–2004), WCD (2007), RCMS (2000).

Table B. Logistic Regression Coefficients by Religious Group Predicting Monthly or Greater Religious Participation—Cross-Sectional Time Series[a]

	Catholic	Christian Orthodox	Protestant	Muslim	Jewish	Buddhist	Hindu	Other Religion	Total Christian	Total Non-Christian
Demographic Predictors										
Age	.037	−.062	.044	−.035	−.929*	−.173*	−.023	−.060	.016	−.072*
Age-squared	.000	.000	.000	.000	.010*	.002*	.000	.001	.000	.001*
Education	.003	−.120**	−.037	.000	.136	.121*	.065†	−.012	−.028*	.046*
Family immigrant	—	—	—	—	—	—	—	—	—	—
Independent immigrant	1.335***	−.153	.026	−.787	.395	.900	.681	−.840	.780**	.229
Other immigrant	.180	.052	.302	−.221	1.667	.568	−.203	−1.226*	.139	−.091
Individual-Level Test Variables										
Gender	−.670***	−.342	−.127	1.442***	.034	1.381**	−.636*	−.524	−.517***	.446*
Spouse	.232†	.059	−.043	−.037	.615	−1.289**	−.023	.290	.105	.238
Children	−.113	−.309	.323†	−.229	3.465	1.094*	−.741*	.014	−.049	−.024
Employment	−.362*	−1.027**	−.626**	−.023	.307	−1.218*	−.444	−.803†	−.581***	−.464*
Contextual-Level Test Variables										
Religious pluralism	.551	−.165	−2.458**	−.623	−1.180	−.874	1.596	2.012	−.637†	−.572
Religious concentration	.954**	−1.436*	−.526	−.395	−2.200	1.650*	−.436	−1.474	−.367†	−.273

Table B. (*Continued*)[a]

	Catholic	Christian Orthodox	Protestant	Muslim	Jewish	Buddhist	Hindu	Other Religion	Total Christian	Total Non-Christian
Time Period										
Postmigration (ref = premigration)	-1.923***	-2.713***	-1.360***	-1.812***	-1.334	-.561	-2.276***	-2.181**	-1.783***	-1.692***
Intercept	.365	5.825***	2.600***	-.434	14.335	-.091	2.901†	3.225	2.236***	-1.010
df	14	14	14	14	14	14	14	14	14	14
Category *N*	1,229	442	549	383	29	177	236	78	2,220	903

†p < .10; *p < .05; **p < .01; *** p < .001, one-tailed.
[a]Sample restricted to permanent residency visa nonadjusters (i.e., immigrants not already living in the United States).
Sources: NIS Wave 1 (2003–2004), WCD (2007), RCMS (2000).

[2]

"You Know, Abraham Was Really the First Immigrant": Religion and Transnational Migration

Peggy Levitt
Wellesley College and Harvard University

The purpose of this article is to summarize what we know about the role that religion plays in transnational migration and to outline a strategy for further research in this area. While migration scholars now generally acknowledge the salience of migrants' economic, social, and political transnational activities, we have largely overlooked the ways in which religious identities and practices also enable migrants to sustain memberships in multiple locations. My goals in this article are threefold. First, I provide a brief overview of related bodies of work on global, diasporic and immigrant religion and differentiate them from studies of migrants' transnational religious practices. Second, I selectively summarize what we have learned about the role of religion in transnational migration from prior research. Finally, I propose an approach to future research on these questions.[1]

GLOBAL, DIASPORIC AND TRANSNATIONAL RELIGION VS. THE RELIGIOUS PRACTICES OF TRANSNATIONAL MIGRANTS – WHAT IS THE CONNECTION?

The study of world or global religions has a long history. Much of this work grew out of the West's attempt to make sense of non-Christian or Eastern religions. With the exception of research on the Catholic Church, most of these studies focus on specific religious traditions in a single setting rather than on

---

[1]My thanks to Josh DeWind, John Eade, Sarah Mahler, Manuel Vásquez, and an anonymous reviewer for their insightful comments on earlier drafts of this paper. The names of respondents are all pseudonyms. My focus is on the United States because, to the best of my knowledge, no systematic attempt has been made to summarize the scholarship on the transnational religious practices of migrants to this region. In addition, much of the literature on the religious lives of North American and European migrants focuses primarily on the receiving country (*i.e.*, Metcalf, 1996; Clarke, Peach, and Vertovec 1990; Vertovec and Peach, 1997; Ebaugh and Chafetz, 2002; Warner and Wittner, 1998; and Schiffauer, 1988. Selective notable exceptions include Gardner, 1995; Huwelmeier, 2001; Eickelman and Piscatori, 1990; and Sahin, 2001). By purposely narrowing my focus, I do not wish to suggest that European and U.S. scholarship should be considered separately. In fact, one goal of the conference that produced this volume was to explore the continuities and discontinuities between the two.

the cross-border connections that like communities share. Recent work on global religions brings to light the ways in which they create international connections that engender universal identities. Because, as Beyer (2001) argues, religion is a global societal system as transnational in its operation as the economy or the nation-state, it is no surprise that migrants use religious institutions to live their transnational lives. Religion and, in particular, religious movements operating in broad geographic contexts, engage in increasingly homogenized forms of worship and organization creating global communities that locals then join. Followers can choose from an array of membership options which reach far beyond their communities and cultures and transform local religious life (Van Dijk, 1997).

A second body of work concerns religion's role in heightened globalization. These researchers debate whether religion functions as a discrete, homogenizing force in its own right or if it is an arena within which individuals assert particularistic, localized identities in the face of globalization. Neo-institutionalists, such as John Meyer and his colleagues (1997), describe globally-diffused models of cultural, political and economic organization which limit the construction of difference. In contrast, Robertson (1991) argues that globalization allows for greater religious diversity because individuals construct local religious identities in relation to the world as a whole rather than in response to their small corner of it.

Studies of diasporic religion or religion in the diaspora grew out of heightened scholarly interest in diasporas in general. This work responds to the widespread recognition that social, economic and political life increasingly transcend national borders and cultures and that individuals sustain multiple identities and loyalties and create culture using elements from various settings (Cohen, 1999). Notions of diaspora and diasporic religion have played a more central role in European scholarship than they have in the United States.[2] The distinct intellectual traditions these conversations build upon partially explains this difference. The Birmingham School, for example, explores identity construction and the role of consciousness and subcultures in encouraging collective solidarity at the social margins. Postcolonial studies, with its emphasis on the continuing legacy of empire, has also strongly influenced diaspora studies. These explore how discursive practices and identities are constructed and imagined during the colonial, national and post-colonial periods. While this work generally tells us a lot about the trans-

---

[2]Exceptions are U.S.-based scholars of diaspora and postcolonialism such as Kachig Tololyan, James Clifford, and Arjun Appadurai who are also important contributors to these debates.

formation of religious life in the immigrant context, it has less to say about the ways in which migration continues to transform sending-country life. It tends to treat migrant and nonmigrant religious life as discrete entities rather than as occurring within the same transnational social field and influencing each other.

In contrast, studies of transnational migration are largely an American product that are, in part, intended to counterbalance race and ethnic and immigration scholarship's focus on immigrant incorporation. These researchers seek to challenge conventional wisdom about immigrant political and economic integration by demonstrating that individuals stay connected to their host communities even as they put down roots in the United States. The role that religion plays in enabling transnational membership has only recently begun to be taken into account. For instance, Rudolph and Piscatori's *Transnational Religion and Fading States* (1997), one of the few books employing a vocabulary of transnational religion, has little to do with immigration. Instead, "transnational" is used to capture the ways in which global or world religions create a transnational civil society that challenges nation-states and security interests as they have been traditionally understood (Eickelman, 1997; Levine and Stoll, 1997) Another set of articles documents the macro-level connections between global religious actors that cross national boundaries (Baker, 1997; Della Cava, 1997).

Research on the religious practices of transnational migrants are connected to the literature on global and diasporic religion because transnational migration households, congregations and communities are sites where diasporic, global and transnational religions are created. The hybridized or creolized religious beliefs and practices that the migration experience gives rise to emerge where local and global religious influences converge. Global religious institutions shape the transnational migration experience at the same time that migrants chip away at and recreate global religions by making them local and then starting the process anew. Transnational migrants bring particular incarnations of global religion with them, create new forms by combining what they bring with what they encounter, and then reintroduce these ideas, practices, identities, and social capital – or what I call social remittances – back to their sending communities (Levitt, 1999). Furthermore, migrant religious institutions are also sites where globally-diffused models of social organization and local responses come together to produce new mixes of religious beliefs and practices. The study of transnational migration and religion, therefore, provides an empirical window onto one way in which religious globalization actually gets done.

One of the reasons the connections between these bodies of work have been underdeveloped in much of the literature is that the levels, scope and sites of transnational migration and their position within the global arena have not been well specified. Let me suggest one mapping of this terrain. My comments are summarized in Table 1.

TABLE 1
LEVELS AND COMPONENTS OF THE TRANSNATIONAL RELIGIOUS FIELD

1. Individual transnational religious practices, including such things as formal and informal devotional practices enacted alone or in groups and in popular and institutionalized settings, tithing or periodic contributions to home-country religious groups, fundraising, hosting visiting religious leaders, consulting home-country religious leaders, and pilgrimages. Both the objective and subjective dimensions of the religious experience must be taken into account.
2. The organizational contexts in which transnational migrants enact their religious lives.
3. The ties between local transnational organizations and their host and home-country regional, national, and international counterparts.
4. The role of states.
5. The role of global culture and institutions.

Transnational migrants are individuals who live aspects of their social, economic and political lives in at least two settings. They establish themselves in their host countries while they continue to earn money, vote and pray in their countries of origin.   In certain settings, the impact of these activities is felt primarily by those who actually move, while in others their strength and scope is so powerful and widespread that aspects of nonmigrants' lives are enacted transnationally as well. Some migrants participate in transnational activities on a regular basis while others do so only occasionally, in response to a crisis or special event. Some migrants engage in a wide range of economic, social and political transnational practices, while others confine their activities to a single arena of transnational activism. They have business interests in their sending communities but belong to religious organizations and participate in political activities that firmly locate them in the countries where they now reside (Levitt, 2001a).

The targets of these activities also vary. Some migrants participate in practices directed at local, bounded communities in their home and host countries, while the transnational practices in which others engage reinforce their membership in the sending country as a whole. For example, Dominican migration to the Jamaica Plain neighborhood of Boston from the sending community of Miraflores created a transnational village to which nonmigrants and migrants belonged. Many of the economic, social and political transnational activities in which these individuals participated   were directed toward these local sites (Levitt, 2001b). In contrast, other migrants engage in transnational practices which attest to their continued membership in the broader sending nation. When Irish Catholic migrants from the Inishowen Peninsula, who have settled in Boston, attend church and receive services from the Irish-government-supported Irish Pastoral Center, these activities do more to reinforce their ties to the broader nation of Ireland than to specific local settings.

One way that migrants stay connected to their sending communities is through transnational religious practices. These practices exhibit the same variations in form, intensity, target and scope that I have described. They are also reinforced by and give rise to religious organizations that may, in turn, assume transnational properties of their own. For example, some migrants sustain long-term, long-distance memberships in the religious organizations to which they belonged prior to migration. They still make significant financial contributions to these groups, raise funds to support their activities, host visiting religious leaders, seek long-distance spiritual and practical guidance from them, participate in worship and cultural events during return visits, and are the subject of nonmigrants' prayers in their absence. Other migrants participate in religious pilgrimages, worship particular saints or deities, or engage in informal, popular religious practices that affirm their continued attachments to a particular sending-country group or place.

Transnational religious identities and practices have both objective and subjective dimensions. The unobservable dimensions of religious life have often been given short shrift because the analytical tools we have to study them are undeveloped and undervalued. Religion plays a critical role in identity construction, meaning making, and value formation. Migrants also use religion to create alternative allegiances and places of belonging. The ways in which memory and imagination are used to create transnational identities must be taken into account.

The transnational religious practices of individuals are often reinforced by the organizational contexts within which they take place. For example, migrants may belong to host-country religious institutions that have formal ties to a home-country "sister congregation." They may belong to a group that functions as a franchise or chapter of a sending-country group that is regularly supervised and funded by home-country leaders. Or, the denomination that they belong to may form part of a worldwide religious institution that accepts them as members wherever they are.

To understand the role of religion in transnational migration, then, we must build from the ground up. We need to start by examining the ways in which ordinary individuals live their everyday religious lives across borders, explore the ways in which these activities influence their continued sending and receiving-country membership, and analyze the relationship between cross-border religious membership and other kinds of transnational belonging. We need to understand what difference it makes for sending and receiving-country communities when migrants express their continued allegiances through religious rather than ethnic or political arenas. We need to explore these changes in both the home and host-country contexts and observe the ways in which they iteratively transform one another over time.

Research on the religious lives of transnational migrants must also be concerned with how local sending and receiving-country religious organizations respond to migration and with what changes, if any, these trigger at the regional, national and international organizational levels. For example, localized connections emerging between members and leaders of Brazilian Baptist churches in Governador Valadares in Brazil and in Framingham, Massachusetts must be analyzed within the context of the broader national and international denominational connections within which they emerge. This context-specific approach is particularly important when studying religious traditions not characterized by a unitary set of beliefs and practices, and with no central authority, because these vary considerably across settings.

Transnational migrants clearly live in multilayered global worlds. So while research on religion and transnational migration focuses on individuals and the local, regional and national organizations in which they participate, it must nest these processes within the multilayered social fields in which they take place. Of singular importance is the role of states, which regulate movement and religious expression and thereby strongly influence the magnitude and character of migrants' transnational religious practices.[3] The religious institutions created by Turkish migrants in Belgium, for example, are fostered by the almost wholesale transplantation of the Turkish religious infrastructure via official Belgian-Turkish channels. In his comparison of Moroccan (primarily Berber) and Turkish migrants in Belgium, Lesthaeghe (2002) found that Turkish migrants and their children were much more likely to engage in transnational practices, such as home ownership in Turkey or returning to Turkey to find a marriage partner, than their Moroccan counterparts. He partially attributes this difference to the Turkish government's ongoing involvement in the religious lives of its emigrants.

[3]Faist (2000), Menjívar (2002), and Smith (1995), among others, also stress the role of the state in shaping transnational activities.

Moroccans, in contrast, encountered a religious vacuum that was initially filled by Saudi-sponsored Islamic cultural activities and later by a range of cross-cutting fundamentalist influences. The net outcome for second generation Moroccans is that they form few religious or political linkages to their ancestral home and that the immigrant community is characterized by a high degree of secularism and religious fragmentation.

A second example of state influence becomes evident when we think about migrants from countries with little separation between church and state and contrast them with those who come from countries with greater religious pluralism. In countries such as Ireland or Pakistan, migrants are often hardpressed to separate what is Pakistani or Muslim or Irish or Catholic about them. Religion and nationality reinforce one another. Such individuals are more likely to be transnational activists because two allegiances motivate their continuing identification.

Finally, global culture and institutions clearly shape migrants' transnational religious practices. Widely available and accepted models of religious institutionalization strongly influence the ways in which migrants combine host and homeland traditions. Because the "model" for praying and for administering Pentecostal churches is recognizable around the world, migrants can locate themselves in almost any church, no matter of where they are. They also have access to a familiar and agreed upon set of tools with which to organize their collective religious lives. That the tradition of pilgrimages or establishing holy sites is also readily recognizable and replicable is another way in which global religious institutions provide migrants with the tools and language they need to assert transnational belonging.

Again, this mapping of the transnational religious field that I have proposed tries to make explicit the link between studies of global and diasporic religion and studies of the religious practices of transnational migrants. Having said this, relatively little work has been done that directly examines the relationship between transnational migration and religion. In the following section, I selectively review research on three aspects of the religious lives of transnational migrants: their organizational dimensions, the relationship between transnational religious space and other forms of belonging, and the relationship between transnational religion and politics.

VARIATIONS IN TRANSNATIONAL MIGRANTS' RELIGIOUS ORGANIZATIONS

Many transnational religious activities take place in individualized, informal settings. They combine formal religious elements with popular folk practices. But an important part of transnational religious life occurs within organizational contexts. When migrants turn to religious arenas to assert their memberships, religious organizations change in response. The more these groups are structured, led and financed transnationally, the more they facilitate transnational practices. Researchers have suggested several approaches to categorizing transnational religious groups.

Ebaugh and Chafetz (2002) propose using network analysis to understand religious connections across boundaries. They argue for studies that examine variations in the density of network nodes and ties, the direction of material and social flows, and the intensity of these flows. Their research examined the relationship between network ties between individuals, local-level corporate bodies, and international religious bodies and found that ties frequently crossed between various types of nodes. For example, at one end of their proposed spectrum, ties between a Mexican Catholic Church in Houston and its sending community of Monterrey were almost completely interpersonal, although they formed within the context of a vast international organization. At the other extreme, Vietnamese Catholics and Buddhists in Houston formed transnational connections to their homelands based solely on institutional, as opposed to, interpersonal connections. These authors conclude that socioeconomic status, legality, distance from the homeland, the geographic dispersion of the immigrant community and English language fluency influence network types.

Yang (2001) also uses a network approach to analyze transnational Chinese Christian communities. He finds three-layered trans-pacific networks formed by contacts between individuals, single churches and parachurch international organizations. These connect migrants in Taiwan, Hong Kong and Mainland China to their counterparts located primarily in the United States and Canada. Political and economic instability in Asia propels individuals and institutions to create transnational ties. These networks also arise because the absence of a strong denominational infrastructure in China encourages the emergence of loose associations between local congregations.

My own work reveals at least three types of transnational religious organizational patterns[4] The first, exemplified by the Catholic Church, is an

---

[4]My research is an ongoing study of transnational migration among Dominicans, Irish, Indians, Brazilians, and Pakistanis to the greater Boston Metropolitan area. Findings from my work on Dominicans from the village of Miraflores who live in the Jamaica Plain neighborhood of Boston, Irish from the Inishowen Peninsula who live in Dorchester, Indians from the Baroda District of Gujarat State who have settled around the city of Lowell, and Brazil-

extended transnational religious organization.[5] From the mid 1800s to the present, the Catholic church has sent out religious orders, mounted missionary campaigns, operated schools, built pilgrimage shrines, and organized international encounters that produced a vast, interconnected network of transnational activities (Casanova, 1994). When transnational migrants circulate in and out of parishes or religious movement groups in the United States, Ireland, the Dominican Republic or Brazil, they extend and tailor this already global religious system into a site where membership in both the sending and receiving communities is expressed.

These intensified connections are evident in the Brazilian, Dominican and Irish communities in the Boston Metropolitan area that I study and in the work of other scholars of immigrant religion. They grow out of interpersonal ties between individuals and clergy in the home and host countries. They also arise because migrants and nonmigrants sometimes participate in parallel social and religious activities, and use the same worship materials, all within the context of an institution that espouses universal Catholicism. For example, several priests in Governador Valadares (where many of the Brazilians in the Boston area come from) said they received frequent requests to say prayers or dedicate masses to their emigrant parishioners. Brazilian immigrant Apostolate churches in Massachusetts read from the same handout of weekly prayers and hymns used in Brazil (printed in Brasilia, the Brazilian capital) and organized mission campaigns that corresponded to those taking place in Brazil. When the National Conference of Brazilian Bishops launched a year-long campaign against homelessness, Brazilian immigrant churches undertook a campaign for better housing and stronger neighborhoods. Religious leaders chose these activities because they resonated with those undertaken in Brazil, while more directly addressing the problems facing immigrants in Boston. Brazilian and U.S. Church leaders have also explored ways to coordinate staffing and training with one another,

ians from Governador Valadares who live in Framingham are discussed in this paper. The project research team includes myself, colleagues in each sending country, and a group of graduate and undergraduate researchers. In the United States, we collect data by interviewing first and second-generation individuals and organizational leaders, observing meetings and special events, and reviewing pertinent documents. After each interview in Boston, we ask for the names of nonmigrant family members to contact. We then travel to each sending country and work with colleagues there to conduct a parallel set of interviews with individuals and organizational leaders at the local, regional, and national level.

[5]I propose these types as heuristic tools. They are not static, impermeable categories. In fact, religious institutions may pass from one form to another over time.

including a 1999 Brazilian Bishops' plan to expand their Pastoral for Immigrants to Brazilians around the world.

In the case of Dominicans from Miraflores who migrated to Massachusetts, the parish-to-parish connections which developed between the United States and the Dominican Republic mutually transformed sending and receiving-country religious life. New immigrants were incorporated into multi-ethnic congregations which used a generic "Latino" worship style that included many familiar elements while excluding those that were uniquely Dominican. They told those at home about these changes in their religious practices and beliefs. Subsequent migrants arrived already pre-socialized into many elements of U.S. Latino Catholicism. They continued to infuse fresh "Dominicanness" into the church, though it was a "Dominicanness" that was each time more pan-Latino in tone. Continuous, cyclical transfers ensued which consolidated these pan-ethnic practices while blanching out their nation-specific elements. In this way, transnational ties both reinforced religious pluralism and abbreviated its scope (Levitt, 2001b).

McAlistar's (2002) work also highlights how Catholic and voodoo practices make transnational lifestyles possible and how the Haitian community uses these to make a space for themselves in the United States. Many of the Haitian migrants in New York that she studied live transnational lives. They work to support households in Haiti, send their children to school in Haiti, or return to Haiti for extended periods to rest. Religious pilgrimages, processions and rituals are just some of the ways that these migrants express their enduring attachments to Haiti. The Feast of our Lady of Miracles, for example, is commemorated in the United States at the same time that it is commemorated in Haiti. It signifies migrants' continued attachment to Haiti and serves to differentiate them from the African-American community in the United States.

Not all migrants take part in transnational religious practices, even when the organizations they belong to redefine their constituencies as those living within and outside of national borders. Menjívar (1999) found that Catholic church membership was far less conducive to transnational activism than membership in Evangelical churches. Because the Catholic Church in Washington, D.C. wanted to develop a sense of pan-ethnic identity among its new immigrant members, it emphasized common projects and discouraged activities directed at particular home communities. Religious leaders also feared that homeland-oriented activities would politicize and divide the Salvadoran community.

The Charismatic, Neucatecumenal, and Cursillo movements that are associated with the Catholic Church also expand the radius of Catholic activities across borders. These groups articulate a life view that is disseminated globally through international conferences, fellowship meetings, prayer links, and the media (Peterson and Vásquez, 2001). Research on these groups provides mixed evidence about their role in promoting transnational belonging. Charismatic groups formed by migrants and nonmigrants in Boston and the Dominican Republic worked in partnership with one another. Migrants visiting Miraflores, and nonmigrants visiting Boston, were warmly welcomed at meetings. This access to "a membership card that works everywhere" encouraged participants' sense of transnational membership and constantly reminded nonmigrants that they too belonged to a social and religious cross-border community (Levitt, 2001b).

Peterson and Vásquez's (2001) work on the Charismatic Catholic Renewal Movement (CCR) in El Salvador and among Central American migrants in Washington revealed different effects. Many of the leaders of the immigrant community in Washington were active in the Charismatic movement in El Salvador. They brought this experience to bear on their lives in Washington, and when they visited El Salvador they also participated in CCR activities. Some members became transnational activists in response to the personal transformations they experienced by joining the CCR. Because of their new religious outlook, they began to send remittances to their families and money for community development projects. But these changes produced few organized transnational activities. Peterson and Vásquez found no connections between religious groups in El Salvador and Washington and no transnational missions. They conclude that the individual transnational allegiances prompted by religion do not necessarily translate into collective efforts.

Protestant churches with affiliates in the United States and in Latin America typify a second type of negotiated transnational religious organization. These groups also extend and deepen organizational ties already in place but within the context of less-hierarchical, decentralized institutional structures. Instead, flexible partnerships that are not already pre-established need to be worked out. I focus on Brazilian immigration to the Boston Metropolitan area as a case in point.

Protestantism has grown tremendously in Latin America, and particularly in Brazil, in the last four decades. In 1997, Governador Valadares, a city of approximately 300,000, had an estimated 430 Protestant churches (Levitt,

2003). These congregations ranged from Mainline Protestant denominations to start-up Pentecostal groups. They prayed in modest private homes and storefronts as well as in large, elegant churches that seat hundreds. Even some of the smallest, most incipient groups, however, had plaques outside their doors indicating that they belonged to larger organizations with chapters in the United States.

Both interpersonal and organizational ties produce this negotiated transnational religious space. As in the Catholic Church, individual migrant and nonmigrant church members and religious leaders often kept up relations with one another. Organizational connections ranged from narrowly-focused ties between the sending-country congregations that migrants used to belong to and the churches where they currently worship to newly-mediated arrangements between sending and receiving-country denominational branches with long histories of missionary work in Brazil.

Like the Catholic Church, relations between Protestant individuals and churches also broaden and thicken what, in some cases, are already global institutions or, in other cases, create new global connections. In contrast to the Catholic case, however, these are negotiated with respect to authority, organization and ritual. There is no leader or administrative hierarchy to set policy and dictate how things are done. When transnational migrants deepen these cross-border connections, issues like power sharing, financing, and administrative practice must be worked out. These negotiations produce a diverse, diluted set of partnerships that are unstable and shift over time. They function like what Manuel Castells (2000) has called a network society – decentralized, flexible yet connected networks providing customized services and goods. Just as decentralized, adaptive modes of production are better suited to compete within the global economy, so flexible production and dissemination of religious goods may be better suited to serve contemporary religious consumers.

Several studies support this view. Wellmeier (1998) argued that because Guatemalan Mayans belonged to independent storefront ministries that were ethnically homogeneous, it was easier for them to devote their energies toward improvements in their hometowns. Because the evangelical church that León (1998) studied formed part of a network of more than twenty-five churches in the United States, Spain, and Mexico, members felt like they belonged to a broad, powerful supranational movement that could sustain their interest and support. Menjivar's (1999) work also lends credence to this view. In contrast to their Salvadoran Catholic counterparts, the Protestant churches she studied were not restrained by an extensive and demanding formal institutional network. They did not have to create new, more inclusive identities to encourage newcomers to feel like they belonged to the U.S. church. Instead, because leaders and members often came from the same regions of El Salvador and because they were all Christians, engaging in home-country oriented activities produced little conflict. In fact, one migrant church in Washington had sister churches in Maryland, Virginia, North Carolina and eastern El Salvador. They broadcast a two-hour radio program in El Salvador at least three times a week, including a call-in component so listeners could hear friends and relatives from back home. According to one member, "We are related to the church there in El Salvador spiritually and in practice. We are oriented to them and they are to us. It's like one church in two places" (Menjivar, 1999:605).

The experiences of Gujarati Hindus from the Baroda district in India, suggest a third type of recreated transnational religious organization.[6] Migrants had to start their own religious groups when they came to the United States because there were few Hindu organizations when they first arrived. Some migrants initiated this process on their own and then sought direction from homeland religious leaders. In other cases, Indian religious leaders came to areas where there were large numbers of migrants and identified individuals who could help them establish themselves in the United States. Most of these groups now function like franchises or chapters of their counterpart organizations in India. Franchises are run primarily by migrants who receive periodic support, resources and guidance from sending-country leadership while chapters receive regular support and supervision from sending-country leadership.

The Devotional Associates of Yogeshwar, or the Swadhyaya movement, is an example of a group that was recreated in the United States. Swadhyaya groups in Baroda are organized informally.   According to Didiji, the group's leader in Bombay, leadership emerges consensually; those who are most knowledgeable or experienced become the *motobhais* or elder brothers of each chapter. In the United States, however, such groups need to look and act like formal congregations to be able to raise funds, obtain tax exempt status, or rent meeting halls (Warner and Wittner, 1998). In response, the organi-

---

[6]Williams (1988:230) calls these Hindu Organizations of Indian Americans "made in the U.S.A. ... assembled in the U.S. from imported components by relatively unskilled labor (at least unskilled by traditional standards) and adapted to fit new designs to reach a new and growing market."

zation in America is divided into nine geographic regions, each with its own coordinator. Although these leaders are allowed to make decisions on their own, they say that they consult with officials in Bombay on a regular basis.

Gibb (1998) described Harari Muslims in Ethiopia and Canada whose experience of diaspora prompted them to construct an identity that could be meaningful transnationally. To reinforce group cohesion over time and space, they felt that they needed to articulate values that were relevant in both the home and host country. Although Harari ethnicity was constructed within the context of a transnational movement, and in response to pressures from the Ethiopian and Canadian states, the meaning of "Muslimness" is no longer local and culturally-specific but instead reflects a more homogenized, globalized tradition that is similar to that of other Muslims in Canada. As a result, Hararis are more oriented toward other Canadian Muslims than to other Ethiopian groups. By developing a pan-Muslim identity, they can communicate with a wider community based on their shared religious traditions.

Because few of the studies I describe here are longitudinal, they tell us little about how transnational religious organizations change over time. Work on the Soka Gakkai International (SGI-USA), a Japanese Buddhist group, is one exception. At first, most members were Japanese immigrants married to American military personnel. They relied heavily on the organization in Japan for practical and financial support. Initially, SGI-USA maintained much of its Japanese character – it was organized hierarchically, leaders achieved their posts based on personal mentor-disciple relations, and women were excluded from holding office. Taking part in religious pilgrimages to the principal Nichiren Shoshu temple reinforced members' attachments to Japan. Until temples were constructed in the United States, new converts either had to travel to Japan or wait until priests came to the United States to become official members of the group. The subsequent influx of U.S. converts, who quickly predominated, transformed the SGI-USA. The group began holding its meetings in English, and Japanese customs, such as kneeling and taking one's shoes off during worship, were abandoned in favor of more American worship styles. When the Japanese organization became embroiled in scandal, the U.S. chapter, which until then relied heavily on the mother temple, formally separated itself from its Japanese leaders. Becoming more American was also a way to avoid falling victim to the anti-cult fever spreading through the United States (Machacek, 2000).

The research I have summarized highlights variations in migrants' transnational religious organizations. But migrants' transnational religious practices are also frequently enacted outside of organized settings. We must therefore examine the ways in which believers use symbols and ideas to imagine and locate themselves within religious landscapes and analyze how religious and political geographies overlap with one another. The following section lays out these issues in greater detail.

TRANSNATIONAL RELIGIOUS SPACE AS AN ALTERNATIVE LANDSCAPE

Ancient pilgrims traveling from one sacred landmark to another, and their contemporary counterparts, create imaginary religious topographies whose boundaries are delineated by these holy places (Eickelman and Piscatori, 1990). Transnational migrants also use religion to delineate an alternative cartography of belonging. Religious icons and sacred shrines, rather than national flags, mark these spaces. The imagined moral and physical geographies that result may fall within national boundaries, transcend but coexist with them, or create new, alternative spaces that, for some individuals, have greater salience and inspire stronger loyalties than politically-defined terrain.

For example, Haitian migrants in New York simply added Harlem to the roster of places where they carry out their spiritual work. By doing so, they extended the boundaries of their spiritual practices and superinscribed them onto the actual physical landscape where they had settled (McAlister, 2002). By building and conducting rituals at a shrine to their national patron saint, Cuban exiles in Miami created what Tweed (1999) calls transtemporal and translocative space. These rituals allowed migrants to recover a past when they were still in Cuba and to imagine a future when they would return. Through these enactments, migrants also asserted their enduring membership in their community of origin. Families brought their newborns to the shrine to formally transform those born in America into citizens of the imagined Cuban nation. In this way, the community used religion to extend the boundaries of Cuba to incorporate those living outside it.

Haitian migrants from Ri Rivyé who settled in Palm Beach County not only use religion to locate themselves within an alternative sacred landscape, but to extricate themselves from it as well (Richman, 2002). Although most of the members of this community are Catholic, many also believe in *lwas* or "saints" who can afflict and protect members of the descent groups to which they belong. *Lwas* must be fed, entertained, and lavished with copious offerings because when they feel neglected or ignored by their heirs, they often retaliate by afflicting illness, hardship, or property loss.

According to Richman (2002:14)

> Although they are characterized as ancient, immutable symbols of "African" tradition, the Iwa have shown that they can be most adaptable to changing conditions of global reproduction. With so many of their "children" now living and working "over there" the Iwa is busier than ever. I once had the opportunity to interview a spirit about her protection of migrants. The female spirit was possessing a male ritual leader, who was conducting a healing rite for an absent migrant in the presence of the migrants' parents and myself. The spirit, whose name is Ezili Dantó/ Our lady of Lourdes, said to us, "Every three days I am in Miami…I have to keep watch over everything that goes on. Miami is where the core is…like all of the spirits whose movements are said to be like the wind, Ezili Dantó can instantly traverse these international boundaries.

Those who believe in these saints situate themselves in a ritual space transcending political boundaries where spirits easily move back and forth to take care of them. In return, they must continue to take care of their *Iwa*, often at tremendous expense and effort. While some see their success in Miami as proof of the *Iwa's* intervention on their behalf, others feel that too many of their remittances are wasted on the *Iwa's* care. They convert to Protestantism as a way to extricate themselves from this system of kinship and ritual obligation.

Suh's (2002) work brings to light the complex relationship between ethnic and religious transnational landscapes. The Korean American Buddhists in her study use religion to locate themselves more centrally with respect to both Korea and the United States and, in particular, in relation to their Korean-American Christian counterparts. Many of the Buddhists in her study associate Buddhism with a nationalistic sense of belonging to Korea. They see Buddhism as an authentic marker of Korean identity and use it to construct a barrier against the undesired Westernization and Americanization that, from their perspective, characterizes the Korean-American Christian experience. At the same time, they claim that Buddhism makes them better Americans because Buddhist doctrines of self-enlightenment are more in line with American democracy than the Christian doctrines they associate with a lack of free will.

Suh argues that Chogye temple membership reinforces homeland ties, even if members never return to Korea. The group hosts numerous Korean monks who give lectures and train members. Because religious leaders travel frequently to Korea, there is always news from the Order back home. The main order of the Chogye established a Los Angeles Branch of Seoul-based

Eastern Mountain Buddhist College, which offers a two-year certificate course in Buddhist Studies to lay members. Although the Sa Chal Temple is run independently, unlike many other U.S.-based groups which are still officially administered by leaders in Seoul, Abbot Lee, the group's leader, still feels that his ties to Korea are crucial to the development of Buddhism in the West.

Many of the Salvadoran youth that Gomez and Vásquez (2001) studied felt they belonged neither in the United States nor in El Salvador. They joined transnational gangs which provided them with a close, tight-knit community and helped counteract their feelings of marginality in the society at large. Gang members shared many of the characteristics of transnational migrants because they acted, made decisions, and developed identities shaped by relationships and resources that crossed borders. In fact, when the Salvadoran peace accords were signed in 1992, they were approved in El Salvador as well as Los Angeles.

The appeal of gang life gradually wore thin when some members became involved in drug trafficking and gangs became a less effective safe haven for adolescents trying to fit in. Pentecostal churches stepped in to fill this gap. They functioned much like gangs, "saving souls transnationally" by using contacts in El Salvador and the United States to reach potential converts. These efforts worked because they "combined deterritorialization (the operation of transnational webs) with reterritorialization (re-centering of self and community)" (Vásquez et al., 2001:34). Religion engendered an alternative, ultimately more satisfying space, because it successfully synthesized self and community.

Some of the Brazilians and Pakistanis I am studying in Massachusetts also use religion to create alternatives places of belonging. Some imagine themselves within global Muslim or Christian denominational communities which are grounded in particular national contexts by their ties to particular sending and receiving churches. Others locate themselves within global religious communities that supercede national boundaries. Pastora Eliana, a leader of a renewed Brazilian Baptist church in Watertown, Massachusetts, said she felt invisible when she first came to the United States because the state offered her no official category to express her Brazilianness. She began to feel she belonged in the United States only when her church formed a partnership with the American Baptist Convention (ABC). It is through her identity as a Baptist, rather than as a Brazilian American, that she began the process of integration into the United States. But her Baptist identity also firmly grounds her in a global religious community that welcomes and empowers her as well.

> Q.: Why wouldn't one be a Baptist? Could you imagine a world where the salient identity would be a Baptist rather than Brazilian or American?
>
> I think that this identity already exists. I mean being a Brazilian person and being a Baptist is synonymous with being smart. It is synonymous with wisdom because among us we know that Baptists are capable of thinking or being in a relationship with one another, of having disagreements but at the same time finding solutions and agreement among ourselves. Calling ourselves Baptists is something that we as a community are proud of. When the denomination (the American Baptist Convention) showed that it was open to establish this relationship with us, giving recognition to us, it was something that we celebrated because it means that we are no longer invisible. So far, we have been an invisible culture without any connection with the new system that we are in. But now, this kind of feeling is so strong because we really feel that we are becoming family in a very constructive way.

Being a Baptist enabled Pastora Eliana to find a place for herself in the United States. But because her religious life takes place within an ethnic Brazilian context, being a Baptist also reinforces her ties to Brazil. The religious landscape she creates fits within and grounds her within the Brazilian-American transnational landscape. Her religious identity inscribes her in a global religious community that is strongly rooted in the United States and in Brazil.

In contrast, Pastor Luis of the Brazilian International Church of the Four Square Gospel categorically tells his followers that they live in the Kingdom of God. One becomes a good citizen, he says, by becoming a good Christian. The main point, Pastor Luis says, is that

> ... when they are good Christians, they are good citizens. So when we teach them to be consistent in their faith, they will be, at the same time, good people, good husbands, good people in the sense that they will try to help others, to try to make a difference in their neighborhoods. They will be concerned about other's well-being. So it's not necessary to become legal and become naturalized and so forth. But in the Bible itself, in the way that Christians should be, would be enough for them to be good citizens .... There are a set of ways of being in the world that have nothing to do with whether you are Brazilian or whether you are from the U.S. but that have more to do with faith in Christ. I teach my followers that they have a responsibility to all mankind but especially to their fellow Christians. We live in a world where Christ is the king, not George Bush or Fernando Colar.

For Pastor Luis' followers, religious membership takes precedence over dual political membership. Believers inhabit a Christian world where God and Christ come before elected officials. This is not to say that national boundaries disappear – political as well as religious landmarks populate this religious space and the rules of national citizenship still apply. But Christian rather than civic values form the basis for membership-in-good-standing in local, national, and transnational political communities. Unlike Pastora Eliana, whose membership in a global religious community reinforces her dual national identity, the religious landscape for Pastor Luis and his followers forms the basis for national and ethnic membership.

RELIGION AS A GUIDE TO TRANSNATIONAL CIVIC ENGAGEMENT

Just as religion furnishes the elements from which an alternative geography is created, so it guides believers about their collective rights and responsibilities. Religious institutions differ from other immigrant institutions in that they see themselves as embodying universal and timeless truths. They provide members with moral compasses and orient them to act upon these values in particular settings in particular ways. As global interconnectedness expands, to what extent do religious traditions articulate globally-oriented theologies? What lessons do transnational religious groups disseminate to members about the rights and duties of transnational, if not global, citizens?

Many assume, for instance, that Pentecostals are apolitical with respect to both transnational and national concerns. But despite what may be the apolitical or anti-political nature of their message, several researchers suggest that Pentecostal communities influence the secular settings in which they are located. The Salvadoran Pentecostal churches in Washington that Menjívar (1999) studied kept in close touch with their sister congregations in El Salvador. They supported community development projects in their home communities, sponsored speaking exchanges between sending and receiving-country pastors, shared a monthly newspaper, held conventions that brought congregations together, and participated in international Evangelical church councils. Evangelization rather than community development motivated these efforts. Members' primary goal was to strengthen and extend the community of God and any political or civic achievements were of secondary importance.

Peterson *et al.* (2001) lend support to this view. Pentecostal communities can erect clear boundaries between the safe, sanctified world of faith and its dangerous, violent secular counterpart with only partial success. Because members fulfill multiple roles and participate in multiple settings they influence the secular world and it continues to influence them. Pentecostal churches also reproduce patterns of domination and exclusion. Their rhetoric of spiritual warfare creates a "terrain of control" that is difficult to challenge.

> Since this closed social terrain is ultimately grounded in the radical deterritorializa-tion demanded by the reign of God, it mirrors the erasure of borders and identities that is central to globalization. In other words, for all its emphasis on the self, Pen-tecostalism, like global capitalism, homogenizes, making particularity only a strate-gy or stepping stone toward the production of globality/universality (Peterson *et al.*, 2001:40).

Peruvian migrants in the United States, Spain, Argentina, and Japan brought images of their patron saint with them to their new homes, raised funds for ritual celebrations, and conquered host-country public spaces by organizing annual processions (Paerregaard, 2001) Although some of these activities involved initial communication with the Mother Church in Lima, homeland ties gradually weakened. There was little evidence of coordination between Brotherhoods in the same receiving country or between different host country contexts. Instead, Paerregaard argues, members used religious engagement to pursue host-country-oriented goals such as carving out a place for themselves in the public sphere and differentiating themselves from other minorities. Transnational religious activities, to the extent that they took shape, promoted host-country political integration.

My work suggests a number of variations in the forms and conse-quences of religiously-motivated transnational politics. When new Irish, Dominican, and Brazilian migrants extend the global Catholic church through their homeland ties, they become part of powerful, resource-rich networks that are potential venues for protection and representation in their home and host communities. When Irish migrants attend church, for exam-ple, they learn about social and legal services that are available to them. Their native-born priests give them indirect classes in local community problem solving and mobilization. At the national level, the Irish Apostolate U.S., an umbrella organization which brings together Irish pastoral workers around the country, has joined forces with a coalition of Irish Immigration Centers and created an informal political action committee to advocate for immigrant rights and amnesty. The Irish Apostolate also functions as the Irish govern-ment's window onto the emigrant community in the United States.

> The Minister of Foreign Affairs came here three years ago and the Minister for Social Welfare came last year. Any time a President comes, like Mary Robinson or Mary McCalese, they come and talk to us. Mary Robinson came and talked to us at lunch

and asked us about the different issues we confront. We also visit Irish prisoners here
and we keep the government informed about whether they are being treated properly, what their sentences are, whether they can be sent back home. We are the voice
of the immigrant community for the Irish government (Father Mike, Boston, 2001).

The clergy working for the Irish Apostolate in the United States and
their counterparts in Ireland also represent Irish emigrants to the Irish public. They receive a yearly grant from the Irish government and must report
back to their legislators about their activities. Father Ronald of the Irish
Episcopal Commission for Emigrants in Dublin, who supervises the priests
working outside of Ireland, sees himself as an advocate for the diaspora. The
commission is one of the few institutions, he says, that fights to keep emigrants on the public's radar screen.

The Irish Catholic experience represents one way in which the relationship between transnational religion and politics plays out. Churchgoing
introduces migrants to U.S. political culture and practices. It is a potential
springboard to civic engagement because it exposes migrants to political
issues and teaches them tools to address them. At the same time, the Irish
government and church officials still see themselves as responsible for their
emigrant flock. The personal and organizational ties connecting the United
States and Ireland are designed to reinforce migrants' continued sense of
attachment to the Irish national and religious community.

The Protestant churches in my study also deliver services to, advocate
for, and politically socialize their members but, within the context of weaker organizational networks. Most of these pastors work individually with
their members to get jobs, find housing, or regularize their immigration status. The message of living "in God's Kingdom," though, produces different
views on appropriate civic engagement.

Some churchgoers believe that their faith teaches them to go outside
religious arenas and make a difference. They get involved because they take
religious teachings as a call to exercise substantive citizenship and as a guide
for how to do so.

> I know there are some people who think of themselves as living in the Kingdom of
> Christ. Pastor Manuel talks about that a lot. But I see myself as firmly planted on
> the ground. My life is here and in Brazil. I feel very strongly about my church and
> about the lessons it teaches. But I see these lessons as telling me to get involved in
> the world around me. So when the police want to meet with the Brazilian com-
> munity to understand us better or there are meetings to try to get people driver's
> licenses (which is illegal without a social security card), I go. My God tells me to be
> there and to help out (Umberto, 52-year-old migrant, Framingham).

For others, who locate themselves within a Christian geography, civic engagement is motivated by religious identities and beliefs more than a sense of ethnic pride or patriotism.   Like the evangelical churchgoers studied by Menjívar (1999) and Peterson *et al.* (2001), these migrants worked with civic groups because this was what was available although they would rather have worked for religious groups. They are doing the work of God because they identify as Christians,   although their actions may also happen to be political.

> When I volunteer at the soup kitchen or at my child's school, it is because this is what God would want me to do. I am not guided by what the Worker's Party has to say about Brazil or the Democratic Party has to say about here. I live in a Christian world that just happens to have national borders criss-crossing it. If what I do helps bring about political change, that's okay with me, but that's not my primary goal (Lourdes, 47-year-old migrant, Framingham).

CONCLUSION AND FUTURE DIRECTIONS

This paper proposes an approach to the study of one aspect of global religious life – migrants' transnational religious practices. I suggest that studies of transnational migration and religion focus on the everyday, lived practice of migrant religion in at least two locations. I propose that they examine the ways in which host country incorporation changes religious ideas and practice, how these changes affect sending-country religious life, and how these changes mutually reinforce one another over time. Research on migrants' transnational religious practices are not only about organizational manifestations of faith. They are also about the alternative places of belonging that religious ideas and symbols make possible and about the ways in which these sacred landscapes interact with the boundaries of political and civic life.

Clearly, there is much work to be done. This article offers only a brief, selective sketch of what is known about migrants' transnational religious practices based on the U.S. experience. This article is intentionally short on conclusions and long on calls for more empirical, grounded work. Many more studies are needed to flesh out how migrants' transnational religious practices are actually enacted, what their impacts are, what explains the variations between them, how transnational religious life differs from transnational life in other social arenas, and what these dynamics means for home- and host-country life.

These tasks pose methodological and epistemological challenges. How do we make concrete the landscapes and communities that people imagine? How can we move from the in-depth, grounded case studies we need to understand the complexity of experience to be able to make comparisons across groups? How would our questions change if we shifted the central organizing principle from nation to faith community – if we took seriously, as many respondents do, a world that is primarily organized around Islamic, Hindu, or Baptist identities rather than ethnic or national affinities, and that is built upon religious principles rather than civic ones?

The study of religious and cultural life across borders raises particular challenges not posed by the study of economics or politics. Religion is not a fixed set of elements but a dynamic web of shared meanings used in different ways in different contexts (Gardner, 1995). It is as much, it not more, about individualized, interior, informal practices and beliefs as it is about formal, collective manifestations of faith carried out in institutional settings. Since so many features of religious life are imagined, it is difficult to hold them constant or to determine where they begin and end. They are deeply felt but often difficult to express. Many of the studies cited in this article speak to the complex relationship between religion and ethnicity. A very interesting, potentially-promising set of research questions would untangle this relationship and explore the unique properties of ethnic and religious identities in enabling transnational belonging and the possible synergistic relationship between them.

On the other hand, several studies indicate parallels between transnational religious, economic and political practices. Like economic and political transnational practices, religion plays a role in transnational community creation and perpetuation (Espinosa, 1999; R.C. Smith, 1995). Religious festivals, and particularly Patron Saint Day celebrations, have always been important sites of contact, maintenance, and renewal of relations between migrants and nonmigrants. Immigrants churches often contribute significant sums of money to community development in their sending communities. Furthermore, migrants' transnational religious practices also generate the same kinds of conflicts over legitimate membership and status between migrants and nonmigrants that others have described (Goldring, 1998; Levitt, 2001b; Espinosa 1999). We need to sort out what is unique about transnational life in the religious sphere and to systematically compare religious transnational practices to transnational activities in other arenas.

What also becomes clear from this overview is how the local "fights back" and continues to challenge global religious homogenization. The same global religious institution is organized very differently in local contexts, making different kinds of demands on its immigrant members, with very different consequences for the relationship between religion, immigrant incorporation, and enduring transnational belonging. Again, additional work on how migrants actually globalize religion can shed light on these broader debates in the field.

As the title of this article implies, the relationship between religion and migration has a long history. Abraham began a journey, guided by his faith, that millions have followed. The intensification of life across borders will only increase the numbers for whom social, political, and religious membership is decoupled from residence. It is time we put religion front and center in our attempts to understand how identity and belonging are redefined in this increasingly global world.

REFERENCES

Baker, D.
1997 "World Religions and National States: "Competing Claims in East Asia." In *Transnational Religion and Fading States*. Eds. S. H. Rudolph and J. Piscatori. Boulder, CO.: Westview Press.

Beyer, P.
2001 "Introduction" In *Religion in the Process of Globalization*. Ed. P. Beyer. Wurzburg, Germany: Ergon Verlag.

Casanova, J.
1994 *Public Religions in the Modern World*. Chicago: University of Chicago Press.

Castells, M.
2000 *End of Millenium*. Oxford, England: Blackwell Publishers.

Clarke, C., C. Peach, and S. Vertovec.
1990 *South Asians Overseas*. New York and Cambridge: Cambridge University Press.

Cohen, R.
1999 *Global Diasporas: An Introduction*. Seattle: University of Washington Press.

Della Cava, R.
1997 "Religious Resource Networks: Roman Catholic Philanthropy in Central and East Europe. In *Transnational Religion and Fading States*. Ed. S. H. Rudolph and J. Piscatori. Boulder, CO.: Westview Press.

Ebaugh, H.R. and J. Chafetz.
2002 *Religion Across Borders: Transnational Religious Networks*. Walnut Creek: Altamira Press.

Eickelman, D.
1997 "Trans-state Islam and Security" In *Transnational Religion and Fading States*. Ed. S. H. Rudolph and J. Piscatori. Boulder, CO: Westview Press.

Eickelman, D. and J. Piscatori, eds.
1990 *Muslim Travelers: Pilgrimage, Migration and the Religious Imagination*. London: Routledge and Berkeley and Los Angeles: University of California Press.

Espinosa, V.
1999 "Negociando la Pertenencia en un Contexto Transnacional: Iglesia, Migracíon a Estados Unidos y Cambio sociocultural en un pueblo Mexicano," *Revista Estudios Sociologicos*. No. 50.

Faist, T.
2000 *The Volume and Dynamics of International Migration and Transnational Social Spaces.* Oxford: Oxford University Press.

Gardner, K.
1995 *Global Migrants, Local Lives.* Oxford, England: Clarendon Press.

Gibb, C.
1998 "Religious Identification in Transnational Contexts: Being and Becoming Muslim in Ethiopia and Canada," *Diaspora,* 7(2):247-267.

Goldring, L.
1998 "The Power of Status in Transnational Social Spaces." In *Transnationalism from Below Comparative Urban and Community Research.* Volume 6. Ed. L. Guarnizo and M.P. Smith. New Brunswick, NJ: Transaction Press.

Gómez, I. and Vásquez, M.,
2001 "Youth Gangs and Religion among Salvadorans in Washington and El Salvador. In *Christianity, Social Change, and Globalization in the Americas.* Ed. A. Peterson, P. Williams and M.Vásquez. New Brunswick, New Jersey: Rutgers University Press.

Huwelmeier, G.
2001 "Women's Congregations as Transnational Communities." Working Paper Transnational Communties Program 2K-13.

León, L.
1998 "Born Again in East LA: The Congregation as Border Space." In *Gatherings in Diaspora: Religious Communities and the New Immigration.* Ed. R.S. Warner and J. Wittner. Philadelphia: Temple University Press. Pp. 163-196.

Lesthaeghe, R.
2002 "Turks and Morrocans in Belgium: A Comparison." Seminar presented at the Center for Population and Development Studies, Harvard University.

Levine, D.H. and D. Stoll.
1997 "Bridging the Gap Between Empowerment and Power in Latin America." In *Transnational Religion and Fading States.* Ed. S. H. Rudolph and J. Piscatori. Boulder, CO: Westview Press. Pp. 63-104.

Levitt, P.
1999 "Social Remittances: A Local-Level, Migration-Driven Form of Cultural Diffusion," *International Migration Review,* 32(4):926-949.

———
2001a
"Transnational Migration: Taking Stock and Future Directions," *Global Networks* 1(3): 195-216.

———
2001b
The Transnational Villagers. Berkeley and Los Angeles: University of California Press.

———
2003 "They Prayed in Boston and It Rained in Brazil: The Institutional Character of Transnational Religious Life," *Sociology of Religion.* Forthcoming.

Machacek, D.
2000 "Organizational Isomorphism in SGI-USA." In *Global Citizens: The Soka Gakkai Buddhist Movement in the World.* Ed. D. Machacek and B. Wilson. New York and London: Oxford University Press.

McAlister, E.
2002 *Rara! Vodou, Power, and Performance in Haiti and its Diaspora.* Los Angeles and Berkeley: University of California Press.

Menjívar, C.
1999 "Religious Institutions and Transnationalism: A Case Study of Catholic and Evangelica; Salvadoran Immigrants," *International Journal of Politics, Culture, and Society,* 12(4):589-611.

2002 "Living in two Worlds? Guatemalan-Origin Children in the United States and Emerging Transnationalism, *Journal of Ethnic and Migration Studies,* 28(3):531-552.

Metcalf, B., ed.
1996 *Making Muslim Space in North America and Europe.* Berkeley and Los Angeles: University of California Press.

Meyer, J., W. J. Boli, G. M. Thomas, and F. O. Ramirez.
1997 "World Society and the Nation-State," *American Journal of Sociology,* 103(1):144-181.

Paerregaard, K.
2001 "In the Footsteps of the Lord of Miracles: The Expatriation of Religious Icons in the Peruvian Diaspora." Working Paper Transnational Communities Programme.

Peterson, A. and M.Vásquez.
2001 "Upwards, Never Down: The Catholic Charismatic Renewal in Transnational Perspective." In *Christianity, Social Change, and Globalization in the Americas.* Ed. A. Peterson, P. Williams and M. Vásquez. New Brunswick, New Jersey: Rutgers University Press.

Richman, K.
2002 "Anchored in Haiti and Docked in Florida." Paper prepared for the SSRC Working Group on Religion, Immigration, and Civic Life Meeting in Seattle, Washington.

Robertson, R.
1991 "The Globalization Paradigm: Thinking Globally." In *New Developments in Theory and Research: Religion and the Social Order.* Volume 1. Ed. David G. Bromley. Greenwich, Connecticut: JAI, Press.

Rudolph, S.H. and J.Piscatori., eds.
1997 *Transnational Religion and Fading States.* Boulder, Colorado: Westview Press.

Sahin, S.
2001 "The Alevi Movement: Transformation from Secret Oral to Public Written Culture in National and Transnational Culture in National and Transnational Public Spaces." Unpublished Doctoral Dissertation, New School for Social Research.

Schiffauer, W.
1988 "Migration and Religiousness." In *The New Islamic Presence in Western Europe.* Ed. T. Gerholm and Y.G. Lithman. London and New York: Mansell.

Smith, R. C.
1995 "Los Ausentes Siempre Presentes: The Imagining, Making and Politics of a Transnational Community between Ticuani, Puebla, Mexico and New York City." Ph.D. Dissertation, Columbia University.

Suh, S.
2002 "Buddhism, Rhetoric, and the Korean American Community: The Adjustment of Korean Buddhist Immigrants in the U.S." Paper presented at SSRC Working Group on Religion, Immigration, and Civic Life Conference, Seattle Washington.

Tweed, T.
1999 *Our Lady of Exile.* New York: Oxford University Press.

Van Dijk, R.
1997
"From Camp to Encompassment: Discourses of Transsubjectivity in the Ghanaian Pentecostal Diaspora," *Journal of Religion in Africa,* 27(2):135-159.

Vertovec, S. and C. Peach.
1997 *Islam in Europe: The Politics of Religion and Community.* London: Macmillan Press, Ltd.

Warner, R. S. and J. Wittner.
1998 *Gatherings in Diaspora.* Philadelphia: Temple University Press.

Williams, R.
1988 *Religions of Immigrants from India and Pakistan: New Threads in the American Tapestry.* New York: Cambridge University Press.

Wellmeier, N. J.
1998 "Santa Eulalia's People in Exile: Maya Religion, Culture, and Identity in Los Angeles." In *Gatherings in Diaspora: Religious Communities and the New Immigration.* Ed. R. S. Warner and J. Wittner. Philadelphia: Temple University Press.

Yang, F.
2002 Chinese Christian Transnationalism: Diverse networks of a Houston church. In *Religions Across Borders: Transnational religious networks.* Ed. H.R. Ebaugh and J. Chafetz. Walnut Creek: Altamira Press.

Part II
Historical Perspectives

[3]

By arrangement with the COLONIAL SOCIETY OF MASSACHUSETTS,
the editors of THE NEW ENGLAND QUARTERLY
are pleased to publish the winning essay
of the 1984
Walter Muir Whitehill Prize in Colonial History

Migrants and Motives: Religion and the Settlement of New England, 1630–1640

VIRGINIA DEJOHN ANDERSON

N O man, perhaps, would seem to have been an unlikelier
candidate for transatlantic migration than John Bent. He
had never shown any particular interest in moving; indeed, in
1638, at the age of forty-one, Bent still lived in Weyhill,
Hampshire, where both he and his father before him had been
born. Having prospered in the village of his birth, John Bent
held enough land to distinguish himself as one of Weyhill's
wealthiest inhabitants. One might reasonably expect that
Bent's substantial economic stake, combined with his growing familial responsibilities—which by 1638 included a wife
and five children—would have provided him with ample
incentive to stay put. By embarking on a transatlantic voyage—moving for the first time in his life and over a vast
distance—Bent would exchange an economically secure
present for a highly uncertain future and venture his family's
lives and fortunes no less than his own. Yet in the spring of
1638, Bent returned his Weyhill land to the lord of the manor,
gathered his family and possessions, and traveled twenty-five
miles to the port of Southampton. There, he and his fam-

340   THE NEW ENGLAND QUARTERLY

ily boarded the *Confidence*, bound for Massachusetts Bay.[1]

In doing so, the Bent family joined thousands of other men, women, and children who left for New England between 1630 and 1642.[2] We know more about John Bent than about the vast majority of these other emigrants because certain information has fortuitously survived. Bent's name appears on one of the few extant ship passenger lists of the Great Migration, and genealogists and local historians have compiled enough additional data to sketch in the outlines of his life in Old and New England. Yet despite this rare abundance of information, John Bent's reasons for moving to Massachusetts remain obscure. In fact, the surviving biographical details render the question of motivation all the more tantalizing because they provide no identifiable economic reason for leaving but rather depict a man firmly rooted in his English homeland.

Most accounts of early New England include a general discussion of the emigrants' motivations, but none has dealt with the issue systematically. If we are ever to comprehend the nature and significance of the Great Migration, however, we must understand why men like John Bent left their homes. The Great Migration to New England, unlike the simultaneous outpouring of Englishmen to other New World colonies, was a voluntary exodus of families and included relatively few indentured servants. The movement, which began around 1630, effectively ceased a dozen years later with the outbreak of the English Civil War, further distinguishing it

---

[1] Allen H. Bent, "The Bent Family," *New England Historical and Genealogical Register* (hereafter *NEHGR*) 47 (1894): 288–96; E. C. Felton, "The English Ancestors of John Bent, of Sudbury," *NEHGR* 48 (1895): 66; Sumner Chilton Powell, *Puritan Village: The Formation of a New England Town* (Middletown, Conn.: Wesleyan University Press, 1963), p. 8. The passenger list for the *Confidence* is printed by Henry Stevens, in "Passengers for New England, 1638," *NEHGR* 2 (1848): 108–10, with corrections by H. G. Somerby in *NEHGR* 5 (1851): 440.

[2] Estimates of the total number of emigrants vary. In 1651 Edward Johnson, a participant in the Great Migration, calculated a total of 21,200 persons. Recent research, however, suggests that Johnson's figure may be as much as a third too large. See J. Franklin Jameson, ed., *[Edward] Johnson's Wonder-Working Providence, 1628–1651* (New York: Charles Scribner's Sons, 1910), p. 58; Henry A. Gemery, "Emigration from the British Isles to the New World, 1630–1700: Inferences from Colonial Populations," *Research in Economic History* 5 (1980): 180, 197–98, 212.

MIGRANTS AND MOTIVES 341

from the more extended period of emigration to other colonies.

These two factors—the emigrants' voluntary departure and the movement's short duration—suggest that the Great Migration resulted from a common, reasoned response to a highly specific set of circumstances. Such circumstances must have been compelling indeed to dislodge a man like John Bent from a comfortable niche in his community. And while Bent and his fellows could not have known it, their reasons for embarking for New England would not only change their own lives but also powerfully shape the society they would create in their new home.

I

Although modern commentators have disagreed over why New England's settlers left the mother country, none of the original chroniclers ever suggested that motivation was an open question. Edward Johnson, for example, knew exactly why the Great Migration occurred. The author of *The Wonder-Working Providence of Sion's Saviour in New England*, who first sailed to Massachusetts in 1630, announced that he and his fellow emigrants left England to escape the evils generated by "the multitude of irreligious lascivious and popish affected persons" who had spread "like Grashoppers" throughout the land. As England strayed from the paths of righteousness, the Lord had sought to preserve a saving remnant of His church by transferring it to an untainted refuge. Johnson adopted a military metaphor to describe the process: the decision to emigrate constituted a voluntary enlistment in Christ's Army, the instrument with which He would "create a new Heaven, and a new Earth in, new Churches, and a new Common-wealth together."[3] Other writers concurred with Johnson's providentialist interpretation. Nathaniel Morton and William Hubbard, both of whom emigrated as children, likewise believed the founding of Massachusetts to be the center-

[3] *Johnson's Wonder-Working Providence*, pp. 23, 25.

342   THE NEW ENGLAND QUARTERLY

piece of a divine plan to preserve the Gospel and proper forms
of worship.[4] The most emphatic explication of the settlers'
religious motivation, however, came not from a participant in
the Great Migration but from a descendant of emigrants. Cotton Mather never doubted that the Lord "carried some Thousands of *Reformers* into the Retirements of an *American Des-
art,* on purpose," that "He might there, *To* them first, and
then *By* them, give a *Specimen* of many Good Things, which
He would have His Churches elsewhere aspire and arise
unto."[5]

Few modern scholars have shared the steadfast conviction
of Mather and his predecessors, but it was not until 1921 that
the emigrants' religious motivation was seriously questioned.
In that year, James Truslow Adams suggested that most New
England settlers—if not their leaders—emigrated "for the
simple reason that they wanted to better their condition." By
leaving England, colonists escaped "the growing and incalcu-
lable exactions of government" while at the same time they
enjoyed unprecedented opportunities for freeholdership.
Adams felt compelled to discount the colonists' religious motivation because so few became members of New England
churches. His thesis soon provoked a spirited response from
Samuel Eliot Morison, who questioned Adams's statistics on
church membership and pointed out that conversion was no
easy process. An excess of piety, rather than a lack of it, might
as readily dissuade individuals from claiming fellowship with a
church's "visible saints."[6]

For some time the work of Adams and Morison defined the
terms of the historical debate as other scholars weighed in
with arguments supporting either economics or religion as the

[4] Nathaniel Morton, *New-Englands Memoriall* (originally published 1669; facsimile
ed., Boston: Club of Odd Volumes, 1903), p. 83; Rev. William Hubbard, *A General
History of New England, from the Discovery to MDCLXXX,* 2d ed. (Boston, 1680),
reprinted in *Massachusetts Historical Society Collections,* 2d ser. 5 (1848): 109.

[5] Cotton Mather, *Magnalia Christi Americana* (1702), ed. Kenneth B. Murdock,
books I and II (Cambridge: Harvard University Press, 1977), p. 93.

[6] James Truslow Adams, *The Founding of New England* (Boston: Atlantic Monthly
Press, 1921), pp. 121–22; Samuel Eliot Morison, *Builders of the Bay Colony* (Boston:
Houghton Mifflin Co., 1930; pbk. ed., 1958), pp. 379–86.

MIGRANTS AND MOTIVES 343

principal force propelling Englishmen from the Old World to the New.[7] More recent writers, however, have woven a more complex web of causality. In his extensive discussion of the background of the emigration from East Anglia, N. C. P. Tyack concluded that economic, religious, and political factors all influenced individual decisions to move.[8] Timothy Breen, Stephen Foster, and David Grayson Allen have likewise suggested that the time has come to cease attempting to "separate the historically inseparable" and to begin examining the interrelationships of various motives. It is quite possible, they have argued, that the emigrants themselves would not have been able to distinguish among a variety of highly localized factors—such as economic distress, religious persecution, the exhortations of a charismatic Puritan leader, or even an outbreak of the plague—and choose the single reason that convinced them to leave their homes.[9]

These scholars have applied a much-needed corrective to what had become a rather stale debate by reminding us that deciding to emigrate was a complicated and highly individualistic affair. But their conclusions are, in the end, disappointing, for they suggest that we must accept the notion that the motives for emigration were so complex as to be irrecoverable. If we examine more closely the lives of the emigrants themselves, we may yet find clues that reveal a common incentive underlying the Great Migration.

In seeking to identify emigrants and explore their motives

[7] See, e.g., Charles E. Banks, "Religious 'Persecution' as a Factor in Emigration to New England, 1630–1640," *Massachusetts Historical Society Proceedings* 43 (1930): 136–51, with a comment by Samuel Eliot Morison on pp. 151–54; Nellis M. Crouse, "Causes of the Great Migration, 1630–1640," *New England Quarterly* 5 (1932): 3–36.

[8] N. C. P. Tyack, "Migration from East Anglia to New England before 1660" (Ph. D. diss., University of London, 1951). In a recent article, Tyack argues that religion may well have been the primary cause of the emigration of the "humbler folk" from one English region; see his "The Humbler Puritans of East Anglia and the New England Movement: Evidence from the Court Records of the 1630s," *NEHGR* 138 (1984): 79–106.

[9] T. H. Breen and Stephen Foster, "Moving to the New World: The Character of Early Massachusetts Immigration," *William and Mary Quarterly*, 3d ser., 30 (1973): 189–220; David Grayson Allen, *In English Ways: The Movement of Societies and the Transferal of English Local Law and Custom to Massachusetts Bay in the Seventeenth Century* (Chapel Hill: University of North Carolina Press, 1981), pp. 163–204.

for moving, historians have received invaluable assistance from none other than Charles I. Not long after the exodus to Massachusetts began, the king and his archbishop of Canterbury became increasingly concerned about the departure of so many English folk for wilderness homes across the seas. On 21 July 1635, in an attempt to keep track of the movement, Charles I issued a proclamation requiring all those who wished to leave the realm to obtain a special license from the Privy Council. Customs officers were instructed to obtain certain information from prospective emigrants aboard each ship, including name, residence, occupation, age, and destination.[10] Although the royal edict was loosely enforced and the passage of more than three centuries has inevitably reduced the amount of extant information, several of these ship passenger lists do survive, and they provide a unique opportunity to examine the lives of ordinary emigrants.

Seven ship passenger lists, which together include the names of 693 colonists, provide the information upon which this essay is based. These appear to be the only lists that have been published in their entirety from surviving documents.[11]

[10] Charles Boardman Jewson, ed., *Transcript of Three Registers of Passengers from Great Yarmouth to Holland and New England*, Norfolk Record Society Publications 25 (1954): 6–7. See also Ann N. Hansen, "Ships of the Puritan Migration to Massachusetts Bay," *American Neptune* 23 (1963): 62–66.

[11] All of the lists used here, along with many others, appear in Charles Edward Banks, *The Planters of the Commonwealth* (Boston: Houghton, Mifflin Co., 1930). Banks's work, however, is not particularly reliable because he usually reordered the lists and often omitted certain information, such as servant status or birthplace, mixed up family or household groups, or added persons whom he thought belonged to a particular ship even though the names were not listed. I have chosen, therefore, to obtain lists from the following sources:

The *Hercules* (Sandwich, 1635) and a Sandwich ship of 1637: Eben Putnam, "Two Early Passenger Lists, 1635–1637," *NEHGR* 75 (1921): 217–27, with corrections by Elizabeth French Bartlett in *NEHGR* 79 (1925): 107–9.

Weymouth ship, 1635: William S. Appleton, "More Passengers for New-England," *NEHGR* 25 (1871): 13–15.

The *James* (Southampton, 1635): Louise Brownell Clarke, *The Greenes of Rhode Island, with Historical Records of English Ancestry, 1534–1902* (New York: Knickerbocker Press, 1903), pp. 768–69.

The *Rose* and the *Mary Anne* (Great Yarmouth, 1637): *Transcript of Three Registers*, pp. 21–23, 29–30.

The *Confidence* (Southampton, 1638): see n. 1.

The two Yarmouth lists and the Sandwich list of 1637 were examined by Breen and

MIGRANTS AND MOTIVES 345

All the lists contain the names of emigrants; most also include occupation (for adult males), residence, age, and evidence of family structure. In other words, each list provides sufficiently specific information to permit accurate tracing of individual passengers in the New World. The lists themselves, of course, can only tell us about the emigrants at one moment in time, the date of registration for the voyage, but an astonishingly large amount of additional information can be found in genealogies and local histories. Using these materials, it has been possible to reconstruct the New England careers of 578 emigrants, or 83.4 percent of those included on the lists.

Since no comprehensive record of the total emigrant population exists, one cannot determine the "representativeness" of these seven lists. Certain evidence, however, does suggest their reliability. According to John Winthrop's record of arriving ships, the three busiest years of the migration were 1634, 1635, and 1638; four of the emigrant groups examined here arrived in those years.[12] Both Winthrop's account and the research of Charles E. Banks, one of New England's most productive genealogists, indicate that most ships sailed from ports in southern and eastern England. The ships included here also came from this general area: two each sailed from Great Yarmouth in Norfolk, Sandwich in Kent, and Southampton in Hampshire, while the other left from Weymouth in Dorset. In addition, although information on numbers of passengers is incomplete, it seems that these ships, which carried between 75 and 119 emigrants, were typical. Winthrop noted the arrivals of 47 ships carrying between 80 and 150 people, with an average of about 110 passengers. In numbers of passengers, as well as in ports of origin and timing of departure,

---

Foster in "Moving to the New World," pp. 189–220. All seven ships sailed to Massachusetts Bay; although the exact ports of arrival are not known, Salem or Boston are likeliest.

[12] Of 106 ships mentioned by Winthrop, 27 came in 1634, 21 in 1638, and 17 in 1635; see John Winthrop, *The History of New England from 1630 to 1649*, ed. James Savage, 2 vols. (Boston, 1825), vol. 1, passim. The other three ships in this study sailed in 1637. Because Winthrop's record of arrivals was not systematic, 1637 may have been either a year of lighter traffic or simply one of lighter documentation.

346   THE NEW ENGLAND QUARTERLY

then, the ships examined here do reflect the patterns established by other sources.

Evidence from these lists suggests that although few emigrants left explicit records of their reasons for moving, the motives of the majority need not remain a mystery. Analyzing the lists in light of supporting genealogical materials enables us to construct a social profile of the emigrants, which can then be compared with that of the English population at large. This comparison in turn suggests that once we know who the emigrants were, we can begin to understand why they came.

II

The New England settlers more closely resembled the non-migrating English population than they did other English colonists in the New World. The implications of this fact for the development of colonial societies can scarcely be overstated. While the composition of the emigrant populations in the Chesapeake and the Caribbean hindered the successful transfer of familiar patterns of social relationships, the character of the New England colonial population ensured it. The prospect of colonizing distant lands stirred the imaginations of young people all over England but most of these young adults made their way to the tobacco and sugar plantations of the South. Nearly half of a sample of Virginia residents in 1625 were between the ages of twenty and twenty-nine, and groups of emigrants to the Chesapeake in the seventeenth century consistently included a majority of people in their twenties.[13] In contrast, only a quarter of the New England settlers belonged to this age group (table 1).[14]

[13] James Horn, "Servant Emigration to the Chesapeake in the Seventeenth Century," in *The Chesapeake in the Seventeenth Century: Essays on Anglo-American Society and Politics,* ed. Thad W. Tate and David L. Ammerman (New York: W. W. Norton & Co., 1979), pp. 61–62; Edmund S. Morgan, *American Slavery, American Freedom: The Ordeal of Colonial Virginia* (New York: W. W. Norton & Co., 1975), p. 408. See also Richard S. Dunn, *Sugar and Slaves: The Rise of the Planter Class in the English West Indies, 1624–1713* (Chapel Hill: University of North Carolina Press, 1972), p. 53.

[14] All the aggregate information is derived from a computer-aided analysis (using the Statistical Package for the Social Sciences) of 693 emigrants. Although some

MIGRANTS AND MOTIVES   347

TABLE 1
DISTRIBUTION OF AGES OF NEW ENGLAND EMIGRANTS

Age (in years)	N	%
0–10	98	23.7
11–20	102	24.7
21–30	102	24.7
31–40	71	17.2
41–50	29	7.0
51–60	10	2.5
61–70	1	0.2
Total	413	100.0

The age structure of New England's emigrant population virtually mirrored that of the country they had left (table 2). Both infancy and old age were represented: the *Rose* of Great Yarmouth carried one-year-old Thomas Baker as well as Katherine Rabey, a widow of sixty-eight. The proportion of people over the age of sixty was, not surprisingly, somewhat higher in the general English population than among the emigrants. Although Thomas Welde reported in 1632 that he traveled with "very aged" passengers, "twelve persons being all able to make well nigh one thousand years," a transatlantic voyage of three months' duration was an ordeal not easily undertaken, and the hardships involved in settling the wilderness surely daunted prospective emigrants of advanced years.[15] On the whole, however, New England attracted people of all ages and thus preserved a normal pattern of intergenerational contact.

---

information was available for nearly every emigrant, the mix of data varied for each individual; therefore, the totals will vary in different tables. The coverage for some major variables is as follows: sex, 97.9% (679/693); age at migration, 59.6% (413/693); English town or parish of residence, 85.1% (590/693); occupation [for adult males], 77.7% (139/179).

[15] Thomas Welde to his former parishioners at Tarling, June/July 1632, in *Letters from New England: The Massachusetts Bay Colony, 1629–1638*, ed. Everett Emerson (Amherst: University of Massachusetts Press, 1976), p. 95. Welde also mentioned that several other passengers were infants.

TABLE 2

AGE STRUCTURE OF THE EMIGRANT POPULATION
AND ENGLAND'S POPULATION IN 1636

Age (in years)	New England Emigrants		English Population, 1636
	N	%	%
0–4	48	11.62	12.40
5–14	81	19.61	19.73
15–24	108	26.15	17.72
25–59	172	41.65	42.03
60+	4	00.97	08.12
Total	413	100,00	100.00

SOURCE: For English figures, see table A3.1, Wrigley and Schofield, *Population History of England*, p. 528.

Similarly, the sex ratio of the New England emigrant group
resembled that of England's population. If women were as
scarce in the Chesapeake as good English beer, they were
comparatively abundant in the northern colonies. In the second decade of Virginia's settlement, there were four or five
men for each woman; by the end of the century, there were
still about three men for every two women.[16] Among the
emigrants studied here, however, nearly half were women
and girls. Such a high proportion of females in the population
assured the young men of New England greater success than
their southern counterparts in finding spouses (table 3).[17]

These demographic characteristics derive directly from the
fact that the migration to New England was primarily a transplantation of families. Fully 87.8 percent (597 out of 680) of

[16] Morgan, *American Slavery, American Freedom*, p. 111 n. 16, p. 336. See also
Russell R. Menard, "Immigrants and Their Increase: The Process of Population
Growth in Early Colonial Maryland," in *Law, Society, and Politics in Early Mary-
land*, ed. Aubrey C. Land, Lois Green Carr, and Edward C. Papenfuse (Baltimore:
Johns Hopkins University Press, 1977), p. 96.

[17] The ratio varied somewhat among individual ships. The *Rose* was the only vessel
carrying a majority of women (sex ratio=84), while the *James*, with nearly two men
for every woman, had the most unbalanced ratio, 184.

MIGRANTS AND MOTIVES   349

TABLE 3
SEX RATIO FOR NEW ENGLAND EMIGRANTS

	N	%
Male	386	56.8
Female	293	43.2
Total	679	100.0

NOTE: Sex ratio=132

the emigrants traveled with relatives of one sort or another (table 4). Nearly three-quarters (498 out of 680) came in nuclear family units, with or without children. Occasionally, single spouses migrated with their children, either to meet a partner already in the New World or to wait for his or her arrival on a later ship. Grandparents comprised a relatively inconspicuous part of the migration, but a few hardy elders did make the trip. In 1637, Margaret Neave sailed to Massachusetts with her granddaughter Rachel Dixson, who was probably an orphan. In the following year, Alice Stephens joined her sons William and John and their families for the voyage to New England. More frequently, emigrant family structure extended horizontally, within a generation, rather than vertically, across three generations. Several groups of brothers made the trip together, and when the three Goodenow brothers decided to leave the West Country, they convinced their unmarried sister Ursula to come with them as well.

Thus, for the majority of these New England settlers, transatlantic migration did not lead to permanent separation from close relatives. Some unscrupulous men and women apparently migrated in order to flee unhappy marriages, but most nuclear family units arrived intact. When close kin were left behind, they usually joined their families within a year or so.[18]

[18] In about 80 percent of the cases for which there is information (61 of 77), nuclear families moving to New England brought all of their members along. Only eight families—about 10 percent—are known for certain to have left members behind in

350   THE NEW ENGLAND QUARTERLY

TABLE 4

THE STRUCTURE OF HOUSEHOLD GROUPS AMONG NEW ENGLAND EMIGRANTS

Categories	Classes	Without Servants	With Servants	Total	%	No. of Emigrants in Each Group Category	
Solitaries	(a) Widowed	2	0	2		2	
	(b) Single/unknown marital status	56	5	61	38.0	73	11.0%
No family	(a) Co-resident siblings	3	0	3		6	
	(b) Co-resident relatives of other kinds	1	0	1	2.4	2	1.2%
Simple family households	(a) Married couples, alone	4	6	10		36	
	(b) Married couples, with children	32	42	74		462	
	(c) Husband with children	1	3	4	54.8	28	79.4%
	(d) Wife with children	0	1	1		8	
	(e) Widow with children	2	0	2		6	
Extended family households	(a) Extended laterally						
	(1) Brothers	2	1	3		18	
	(2) Other kin	2	0	2		16	
	(b) Combinations						
	(1) Nuclear family and servant's family	0	1	1	4.8	7	8.4%
	(2) Nuclear family with others of unknown relationship	1	0	1		10	
	(3) Brothers and families with mother	0	1	1		6	
Total number of groups:				166	100.0		
Total number of emigrants in all groups:						680	100.0%

NOTE: This table is modeled on that in Laslett, *Family life and illicit love*, pp. 96–97.

MIGRANTS AND MOTIVES   351

Samuel Lincoln, for instance, who traveled aboard the *Rose* in 1637, soon joined his brother Thomas, who had settled in Hingham in 1633. Another brother, Stephen, arrived in the following year with both his family and his mother. Edward Johnson, who had first crossed the ocean with the Winthrop fleet in 1630, returned to England in 1637 to fetch his wife and seven children. For Thomas Starr, who left Sandwich in 1637, migration meant a reunion with his older brother Comfort, a passenger on the *Hercules* two years earlier. Although some disruption of kin ties was unavoidable, it was by no means the rule.

The average size of migrating households was 4.07 persons, which again resembled conditions in the mother country; mean household size in a sample of 33 seventeenth-century English parishes was 4.60 persons.[19] The proportion of single people aboard the ships was, however, higher than that in the English population at large, a fact that substantially reduced the mean household size. The four-person mean therefore tends to obscure the fact that fully 20 percent of the emigrants traveled in family groups of six persons and over 10 percent in groups of eight or more (table 5). The "mean experienced household size"—that is, the household size familiar to the average individual—was a considerably larger 6.31 persons.

Further exploration of demographic patterns reveals other subtle but significant differences between the migrating population and that of England. These differences illustrate the important fact that migration was a selective process; not all people were equally suited to or interested in the rigors of New World settlement. Since the movement to New England

---

England. Seventeenth-century court records are interspersed with orders for husbands and wives to rejoin their spouses either in England or New England; see, e.g., George Francis Dow, ed., *Records and Files of the Quarterly Courts of Essex County, Massachusetts*, 8 vols. (Salem: Essex Institute, 1911–75), 1:123–24, 137, 159, 160, 166, 208, 228, 229, 231, 244, 245, 274, 275, 306, 360.

[19] Peter Laslett, "Mean household size in England since the sixteenth century," in *Household and Family in Past Time: Comparative studies in the size and structure of the domestic group over the last three centuries in England, France, Serbia, Japan and colonial North America, with further materials from Western Europe*, ed. Peter Laslett and Richard Wall (Cambridge: Cambridge University Press, 1972), p. 130.

352   THE NEW ENGLAND QUARTERLY

TABLE 5

SIZE OF EMIGRANT GROUPS TRAVELING TO NEW ENGLAND

Size of Group	N of Groups	% of Groups	N of People in Groups of This Size	% of People in Groups of This Size
1	56	33.5	56	8.2
2	13	7.8	26	3.8
3	9	5.4	27	4.0
4	16	9.6	64	9.4
5	18	10.8	90	13.3
6	23	13.8	138	20.3
7	13	7.8	91	13.4
8	7	4.2	56	8.2
9	3	1.8	27	4.0
10	4	2.4	40	5.9
11	1	0.6	11	1.6
12	2	1.2	24	3.5
13	1	0.6	13	1.9
16	1	0.6	16	2.4
Total	167	100.1	679	99.9

was a voluntary, self-selective affair, most of this winnowing-out process occurred before the hearths of English homes, as individuals and families discussed whether or not to leave.

Although family groups predominated within the emigrant population, many individuals came to New England on their own.[20] The vast majority of these solitary travelers were male—men outnumbered women by a factor of ten to one—and together they constituted 38 percent of the emigrant households (table 4). This figure stands in sharp contrast to England's population, where only about 5 percent of all households were composed of one individual.[21] About one in

[20] Servants are not included in this category; they are included in the household with which they traveled.

[21] The figure is based on Laslett's calculations for 100 English communities for the period 1574–1821; see table 4.8 in his "Mean household size," p. 146.

six emigrants aged twenty-one to thirty sailed independently, perhaps drawn to New England by hopes of employment or freeholdership. These men were hardly freewheeling adventurers; instead, they provided the new settlements with skilled labor. The unaccompanied travelers included shoemakers, a carpenter, butcher, tanner, hempdresser, weaver, cutler, physician, fuller, tailor, mercer, and skinner. Some were already married at the time of the voyage, and those who were single seldom remained so for more than a couple of years after their arrival. Through marriage, the men became members of family networks within their communities. Within a few years of his arrival in 1635, for instance, Henry Ewell, a young shoemaker from Sandwich in Kent, joined the church in Scituate and married the daughter of a prominent local family. William Paddy, a London skinner, managed to obtain land, find a wife, and get elected to Plymouth's first general court of deputies within four years of his voyage.[22]

Analysis of the composition of migrating families reveals other important differences between the colonizing population and that of England. Children were a less ubiquitous component of emigrating household groups than they were in the general English population. Between 1574 and 1821, for example, it seems that not less than three-quarters of English households included children. For the New England emigrants at the time of their departure, the figure was just over half of all households (90 of 166). Yet 90 out of 99 emigrating *families* had children, and within these families, children were a conspicuous presence indeed. Most emigrant families that had children had three or more (table 6). The average number of children per family was 3.08, compared to an aver-

[22] For Henry Ewell, see James Savage, *A Genealogical Dictionary of the First Settlers of New England, Showing Three Generations of Those Who Came before May, 1692, . . .* , 4 vols. (Boston, 1860–62), 2:132; C. F. Swift, *Genealogical Notes of Barnstable Families, Being a Reprint of the Amos Otis Papers, Originally Published in the Barnstable Patriot*, 2 vols. (Barnstable, Mass., 1888), 1:359. For William Paddy, see Savage, *Genealogical Dictionary*, 3:328–29; Charles Henry Pope, *The Pioneers of Massachusetts, A Descriptive List, Drawn From Records of Colonies, Towns, and Churches, and Other Contemporaneous Documents* (Boston: the author, 1900), p. 338.

354   THE NEW ENGLAND QUARTERLY

TABLE 6

DISTRIBUTION OF HOUSEHOLDS IN ENGLAND AND NEW ENGLAND

No. of Children	Groups with This Number of Children		Number of Children in Groups of This Size		
	New England		New England		Sample of 100 English Parishes
	N	%	N	%	%
1	14	16.1	14	5.2	11.2
2	25	28.7	50	18.7	18.4
3	17	19.5	51	19.0	23.1
4	13	14.9	52	19.4	18.1
5	12	13.8	60	22.4	13.4
6	2	2.3	12	4.5	7.7
7+	4	4.7	29	10.8	7.2
Total	87	100.0	268	100.0	99.1

SOURCE: For English figures, see Laslett, "Mean household size," p. 148.

age of 2.76 for a sample of 100 English communities.[23] Emigrating children did not suffer for lack of playmates aboard ship or in the New World; over half of them came in groups including four or more children.

New England clearly attracted a special group of families. The average age of emigrant husbands was 37.4 years (N=81); for their wives the average was 33.8 (N=55). The westward-bound ships carried couples who were mature, who had probably been married for nearly a decade, and who had established themselves firmly within their communities. The typical migrating family was complete—composed of husband, wife, and three or four children—but was not yet completed. They were families in process, with parents who were at most halfway through their reproductive cycle and who would continue to produce children in New England. They would be responsible for the rapid population growth that

[23] Figures for English households are from Laslett, "Mean household size," p. 148.

MIGRANTS AND MOTIVES   355

New England experienced in its first decades of settlement. Moreover, the numerous children who emigrated with their parents contributed their efforts to a primitive economy sorely lacking in labor.

The task of transforming wilderness into farmland, however, demanded more labor than parents and their children alone could supply, and more than half of the emigrating families responded to this challenge by bringing servants with them to the New World (table 4). Perhaps some had read William Wood's advice in *New England's Prospect* and learned that "men of good estates may do well there, always provided that they go well accommodated with servants." In any case, servants formed an integral part, just over 17 percent, of the colonizing population and in fact were at first somewhat more commonplace in New England than in England.[24] Most were males (80 of 114) and labored alongside their masters, clearing land, planting corn, and building houses and barns. Their presence substantially increased the ratio of producers to consumers in the newly settled towns.[25]

Household heads, however, knew that servants might easily become a drain on family resources in the critical early months of settlement. Their passages had to be paid and food

[24] William Wood, *New England's Prospect*, ed. Alden T. Vaughan (Amherst: University of Massachusetts Press, 1977), p. 70; Laslett, "Mean household size," p. 152. Ann Kussmaul, in examining the prevalence of servants in husbandry (not domestic servants) found that they comprised 1 to 13 percent of the population in a sample of six seventeenth-century parishes; see her *Servants in Husbandry in Early Modern England* (Cambridge: Cambridge University Press, 1981), p. 12. Peter Laslett calculated that in Clayworth in 1676, servants were present in 31 percent of the households, and comprised 16.7 percent of the parish's population; see Peter Laslett, *Family life and illicit love in earlier generations* (Cambridge: Cambridge University Press, 1977), p. 90. Since the vast majority of New England servants were male, Kussmaul's figures may provide the more relevant comparison here; that comparison indicates that servants in early New England may have been up to twice as common as in England.

[25] Wrigley and Schofield calculated the "dependency ratio" for England over five-year intervals for the period from 1541 to 1871. This ratio measures the numbers of persons aged 0 to 14 years and over 60 years—presumably those too young or too old to provide much productive labor—as a proportion of every 1,000 persons in the general population. In England in 1636, the dependency ratio was 674 per 1,000; among the New England emigrants studied here, the comparable figure was a considerably lower 475 per 1,000. See E. A. Wrigley and R. S. Schofield, *The Population History of England, 1541–1871: A Reconstruction* (Cambridge: Harvard University Press, 1981), p. 528.

and shelter provided at a time when those commodities were at a premium. Hence, when arranging for a suitable labor supply, masters heeded the advice of writers like William Wood, who emphasized that emigrants should not take too many servants and should choose men and women of good character. "It is not the multiplicity of many bad servants (which presently eats a man out of house and harbor, as lamentable experience hath made manifest)," he warned, "but the industry of the faithful and diligent laborer that enricheth the careful master; so that he that hath many dronish servants shall soon be poor and he that hath an industrious family shall as soon be rich."[26] Most families attempted to strike a balance between their need for labor and available resources by transporting only a few servants. Nearly half of the families brought just one and another quarter of them brought only two.

III

Before departing for New England, the emigrants had called a wide variety of English towns and villages their homes (see fig. 1). Most lived in the lowland area of England, a region that extends south and east of a line drawn diagonally from Teesmouth in the northeast to the port of Weymouth on the Dorset coast. The lowlands in general enjoyed a more even topography, drier climate, and richer soil than did the highlands to the north and supported the bulk of the country's population.[27] Within this expanse of southeastern England, those who chose to emigrate had known many different forms of social organization, agricultural practice, industrial development, and local government. At one end of the spectrum, Parnell Harris, William Paddy, and Edmund Hawes all left the burgeoning metropolis of London, which was about to overtake Paris as the largest city in Europe; at the other, the widow Emme Mason left the tiny Kentish parish of Eastwell,

[26] Wood, *New England's Prospect*, pp. 70–71.

[27] Joan Thirsk, "The Farming Regions of England," in *The Agrarian History of England and Wales*, vol. 4, 1500–1640, ed. Joan Thirsk (Cambridge: Cambridge University Press, 1967), pp. 2–15.

MIGRANTS AND MOTIVES   357

Figure 1
**English Origins of Passengers
on Seven Ships to Massachusetts, 1635–1638**

The numbers of passengers from each county (and London) are as follows —
Berkshire: 6, Dorset: 18, Hampshire: 54, Kent: 182, London: 3, Middlesex:
1, Norfolk: 152, Oxford: 20, Somerset: 33, Suffolk: 36, Wiltshire: 86,
Worcestershire: 1. English residences were unknown for 101 passengers.
After a map by Richard Stinely in David Grayson Allen, *In English Ways:
The Movement of Societies and the Transferal of English Local Law and
Custom to Massachusetts Bay in the Seventeenth Century* (Chapel Hill:
University of North Carolina Press, 1981), p. 17. Published for the Institute
of Early American History and Culture. Used with permission.

358   THE NEW ENGLAND QUARTERLY

which was "not more than a mile across each way" and whose
church in 1640 counted just 55 communicants.[28]

A relatively large proportion of the New England settlers
dwelled in urban areas prior to their emigration. In addition to
London, substantial towns such as Norwich in Norfolk,
Canterbury in Kent, and Salisbury in Wiltshire were residences for scores of prospective colonists. In the mid-seventeenth century, only about one out of five Englishmen was a
town-dweller, whereas at least one of three emigrants had
lived in a community with three thousand or more inhabitants. Fully 60 percent of the future New Englanders came
from market towns. Although these communities were not
"urban" on the same scale as a large provincial capital like
Norwich or Canterbury, they differed qualitatively from their
neighboring communities. Each served as a focus for networks
of trade and distribution, and often for the social life, of its
surrounding region.[29]

New England would never offer its first generation of settlers anything approaching the bustle and complexity of the
urban centers they had abandoned. But large towns best furnished prospective emigrants like the locksmith William Ludkin or the cutler Edmund Hawes with markets for their specialized skills. Emigrants involved in trade resided in sizable
towns like Norwich, Romsey, or Sandwich, which provided
access to important commercial networks. Likewise, prospective settlers who made their livings in the cloth industry fre-

[28] E. A. Wrigley, "A Simple Model of London's Importance in Changing English
Society and Economy, 1650–1750," *Past and Present* 37 (1967): 44; Edward Hasted,
The History and Topographical Survey of the County of Kent, 2d ed., 12 vols.
(Canterbury, 1797–1801), 7:399, 411. For the most recent discussion of the diversity
of New Englanders' origins, see Allen, *In English Ways*; see also Powell, *Puritan
Village*.

[29] Two hundred emigrants, out of 590 with known English residences, came from
the seven towns of Canterbury, Dover, Great Yarmouth, London, Maidstone, Nor-
wich, and Salisbury. Population figures for these towns are in John Patten, *English
Towns, 1500–1700* (Folkestone: Dawson, 1978), pp. 106, 111–12, 251; Wrigley, "A
Simple Model," p. 44; C. W. Chalklin, *Seventeenth-Century Kent: A Social and
Economic History* (London: Longmans, 1965), pp. 30–31. For market towns, see
Alan Everitt, "The Marketing of Agricultural Produce," in *Agrarian History*,
4:470–75, 488–90.

MIGRANTS AND MOTIVES   359

quently depended on the manufacturing and marketing amenities of large towns such as Norwich, Salisbury, Canterbury, and Sandwich. Weavers from these towns acquired yarn from local spinners, produced a multitude of different fabrics, and often sold them as well.[30]

Town life also equipped future emigrants with complex and regionally distinctive experiences of local government. Most incorporated boroughs were run by an annually elected mayor, but the numbers and duties of subsidiary officeholders varied widely.[31] Admission to a town's body of freemen—which often brought enfranchisement and eligibility for officeholding—was based on different criteria in different places. In Norwich, Nicholas Busby and William Nickerson probably achieved freeman status by completing seven-year apprenticeships and proving competence in their craft as weavers. Henry Bachelor and Nathaniel Ovell, two emigrants from Dover, however, would have had to demonstrate that their lands were worth at least five pounds a year.[32] Electoral practices also varied. In Reading, home of the emigrant Augustine Clement, the town's aldermen selected the mayor; in Salisbury, the mayor was chosen by the common council. In

[30] K. J. Allison, "The Norfolk Worsted Industry in the Sixteenth and Seventeenth Centuries [Part I]," *Yorkshire Bulletin of Economic and Social Research* 12 (1960): 73–78; G. D. Ramsay, *The Wiltshire Woollen Industry in the Sixteenth and Seventeenth Centuries*, 2d ed. (London: Oxford University Press, 1965), pp. 2–19; Chalklin, *Seventeenth-Century Kent*, pp. 123–26.

[31] In addition to a mayor, Dover had 12 *jurats* and a 36-member common council. Southampton had 9 justices, a sheriff, 2 bailiffs, and 24 common councilmen, plus an equal number of burgesses, while Newbury had a high steward, a recorder, 6 aldermen, and 24 capital burgesses, and Canterbury had a recorder, 12 aldermen, and 24 common councilmen. See Rev. John Lyon, *The History of the Town and Port of Dover, and of Dover Castle; with a Short Account of the Cinque Ports*, 2 vols. (Dover, 1813–14), 1:218; Richard Warner, *Collections for the History of Hampshire, and the Bishopric of Winchester* . . . , 5 vols. (London, 1795), 1:179; anon., *The History and Antiquities of Newbury and Its Environs, Including Twenty-Eight Parishes, Situate in the County of Berks* . . . (Speenhamland, 1839), p. 129; Hasted, *History and Topographical Survey* . . . *of Kent*, 11:28.

[32] Both Busby and Nickerson were freemen; whether Bachelor and Ovell were also is unknown. See Jewson, *Transcript of Three Registers*, pp. 21–22; John Evans, *Seventeenth-Century Norwich: Politics, Religion, and Government, 1620–1690* (Oxford: Clarendon Press, 1979), p. 8; Lyon, *History of the Town and Port of Dover*, 1:22.

360   THE NEW ENGLAND QUARTERLY

Norwich, freemen voted in both municipal and parliamentary contests.[33] Each borough had its own distinct political calendar regulating its citizens' participation in local affairs, often in accordance with liturgical cycles inherited from pre-Reformation days. Mayors were chosen on the Feast of the Nativity of Our Lady (2 February) in Dover, on the first of May in Norwich, on St. Matthew's Day (21 September) in Newbury, All Souls' (2 November) in Maidstone, and on the Monday after St. Andrew's Day (30 November) in Sandwich.[34]

In addition, seventeenth-century English towns, especially the larger ones, often encompassed a multiplicity of civil and ecclesiastical jurisdictions. If Edmund Batter, Michael Shafflin, or any of the other emigrants from Salisbury lived in the cathedral close, their neighborhood was administered by the diocesan dean and chapter, who clashed at times with the municipal government.[35] Provincial centers such as Canterbury and Norwich were divided into several parishes; the Kentish city had at least eight in 1640, while the East Anglian capital boasted thirty-four parishes.[36] Moreover, town-dwellers lived in the midst of a more heterogeneous population than did persons who resided in the countryside. Major textile manufacturing centers received an influx of foreign artisans in the late sixteenth and early seventeenth centuries. The newcomers, mainly Dutch and Walloon tradesmen, settled primarily in Kent and East Anglia and helped to revitalize the depressed cloth industry in those areas. Their congregations

[33] Rev. Charles Coates, *The History and Antiquities of Reading* (London, 1802), p. 65; Mary E. Ransome, "City Government, 1612–1835," in *A History of Wiltshire*, ed. R. B. Pugh and Elizabeth Crittall, 12 vols., The Victoria History of the Counties of England (London: Oxford University Press, for the University of London Institute of History, 1956–75), 6:105; Evans, *Seventeenth-Century Norwich*, p. 7.

[34] Lyon, *History of the Town and Port of Dover*, 2:267, 287; Evans, *Seventeenth-Century Norwich*, p. 57; *History and Antiquities of Newbury*, p. 129; William Newton, *The History and Antiquities of Maidstone, the County-Town of Kent* (London, 1741), p. 27.

[35] Paul Slack, "Poverty and Politics in Salisbury, 1597–1666," in *Crisis and Order in English Towns, 1500–1700: Essays in Urban History*, ed. Peter Clark and Paul Slack (London: Routledge and Kegan Paul, 1972), pp. 187–88.

[36] Hasted, *History and Topographical Survey . . . of Kent*, 11:214–86; Breen and Foster, "Moving to the New World," p. 199 n. 27.

MIGRANTS AND MOTIVES 361

grew rapidly and often gained important concessions from local authorities—such as permission to worship separately —which helped both to maintain their sense of identity and to impart a more cosmopolitan flavor to the towns in which they lived.[37]

In the countryside, although the contrasts were perhaps less striking, villages also differed significantly from one another. Much of seventeenth-century England was an intricate patchwork of parishes with particular local customs dating from time out of mind. Ancient practice often dictated the shape of the landscape, patterns of settlement, modes of landholding, and rituals of agrarian activity. Even within a single county, substantial variation was evident. The emigrant Nathaniel Tilden's home in Tenterden lay in the densely wooded Wealden region of southern Kent, where most of the land was devoted to pasture. He probably spent much of his time tending cattle and perhaps a few sheep and pigs. Many Wealden farms contained dairy houses and cheese chambers; Lydia Tilden and her daughters may have supplemented the family's diet and income by converting some of their herd's milk into cheese and butter. In addition, the Tildens and their servants, like other Wealden farmers, probably cultivated a dozen or so acres of wheat, oats, and peas for domestic use. Since mixed farming of this sort left farmers and their families with spare time at certain periods of the year, some Tildens may have turned to by-employments, like spinning for local cloth producers, to keep themselves busy and to earn a few shillings during the slack months.[38]

Thomas Call and his family, who sailed to New England in 1637, lived only twenty-odd miles north of the Tildens, but their agricultural routine would have been quite different. The Calls lived in Faversham, a village of about a thousand

[37] K. J. Allison, "The Norfolk Worsted Industry in the Sixteenth and Seventeenth Centuries [Part 2]," *Yorkshire Bulletin of Economic and Social Research* 13 (1961): 61–69; Dorothy Gardiner, *Historic Haven: The Story of Sandwich* (Derby: Pilgrim Press, 1954), pp. 182–85; Chalklin, *Seventeenth-Century Kent*, pp. 123–24.

[38] Thirsk, "Farming Regions of England," pp. 57–59; Chalklin, *Seventeenth-Century Kent*, pp. 75–82.

362   THE NEW ENGLAND QUARTERLY

inhabitants located in the northern part of the county near the
coast. Here, unlike the region around Tenterden, the country
was "a fine extended level, the fields of a considerable size,
and most unincumbered with trees or hedgerows."[39] Because
of its fertile soil and easy access by water to London, north
Kent had become an important supplier of the city's food.
Thomas Call's neighbors concentrated on the production of
wheat and, to a lesser extent, barley. Much of the grain harvested from their fields was shipped either to the metropolis
or, if of lower quality, sent along the coast to other parts of the
country. In addition, Call probably grew a crop of beans or
peas as fodder for his animals. Since north Kentish farms
tended to be larger than those in the Weald, Call was likely to
have owned more land than Nathaniel Tilden did in Tenterden. Perhaps he used some of his acreage to plant an orchard;
by the middle of the seventeenth century, farmers in his
neighborhood had begun to produce large quantities of cher-
ries for market.[40]

Agricultural diversity likewise prevailed in the county of
Norfolk, where Henry and Elizabeth Smith of New Bucken-
ham lived with their two sons. Norfolk's wood pasture region,
like the Kentish Weald, supported a considerable population
of small farmers engaged in stock rearing and dairying. Large
hedges marked the boundaries of enclosed fields where cattle
grazed and farmers cultivated small plots of barley, wheat, and
rye, and perhaps some oats and peas, for household consumption. In these wooded regions in both counties, manorial organization was weak, its function reduced to intermittent financial and legal administration which intruded only sporadically
into inhabitants' daily lives. The Smiths, like the Tildens, may
also have engaged in by-employments, such as combing wool
or weaving flax, during the winter months.

But the Moulton, Page, and Dow families, who emigrated

---

[39] Hasted, *History and Topographical Survey . . . of Kent*, 6:319.

[40] F. J. Fisher, "The Development of the London Food Market, 1540–1640," in
Essays in Economic History, ed. E. M. Carus-Wilson, 3 vols. (London: E. Arnold,
1954–62), 1:136, 138–42; Chalklin, *Seventeenth-Century Kent*, pp. 74–82, 90;
Thirsk, "Farming Regions of England," pp. 56–57, 62.

MIGRANTS AND MOTIVES   363

from the small coastal village of Ormsby, knew a different Norfolk. They lived and worked in a district devoted to the twin agricultural pursuits of grain cultivation and sheep rearing. Barley, rye, and wheat were again the main crops but here were grown for market. Sheep provided fertilizer as they were bred and fattened for sale. Manorial structure maintained its hold; inhabitants lived in nucleated villages and often farmed cooperatively in open fields. The lords of the manors, who stood at the apex of society in this sheep-corn region, grazed their flocks on tenants' harvested and fallow fields and dominated the local sheep market. As husbandmen, John Moulton, Robert Page, and Henry Dow may not have owned any sheep themselves but might have preferred instead to leave that enterprise to the local gentry while they concentrated on planting cereals. Although arable regions did not generally sustain much local industry, northern Norfolk was unusual in that several of its villages supported worsted cloth manufacture. The three Ormsby families who emigrated may well have spun yarn or have woven fabric in addition to farming.[41]

Other rural routines regulated the lives of emigrants from southwestern counties. Peter Noyes and John Bent followed ancient custom when they returned their lands to the lord of the manor in the open-field parish of Penton in Hampshire before embarking for New England. Property-holding in this grain-growing and sheep-rearing downland enmeshed farmers in a network of feudal dues and practices.[42] Dorsetshire farmers such as Edmund and William Kerley labored in a pastoral region of dairying and pig raising dominated by the local manor, while across the border in southern Wiltshire, Edmund and John Goodenow farmed in another common-field district devoted to sheep-and-corn husbandry. To the west, Robert and Joan Martin worked in Batcombe, Somerset, a small village where the "lands are all enclosed, but not

[41] Thirsk, "Farming Regions of England," pp. 46–49, 42–46; K. J. Allison, "The Sheep-Corn Husbandry of Norfolk in the Sixteenth and Seventeenth Centuries," *Agricultural History Review* 5 (1957): 12–30.

[42] Powell, *Puritan Village*, pp. 3, 7–10.

364   THE NEW ENGLAND QUARTERLY

crouded with wood; and there is a greater proportion of pasture than tillage."[43] In the migration to New England, then, not only would villagers and townsfolk intermingle but farmers would also encounter other countrymen with very different experiences of rural life.

IV

The diversity of the emigrants' English backgrounds—and their urban origins in particular—influenced the distribution of their occupations. Virtually the same number of men were engaged in farming and in artisanal trades not involved with cloth manufacture; slightly fewer earned their livings in the textile industry (table 7).[44] Most of the cloth workers emigrated from cities well known for their textile manufacture; half of the fourteen weavers left Norwich, while five of the sixteen tailors had lived in Salisbury. The geographical distribution of the other artisans was more even, yet many also had congregated in urban areas. Ten of the eleven shoemakers came from Norwich, Great Yarmouth, Sandwich, and Marlborough, while the only two joiners had lived in Canterbury and Norwich. Nearly all of the men with highly specialized

[43] Thirsk, "Farming Regions of England," p. 4; Powell, *Puritan Village*, fig. 2; Eric Kerridge, "Agriculture *c*. 1500–*c*. 1793," in the Victoria *History of Wiltshire*, 4:43–45; quotation from John Collinson, *The History and Antiquities of the County of Somerset* . . . , 3 vols. (Bath, 1791), 3:466; Thomas G. Barnes, *Somerset 1625–1640: A County's Government During the "Personal Rule"* (Cambridge, Mass.: Harvard University Press, 1961), p. 4.

[44] In the category "agriculture" (33.8% of the total of men with listed occupations), I have included 30 husbandmen, 5 yeomen, 6 laborers, and 6 men called "husbandmen or laborers," a dual label retained in the coding. "Cloth trades" includes 1 clothier, 14 weavers, 16 tailors, 2 mercers, a calenderer, and a fuller (25.2%). "Other artisans" consists of 1 hempdresser, 13 shoemakers, 2 tanners, 1 skinner, 12 carpenters, 1 sawyer, 3 joiners, 3 coopers, 1 "moulter," 2 butchers, a brewer, a painter, a cutler, 2 ropers, a chandler, and a locksmith (33.1%). "Trade" includes 2 merchants and a grocer (2.2%); "Maritime" includes 2 mariners and a fisherman (2.2%); and "professional" includes 2 surgeons, 2 ministers, and a schoolmaster (3.6%). This occupational distribution is roughly similar to that obtained by N. C. P. Tyack for 147 East Anglian emigrants. He found 16.3% of his sample in agriculture, 23.1% in cloth trades, 26.5% in other artisanal trades, 3.4% each in trade and maritime occupations, and 27.2% in the professions. This last figure includes a large number of ministers leaving East Anglia in the early 1630s. See Tyack, "Migration from East Anglia," appendix 3.

MIGRANTS AND MOTIVES 365

TABLE 7
OCCUPATIONAL DISTRIBUTION OF ADULT MALE EMIGRANTS

Category	N	%
Agriculture	47	33.8
Cloth trades	35	25.2
Other artisans	46	33.1
Trade	3	2.2
Maritime	3	2.2
Professional	5	3.6
Total	139	100.1

skills lived in large towns; the locksmith William Ludkin in Norwich, the cutler Edmund Hawes in London, the surgeon John Greene (who appears to have been a physician, not a barber-surgeon) in Salisbury. Artisans, both in the cloth trades and in other pursuits, formed a greater proportion of the emigrant population than tradesmen did in the English population as a whole. In 1696, Gregory King estimated that "freeholders" and "farmers" outnumbered "artizans and handicrafts" by a factor of more than seven to one; among the emigrants to New England, however, artisans predominated by a ratio of nearly two to one.[45]

The occupational spectrum of future New Englanders placed them at the more prosperous end of English society. As farmers and artisans, prospective emigrants belonged to that part of the population that—according to Gregory King—"increased the wealth of the kingdom." Yet in striking contrast to Virginia, where, at least initially, the population included "about six times as large a proportion of gentlemen as England had," New England attracted very few members of the upper class.[46] Sir Henry Vane and Sir Richard Saltonstall were

[45] Charles Wilson, *England's Apprenticeship, 1603–1763* (London: Longman, 1965), p. 239.

[46] Wilson, *England's Apprenticeship*, p. 239; Morgan, *American Slavery, American Freedom*, p. 84.

unique among the leaders of the migration, and for the most part even they submitted to government by such gentle but untitled figures as John Winthrop and Thomas Dudley. On the whole, emigrants were neither very high nor very low in social and economic status. Husbandmen predominated among the farmers who came to Massachusetts; thirty of them emigrated compared to just five yeomen.[47] By the seventeenth century, the legal distinctions between the status of yeoman and that of husbandman had largely eroded and evidence indicates that the labels generally denoted relative position on the economic and social ladder. Both groups primarily made their livings from the land, but yeomen were generally better off. New England, however, was peopled by less affluent—but not necessarily poor—husbandmen.[48]

Emigrant clothworkers practiced trades that also placed them on the middle rungs of the economic ladder. Textile manufacturing in the early seventeenth century employed the skills of dozens of different craftsmen, from the shearmen, carders, and combers who prepared wool for spinning to the wealthy clothiers who sold the finished product. But the emigrant clothworkers did not represent the entire spectrum of skills; most were weavers and tailors who made a modest living at their trade. While it is true that, during his impeachment trial, the former bishop of Norwich was accused of harrying some of the city's most important and prosperous tradesmen—including the weavers Nicholas Busby, Francis Lawes, and Michael Metcalf—out of the land, these emigrants' economic status was probably exaggerated.[49] Most urban weavers

[47] Tyack found a similar result: twenty-two husbandmen, one yeoman, and one "farmer"; see "Migration from East Anglia," pp. 54–56, and appendix 3, vi–via.

[48] Mildred Campbell, *The English Yeoman in the Tudor and Early Stuart Age* (New Haven: Yale University Press, 1942), pp. 11–13, 23–33; Gordon Batho, "Noblemen, Gentlemen, and Yeomen," in *Agrarian History*, 4:301–6; Margaret Spufford, *Contrasting Communities: English Villagers in the Sixteenth and Seventeenth Centuries* (Cambridge: Cambridge University Press, 1974), pp. 37–39. Husbandmen could, in fact, be quite well-off. Benjamin Cooper, a husbandman who sailed on the *Mary Anne*, died during the voyage in 1637. An inventory of his estate, recorded in Massachusetts that September, amounted to £1,278.12.00; Probate docket no. 4, Suffolk County Registry of Probate, Boston, Mass.

[49] John Browne, *History of Congregationalism and Memorials of the Churches in Norfolk and Suffolk* (London, 1877), p. 89.

MIGRANTS AND MOTIVES   367

from Norfolk in this period had goods worth no more than £100, and one out of five did not even own his own loom.[50] Among the non-clothworking artisans, shoemakers and carpenters predominated, and they too worked in trades that would bring comfort, if not riches. All in all, the New England–bound ships transported a population characterized by a greater degree of social homogeneity than existed in the mother country. Despite Winthrop's reminder to his fellow passengers on the *Arbella* that "some must be rich some poor, some highe and eminent in power and dignitie; others meane and in subieccion," New Englanders would discover that the process of migration effectively reduced the distance between the top and the bottom of their social hierarchy.[51]

V

In a letter to England written in 1632, Richard Saltonstall commented on the social origins of New England's inhabitants. "It is strange," he wrote, "the meaner sort of people should be so backward [in migrating], having assurance that they may live plentifully by their neighbors." At the same time, he expressed the hope that more "gentlemen of ability would transplant themselves," for they too might prosper both spiritually and materially in the new land. For young Richard, the twenty-one-year-old son of Sir Richard Saltonstall, New England promised much but as yet lacked the proper balance of social groups within its population that would ensure its success. The migration of the "meaner sort" would help lower the cost of labor, while richer emigrants would "supply the want we labor under of men fitted by their estates to bear common burdens." Such wealthy men would invest in the colony's future even as they enhanced their own spiritual welfare by becoming "worthy instru-

---

[50] Allison, "Norfolk Worsted Industry [Part I]," pp. 76–77. Lack of suitable records makes it nearly impossible to assess the emigrants' economic positions prior to their voyages; even the few extant tax lists are inaccurate measures of total wealth. See Breen and Foster, "Moving to the New World," pp. 198–99 n. 27.

[51] "A Modell of Christian Charitie," *Winthrop Papers*, 5 vols. (Boston: Massachusetts Historical Society, 1929–47), 2:282.

368   THE NEW ENGLAND QUARTERLY

ments of propagating the Gospel" to New England's natives.[52]

Saltonstall wrote early in the migration decade, but the succeeding years did little to redress the social imbalance he perceived in Massachusetts. Two years later, William Wood could still write that "none of such great estate went over yet."[53] Throughout the decade of the 1630s, New England continued to attract colonists who were overwhelmingly ordinary. Demographically they presented a mirror image of the society they had left behind, and socially and economically they fairly represented England's relatively prosperous middle class. The question is inescapable: why did so many average English men and women pass beyond the seas to Massachusetts' shores?

Whether or not they have assigned it primary importance, most historians of the period have noted that economic distress in England in the early seventeenth century must have been causally related to the Great Migration. These were years of agricultural and industrial depression, and farmers and weavers were conspicuous passengers on the transatlantic voyages. A closer examination of the connections between economic crisis and the movement to New England, however, indicates that the links were not as close as they have been assumed to be.

Agriculture—especially in the early modern period—was a notoriously risky business. Success depended heavily upon variables beyond human control. A dry summer or an unusually wet season rendered futile the labor of even the most diligent husbandman, and English farmers in the early seventeenth century had to endure more than their share of adversity. While the decade of the 1620s began propitiously, with excellent harvests in 1619 and 1620, the farmers' luck did not hold. The next three years brought one disastrous harvest after another; improvement in 1624 was followed by dearth in 1625. The beginning of the 1630s, especially in the eastern

[52] Richard Saltonstall to Emmanuel Downing, 4 February 1631/2, in *Letters from New England*, p. 92.

[53] Wood, *New England's Prospect*, p. 68.

MIGRANTS AND MOTIVES   369

counties, was marked by further distress; in 1630, the mayor of Norwich complained that "scarcity and dearth of corn and other victuals have so increased the number and misery of the poor in this city" that civic taxes had to be boosted to unprecedented heights and the city's stock of grain dwindled dangerously. In 1637, a severe drought spawned further hardship.[54]

Although this period of agricultural depression undoubtedly touched the lives of many English families, it did not necessarily compel them to emigrate. The worst sustained period of scarcity occurred in the early 1620s, a decade or so before the Great Migration began; if agrarian distress was a "push" factor, it produced a curiously delayed reaction. Furthermore, annual fluctuations were endemic in early modern agriculture. Englishmen knew from experience that times would eventually improve, even if that day were unpleasantly distant; moreover, they had no reason to suppose that farmers in New England would somehow lead charmed lives, exempt from similar variations in the weather. In addition, dearth was not an unmitigated disaster for families engaged in husbandry: as supplies of grain and other products shrank, prices rose. In 1630, a year with one of the worst harvests in the first half of the seventeenth century, the price of grain was twice what it had been in the more plentiful years of 1619 and 1620. Thus for farmers involved in market agriculture, a bad year, with half the yield of a good one, could still bring the same income.[55] As the Norwich mayor's lament amply demonstrates, the people really hurt in times of scarcity were city-dwellers dependent on the countryside for their food. That urban dwellers left for New England to assure themselves of a steady food supply, however, is highly unlikely. Emigrants would

---

[54] B. E. Supple, *Commercial Crisis and Change in England, 1600–1642: A Study in the Instability of a Mercantile Economy* (Cambridge: Cambridge University Press, 1959), pp. 55, 57, 101, 110–11; Peter Bowden, "Agricultural Prices, Farm Profits, and Rents," *Agrarian History*, 4:623–32; Tyack, "Migration from East Anglia," pp. 124–37; and "Grain Shortages in 1630–31 and the Measures Taken in Somerset, Derbyshire, Nottinghamshire, and Norwich," in *Seventeenth-Century Economic Documents*, ed. Joan Thirsk and J. P. Cooper (Oxford: Clarendon Press, 1972), pp. 37–38.

[55] Thirsk, *Agrarian History*, vol. 4, Statistical Appendix, table 6, pp. 849–50.

surely have anticipated the primitive state of the region's agriculture; reports of scarcity at Plymouth and the early Massachusetts Bay settlements had quickly filtered back to England. Moreover, emigrating urban artisans certainly understood that, in the New World, responsibility for feeding their families would lie in their own hands—hands more accustomed to the loom or the last than the plow.

The slump in England's textile industry has also been accounted an incentive for emigration. The industry was indeed mired in a severe depression in the early seventeenth century; it is true as well that a quarter of the adult male emigrants were employed in a trade related to cloth manufacture. The weavers Nicholas Busby, Francis Lawes, and Michael Metcalf of Norwich all completed their apprenticeships at a time when the textile trade "like the moon [was] on the wane," and the future of Norfolk's preeminent industry was growing dimmer each year.[56] Throughout the sixteenth century, the county's traditional worsted manufacture had steadily lost ground in its European markets to a developing continental industry. In southern England and the West Country, broadcloth producers suffered reverses as well. In 1631, the clothiers of Basingstoke, Hampshire—a town about fifteen miles southwest of the home of the emigrant weaver Thomas Smith of Romsey— informed the county's justices that the "poor do daily increase, for there are in the said town 60 householders, whose families do amount to 300 persons and upwards being weavers, spinners, and clothworkers, the most of them being heretofore rated towards the relief of the poor, do now many of them depend upon the alms of the parish" and begged for some kind of relief.[57]

The decline in sales of the white, undressed fabric that had

[56] The quotation is from a parliamentary debate of 1621, in Supple, *Commercial Crisis and Change*, p. 54.

[57] Allison, "Norfolk Worsted Industry [Part I]," pp. 73, 78–80; Chalklin, *Seventeenth-Century Kent*, pp. 121–22; Peter Clark, *English Provincial Society from the Reformation to the Revolution: Religion, Politics, and Society in Kent, 1500–1640* (Hassocks, Sussex: Harvester Press, 1977), p. 356; quotation from "Depression in the Hampshire Cloth Industry, 1631," in *Seventeenth-Century Economic Documents*, pp. 38–39.

been the mainstay of English clothiers proved to be irreversible. At the same time, however, certain sectors in the textile industry recovered by switching over to the production of "new draperies." These fabrics, lighter in weight and brighter in color than the traditional English product, were made from a coarser—and therefore cheaper—type of wool. They were introduced in England largely by immigrant Dutch and Walloon artisans, who were frequently encouraged by local authorities to take up residence in England. East Anglia and Kent became centers of the revitalized industry; the cities of Norwich, Canterbury, and Sandwich counted scores of these north European "strangers" among their inhabitants. With the end of hostilities between England and Spain in 1604, trade expanded, and the new fabrics found ready markets in the Mediterranean and the Levant. By the mid-seventeenth century, the production of Norwich stuffs—new versions of worsted wool—had "probably raised the prosperity of the industry to an unprecedented level" and brought renewed prosperity to a number of beleaguered artisans as well.[58]

We cannot know whether worsted weavers like Nicholas Busby, William Nickerson, or Francis Lawes adapted to prevailing trends in their trade, but they seem not to have been in serious economic straits at the time they decided to go to Massachusetts. The identification of Busby, Lawes, and Michael Metcalf among Norwich's most important tradesmen at Bishop Wren's impeachment trial, even if those claims were somewhat exaggerated, attested to their standing in the community. Busby's service as a *jurat* responsible for checking the quality of worsted wool produced in the city certainly indicated that he had achieved considerable status in his profession. Economic advancement attended professional prominence: before their departure for the New World, Busby and his wife owned a houselot in a prospering parish in the northern part of the city. In the countryside as well, some cloth

[58] Allison, "Norfolk Worsted Industry [Part 2]," pp. 61–77, quotation from p. 77; Supple, *Commercial Crisis and Change*, pp. 136–62; Chalklin, *Seventeenth-Century Kent*, pp. 123–36; Evans, *Seventeenth-Century Norwich*, p. 16; Ramsay, *Wiltshire Woollen Industry*, 2d ed., pp. 65–84, 101–21.

372   THE NEW ENGLAND QUARTERLY

workers managed to make a good living in hard times. Thomas
Payne, a weaver from the village of Wrentham in Suffolk,
emigrated to Salem in 1637 but died soon thereafter. His will,
written in April 1638, not only listed property recently acquired in Salem, but also mentioned his share in the ship
Mary Anne, on which he had sailed to Massachusetts. At the
time of his departure from Suffolk, then, Payne could not only
afford his family's transportation costs but also had funds to
invest in the New England enterprise.[59]

Even if evidence did suggest that emigrant weavers were
compelled by economic adversity to leave their homeland,
Massachusetts would not have been a wise choice of destination if they hoped to continue in their trade. Flight to the
Netherlands, a place with a well-developed textile industry,
would have been a more rational choice for artisans worried
about the fate of their trade in England and anxious to per-
sist in its practice. Massachusetts lacked both the wool supply and the intricate network of auxiliary tradesmen—such
as combers, carders, calenderers, fullers, dyers, etc.—upon
which England's weavers depended. Several of the emigrants
packed up their looms along with their other belongings, but
there is little evidence that they were able to earn their livings
in Massachusetts solely by weaving.[60]

Arguments linking the Great Migration to economic hardship in England all share an important weakness. Although
historians have discovered that many *places* from which emigrants came suffered from agricultural or industrial depression, they have had little success in connecting those unfavor-
able economic circumstances to the fortunes of individual
emigrants. On the contrary, it appears that the families that

[59] Evans, *Seventeenth-Century Norwich*, pp. 18, 21–22; William L. Sachse, ed.,
Minutes of the Norwich Court of Mayoralty, Norfolk Record Society Publications 15
(1942): 68; Anna C. Kingsbury, *A Historical Sketch of Nicholas Busby the Emigrant*
(n.p., 1924), pp. 5–8; Nathaniel E. Paine, *Thomas Payne of Salem and His Descendants: The Salem Branch of the Paine Family* (Haverhill, Mass.: Record Publishing
Co., 1928), p. 16.

[60] Jewson, *Transcript of Three Registers*, contains lists of East Anglians heading for
Holland. Most appear to have been going for short periods of time—to visit friends
or to enter military service—and not to pursue their trade.

MIGRANTS AND MOTIVES   373

went to New England had largely avoided the serious setbacks that afflicted many of their countrymen during those years.

An alternative interpretation of the colonists' economic motivation has recently been proposed by Peter Clark, who discovered similarities between the New England settlers and "betterment migrants" traveling within the county of Kent during the decades preceding the English Civil War. Betterment migrants, like the New England colonists, were persons of solid means who, Clark argues, sought further to improve their economic positions. Most betterment migrants traveled only a short distance, usually to a nearby town; the New Englanders differed from them primarily through the immense length of their transatlantic journeys. On the whole, betterment migrants were not especially mobile; in their search for opportunity, they generally moved just once in their lives. New England emigrants like John Bent, while they lived in England, also tended to be geographically stable. In addition, betterment migrants shared with the Massachusetts settlers a tendency to rely on kin connections in their choice of destinations.[61]

Clark's model of betterment migration fits the New England movement in certain particulars, but it makes little sense within the larger context of the transatlantic transplantation. If migration to New England was not a sensible economic decision for farmers or weavers hurt by hard times in England, it was even less sensible for people doing well. Most emigrants exchanged an economically viable present for a very uncertain future. As we have seen, nearly one in ten was over forty years old at the time of the migration and had little reason to expect to live long enough to enjoy whatever prosperity the New World might bring. The emigrant groups studied here all left England five or more years after the Great Migration had begun and a decade and a half after the landing at Plymouth; they surely heard from earlier arrivals that New England was no land of milk and honey. If any had a chance to read Edward

---

[61] Clark, *English Provincial Society*, pp. 372–73, and "The migrant in Kentish towns 1580–1640," in *Crisis and Order in English Towns*, pp. 134–38.

374   THE NEW ENGLAND QUARTERLY

Winslow's *Good Newes from New England,* published in
1624, he or she would have learned that the "vain expectation
of present profit" was the "overthrow and bane" of plantations.
People might prosper through "good labor and diligence," but
in the absence of a cash crop, great wealth was not to be expected. The message of William Wood's *New England's Prospect,* published a decade later, was similar. Some colonists
were lured westward by descriptions of plenty, Wood acknowledged, but they soon fell to criticizing the new society,
"saying a man cannot live without labor." These disgruntled
settlers "more discredit and disparage themselves in giving
the world occasion to take notice of their dronish disposition
that would live off the sweat of another man's brows. Surely
they were much deceived, or else ill informed, that ventured
thither in hope to live in plenty and idleness, both at a time."
Letters as well as published reports informed would-be settlers that New England was not a particularly fertile field for
profit. In 1631, one young colonist wrote to his father in Suffolk, England, that "the cuntrey is not so as we ded expecte
it." Far from bringing riches, New England could not even
provide essentials; the disillusioned settler begged his father
to send provisions, for "we do not know how longe we may
subeseiste" without supplies from home.[62]

If prospective emigrants were not hearing that New England offered ample opportunities for economic betterment,
they *were* informed that life in Massachusetts could bring
betterment of another sort. When Governor Thomas Dudley
provided the countess of Lincoln with an account of his first
nine months in New England, he announced that "if any come
hether to plant for worldly ends that canne live well at home
hee comits an errour of which he will soon repent him. But if
for spirituall [ends] and that noe particular obstacle hinder his
removeall, he may finde here what may well content him."

[62] Edward Winslow, *Good Newes from New England: or a true Relation of things
very remarkable at the Plantation of Plimoth in New-England* (London, 1624), reprinted in *Chronicles of the Pilgrim Fathers of the Colony of Plymouth, from 1602 to
1625,* 2d ed., ed. Alexander Young (Boston, 1844), pp. 272–73, 370–71; Wood, *New
England's Prospect,* p. 68; [?] Pond to William Pond, *Winthrop Papers,* 3:18.

MIGRANTS AND MOTIVES   375

Dudley worried that some might be drawn to Massachusetts by exaggerations of the land's bounty and wanted to make clear who would benefit most from emigration. "If any godly men out of religious ends will come over to helpe vs in the good worke wee are about," the governor wrote, "I think they cannot dispose of themselves nor of their estates more to God's glory and the furtherance of their owne reckoninge."[63] New England promised its settlers *spiritual* advantages only; men merely in search of wealth could go elsewhere. Emmanuel Downing, in a letter to Sir John Coke, clarified the important difference between New England and other colonial ventures. "This plantation and that of Virginia went not forth upon the same reasons nor for the same end. Those of Virginia," he explained, "went forth for profit. . . . These went upon two other designs, some to satisfy their own curiosity in point of conscience, others . . . to transport the Gospel to those heathen that never heard thereof."[64]

Both published tracts and private correspondence advertised New England's religious mission. In *The Planter's Plea*, Rev. John White proclaimed that "the most eminent and desirable end of planting Colonies, is the propagation of Religion." Prospective emigrants learned from the Rev. Francis Higginson's *New-England's Plantation*, published in 1630, that "that which is our greatest comfort . . . is, that we haue here the true Religion and holy Ordinances of Almightie God taught amongst us: Thankes be to God, we haue here plentie of Preaching, and diligent Catechizing, with strickt and carefull exercise, and good and commendable orders to bring our People into a Christian conuersation with whom we haue to doe withall."[65] Indeed, New England's Puritan predilections

[63] "Gov. Thomas Dudley's Letter to the Countess of Lincoln, March, 1631," in *Tracts and Other Papers Relating Principally to the Origin, Settlement, and Progress of the Colonies in North America, From the Discovery of the Country to the Year 1776*, ed. Peter Force, 4 vols. (Washington, D.C., 1836–46), 2:12.

[64] This letter is quoted in *Letters from New England*, p. 93. For a similar statement, see John Winthrop's "General Observations: Autograph Draft," *Winthrop Papers*, 2:117.

[65] John White, *The Planter's Plea* (London, 1630), reprinted in *Tracts and Other Papers*, 2:12; Rev. Francis Higginson, *New-England's Plantation with The Sea Jour-*

were so well known that colonial leaders feared retribution from the Anglican establishment in England. *The Planter's Plea* specifically sought to dispel rumors that Massachusetts was overrun with Separatists, and, during the early 1630s, Edward Howes maintained a steady correspondence with John Winthrop, Jr. concerning similar allegations of New England radicalism. In 1631, Howes reported that "heare is a mutteringe of a too palpable seperation of your people from our church gouernment." The following year, he again informed Winthrop of claims that "you neuer vse the Lords prayer, that your ministers marrie none, that fellowes which keepe hogges all the weeke preach on the Saboth, that euery towne in your plantation is of a seuerall religion; that you count all men in England, yea all out of your church, and in the state of damnacion." Howes knew such rumors were false but feared that many other Englishmen believed them. The spread of such lies endangered not only the colony's reputation but perhaps its very survival as well.[66]

Prospective emigrants, then, could hardly have been unaware of the peculiar religious character of New England society. Accounts of the region's commitment to Puritanism were too numerous to be overlooked; those who made the voyage had to know what they were getting into. Adherence to Puritan principles, therefore, became the common thread that stitched individual emigrants together into a larger movement. As John White declared, "Necessitie may presse some; Noveltie draw on others; hopes of gaine in time to come may prevaile with a third sort: but that the most and most sincere and godly part have the advancement of the *Gospel* for their maine scope I am co[n]fident."[67]

White's confidence was by no means misplaced. The roster

---

nal and Other Writings (facsimile, Salem: Essex Book and Print Company, 1908), p. 108. See also the letter from Edward Trelawney to his brother Robert in *Letters from New England*, pp. 175–78.

[66] White, *Planter's Plea*, pp. 33–36; Edward Howes to John Winthrop, Jr., 9 November 1631 and 28 November 1632, *Winthrop Papers*, 3:54, 100–101.

[67] White, *Planter's Plea*, p. 36.

MIGRANTS AND MOTIVES　　　377

of passengers to New England contains the names of scores of otherwise ordinary English men and women whose lives were distinguished by their steadfast commitment to nonconformity, even in the face of official harassment. The *Hercules* left Sandwich in 1635 with William Witherell and Comfort Starr aboard; both men had been in trouble with local ecclesiastical authorities. Anthony Thacher, a nonconformist who had been living in Holland for two decades, returned to Southampton that same year to embark for New England on the *James*. Two years later, the *Rose* carried Michael Metcalf away from the clutches of Norwich diocesan officials. Metcalf had appeared before ecclesiastical courts in 1633 and again in 1636 for refusing to bow at the name of Jesus or to adhere to the "stinking tenets of Arminius" adopted by the established Church. Before his departure, Metcalf composed a letter "to all the true professors of Christs gospel within the city of Norwich" that chronicled his troubled encounters with church officials and explained his exclusively religious reasons for emigration. Thomas and Mary Oliver, Metcalf's fellow parishioners at St. Edmund's in Norwich, had also been cited before the archepiscopal court in 1633 and set sail for Massachusetts the same year as Metcalf. Other emigrants leaving in 1637 were John Pers and John Baker, two Norwich residents evidently also in trouble with church officials; Joan Ames, the widow of the revered Puritan divine William Ames, who had only recently returned from a lengthy stay in Rotterdam; and Margaret Neave and Adam Goodens, whose names appeared on Separatist lists in Great Yarmouth. Peter Noyes, who emigrated in 1638, came from a family long involved in nonconformist activities in England's southwest.[68]

Although New England was not populated solely by unsuc-

[68] Clark, *English Provincial Society*, p. 372; Savage, *Genealogical Dictionary*, 4: 270–71; Breen and Foster, "Moving to the New World," pp. 202–3, 207 n. 37; Jewson, *Transcript of Three Registers*, p. 8; Champlin Burrage, *The Early English Dissenters in the Light of Recent Research, 1550–1641*, 2 vols. (Cambridge: Cambridge University Press, 1912), 2:309; Powell, *Puritan Village*, p. 4; "Michael Metcalfe," *NEHGR* 16 (1862): 279–84. The incomplete survival of ecclesiastical records in England makes it impossible to discover the full extent of colonists' troubles with the authorities.

cessful defendants in ecclesiastical court proceedings, the nonconformist beliefs of other emigrants should not be underestimated merely because they avoided direct conflict with bishops and deacons. John Winthrop's religious motivation has never been in doubt even though he was never convicted of a Puritan offense. Winthrop's "General Observations for the Plantation of New England," like Metcalf's letter to the citizens of Norwich, emphasized the corrupt state of England's ecclesiastical affairs and concluded that emigration "wilbe a service to the church of great consequens" redounding to the spiritual benefit of emigrants and Indians alike. Those few men who recorded their own reasons for removal likewise stressed the role of religion. Roger Clap, who sailed in 1630, recalled in his memoirs that "I never so much as heard of *New-England* until I heard of many godly Persons that were going there" and firmly believed that "God put it into my Heart to incline to Live abroad" in Massachusetts. John Dane, who seems to have spent most of his youth fighting off his evil inclinations, "bent myself to cum to nu ingland, thinking that I should be more fre here then thare from temptations." Arriving in Roxbury in the mid-1630s, Dane soon discovered that relocation would not end his struggle with sinfulness; the devil sought him out as readily in the New World as in the Old.[69]

To declare that most emigrants were prompted by radical religious sentiment to sail to the New World, however, does not mean that these settlers resembled Hawthorne's memorable "stern and black-browed Puritans" in single-minded pursuit of salvation. The decision to cross the seas indelibly marked the lives of those who made it. Even the most pious wrestled with the implications of removal from family, friends, and familiar surroundings. Parents often objected to the departure of their children; a son following the dictates of his conscience might risk the estrangement of a disappointed

---

[69] *Winthrop Papers*, 2:111; "Memoirs of Roger Clap," *Dorchester Antiquarian and Historical Society Collections* 1 (1844): 18–19; "John Dane's Narrative, 1682," *NEHGR* 8 (1854): 154.

MIGRANTS AND MOTIVES   379

father.[70] Although religious motivation is the only factor with sufficient power to explain the departure of so many otherwise ordinary families, the New England Puritans should not be seen as utopians caught up in a movement whose purpose totally transcended the concerns of daily life.

Solitary ascetics can afford to reject the things of this world in order to contemplate the glories of the next; family men cannot. Even as prospective settlers discussed the spiritual benefits that might accompany a move to New England, they worried about what they would eat, where they would sleep, and how they would make a living. In the spring of 1631, Emmanuel Downing wrote with considerable relief to John Winthrop that the governor's encouraging letters "haue much refreshed my hart and the myndes of manie others" for "yt was the Iudgement of most men here, that your Colonye would be dissolved partly by death through want of Food, howsing and rayment, and the rest to retorne or to flee for refuge to other plantacions."[71] Other leaders and publicists of the migration continued both to recognize and to sympathize with the concerns of families struggling with the decision of whether or not to move, and they sought to reassure prospective settlers that a decision in favor of emigration would not doom their families to cold and starvation in the wilderness. At the same time, the way in which these writers composed their comforting messages to would-be emigrants underscored the settlers' understanding of the larger meaning of their mission.

Although several of the tracts and letters publicizing the migration contained favorable descriptions of the new land, they were never intended to be advertisements designed to capture the interest of profit-seekers. When John White, Thomas Dudley, and others wrote about the blessings of New

[70] See, e.g., the story of Samuel Rogers in Kenneth W. Shipps, "The Puritan Emigration to New England: A New Source on Motivation," *NEHGR* 135 (1981): 83–97. Both Roger Clap and John Dane noted that their fathers, at least initially, protested their emigration; see "Memoirs of Roger Clap," p. 18; "John Dane's Narrative," p. 154.

[71] Edward Downing to John Winthrop, 30 April [1631], *Winthrop Papers*, 3:30.

England's climate, topography, and flora and fauna, they simply hoped to assure godly English men and women that a move to the New World would not engender poverty as well as piety. In *The Planter's Plea,* John White succinctly answered objections that New England lacked "meanes of wealth." "An unanswerable argument," White replied, "to such as make the advancement of their estates, the scope of their undertaking." But, he added, New England's modest resources were in "no way a discouragement to such as aime at the propagation of the Gospell, which can never bee advanced but by the preservation of Piety in those that carry it to strangers." For, White concluded, "nothing sorts better with Piety than Compete[n]cy." He referred his readers to Proverbs 30:8—"Remove far from me vanity and lies: give me neither poverty nor riches; feed me with food convenient for me." Thomas Dudley in effect explicated the meaning of "competency" in a New England context when he listed such goods as "may well content" a righteous colonist. In Massachusetts, Dudley noted, settlers could expect to have "materialls to build, fewell to burn, ground to plant, seas and rivers to ffish in, a pure ayer to breath in, good water to drinke till wine or beare canne be made, which togeather with the cowes, hoggs, and goates brought hether allready may suffice for food." Such were the amenities that emigrants not only could but should aspire to enjoy.[72]

John White repeatedly assured his readers that "all Gods directions"—including the divine imperative to settle New England—"have a double scope, mans good and Gods honour." "That this commandement of God is directed unto mans good *temporall and spirituall,*" he went on, "is as cleere as the light."[73] The Lord, in other words, would take care of His own. To providentialists steeped in the conviction that God intervened directly in human lives, that divine pleasure or disapproval could be perceived in the progress of daily events,

[72] White, *Planter's Plea,* p. 18; "Dudley's Letter to the Countess of Lincoln," p. 12. See also Wood, *New England's Prospect,* p. 68.

[73] White, *Planter's Plea,* p. 2; italics added.

MIGRANTS AND MOTIVES   381

White's statement made eminent sense. If emigrant families embarked on their voyages with the purpose of abandoning England's corruption in order to worship God according to biblical precepts in their new homes, and if they adhered to this purpose, they might expect as a sign of divine favor to achieve a competency, if not riches. Thus John Winthrop could assert that "such thinges as we stand in neede of are vsually supplied by Gods blessing vpon the wisdome and industry of man." The governor's firm belief in the connection between divine favor and human well-being explains why in his "Particular Considerations" concerning his own removal out of England, he admitted that "my meanes heere [in England] are so shortned (now my 3 eldest sonnes are come to age) as I shall not be able to continue in this place and imployment where I now am." If he went to Massachusetts, Winthrop anticipated an improvement in his fortunes, noting that "I [can] live with 7. or 8: servants in that place and condition where for many years I have spent 3: or 400 *li*. per an[num]." Winthrop, despite these musings on his worldly estate, did not emigrate in order to better his economic condition. Rather, he removed in order to undertake the "publike service" that God had "bestowed" on him and hoped that God might reward him if his efforts were successful. In similar fashion, thousands of other emigrants could justify their decisions to move to New England. They believed that, by emigrating, they followed the will of God and that their obedience would not escape divine notice. In return for their submission to His will, the emigrants sincerely hoped that God might allow them—through their own labor—to enjoy a competency of this world's goods.[74]

Historians have generally agreed that early New England displayed a distinctive social character. The first colonists, after all, succeeded in creating a remarkably stable society on the edge of a vast wilderness. But stability alone does not sum up the New Englanders' achievement, for colonists who went

[74] *Winthrop Papers*, 2:143–44, 126.

to other parts of North America also established lasting settlements. What set New England society apart was its Puritan heritage. Religious and social ideals became inextricably intertwined as settlers applied the Puritan concept of the covenantal relationship between God and man to their temporal as well as religious affairs. When New Englanders pledged themselves to God in their churches and to each other in their towns, they imbued their society with a deeply spiritual significance. Other British colonists would also strive to create social harmony, but none would do so with the same intensity of religious purpose as New England's founding generation.[75]

Ironically, the scholarly portrait of New England society has largely been drawn without reference to the identity of the emigrant population. Historians have instead turned to the writings of religious leaders and to the formulaic language of town covenants in order to explicate the meaning of the New England experiment. And while their efforts have produced a most coherent and convincing analysis of that society and culture, their conclusions are rendered even more compelling when the character and motivation of the emigrants themselves are also taken into account. For then it becomes clear that the predilections of the emigrants were just as important as the prescriptions of the clergy in shaping New England society.

At the heart of the colonists' achievement lies an apparent

---

[75] Some of the major works on New England Puritanism and its relationship to social stability include Perry Miller, *Errand into the Wilderness* (Cambridge: Harvard University Press, 1956); Kenneth Lockridge, *A New England Town: The First Hundred Years* (New York: W. W. Norton and Co., 1970); Timothy Breen and Stephen Foster, "The Puritans' Greatest Achievement: A Study of Social Cohesion in Seventeenth-Century Massachusetts," *Journal of American History* 60 (1973): 5–22. In their recent work on early Virginia, Darrett and Anita Rutman have argued that communalism also characterized English colonies in the Chesapeake region and was not specifically a function of religious belief. David Allen has also suggested that much of what we have assumed to be distinctively Puritan in Massachusetts in fact represents transplanted local English customs. Yet for reasons that I hope are clear from this essay, I believe that New England culture was indeed distinguished by its Puritan character and that its pervasive Puritanism resulted from the shared beliefs of the emigrants themselves. See Rutman and Rutman, *A Place in Time: Middlesex County, Virginia, 1650–1750* (New York: W. W. Norton & Co., 1984); Allen, *In English Ways*.

MIGRANTS AND MOTIVES   383

paradox. Settlers in Massachusetts, Plymouth, and Connecticut created a remarkably unified culture and a homogeneous society in a setting where the power of central authorities was exceedingly weak. Preachers and magistrates could have expended every effort extolling the virtues of communal and spiritual harmony and yet failed miserably had not their audience shared in their aspirations. But since the majority of emigrants responded to a common spiritual impulse in moving to New England, they readily accepted the idea of the covenant as the proper model for their social as well as spiritual relationships. Indeed, covenants, because of their voluntary nature, provided the only truly effective means of maintaining social cohesion where coercive power was limited. The social homogeneity of the emigrant population— the absence of both rich and poor folk—unintentionally reinforced covenantal ideals by reducing the differences in status among partners. In this way, social fact joined with communal ideals to create a society of comparative equals pledged to one another's support. At the same time, social and religious covenants helped settlers from diverse geographical and occupational backgrounds to come to terms with their new common enterprise. Emigrants concerned solely with their own material improvement would scarcely have acceded so readily to an ideal of mutual cooperation. It is only because most colonists (at least initially) placed the good of their souls above all else and trusted in the Lord to provide for them that the story of New England's origins occupies a unique place in American history.

Virginia DeJohn Anderson *is an Assistant Professor of History at the University of Colorado, Boulder.*

[4]

Journal of Muslim Minority Affairs, Vol. 29, No. 4, December 2009

Ｒ Routledge
Taylor & Francis Group

The "New" Muslim Minorities in Greece: Between Emigration and Political Participation, 1881–1886

NICOLE IMMIG

Abstract

The withdrawal of the Ottoman Empire and the establishment of new nation-states in South-Eastern Europe brought about significant changes in the relations between the region's ethnic groups, caused by military conflict, expulsions and other forms of forced migrations. Whereas in Serbia and Bulgaria the establishment of new nation states and their legal systems lead to significant restrictions in the juridical status of the formerly-privileged Muslim populations, in Greece the government—at least officially—attempted to integrate these "new" Muslim minorities into the new nation-state. However, by the end of the twentieth century most of the Muslim population in recently-acquired regions such as Thessaly and Epirus had left Greece for regions still under Ottoman governance. In this paper we shall explore not only the sociological situation of Muslim populations in Thessaly and the challenges for both Muslims and the Greek government involved in incorporating them into the new Greek nation-state, but also their ultimate motives for emigration. I shall argue that Muslims emigrated from Greece primarily due to social and economic reasons rather than as a result of discrimination or ethnic violence. I will confine my analysis to the first five years of the incorporation of the region, from 1881 to 1886.

Introduction

The history of South-Eastern Europe at the end of the nineteenth and at the beginning of the twentieth centuries can be characterized by a massive transformation in the political status of the region. In the course of the withdrawal of the Ottoman Empire and the establishment of the new nation states in South-Eastern Europe, the region was undergoing not only a formidable change in the political sense but also an enormous transformation in the composition of ethnic, cultural and linguistic mix. Due to military conflicts, expulsions, state-directed population-transfers, people were often forced to leave the territory they used to perceive as their home.[1] In many parts of the former European provinces of the Ottoman Empire, the so-called "European Turkey", political decisions and their territorial implications resulted in a total reversal of the population structure. In many cases, majority populations became minorities and *vice versa*, if they did not seek refuge in neighbouring countries or states they were expected to belong to. Among the most controversial of these migrations in south-eastern Europe at the end of the nineteenth and at the beginning twentieth centuries are the population transfers of Muslims—which by no means formed a linguistically, ethnically or socially homogenous group—now living on the territories of the emerging nation states.[2]

ISSN 1360-2004 print/ISSN 1469-9591 online/09/040511-12 © 2009 Institute of Muslim Minority Affairs
DOI: 10.1080/13602000903411408

512   *Nicole Immig*

Historiography of Muslim Migration in Europe

Many historians working on migration in South-Eastern Europe mostly place the population transfers of Muslims in the context of "forced migrations" in South-Eastern Europe at the end of the nineteenth and the beginning of the twentieth centuries. Declaring the expulsion of Muslims in the new Balkan states as a "continuum" in South-Eastern European History valid for all new Balkan states, the expulsion of the Morea Muslims in Peloponnes in the frame of the Greek Revolution 1821–1827 is considered as the beginning of forced migrations of Muslims in South-Eastern Europe. As Justin McCarthy states in his often-cited book "Death and Exile":

> ... The Greek rebellion was the first of the movements that identified them-selves by the murder and expulsion of Muslims from their land. (...) The Greek revolution set a pattern for future revolutions in the Balkans. The policy of ridding regions of their Turkish population in the name of national independence was seen again in the wars of 1877–78, 1912–13, and 1919–23.[3]

Bilal Şimşir, Kemal Karpat and others have done extensive research on the expulsions of Balkan Muslims towards the end of the nineteenth century showing that with the with-drawal of the Ottoman Empire the newly established Nation States as Bulgaria, Serbia as well as Montenegro, fostered emigrations of Muslims with every military conflict in the region.[4] Striking is the fact that Muslim emigration from Greece in the late nineteenth century is often discussed in the same context as forced migrations of their co-religionists in the neighbouring states of Serbia and Bulgaria in roughly the same period without referring to any examples from the Greek case or using instances from the period of the Greek Revolution.[5] Although nearly no research has been done—especially not in an international frame—on the Muslim Populations in Greece and their political and sociological situation before the Balkan Wars, it is often argued that after the political changes of the Berlin Treaties in the framework of the Congress of Berlin in 1878, or respectively the Convention of Constantinople in 1881, it was clear "that the successful establishment of national states depended on the liquidation of the muslim element or, at least, on the reduction of the Muslims to the status of a politically and economically harmless minority".[6]

In this article I shall focus on the region of Thessaly after the incorporation of this territory into the Greek Kingdom in 1881 specifically in the context of the political and territorial changes of the Congress of Berlin in 1878. I will try to analyze the situation of Muslims—formerly living as a privileged majority and now having been minimized to a "new" minority in the young Greek nation state—in Thessaly in the first years of the cession of the region to Greece 1881–1886. Investigating the challenge for both, Muslim communities and the Greek Government involved in integrating them into the new nation-state, I hope to contribute to the academic discourse on forced migrations in South-Eastern Europe. An in-depth reading of source material from Thes-saly and Epirus suggests that the idea of a distinct state-directed policy by the Greek State, which aimed either at a total expulsion or a massive reduction of Muslims to a "harmless minority", as assumed by the mentioned historiography, must be seriously reconsidered. Ongoing research is rather showing that Muslims continued to participate on all political and socioeconomic levels. Nevertheless, it is also a matter of truth that in the examined period Muslim population emigrated from the region. It is argued that

Muslim emigration from Greece, in contrast to that of Muslims from neighbouring states, was in fact prompted by different experiences. My research suggests so far that Muslims emigrated from Greece primarily due to social and economic reasons rather than as a result of open discrimination or ethnic violence.

Emigration as Consequence of Political and Territorial Transformation

In the search for interconnections between emigration and politics in South-Eastern European history, international research characterizes the political and sociological environment, from which emigration arises, as follows:[7] In the case of Muslim populations, for example emigration was above all, the result of military conflicts between the European states or rather the new Christian Nation States and the Ottoman Empire. Secondly emigration was furthermore dependant on the political and legal status of Muslim populations in the newly formed State, perhaps even a reaction to the prevailing dimensions of discrimination or intolerance and the respective politics concerning the new minority populations of non-Christian faith. Emigration of Muslims is furthermore often based on the assumption that the life of Muslim populations is characterized by high incidence of migration and "ethnic mobilisation" as a means to escape violence.[8] National historiography from South-Eastern Europe as well as from Turkey often considers migration of Muslim populations to the Ottoman Empire as "remigration", as going back to the "ancestral homeland" they came from, implying a long desired wish of the Balkan-Muslims to leave the region.[9] Explaining motives of emigration, Muslim populations are often pictured as politically and/or religiously extreme and highly religiously fanaticized.[10] This is also related to the argument that Muslims are strongly attached to Islam which is used to strengthen the case for explaining emigration of Muslims from Greece at the end of the nineteenth century.

Focusing at the first two points in the case of Greece—in comparison to other Balkan States—these characteristics may only be applicable with some modifications. The Congress of Berlin had decided in separate meetings after 1878 that the Ottoman Empire and Greece should settle their borders. Greece had not actively participated in the military actions in frame of the Ottoman-Russian War of 1876–1878. The bilateral negotiations between the Greek Kingdom and the Ottoman Empire proved to be of rather complicated character.[11] After long and enduring proceedings, which lasted nearly two years, and under the intervention of the European Powers, the negotiations finally led to the Convention of Constantinople on 24th of May 1881. The Convention determined that the Sandschak of Thessaly and a part of Epirus, the town of Arta, should be ceded to Greece.[12] Whereas in Bulgaria armed hostilities had pushed the Ottoman Empire to retreat and the region was heavily devastated by military action, in Greece the cession of Thessaly and Arta was negotiated and decided by the Ottoman Empire and Greece and the European Powers "on paper". In the case of Bulgaria and Serbia it can be stated that a large segment of the Muslim population left the Bulgarian lands as a consequence of military operations and accompanying violence.[13] In the case of Thessaly, Greek troops had however crossed the Greek-Ottoman border, invading smaller parts of Thessaly in 1878 and 1880 as means of pressure to achieve a more favourable agreement and as a result of the delay of the diplomatic negotiations, only to be recalled two days later.[14] But the regions of Thessaly and Epirus were not a military battle field when talking in terms of war. What is more likely to be seen as a threat for the Thessalian—Christian and Muslim—population is another fact: Thessaly was suffering heavily from devastating brigandage and roving bands of irregulars, which left the provinces in a state of great insecurity.[15] Affected was the entire population of Thessaly including Muslim and Christian families as well. But it is questionable, whether the provinces had experienced such violence that stimulated or fostered emigration Muslims from the region as a result of the open military conflict.

With the final agreement of ceding the provinces of Thessaly and the town of Arta to Greece, an exact plan for the Ottoman evacuation and the occupation of the territory by the Greek state was elaborated. The plan directed the military takeover by Greek troops and administration. The supervision of the territory transfer was assigned to a commission of the Great Powers, which should guarantee the peaceful handover of the provinces. The Greek Government assured the European diplomats before the Greek takeover of the region that

> ... at the desire of his Majesty the King of Greece some time ago instructed the Agents of the Greek Government in Thessaly to spare no pains in assuring the Musulman population about to be incorporated within the limits of Greece that they need harbour no fear nor apprehension with regard to their future and condition which would be seriously respected and attended to by the New Government (. . .).[16]

According to the Greek press, the foreign diplomats, and also accounts of Ottoman officials, the Greek occupation was conducted in a quiet and peaceful manner.[17] In the Athenian newspaper *Aion* the mayor of the Trikala, Kadri Bey, announced the unification of "our homeland *(tis patridas imon)* with Greece" and confirmed the calm and orderly takeover of the town.[18] Similar statements were issued in other Athenian newspapers such as the *Ethnikon Pnevma*, which published telegrams by various Ottoman mayors of the Thessalian towns as Fersala and Trikala, as well as the religious leaders of both communities, the *mufti* of Fersala and the Archbishop of Trikala, who welcomed the new Greek administration.[19] In order to prevent every possible disturbance which could be taken as a reason for troubles, the Greek Government enabled measures concerning the practical order of the evacuation and occupation of Thessaly by military action. The Greek population of the region was further requested to refrain from every major celebration in favour of the Greek troops, a directive, which was followed only to a certain degree.[20] The same was demanded also in conjunction with the official visit of the Prime-Minister and the King of Greece in the month after the occupation of Thessaly. In preparation for visiting the towns with Muslim communities the Prime-Minister as well as the King attached great importance to meeting primarily the deputies of the Muslim communities and afterwards the Greek officials.[21] In the towns of Larissa, Trikala and Volos, where a great number of Muslims were living, the King and the Prime-Minister were welcomed either by the Ottoman representatives of the Muslim communities and/or by the Muslim mayors, who continued to be in office after the assumption of the territory.[22] In Larissa, which had the biggest Muslim population in comparison to other Thessalian towns, the Greek Prime-Minister Koumoundouros was first welcomed by the Ottoman Beys of the city and then by the Greek officials and military. Asked by the British diplomat-agent of Larissa towards their future plans, the numerous Muslim Beys of the town assured "that they would gain rather than lose by entrusting him with their social and political interests"[23] It seems that the Greek side was basically interested in preventing everything which could shed a negative light on the Greek takeover. An article in the Greek newspaper "*Aion*" in the first month of the occupation of Thessaly states that, although the Ramadan was announced by cannon shooting by the Greek army, the public announcement of religious Christian celebrations was strictly forbidden.[24]

The Convention of Constantinople and the Implications for Muslims in Thessaly

Incorporating the regions of Thessaly and Arta not only meant considerable enlargement of the Greek territory but involved the integration of non-Christian minorities which, for the first time, reached almost 10% of the total population. About 8.2% of the population of Greece was now of Muslim faith and 1.1% belonged to the Jewish communities of Thessaly. The numbers given vary from 290,000 to 330,000 for the whole population, including 35,000–40,000 Muslims and 4,000–6,000 Jews in the year after the cession to the Greek State.[25] Muslim populations were scattered in the towns and in the plains of Thessaly, Larissa, Trikala, Tyrnavos, Almyro; and in Larissa (Yenişehir), the capital of Thessaly, they were in the majority.

While in the first Constitutions after the Greek War of Independence religion was the determining criterion of Greek national identity ('those indigenous inhabitants of the realm of Greece who believe in Christ are Greeks', Art. 2),[26] which was later enlarged by the criterion of language, the Convention of Constantinople, of May 24th 1881 set the pattern for religious and political rights of non-Christian populations in Greece at least until 1913.[27] The Convention, which was ratified by the Greek parliament in June 1882, not only guaranteed the Muslims freedom of religion and the right to practise their religion, it also assured the autonomy and hierarchical organization of the Muslim communities without any interference from the Greek State. Article 8 of the Convention further respected the religious jurisdiction of the *shariah*-courts. It also laid down the protection of their belongings since it included the assurance on the property rights for Muslims, who decided to stay and as well for those who emigrated.[28] The Greek government granted the Muslims the right to opt for the Ottoman or the Greek citizenship within a time of three years, a period of time which was extended later until the year 1889.[29] Pushed by the European Powers or not, the Convention of Constantinople included a number of minority rights for the Muslim communities of Thessaly, whereas in Serbia and Bulgaria the establishment of new nation states and their legal codes in the 1880s brought about significant restrictions in the juridical status of the formerly-privileged Muslim populations.[30] It seems that in Greece the government intended to convince the Muslim communities to stay in the provinces, and attempted to integrate—at least officially—Muslim communities into the new nation-state. Debates in local and Athenian newspaper point to the fact that the Greek government was sufficiently aware of the economic consequences mass emigration of the Muslim population could imply for the region. According to some this could lead to a total economic breakdown in Thessaly.[31] Furthermore it must be taken into consideration that the Greek government was experiencing a difficult inner political stage in Athens and feared to loose in the next elections.[32] On this account, conceivably the prospect of votes from several thousand Muslims from Thessaly could have helped it to remain in power. It can be suggested that a positive political account on minority issues towards Muslim populations could also contribute in securing the approval of the European Powers in further expansion-projects of the Greek Kingdom. However, by the end of the twentieth century most of the Muslim population in recently-acquired regions such as Thessaly and Epirus had left Greece for regions still under Ottoman governance.

Motives for Emigration

In their quest to establish motivations for Muslims in their preference to migrate rather than to remain in Thessaly, Greek and also European nationally perceived historiography suggests that emigration of the Muslim populations after the assumption of control in Thessaly can be interpreted by the "naturalness of things", so to say a "physical reaction" of Muslims due to the recent political changes, determined by the "path of history" and therefore generally expected. Their migration is perceived as a natural "return" or "remigration" of those populations.

However, based on the assumptions concerning mass expulsions of Muslims in Bulgaria and Serbia in 1878–1879 and in the frame of the Balkan Wars of 1912–1913—the reasons for Muslim emigration are exclusively to be found in ethnic conflict. In a recently published book on the history of Thessaly, Angeliki Sfika-Theodosiou assumes that the Ottoman nobles of the town, although they welcomed the political and administrative representatives of the new Government, were full of contempt, disrespect and grave animosity.[33] Motives for Muslim emigration are furthermore found by Greek historiography in the religious fanaticism of the Balkan Muslims. Muslim populations are often pictured as religiously and/or politically extreme assuming a strong political affinity to the Ottoman Empire and to Islam.[34] As Sfika-Theodosiou states, without giving any references: "the feelings of the Muslims were to such a degree hostile, that there existed a permanent threat of clash/collision".[35]

It is therefore not surprising that in the search for establishing the motivations for the Muslims to emigrate, scholars come to the conclusion that it could be ascribed to the reluctance on the part of Muslims to be ruled by Christians and their inability to cope with the new political situation.[36] This seems to be in accordance with the assessments of Athenian politicians of the same period around this issue. The Greek Prime-Minister Koumoundouros as well as his successor Trikoupis, who officially supported the non-emigration of Muslims from Thessaly, nevertheless expected their departure or rather their "return" to the Ottoman Empire, "where they would be able to live under institutions more congenial to their tastes and habits".[37] Within many Greek political circles the fate of Muslims in Thessaly was generally understood as a "somewhat anomalous position the Turks would occupy in a country which would soon adopt the manners and customs of the civilization of the Western Europe and that the feeling of equality amongst the different classes of society which existed in so high a degree in Greece was not likely to be appreciated or even understood by a Turkish population".[38] In this the Greek Prime Minister was in agreement with many European scholars, who predicted the total emigration of Muslims of European Turkey until the end of the twentieth century and therefore an easy solution of the "Muslim Question" in South-Eastern Europe, since it was generally believed that a long-term coexistence between Muslims and Christians was impossible, because their "religious and cultural differences were thought too antagonistic".[39]

Social Changes and Socio-Political Participation

In the search for explanations for emigration of Muslims despite the above mentioned criteria it seems that analyzing the juridical and political status does not give a satisfactory explanation for mass emigration of Muslims from Greece. Research has focused overwhelmingly on the diplomatic and military situation in Greece and its impact on the political, social and economic situation of the Greek population. The social and economic situation of Muslim populations in reaction to the principal political changes after 1881; the practical consequences of political decisions and territorial agreements for the Muslim communities in everyday life; as well the challenges for both Muslims and the Greek governments involved in incorporating them into the new Greek nation-state were rather neglected. In the case of the Bulgarian Muslims it has been suggested that—leaving aside mass emigrations caused by military actions and accompanying acts of violence, which caused or stimulated emigration to territories still under Ottoman governance—"rather than any 'political oppression' or legal discrimination, what most effected the Turkish and Muslim community at this time was the general trend of social change",[40] so to say the lingering change of the environment in general, the slow altering of the mutual cultural environment ("*kultureller Lebensraum*"[41]). This can be suggested also for the Muslim communities of Thessaly. Since the political and juridical status of the "new" Muslim minority in Greece does include fundamental minority regulations stipulated by the Convention of Constantinople, it must be questioned, if the socio-economic situation of Muslim populations in Thessaly equates the promulgated policy of the Greek Kingdom.

Research indicates that the situation of Muslims in the region was quite ambivalent during the early years (1881–1886) after the incorporation of Thessaly. At hand many examples exist proving that the political and religious rights of Muslims were officially respected. The fact that in the general elections of December 1881 two Muslim MPs were elected in the Greek parliament exemplifies that many Muslim voters did participate in the general election. Though it was not the norm, the Muslim MPs from Thessaly swore on the Qura'n in the Parliament which was not even debated in the Greek press— and pledged their loyalty to the Greek King.[42]

Striking nevertheless is the fact that the two delegates did not actively participate in any political parliamentary debate at the state level, although many issues were concerning the Muslim populations in Thessaly, as for instance the agrarian question, which was a heavily drawn-out issue in the 1880s.[43] Regarding the election campaign participation of Muslims becomes also apparent by the study of a few preserved electoral registers and published lists in the local and Athenian press.[44] However, from the analysis of diplomatic records and local and Athenian newspapers it can be determined that in the elections many Muslim voters in Thessaly were either actively prevented from going to the polling places by force—especially in smaller villages—or did not find their names on the voting lists.[45] In a letter to the Athenian Newspaper "*Proia*", Tahir Bey, a Muslim from Trikala describes, how Muslim, as well as Jewish voters, were violently restrained from entering the polling stations and thus they could not exercise their electoral rights. Although the persons concerned complained to the Kings Representative in Trikala, who nevertheless supported their request, public authorities were not willing to allow the Muslims and the Jews to participate in the elections.[46]

In 1885 the Greek Parliament discussed critical incidents within the elections in the newly ceded provinces, where it was stated that more and more pressure was imposed on members of minorities against participation in state elections. In Domokos, Fersala and other villages Muslims and Gypsies were threatened by the Prefect (Nomarchis) and the local authorities or even locked in their own houses by Greek inhabitants to deter them from going to the polling stations.[47] Furthermore, there is evidence that in some regions in the newly ceded provinces, separate polling stations for Muslim voters were established.[48] In this respect there has to be mentioned that on the local level some confusion seemed to have prevailed about the realization and the execution of the elections in the newly acquired provinces.[49] It seems furthermore that it was unclear if Muslims who wanted to participate in the elections had first to become Greek citizens or not, although this condition had previously been announced by the Greek government.[50] The same confusion prevailed as well with regard to eligibility for an office, which means, the right to be elected and the way this was to be proven and/or documented by the candidates.[51] Additional disturbance was raised by the position of the Ottoman Consulates towards the participation of "Ottoman Muslims" in the elections in Thessaly. In accordance with the local newspaper from Larissa *Anexartisia* the Ottoman authorities claimed that Muslims who ran for office in Thessaly would loose automatically the Ottoman citizenship.[52]

Regarding official representation of Muslims after the incorporation of Thessaly into the Greek Kingdom it can be stated that in many Thessalian towns the Muslim mayors remained in office only until the next elections, and in smaller villages with a high percentage of Muslim population, some mayors of Muslim faith were even confirmed in office. Although reports of emigrating Muslim families in the local and Athenian press are numerous—especially in the first years after the cession to the Greek Kingdom—, Muslims did not cease totally to participate in political, social and economic live of the towns and cities. On the political level representatives of Muslim communities in Thessaly appear—at least until 1886—as deputies in city-councils. Unfortunately not many documents of city-councils in Thessaly at that time have survived, but at least in Larissa records show that there were three constant members of the city-council, who actively engage in public affairs and matters pertaining to requirements of the religion even after 1886.[53] Because there were so many Ottoman fellow citizens interested in the local news, the local newspaper from Larissa, *Anexartisia*, announced during the first month after the occupation, that they would provide a part of the news in Turkish language written in Greek alphabet.[54]

Muslims were also participating in many ways in the social and political life of the community. At the inauguration of the new railway line in Thessaly the representatives of the three religious Communities in Larissa—Orthodox, Jews, Muslim—were present and Muslim deputies were consulted on other official events.[55] This is also the case concerning educational issues. At the board of education commission which was set up by the prefecture of Thessaly, delegates from the Muslim communities—at least in Larissa and Volos—were also involved. In Larissa two basic Turkish schools were operational as well as one girls' school, where the teachers were appointed and paid for by the Greek State.[56] The establishment of new Turkish schools was allowed only with the restriction that the community must contain at least 1,000 persons.[57]

Muslim presence can also be noticed in the field of economy of the region. However, official national Greek historiography on the years after the Congress of Berlin and before the Balkan Wars 1878–1912, often ignores the existence of Muslim Populations in the newly-acquired regions. A common justification for neglecting Muslim presence, conveyed by many scholars is, that the Muslims, meaning mostly to the great land owners, had already left the region in the years 1876–1878 having sold their propertirs at extensively low prices because of fear of the takeover of the region by the Greek State.[58] Since research has shown that the presumptions made by most scholars concerning the political circumstances as well as the political and social consequences arising for Muslim populations in the Greek case are not similar to those in the neighbouring states at the same period of time, the assumptions concerning economic anticipation of Muslims in the region have to be closely re-examined. Vangelis Prontzas has shown that many Muslim landowners—even though they had migrated to regions still under Ottoman Governance—nevertheless kept their estates and were also involved in the newly established banking-system by taking out loans from Greek Banks in Thessaly.[59] In Larissa Muslims are also engaged in the resident "Farmers' Association", which is dominated by Christian landowners of the region.[60] The study of a large number of notarial documents found in several archives in Greece shows that many estates were often administered through Muslim, but also Greek confidants living in Thessaly. In these documents Muslim inhabitants, mostly of towns in Thessaly as Larissa, Trikala and Karditsa do not only act as trustees to notaries, but functioned also as money-lenders, buyers and sellers of property or real estates in the region.[61]

Although Muslim participation can be noticed in all fields of political and socio-economic levels, there seems to have prevailed an ambivalent atmosphere towards the "new" Muslim minority. The example of the Muslim mayor of Larissa, who was involved in a political scandal after 1881, illustrates the two faces of Greek society. The Muslim mayor was confirmed in his position at least until August 1882. Then he retreated from the mayor's office together with all his staff. Until then Halil Bey had represented the main town of Thessaly on all official occasions. In a letter to the Athenian newspaper "*Paliggenisia*", which had reported that the mayor had been forced to retreat from his position, because of suspicions in connection to the Ottoman Empire, the Mayor accused the newspaper of spreading rumours. These were "not only discouraging for Muslims and therefore frustrating, but would also lead to mistrust not only in the Greek but as well in the Muslim population". Halil Bey stated that the newspaper referred to the Muslims in Thessaly as "our Ottoman fellow citizens", although at the same time treating them and the Mayor, as "total strangers in spite of their strong and long-lived affinity to the region. This would rather help to empoisen [sic.] the situation in Thessaly".[62]

Conclusion

The political and territorial transformation of South-Eastern Europe at the end of the nineteenth century had wide implications for Muslim populations living in the new nation states, since they—as a formerly privileged majority—had now become a minority group in a Christian society. In Greece the 1881 Convention of Constantinople granted Muslim populations in the newly acquired regions such as Thessaly, fundamental minority rights. Although Muslims participated in all political and socioeconomic fields, it seems that at least on a local level the implementation and execution of a policy, which tried to prevent Muslims from emigrating, could not be realized. By 1913 at the latest, and more likely as early as the Greek-Turkish War of 1897, most of the Muslim population had left Thessaly for regions still under Ottoman Governance. Nevertheless, the widely held belief that the Greek government pursued a clear policy, which aimed at total expulsion of Muslims and the homogenization of the populations living in Greece, must be reconsidered.

NOTES

1. There is an ongoing discussion about the terminology in migration studies towards classifying migrations as "forced" or "voluntary" migrations. Included here should be all forms of migration without implying any judgement in the utilization of the expressions. The use of the terms "exit" and "emigration" is also applied, while "flight"and "escape" are referred mostly to as refugee-movements, as "classical forms" of "forced migrations". The term "ethnic cleansing", which is also part of current debates, but mostly refers to the twentieth century, will be avoided. Concerning "forced migrations" and "ethnic cleansing" see Ph. Ther, "A Century of Forced Migration: The Origins

520   *Nicole Immig*

and Consequences of 'Ethnic Cleansing'", in *Redrawing Nations: Ethnic Cleansing in East-Central Europe, 1944–1948*, eds Ph. Ther and A. Siljak, Oxford: Rowman and Littlefield, 2001, pp. 43–72; H. Sundhaussen, "Prolegomena zu einer Geschichte der Vertreibungen und Zwangsumsiedlungen im Balkanraum" (Preamble to a history of forced migrations and involuntary resettlements in the Balkans) in *Vertreibungen europäisch erinnern? Historische Erfahrungen. Vergangenheitspolitik—Zukunftskonzeptionen* (Forced Migrations remembered in a European perspective? Historical Perceptions, Politics of Remembrance, Visions of the Future), eds D. Bingen, W. Borodziej and S. Troebst, Wiesbaden: Harrassowitz, 2003, pp. 44–53.

2. In this article, the term "Muslim" will be used, although it refers to a variety of ethnicities of followers of the Muslim faith living in South-Eastern Europe. This is related to the utilization of the term in most of the sources referred to. Here the terms "Muslim", "Ottoman" and "Turk" are used without pointing to any specific ethnicity. It can be assumed however that for the case of Thessaly, it also includes Albanian, and in very small numbers Circassian and Yürük Muslims as well as so-called "Koniaroi-Turks". See A. Tourmakine, *Les Migrations des Populations Musulmanes Balkaniques en Anatolie (1876–1913)* (Migrations of Muslim Populations to Anatolia), Istanbul: Isis, 1995. For the Koniaroi-Turks, see the critical perception of Kiel in: M. Kiel, "Das türkische Thessalien: Etabliertes Geschichtsbild versus Osmanische Quellen" (Turkish Thessaly: Established historical perception versus Ottoman Sources) in *Die Kultur Griechenlands in Mittelalter und der Neuzeit* (The Culture of Greece in the Middle Ages and Modern Times), eds R. Lauer and P. Schreiner, Göttingen: Vandenhoeck & Ruprecht, 1996, pp. 162–185.

3. J. McCarthy, *Death and Exile: The Ethnic Cleansing of the Ottoman Muslims 1821–1922*, Princeton, NJ: Darwin Press, 1995, p. 12.

4. B. Şimşir, ed., *Rumeli'den Türk Göçleri* (Turkish Emigrations from the Balkans. Documents), Vol. I–III, Ankara: Türk Tarih Kurumu (1968–1970); K. Karpat, ed., *The Turks of Bulgaria, the History, Culture and Political Fate of a Minority*, Istanbul: ISIS, 1990; K. Karpat, *Ottoman Population 1830–1914. Demographic and Social Characteristics*, Madison, WI: University of Wisconsin Press, 1985; B. Lory, *Le sort de l'Heritage Ottoman en Bulgarie: l'Exemple des Villes Bulgares 1878–1900* (The Type of Ottoman Heritage in Bulgaria: The Case of Bulgarian Cities, 1878–1900), Istanbul: Editions Isis, 1985.

5. J. McCarthy, *Death and Exile, op. cit.*; K. Karpat, *Ottoman Population 1830–1914, op. cit.*

6. K. Karpat, *Ottoman Population 1830–1914, op. cit.*

7. W. Höpken, "Flucht vor dem Kreuz? Muslimische Emigration aus Südosteuropa nach dem Ende der osmanischen Herrschaft (19./20. Jahrhundert)" (Escape from the Cross? Muslim Emigration from South-Eastern Europe at the end of the Ottoman Empire (19th/20th century)), in *Zwangsmigrationen in Mittel- und Südosteuropa* (Forced Migrations in Central- and South-Eastern Europe), *Comparativ*, Vol. 6, No.1, 1996, pp. 1–24, 6; A. Tourmakine, *Les Migrations des Populations Musulmanes Balkaniques en Anatolie (1876–1913)* (Migrations of Muslim Populations to Anatolia), Istanbul: Isis, 1995, p. 67.

8. W. Höpken, "Flucht vor dem Kreuz, op. cit.*, pp. 1–24, 4; G. F. Kennan, ed., *The Other Balkan Wars: A Carnegie Endowment Inquiry in Retrospect with a New Introduction and Reflections on the Present Conflict*, Washington, DC: Carnegie Endowment for International Peace, 1993 (Reprint 1914), p. 72.

9. As Koliopoulos and Veremis state towards this historiographical perception: The Turks "had invaded the Greek lands and were temporarily 'camping' in them". See J. Koliopoulos, and Th. Veremis, *Greece: The Modern Sequel: From 1821 to the Present*, London: Hurst, 2002, p. 256.

10. A. Sfika-Theodosiou, *I Prosartisi tis Thessalias: I proti fasi stin ensomatosi mias ellinikis eparchias sto elliniko kratos (1881–1885)* (The Cession of Thessaly: The first phase of the incorporation of a Greek region into the Greek State, Salonica: Aristoteleio Panepistimio Thessalonikis, 1989, p. 33.

11. Concerning the negotiations see A. Sfika-Theodosiou, "I entaksi tis thessalias sto elliniko kratos (1878–1881)" (The incorporation of Thessaly into the Greek State), in *Thessalia: Themata Istorias* (Thessaly:Historical Issues), Vol. 1, Larissa: TEDK Thessalias 2006; R. Davison, "The Ottoman-Greek Frontier Question, 1876–1882: From Ottoman Records", in *Praktika: I teleutaia fasi tis anatolikis kriseos kai o ellinismos (1878–1881)* (Papers: The last phase of the Eastern Question and Hellenism), Athens: Diethnēs Enōsē Notioanatolikēs Eurōpēs (International Union of Southeastern Europe), 1983, pp. 185–204.

12. Ministère des Affaires Étrangères de la République Française, *Documents Diplomatiques, Affaires de Grèce, 1880–1881*(Ministry of Foreign Affaires of the French Republic, DiplomaticRecords, Greece, 2nd part), deuxième partie, Paris, 1881; *Accounts and Papers (British Parliamentary Papers)*, Greece, Vol. 7, London: Harrison, 1881; G. Noradounghian, *Recueil d'actes internationaux*

  de l'Empire ottoman (Collection of International Papers on the Ottoman Empire), Vol. 4, Paris: [s.n] (no publisher), 1903.

13. J. McCarthy, *Death and Exile, op. cit.*, especially the chapter on Bulgaria, pp. 59–108.

14. Academy of Athens, *Istoria tou ellinikou ethnous* (History of the Greek People), Vol. 14, Athens: Ekdotiki Athinon, 1977.

15. J. S. Koliopoulos, *BrigandswWithout a Cause: Brigandage and Irridentism in Modern Greece: 1821– 1912*, Oxford: Clarendon Press, 1987.

16. FO 32 530 (June 19, 1881), Letter from Ford to Granville.

17. FO 32 530 (Sept. 9, 1881), Letter from Ford to Granville.

18. *Aion* (Century), Aug. 27, 1881.

19. *Ethnikon Pnevma* (National Spirit), Aug. 26, 1881.

20. See, for example, the entry of Greek military forces in Domokos on 8th of August 1881, which states, that the Greek flag was raised secretly and in total silence in order not to provoke any disturbances by the Turks. (*Paliggennisia* (Regeneration), Aug. 18, 1881). This is also documented in FO 286 342 (Embassy Greece, Aug. 25, 1881), Letter from Ford to Granville.

21. This request was assailed by the Greek Press, see Paliggenisia, Oct. 17, 1881.

22. See reports in a variety of local and national newspapers in October 1881.

23. FO 286 342 (Embassy Greece, Oct. 12, 1881), Letter from Longworth to Dufferin.

24. *Aion*, Aug. 22, 1881.

25. The data regarding the size of the new minority varies depending on the sources consulted. Quantitative records of the population of the new provinces in the years 1878 until 1881 can be found in a variety of sources and statistics which cannot be discussed here. See *Istoria tou ellinikou ethnous, op. cit.*; M. Sivignon, *Thessalia, Geografiki analysi mias ellinikis periphereias* (Thessaly: Geographical Analysis of a Greek Periphery), Athens: Morfotiko Instituto Agrotikis Trapezas, 1992; I. Banco, *Studien zur Verteilung und Entwicklung der Bevölkerung von Griechenland* (Studies of the Dispensation and Development of the Population of Greece), Bonn: Dümmler, 1976. For critics on the statistics, see M. Kiel, "Das türkische Thessalien", *op. cit.*, pp. 109–196.

26. See J. Koliopoulos, and Th. Veremis, *Greece: The modern sequel, op. cit.*, p. 250.

27. For the first half of the nineteenth century, see Bogli, Elpida, *"Ellines to genos": I Ithageneia kai I tavtotita sto ethniko kratos ton Ellinon (1821–1844)* (Greeks by Descent: Citizenship and Identity in the Greek State), Irakleio: Panepistimiakes Ekdoseis Kritis, 2008. Theoretically, this followed the thoughts of an enlarged Greek citizenship in 1835, opening the Greek citizenship for foreigners who would like to settle down in Greece after having spent more than three years in Greece.

28. A. Popovic, *L'islam balkanique: les musulmans du sud-est européen dans la période post-ottomane* (Balkan Islam: the Muslims of South-Eastern Europe in the post-ottoman period), Wiesbaden: Harrassowitz, 1986; G. Nakos, *To nomiko kathestos ton teos dimosion othomanikon gaion: 1821–1912* (The Juridical System of Ottoman State Property), Thessaloniki: University Studio Press, 1984.

29. The right to opt for the Greek citizenship is discussed in: H. Sundhaussen, "Unerwünschte Staatsbürger: Grundzüge des Staatsangehörigkeitsrechts in den Balkanländern und Rumänien" (Undesirable Citizens: Main Features of the Citizenship Law in the Balkans and Rumania), in *Staatsbürgerschaft: Historische Erfahrungen und aktuelle Debatten* (Citizenship: Historical Dimensions and Actual Debates), eds Ch. Conrad and J. Kocka, Hamburg: Ed. Körber Stiftung, 2001, pp. 193–215.

30. For the case of Serbia, see D. Müller, *Staatsbürger auf Widerruf: Juden und Muslime als Alteritätspartner im rumänischen und serbischen Nationscode: ethnonationale Staatsbürgerschaftskonzepte 1878–1944* (Citizens on repeal: Jews and Muslims as Partners of "the Others" in Rumanian and Serbian National-Codes), Wiesbaden: Harrassowitz, 2005.

31. *Paliggenisia*, Nov. 30, 1881, which states that due to massive emigration from Thessaly, many of the estates are not cultivated.

32. Gunnar Hering, *Die politische Parteien in Griechenland: 1821–1936* (The political parties in Greece), Vol. 1, München: Oldenbourg, 1992, pp. 494–499.

33. A. Sfika-Theodosiou, "I entaksi tis thessalias sto elliniko kratos (1878–1881)", *op. cit.*

34. E. Allamani, "I Thessalia sta televtaia peninta chronia tis tourkikis kyriarcheias (1832–1882)" (Thessaly in the last 50 years of Ottoman Dominion), in *Praktika, I televtaia fasi tis anatolikis kriseos kai o ellinismos (1878–1881)* (Papers: The last phase of the Eastern Crisis and Hellenism), Athens: Diethnēs Enōsē Notioanatolikēs Eurōpēs (International Union of Southeastern Europe), 1983, pp. 75–101, 86; M. Sivignon, *Thessalia, Geografiki analysi, op. cit.*, p. 150.

35. A. Sfika-Theodosiou, *I Prosartisi tis Thessalias, op. cit.*, p. 33.

36. Sivignon, *Thessalia, Geografiki analysi, op. cit.*

37. FO Greece Nr. 1 (Oct. 24, 1881) Letter from Ford to Granville. Also two years later the Greek Premier Trikoupis with the same attitude towards Muslim emigration from Greece, see FO Greece (May 16, 1883), Letter from Ford to Granville.

38. FO Greece (May 16, 1883), Letter from Ford to Granville.

39. W. Höpken, "From Religious Identity to Ethnic Mobilisation", in *Muslim Identity and the Balkan State*, eds Hugh Poulton and Suha Taji-Farouki, New York: New York University Press, 1997, pp. 54–81, 59.

40. *Ibid.*

41. R. Vierhaus, *Wege zu einer neuen Kulturgeschichte* (Ways to a new Cultural History), Göttingen: Wallstein, 1995.

42. *Efimeris ton syzitiseon tis voulis* Th'A' (Journal of Parliamentary Debates), Jan. 18, 1882.

43. L. Arseniou, *I Thessalia stin Tourkokratia* (Thessaly under Ottoman Rule), Athens: Epikairotita, 1984 and still valid; D.K. Tsopotos, *Gi kai georgoi tis Thessalias kata tin tourkokratian* (Soil and peasants of Thessaly under Ottoman Rule), Athens: Epikairotita, 1983.

44. The newspaper *Aion* (Dec. 12, 1881) mentioned two Muslims listed as candidates in the electoral register for Almyro. For Trikala one Muslim Bey is reported in Paliggenisia (Dec. 4, 1881). In Arta, several Muslims appear in preserved voting lists of 1881; see *Politikes Apofaseis 1881* (Political Decisions of 1881) Genika Archeia tou Kratous Arta (General State Archives).

45. This is indicated in an article from the 28th of Dec. sent to the newspaper from Larissa. In the same article, the author states that the Muslims of Thessaly were threatened by Turkish Officials of the neighboring Ottoman Provinces not to participate in the Greek elections. *Paliggenesia*, Jan. 1, 1882.

46. *Proia*, Dec. 22, 1881.

47. See the parliamentary debate in: *Efimeris ton syzitiseon tis* voulis *I'A'* (Journal of Parliamentary Debates), June 10, 1885.

48. See G. Hering, *Die politischen Parteien in Griechenland 1821–1936* (The Political Parties of Greece), Vol.1, München: Oldenbourg Verlag, 1992, with a link to K. Gardika, "Politics and Parties in Greece, 1875–1885", unpublished PhD Dissertation, Kings College, London, 1988.

49. *Aion*, Dec. 18, 1881.

50. An article in *Paliggenisia* (Oct. 19, 1881) informs about the decision of the Government.

51. This is documented in an article in the newspaper *Aion* of the 25th of Oct. 1882, which states that the listed persons, including three Muslims, who where nominated for election and proclaimed representatives of the town of Tyrnavo, are not elected due to irregularities in the nominations.

52. *Aion*, Dec. 26, 1881.

53. *Praktika Dimotikou Symvouliou Larissas* (Papers of the city-council of Larissa) (1882–83, 1884–1886), (Genika Archeia tou Kratous Larissa, ABE 447) (General State Archives Larissa).

54. *Anexartisia*, Nov. 2, 1881. It is not clear if this happened.

55. *Astir tis Thessalias*, May 13, 1884.

56. *Paliggenisia*, Dec. 10, 1882.

57. FEK (Fyllo Efimeridos tis Kyverniseos) (Governmental Gazzette) No. 188, 1–131 (1882), (June 18, 1882).

58. E. Allamani, "I Thessalia sta televtaia peninta chronia tis tourkikis kyriarcheias (1832–1882), *op. cit.*, p. 87. This presumption has to be critically reconsidered because in the negotiations, the incorporation of the town of Larissa, a city with a high percentage of Muslim population, into Greece was not to be foreknown, but arose within the proceedings. See R. Davidson, "The Ottoman-Greek Frontier Question", *op. cit.*, pp. 185–204.

59. V. Prontzas, "Trapeza kai tsifliki" (Bank and Tsiflik), *Ta Istorika* (Historical), Vol. 3, No. 6, Dec. 1986, pp. 315–348.

60. *Astir tis Thessalias*, 8 März, 1884.

61. See the archives of Ioannidis and Skamvougeras in the General State Archives Larissa. These notary archives contain a rich number of documents that show Muslim economic participation in the region. GAK (General State Archives Larissa) Ioannidis Documents, No. 235 (1882), No. 4552 (1885); Skamvougeras Documents, No. 213 (1881), No. 12462 (1890).

62. *Paliggenisia*, Oct. 5, 1882.

[5]

BARBARA DIETZ

Jewish Immigrants from the Former Soviet Union in Germany: History, Politics and Social Integration

Emigration from the former Soviet Union (FSU) was kept under strict control by the Soviet authorities until the late 1980s. The rarely granted right to leave the country was basically limited to family reunification for certain ethnic groups, including Jews, Germans, Armenians and Greeks. During the Soviet period almost all Jewish emigrants from the Soviet Union went to Israel or the United States. Following the policy of *perestroika* and the subsequent break-up of the Soviet Union, emigration restrictions were relaxed. On account of this relaxation, growing anti-Semitic sentiment and the economic, social and political disintegration of the FSU, the emigration of Jews increased considerably. The most important receiving country, after Israel and the United States, was Germany.

In the following pages the history and politics of Jewish emigration from the FSU to Germany will be analysed as will the integration of Jewish immigrants into German society. First, this article looks at Jewish emigration from the FSU, exploring the history, demography and identity of the Jewish population; the Jewish migration to Germany will then be evaluated in the framework of Germany's admission policy. Second, the motivations of the emigrants, the socio-demographic background and the identity formation of Jewish immigrants in Germany will be examined. The final part of the article will look at the integration patterns of Jewish immigrants from the FSU in German society. In addition, it will be asked whether, and in which ways, post-Soviet Jewish immigrants are reshaping Jewish communities in Germany and their relations with German institutions.

Jewish emigration from the FSU: history, receiving states and politics
In looking at Jewish emigration from the FSU, it is crucial to understand the self-definition and ethno-national boundaries of the Jewish population. From the beginning, the Soviet state defined the Jewish population in ethno-national, not in religious terms. In the post-Second World War censuses

East European Jewish Affairs, Vol.33, No.2, Winter 2003, pp.7–19
ISSN 1350-1674
DOI: 10.1080/1350167032000217480 © 2003 Taylor & Francis Ltd.

8   History, Politics and Social Integration

(1959, 1970, 1979, 1989) Jews, like other Soviet citizens, were documented in accordance with their ethnic self-identification.[1] In this respect, the Soviet Union's definition of Jewish citizens comes close to the concept of the 'core Jewish population' suggested by Kosmin *et al*.[2] According to this perception, Jews are documented by self-identification, irrespective of a commitment to the Jewish religion, culture or community affiliation.[3]

In contrast to the Soviet census definition, the mandatory nationality registration in the internal passport of the Soviet Union and other official documents was based on the Jewish background of at least one parent.[4] Although this definition is related to normative criteria, it does not coincide with the *Halakha* (rabbinical law), which accepts as Jews only those who have a Jewish mother or have undergone a formal conversion.

Beyond population statistics and the nationality identification in official documents, what does it mean to be Jewish in post-Soviet societies? First of all, the ethnic identity of many Jews is defined from outside – by state politics, authorities and public perceptions.[5] A second determinant of Jewish identity is the experience of discrimination and anti-Semitism in everyday life.

Active preservation of religious or cultural practices or of Hebrew- or Yiddish-language competence is rare. In some cases, a sense of identification with the Jewish religious and cultural traditions is found in Jewish families. A survey conducted in 1993 concluded:

Fewer than a fifth of Jews in Moscow, Kiev and Minsk have a working knowledge of Hebrew or Yiddish, belong to or participate in a Jewish organization, have a Jewish upbringing, are giving a Jewish upbringing to their children or celebrate the Sabbath or the High Holy Days ... These results indicate that the cultural and organizational infrastructure of the Jewish communities embraces only a small fraction of the Jewish population.[6]

Obviously, the minor role played by Jewish religious and cultural practices in everyday life reflects a long history of repression and, sometimes, of state-supported anti-Semitism.[7] But, although Jewish religion and Jewish culture were, for a long time, to a great degree forbidden, the Jewish population of the FSU remained identifiable through formal structures, for instance the nationality entry in the internal passport. In recent years, though, there has been a revival of Jewish religious and cultural traditions in the former Soviet states, especially Russia.[8]

Against the background of these forms of self-definition, it is clear that the Jewish population of the FSU is not always well defined, and that ethnic boundaries are flexible, especially in the case of mixed families.

The Jewish population in Russia and the FSU: social background
Emigration decisions of individuals or population groups and their integration patterns in the receiving countries are usually closely related to their living

conditions in the sending areas. The history and home country experiences of the Jewish population in Russia and the FSU, then, are seen as a precondition for understanding their migration and integration processes.

At the turn of the nineteenth century 5,216,000 Jews lived in the Russian Empire, representing some 4 per cent of the population.[9] Restrictive laws and anti-Jewish pogroms at the end of the nineteenth and the beginning of the twentieth century adversely affected the living conditions of the Jewish population of Russia.[10] In the final decades of the tsarist regime the Jews belonged to the most oppressed population groups. The October Revolution ended the official discrimination against Jews and brought about the abolition of the Pale of Settlement.[11] The new Soviet government declared equal rights for all citizens, irrespective of national or religious affiliation.

With the end of the restrictive settlement laws and the opening up of new possibilities for employment and social mobility, many Jews migrated from rural areas and small towns in the western frontier regions of the new Soviet state to the larger cities in the centre.[12] As a result, the Jews of the Soviet Union became a population of city-dwellers, concentrated in metropolitan areas and large cities. The 1926 population census reveals that 82.4 per cent of Soviet Jewry lived in towns, compared to only 18.9 per cent of the total population of the USSR.[13] In 1989 the urbanisation rate had reached 99 per cent. In Russia, more than half (52.3 per cent) of the Jewish population was concentrated in Moscow and St Petersburg.

Traditionally, the Jewish population of the Soviet Union settled in the European part of Russia – in Ukraine, Byelorussia, Moldova, Latvia and Lithuania. A small Jewish population also lived in the Caucasus – in Georgia and Azerbaijan and in Central Asia – in Uzbekistan, and in southern Kazakhstan.

From the late 1930s onwards the Jewish population of the USSR underwent a permanent decline. Whereas more than 3 million Jews resided in the USSR in 1939, in 1959 only 2.2 million lived there. This sharp decrease must be attributed to the consequences of the Stalinist terror, the war and the Holocaust.[14] But even after the 1950s the decline of the Jewish population continued: in 1989 there were only 1.4 million Jews in the Soviet Union, while in 1998 only 540,000 lived in its successor states. The dramatic reduction of the Jewish population was the result of emigration, a negative vital balance and assimilation processes.[15] Because mixed marriages in the Jewish population had increased considerably since the Second World War, assimilation processes were reinforced, especially in the second generation.[16]

Besides a very low fertility rate, the age structure of the Jewish population of the FSU reveals a disproportionately large number of older people. According to the Russian micro-census of 1994, the median age of the Jewish population was 52.8 years compared to 36.2 years for the Russian population

10   History, Politics and Social Integration

and 36.1 years for the total population.[17] According to Tolts,[18] the Jews of the FSU have reached the terminal stage of demographic evolution, if one looks at the development of their demographic indicators in the 1990s.

The emigration of Jews from the FSU

As we have mentioned, it was primarily for the purpose of reuniting families that Soviet citizens were allowed to emigrate.[19] In this context, the intervention of foreign states on behalf of groups wishing to emigrate played an important role. The main beneficiaries of this policy were Jews, Germans, Armenians and Greeks, whose families had been separated by the events of the Second World War and whose potential receiving countries (the USA, Israel, Germany, Greece and France in the case of Armenians) supported their cause.[20]

In May 1991 the Soviet Union adopted a new emigration law, which recognised the individual right to travel. This allowed Jews, among other citizens, to leave the country without restrictions.

Until the mid-1970s practically all Jewish emigrants from the FSU went to Israel. In subsequent years the migration changed: between 1980 and 1989 only 25.9 per cent of all Jewish emigrants moved to Israel, 72.5 per cent preferred the USA, and a small minority settled in other countries, primarily Canada and a number of European states.[21]

Already in the 1980s a number of Jewish emigrants from the Soviet Union who had applied for an exit visa to Israel remained in large European capitals such as Vienna or Rome. Some moved on to West Germany, mainly to West Berlin.[22] As these individual cases turned into a movement, the Israeli government urged West European states not to accept Jewish immigrants from the USSR as refugees, arguing they should go to Israel.[23] Most West European governments accepted Israel's request, but Germany contended that, because of its 'historical responsibility' with regard to the Holocaust, it could not reject Jewish immigrants. This was the beginning of a Jewish migration movement to Germany, which became increasingly relevant in the 1990s.

Jewish migration from the FSU to Germany: admission policy

In July 1990 the last GDR government granted asylum to Jewish citizens from the Soviet Union who were threatened by persecution or discrimination.[24] A number of Jews from the USSR took advantage of this offer and moved to East Germany, mainly to East Berlin. Nearly all of them travelled with a tourist visa. Following German reunification, all Jewish immigrants who had come to Germany between 1 June 1990 and 15 February 1991 were recognised retroactively as 'quota refugees.'[25]

In the early 1990s the admission of immigrants to Germany was severely restricted. Germany did not even consider itself a country of immigration. This situation obviously shaped the discussion on the admission of Jewish

immigrants from the FSU and there are a number of reasons for the
acceptance of Jewish immigrants at a time when Germany was deeply
unsympathetic towards immigration. As mentioned above, the German
government invoked its 'historic responsibility' with respect to the
Holocaust, arguing that the immigration of Jews into Germany could be seen
as a basis for the renewal of German–Jewish relations. On the other hand, the
Jewish communities in Germany, which were small and ageing in the early
1990s, saw a revival of Jewish life in this immigration and thus fully
supported it.

Since the final decision of the German government to admit Jews from the
FSU in 1991, immigrants can no longer arrive with a tourist visa: they must
apply for an entry permit at German embassies in their countries of origin.
There the prospective immigrants must submit an application form together
with proof of Jewish identity. The application is then sent to the Federal
Administration Office in Germany, which distributes it among the *Länder* in
accordance with the quota system. The interior ministry in each of the *Länder*
decides whether the applicant will be admitted.[26] After the application form is
returned to the embassy in the country of origin, the prospective immigrant
may apply for an exit visa. The emigration has to be completed within a year
or the entrance permit will expire.

With regard to the number of Jewish immigrants from the former USSR
in Germany, two approaches exist: that of the German Federal Administration
Office and that of the Jewish communities. The Federal Administration Office
includes in the Jewish quota refugee regulation all immigrants who are Jewish
according to the documents of the post-Soviet administration or who belong
to the group of non-Jewish spouses and relatives of Jewish immigrants. In
contrast, the Jewish communities invoke Jewish religious law (*Halakha*) and
accept as Jewish only those who have a Jewish mother or have converted to
Judaism.[27]

The different classifications result in remarkable differences in the
immigration figures. As Table 1 shows, according to the Federal
Administration Office, 164,492 Jewish quota refugees arrived between
January 1990 and December 2002; according to the Jewish communities,
77,642 arrived in that period. In the light of these differences one might argue
that approximately 50 per cent of the Jewish immigrants in Germany are
either non-Jewish relatives or Jews who are not members of the Jewish
communities.

With respect to recent data of the Federal Administration Office, it is
evident that more Jewish emigrants from the FSU are moving to Germany
than to Israel or the United States. In 2002 19,262 Jewish immigrants from the
successor states of the Soviet Union came to Germany, 18,878 went to Israel,
and only 2,494 went to the United States (figures supplied by HIAS).[28]

12   History, Politics and Social Integration

TABLE 1

IMMIGRATION OF JEWS FROM THE FSU TO GERMANY, 1990–2002

Year	Federal Administration Office	Central Welfare Board of Jews in Germany
1990		1,008
1991		5,198
1992		3,777
1993	16,597*	5,205
1994	8,811	5,521
1995	15,184	8,851
1996	15,959	8,608
1997	19,437	7,092
1998	17,788	8,299
1999	18,205	8,929
2000	16,538	7,405
2001	16,711	7,152
2002	19,262	6,597

*This figure includes all Jewish immigrants who came to Germany between 1990 and 1993.

Sources: Federal Administration Office; Central Welfare Board of Jews in Germany.

Jewish immigrants in Germany: motivation of emigrants, socio-demographic background, and identity formation

Why do Jews leave the FSU and why has a considerable number of recent Jewish emigrants come to Germany instead of Israel and the United States? These questions are discussed frequently, in the context of why Jewish emigrants intentionally move to the 'land of the Holocaust.'[29]

If one turns first to the reasons why Jews emigrate from the FSU, several arguments seem to be relevant. First, overt as well as latent anti-Semitism have been push factors. Second, economic crisis, political instability, ecological catastrophe and ethnic tensions in the successor states of the USSR have contributed to the emigration.[30] In some cases, career advancement, the future of the children, or health problems are decisive factors.

Yet, in reviewing the reasons for choosing a destination, next to individual motivation admission policies play a role. When the FSU authorities accepted freedom of movement, many Western states, like the United States, closed their borders to immigrants from this area or reduced their immigration quotas. While Israel kept its doors open to Jewish immigrants from the FSU, Germany introduced a new admission procedure for this group in 1991.

From what is known of the motivation of Jewish immigrants to Germany, various reasons played a role. In many cases, emigrants felt insecure about going to Israel for economic, political, religious or social reasons.[31] Living in a mixed family too may have strengthened the preference for Germany. In other cases, emigrants were unable to obtain a visa for the United States and opted for Germany as second choice. Additional arguments were: economic improvement, escape from anti-Semitic discrimination, and a desire to live free of political insecurities.[32] For some emigrants, the narrower cultural and linguistic distance in Germany compared to Israel also played a role. And some Jewish emigrants already had relatives, friends or acquaintances in Germany which made it easier for newcomers to adapt to the German economy and society.[33] Finally, spreading migrant networks obviously supported Jewish emigration to Germany.

What can be said of the demographic and social characteristics of recent Jewish immigrants in Germany? A very high percentage came from the European part of the former USSR – from Russia, Ukraine, the Baltics, Belarus and Moldova. As is typical of the Jewish population of the FSU, nearly all had lived in an urban area. In addition, the Jewish immigration consisted of a relatively high number of people over 50.[34] Yet, on average, immigrants were still younger than the Jewish population who remained in the USSR successor states.[35] This is characteristic of family migrations with an ethno-national background, where migrants leave the home country without a return option.

Jewish immigrants from the FSU to Germany are well educated. Several surveys found that over 70 per cent of them had a university or college education.[36] Many had extensive professional experience, as academics, scientists or technicians. In most cases, however, this high level of human capital cannot be transferred to the German labour market. Among other reasons, incompatibilities in educational attainment and professional experience and the lack of German-language competence are responsible for this.[37]

With respect to Jewish religious practice and cultural traditions, many Jewish immigrants express ambivalence following their arrival in Germany.[38] As mentioned above, Jews in the FSU were defined primarily in terms of Soviet nationality policy and anti-Semitism. Apart from minor elements of Jewish religious and cultural practices, Jewish immigrants are deeply influenced by the system, culture and social norms of post-Soviet society.[39] In most cases, their first language is Russian: German, Hebrew and Yiddish have not been a part of their education and upbringing.

How German society responds to Jewish immigrants depends mostly on the social setting. In the view of German authorities, Jews from the FSU are seen first and foremost as immigrants whose admission is based on their Jewish background. By contrast, many Germans view them as Russians because of their country of origin and their use of Russian in daily life. Finally, Jewish communities in Germany consider the Jewish background of recent immigrants and try to improve their knowledge of Jewish religious and cultural practices.[40]

14   History, Politics and Social Integration

A new Jewish life in Germany? Social integration patterns of Jewish immigrants from the FSU

Having arrived in Germany, Jewish immigrants are faced with wide-ranging problems of integration.[41] They not only have to learn the German language and seek housing, employment and schools for their children, but also to integrate into German society, especially with respect to Germany's Jewish communities. The importance of the Jewish communities to recent Jewish immigrants cannot be overestimated.[42] Not only are they responsible for assistance, primarily with social integration, they also support and legitimise the immigration and integration procedure.[43]

When looking at the social integration of recent Jewish immigrants in Germany, some theoretical considerations should be mentioned. With reference to the seminal survey of integration literature,[44] the most important indicators of social integration are acculturation, meaning the ability of migrants or minorities to adapt to the language and culture of the receiving society, and socio-structural integration, indicating the entrance of immigrants into the social organisations, institutions and neighbourhoods of the new country. A number of studies have demonstrated that not all categories of social integration may be achieved at once: immigrants may acculturate but still not take part in institutions or social organisations of the receiving society, or come into close contact with the majority population. In this context, there have been discussions on to which part of the receiving society and to which cultural patterns immigrant groups integrate.[45] These issues have become especially relevant with regard to societies which vary considerably in terms of social class, include immigrant or minority cultures, and have become increasingly pluralistic in ethnic, linguistic, religious and cultural terms, mainly because of immigration.[46] Specialists on integration agree that social integration usually takes time – one generation at least – and that it changes not only the immigrants but also the majority societies.

To evaluate the social integration of recent Jewish immigrants in Germany, the criteria cited above – acculturation and socio-structural integration – must be examined. As with many immigrant groups, learning German is a lengthy process for Jewish immigrants in Germany. Only 15 per cent of the respondents in a national survey in 1998 reported a good or very good knowledge of German.[47] In daily life, many Jewish immigrant families speak Russian, which is also the common language in Jewish immigrant networks. Comparatively slow language acquisition is typical of first-generation immigrants.

With respect to the socio-structural integration of recent Jewish immigrants, the relationship to Jewish communities must be mentioned first. Independent of the strength of their religious affiliation, many Jewish immigrants become members of the Jewish communities in Germany.[48] Due to a loss of Jewish cultural and religious traditions, Jewish immigrants introduce secular elements into Jewish communities.[49] Referring to a subjective Jewish identification in connection with strong ties to the culture and traditions in their former home, a considerable number of Jewish immigrants form Russian-speaking networks in the Jewish communities in Germany. Obviously these behaviour patterns set them apart from local Jewish community members. In addition, the self-conception of Jews in Germany differs from that of the new Jewish immigrants. Most importantly, the identity of Jews in Germany remains deeply influenced by memory of the Holocaust.[50] Carlebach writes:

Germans may wish to dissociate themselves from a sense of guilt in connection with the Holocaust, but no Jew living in Germany is able to escape it ... The physical proximity of victim to perpetrators and their respective descendants can distort relationships on both sides; the meaning of a Jewish identity is obscured through the intervention of incomprehensible realities which a Jew outside Germany does not have to face.[51]

By contrast, the trauma of the Stalinist purges is much more present in the memory and identity of Jewish immigrants from the FSU. In the face of considerable differences in socialisation, tradition and self-identification, the integration of Jewish immigrants into Jewish communities is far from easy. Many communities have managed the integration of newcomers from the FSU quite successfully but, in some cases, tensions are visible in the interaction between local and immigrant Jewish community members.[52]

Although they are of a Jewish background, some immigrants from the FSU do not participate in Jewish communities but are active in their own, newly established self-help organisations. Usually these organisations are less formal and pursue integration-related goals, for example housing and jobs or leisure activities.[53] Sometimes newcomers join groups which have been formed by secular Jews outside the Jewish communities, thus contributing to the heterogeneity of Jewish life.[54]

Beyond the Jewish communities, the integration of Jewish immigrants into German neighbourhoods or institutions seems to have been rather limited so far. In a recent national survey[55] 70 per cent of the respondents rarely or never met non-Jewish Germans for leisure activities. A similarly high percentage (70 per cent) described their contacts with Germans as discouraging.[56] In their free time, most Jewish immigrants are engaged in family and friendship networks. But, regardless of the obviously slow integration process, a considerable number of Jewish immigrants, especially of the younger generation, express a certain satisfaction with their decision to emigrate.

What are the implications of the recent Jewish immigration for the Jewish communities and Jewish life in Germany? Are there any indicators that post-

16   History, Politics and Social Integration

Soviet Jewish immigrants reshape Jewish communities and their interaction with German institutions? First of all, the immigration of Jews from the FSU has contributed to a remarkable growth of the Jewish communities, as Table 2 indicates:

TABLE 2

MEMBERS OF JEWISH COMMUNITIES IN GERMANY,
01/01 OF THE RESPECTIVE YEAR

Years	Members	Years	Members
1988	27,684	1996	53,797
1989	27,552	1997	61,114
1990	27,711	1998	67,471
1991	29,089	1999	74,289
1992	33,692	2000	81,739
1993	36,804	2001	87,756
1994	40,917	2002	93,326
1995	45,559	2003	98,335

Source: Central Welfare Board of Jews in Germany.

While there were only 27,684 community members in 1988, this number increased to 98,335 in 2003, turning Germany into the only country in Europe with an expanding Jewish population. This is an unexpected development, especially if one looks at a discussion in 1987 when Bensimon[57] noted that the German Jewish population seemed to lack the demographic forces for self-renewal. In addition to the growth of Jewish communities, the Jewish population in Germany began to be rejuvenated in the early 1990s, although this process has slowly reversed due to a continued low fertility rate.[58] The immigration of Jews from the FSU may reduce the problems of an ageing Jewish population in Germany but cannot guarantee its long-term rejuvenation.

Besides the demographic impact, recent Jewish immigrants have introduced new social and political elements into Jewish communities. Their more secular background, their language, their close proximity to some post-Soviet and Russian cultural traditions, their distance from the established German/Jewish discourse – all these elements reshape Jewish communities in Germany, also making them, in all probability, less traditional and more pluralistic in the long run.

The author acknowledges helpful comments by Robin Ostow. The article is based on research carried out in the framework of the Forschungsverbund Ost- und Südosteuropa (forost). Financial support from forost is gratefully acknowledged.

B. DIETZ   17

NOTES

1 R. Karklins, *Ethnic Relations in the USSR: The Perspective from Below* (Boston, 1986).
2 B. A. Kosmin, S. Goldstein, J. Waksberg, N. Lerer, A. Keysar, J. Schleckner, *Highlights of the CJF 1990 National Jewish Population Survey* (New York, 1991).
3 S. Della Pergola, 'World Jewish Population, 2001', in *American Jewish Year Book 2001*(New York: American Jewish Committee, 2001).
4 Children of Jewish parents were registered as Jews while children of Jewish–non-Jewish marriages could, if they wished, choose their parents' nationality. Due to latent anti-Semitism, children in 'mixed' marriages often opted for the nationality of the non-Jewish parent.
5 I. Oswald and V. Voronkow, 'Die jüdische Gemeinde in St. Petersburg. Zwischen Assimilation und neuem Selbstbewußtsein', in M. Hausleitner and M. Katz (eds.), *Juden und Antisemitismus im östlichen Europa* (Wiesbaden, 1995), 93–108.
6 R. Brym and R. Ryvkina, *The Jews of Moscow, Kiev and Minsk: Identity, Antisemitism, Emigration* (London: Macmillan, 1994), 26.
7 See, for example, Pinkus (note 10 below) or S. Margolina, *Das Ende der Lügen. Rußland und die Juden im 20. Jahrhundert* (Siedler: Berlin Margolina, 1992).
8 P. Polian, 'Geschichte und Soziologie einer Emigration', in J. Schoeps, K. E. Grözinger, G. Mattenklot (eds.), *Menora. Jahrbuch für deutsch-jüdische Geschichte 1999* (Potsdam, 1999).
9 These data are based on the 1897 Russian population census.
10 B. Pinkus, *The Jews of the Soviet Union: The History of a National Minority* (Cambridge, 1988), 25.
11 On the Pale of Settlement, see ibid., 21ff.
12 M. Altshuler, 'Demographic Trends in Soviet Jewry', in A. Greenbaum (ed.), *Minority Problems in Eastern Europe between the World Wars with Emphasis on the Jewish Minority* (Jerusalem, 1988), 110.
13 G. Simon, *Nationalism and Policy Toward the Nationalities in the Soviet Union: From Totalitarian Dictatorship to Post-Stalinist Society* (Boulder, 1991), 390.
14 At least 700,000 Soviet Jews in the USSR perished in the Holocaust – see Polian, 'Geschichte und Soziologie einer Emigration'.
15 M. Tolts, 'Jews in the Russian Federation: A Decade of Demographic Decline', *Jews in Eastern Europe*, No. 3 (40), 1999, 5–36.
16 M. Tolts, 'Jewish Marriages in the USSR: A Demographic Analysis', *East European Jewish Affairs*, Vol. 22, No. 2, 1992, 3–20; M. Tolts, 'Demographic Trends among the Jews in Three Slavic Republics of the Former USSR: A Comparative Analysis', *Jewish Population Studies*, No. 27, 1997, 171.
17 *Goskomstat Rossii: Raspredelenie naseleniia Rossii po vladeniiu iazykami* (State Committee of Statistics of Russia: Distribution of the Population of Russia by Language Competence) (Moscow, 1995), 151, 160.
18 M. Tolts, 'Demographic Trends', 166.
19 S. Heitman, 'The Third Soviet Emigration: Jewish, German and Armenian Emigration from the USSR since World War II', *Berichte des Bundesinstituts für ostwissenschaftliche und internationale Studien*, No. 21, 1987, 14–15.
20 V. Zaslavsky and R. Brym, *Soviet Jewish Emigration and Soviet Nationality Policy* (London, 1983).
21 E. F. Sabatello, 'Migration from the Former Soviet Union to Israel', in H. Fassmann and R. Münz, *European Migration in the Late Twentieth Century: Historical Patterns, Actual Trends and Social Implications* (Aldershot: Edward Elgar, 1994), 262.
22 E. Leshem, Y. Rosenbaum, O. Kashanov, 'Drop-outs and Immigrants from the Soviet Union', in T. Horowitz (ed.), *The Soviet Man in an Open Society* (Lanham, New York, London, 1989), 57–63.
23 The Israeli government argued that, given the existence of the Israeli state, Jewish migrants were no longer refugees: the 'right of return' allows every Jew to come to Israel.
24 Beauftragte der Bundesregierung für Ausländerfragen (ed.), *Migration und Integration in Zahlen. Ein Handbuch* (Berlin, 1997), 307.
25 The quota refugee regulation is based on a law (*Kontingentflüchtlingsgesetz*) adopted in 1980

18   History, Politics and Social Integration

for the admission of refugees from South-East Asia to Germany. The law regulates the admission and distribution of refugees according to a quota system throughout the *Länder*.

26   Until now the admission of Jewish immigrants from the former USSR has been refused only in very rare cases.

27   J. Kessler, 'Jüdische Immigranten seit 1990', *Zeitschrift für Migration und soziale Arbeit*, No. 1, 1997, 40–47.

28   According to data provided by the Jewish communities, 6,597 Jewish immigrants from the FSU entered Germany in 2002. Because Israel and the United States accept spouses, children and close relatives of Jewish immigrants, a comparison with data supplied by the Federal Administration Office seems reasonable.

29   A. Silbermann and H. Sallen, *Juden in Westdeutschland. Selbstbild und Fremdbild einer Minderheit* (Cologne, 1992).

30   J. Doomernik, *Going West: Soviet Jewish Immigrants in Berlin since 1990* (Aldershot: Edward Elgar, 1997), 19; J. H. Schoeps, W. Jasper, B. Vogt, *Ein neues Judentum in Deutschland. Fremd- und Eigenbilder der russisch-jüdischen Einwanderer* (Potsdam: Verlag für Berlin-Brandenburg, 1999), 150.

31   Doomernik, *Going West*, 81; Y. Schütze, 'Warum Deutschland und nicht Israel? Begründungen russischer Juden für die Migration nach Deutschland', *BIOS Zeitschrift für Biographische Forschung*, Vol. 10, No. 2, 1997, 186–208.

32   S. Gruber and H. Rüßler, *Hochqualifiziert und arbeitslos. Jüdische Kontingentflüchtlinge in Nordrhein-Westfalen* (Opladen: Leske+Budrich, 2002), 15.

33   Schütze, 195.

34   Doomernik, *Going West*, 74; Schoeps *et al*, *Ein neues Judentum in Deutschland*, 41.

35   M. Tolts, 'Jews in the Russian Federation', 5–36.

36   Doomernik, 85; Schoeps *et al.*, *Russische Juden in Deutschland*, 42; Schoeps *et al.*, *Ein neues Judentum in Deutschland*, 44.

37   According to the recent survey by Schoeps *et al.*, *Ein neues Judentum in Deutschland*, 66, almost half (48 per cent) of the able-bodied Jewish immigrant population was unemployed in 1999, a figure which exceeded by more than four times the overall unemployment rate in Germany. Other surveys found similar results (Gruber and Rüßler, *Hochqualifiziert und arbeitslos*).

38   F. Becker, *Ankommen in Deutschland. Einwanderungspolitik als biographische Erfahrung im Migrationsprozeß russischer Juden* (Berlin: Dietrich Reimer Verlag, 2001).

39   M. Tress, 'Soviet Jews in the Federal Republic of Germany: The Rebuilding of a Community', *The Jewish Journal of Sociology*, Vol. 37, No. 1, 1995, 39–54, 48.

40   Kessler, 40–47.

41   Jewish immigrants are a comparatively privileged group in Germany. They receive an unlimited residence permit, permission to work, initial housing support, and absorption assistance for a maximum of six months, along with a state-provided German-language course for a maximum period of half a year. In cases where the education or the professional background of the immigrants does not meet the requirements of the German labour market, a retraining course may be offered. Furthermore, Jewish immigrants are eligible for social security benefits if they have not been able to find work after the absorption assistance has expired (M. Tress, 'Foreigners or Jews? The Soviet Jewish Refugee Population in Germany and the United States', *East European Jewish Affairs*, Vol. 27, No. 2, 21–38, 33).

42   P. A. Harris, 'Russische Juden und Aussiedler: Integrationspolitik und lokale Verantwortung', in K. J. Bade and J. Oltmer (eds.), *Aussiedler: deutsche Einwanderer aus Osteuropa* (Osnabrück: Rasch, 1999), 247–64.

43   Jewish communities in Germany are heavily involved in the social, economic, religious and cultural integration of Jewish immigrants (Harris, 'Russische Juden und Aussiedler', 259; Kessler). Besides the integration measures of the German state, they provide assistance in the form of additional German-language training, immediate housing support, instruction in Jewish culture and religion, and in counselling.

44   R. Alba, 'Rethinking Assimilation Theory for a New Era of Immigration', *International Migration Review*, Vol. 31, No. 4, 1997, 826–74, 829.

45   Ibid, 832.

46 See also Oliver Lubrich, 'Are Russian Jews Post-colonial? Vladimir Kaminer and Identity Politics' in this issue.
47 Schoeps *et al.*, *Ein neues Judentum in Deutschland*, 77.
48 Schoeps *et al*, *Russische Juden in Deutschland*, 20.
49 Robin Ostow, 'The Post-Soviet Immigrants and the *Jüdische Allgemeine* in the New Millennium: Post-Communism in Germany's Jewish Communities' in this issue.
50 M. Bodemann, 'A Reemergence of German Jewry?', in S. L. Gilman and K. Remmler (eds.), *Reemerging Jewish Cultures in Germany: Life and Literature since 1989* (New York, London: New York University Press, 1994), 46–61; F. Becker, *Ankommen in Deutschland*.
51 J. Carlebach, 'Jewish Identity in the Germany of a New Europe', in J. Webber (ed.), *Jewish Identities in the New Europe* (London, Washington, 1994), 205–18, 207.
52 M. Tress, 'Soviet Jews in the Federal Republic of Germany' 50; Schoeps *et al.*, *Ein neues Judentum in Deutschland*, 105.
53 Gruber and Rüßler, *Hochqualifiziert und arbeitslos*.
54 M. Bodemann, 'A Reemergence of German Jewry?', 46–61.
55 Schoeps *et al*, *Ein neues Judentum in Deutschland*, 81.
56 Ibid, 86.
57 D. Bensimon, 'Demographical Trends of the Western European Jewish Population', in S. Della Pergola and L. Cohen (eds.), *World Jewish Population: Trends and Policies. Selected Proccedings of a Conference on the World Jewish Population* (Jerusalem, 1992).
58 B. Dietz, U. Lebok, P. Polian, 'The Jewish Emigration from the Former Soviet Union to Germany', *International Migration*, Vol. 40, No. 2, 2002, 29–48.

[6]

Latter-day Saint Scandinavian Migration through Hull, England, 1852–1894

Fred E. Woods and Nicholas J. Evans

Nearly one hundred thousand Latter-day Saints made the journey across the Atlantic during the nineteenth century. Both contemporary commentators and Mormon historians alike have described these ocean crossings extensively. Yet the journey from Liverpool to America was but one segment in the much longer gathering process for over twenty-four thousand Scandinavian Mormons who migrated to Utah during this period. Scandinavians represented the second-largest ethnic group of Saints gathering to Zion between 1852 and 1894. During these years, nearly two hundred vessels carrying Latter-day Saints (fig. 1) left Scandinavia bound for Hull, an important port on the east coast of England.[1] The emigrants then made the overland railway crossing from Hull to Liverpool, where the headquarters of the British and European Missions were situated.[2] Only once they had completed the journey to Liverpool could the transatlantic crossing commence. Our study of the migrant journeys made during these years seeks to explain the patterns of migration along established trade routes through the British port of Hull.

The Call to Gather and the Founding of the Hull Conference

Less than six months after the founding of The Church of Jesus Christ of Latter-day Saints, the Prophet Joseph Smith announced that he had received a revelation calling for a gather of the Saints: "And ye are called to bring to pass the gathering of mine elect; … they shall be gathered in unto one place upon the face of this land" (D&C 29:7–8). Latter-day Saint immigration to America commenced a decade later when the Latter-day Saint missionaries who had first arrived in Britain in 1837 reaped a rich harvest of converts in the British Isles.[3] [75]

During this period, 1837–41, the missionaries baptized thousands throughout Great Britain, necessitating the organization of various conferences (ecclesiastical units). Each conference comprised several branches (smaller ecclesiastical units). Among the larger units was the Hull Conference, established in 1843.[4] By December 1847, its membership had reached 65, "including 1 high priest, 3 elders, 5 priests, 3 teachers, and 2 deacons."[5] Eight months later, the conference had reportedly increased to 163.[6] By 1851, the Hull Conference had grown to 318 members.[7] By the mid-nineteenth century, the Latter-day Saints in the Hull region were

Publisher's note:
Image removed due to copyright restrictions.

Fig. 1. SS *Lion*, by Carl Baargoe. Oil on canvas. Hull Maritime Museum: Hull City Museum and Art Gallery. Used by permission. The SS *Lion* transported the first large company of Scandinavian Latter-day Saints that migrated through Hull across the North Sea in December 1852. Built at Hull in 1841, the SS *Lion* was two hundred feet in length and 627 gross tons. Although the ship derived most of its income through the shipment of goods across the North Sea, the owners supplemented the ship's income through the transportation of passengers of all classes. Migrants would have been transported in third-class quarters in the 'tween deck (the area just below the main deck of the ship).

in a position not only to observe and proselytize the inhabitants of England's third largest port but also to offer support to their fellow Saints who were immigrating through the port en route to America. [76]

Hull as a Way Station for Converts in Eastern England

The first known Saints who migrated to America through Hull were a group of five families from the Louth Branch in Lincolnshire (then part of the Hull Conference).[8] The members of this group made their way through Hull before traveling by rail to Liverpool and then crossing the Atlantic en route to Utah via New Orleans.[9] One teenage member of the group recalled:

> On the 16th of January, 1849, we left Louth by the morning train and although it was quite early in the morning, the station house was crowded with our friends and associates who were there to say farewell. ... The departure of these leading families of the Louth Branch left it in a disorganized condition, from which it has not since recovered. [77]
> Our journey from Louth to Hull on the 16th, and from Hull to Liverpool on the 17th January was full of interest to me, a boy of 16 years of age, when I could appreciate to some extent the many strange, interesting, and delightful scenes we witnessed.[10]

The use of the port of Hull as an entrepôt for gathering Saints increased as rates of conversion in the hinterlands of Hull, the East Riding of Yorkshire, and nearby North Lincolnshire accelerated. But Hull and its surrounding region would never harvest the large numbers of converts that the West Yorkshire and Lancastrian towns yielded.[11] In this aspect, Hull would remain a relatively insignificant branch of the Church throughout the 1840s. Hull's important role in Latter-day Saint history grew not from the region's harvested souls but through the large numbers of Latter-day Saint emigrants who migrated through the port en route to Utah. Hull's location as a harbor with railway access to Liverpool allowed the Church an economically feasible yet quick option in assisting the newly converted migrants who passed through the port each year.

Early History of the Latter-day Saint Scandinavian Mission

Having already established a secure foothold in Britain, the Church began planning to expand missionary work into parts of mainland Europe. The funds needed for missionary work and for helping converts migrate came from the trade generated by prospectors passing through Utah in 1849.[12] During the same year, King Frederick VII of Denmark signed a new constitution, which granted religious toleration to its citizens and enabled the Danes—who were the largest port of Scandinavian Latter-day Saint converts—the opportunity to hear the restored gospel.[13]

Four months after this declaration of religious tolerance, the fall general conference say several Mormon elders called to various missions on October 6–7, 1849.[14] Among them was Elder Erastus Snow, called to Denmark, with Elders Peter O. Hansen and John E. Forsgren called to work under his direction in Denmark and Sweden.[15] Hasty preparations were made for the missionaries' late-season journey across America. They left their wives and children to perform the household chores and prepare for the crop harvest, while they departed to Europe to harvest souls.

On October 19, 1849, the missionaries gathered east of the Salt Lake Valley "at the mouth of Emigration Canyon," where they were met by Brigham Young, who bade farewell to a company consisting of "twelve wagons, forty-two horses and mules, one carriage, and thirty-five men." By December 7, 1849, despite terrible mountain snowstorms, they reached the Missouri River and were warmly gretted by friends at Kanesville, Iowa. [78] From Kanesville, the missionaries took different routes and visited local groups of Saints the cities they passed through, such as St. Louis, New Orleans, and Boston. They preached the gathering and received liberal contributions to their missions in each of the places they visited.[16] In spring 1850, they finally set sail for Liverpool.[17]

Once in Britain, the three elders traveled extensively, preached to local Saints, and received much-needed financial assistance for their forthcoming missionary work in Scandinavia. They added to their number George Parker Dykes, a Latter-day Saint missionary already serving in Britain who had earlier ministered among Norwegian immigrants in Illinois. Peter O. Hansen "proceeded alone to his native land, Denmark," arriving in Copenhagen on May 11, 1850.[18] The others followed from Hull on June 14, on board the steamer *Victoria*.[19] Once the missionaries were reunited, their important work could commence, and they began to introduce the gospel in Scandinavia.

During the earliest days of the Scandinavian Mission, Elder Snow (who served as Scandinavian Mission president) urged postponing baptisms until converts had thoroughly investigated the Church. The Lord, however, warned him in a dream to move ahead with baptisms. As a result, the first fifteen Danish Latter-day Saint converts were baptized on August 12, 1850, just two months after the missionaries arrived in Copenhagen.[20] The first fruits of preaching the restored gospel in Denmark were now realized, and the first Danish branch was organized in Copenhagen on September 15, 1850.[21]

Just as in America in the 1830s and then Britain in the later 1830s and '40s, the early successes of missionary work enabled the mission to spread. The Scandinavian Mission expanded throughout Denmark and then to Sweden and Norway. Though the Latter-day Saint missionaries encountered difficulties throughout Scandinavia, they successfully established branches of The Church of Jesus Christ of Latter-day Saints in each of the countries that they visited. As the Scandinavian Mission grew, the need to organize the gathering escalated.

The Beginnings of Latter-day Saint Scandinavian Emigration

Each Scandinavian convert represented a potential emigrant. Between 1850 and 1905, just under 49 percent of the Scandinavian converts emigrated[22] (fig. 2). Unlike the British emigrants from Liverpool, no Scandinavian convert would travel a direct course to America but instead made a "series of journeys."[23] As William Mulder explained:

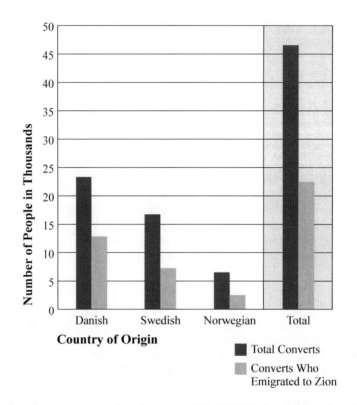

Fig. 2. Scandinavian converts and emigrants, 1850–1905. Information taken from William Mulder, *Homeward to Zion: The Mormon Migration from Scandinavia* (Minneapolis: University of Minnesota Press, 1957; reprinted, Provo, Utah: BYU Studies, 2000), 107.

Going to America involved a whole series of journeys. The proselytes first had to make their way to Copenhagen [the] main assembly point. … [79] From Copenhagen they took a steamer to Kiel or Lübeck on the German portion of the peninsula, continuing by rail to Altona, within walking distance of Hamburg, or Glückstadt, a little farther down the Elbe. Except for the years 1862, 1865, and 1866, when parties went directly from Hamburg to America, the emigrants moved straight across the North Sea to Grimsby or Hull and entrained for Liverpool along with whatever Norwegian Saints had come directly from Christiania or Stavanger.[24]

The First Scandinavian Migrants.

The first Mormon Scandinavian migrants, consisting of a small group of nine converts, left Copenhagen on January 31, 1852, and traveled to Liverpool via Hamburg and London. They Arrived on February 7, too late for the voyage of the *Ellen Maria*, and so had to wait over a month in Liverpool for the chance to leave on another Latter-day Saint–chartered vessel.[25] During this time, Elder Erastus Snow arrived [80] from Copenhagen with another group of nineteen Scandinavian converts. The combined group of twenty-eight emigrants left Liverpool on the ship *Italy* on March 11, 1852, in the care of Ole U. C. Mönster.[26]

With the first group of converts now sailing to Zion, the Scandinavian Mission commenced arrangements for the transportation of future emigrating companies along the migrant route (via Hull and Liverpool) used by thousands of non–Latter-day Saint European emigrants. As historian Phillip A. M. Taylor noted:

> In 1852, Appleton Harmon made enquiries about the cost of bringing over the very first company of Scandinavian Mormons. He found that Gee and Company of Hull would charge a guinea a head from Copenhagen for deck or steerage passage, or would provide a whole ship for three or four hundred people, at £1. 10[s].0*d*. each [per shipload].[27]

Many steamship operators of the time were willing to transport passengers on the routes their ships plied regularly, but transporting the large companies of emigrating Saints necessitated special arrangements between the shipping agent and the mission leaders. Furthermore, the leaders of the Scandinavian Mission in Copenhagen and the British Mission in Liverpool sought to charter such vessels for their exclusive use, enabling the allocation of more space (per passenger) than was normally provided for third-class passengers traveling during this period.[28]

Such arrangements required careful negotiation, but the business was competitive. By fall 1852, Morris and Company of Hamburg had outbid the competing companies and accordingly received the contract to carry the first large company, the John Forsgren Company, of Scandinavian Latter-day Saint converts from Copenhagen, through various cities and finally to New Orleans.[29] With this contract in place, the emigration of Latter-day Saint converts commenced en masse. Each group of emigrating Saints gathered in Copenhagen, then traveled to Hamburg or Glückstadt, before journeying to Liverpool via Hull or Grimsby.[30]

The John Forsgren Company.

The first large company of Mormon Scandinavians to embark from Copenhagen—led by Elder John E. Forsgren, one of the original four missionaries sent to Scandinavia—consisted of "199 adults and 95 children under [the age of] twelve."[31] These Latter-day Saint converts voyaged from Copenhagen to Kiel, Germany, on the steamer *Obotrit*. After taking a train to Hamburg, they voyaged down the Elbe River and into the North Sea on the *Lion* (see fig. 1). Here they abruptly encountered the most difficult part of their journey westward when a terrible winter storm enveloped them in the night. One Danish Saint wrote in his journal on Sunday, December 26, 1952: "Toward midnight [81] a terrific storm arose and the great waves broke over the ship in quick succession, and frequently the water poured down upon us in the hold."[32] The "Manuscript History of the John H. Forsgren Emigrating Company' entry for Tuesday, December 28, verifies this event:

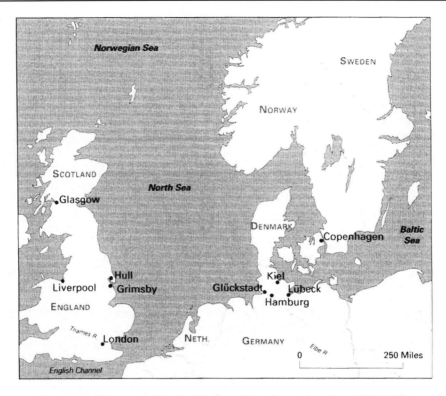

European cities associated with Scandinavian migration, 1852–1894

> After sailing all of Sunday and Monday, and most of today we arrived through the grace and kindness of God at Hull, England, at 5 o'clock in the evening. We had come through a storm the like of which the captain of the ship said he had never been out in. Some of the ship's cargo was ruined, and the wind was so strong that our clothes were nearly blown overboard. The Lord helped and strengthened all of us both in body and soul so that we could continue our journey without delay.[33]

The hurricane conditions experienced on this North Sea crossing were some of the worst in the area for over thirteen years. The local press described the storm and its aftermath: "On Saturday, Sunday, and Monday last, this island was visited by terrific gales of wind, approaching, in fact, to a perfect hurricane. As a matter of course, the wrecks upon our coast have been frightfully numerous, and, what is still worse, they have been accompanied [82] with a shocking loss of human life."[34] The John Forsgren Company suffered no loss of life and landed at the Steam Packet Wharf in Hull on Tuesday, December 28, where they were met by Richard Cortis, one of Hull's emigration agents[35] (fig. 3).

On the morning of Wednesday, December 29, 1852, having stayed overnight in a nearby lodging house, the migrants made the one-and-a-half-mile journey on foot to the Paragon Railway Station.[36] From this station, the Scandinavian Saints traveled on a specially chartered train that took them all the way to Liverpool. There, the Forsgren Company remained in another lodging house while awaiting their departure on the *Forest Monarch*, which sailed on January 16, 1853, with 297 Saints on board.[37]

Publisher's note:
Image removed due to copyright restrictions.

Fig. 3. *Hull from the Humber* (detail), by John Ward (1798–1849). Oil on canvas, 48.3 cm x 91.4 cm, ca. 1837. Ferens Art Gallery: Hull City Museums and Art Gallery. Used by permission. This rendering of the Hull waterfront about 1837 would have been one of the first views Latter-day Saint pioneers saw of the port of Hull. The Trinity House yacht *Zephyr* is moored in front of the ferryboat pier.

The migration route of the Forsgren Company from Copenhagen to Liverpool (via Hull) established the primary pattern that would be followed by Scandinavian concerts for the subsequent forty-one years. Though 3,175 immigrating Saints would arrive in Liverpool via Grimsby, 4 via Newcastle, and 9 via London, it would be Hull that received most of the Saints destined for Utah, with 21,243 (87 percent) arriving there between 1852 and 1894.[38]

Trade Agreements and Migration through Hull

The Latter-day Saint Scandinavians who emigrated between 1852 and 1894 represent only a small fraction of the many Europeans who migrated [83] to America. Between 1836 and 1914, an estimated thirty million Europeans immigrated to the United States.[39] About four million of these migrated through the United Kingdom "via the eastern ports of Harwich, Hull, Grimsby, Leith, London, Newcastle and West Hartlepool." Having arrived at an east coast port, the "transmigrants were then transported by train to the ports of Glasgow, Liverpool, London, and Southampton."[40] Even though London was used as the primary port of entry for European immigrants who settled in Great Britain, the ports of Hull and Grimsby were used by about three million (75 percent) of the European migrants destined for America and Canada because the distance between the River Humber and Liverpool by rail was the shortest. Of these migrants, about 2.2 million (73 percent) favored Hull over Grimsby.

British ship owners, and later the railway companies, developed an effective system of organization for migrant shipping. As steamships replaced sailing vessels, trade agreements between steamship companies and rail operators became stronger, led by the Wilson shipping

Publisher's note:
Image removed due to copyright restrictions.

Fig. 4. *Portrait of Thomas Wilson, Founder of the Wilson Line*, by William Hill. Engraving on paper. Hull Maritime Museum: Hull City Museum and Art Gallery. Used by permission. Thomas Wilson (1792–1869) was the founder of the Wilson line. This Hull-based company came to dominate the North Sea migrant trade and transported the majority of Scandinavian Saints to Britain.

Fig. 5. *The Railway Dock*, by F. S. Smith (1860–1925). Watercolor on paper, ca. 1885. Wilberfore House: Hull City Museums and Art Gallery. The Railway Dock, so called because Hull's first railway station was located nearby, opened in 1846. Shipping lines such as the Wilson Line built their warehouses around the dock to facilitate the speedy movement of goods from ship to shore (and vice versa). Between 1864 and 1894, nearly all the vessels carrying Latter-

Courtesy Hull Museums, UK

day [86] Saint Scandinavian emigrants to Britain landed via the Railway Dock, as the Wilson Line's vessels carried commercial goods that needed to be unloaded as soon as the vessel moored at its berth. The emigrants then made a one-mile journey to the Paragon railway station before boarding the train for Liverpool. [87]

line of Hull, the North Eastern Railway, and (later) the Guion shipping line of Liverpool. Trade agreements between shipping and railway operators were essential because they enabled the British operators to lower the price of direct migration. Cheap, safe, and reliable travel encouraged millions of Europeans to travel via Britian.

Morris and Company.

From 1852 to 1869, Morris and Company provided good service for the European Latter-day Saint migrants. Although Morris and Company chartered only sailing vessels to transport Saints on the Atlantic crossing from Liverpool, they were able to use the steamers of the Wilson Line, owned by the Hull-based Thomas Wilson (fig. 4), Sons and Company and other North Sea operators, on the North Sea crossing.[41] The success of the Wilson Line's passenger operations was based upon its ability to supply Liverpool shipping operators with the large numbers of third-class passengers needed to fill the vessels that ferried passengers across the North Atlantic. But beginning in 1867, Morris and Company gradually lost the "Mormon Contract" to transport Saints to Zion when the Guion Line began transporting Saints across the North Atlantic on steamships instead of sailing vessels. After three sailing vessels (probably belonging to Morris and Company) of Latter-day Saint immigrants were sent the following year (1868), an agreement was made between the Church and the Guion Line to transport the remaining Mormon migrants for the remainder of the year.[42]

The Guion and Wilson Lines.

The Guion Line's steamships drastically reduced the time involved in gathering to Zion, shortening the length of the [84] Atlantic crossing from 32–36 days to 10–16 days.[43] Although the Mormons contracted solely with the Guion Line for the transport of all their European converts, the Liverpool-based company subcontracted the Wilson Line to carry the European converts across the North Sea to Hull (as the Wilson Line had successfully done for Morris and Company). After the Church signed a new emigrant contract with Guion for a company traveling in 1869, Mormon converts traveled on a Wilson Line steamer to Hull (fig. 5) and journeyed across England to Liverpool by the North Eastern Railway's trains before they were allocated a berth on a steamship of the Guion Line for their transatlantic passage. This integrated service utilized the successful operations of large-scale transport companies on chartered (not scheduled) services and demonstrated how organized groups could form successful partnerships that were beneficial to all parties concerned. In addition, organized groups, such as the Mormons, were able to obtain a reduction in price by purchasing their tickets in bulk.

On May 13, 1869, George Ramsden, agent of the Guion Line, met with British Mission President Albert Carrington in Liverpool to arrange transatlantic transport for a company of Mormon converts aboard the *Minnesota*.[44] According to their plan, the Saints boarded the *Minnesota* in Liverpool on June 1, 1869. The British Mission history records:

> On their arrival on board they were provided with tea, and everything was done by the manager, Mr. G. Ramsden, for the comfort of the Saints. They had the best part of the steamer entirely for themselves and could use the aft part of the ship in common with the cabin passengers.[45]

The successful partnership between the Church and the Guion line lasted for a quarter of a century (1969–94). The relationship of Guion agent [85] George Ramsden with the Mormons was extraordinary. In praise of the trust Ramsden enjoyed with the Saints, British Mission President Anthon H. Lund pointed out that Ramsden worked for decades with the Church without a written contract.[46]

For its part, the Wilson Line provided a standard of steamer that surpassed most of its North Sea rivals.[47] The Guion Line (fig. 6), for its agreed responsibilities, hired the services of Charles Maples, a Hull-based emigration agent, who met the migrants on arrival in port and escorted them safely to the railway station.[48] Maples, like this counterparts at Liverpool, was noted by Latter-day Saint migrants for the help he provided in assisting the foreign concerts en route to Liverpool.[49]

Fig. 6. Guion Line advertisement, 1886–87. Beginning in 1867, the Church used the Guion Line to transport emigrants to the United States. This advertisement, claiming "the safest route to New York," lists the sailing dates of various ships leaving Liverpool.

Not only did the Saints receive a good standard of service from these shipping lines, but they were also assisted by their fellow Saints en route. Scandinavian Saint Peter O. Hansen noted on arrival at Hull in 1855 that the company he traveled with was "very kindly greeted by the Hull Saints."[50] Four years later, another Mormon migrant wrote: "At the landing place, 18 brethren and sisters picked us up, who accompanied us to our inn where they entertained us greatly with their song."[51]

Those who could not afford to emigrate often sought assistance through the Perpetual Emigrating [88] Fund, a revolving fund that assisted Saints migrating to Utah. Others sold their goods in order to pay for the cost of the long journey westward. Unlike previously used shipping lines, the Wilson Line offered services from numerous ports in Europe. Eventually a system was established in which Saints would journey to Hull from their local port in Norway, Sweden, or Denmark without having always to gather at the Scandinavian Mission headquarters in Copenhagen. Although this system increased the number of European ports from which the Saints could embark, Wilson's base in Hull ensured that Grimsby would no longer be used by the Saints as a port of entry into Britain. Hull would now monopolize the Latter-day

Saint migrant trade to Liverpool as Copenhagen once had. Hull would retain this role until 1894, when the Guion Line folded.

The Rail Journey from Hull to Liverpool

From Hull, the Latter-day Saint migrants traveled by train to Liverpool. A fifteen-year-old Mormon convert who traveled in 1888 described the train:

> The passenger trains were different then any I had seen before. The coaches were divided into compartments that would accommodate from 6 to eight passengers; they would be locked in. A running board on the outside of the train that the conductor used to go from compartment through the whole train. I thought it a practical way to check all passengers with out disturbing those already checked.[52]

Rail services from Hull to Liverpool had been established in 1840 when the rail line between Liverpool and Selby was extended all the way to Hull.[53] The North Eastern Railway, which took over control of this route in 1851, chartered trains from Hull to Liverpool for emigrants when trade necessitated. As the scale of the migration grew, so the facilities improved. An emigrant waiting room was provided at the Paragon Railway Station in Hull from 1871 and extended in 1881 (fig. 7). It provided the migrants with a warm room, limited washing facilities, and seats to rest on while waiting for the train tickets for their railway journey across the Pennines to Liverpool.[54] The journey to Liverpool lasted up to six hours.

Courtesy Nicholas J. Evans

Fig. 7. Emigration Waiting Room, Paragon Station, Hull, England, 2002. Built in 1871 by the North Eastern Railway, the one-story emigrant waiting room ran adjacent to the main railway station but was sufficiently separated to reduce the interaction of migrant and "normal" railway passengers. Such isolation was seen as necessary to reduce the possible introduction of contagious diseases such as cholera, small pox, and trachoma.

The rail route out of Hull varied according to arrangements made in advance between the railway and steamship companies and the agents for the Latter-day Saints. The majority traveled on the North Eastern Railway's trains via Leeds, Manchester, and Bolton before arriving at Liverpool's Lime Street Station. Most migrating Saints saw little of the port of Hull. As one passing Saint recorded:

> I did not see anything of Hull beyond the streets through which we went to reach the railway station. The railway station itself was beautiful [89] and imposing. We left for Liverpool on a special train at 3 o'clock in the afternoon, and came through the towns of Howden, Selby, Normington [Normanton], Brandford [Bradford], Leeds Hudbersfild [Huddersfield], Manchester and Bolton to Liverpool. But as it became dark at an early hour, I saw little or nothing at all of the cities and the country we passed through. The country around Hull was pretty, flat and fertile. Farther away it was more mountainous. The railway was frequently on a higher level than the towns and villages, and sometimes it also went along below the surface at considerably long stretches.[55]

Passengers arriving in England via Grimsby in the 1850s and 1860s waited at the Manchester, Sheffield, and Lincolnshire Railway's dock terminus in Grimsby. Located near to the landing stage where the migrants had arrived, they slept overnight in a large dining-cum sleeping room before traveling to Liverpool via Sheffield, Manchester, and seven tunnels.[56]

Regardless of the route they took, all migrants traveled the 140-mile journey to Liverpool by steam train. The scenery they passed through varied as greatly as the diverse backgrounds of the passengers on board. From the flat hinterlands of the Humber to the rugged terrain of the Pennines, the journey was an experience they would never forget—especially [90] for those like Joseph Hansen and his father. Joseph wrote that "this was the first and only time that my father rode in a railroad train."[57]

The Arrival in Liverpool

At Liverpool, the Mormon converts were greeted by the agents of the shipping company with which they were booked to cross the Atlantic as well as with Church-appointed emigration agents. As the primary port of Mormon embarkation, Liverpool launched most of the international emigration-voyages made to America in the nineteenth century. It was not only the home of the British Mission and the administrative headquarters for the Church in Europe,[58] but it was also (by the time Mormon emigration was launched in 1840) considered the most active international port of emigration in the world. With two thousand public houses, it was considered a sailor's paradise. Its prominence derived from its prime location for rail connections in the British Isles and from its excellent navigable channels in the Mersey River.[59] Though Scandinavian Latter-day Saint emigrants would join other European converts (mostly British) who were also emigrating to Zion, the cosmopolitan nature of Britain's second largest port left a permanent impression upon those traveling via the Atlantic port.

The Mormon emigrants' stay in Liverpool was often shorter than that of their non-Latter-day Saint counterparts. When Morris and Company (based in Hamburg) had the Mormon contract, emigrants usually spent anywhere from a few days to a few weeks here. Once Guion (based in Liverpool) had taken over the business of shipping Latter-day Saint emigrants, the waiting time was reduced to a day or two. After gathering their luggage from the railway station, a lodging house, or the mission headquarters, the Scandinavian pioneers joined their fellow travelers on board vessels that would transport them across the Atlantic. Having traversed the North Sea and Britain, the Saints had overcome the first stage in their lengthy journey west.

Conclusion

During the latter half of the nineteenth century, the Scandinavian Mission sent off over twenty-four thousand Latter-day Saint immigrants.[60] Each detail of their journey from Europe to America was planned in advance by Church leaders, shepherding missionaries, and the providers of chartered transport. Leaders arranged for agents, located from Copenhagen to Liverpool, to meet each group of Saints at each stop on their epic journeys west.

Throughout the period of gathering, Church leaders took advantage of the latest developments in technology to transport the foreign converts in [91] as comfortable and efficient a way as possible. Though Latter-day Saints are generally aware of European converts crossing the Atlantic from Liverpool, it was the transit arrangements at Copenhagen, Hamburg, Grimsby, and Hull that ensured that the Scandinavian converts would reach Utah. These "feeder ports" each had a pivotal role in this process, but it would be Hull that sent more Latter-day Saint Scandinavian migrants on to Liverpool than any other port in this era of gathering.

Hull's role was not determined by geographic location alone. More important, the links fostered between the Church leaders in Copenhagen and Liverpool and specific steam and rail operators accounted for Hull's significant role in transporting Latter-day Saint converts to America. Such operators proved they could provide a level of service and integrated transportation systems that would efficiently convey the migrants to the vessels moored in Liverpool. Such services led Church leaders in Europe to direct the majority of Scandinavia's Mormon emigrants to the ships chartered by Morris and Company and later the Guion Line. Both shipping lines chartered ships to transport the Saints across the North Sea from various parts of Europe to the European Mission headquarters in Liverpool. Between 1867 and 1894, all these feeder services would be provided by the Wilson Line of Hull and the rail services of the North Eastern Railway.

The revolution in steam technology drastically reduced the time needed to make the journey from mainland Europe to the great Mormon gathering place in the Salt Lake Valley. This change, coupled with competition between rival steamship operators and Church financial assistance, put Zion within easier reach of European disciples.

Though traveling was a drawn-out affair, almost every one of Zion's gatherers knew it would be worth it. This determination to reach Zion is perhaps best exemplified by the journal of Jane C. Robinson Hindley, who in 1855 wrote:

> I believed in the principle of the gathering and felt it my duty to go altho it was a severe trial to me in my feelings to leave my native Land and the pleasing associations I had formed there, but my heart was fixed I knew in whom I had trusted and with the fire of Israels God burning in my bosom, I forsook my home.[61] [92]

Authors

Fred E. Woods (fred_woods@byu.edu) is Associate Professor of Church History and Doctrine at Brigham Young University. He received his B.A. and M.A. from BYU and his Ph.D. from the University of Utah. In 2002 he was awarded the Richard L. Anderson Distinguished Research Award by Religious Education.

Nicholas J. Evans is Caird Doctoral Fellow at the Maritime Historical Studies Centre, University of Hull, England. He received his B.A. in history from Leicester and is currently completing a Ph.D. on European migration via the United Kingdom, 1836–1916.

Notes

1. See Gordon Jackson, "The Ports," in *Transport in Victorian Britain*, ed. Michael J. Freeman and Derek H. Aldcroft (Manchester: Manchester University Press, 1988), 218–52. The city of Hull is officially styled Kingston upon Hull, which is derived from the fact that Hull was founded by King Edward I and was situated upon the River Hull.

2. Most of the Scandinavian converts embarked from Copenhagen, headquarters of the Scandinavian Mission. This information has been culled from the *Mormon Immigration Index* CD (Salt Lake City: Family History Department of The Church of Jesus Christ of Latter-day Saints, 2000); British and Scandinavian Mission Records; and Customs Bills of Entry in the City of Hull, England. For information concerning vessels carrying Mormon Scandinavian converts from Copenhagen, see Shauna C. Anderson, Ruth Ellen Maness, and Susan Easton Black, *Passport to Paradise: The Copenhagen "Mormon" Lists*, 2 vols. (West Jordan, Utah: Genealogical Services, 2000), vols. 1–2, covering the years 1872–94.

3. The gathering from distant lands did not commence until the necessary priesthood keys of the gathering were restored in 1836 (D&C 110:11). The following year, Apostle Heber C. Kimball was called by Joseph Smith to lead a mission to England. Accompanied by Apostle Orson Hyde, Elder Kimball led a small group of missionaries who found great success in the British Isles. They had been warned by Joseph to "remain silent concerning the gathering ... until such time as the work was fully established, and it should be clearly made manifest by the Spirit to do otherwise." See Joseph Smith Jr., *History of The Church of Jesus Christ of Latter-day Saints*, ed. B. H. Roberts, 2d ed. rev., 7 vols. (Salt Lake City: Deseret Book, 1971), 2:492. Their groundbreaking work was greatly augmented by the mission of the Twelve in 1840–41. For excellent information on these early missions, see James B. Allen, Ronald K. Esplin, and David J. Whittaker, *Men with a Mission, 1837–1841: The Quorum of the Twelve in the British Isles* (Salt Lake City: Deseret Book, 1992); and James B. Allen and Malcom R. Thorp, "The Mission of the Twelve to England, 1840–1841: Mormon Apostles and the Working Classes," *BYU Studies* 15, no. 4 (1975): 499–526.

4. Andrew Jenson, *Encyclopedic History of the Church* (Salt Lake City: Deseret News Publishing, 1941), 346, notes:

    The Hull Conference, or District, of the British Mission, dates back to 1843 and continued under that name until 1868, when it became a part of the Leeds Conference. When the Grimsby Conference was organized in 1900 the branches formerly belonging to the Hull Conference constituted this new conference which continued until 1910, when the Grimsby Conference became the Hull Conference, consisting of the Latter-day Saints residing in the city of Hull and vicinity in Yorkshire, England with headquarters at Hull. [93]

    See also Jack Spurr, ed., *A History of The Church of Jesus Christ of Latter-day Saints in the Hull Area, 1844–1973* (Hull, England: By the editor, 1973).

The Hull Conference and its local branch in Hull developed in a region that had experienced the large-scale growth of nonconformist religious groups during the eighteenth and early nineteenth centuries. By 1851, membership and attendance at nonconformist churches, chapels, and mission halls in this important maritime center had eclipsed that of England's state church, the Church of England. See David Neave, *Lost Churches and Chapels of Hull* (n.p.: Hutton Press, Cherry Burton, 1991), 7.

5.   James Ure and Charles Barnes, "Conference Minutes. Hull," *Millennial Star* 10 (May 1, 1848): 134.

6.   Orson Pratt, "Conference Minutes. General Conference," *Millennial Star* 10 (August 15, 1848): 252, reported that by August 14, 1848, the Hull Conference had 7 branches and 163 members, including 11 elders, 10 priests, 6 teachers, and 5 deacons. These statistics were also quoted in "Latter-day Saints," *Hull Advertiser*, September 29, 1848, 5, which also noted they held their meeting in the Temperance Hall, Paragon Street.

7.   Spurr, *Latter-day Saints in the Hull Area*, 2.

8.   Ure and Barnes, "Conference Minutes. Hull," 134, noted that a conference was held in Hull on December 26, 1847, in the "Temperance-Hall on Blanket-row." At this conference, a representation of the branches was called for which included the Louth Branch among several others. It said the "Louth Branch, [was] represented by letter, [and consisted] of 36 members, including 3 elders, 3 priests, 1 teacher, and 1 deacon."

9.   They traveled by the East Lincolnshire Railway from Louth to Grimsby before joining the train of the Manchester, Sheffield and Lincolnshire Railway from Grimsby to New Holland (on the south bank of the River Humber). At New Holland, they boarded a steam packet belonging to the Manchester, Sheffield and Lincolnshire and sailed to nearby Hull. This group of Saints from Lincolnshire sailed across the Atlantic on the *Zetland*. See Conway B. Sonne, *Saints on the Seas: A Maritime History of Mormon Migration, 1830–1890* (Salt Lake City: University of Utah Press, 1983), 149. For first-person accounts of this voyage, see the winter voyage of the *Zetland* on the *Mormon Immigration Index* CD.

10.   "Autobiography of Thomas Atkin Jr.," typescript, 4, Church Archives, The Church of Jesus Christ of Latter-day Saints, Salt Lake City. Other converts from Hull and the British Isles gathered to Zion for spiritual as well as temporal reasons. Letters posted in Hull's local newspaper created an additional stir about immigration to Utah. For example, in an article titled "The Great Salt Lake Valley," *Hull Advertiser*, July 26, 1850, 7, the editor posted a letter composed by a British convert who, on his way to Utah, had written to his brother, a tradesman in Hull. Among other things, the convert reported that the Salt Lake Valley had been said to be "the most healthy climate in the world, the country most beautiful, and that that people will eventually be the richest on earth." A few years later, a Latter-day Saint convert from Hull named Mr. Wm. Brown wrote in an article titled "Letter from a Hull Mormon in America," *Hull Advertiser*, December 6, 1856, 1, the following description of Springville, Utah:

> I enjoy the best kind of health here amongst the mountains. I am quite happy, and rejoice in God that ever I was led to hear the Latter Day Saints [94] preach to Gospel, and that I left England to travel this place. ... We are living in the last days. ... I should impress upon your mind the necessity of obeying the gospel that is taught by the Mormons.

11.   Phillip A. M. Taylor, *Expectations Westward: The Mormons and the Emigration of Their British Converts in the Nineteenth Century* (Edinburgh, Scotland: Oliver and Boyd, 1965), 248–49, shows that for the period 1863 to 1870, British Mormon emigrants from the Hull Conference numbered only 94 (out of a periodic total of 10,742 emigrants from all conferences in England). For the earlier and later peiods of British Mormon emigration (1850–62 and 1874–90), the number of emigrants from the Hull Conference had been included in either the figures for Mormon Emigration from Yorkshire (1,203 out of 12,618 total English Latter-day Saint emigrants between 1850 and 1862) or from the Leeds Conference (474 out of 11,168 between 1874 and 1890).

12.   Leonard J. Arrington, *Great Basin Kingdom: An Economic History of the Latter-day Saints, 1830–1890* (Lincoln: University of Nebraska Press, 1958), 64. To help assist the poor international

Saints who desired to emigrate, Church leaders created a revolving fund called the Perpetual Emigrating Fund, which the Saints sustained in the October 1849 general conference held in Salt Lake City. John D. Unruh Jr., *The Plains Across: The Overland Emigrants and the Trans-Mississippi West, 1840–60* (Urbana: University of Illinois Press, 1993), 303, states that over ten thousand gold seekers made a detour through Utah in 1849 and thousands more in the immediate years that followed. See Fred E. Woods, "More Precious than Gold: The Journey to and through Zion in 1849–§850," *Nauvoo Journal* 11 (spring 1999): 109, for the story of Saints who gathered to Utah instead of the California gold fields.

13.   Richard L. Jensen noted in his critique of an earlier version of this article that "while there may have been official tolerance on the part of the government, much of the Danish populace was far from tolerant where religion was concerned. Many Mormons were persecuted in Denmark despite the provisions of the constitution." Jensen also emphasized that religious freedom was even more limited in Norway and Sweden. Richard L. Jensen, email to author, October 9, 2002.

14.   Marius A. Christensen, "History of the Danish Mission of The Church of Jesus Christ of Latter-day Saints, 1850–1964" (master's thesis, Brigham Young University, 1966), 6–8.

15.   For a list of various places these missionaries were assigned, see Thomas Bullock, "Minutes of the General Conference, Held at the Great Salt Lake City," *Millennial Star* 12 (May 1, 1850): 133.

16.   Andrew Jenson, "The Gospel in Denmark," *Contributor* 16 (November 1894): 45.

17.   Elder Erastus Snow left Boston on April 4, arriving at Liverpool on April 16 on board the *Niagra*; Elder Peter O. Hansen arrived April 8; and John E. Forsgren arrived on April 19. Andrew Jenson, *History of the Scandinavian Mission* (Salt Lake City: Deseret News, 1927), 3.

18.   Jenson, *History of the Scandinavian Mission*, 3.

19.   Gerald Myron Haslam, *Clash of Cultures: The Norwegian Experience with Mormonism, 1842–1920* (New York: Peter Land, 1984), 10; Jenson, "Gospel in [95] Denmark," 46; Jenson, *History of the Scandinavian Mission*, 4. According to Freebody's *Directory of Hull* (Hull, England: J. Pulleyn, 1851), 87, the cost of travel on board the *Victoria* was "6 shillings 6 pence Best Cabin Fare and 4 shillings for second Cabin." Latter-day Saint missionaries in Europe nearly always traveled second class, thus enjoying the privacy of their own cabin, while presidents of the European Mission traveled first class. Elder Erastus Snow and his companions were met at the docks of Copenhagen by Peter O. Hansen and taken to a very noisy local hotel. The next day they found better lodgings at the home of Mr. Lauritz B. Malling. On their third day, they visited the meeting of a reformed Baptist minister named Peter C. Mönster, who was initially warm to the elders and allowed them to preach to his congregation. Mönster's attitude soon hardened when he realized they were going to decrease the numbers of his flock by preaching the word of the restored gospel and not that of the Baptist persuasion. Jenson, *History of the Scandinavian Mission*, 4–7.

20.   Jenson, *History of the Scandinavian Mission*, 4–9.

21.   Jenson, *History of the Scandinavian Mission*, 10.

22.   William Mulder, *Homeward to Zion: The Mormon Migration from Scandinavia* (Minneapolis: University of Minnesota Press, 1957; reprinted, Provo, Utah: BYU Studies, 2000), 107. For a general overview of the Scandinavian Mission, see Jenson, *History of the Scandinavian Mission*; and Christensen, "History of the Danish Mission." For brief early histories of the restored Church in Sweden and Norway, see Andrew Jenson, "Scandinavian Reminiscences," parts 2 and 5, *Contributor* 16 (March 1894): 94–100; (December 1894): 297–300. Mulder reports that a small fraction of the Scandinavian emigrants were Icelandic (p. 107). For a more extensive treatise of the Latter-day Saint Norwegian experience, see Haslam, *Clash of Cultures*. For an overview of the early history of the Church in Iceland, see Fred E. Woods, "Fire on Ice: The Conversion and Life of Gudmundur Gudmundsson," *BYU Studies* 39, no. 2 (2000): 57–72; Fred E. Woods, "A Sesquicentennial Sketch of Latter-day Saint Icelandic Emigration and Conversion," forthcoming in *Regional Studies in Latter-day Saint Church History: Europe*, ed. Donald Q. Cannon (Provo, Utah: Department of Church History and Doctrine, Brigham Young University, 2001).

23.   William Mulder, "Mormons from Scandinavia, 1850–1900: A Shepherded Migration," *Pacific Historical Review* 23 (1954): 237, notes that Scandinavian converts from Norway sometimes voyaged directly across the North Sea from Christiana or Stavenger to Liverpool, whereas the Swedes and especially the Danes cam primarily through the port of Hull and secondarily through

Grimsby. The Saints from Iceland were an exception, as evidence reveals that some voyaged from their homeland via Leith, Scotland, and others voyaged direct to Liverpool. See Woods, "Sesquicentennial Sketch," 8.

24. Mulder, "Mormons from Scandinavia," 237. According to the *1997–1998 Church Almanac* (Deseret News: Salt Lake City, 1996), 162–63, during the years of embarkation from Hamburg (1862, 1865, and 1866), over three thousand Latter-day Saint converts voyaged on eight sailing vessels to gather to Zion. Mormon embarkation using the Morris Line's sailing vessels from Hamburg was discontinued in 1866. The primary reason for this discontinuation stems from the fact that the following year, the Church decided to no longer send Latter-day Saint immigrants via sailing vessels. Commencing in 1867, all Mormon migrants were to be transported by steamers. It was also decided in this same year that Church teams [96] would not be sent to the frontier. See "Church Emigration to Utah in 1867," in "Church Emigration Book, 1862–1881," Church Archives. Furthermore, Sonne, *Saints on the Seas*, 187, points out that in a letter to British Mission President Franklin D. Richards dated May 23, 1868, Brigham Young reaffirmed the decision to use steamships: "To enable our immigration to avail themselves of the healthiest portion or portions of the year … employ none but steamships." Thus, the port of Hamburg seems to have been discontinued due to the decision to no longer use sailing vessels. Apparently it was advantageous to take the indirect route to Liverpool wherein different steam shipping lines were employed. Vessels from the port of Liverpool transporting passengers to New York were of a higher caliber than those provided by Morris and Company in Hamburg. Furthermore, vessels from Liverpool were filled with British and European Latter-day Saints, providing more bargaining power and enabling cheaper rates when the Church chartered transatlantic vessels. Finally, shipping was cheaper from Liverpool due to greater competition.

   Hundreds of Swiss-German Latter-day Saints migrated through Hull in the nineteenth century, representing a small portion of the total number of European converts. These migrants were similarly conveyed via Britain, essentially as their numbers were so insignificant that there was no fiscal advantage for the Swiss-German Mission to charter a transatlantic vessel for their sole use. For information on the Swiss-German emigrants, see Douglas D. Alder, "The German-Speaking Migration to Utah, 1850–1950" (master's thesis, University of Utah, 1959). Migrants arriving via the Port of Grimsby, as well as those who had arrived at Hull and then traversed the River Humber to Grimsby, had the added advantage of staying in the Manchester, Sheffield, and Lincolnshire Railway Emigrants' Home that opened in 1854 in a former dockside passenger station. The shelter provided a single mixed-sex dormitory-cum-dining room where the migrants slept overnight under the supervision of Isaac Freeman, the railway's interpreter. From immediately outside this dockside shelter, migrants boarded the train that took them to Liverpool. Freeman and his wife provided a high level of service for migrants arriving at the port. In 1871, *The Grimsby Observer* noted, "Mr. Freeman, the port interpreter, who speaks several languages, is the manager of this important establishment, and it speaks well for its conduct that we have never heard a complaint against it, but very many instances of kindness, sympathy, and consideration for the strangers have reached us." "The Emigrants Home," *Grimsby Observer*, October 25, 1871, 4. For more information on the development by railway companies of facilities for emigrants, see Nicholas J. Evans, "A Roof over Their Heads: The Role of Shelters in Jewish Migration via the UK, 1850–1914," in *Shemot* 9 (March 2001): 11–15.

25. Jenson, *History of the Scandinavian Mission*, 46–47, states that upon their arrival in Liverpool the Saints "were informed that they were too late to sail on the 'Ellen Marian,' … for that ship had just cleared port the same day." Sonne, *Saints on the Seas*, 150, notes that the *Ellen Maria* departed from Liverpool on February 10, 1852, with 369 Latter-day Saint passengers on board.

26. Jenson, *History of the Scandinavian Mission*, 46–47; Sonne, *Saints on the Seas*, 150.

27. Taylor, *Expectations Westward*, 162. The transportation price of £1. 10.s. 0d. is significantly more than a guinea. Gee and Company were a Hull-based shipping line that ran steamers between Hull and the continental ports of Antwerp, Copenhagen, [97] Hamburg, and St. Petersburg. "Diary of Appleton Harmon," 1850–52, typescript, 84, L. Tom Perry Special Collections, Harold B. Lee Library, Brigham Young University, Provo, Utah, notes that on September 29, 1852, Harmon and a Brother Hardy made arrangements with the Gee and Company to bring Scandinavian converts

from Copenhagen to Hull. Hardy forwarded the arrangements to a Brother Hasgreen in Copenhagen in which it was noted, "'Emegrants from Copenhagah on the Steam ship Emperor-Deck or in the Hold of Room' £1..1..0.. or they would send a Steamer on purpose to fetch from 3 to 4 hundred for £ 1..10..0 per head."

28. "Epistle of the Twelve," *Millennial Star* 1 (April 1841): 311, states, "It is also a great savings to go in companies, instead of going individually. ... [A] company can charter a vessel, so as to make the passage much cheaper than otherwise."

29. Willard Snow, Journal, October 16, 1852, 101, Church Archives, states:

> About the middle of Oct[ober] we received a proposition from Mr Morris + Co. from Liverpool through their agent, Mr Carl Rydhing in Copenhagen to the following effect that they would take Emigrants from Hamburgn to [New] Orleans via Hull & Liverpool on the following conditions: 2d Cabin 80 [rigsdaler,] 3d cabin 60 [rigsdaler,] & steerage 46 [rigsdaler] children between twelve and one 8 doll [dollars] less.

> A week later (October 23, 1852), Snow wrote: "Held a conversation with Mr Morris in person who happened to be in the city & he made another proposition to take us for 52 rigsdaler from this city" to New Orleans. Three and a half weeks later, Snow wrote:

> On the 16th closed the contract with Mr Morris & Co for to transport our emigration from Copenhagen by steam to Kiel by Railway from Kiel to Hamburgn and by steamer from Hamburgn to Hull and by Railway from Hull to Liverpool and by ss first rate sailing vessel from Liverpool to New Orleans for fifty two dollars a passenger children under twelve eight dollars less sucklings under one.

30. Mulder, *Homeward to Zion*, 139–41, further notes that the Latter-day Saints used Morris and Company from 1852 to 1869. The Guion Line then became the preferred shipping company because of its superior steam vessels for which the sailing vessels provided by Morris and Company were no match.

31. Mulder, *Homeward to Zion*, 158.

32. Scandinavian Mission, "Manuscript History," vol. 8 (1850–55), December 20, 1852, Church Archives, extracted this journal entry from the journal of Herman Julius Christensen, December 26, 1852. On the following day, this same passenger noted, "The captain, who had been a seafaring man for 25 years, declared that in all his previous voyages he had never experienced a worse storm."

33. "Manuscript History of the John H. Forsgren Emigrating Company," 1, Church Archives. The maritime safety record of the Latter-day Saint immigrants in the nineteenth century was most impressive. There were no known lives lost because of shipwreck across the North Sea or the Atlantic, and the only one known shipwreck occurred on the Pacific. This is in sharp contrast to the fact that at least fifty-nine immigrant ships were lost crossing the Atlantic between 1847 and 1853. See Sonne, *Saints on the Seas*, 138–39. [98]

34. On Tuesday, December 31, 1852, the *Hull Packet* reported that "three hundred Mormons, from Norway and Denmark, arrived on the *Lion*, from Hamburg, on Tuesday night, and were forwarded by Mr. R. J. Cortis, the agent, to Liverpool, en route to New Orleans and the Salt Lake." "Great Loss of Life," *Hull Advertiser*, December 31, 1852, 5. The *Master's Declaration* (return of aliens) for this first group of Saints recorded "two hundred and ninety nine passengers, emigrants on their way to America via Liverpool," arrived on board the *Lion*, mastered by Mr. John Frederick Kruger at Hull from Hamburg, on December 28, 1852. "Return of Alien Passengers Made by Masters of Chips," HO/3/67, Public Record Office, Kew, London. The Customs Bills of Entry, a document produced weekly that provided information for merchants interested in the commerce of the port, similarly noted that along with passengers, the *Lion* was laden with a cargo of metal, pork, wool, and linseed. Customs Bills of Entry, no. 12, January 1, 1853, Hull Central Library, Hull, England.

35. "Local Intelligence," *Hull Packet*, December 31, 1852, 5. The pier has been referred to by numerous names during the past century. During the period in question, the pier was most frequently referred to as the "Humber Pier." Richard Cortis was a one-man business who worked as an emigration

agent. He worked alongside other agents who worked for various Atlantic lines—with each agent working exclusively for different Liverpool-based shipping lines. Information on Cortis can be found in various commercial directories for the port and town of Kingston upon Hull, Hull Central Library, Hull, England. For further information on the role of port-based emigration agents on the east coast of Britain, see Nicholas J. Evans, "Aliens En Route: European Migration through Britain, 1836–1914" (Ph.D. diss., University of Hull, forthcoming).

36. Hull had two railway stations. The first was situated at Wellington Street and opened in 1840. The second was at the end of Paragon Street and begain operating in 1849. European migrants used only the Paragon Street terminus to Liverpool.

37. Sonne, *Saints on the Seas*, 150.

38. For analysis of the number of Saints migrating through Britain, see Evans, "Aliens En Route." Details of the ports used by migrating Saints can be gleaned through the personal accounts of those Saints journeying to Zion. See the *Mormon Immigration Index* CD. As previously note, the *1997–1998 Church Almanac*, 162–63, indicates that over three thousand Mormon immigrants voyaged to America from Hamburg on eight vessels during the years 1862, 1865, and 1866.

39. Statistical analysis of immigration into America is provided by numerous scholars and their publications. E. A. Ross, *The Old World in the New: The Significance of Past and Present Immigration to the American People* (New York: Century, 1914), 307–10, states that the total number of immigrants for the period 1835–1914 was 30,245,034. British and Scandinavian Mission records reveal that over one hundred thousand European Mormon converts gathered to America from 1840–1914, of which at least one fourth were Scandinavians, while the majority were British.

40. Nicholas J. Evans, "Indirect Passage from Europe: Migration via the UK, 1836–1914," *Journal for Maritime Research* (June 2001): 2.

41. For details of the vessels chartered for transatlantic travel during the period when Morris and Company enjoyed the "Mormon contact," see the appendix of Sonne, *Saints on the Seas*. For details of the vessels used on the North Sea crossing, [99] see the *Mormon Immigration Index* CD. This latter source also refers (along with Jenson, *History of the Scandinavian Mission*) to the problems encountered with vessels chartered to sail directly to America from the port of Hamburg. Comparative analysis of the time taken on the direct and indirect journeys from the European port of embarkation to the American port of arrival are included in Evans, "Aliens En Route."

Thomas Wilson was a Hull-based merchant who had previously worked in the offices of Whitaker, Wilkinson and Company, Hull's largest importer of Swedish iron ore, before setting up in partnership in 1822 as Beckinton, Wilson and Company. In 1831, he established his second company under the name of Wilson, Hudson and Company, and then, in 1841, he founded his own firm—Thomas Wilson, Sons and Company. The company was centered in the Scandinavian and North Sea trades and quickly expanded as trade along this route, coupled with the Swedish Royal Mail Contract, generated good financial returns for the company. Wilson managed the day-to-day operations himself until 1866, when the company became jointly managed by his sons, Charles Henry Wilson and Arthur Wilson. Under their direction, the company continued to expand and by 1903 included over one hundred vessels, making it the largest privately-owned shipping company in the world. See J. Harrower, *Wilson Line* (Gravesend, Kent, U.K.: World Ship Society, 1998); Arthur Credland, *The Wilson Line* (Stroud, G.B.: Tempus, 2000).

42. Sonne, *Saints on the Seas*, 118. Herein, Sonne further notes that the name of the first Guion vessel that transported the Latter-day Saint immigrants in 1867 was the *Manhattan*.

43. See Evans, "Aliens En Route." Sonne, *Saints on the Seas*, 117, indicates that the Fuion Line carried over forty thousand Latter-day Saint converts across the Atlantic, which amounted to about 98 percent of all Mormon emigrants who voyaged by steamship from Liverpool to New York. The Latter-day Saints used the Guion Line consistently from 1869 to 1894, at which time the company was liquidated. For more information on the Guion Line, see "Rise and Fall of the Guion Line," *Sea Breezes* 19 (1955): 190–216.

Anthon H. Lund, Journal, June 30, and July 2, 5–7, 1894, Church Archives, notes that arrangements were made by British Mission President Anthon L. Lund for the European converts to travel with the Anchor Line, based in Glasgow. Converts were thus rerouted through Glasgow before going on to New York. President Lund made these new arrangements known to President

Sundwall of the Scandinavian Mission, President Naegle of the Swiss German Mission, and Church President Wilford Woodruff.

44. British Mission, "Manuscript History," vol. 24 (1869–71), May 13, 1869, Church Archives.

45. British Mission, "Manuscript History," June 1, 1869. However, the Guion Line did not provide food at Hull for their passengers as other shipping lines did. This is one way the Guion Line was able to cut the cost of the trip.

46. Perhaps, after the initial contract of 1869, both parties no longer felt a need for a written contract due to the relationship of trust that developed between the Guion agent George Ramsden and the Church. Praiseworthy remarks made by Anthon H. Lund at the time of Ramsden's death are noted in "A Good Friend Gone," *Millennial Star* 58 (June 4, 1896): 360–62. For an excellent discussion of the [100] relationship between the Guion Line (especially their agent George Ramsden) and the Saints, see Richard L. Jensen, "Steaming Through: Arrangements for Mormon Emigraton through Europe, 1869–1887," *Journal of Mormon History* 9 (1982): 5–8. When the Guion Company was liquidated in 1894, Ramsden helped Lund with arrangements for the Saints to transfer their business to the Anchor Line, which ran its operations out of Glasgow. See British Mission, "Manuscript History," 34 (1891–96), June 30, 1894. Although the Anchor Line is mentioned herein, not only for the date of June 30, but also for the dates of July 5–6, and September 20, 1894, it is most probable that it is rather the Allan Line that was the shipping company run from Glasgow at this time. This change rerouted the Mormon converts from the Scandinavian and Swiss-German Missions through the port of Leith to Glasgow, where they began the transatlantic voyage to New York.

47. In 1866 increasing alarm at the standard of accommodation provided for third-class or steerage passengers prompted the Hull Town Council to interview Charles Wilson, who was a member of Parliament representing Hull and the managing director of the Wilson Line. This action led to an improvement in the standard of accommodation provided for passengers carried by the Wilson Line but not by other European shipping operators. The condition of emigrants who arrived into Hull were reported in numerous reports by the Medical Officer of Health for the Hull Board of Health. The volume for 1866 can be found in Kingston upon Hull City Archives, Hull, England.

48. The 1881 British census documents that Maples was born in Thorne, a town thirty miles west of Hull. Since his wife and daughter were born in Australia, it can be assumed that Maples gained his knowledge of the emigration business through his own personal experiences in emigrating to Australia. Maples had returned to Hull during the early 1850s and established himself as an emigration agent working alongside Richard Cortis. Later, Cortis and Maples would combine their business, with Maples taking sole control upon the death of the former. *1881 British Census and National Index: England, Scotland, Wales, Channel Islands, Isle of Man, and Royal Navy*, 24 CDs (Salt Lake City: The Church of Jesus Christ of Latterday Saints, 1999).

49. Latter-day Saint migrant Jesse N. Smith recalled, "Mr. Maples on behalf of the forwarding Company furnished a meal for the emigrants and sent all forward the same evening to Liverpool." Jesse N. Smith, Autobiography and Journal, 1855–1906, July 15, 1870, 259, Church Archives. Another passing migrant noted, "Mr. Maples, the Guion Agt, came on board and got the list of Emigr[ants]." Hans Jorgenson, Reminiscences and Journal, 174, Church Archives.

    Apparently this line had many staff members who also provided excellent service. Another Guion agent who is praised in several Latter-day Saint immigrant accounts is a Mr. Gibson. See, for example, E. L. Sloan to President Geo. Teasdale, *Millennial Star* 51 (November 25, 1889): 749; George Romney Jr. to President George Teasdale, *Millennial Star* 51 (December 23, 1889): 811; L. F. Monch to President George Teasdale, *Millennial Star* 50 (December 24, 1888): 829. However, the agency was apparently not without some criticism by the British government. According to government inspector W. Cowie, while other Atlantic passenger lines provided temporary lodging and meals for passing emigrants at Hull, the Guion Line transferred its passengers directly to the rails "so that those people are the greater portion of the day without a meal." See *Reports Received by the Board of* [101] *Trade and the Local Government Board Relating to the Transit of Scandinavian Emigrants through the Port of Hull*, July 11, 1882, 9. Yet for those traveling to Utah, such speed was often welcomed, because it shortened the long journey.

50. P. O. Hansen to President F. D. Richards, *Millennial Star* 17 (February 3, 1855): 71.

51.   Heinrich Hug, Journal, August 13, 1859, in possession of Kent Hug, translated from German by Brooks Haderlie. According to his journal entry, Hug arrived with a company of Swiss Latter-day Saint immigrants in Hull on August 13, 1859. Although Hansen and Hug are the only known European Saints to mention the reception provided by the Hull Saints, these local Saints were probably instrumental in assisting other Latter-day Saint companies who passed through.
52.   Frederick Zaugg, Autobiography, 25, original in private possession.
53.   Edward Gillett and Kenneth A. MacMahon, *A History of Hull* (Hull, England: University of Hull Press, 1989), 303.
54.   Plans of the North Eastern Railway's emigrant waiting room can be seen at the Hull City Archives (OBL/M/2585 and OBL/M/6328). The Pennines are a mountain chain known as the backbone of England because they are so hilly.
55.   Hans Hoth, Diary, typescript, 3–4, December 27, 1853, translated from German holograph by Peter Gulbrandsen, Bancroft Library, University of California, Berkeley.
56.   Ove Christian Oveson, "Sketch of the Life of Ove Christian Oveson," typescript, April 26, 1864, 22, Church Archives.
57.   Joseph Hansen, Hansen Family History, December 1852, 7, Church Archives.
58.   The British Mission became the administrative center for the Church in Europe commencing June 28, 1854, under the direction of Franklin D. Richards. Richards also served at this time as the president of the British Mission. Subsequent presidents of the British Mission also had stewardship over all other missions in Europe during their various terms of service.
59.   Conway B. Sonne, "Liverpool and the Mormon Emigration," paper presented at the Mormon History Association Conference in Liverpool, England, on July 10, 1987, 2–5. Note that the public houses were also known as "pubs." These facilities were not hotels but were establishments licensed to sell alcoholic beverages. For more information on Liverpool and Mormon emigration, see Fred E. Woods, *Gathering to Nauvoo* (American Fork, Utah: Covenant Communications, 2002), 42–51.
60.   Jenson, *History of the Scandinavian Mission*, 533, provides statistical evidence that over twenty thousand Saints emigrated from the Scandinavian Mission between 1852 and 1894. As noted earlier, Mulder, *Homeward to Zion*, 107, maintains that 22,653 of the 46,497 Scandinavian converts immigrated to America between 1850 and 1905. These two estimates are less than the total of 24,431 Scandinavian migrants that we estimated. Our figure was based on several sources including the following: The *Mormon Immigration Index* CD; Jenson, *History of the Scandinavian Mission*; local Grimsby newspapers (1954–68); Grimsby Library Customs Bills of Entry in Hull, Hull Central Library Customs Bills of Entry (Hull), 1852–60; Hull City Archives Master's Declaration, HO/3/1–120, Public Record Office, Kew, London.
61.   Jane Charter Robinson Hindley, "Journals 1855–1905," February 16, 1855, Church Archives. [102]

Part III
Transnational and Global Dimensions

[7]

Turkish Studies,
Vol. 6, No. 2, 201–213, June 2005

Religion, Transnationalism and Turks in Europe

GAMZE AVCI

Department of Turkish Studies, Leiden University, The Netherlands

ABSTRACT   *This essay focuses on organizations of Turkish labor migrants in the Netherlands from 1960 onwards. It seeks to analyze how the orientations of migrant organizations have changed over time by religion-based organizing principles. The study distinguishes between organizations operating directly out of the sending country and organizations arising out of the political and cultural opportunity structure in the destination country. The ultimate aim is to explore to what extent "religion" matters for immigrant organizations and how those in turn may influence the role immigrant organizations play in the integration of migrants.*

Introduction

Immigrants in Europe are no longer just targets of immigration policies but have become increasingly political actors themselves. Their activities have been manifested in different spheres of life in the receiving countries. An important means and platform for their activities have been immigrant organizations. Immigrants have found refuge in these organizations based on nationality, religion or both. These immigrant organizations are not isolated from the outside world. They operate with and are increasingly involved in the politics of their home societies as well as their host country. In other words, these organizations transgress national boundaries; they operate at multiple sites and across a geographic scope ranging from the local to the global. In this sense, they are truly "transnational."

The transnational transactions of immigrant organizations and immigrants are not confined to the economic and political realm. Religion plays a decisive role in many cases.[1] This essay is based on a larger ongoing research project of the author that aims to explore the overall extent, implications and determinants of cross-border political relationships initiated and maintained by Turkish immigrant organizations in the Netherlands (and Germany) with their home country.[2] This essay draws on the evolution of specific Turkish *religious* immigrant organizations in the Netherlands to highlight the type and scale of influence of the home countries on immigrant organizations in the host countries. This essay concentrates on two case studies, covering the period 1960–2000. The case studies have been selected on the basis of how these

Correspondence Address: Gamze Avcı, Department of Turkish Studies, Leiden University, P.O. Box 9515, 2300 RA Leiden, The Netherlands. Email: g.avci@let.leidenuniv.nl

ISSN 1468-3849 Print/1743-9663 Online/05/020201-13 © 2005 Taylor & Francis Group Ltd
DOI: 10.1080/14683840500119536

202   *G. Avcı*

organizations have emerged in the context of political and institutional opportunity structures in the receiving country. The selected cases are *Diyanet* (operating from Turkey) and *Milli Görüş* (emerged from political opportunity structure in the Netherlands). These two cases represent the major groups of Turkish-Islamic associations in Europe: those that are advocating a more orthodox conservative vision and those controlled by the Turkish General Directorate for Religious Affairs, which represents the official secular line in Turkey. The essay will first outline the relevant literature on immigrant organizations; second, discuss the general characteristics of Turkish migrant organizations in Europe and the Netherlands in particular, and finally map out the two case studies in the Netherlands.

Literature Review of Immigrant Organizations

According to the immigration literature, immigrant organizations fulfill many functions.[3] Yet, it is still unclear whether and what kind of role they play in immigrant integration. Thus, the word is still out on whether they function like or serve as a *bastion* (stronghold) or else a *bindmittel* (adhesive) in the host society.[4] One of the prime reasons for their controversial role in integration is the links they sustain with their respective home countries.[5]

A large extent of the discussions on immigrant organizations takes place in the theoretical context of transnationalism and transnationalization.[6] The consequences and impact of transnational activities on integration are disputed. Some argue that transnational political loyalty and political incorporation are not mutually exclusive,[7] though still others argue that immigrant organizations inhibit integration.[8]

Immigrants' involvement in politics "here" and "there" is referred to as "political" transnationalism. This involves the political activities of party officials, governmental functionaries, or community leaders whose main goals are the achievement of political power and influence in the home or host country.[9] In general, the relationship between countries of origin and voluntary associations, as well as political integration, is rarely discussed in the context of multicultural societies in Europe. Theorization on the topic within the transnational literature has been confined mostly to the United States.[10] Within this literature, there is no agreement on whether immigrants who have stronger ties to their countries of origin end up less integrated or not. Frequently, the pull to "home" is seen as transnationalism, which serves to give immigrants a sense of empowerment.[11] The discussion on how the "new" generations of immigrants will fare is open-ended and undecided.[12] Within these studies, the role of the country of origin has been particularly highlighted. It has been claimed that migrants are often subject to considerable political pressure by the institutions of the country of origin.[13]

The influence that the institutions in the country of origin exercise on migrant organizations manifests itself in a variety of ways. Some countries seek to hold onto "their" migrants for the sake of the nation, and thus "sell" nationalism abroad. Other regimes oppose and hold up their emigrants, especially those who are disapproving of the regime in their country of origin, or who even reject or resist the state itself.[14]

Hence, some researchers in the United States have worked on delineating the differences between policies of the home countries *vis-à-vis* their immigrants abroad.[15] Others have taken this further by questioning whether there is such a thing as a class of political "transmigrants," i.e., immigrants who become involved in their home country politics on a regular basis.[16]

The host society has also been targeted in studies on immigrant organizations. Some argue that host societies are critical in shaping the collective organization of migrants,[17] yet others claim that when the "transnational element" is included, the differentiation between inclusive/exclusive political structures in the host society does not hold (i.e., these people involved in immigrant organizations will not be politically promoted in mainstream politics).[18] Thus local institutional structures are perceived as obstacles to "transnational" political practices among immigrant organizations.

Turkish Immigrant Organizations Abroad

The general landscape of Turkish immigrant organizations in Europe has been mapped out in depth.[19] *Diyanet* and its network in the Netherlands and Germany,[20] and *Milli Görüş* in Germany,[21] have been subjects for case studies. Comparative work is rare, though, and this will be undertaken in the current essay.[22] Transnational features have been examined also in the Turkish context.[23] Similar to other migrant communities, Turkish transnational activities have emerged because they are sources of information and offer opportunities for political mobilization despite existing barriers.[24] In particular, religion has been analyzed as a transnational factor.[25] Studies have also focused on Turkish political Islam and the transnational dimension of Turkish Islamic organizations.[26]

Differentiation of migrant organizations can be based on a number of factors.[27] In the case of Turkish migrant organizations certain characteristics are underlined. A 2003 study emphasizes that in Germany, traditional class-based imported factions were popular in the 1960s, 1970s and 1980s, but in the 1990s there was a tendency towards local collective action associations with ethnocultural orientations (ethnocultural organizations increase at the expense of class ideology).[28] There is significance to the type of migrants involved.[29] Political migrants mostly control the leadership positions in these organizations and a strong element of competition among the organizations remains.[30] Research in the Netherlands underlines the interconnectedness of migrant organizations (through board members) and their high density. It is also pointed out that in the Netherlands, the political opportunity structure for migrant organizations emerged in the 1980s, as financial support became available and there was increased legitimacy for these organizations.[31] Continual organizational growth is observed as well.[32] In terms of development, it is claimed that many of them are still at a "preliminary" stage of development and have not fully "matured" yet. Inter-generational conflict and political divisions haunt them and have led to the decline of many immigrant organizations.[33] When it comes to policies related to the host state, a so-called "ideological convergence" is visible.[34] This means that many of the organizations have similar attitudes towards the host country. Their influence on the host country remains limited, however.[35] In countries like Germany, in particular, the difficulty of obtaining citizenship and the lack of access to policymaking through corporatist channels weakens their influence.[36]

There is high organizational fragmentation among Turkish immigrant organizations in the host countries. In addition, organizations have difficulties to overcome their differences. Orientation-wise, organizations mimic/parallel the situation in their homeland and are largely patterned along the lines of political and religious cleavages in Turkey. Size-wise, Turkish immigrant organizations are much larger in Germany and are perceived as agenda-setters for Turkish organizations in the Netherlands or a potential source of domination among them. The activities and orientations of immigrant organizations attract a lot of attention, in particular; the question on whether these organizations concentrate on "immigrant politics," "homeland politics" or have a dual agenda.[37] It is argued frequently that Turkey sets the agenda of Turkish immigrant organizations abroad.[38]

Turkish Migrants and their Organizations in the Netherlands

Turkish migration to the Netherlands began in the 1960s. It was first reported by Statistics Netherlands (*Centraal Bureau voor de Statistiek*, CBS) in 1960. There were 100 Turkish immigrants in 1960, compared to 341,000 today. Initially it was labor migrants that came. This was based on the agreement signed by the Dutch and Turkish governments in 1964. With the economic recession in the mid-1970s, the demand for labor slowed down and resulted in an official stop to migration in 1974. Yet, family reunification and formation schemes led to an increase in the numbers of women and children. Furthermore, in the 1980s, political refugees came. Most of them chose Amsterdam, Rotterdam, Utrecht, Twente and cities in mid-Brabant, where the demand for unskilled labor was the highest in the 1960s and 1970s. Most of the Turks (about 96 percent) consider themselves Muslims, although there are differences among them. It is estimated that 15–35 percent are Alevites. Most of the Turkish migrants in the Netherlands come from small villages in the central part of Turkey or the Black Sea coast. The Turkish migrants that come from the big cities (Istanbul, Izmir and Ankara) are a minority. Two hundred thousand have dual nationality.[39]

Over the years, Dutch integration policy has received a series of different mandates as to the course it should take. The so-called minorities' policy of the 1980s targeted the promotion of integration whilst retaining one's own culture and identity, which promoted in turn the development of ethnic self-organizations. The idea was to promote and conserve cultural identities, emancipate their constituency and function as a pressure group. From the middle of the 1990s onwards, the term "active citizenship," with its concomitant rights and duties, was regarded as the decisive guideline for immigrants' participation in society. Greater emphasis was also placed on individual integration into mainstream institutions.

The Turks have been very active in the formation of organizations. The Institute for Migration and Ethnic Studies (IMES) of the University of Amsterdam lists 1,126 different Turkish migrant organizations.[40] Turks began to build their ethnic community around 1978 and their organization density increased almost every year.[41] These organizations reflected the political and religious cleavages in the home country. At times they emerged due to the opportunities in the host country or otherwise as a reaction to the home country. Some were established by the host country as a platform. A large number of them happen to be religiously oriented.

The largest part of the mosques are connected to the *Diyanet* and are members of the Foundation of the Turkish-Islamic Cultural Federation (*Stichting Turks-Islamitische Culturele Federatie*, TICF) and the Islamic Foundation Netherlands (*Islamitische Stichting Nederland*, ISN). *Diyanet* represents the official Islam of Turkey and is regulated by the Turkish government. The so-called parallel Islam is reflected in *Milli Görüş* (MG) and the Foundation of the Islamic Center Netherlands (*Stichting Islamitisch Centrum Nederland*, SICN). The Alevites and Bektaşis are united in the Federation of Alevite and Bektaşi Associations (*Federatie van Alevitische en Bektashistische verenigingen*, HAK-DER) and represent a more liberal Islamic stream. On the left side of the political spectrum are the HTIB (which was until the end of the 1980s the most influential Turkish organization), the women's organization HTKF and the smaller DSDF. On the right side of the political spectrum are the umbrella organization Turkish Federation Netherlands (*Turkse Federatie Nederland*, HTDF, officially *Federatie van Idealistische Democratische Turkse Organisaties in Nederland*, the Federation of Idealistic Democratic Turkish Organizations in the Netherlands) and the Turkish Islamic Federation (*Turks Islamitische Federatie*). It is claimed that the latter have close ties with the unofficial militant arm of the National Movement Party (*Milliyetçi Hareket Partisi*, MHP) known as the Grey Wolves. Lastly, there is the Federation of Turkish Sports and Culture in the Netherlands (*Federatie van Turkse Sport en Cultuur in Nederland*). Most of these organizations are represented in the *Inspraak Orgaan Turken* (IOT). These are only the main organizations. There are many other smaller ones.

Milli Görüş

Milli Görüş is among the leading Turkish migrant organizations in Europe.[42] Still, the organization is viewed differently in each host country. While it is considered a constitutional threat in Germany,[43] it is more accepted in the Netherlands. The organization's vision has its roots in Turkey and many developments within the organization have reflected and reacted to political changes in Turkey. The term "*Milli Görüş*" (National Vision) reflects a nationalistic-religious vision and has been the key concept in the ideology of Islamic parties in Turkey. It is openly critical of the secular system in Turkey and has been known to advocate the *shari'a*.

Milli Görüş in the Netherlands (initially Federation of Associations and Communities of Muslims, *Federatie van Verenigingen en Gemeenschappen van Moslims*, later in May 1987 renamed Netherlands Islamic Federation, *Nederlandse Islamitische Federatie*, NIF) began its activities in Rotterdam in 1975. The Dutch *Milli Görüş* distances itself from the German *Milli Görüş* because the German counterpart is

206   *G. Avcı*

considered to be a "constitutional threat" in Germany. *Milli Görüş* in the Netherlands also denies any links to political parties in Turkey. Since 1997, *Milli Görüş* has been divided into two regional organizations reflecting similar divisions as in Turkey: *Zuid-Nederland* (South Netherlands) and *Noord-Nederland* (North Netherlands). Although the two political streams (the AKP versus the SP-line) in Turkey cannot be necessarily distinguished on a regional basis, the similarity is in that we see a more progressive and a more conservative branch. *Milli Görüş Zuid-Nederland* has a network of 18 mosque organizations and about 40 youth and women's associations. *Milli Görüş Noord-Nederland* has about 20 local associations linked to it, mostly mosque associations. Hacı Karacaer, the director of MG North Netherlands, appears as the new, moderate face of *Milli Görüş*, although some politicians and journalists in the Netherlands remain skeptical because it is unknown whether his tolerant opinions (on integration in the Netherlands or emancipation, for example) are also shared by MG supporters, or whether this is a one-man show.

Necmettin Erbakan, who is considered the ideologue of the "national vision," has frequently visited the European branches and is in particular supported by the South Netherlands branch of the organization. It is known that the European wing of the organization has provided funds and massive moral support for Erbakan over the years. There is political intertwining between *Milli Görüş* Europe and Turkey. *Milli Görüş* members have run for political office in Turkey and members of the movement in Turkey have joined the ranks within *Milli Görüş*, especially in Germany.[44]

At this point it is relevant to look closely at what the movement has advocated. The political vision of the Islamist parties in Turkey is based on a certain way of interpreting Muslim history and Western influence in the world. They argue that the Muslim World has experienced a decline for several centuries, although it used to be more advanced than the West. They explain their greatness with the moral and spiritual strength that comes from the nation's faith (*iman*). As Turkey has imitated Western values and utilized inappropriate Western technology by a Western-oriented elite it has fallen behind. They point to a better future when Turkey properly blends and synthesizes moral-spiritual (Islam) and material development.

Political movements or organizations of Turkish migrants abroad are closely tied to Turkish politics. In the case of *Milli Görüş* there are close ties to some political parties in Turkey. *Milli Görüş*'s vision is linked strongly to political parties associated with a political Islamic tradition, starting with the National Salvation Party (*Milli Selamet Partisi*, MSP), the Welfare Party (*Refah Partisi*, RP), the Virtue Party (*Fazilet Partisi*, FP) and the Felicity Party (*Saadet Partisi*, SP). The FP, which was closed down in 2001, split into two parties. SP is under the control of the traditionalists (*gelenekçiler*), whereas the second party, the Justice and Development Party (*Adalet ve Kalkınma Partisi*, AKP) is seen as the reformist (*yenilikçi*) wing of the movement. The AKP has taken a different approach to political Islam than the classical line. Their discourse is more sophisticated; they avoid confrontational rhetoric and plead for democracy and human rights.

This development—where SP and AKP have split the one Islamic party tradition in Turkey—is quite important, as it seems to be paralleled by the movement in the

Netherlands, although it should be noted that rather than mimicking what has been happening in Turkey, the role of Hacı Karacaer and other *Milli Görüş Noord* members has been crucial. In other words, rather than following developments within the religious-conservative movement in Turkey, these people may have been crucial in inducing change independently within their organization in the Netherlands. Secondly, it is important as the AKP, which has been in government since 2002, has sustained its sympathy to *Milli Görüş*. In 2003, under the AKP government, the Foreign Ministry issued a memorandum to Turkish embassies that said they should cooperate with *Milli Görüş*. This was a critical change as *Milli Görüş* has always been considered an unacceptable movement to the establishment in Turkey.

A significant re-styling emerged in the late 1980s, when more emphasis was placed on problems related to the host country rather than to the country of origin. In terms of activities, *Milli Görüş* offers a broad range of services such as Koran courses, religious education to children and youth, homework help, language courses, orientation courses, mosque services, weddings, funerals, Friday prayers, *hajj* pilgrimages, religious books, moral support, sports activities, support for women, assistance for mothers. They have also established their own schools. In their efforts, they strive for more political participation and influence in decision-making. Their rhetoric focuses on education, dialogue and the permanent presence of Islam. Increasingly they do this in Dutch, and involve increasingly the second generation of migrants. Their evolution has been described as one where, "As the political space expanded, along with the weakening of the state, *Milli Görüş* evolved from [an] anti-capitalist, anti-Zionist, and anti-Western movement into [a] pro-capitalist, pro-democratic and pro-European Union movement."[45] Their dilemma, however is that often they are not seen as sincere, but as having a dual agenda or two faces: "The movement has two faces: one modern, friendly, particularly focused on the consultation with and social elevation of Turkish youth and an intolerant, orthodox, anti-Western face."[46]

Diyanet

Diyanet (Directorate for Religious Affairs),[47] the largest Turkish organization in the Netherlands, is based on two organizations: TICF (Turkish Islamic Cultural Federation, *Turks Islamitisch Culturele Federatie*) and ISN (Islamic Foundation Netherlands, *Islamitische Stichting Nederland*). TICF was established in January 31, 1979 with 17 mosque organizations as an organization close to *Diyanet*. The aim was to sustain contacts with *Diyanet* in Turkey, support mosque associations and spread Islam in the Netherlands, but it was also clearly meant as a reaction to the *Süleymancılar*, a rival of *Diyanet*'s and a Sufi-based religious order.[48] The ISN, the Dutch branch of *Diyanet*, was established in 1982. ISN and TICF work closely together. Today there are 143 mosque associations as members. There is some sort of division of labor between the two organizations. TICF focuses on social and cultural affairs, whereas ISN deals with religious matters. This division, referred to as the external versus internal face,[49] is to counter criticism that it is an instrument of the Turkish government.[50]

208   G. Avcı

Diyanet was founded as a reaction to the formation of extremist Islamist organizations abroad and reflects the more "secular" approach of the Turkish state. *Diyanet* uses a "franchised authority structure to promote Kemalist-Islamic identity compatible with the Turkish regime."[51] This makes it on the one hand an extension of the Turkish state abroad and at the same time very vulnerable to changes and movements within the Turkish polity. The activities of *Diyanet* are geared towards the preservation of the cultural and religious identity of Turks abroad. Since 1985 its main seat has been in Cologne. Besides members' contributions it is largely funded by the Turkish state.

Diyanet in the Turkish context can be considered to have a monopoly over religious activities. In that sense certain religious movements (e.g., *Süleymancılar*, *Milli Görüş*), which found more operating space in Europe, have presented a challenge to *Diyanet*. Before the 1980s there was little interest (in *Diyanet*) outside of Turkey. A new role was given to *Diyanet* in the 1980s when it emerged that anti-Kemalist movements were freely active in Europe and had an impact on politics in Turkey. In that sense when *Diyanet* came to the Netherlands in the 1980s and also in latter moves, its style has been mostly "reactive."[52] *Diyanet* aims to encourage the full integration of Turkish Muslims within the host society.[53]

Structure-wise, *Diyanet* abroad is guided by the religious affairs unit (*Din Hizmetleri Müşavirlikleri*) of the Turkish Embassies or the Religious Services Attaches of the Consulates. *Diyanet* abroad has been susceptible to changes in the mother country. The growth of *Diyanet* in Turkey is also paralleled by the growth of *Diyanet* abroad. In Turkey, *Diyanet* employed 53,000 personnel in 1980 and 90,000 in 1995. In 1981, *Diyanet* had 81 personnel abroad compared to 600 in 1989.[54] In 1995, the number of paid *imams* was 750.

Diyanet abroad has the same function as in Turkey. In other words, it is active in building, maintaining and operating mosques and it employs *imams*. Their activities also include: organization of religious events (*hajj/ümre*, *kurban*, burial funds and religious education), sociocultural activities (conferences, inter-faith dialogues, exhibitions, soccer matches, national and religious celebrations) and courses geared towards literacy, computer use, hobbies, language and professional education, wrestling competitions and maintaining a library.

It is often argued that the Turkish government exercises influence in the Netherlands through *Diyanet*, which is permitted to appoint *imams* for the 140 Turkish mosques in the country. These *imams* are Turkish civil servants and complete their training in Turkey, after which they are usually dispatched for four years to the Netherlands. The discussion on the role *imams* have held has been ongoing since the 1980s. The questions converge around whether non-integrated *imams* can fulfill these functions and secondly whether *imams* who work in Dutch mosques should be educated in the Netherlands, or in the countries of origin. The Dutch Government has decided that all *imams* and other spiritual leaders recruited in Islamic countries must first follow a one-year integration course before they are allowed to practice in the country. Another issue of concern has been that the texts for Friday prayers originate from Turkey and present an unwanted foreign influence.

Conclusion

The expression of transnationalism can have many dimensions and meanings. The intensification of transport and communication, availability of mass media, remittances to the home country, and dual citizenship are classically cited as such. Immigrant organizations happen to be another element of transnationalism. They are also in a position to constantly evolve, as constellations in the home country, the receiving country and the migrant population change.

This essay has looked at two Turkish migrant organizations in the Netherlands: one established as an Islamic movement operating in the Netherlands (*Milli Görüş*), the other an organization that is an extension of a bureaucratic unit of the Turkish government (*Diyanet*). Given the complex web of characteristics and intertwining relationships of Turkish organizations in the Netherlands, certain findings can be pointed out.

Milli Görüş has evolved out of a continuing political Islamic movement in Turkey. Throughout its existence in Europe, its interlocking politics or political involvement with Turkey has continued. As the left–right polarization among Turkish organizations has diminished, it has evolved into a stronger movement in the Netherlands and in Europe using its own philosophy. Islam has helped to mobilize people for the organization. However, over time, its emphasis has shifted more towards the issues surrounding migrants in the Netherlands rather than "home country oriented politics." It has always emphasized religion in its activities and Islamic rhetoric rather than Turkish nationality, although it has toned down the more "radical" elements. The split between a more traditional and a more reformist *Milli Görüş* that occurred in the Netherlands (along the regional lines) resembles much of the split between the AKP and SP in Turkey. The more progressive approach of Hacı Karacaer of *Milli Görüş*, which evolved from *Noord-Nederland*, reflects a more modern and softer version of the National Vision movement as opposed to the *Zuid-Nederland* branch. This, in many ways, seems to parallel the AKP's route in Turkey.

Milli Görüş's emphasis on religion rather than nationality has been different from *Diyanet*. If one would have to differentiate between *Diyanet* and *Milli Görüş*, it could be said that the rank order for *Diyanet* has been first Turkish then Muslim (or at least it focused on Turkish Muslims), whereas *Milli Görüş* has been focusing on being primarily Muslim; ethnicity and nationality are of lesser importance. *Diyanet* by definition is "objective" and not necessarily close to any political party or movement. However, the position of *Diyanet* has always been discussed in Turkey (as it is in the Netherlands). For secularists it is never secular enough, for more religious Turks it is never religious enough. Since the AKP's ascent to power in 2002, given that some of its leaders have *Milli Görüş* roots, the position of *Diyanet* may change in Turkey. It has the potential to become more of a conservative religious force under the AKP and may lose out on its position of being the "protector" of secular principles. Although marginal, this change is already felt in certain ways and has repercussions for *Diyanet* abroad as well. On the other hand, with the

210   *G. Avcı*

ongoing EU–Turkey rapprochement, *Diyanet* may obtain a more independent position in Turkish politics and reach out to other organizations and movements.

An interesting development has been that the organizations of *Milli Görüş* in Europe, due to the changing political circumstances in Turkey, are now more of an acceptable partner for the Turkish state. This may also turn the relationship between *Milli Görüş* and *Diyanet* into less of an "adversarial" relationship. In that sense, it is clear that political changes in the home country can make or break the relationship between organizations abroad. They can also "redefine" the relationship towards the home country. The rapprochement between the "official" (supported by the state) and the "parallel" Islam in Europe could be one of the outcomes. Furthermore, the Welfare Party at some point advocated the privatization of *Diyanet*.[55] Today the AKP can do this under the banner of the EU and establish an independent *Diyanet*. This would also change *Diyanet*'s position abroad.

The changes in the political climate in the Netherlands present a challenge to both organizations. Financially, *Milli Görüş* is more independent than *Diyanet*. The Turkish government financially backs *Diyanet* and its political strength depends on the continued official dialogue with the government. Furthermore, *Diyanet* competes with and contains "conservative-religious" elements. Finally, we see that each organization continues to offer its own activities and courses with its distinctive flavors. This is not too foreign to Dutch politics, where there was a tradition of institutionalizing religious and cultural interests on a group basis. The question is how representative these Turkish migrant organizations are and whether this will work in a "depillarizing" society like the Netherlands.

Notes

1.   Peggy Levitt, "'You Know, Abraham Was Really the First Immigrant': Religion and Transnational Migration," *International Migration Review*, Vol.37 No.3 (2003), pp.847–73; Peggy Levitt, "Local-Level Global Religion: U.S.–Dominican Migration," *Journal for the Scientific Study of Religion*, Vol.37 (1998), pp.74–89; Susanne H. Rudolph and James Piscatori (eds.), *Transnational Religion and Fading States* (Boulder, CO: Westview Press, 1997).

2.   This essay is based on an ongoing larger project—funded by the Netherlands Scientific Council—that aims to explore the extent, implications and determinants of cross-border political relationships initiated and maintained by Turkish immigrant organizations in the Netherlands (and Germany) with their home country.

3.   Marlou Schrover, "Immigrant Organizations in the Netherlands, Then and Now," Paper for the Workshop "Paths of Integration: Similarities and Differences in the Settlement," Osnabrück, June 19–21, 2003, ⟨http://www.imis.uni-osnabrueck.de/biling/papers/schrover.pdf⟩.

4.   Rinus Penninx and Marlou Schrover, *Bastion of Bindmiddel? organisaties van immigranten in historisch perspectief* (Amsterdam: Het Spinhuis, 2001).

5.   Nedim Ögelman, Jeannette Money and Philip Martin, "Immigrant Cohesion and Political Access in Influencing Foreign Policy," *SAIS Review*, Vol.22, No.2 (2002); Nedim Ögelman, "Documenting and Explaining the Persistence of Homeland Politics Among Germany's Turks," *International Migration Review* (2003), pp.163–93; Eva K. Østergaard-Nielsen, *Trans-State Loyalties and Politics of Turks and Kurds in Western Europe* (London: Routledge, 2003).

6.   Thomas Faist, *The Volume and Dynamics of International Migration and Transnational Social Spaces* (Oxford: Oxford University Press, 2000); Al-Ali Nadje and Khalid Koser (eds.), *New*

Religion, Transnationalism and Turks in Europe   211

Approaches to Migration: Transnational Communities and the Transformation of Home (London: Routledge, 2002); Peter Kivisto, "Theorizing Transnational Immigration: A Critical Review of Current Efforts," *Ethnic and Racial Studies*, Vol.24, No.4 (2001), pp.549–77; Steven Vertovec, "Transnationalism and Identity," *Journal of Ethnic and Migration Studies*, Vol.27, No.4 (2001), pp.573–82.

7. Hassan Bousetta, "Institutional Theories of Immigrant Ethnic Mobilisation: Relevance and limitations," *Journal of Ethnic and Migration Studies*, Vol.26, No.2 (2000), pp.229–45; Meindert Fennema and Jean Tillie, "Civic Community, Political Participation and Political Trust of Ethnic Groups," *Connections*, Vol.23, No.2 (2000), pp.44–59; Anja van Heelsum, "Political Participation of Migrants in the Netherlands," Paper presented at Metropolis Conference, November 13–20, 2000.

8. F. Bilgi, "Milli Görüş und Integration," *Yazinca*, No.17 (1997).

9. J. Itzigsohn, "Immigration and the Boundaries of Citizenship: The Institutions of Immigrants' Political Transnationalism," *International Migration Review*, Vol.34 No.4 (Fall 2000), pp.1126–54.

10. Luis E. Guarnizo, "On the Political Participation of Transnational Migrants: Old Practices and New Trends," in Gary Gerstle and John Mollenkopf (eds.), *E Pluribus Unum? Contemporary and Historical Perspectives on Immigrant Political Incorporation* (New York: Russell Sage, 2001), pp.213–63; L. E. Guarnizo, "The Rise of Transnational Social Formations: Mexican and Dominican State Responses to Transnational Migration," *Political Power and Social Theory*, Vol.12 (1996), pp.45–94; Michael Jones-Correa, "The Study of Transnationalism among the Children of Immigrants: Where We Are and Where We Should Be Headed," in Peggy Levitt and Mary Waters (eds.), *The Changing Face of Home: The Transnational Lives of the Second Generation* (New York: Russell Sage, 2002), pp.221–41; Michael Jones-Correa, *Between Two Nations: The Political Predicament of Latinos in New York City* (Ithaca, NY: Cornell University Press, 1998).

11. Jorge Duany, "Quisqueya on the Hudson: The Transnational Identity of Dominicans in Washington Heights," *Dominican Research Monographs* (New York: CUNY Dominican Studies Institute: 1994).

12. Levitt and Waters (2002).

13. Bryan R. Roberts *et al.*, "Transnational Migrant Communities and Mexican Migration to the US," *Ethnic and Racial Studies*, Vol.22 (1999), p.262.

14. Jones-Correa (1998); for the Cuban example, see Maria de los Angeles Torres, *In the Land of Mirrors: Cuban Exile Politics in the United States* (Ann Arbor, MI: University of Michigan Press, 1999).

15. Peggy Levitt and Raphael de la Dehesa, "Transnational Migration and the Redefinition of the State: Variations and Explanations," *Ethnic and Racial Studies*, Vol.26, No.4 (2003).

16. Luis E. Guarnizo, Alejandro Portes and William Haller, "From Assimilation to Transnationalism: Determinants of Transnational Political Action Among Contemporary Migrants," working paper, Center for Migration and Development, Princeton University, 2002, ⟨http://cmd.princeton.edu/CMD_Working_Papers/wp0107.pdf⟩.

17. Jeroen Doomernik, "The Institutionalisation of Turkish Islam and Germany and the Netherlands: A Comparison," *Ethnic and Racial Studies*, Vol.18, No.1 (1995), pp.46–63.

18. Eva K. Østergaard-Nielsen, "The Politics of Migrants' Transnational Political Practices," WPTC-01-22 (2001), Paper given at "Transnational Migration: Comparative Perspectives", Princeton University, 30 June–1 July 2001, <http://www.transcomm.ox.ac.uk/working%20papers/WPTC-01-22%20Ostergaard.doc.pdf>.

19. Canan Atılgan, "Türkische politische Organisationen in der Bundesrepublik Deutschland," Konrad Adenauer Stiftung Kommunalpolitik Paper No.9, 1999, <http://www.kas.de/upload/kommunalpolitik/materialien_vor_ort/9.pdf>; Özcan Ertekin, *Türkische Immigrantenorganisationen in der Bundesrepublik Deutschland* (Berlin: Hitit, 1992); M. Fennema and J. Tillie, "Ethnic Associations: Creating Networks within the Turkish Community," UNESCO-MPMC Project 1997, <http://www.unesco.org/most/p97.htm>; A. van Heelsum, J. Tillie and M. Fennema, *Turkse organisaties in Nederland: Een Netwerkanalyse* (Amsterdam: Het Spinhuis, 1996); J. Fijalkowski and H.Gillmeister, *Ausländervereine – Ein Forschungsbericht* (Berlin: Hitit, 1997); S. Küçükhüseyin,

212   *G. Avcı*

"Türkische politische Organisationen in Deutschland," Konrad Adenauer Stiftung Zukunftsforum Politik, 2002, <http://www.kas.de/publikationen/2002/855_dokument.html>; Thomas Lemmen, *Türkisch-islamische Organisationen in Deutschland: Eine Handreichung* (Verlag für Christlich–Islamisches Schrifttum Altenberge, 1998).

20. N. Landman, "Sustaining Turkish-Islamic loyalties: The *Diyanet* in Western Europe," in Suha Taji-Farouki and Hugh Poulton (eds.), *Muslim Identity and the Balkan State* (London: Hurst, 1997), pp.214–31; Günter Seufert, "Die Milli Görüş Bewegung," in Günter Seufert and Jacques Waardenburg (eds.), *Turkish Islam and Europe* (Stuttgart: Steiner, 1999), pp.295–322.

21. G. Seufert, "Türkisch-Islamische Union der türkischen Religionsbehörde (DITIB)," in Seufert and Waardenburg (1999), pp.261–92.

22. L. Yalçın-Heckmann, "The Perils of Associational Life in Europe: Turkish Migrants in Germany and France," in Tariq Madood and Pnina Werbner (eds.), *The Politics of Multiculturalism in New Europe* (London: Zed Books, 1998), pp.95–110.

23. Riva Kastoryano, "Transnational Participation and Citizenship: Immigrants in the European Union," Technical Report NEC Paper No.64, National Europe Centre, ANU, 2003.

24. Yalçın-Heckmann (1998).

25. J. Waardenburg, "The Institutionalization of Islam, 1961–1986," In T. Gerholm and Y. G. Lithman (eds.), *The New Islamic Presence in Europe* (London: Mansell, 1988), pp.8–31; P. van Veer, "Transnational Religion," Working Paper No.01-06, Princeton University Center for Migration and Development, 2001, <http://www.cmd.princeton.edu/Papers_pages/trans_mig.htm>; Thijl Sunier, "Explaining the Reactions of Nations to Religious Newcomers," Paper presented at the workshop "Paths of Integration," Osnabrück, June 19–21, 2003, <http://www.imis.uni-osnabrueck.de/biling/papers/sunier.pdf>.

26. Werner Schiffauer, "Islam as a Civil Religion: Political Culture and the Organisation of Diversity in Germany," in Madood and Werbner (1998), pp.147–66; V. Amiraux, "Turkish Political Islam and Europe: Story of an Opportunistic Intimacy," in Stefano Allievi and Jørgen S. Nielsen, *Muslim Networks and Transnational Communities in and across Europe* (London: E. J. Brill, 2003), pp.146–69.

27. Schrover (2003).

28. Ögelman (2003).

29. Yalçın-Heckmann (1998).

30. Ibid.

31. F. Vermeulen, "Immigration Policy and Ethnic Organizations in Amsterdam, 1960–1990: A Local Historical Approach," Paper presented at European Consortium for Political Research meeting in Turin, March 22–27, 2002.

32. Ibid.

33. Yalçın-Heckmann (1998).

34. Ibid.

35. Ögelman (2003).

36. Ögelman, Money and Martin (2002).

37. Østergaard-Nielsen (2003).

38. Ögelman (2003); Yalçın-Heckmann (1998).

39. A. Fermin, H. Hufen and S. Van der Hijden, *Eindrapportage Rol Overheden Landen van Herkomst: Turkije en Marokko*, Aaanvullend bronnenderonderzoek voor de Tijdelijke Commissie Onderzoek Integratiebeleid, Sept. 10, 2003.

40. See <http://www2.fmg.uva.nl/imes/turks.xls>; and Heelsum, Tillie and Fennema (1996).

41. Vermeulen (2002), p.20.

42. Generous estimates claim that it has about 300,000 followers in Europe. Its strongest support is in Germany.

43. Germany's domestic intelligence agency has repeatedly warned about MG's activities, describing the group in its annual reports as a "foreign extremist organization," oriented toward Islamic law "as opposed to ideological pluralism in a secular state."

Religion, Transnationalism and Turks in Europe 213

44. Between 1995 and 1999, Osman Yumakoğullari, a former chair of MG Germany and other known leading members of MG Germany (Azım Genç/Abdullah Gencer and Şevket Yılmaz) became MPs in the Turkish Parliament. Approximately 30 MG Germany members (unsuccessfully) put up their candidacy, Küçükhüseyin (2002). Another intertwining was more on the family level. Mehmet Sabri Erbakan, a nephew of Necmettin Erbakan, led MG Germany between 1996 and 2002.

45. H. Yavuz, "Conversations Within Islam: Culture, Politics and Religion in the Global Public Sphere. A Forum of Leading Younger Islamist Scholars and Activists," Central European University, Budapest, May 29, 2003 <http://www.humanities.uci.edu/history/levineconference/MLbudapesttranscriptedit2.pdf>.

46. Author's own translation, quoted from J. Den Exter, "Turkse organisaties en stromingen," in *Handboek Minderheden 1999*, 7/1050-3-10 (Houten/Lelystad: Bohn Stafleu Van Loghum/Koninglijke Vermande, 1999).

47. Established in Turkey in 1924. It supports Sunni Islam and was established to administer mosques and appoint *imams*.

48. T. Sunier, *Islam in Beweging: Turkse Jongeren en Islamitische Organisaties* (Amsterdam: Het Spinhuis, 1996), p.65.

49. K. Canatan, *Turkse Islam: Perspektieven op organisatievorming en leiderschap in Nederland* (Rotterdam: Proefschrift Erasmus University, 2001).

50. Ibid., p.89.

51. Ögelman (2003), p.169.

52. See Doomernik (1995), p.10.

53. Ibid., p.13.

54. Landman (1997).

55. Sunier (1996), p.58.

[8]

Journal of Ethnic and Migration Studies
Vol. 30, No. 5, September 2004, pp. 879–894

 Carfax Publishing
Taylor & Francis Group

Beyond Migration: Islam as a Transnational Public Space

John R. Bowen

Recent studies of transnational religious phenomena have emphasised the importance of distinguishing between transnational processes of migration and movement on the one hand, and diasporic forms of consciousness, identity, and cultural creation on the other. While this distinction is useful, it risks directing the study of transnational social phenomena in certain, limited directions. Migration and diaspora insufficiently take into account the possibility of quite distinct self-understandings about boundaries and legitimacy on the part of both 'host' countries and 'immigrant' populations. Taking 'Islam in France' as an illuminating case in point because each of its two constitutive terms challenges the possibility of self-defining through migration and diaspora, I argue that transnational Islam creates and implies the existence and legitimacy of a global public space of normative reference and debate, and that this public space cannot be reduced to a dimension of migration or of transnational religious movements. I offer two brief ethnographic examples of this transnational public space, and maintain that even as it develops references to Europe it implies neither a 'Euro-Islam' nor a 'post-national' sense of European membership and citizenship. Rather, current directions of debate and discussion in France are strongly shaped by, first, French efforts to define Islam within national political and cultural boundaries, and, second, efforts by Muslim intellectuals to maintain the transnational legitimacy of Islamic knowledge.

Keywords: Diaspora; France; Islam; Religion; Transnationalism

Recent studies of transnational religious phenomena have emphasised the importance of distinguishing between transnational processes of migration and movement on the one hand, and diasporic forms of consciousness, identity and cultural creation on the other (Levitt 2001a; Vertovec 2000). While this distinction is useful (and subtly deployed by these authors), it risks directing the study of transnational social

John R. Bowen is Dunbar-Van Cleve Professor in Arts & Sciences at Washington University in St. Louis, USA, where he is also Professor of Anthropology and Chair of Social Thought and Analysis. Correspondence to: Prof. John Bowen, Box 1114, Washington University, 1 Brookings Dr, St. Louis MO 63130. E-mail: jbowen@wustl.edu

ISSN 1369–183X print/ISSN 1469–9451 online/04/050879-16 © 2004 Taylor & Francis Ltd
DOI: 10.1080/1369183042000245598
Cafax Publishing

phenomena in certain, limited directions. If 'transnationalism' is mainly about migration and its variable aftermaths, it is a short step to suggesting that it be subsumed under the category of cultural assimilation (as recently advocated by Kivisto 2001), leaving 'diaspora' to designate populations living outside putative 'homelands' as well as the self-understandings held by those populations (Saint-Blancat 2002; Vertovec 1997).

Migration and diaspora do, of course, define a wide range of social processes and experiences, but they do not exhaust transnationality. In particular, they insufficiently take into account the possibility of quite distinct self-understandings about boundaries and legitimacy on the part of both 'host' countries and 'immigrant' populations. I take Islam in France as an illuminating case in point because each of its two terms challenges the possibility of self-defining through migration and diaspora. First, *Islam* complicates current lines of transnational analysis by emphasising its own universal norms and its practices of deliberating about religious issues across national boundaries.[1] Secondly, *France* raises the stakes of diasporic self-definition by challenging the cultural, political, and even religious legitimacy of any sort of extension of a citizen's life beyond state borders. The one resists national assimilation; the other requires it; both question the legitimacy of 'diaspora' as a descriptive term for portions of their membership.

In what follows I argue that transnational Islam creates and implies the existence and legitimacy of a global public space of normative reference and debate, and that this public space cannot be reduced to a dimension of migration or of transnational religious movements. I offer two brief ethnographic examples of this transnational public space, and maintain that even as it develops references to Europe it implies neither a 'Euro-Islam' nor a 'post-national' sense of European membership and citizenship.

Three Transnational Dimensions of Islam

The phrase 'transnational Islam' can be used to refer to a variety of phenomena, among which I would emphasise three: demographic movements, transnational religious institutions, and the field of Islamic reference and debate. I will argue that a focus on the first two, and in general on phenomena of migration and movement, has obscured the importance of the third.

Muslims may move across national borders for social or economic reasons, and in this first respect can be said to participate in transnational movement in precisely the same way as do Haitians who move to North America or middle-class Europeans who live and work in more than one country. There is nothing necessarily 'Islamic' about these attachments and returns, although they *may* define or create trajectories along which religious ideas or forms are carried and changed. Many of the North or West Africans, Turks, or South Asians who migrated to European countries in search of work have remained profoundly attached to their countries of origin. Many of them make frequent trips to these countries; those who retained their original citizenship may return to vote; some have chosen to have their bodies 'repatriated' for burial: and

Journal of Ethnic and Migration Studies 881

in this sense these individuals participate in the transnational movements proposed for anthropology by Glick Schiller (1997), Portes (1999) and others.

Of course, different populations develop distinct trajectories: in France and Italy, West Africans seem to travel more frequently to origin countries than do North Africans, for reasons having in part to do with the greater participation by the former in transnational Sufi movements (Grillo 2001; Riccio 2001). In this respect Senegalese in Italy or France (and Turkish workers in Germany) resemble the now-classic cases of transnational movement between Caribbean countries and the eastern United States (Levitt 2001b; McAlister 1998).[2] To that extent, these Muslim populations fit quite well into the analytical category of transnational demographic movement.

Certain transnational practices *are* tied to religious practice, however, and these transnational religious institutions have been a second focus of study for those interested in 'transnational Islam'. Some Muslims belong to religious organisations that either promote cross-national movement as part of their religious practice, or encompass and promote cross-national communication within their religious hierarchy. One of the most prominent in France and elsewhere in Europe (and North America) is the Tablighi Jama'at (Kepel 1991; Masud 1999; Metcalf 1996, 2001). The movement has its origins and centre in northern India, and sends missions out to urge Muslims residing elsewhere in the world to return to the correct practice of Islam. Diverse Sufi orders also maintain ties and communication between new places of residence and their centres, as they have been doing since the tenth century. Their devotions focus on a living or dead saint, and they carry that devotional orientation with them as they travel. Sufis in Manchester or Paris have local leaders, but they also maintain their ties of devotion to saintly leaders in Pakistan, Senegal, or elsewhere (Riccio 2001; Werbner 2003). These groups maintain particularly strong ties to a homeland and maintain these ties across generations. In that respect these transnational religious movements develop a diasporic character in the form of representations and imaginations of a homeland.

In studies about Islam and transnationalism in Europe, it is these transnational, diasporic religious movements that have received the most attention (Grillo *supra*). In Britain, for example, anthropological and sociological studies of Islam have focused on the perduring ties between local mosques or associations and home-country institutions, particularly those in Kashmir and Bangladesh (Lewis 2002; Werbner 2003). In Germany, a great deal of attention is paid to the ties between Islamic organisations in Germany and Turkish political parties (e.g. Schiffauer 1999). The reasons for this research concentration are probably multiple. These movements provide a sociologically clear entity to study, with members, leaders and group activities. They involve movement and communication across borders, and so are clearly 'transnational' in a way that links their study both to migration literature and to current writing about globalisation. Finally, the Sufi ties of some of these organisations may make them intrinsically more attractive to some anthropologists and sociologists, intellectually so because they have their own rituals and genealogies, and perhaps ethically so to the extent that many social scientists prefer Sufism to the more pared-down versions of Islam associated with modernist and (non-Sufi) reformist movements.

This emphasis within sociological and anthropological studies has led to the relative neglect of a third form of transnational Islam: namely, the development of debates and discussions among Muslims about the nature and role of Islam in Europe and North America. These debates and discussions have led to the creation of networks, conferences, and increasingly formalised institutions for systematic reflection among scholars. These activities and institutions focus on the dilemmas faced by Muslims attempting to develop forms of Islamic life compatible with the range of Western norms, values and laws—in other words, how to become wholly 'here' and yet preserve a tradition of orientation toward Islamic institutions located 'over there' (Grillo 2001).

This third sense of 'transnational Islam' as a public space of reference and debate draws, of course, on Islam's history of movement, communication and institutional innovation. Islam has an intrinsic universality (which it shares with Christian religions) and also more specific universalistic dimensions. The message of the Qur'ân was to turn away from localised deities and worship the transcendent God. The capitals of Islamic polities shifted from one city to another (Baghdad, Damascus, Cairo, Istanbul), meaning the caliphate was and is not limited to one particular region or centre—and indeed in some contemporary imaginings can be entirely deterritorialised (Kahani-Hopkins and Hopkins 2002). Mecca remains the religious focal point of Islam, but the Islamic era began with the flight or migration (*hijra*) from Mecca to Medina (Eickelman and Piscatori 1990).

Other features of Islamic religious practice promote the sense of a worldwide community, the *umma*, among ordinary Muslims. The perduring role of Arabic as the primary language of scholarship and the development of a global jurisprudence (albeit with several schools or traditions) made possible international communication among scholars.[3] The standardisation of the Qur'ân, the requirement to pray in Arabic, and the popular enjoyment of reciting and writing verses of the Qur'ân promote among ordinary Muslims the sense of participation in a universal message (Hirschkind 2001). The annual pilgrimage brings together a sampling of Muslims, and the Saudi government's quota system ensures that pilgrims will meet a geographically wide range of fellow pilgrims. Daily, theoretically five times daily, Muslims turn their bodies in the direction of Mecca in order to carry out the obligatory rituals of worship (*salât*). Even those Muslims who refer to their allegiance to a spiritual leader or to the Shiite legacy of 'Ali more than to their membership in the worldwide *umma* would deny that Islam is or should be defined or bounded by local or national borders. This sense of Islam's transnational character is diffuse but powerful, and it derives its power from the ways in which rituals reproduce, and histories remind Muslims of, the shared duties and practices of Muslims across political boundaries. In its impulse to refuse particularistic loyalties to ethnic groups or to a nation-state, this consciousness first and foremost creates an imagination of an Islamic community transcending specific boundaries and borders.[4]

This consciousness in turn supports the legitimacy and indeed the imperative of searching anywhere in the world for the highest authority on Islamic matters. This imperative creates specific networks of authority, learning and communication that are more historically and sociologically specific than the general sense of global *umma*-hood. Some sources of religious authority—Meccan jurists, Cairene muftis—owe their status to their institutional associations and affiliations; they have been at least recognised, if not always acknowledged, by Muslims throughout the world and over the centuries. Other sources of authority, such as the currently *mediatique* Yûsuf Qardâwî of al-Jazîra television fame, have followed more specific paths to positions of authority, but nonetheless find audiences in many countries. Still others, such as the Syrian father and son al-Bouti mentioned below, have a smaller, but nonetheless enthusiastic body of followers.

The scope of influence of these authorities varies greatly, but in each case, and this is the critical point, it reaches far beyond the borders of the home country. The communications between these sites and Muslims living elsewhere in the world take many forms: newspaper columns, Internet sites, cable television, or books (Eickelman and Anderson 1999). Moreover, links to authority sites often demand a competence in Arabic and a familiarity with the genre conventions of the advice column or the fatwa. These sites are not the only ones available to Muslims, of course, and those in, say, northern India, Iran or Java require additional or distinct linguistic competencies and take different institutional forms. But to claim the highest level of scholarly expertise and authority, one must be able to read texts written in classical Arabic and perhaps be able to recite these texts as well.[5]

This orientation is more specific and can be more particularistic than that toward the *umma*, in that different populations of Muslims pay attention to different sources of authority (and scholars do so more than ordinary people) but it, too, draws on a general feature of Islam, namely, the idea that it is to the most learned, wherever they may reside, that the Muslim ought to listen. It has to do much more with the worldwide communication of ideas than with the movement of populations, and does not depend on it. Muslims may communicate and debate across political boundaries without necessarily migrating or forming transnational religious movements.

For the rest of this paper I wish to consider the implications of this transnational public space for the question of Islam's place in Europe, and I do so for the hardest case, that of France. Because the transnational public space of Islam is based on a set of extra-national social norms—the many interpretations of *shari*ʻa, 'God's plans and commands'—one will expect a higher level of conflict between transnational and national public claims in those states that make the stronger demands on their members for normative conformity or homogeneity. As the first example suggests, the more successful states are in organising Islam internally, the more visible will be those conflicts.

Conflicts of Justification at *Le Bourget*

The scene is the 'Exhibition Park' at the former airport of *Le Bourget*, in April 2003, during the four-day annual assembly of the UOIF, the Union of Islamic Organisations of France (*Union des Organisations Islamiques de France*), an umbrella organisation of mosques and local Islamic associations in France. The UOIF is only one of several such national organisations; its main rivals are a network of mosques under the control of the Paris Mosque, which itself is financed and controlled by the Algerian government, and the FNMF (*Fédération Nationale des Musulmans de France*), controlled by Morocco.[6]

The assembly is part book fair, part marriage market, and part Islamic school, with speakers from several countries talking on spirituality, law and politics (for details see Bowen 2004). This assembly was the twentieth sponsored by the UOIF, and also occurred just after nation-wide elections for a new representative council of Muslims, the *Conseil Français du Culte Musulman* (CFCM). The previous December, the Minister of the Interior (who is also 'Minister of Cults'), Nicolas Sarkozy, had succeeded in convincing the major Islamic organisations to participate in these elections. One of the means by which he did so was to get all parties to agree that the first President of the Council would be the head of the Paris Mosque, Dalil Boubakeur, and that the leaders of the UOIF and the FNMF would supply vice-presidents. At the elections the latter two organisations, in some places in alliance with each other or with other groups (notably the Turks), crushed the Paris Mosque candidates. The UOIF/FNMF victories could be attributed to a number of factors, among them the Moroccan dominance of mosques (the electoral unit) and of Moroccan prominence in both the UOIF and the FNMF. But at Le Bourget the UOIF leadership celebrated the results and the large turnout as a vote of confidence in their organisation's willingness to follow Sarkozy's game.

The high point of this celebration was to be the prime-time moment, Saturday evening, when Sarkozy was to address the gathering—the first such visit by a minister. He arrived punctually and was loudly, repeatedly applauded (27 times, said one source), particularly when he called for treating all citizens equally, whatever their religion. But then came the moment that would dominate public discussion throughout France for the next 10 days (until debates over a new pension reform plan took the stage). Sarkozy said that because all are equal before the law, all must comply with the law that all residents must have their picture taken for identity cards with their heads uncovered: 'nothing would justify women of the Muslim confession benefiting from a different law'.

The booing and whistles took minutes to die down. The statement ruptured the mood, but logically it was merely an application of the general principles applauded moments before. The reasoning was impeccable: Muslims must obey the law, the law says no headcovering on identity cards, Muslim women must untie their scarves at such moments. The Minister simply recited a syllogism, a basic cultural fact of French mental life.

The UOIF officials immediately denounced the law in question, and said it was their right to work to overturn it—one official making the unfortunate comparison with what he saw as a similarly unjust law, the Nazi requirement that Jews wear yellow stars. This remark also was covered in the press. Less remarked on was the equally clear-cut recitation of how Islamic law should be followed that occurred in the same place two

Journal of Ethnic and Migration Studies   885

days after the Minister's speech, delivered as part of the UOIF's report on Islamic law. The organisation's spokesman on Islamic law, Ahmad Jaballah, issued a fatwa on behalf of the UOIF and the broader European network of which it is part, to the effect that Muslim women must wear headscarves. His speech came in response to a question, in the form of question and answer that defines the work of a mufti. The question concerned the obligation to wear 'le *hijâb*', which always means, in these discursive contexts, a headcovering. Jaballah said:

> This question [out the *hijâb*] was invoked earlier and the media have spoken about it. Many families find themselves obliged to have their daughters take off the hijab at work or at school. And as you know, many officials would like to pass a law forbidding it. But I should make several points. First, Islam requires women to wear the hijab, and here all scholars, in the past and today, agree. Secondly, we consider wearing the hijab to be an act of choice by a woman and not something forced upon her. Families should not oblige a girl to wear it if she does not want to. Third, when a Muslim woman wears the headscarf, she does it as an act of faith, and not as a political act or to signal her separate social identity. Fourth, the Conseil d'Etat [France's highest administrative tribunal] has decided that wearing the headscarf is not incompatible with *laïcité* [here, applause from the crowd], and this decision is consistent with the European Charter of Human Rights, where it guarantees the expression of religious beliefs both in private and in public. Many denounce ostentation and proselytism, but these occur only when someone wishes to impose religion on someone else, and such practices are not found in Islam. Fifth, what must be done? Try dialogue and avoid confrontation. Some school principals have interpreted the Conseil's decision in the direction of permitting the headscarf. Cover the maximum possible with the *foulard*, and not just with a bandanna. Don't focus on the issue of its colour; the point is to cover up [more applause]. We need to have Muslim women in every sector of public life. Some work not because they have to but because they received education and want to contribute, and they need to do so with their headscarf. If you have to take it off at work because you are forced to do so, this does not mean that you should leave it off the rest of the time, only when obliged to. Finally, there is a decree regarding the identity cards, but we must emphasise that no statute forbids wearing the headscarf, and legal specialists agree that such a law would be in conflict with the European convention. In 1983 the UOIF asked Gaston Deferre, then the Minister of the Interior, to allow Muslim women to keep their headscarves on when photographed for their identity cards, 'because the foulard is a part of their identity', and he agreed. We have the letter on file and it could become part of the jurisprudence [more applause].

Both Sarkozy and Jaballah were categorical and explicit: each of the two systems of norms, one enforced by the 'chief cop of France', as he had been introduced to the UOIF crowd, the other enforced by God, is absolute. No exceptions or exemptions can be tolerated. Indeed, Jaballah had devoted his own speech, earlier in the meeting, to the precise topic of the conditions under which exemptions can be made to an Islamic rule (*ahkam*), and his exposé did not allow for exemptions in cases such as that of the *hijâb*. It is important to note that the fatwa was not limited to France; it was originally the product of a European assembly of scholars, all individuals of non-European origin, although most now living in European countries, and of which the leader is the Egyptian scholar, resident in Qatar, Yûsuf Qardâwî (on the European council see Caeiro 2003).

What I wish to emphasise here is that the two structures of justification are identical in form, and that they have entirely different starting points. Sarkozy and others in the French government start from the positive laws of France, but quickly proceed to deduce these laws, and perhaps others that need to be passed, from a conception of the Republic. In March 2004 the French National Assembly and Senate passed a law that will forbid public school students from wearing clothing that calls attention to their religious affiliation. The legislators argued that the presence of the scarves contravened norms of gender equality and of *laïcité*, interpreted in the parliamentary debates to mean the absence of religious signs in the public sphere (see Bauberot 2000; Favell 2001). As I argue elsewhere (Bowen 2003), the deductive form taken by French arguments about *laïcité* make for particularly sharp confrontations with alternative ideas of justice or public comportment.

The UOIF, and many other Muslims, start from authoritative interpretations of Islamic norms ('l scholars, in the past and today, agree'). These interpretations are the more authoritative the less bound they are by space or time: better if they reflect the opinions of learned Muslims over the centuries, and across political boundaries. Indeed the more 'liberal' views of Islamic norms urge Muslims to begin their interpretations from the general principles of Islam rather than from the specifics of time and place. The value of generality helps explain why, at the beginning of the Dâr al-Fatwa session at which Jaballah spoke, the moderator was careful to emphasise that the session reflected the opinions of the European Council as well as the French one.

Now, as we saw above, the UOIF spokesman also refers to European norms of human rights and to the French Conseil d'Etat. This sort of reference has led Yasemin Soysal (2002) to argue that Muslims in Europe are justifying their claims to specific rights (to dress, food, or language) on the basis of 'natural' rights of individuals and human rights 'rather than drawing on religious teachings and traditions' (2002: 144). Although she points to occasional 'alternative' references to 'God's law', she states that these should not detract from the 'prevalent universalistic forms of making claims by Muslim groups that are commonly overlooked' (2002: 145). This argument is part of the broader one that groups and states in Europe are moving towards 'post-national' forms of membership in Europe.

Soysal's claim usefully reminds us that some Muslims make such references, as Jaballah's discourse exemplifies. But we must ask what rhetorical position these references occupy in justifications of social claims made by key public Muslim actors. In trying to persuade other Muslims of the truth of their position on various religious matters, do Muslim public intellectuals base their justifications on general human rights grounds or on notions of European citizenship? No, they base them on Islamic norms, as did the UOIF with respect to headscarves. The normative force of wearing the *foulard*, its obligatory quality, comes from scripture, not from human rights, as is true for 'ordinary' women discussing their decisions to wear headscarves or not to do so (Souilamas 2001; Venel 1999). (Similarly, Sarkozy's counter-argument comes from French law, not from European laws or universal rights). The references to non-Islamic normative sources are purely instrumental in Jaballah's speech on behalf of the Dâr al-Fatwa: the Conseil d'Etat has ruled that schoolgirls must be allowed to keep

Journal of Ethnic and Migration Studies   887

their headscarves on, and any new law that said otherwise would contravene the European Convention on Human Rights. These are useful ways to persuade French law-makers and school principals, but the specific norms invoked are entirely a function of the strategic advantages such citations will produce. If focusing on the contingencies of French court decisions best supports the case for the headscarves, then it is to those sources that most Muslim spokespersons and others will point. If that recourse becomes impossible because the law has changed, then the reference will change as well.

In any case, references to non-Islamic normative sources are secondary to a justificatory discourse that is based in Islamic jurisprudence, manifestly transnational, and not European. How precisely one interprets Islamic norms and jurisprudence is, however, open to debate, and Muslim public intellectuals writing and speaking in France have proposed a range of alternative positions, from a traditional reliance on one legal tradition (*madhhab*) to an effort to rethink Islamic norms in terms of broad ethical principles (see Bowen forthcoming). Moreover, Europe may define a set of shared contingencies, as evidenced in the willingness of Qardâwî and his European Council to allow Muslims to take out first mortgages because of the 'necessity' created by high European house rental rates (Bowen forthcoming; Caeiro 2003). However, the space of reference and debate on normative questions is one that includes the sources of greater authority to be found in the Arabic-speaking world.

Speaking Through France in the 19th Arrondissement

Indeed, one sometimes finds debates taking place across Arabic countries, and in the Arabic language, with France providing a location and a public. One setting for such debates is the Adda'wa Mosque in Paris's 19th Arrondisement, presided over by the Algerian-born Larbi Kechat. Kechat has devoted himself both to developing his mosque as an independent force among Muslims in Paris, and to fostering dialogue among Muslims and non-Muslims on current social topics. Since 1995, Kechat has organised and moderated panel discussions on topics ranging from Islamic spirituality to AIDS, and for each of the six or more panels that occur during the year he has recruited French-speaking Muslims, prominent non-Muslim French authorities, and well-known Islamic scholars who speak in Arabic (with French translations). Each session lasts a full afternoon, and offers the 100–300 people who attend the opportunity to write down questions for the moderator; some choose to come forward and speak, and often these disquisitions become mini-seminars themselves. I estimate that nearly everyone attending these sessions could understand the French, and that at least one-half of them also could follow at least some of the Arabic.

On 6 April 2002 the panel was devoted to Islamic jurisprudence; the 'star' speaker of the afternoon was the well-known scholar of Islamic law, Dr. Mohamed Tawfik al-Bouti, the son of the still more famous Sheikh Mohamed Sa'id Ramadan al-Bouti. Tawfik al-Bouti is chair of the Department of Islamic Jurisprudence at the University of Damascus, Syria. Other speakers included Dr. Shayma Sarraf, a woman from Iraq with a French doctorate in Islamic thought, a French legal scholar, and myself (I spoke on Indonesian law). The panel was moderated by a professor from Algeria.

I have described the event in detail elsewhere (Bowen 2004); here I wish to focus not on the formal speeches, but on the ensuing debates that involved members of the audience, and what they can tell us about the transnational character of Islamic debate in France. Al-Bouti set the tone for the afternoon in his Arabic-language talk, emphasising that although Islamic norms do change when new circumstances arise, matters once settled remain settled, and not just anyone may engage in the interpretation of scripture (*ijtihâd*).[7]

> The gates of *ijtihâd* are not closed, but you must only refer to well-qualified experts to carry out *ijtihâd*. *Ijtihâd* should be for new matters, and not for matters which have been examined thoroughly by the experts (the *mujtahîdûn*). ... Another issue regards the rules [al-ahkam] that change according to the social environment, customs ['urf] and interests that change also. As for rules based on the texts, they do not change even if the times change.

After the formal speeches came a series of five long speeches from the floor. The first to speak was a thin, older man, identified later by Larbi Kechat as Dr. Moussa, Dean of the Faculty of Islamic Studies at Oran, Algeria. Moussa argued that we must adapt Islam to a changing world and adopt a '*fiqh* of reality'. He cited, as so many do, the initial revelations of the Qur'ân ('Recite!'), and a *hadîth* of the Prophet Muhammad to the effect that 'the entire Qur'ân directs us toward *ijtihâd*'. He mentioned the case of a young woman working as an engineer who was told she had to remove her headscarf at work; she came to him and he could not resolve the problem. 'These are questions from the real world for which we try *ijtihâd*. ... It is better that I support a clever young Muslim woman at work than cause her to leave her field'. With that Dr. Moussa started to step away from the microphone, but al-Bouti shot him a question: 'Did you give her a fatwa telling her to remove the *hijâb*?' 'No, we told her to wear whatever she could. ... We have to find a solution, it is better'.

The next speaker, an excited young mathematics student from Morocco named Idris, also spoke in Arabic, attacking the tendency to not face squarely the world that one finds in certain Muslim countries, and accusing Syrian scholars (implicitly including al-Bouti) of being corrupt. Another young man, Muhammad, spoke next (again in Arabic).

> When Islam was attacked, mainly by the West, they did not succeed in destroying Islamic faith, but they worked hard on another issue, namely, relating religion to life. ... They started attacking the fixed Islamic rules, and their attack led to *fiqh al-waqi'* [*fiqh* based on circumstances or realism]. We hear these days that some scholars approve of 'making *halal*' things such as going without the *hijâb*, borrowing at interest (*riba*), eating meat that has not been properly killed.

He went on to denounce the idea that one could interpret through *ijtihâd* matters already settled by scripture:

> We cannot say that interest is permitted and that women should not wear the veil, because our religion is obligation, because God will reward you based on how much

Journal of Ethnic and Migration Studies   889

hardship you undergo. Women should not decline to wear the *hijâb*, even if she leaves school and university, because there always are alternatives.

Finally, a woman wearing a long gown with matching headcovering came forward to speak (without giving her name). She began in Arabic but Larbi Kechat, apparently recognising her, told her that she should speak in French (the only time he did this). She is a medical doctor and always has worked wearing her headcovering.

> The easiest solution is to take off the headscarf. ... I had to stop my studies for a year and change towns before I found a situation where I could resume my study covered. ... When looking for work I received a call from a professor of law, and I said excuse me but I wear the *foulard*, and he said that is perfectly alright, and I have lived what God said.

These speakers disagreed among themselves on a range of issues. Dr. Moussa most explicitly disagreed with al-Bouti's statement limiting the range of *ijtihâd*. Indeed, in his response, al-Bouti summarily dismissed everything that Moussa had said:

> Dr Moussa spoke. I allow him to talk about profound medical issues, but when he talks about profound matters of the foundations [the *usûl al-fiqh*] I do not permit him to talk, because this matter has been discussed thoroughly by scholars.

Al-Bouti clearly had been irritated that Moussa would have dared to issue advice to the young woman faced with the question of covering her head at work. Muhammad, by contrast, went even farther than al-Bouti in attacking the idea that Islamic norms should adapt themselves to reality, and referred to the controversial fatwa by Yûsuf Qardâwî permitting mortgages as a prime example of interpretations that simply aid the West in its efforts to destroy Islam (Conseil européen des fatwâs et de la recherche 2001).

Al-Bouti continued the line of reasoning initiated by Muhammad in his own follow-up, attacking the 'illegitimate innovation (*bid'a*) called *ijtihâd al-maqâsid*', that would replace adherence to Islamic rules based on scripture with developing new rules based on the 'principles' (*maqâsid*) of scriptures. The concept of *maqâsid* has become the key category used by French Muslim thinkers, including Larbi Kechat himself, in trying to rethink Islamic norms in a French, or European context (see Bowen forthcoming), and in choosing to formulate his criticism in this way, al-Bouti was subjecting that manner of reasoning to a frontal assault.

What can one learn about 'transnational Islam' from these glimpses into what was a nearly six-hour event? Let me underscore three aspects of the afternoon's conversations. First, the discussions were about the proper way to understand Islamic norms: what is *ijtihâd*? How do you know when a scriptural text is fixed and certain? How do we apply Islamic law to current issues? To some extent this focus was a product of the topic; other panels at the mosque have included more extensive reference to French laws and social norms. And yet it was notable that no one speaking this particular afternoon thought to justify a practice by referring to French, European, or international norms or laws. Secondly, although it was not a topic of the prepared presentations, women's headcoverings continually surfaced as a key example. With one exception (a brief, exasperated remark by Dr. Sarraf, to the effect of 'it's up to each woman'), all speakers emphasised that wearing headcovering of some sort is an obligation for Muslim women. Third, the exchanges among speakers took place mainly in Arabic, and referred widely to events, writers, politicians and places in various Arab-speaking countries. (Intriguingly, the French translations usually omitted the more controversial portions of each speech.)

This event, and the many others occurring weekly in French cities (and elsewhere in Europe) create and sustain a particular sort of transnational Islamic public space, where Arabic serves as the background language, Islamic texts and norms are the starting-point for all discussions, and local issues are discussed against that shared normative and linguistic background. Among those in the audience with whom I have spoken over the years, many live in and around Paris but many others have recently arrived for school or work, and some move back and forth across the Mediterranean. Al-Bouti could assume a rather remarkably high degree of familiarity among at least a good portion of his audience in matters of *ijtihâd*, *maqâsid*, and so forth.

What 'Post-Nationality'?

The two examples presented above indicate that the transnational public space of Islam in France is firmly anchored in Islamic norms of justification. Debates within that sphere concern the proper ways to interpret Islamic knowledge and to apply it to conditions today, in this case in France. Muslims participating in these debates may take account of norms, laws and conditions prevailing in France, as elements that are *normatively external but pragmatically internal* to the debates. Thus, Muslim actors may *not* cite French social and legal norms of gender equality or religious freedom as independent norms that might counter norms derived from scripture. Such an argument would immediately raise charges of seeking to fit Islam to reality, rather than the proper action of using Islam to reshape reality. Not even the most 'liberal' Muslim public intellectuals in France make such arguments (see Bowen forthcoming).

However, Muslims may be motivated by their knowledge of French social life or by their agreement with certain French norms to favour some pathways and strategies of Islamic interpretation rather than others. For example, some Muslim public intellectuals urge Muslims to rethink Islamic practices in terms of the broader objectives of the Qur'ân, or in terms of similarities between Islamic law and European legal systems, e.g., with respect to contracts (see Bowen forthcoming). Alternatively, they may cite features of French life as posing barriers to conduct that become Islamically relevant insofar as they redefine 'social interest' (*maslaha*) or create new forms of 'necessity' (*darurat*), both valid categories in Islamic jurisprudence. Such was Dr. Moussa's approach when he told a young Muslim woman in danger of losing her employment to seek an accommodation with her employer that would allow her some degree of headcovering. It also was the approach adopted by Yûsuf Qardâwî in permitting mortgages on grounds of necessity for Muslims living in Europe.

Finally, French and European norms and laws may become strategically useful in developing arguments for consumption outside the public space of Islamic reference

Journal of Ethnic and Migration Studies   891

and debate. Thus, as do many others, Ahmed Jaballah emphasises that Islam allows free choice, that women are to make their own decisions as to whether or not to wear headcovering, that in this respect Islam is in keeping with European conventions, and that a French law preventing women from exercising such choice would violate those conventions. Yet he also states that wearing such headcovering is an obligation for women. In this view, Islamic norms are clear, but the process of individuals coming to accept them involves choice and freedom.

I have pointed out that this transnational Islamic space of reference and debate extends both across Europe (*vide* the European Council for Fatwa and Research) and beyond it, to include, most importantly, figures of learning and authority from the Arabic-speaking world. It is transnational without being either 'post-national', in the sense of succeeding an earlier space bounded by state boundaries, or 'European', in the sense of delimiting itself to a bounded European entity of normative value. Muslim public intellectuals who are engaged in serious discussions about how to adapt and adopt Islam to Europe are unwilling to cut themselves off from the transnational space that has, since the beginning of Islamic history, been the appropriate sphere for reference and debate.

We might most fruitfully consider this space to provide the social support for an 'alternative cosmopolitanism' (van der Veer 2001) among Muslims. This form of transnationalism differs markedly from the perduring ties to two or three specific places that mark many transnational religious movements (McAlister 1998; Schiffauer 1999; Werbner 2003). Al-Bouti was not present as a link to Syria, and he could have been speaking in Jakarta, Lahore or Chicago (as, indeed, he probably has done). The UOIF places into deep background precisely the bilateral ties or attachments to overseas communities that most transnational movements highlight. Both the UOIF and the Adda'wa mosque seek to develop reference and debate to 'Islam' as a deterritorialised set of norms and traditions, as well as to 'France' as a bounded set of obligations and rights. Sarkozy, Jaballah and al-Bouti all agree that 'French citizenship practices' (*citoyenneté* having this broad sense) are an appropriate, perhaps the only appropriate, intersection of these two conceptions, 'Islam' and 'France'—and it is probably only on this proposition that they could agree (see Favell 2001; Kumar 2002).

Migration and Islamic religious movements have played an obvious and perduring role in developing a Muslim presence in France and elsewhere. Islam's transnational public space is 'beyond migration', however, in that it is dependent neither on specific migration patterns nor on the activities of particularistic transnational movements. This space has existed since the beginning of the Islamic era, and long before it extended to Europe it regularly defined and developed debates and references among scholars and public figures from Indonesia, Pakistan, Egypt and elsewhere. Just as the norms and laws that now define 'Europe' are reshaping the citizenship practices of particular European countries (Soysal 1994), so too the debates and challenges that are nurtured in and emerge from the Islamic transnational sphere already are demanding that state officials rethink what it means to be 'French' or 'German'. These challenges extend far beyond migration.

892   *J. R. Bowen*

Notes

[1]   I should emphasise that the authors referred to here are well aware of these internal formulations within Islam; see Vertovec (2000).

[2]   On the ways in which the movements of Turkish workers, made mainly for economic reasons, nonetheless shape religious consciousness, see Amiraux (2001) and Schiffauer (1999).

[3]   I have been struck by this use of Arabic in what might otherwise be unlikely places. Two examples will illustrate the general point. The Fiqh Council of North America does use English at their meetings but participants are expected to be able to converse in Arabic as well, despite the group's inclusion of American converts and South Asians. In the Gayo highlands of Aceh, Indonesia, where I worked for many years, 'traditionalist' religious scholars, all speakers of the Gayo language, generally write down the conclusions of their meetings in Arabic, a language none of them converse in fluently.

[4]   I omit discussion of the debates among Muslims about the ways to conceive of the 'Islamic world' and the rest: should they be considered as two distinct realms (*dâr*) based on the Islamic character of the society or the government? Or should one focus instead on the degree to which Muslims are free to pursue their religious activities in different countries? For historical and comparative perspectives on this question, see Abou El Fadl (1994); Bowen (forthcoming); Kahani-Hopkins and Hopkins (2002); and Ramadan (2002).

[5]   Zaman (2002) shows how scholarly writing and debates in today's Pakistan take place in Arabic, not in Urdu. Zaman has remarked (personal communication, 2003) that this fact explains the small number of Western scholars of Islam in South Asia competent to master the scholarly communications, in that Arabic has not been a regular part of the training of South Asianists.

[6]   In response to the North African domination of public Islamic activities, immigrants from Turkey formed their own grouping, as did a collection of Muslims from a broad array of places, including the Comoros, the West Indies, and West Africa. Because the strongest rivalries are among the three North African groups, sometimes mosques at which Muslims from more than one of these groups worship will choose someone from a smaller grouping to be the imam or mosque leader. In one mosque south of Paris, men from Algeria and Morocco laughingly (but meaningfully) recounted to me that only a Comoro man could have brought peace to their mosque. Mosques in the Paris region usually are multi-ethnic, and preach in Arabic or French and Arabic; in cities with large populations of non-Arabic speakers such as Marseille one finds ethnic-specific mosques.

[7]   I would like to thank Mahmoud Abdallah for translating the Arabic speeches from my tapes.

References

Abou El Fadl, K. (1994) 'Islamic law and Muslim minorities: the juristic discourse on Muslim minorities from the second/eighth to the eleventh/seventeenth centuries', *Islamic Law and Society*, 1(2): 143–87.

Amiraux, V. (2001) *Acteurs de l'Islam entre Allemagne et Turquie. Parcours militants et expériences religieuses*. Paris: L'Harmattan.

Baubérot, J. (2000) *Histoire de la laïcité française*. Paris: Presses Universitaires de France.

Bowen, J.R. (2003) 'Two approaches to rights and religion in contemporary France', in Mitchell, J. and Wilson, R. (eds) *Rights in Global Perspective*. London: Routledge, 33–53.

Bowen, J.R. (2004) 'Does French Islam have borders? Dilemmas of domestication in a global religious field', *American Anthropologist*, 106(1): 43–55.

Bowen, J.R. (forthcoming 2005) 'Pluralism and normativity in French Islamic reasoning', in Hefner, R. (ed.) *Islam, Pluralism, and Democratization*. Princeton: Princeton University Press (in press).

Caeiro, A. (2003) *La Normativité Islamique à l'Epreuve de l'Occident: le cas du Conseil européen de la fatwa et de la recherche*. Paris: l'Harmattan.

Conseil européen des fatwâs et de la recherche (2001) *Recueil de fatwâs*. Lyon: Tawhid.

Eickelman, D.F. and Anderson, J. (eds) (1999) *New Media in the Muslim World: The Emerging Public Sphere*. Bloomington: Indiana University Press.

Eickelman, D.F. and Piscatori, J. (eds) (1990) *Muslim Travelers: Pilgrimage, Migration, and the Religious Imagination*. Berkeley: University of California Press.

Favell, A. (2001) *Philosophies of Integration: Immigration and the Idea of Citizenship in France and Britain*. Houndmills: Palgrave (2nd edition).

Glick Schiller, N. (1997) 'The situation of transnational studies', *Identities*, 4(2): 155–66.

Grillo, R.D. (2001) *Transnational Migration and Multiculturalism in Europe*. Oxford: Transnational Communities Working Paper WPTC-01-08.

Hirschkind, C. (2001) 'The ethics of listening: cassette-sermon audition in contemporary Egypt', *American Ethnologist*, 28(3): 623–49.

Kahani-Hopkins, V. and Hopkins, N. (2002) '"Representing" British Muslims: the strategic dimension to identity construction', *Ethnic and Racial Studies*, 25(2): 288–309.

Kepel, G. (1991) *Les Banlieues de l'Islam: naissance d'une religion en France*. Paris: Seuil.

Kivisto, P. (2001) 'Theorizing transnational immigration: a critical review of current efforts', *Ethnic and Racial Studies*, 24(4): 549–77.

Kumar, K. (2002) 'The nation-state, the European Union, and transnational identities', in Alsayyad, N. and Castells, M. (eds) *Muslim Europe or Euro-Islam*. Lanham, MD: Lexington Books, 53–68.

Levitt, P. (2001a) *Between God, Ethnicity, and Country: An Approach to the Study of Transnational Religion*. Oxford: Transnational Communities Working Paper WPTC-01-13.

Levitt, P. (2001b) *The Transnational Villagers*. Berkeley: University of California Press.

Lewis, P. (2002) *Islamic Britain: Religion, Politics, and Identity among British Muslims*. London: I.B. Tauris (2nd edition).

Masud, M.K. (ed.) (1999) *Travelers in Faith: Studies of the Tablighi Jamaat as a Transnational Islamic Movement for Faith Renewal*. Leiden: Brill.

McAlister, E. (1998) 'The Madonna of 115th Street revisited: Vodou and Haitian Catholicism in the age of transnationalism', in Warner, R.S. and Wittner, J. (eds) *Gatherings In Diaspora: Religious Communities and the New Immigration*. Philadelphia: Temple University Press, 123–60.

Metcalf, B.D. (1996) 'New Medinas: the Tablighi Jama'at in America and Europe', in Metcalf, B.D. (ed.) *Making Muslim Space in North America and Europe*. Berkeley: University of California Press, 110–27.

Metcalf, B.D. (2001) '"Traditionalist" Islamic activism: Deoband, Tablighis, and Talibs', in Calhoun, C., Price, P. and Timmer, A. (eds) *Understanding September 11*. New York: The New Press, 53–66.

Portes, A. (1999) 'Conclusion: toward a new world—the origins and effects of transnational activities', *Ethnic and Racial Studies*, 22(2): 463–77.

Ramadan, T. (2002) *Dâr Ash-shahâda: L'Occident, espace du témoignage*. Lyon: Tawhid.

Riccio, B. (2001) 'From "ethnic group" to "transnational community"? Senegalese migrants' ambivalent experiences and multiple trajectories', *Journal of Ethnic and Migration Studies*, 27(4): 583–99.

Saint-Blancat, C. (2002) 'Islam in diaspora: between reterritorialization and extraterritoriality', *International Journal of Urban and Regional Research*, 26(1): 138–51.

Schiffauer, W. (1999) *Islamism in the Diaspora: The Fascination of Political Islam Among Second Generation German Turks*. Oxford: Transnational Communities Working Paper WPTC-99-06.

Souilamas, N.G. (2001) *Des "beurettes" aux descendantes d'immigrants nord-africains*. Paris: Grasset.

894 *J. R. Bowen*

Soysal, Y.N. (1994) *Limits of Citizenship: Migrants and Postnational Membership in Europe*. Chicago: University of Chicago Press.

Soysal, Y.N. (2002) 'Citizenship and identity: living in diasporas in postwar Europe?', in Hedetoft, U. and Hjort, M. (eds) *The Postnational Self*. Minneapolis: University of Minnesota Press, 137–51.

van der Veer, P. (2001) *Transnational Religion*. Princeton University Center for Migration and Development Working Paper 01-06h.

Venel, N. (1999) *Musulmanes Françaises: des pratiquantes voilées à l'université*. Paris: L'Harmattan.

Vertovec, S. (1997) 'Three meanings of "diaspora", exemplified among South Asian religions', *Diaspora*, 6(3): 277–300.

Vertovec, S. (2000) *Religion and Diaspora*. Oxford: Transnational Communities Working Paper WPTC-01-01.

Werbner, P.S. (2003) *Pilgrims of Love: Anthropology of a Global Sufi Cult*. London: Hurst & Company.

Zaman, M.Q. (2002) *The Ulama in Contemporary Islam*. Princeton: Princeton University Press.

[9]

Journal of Ethnic and Migration Studies
Vol. 36, No. 9, November 2010, pp. 1499–1518

Migration as Preservation and Loss: The Paradox of Transnational Living for Low German Mennonite Women

Luann Good Gingrich and Kerry Preibisch

Throughout history, conservative groups of Low German-speaking Mennonites have collectively migrated to preserve their religious integrity. However, their contemporary migrations to North America are not collective or church-sanctioned, but primarily economically motivated. This paper explores the intertwined processes of gender and religion in transnational social spaces through the destination experiences of Mennonite women in Canada. The paradoxes of the transnational social field—each simultaneous gain and loss—constitute a double-bind wherein choice is elusive. Caught in the contest between physical and cultural survival, women find themselves in the 'nothing' of in-between, as conflicting social fields and systems of capital—secular and sacred—collide.

Keywords: Gender; Religion; Transnational Migration; Low German Mennonites; Immigrant Integration; Canada

Introduction

For centuries, conservative groups of Low German Mennonites (henceforth LGMs) have maintained a tenacious commitment to a distinct culture that is intensely religious, agrarian and patriarchal. Religion is expressed as a way of life—a system of practices passed down through the generations, seldom articulated in words, as ideas or as beliefs. Rather, religion is lived in the collective re-enactment of seemingly mundane, quotidian rituals, needed to sustain a separate agrarian lifestyle. Yet this people—rooted solidly within highly defined religious principles and a rural livelihood in harmony with the land—has remained unanchored from a single

Luann Good Gingrich is Associate Professor in the School of Social Work at York University, Toronto. Correspondence to: Prof. L. Good Gingrich, Faculty of Liberal Arts and Professional Studies, York University, 4700 Keele Street, Toronto, Ontario M3J 1P3, Canada. E-mail: luanngg@yorku.ca. Kerry Preibisch is Associate Professor in the Department of Sociology and Anthropology at the University of Guelph. Correspondence to: Prof. K. Preibisch, Dept of Sociology and Anthropology, Mackinnon Building, University of Guelph, Guelph, N1G 2W1 Ontario, Canada. E-mail: kpreibis@uoguelph.ca.

ISSN 1369-183X print/ISSN 1469-9451 online/10/091499-20 © 2010 Taylor & Francis
DOI: 10.1080/1369183X.2010.494825

territory or nation-state since its emergence over 400 years ago. Throughout their history, LGMs have criss-crossed the globe, moving from Europe to Russia to North America and then to Latin America, whenever they perceived their religious integrity to be at stake. Thus, when governments imposed assimilation policies on their people through obligatory military service or public school attendance, church leaders moved the colony *en masse* to a country where they could rebuild their separate and closed-colony life.

The most recent migrations of LGMs, however, have not been collective or sanctioned by the church. Since the 1960s, as their rural subsistence economy has been eroded by state policies and global processes that are profoundly anti-agrarian in nature, hundreds of families from Latin American colonies have engaged in independent return migrations to Canada. The entrenchment of economic neoliberalism and its devastating impact on rural livelihoods has only deepened this trend, resulting in a Low German immigrant population of some 60,000 in rural North America, representing almost one-third of all 'old order' Dutch-Russian Mennonites (Loewen 2007).[1] Our paper explores the destination experiences of adult women engaging in migratory flows between Mexico and Canada. We argue that LGM women's contemporary experiences of migration are defined by paradox, whereby gain and loss, preservation and sacrifice are entwined, as that which is protected is at once threatened. Despite various degrees of settlement in Canada, women's daily life practices remain deeply rooted in their colonies in Mexico, while their lives and livelihoods become necessarily transnational, transcultural and even transtemporal. When we consider how religion and gender intersect with the meaning and experience of economic migration, it becomes apparent that this paradox is more than a contradiction in terms; it is the double-bind of transnational livelihoods. Although Canada may offer work, food and opportunity, much of value is threatened: family stability, religious life and cultural preservation. We argue that this seemingly atypical group of economic migrants permits the examination and theorisation of the intertwined processes and structures of gender and religion in transnational social spaces.

Transnational Social Fields as Gendered and Religious Arenas

Research on women, migration and religion is an exercise fraught with contradictions. For many migrant women, movement to a high-income liberal democracy often entails some measure of gender emancipation through employment and protective institutions (Goldring 1996; Hondagneu-Sotelo 1994, 2003; Itzigsohn and Giorguli 2005: 897). Empirical evidence of these trends has led to the enduring, but mistaken 'tendency to link support for women's rights and sexual freedoms to a narrative of Western progress and a submerged assumption that more religious cultures must be encouraged to catch up with the enlightened secularism of the West' (Woodhead 2008: 54). At the same time, most migrants find themselves at the bottom of social, political and economic hierarchies; here, religion becomes

Journal of Ethnic and Migration Studies   1501

particularly significant. Thorny debates around complex social processes, particularly those that involve difficult moral considerations regarding patriarchal practices enshrined in religion, become all the more unnavigable when the academic literature provides little direction. Studies on immigration and transnationalism have largely ignored the relationship between these processes and religion (Levitt *et al.* 2003; Vande Berg and Kniss 2008), not to mention its gendered expressions.

Despite this gap, theoretical advancements in migration studies have been useful in understanding migration as non-linear and at the intersection of multiple social relations. The concept of transnationalism—a process by which social actors maintain connections with their homelands and engender complex identities and relations that span more than one national state—has proved effective in understanding the empirical reality of contemporary migrations and settlements (Basch *et al.* 1994). In a central theoretical shift, transnational theorising has moved beyond notions of immigration focused on assimilation and immigrant incorporation within a single national territory. As Levitt (2003) and others have discerned, however, movement is not a prerequisite to engagement in transnational activities; while transmigrants may travel regularly, there are also those whose lives remain fixed primarily in one location but who are integrally linked to social contexts that occur in another nation-state, as well as those who do not move at all but whose social world has become transnationalised. Comprehending processes that are transnational in scope and the spaces in which they occur has found utility in Bourdieu's concept of social fields (Faist 2000; Glick Schiller 2005; Levitt and Glick Schiller 2004; Peake and Trotz 1999). The notion of social fields emphasises relations of power in social spaces, recognising unique 'rules' of contest and struggle in the acquisition, exchange and convertibility of resources or capital in each social field (Bourdieu 1990; Bourdieu and Wacquant 1992). Transnational social fields are defined and divided by conflicting geographic, economic, social, cultural and symbolic economies and spaces—spaces that are also deeply gendered.

Feminist scholars have made a strong empirical and theoretical case for using gender analysis as a key organising lens in migration and settlement studies (Curran *et al.* 2006), as gender constitutes 'one of the fundamental social relations anchoring and shaping immigration patterns' (Hondagneu-Sotelo 2003: 3). The increased attention to gender can be partly explained by the empirical reality that the numbers of women and men engaging in international migration flows are now virtually equal. But more importantly, 'many migration scholars now insist that migration itself is a gendered phenomenon' (Donato *et al.* 2006: 4). Supporting this resolve, the literature on gender and migration shows abundant evidence that (im)migrants' destination experiences are highly gendered (see Goldring 1996; Hondagneu-Sotelo 1994; Itzigsohn and Giorguli 2005; Preibisch and Hermoso 2006) and that men and women participate differently in transnational spaces (Goldring 1996; Itzigsohn and Giorguli 2005), including engagement in transnational religious practice (Vertovec 2002).

Faith and religion have been neglected within the literatures on both transnationalism and gender and migration. Within the first body of scholarship, the study of transnational and diaspora religion is fairly nascent (Drbohlav 2003; Ebaugh and Chafetz 1999; Levitt 2001, 2003; Vande Berg and Kniss 2008; Vertovec 2002, 2004). Greater understanding of the transnational religious activities must involve not only 'the organizational manifestations of faith but . . . the alternative places of belonging that religious ideas and symbols make possible and . . . the ways in which these sacred landscapes interact with the boundaries of political and civil life' (Levitt 2001: 24). Further, the desire to keep a faith intact may initiate a diasporic movement. Religion has also escaped thorough interrogation within a contemporary context of global migrations that are largely economic in nature, yet studies of religion and migration have shown that women play a key role in reproducing religious practices, particularly within the domestic sphere (Vertovec 2004).

Research on the destination experiences of a group of transmigrant women whose position within the social hierarchy of their host community is largely determined by religious marginalisation in the context of the secular West, calls attention to the intersections between gender, transnational migration and religion. LGMs are not so much transnational as supranational; for these Mennonites who actively resist assimilation into both 'home' and 'host' country, 'home' is not so much a social field associated with a nation-state, but one that has been constructed and protected to exist *despite* the nation-state. Further, LGMs' religious distinctiveness and their class position as economic migrants situate them in the host society within a set of social relations that are mutually reinforcing. While, to the secular West, these migrant women appear enmeshed in a religious culture that is seemingly patriarchal and 'backward', the culture may provide more security, spiritual comfort and value as women than that offered by a host society that consigns them to the margins.

Research Methodology

Our theoretical findings derive from two qualitative studies that conducted a total of 41 in-depth and semi-structured interviews, four life-history interviews, and eight focus groups with LGMs and service-providers working with this population. The focus on women was undertaken as part of the Community University Research Alliance *Rural Women Making Change*, a programme of research that seeks to make visible the challenges facing rural women, to use a rural, gendered analysis to explore the local/global processes from which these challenges stem, and to propose strategies to get rural women's concerns onto policy agendas. LGM women represent a frequently misunderstood but highly targeted group of rural women. Indeed, within their rural communities—whether fixed geographically in Canada or Mexico—women's realities are often the most invisible, in part a result of self-imposed exclusion (Good Gingrich 2006). Despite this invisibility, their gendered responsibilities involve crafting the very survival strategies that underpin their households' material and cultural preservation. Within Canada, moreover, women become the

Journal of Ethnic and Migration Studies   1503

principal targets of state intervention in their lives: on the one hand, through social assistance that supplements their household's seasonal agricultural wages and, on the other, when their children are taken away if they fail to follow prescribed notions of care. Focusing on this group allows us to explore transnational social fields at the intersection of multiple realms—public and private, religious and secular, national and transnational—and allows us to better understand a group of rural women whom others so desire to change, while exploring the broader and increasingly common reality of transnational livelihoods.

The project's first qualitative study was completed in 2003 (Good Gingrich 2006). This was followed by a second phase of in-depth interviews in 2006. Respondents, accessed through key informants and snowball sampling, were all Mexican-born women living in areas of concentrated LGM settlement in Ontario, Canada. These interviews were conducted in Low German by a Mexican-born, Canadian Mennonite woman. The interviewing style, heavily informed by a shared cultural understanding, was crucial—our participants had never been interviewed before.[2] The taped interviews were translated into English and transcribed by another Mennonite Mexican-born woman. Finally, the researchers and the transcriber engaged in a collaborative analysis process to check interpretations, discuss and corroborate findings, and build the conceptual framework.

The Low German Mennonites

The LGMs coalesced in the 1920s as the most conservative among the multifarious Dutch-Russian Mennonite groups, when almost 9,000 unequivocally rejected—through migration to Mexico and Paraguay—compulsory public education for their children in Western Canadian provinces (Loewen 2006).[3] This proved to be a decisive migration, as it has prolonged their diasporic tendencies long after all other Mennonite groups in North America had settled and, mostly, assimilated into the dominant host societies.[4] Maintaining their Low German distinctiveness is a core element of their religious beliefs. Households, composed of nuclear families, are expected to be self-sufficient units encapsulated in the closed community of the colony. The Mennonite colonies in Latin America have attempted to replicate those built by their parents and grandparents in Canada and their ancestors in Russia and Poland. Within these villages, work, church, education and family are inter-dependent, entangled in a singular system, such that change in the organisation and practices in one social arena is consequential for all others. The colony strives for economic, social and religious autonomy and self-sufficiency to ensure that members have minimal engagement with the secular society around them. The ideal is for family members to work together within the colony, providing the necessities of life through farming. Educating children is shared between the home and the church. Young women and girls work inside the home, learning the skills of mothering and homemaking. Boys work outside with their fathers, learning to live from and with the land. The purpose of school, intimately linked to the church, is to teach children the values and beliefs of colony life. This faith-driven education is considered necessary for their continuance as a people. LGMs place great emphasis on 'staying with what we have been taught', which refers largely to preserving all aspects of life, including school, church, clothing, language and work.

Despite high degrees of cooperation among households, social inequality is a dimension of colony life. Households are expected to function as nuclear, self-sufficient agrarian units. Yet an increasing number have been unable to achieve these goals over the last four decades. Beginning in the 1960s, Mennonite families began leaving their colonies in Latin America to engage in circular migration to Canada, travelling overland through the US. Many arrive at the US border with at least one Canadian citizen among them as a result of the years their parents or grandparents spent in Western Canada from 1870 to the early 1920s.[5] Their claim to Canadian citizenship is the crucial factor that makes these individual family migrations possible.

As a result, almost equal numbers of Low German-speaking Mennonites now reside in North America and in Mexico, with an estimated 40,000 in Ontario alone, and another 20,000 in Saskatchewan, Manitoba, Kansas, Oklahoma and Texas (Janzen 1998; Loewen 2007). Some families continue to migrate between North America and their Mexican colony, finding employment on Northern farms and returning south when the work runs out. Others attempt to 'settle' more permanently, returning only for extended winter vacations. And there are some for whom any thought of return, even for a visit, is financially and logistically impossible. Canadian-bound migration by Low German-speaking Mennonites is primarily economically motivated in ways that are both similar to and different from most Latin American economic migrants. While initial migration is about material survival, their long-term aspirations are to preserve a very distinct *via campesina*—one that is both profoundly anti-capitalist and peasant in nature and that fits within the dictates of their religious faith. These migrations, referred to by some church leaders as an 'uncontrolled migration' (Good Gingrich 2006), are in sharp contrast in practice and meaning to the church-led colony migrations and settlements of Mennonite history.

Motivations for 'Uncontrolled' Migrations

A number of structural inequalities have made it difficult for LGM families to sustain themselves in their Mexican colonies. Their migration to Canada seems to be, first and foremost, a strategy for physical survival. In interviews, women related that, in Mexico, their children are hungry, there is no work and often no hope. The life experiences of LGM women highlight the following inter-related factors contributing to their privation. Firstly, while closed Mennonite colonies were able to survive the recurrent agricultural crises that plagued the Mexican countryside throughout the twentieth century to a greater extent than the dominant rural population (Gates 1993), they have not escaped the anti-agrarian impacts of the neoliberal development policies pursued by the Mexican government or the increased vulnerability to the

Journal of Ethnic and Migration Studies   1505

global market facing small producers the world over. Within this context, rural credit is virtually non-existent and rates offered by local moneylenders are usurious. As some creditors obtain their lending capacity from the drug trade, those who default are often threatened by violence. Migration offers an escape from moneylenders and an opportunity to repay. Secondly, this adverse policy environment has been compounded by extreme weather patterns that have severely afflicted Latin America with recurring drought and flooding. Thirdly, colonies are also experiencing demographic pressures: land is limited and the price of even small properties is prohibitive for many newly married couples. Finally, several respondents described Mexico as a society of escalating violence, lawlessness and corruption that only exacerbated their material hardship. In summary, the initial push factors vary: some families migrate to pursue the dream of owning a farm on which to sustain an independent household, others in order to maintain the farm they already own in their Southern colony, and others to escape debt.

Those who migrate to Canada find work in agriculture. This occupational preference is religious, historical and cultural. Men within this group are expected to provide a living from the land; the inability to do so is considered a personal failure. Working outside the colony means engaging with the secular world, which threatens their separate and distinct way of life. In rural Mexico, the material rewards for defying the church in this way are often too low to meet even subsistence needs. In Canada, however, waged agricultural work provides greater returns. Furthermore, since Canadian farmers often employ LGMs as families, households can work together with the land.

Canadian citizenship, while providing LGMs with an alternative labour market and thus a means of supporting their cherished agrarian livelihoods, also allows them to access a relatively well-funded public health-care system. Mexican public health services are inadequate and private care is prohibitively expensive; for low-income households, a health crisis can be the tipping point into marginality. Several respondents explained that the possibility of accessing medical treatment for an ailing family member through the Canadian public health system motivated their migration. In addition to these seemingly economic considerations, however, LGMs engaged in migration as a strategy for optimising their cultural security by maintaining a second citizenship and thus an alternative space of refuge should it become difficult for them to practice their traditions in Mexico. As Ong (1999) has argued, people with multiple passports cultivate potential ties that can be mobilised to expand opportunities or flee insecurity. Increasingly, LGM families find themselves with little alternative but to venture north. The following section traces these gendered experiences.

Experiences of Transnational Migration

Transnational migration offers hope for survival, in all respects. Yet LGM women report that, in their experience of the transnational social field, the survival they seek—stability of the family, continuance of the church and preservation of their way of life—is threatened by the imposed and rigid divisions between home, school, church and work; by geographic, emotional and religious separation from extended family; by laws and interventions that seek to protect women and children; and by the freedom and pressure to conform. Through the act of migration, LGM women come to know the double-bind of transnationalism in their daily lives as work sustains and divides, citizenship unites and jeopardises, life outside the colony isolates and connects, independence liberates and burdens, and migration preserves and destroys.

Work Sustains and Divides

The LGM preference for farm labour is a deeply held conviction. For those who resort to international migration, the religious ideal of the farming life has become a 'broken dream' (interview with Susana, age 24). In Canada, where farm labourers are in demand and the wages considerably higher, making a living becomes *earning a wage*. Traditional gender and generational roles are disrupted when waged labour is the only form of recognised, legitimate work. In closed-colony life, responsibilities are clearly defined according to gender, yet the boundaries between domestic and public realms are fluid and physically proximate. In addition to their domestic responsibilities, women cared for livestock, milked cows, made cheese, baked goods for sale, and gardened. In this way, work at 'home' demanded a broad range of activities that involved social engagement and multiple responsibilities. As Susana said: 'One day you would do laundry and then one day you would work on the field and then another day, we had to grind. And milking in the mornings and evenings'. In Mexico, women's productive and reproductive work has a central role within the family's livelihood strategies.

The transnational social life of LGM families in Canada is organised by labour and consumer markets, with implications for each family member. Women's domestic portfolio becomes more narrowly defined with the disappearance of their gainful activities in subsistence production. Women reported that housework in Canada is more 'routine', 'less interesting' and 'lonely'. Women with access to washing machines and indoor plumbing, however, praised modern conveniences for easing the drudgery of domestic work. Despite being relieved of some of their tasks and the effort required to realise these, because women are required to engage in wage labour in Canada, their work days become extended with the physical separation of reproduction and production; their labour becomes divided between paid and unpaid, caring and sustaining work. Katharina (26 years), explained how private and public activities become split between distinct physical and temporal spaces:

> If you want to be able to get by better, then the female has to go out and get a job plus come home and do all the work. In Mexico, you just have all day to do your work in the house, so you don't have to worry about going and working out yet and then come home and do stuff.

Journal of Ethnic and Migration Studies   1507

In Canada, furthermore, women's private activities no longer contribute directly to the household's livelihood strategies.

When making a living is translated into earning a wage, LGMs cannot practise the gendered divisions of labour to which they are accustomed. In their culture, the religious significance of work requires everyone to contribute to the family livelihood. In Canada, particularly among recently arrived migrants, the entire household must participate in waged labour. This means that girls and women engage in work that is usually considered more appropriate for boys and men, and even young children will work alongside their mothers in the fields. When girls participate in paid work, they have less time to help their mothers with domestic work. Although uncommon, some families find it necessary to expand male responsibilities into the domestic realm.

> *When you worked too, did you have to come home and clean the house?*
> Maria (39): Yes, everything was waiting when we came home. It wasn't very fun when you came home and everything was dirty and everything needs to be done—the food prepared and the cleaning and laundry—everything you had to do. But we would all do it together. We thought if we all worked, then we all had to do the house.
> *The boys did it too?*
> Maria: We all had to help. We have it like that now too. We have it so the boys have to help too, and we have so many boys they have to do their share too.

For others, the demands of waged labour simply mean that women do 'double duty' in the transnational social field. Most women reported that their daily work is harder in Canada than in Mexico, and life more difficult than they expected. Sarah (28) remarked: 'When you have three children and bring them to the babysitter and work and pick them up and have to do everything at home, it is sometimes quite hard'.

Engaging in the Canadian labour market inserts Low German (im)migrants into a new set of productive relations. Firstly, they lose control over their collective labour power. As subsistence farmers in Mexico, Mennonites (particularly men) have a preference to be 'their own boss'. The desire to maintain some autonomy often means they readily agree to work for piece rates—less supervised, but highly precarious. Paid work also redefines the livelihood contributions of family members in highly individualising ways. Furthermore, when farm operators contract the whole family, including children, to harvest, women experience a new set of patriarchal relations in which Canadian employers pay their husbands for the household's collective labour. Unsurprisingly, in those families that can afford it, women prefer to concentrate on their domestic responsibilities. In fact, many women see the social assistance they receive from the Canada Child Tax Benefit (CCTB)[6] as significant income and refer to this monthly cheque as *their* 'earnings'. Low German women are not accustomed to entrusting the care of their children to women outside the extended family or colony. Even though women's caring work does not contribute to the material well-being of the family, the gendered work of social reproduction is valued above all other tasks.

Citizenship Offers Privilege and Vulnerability

Survival—both material and cultural—is closely linked with protecting or acquiring Canadian citizenship. Women expressed concerns about changes in Mexico, including growing violence, rising substance abuse, new laws that threaten their traditions, and the desperate economic environment. Access to rights and services in Canada is tied to citizenship; those families which do not secure regularised status face considerable challenges.

It is clear from the data that engagement in secular Canadian society and learning English is more acceptable (and materially rewarding) than engagement in secular Mexican society. As Susana's husband explained:

> We knew we were coming for our Citizens [sic], so we came for a whole year. We wanted to see if we could make it here. You can never know what you are going to have later. Later we might want to come to Canada if it should not work out in Mexico. And for all those that come after, like the children we may have. If we didn't do it now then our citizenship would all be for nothing and then we wouldn't be able to make our children as citizens. And through that, we came to the decision that we would come here. It is far thinking, but ... (Elias, 26).

The work of acquiring citizenship represents investment in their children's future, in the possibility of preserving their way of life for generations to come.[7] At the same time, some women who are Canadian citizens or could claim citizenship must remain in Mexico because their husbands do not have papers. It is not uncommon for families to be divided by citizenship, and women in these transnational social fields are often separated from parents, siblings and even children. Conversely, a primary motive for continuing circular migration is often reunification of the nuclear or extended family.

For most transnational Mennonite women and their families, invisibility is available through citizenship, permitting them to quietly come and go, to pursue their separate and non-conformist lifestyle largely unnoticed. Yet their invisibility serves to keep them vulnerable. The rural housing commonly offered by Canadian farm employers for the duration of the season is often expensive yet dilapidated. Almost all participants expressed dissatisfaction with these rental arrangements. Some women reported living in dwellings without running water or heat, with broken windows and doors and with rodent infestations. Multiple families often share a single dwelling, compromising family privacy. Substandard housing is rarely reported, as most LGMs prefer the relative safety of invisibility. As Mary (37) disclosed: 'We don't want to have trouble'. Women reported fearing the loss of their jobs or the removal of their children if their housing was deemed to be unsuitable. Despite the state of rural housing, LGM women prefer living in the

Migration and Religion I

Journal of Ethnic and Migration Studies 1509

country, where children can play outside and the family is close to the fields where they work.

Due in part to language and cultural barriers, but also to their racialisation as an ethnic minority, LGMs find themselves in subordinate, weaker social positions when they enter the Canadian labour market. They take up jobs in agriculture that are at the bottom of the occupational hierarchy and, within those jobs, carry out the most undesirable and hazardous tasks, accept working conditions that would be rejected by other Canadian citizens, and agree to work for cash and without benefits—leaving them vulnerable to exploitation. As Canadian citizens who refuse to look or behave as the dominant majority, LGMs lack legitimacy in the transnational social fields they occupy in the North. They are not counted as immigrants, economic refugees or migrant workers. Negatively racialised as outsiders, they are not quite 'white' Canadians.

Laws and Social Services Protect and Threaten

Deepening global social and economic divisions have permeated the Mennonite colonies in Mexico. Women related personal experiences of conflict and corruption, both in secular Mexican society and within colonies and families. Many expressed appreciation for Canadian laws that protect their families, their children, and themselves as women, which they perceive as a sense of security not possible in Mexico. In addition, women conveyed gratitude for welfare and disability benefits, particularly immediately following their arrival, when steady work is hard to find or when physical decline resulting from disease or years of manual labour makes working in the fields impossible. Social assistance and food banks—non-existent in Mexico—protect women and their families from desperate poverty.

Yet these same 'protective' social and legal institutions also threaten LGMs' existence as a people. Women are subject to laws that go against their traditions. A poignant example, reminiscent of their religious migration history, is the requirement to enrol their children in the public, secular education system. It was reported that some families—especially those engaging in circular migration on an annual basis—send their children to school only if 'caught' by truancy officers. Some—even illiterate—mothers attempt to meet the requirements of Canadian laws by home-schooling their children. When financially feasible, others devote a significant portion of their income to educate their children in a private, unaccredited Low German Old Colony school, where the curriculum is infused with their religious tradition and the school year allows children to participate in fieldwork.[8] Our interviewees made clear that this does not necessarily represent disregard for the value of education, but rather a commitment to preserving the lifestyle of their faith tradition. Tina (44) expressed appreciation for the formal schooling her daughters receive in Canada, but reflected on the sacrifices outside the integrated life of the colony: 'In Mexico it isn't so common that the girls go to work. They just do housework with their moms. I believe the girls get taught more over there than here in Canada'. Furthermore, provincial laws requiring regular school attendance for all children aged five to 18 have significant implications for family income, women's role as mothers, and religious preservation. For LGM women, sending their children to school is to risk losing them to the world and to the hope of preserving their church and people.

Participation in the secular sphere—through accessing public health-care services or education, accepting government benefits, or involuntary subjection to professional intervention—initiates procedures of constant scrutiny and regulation. For example, it was reported that social assistance caseworkers 'want to know everything' about matters that are customarily kept private. While Mennonites demonstrate greater confidence in 'English' authorities in Canada than in 'Spanish' authorities in Mexico, they experience the 'English' to be much more intrusive in their daily lives and practices. LGM families hear about 'Children's Aid'—a provincially funded community-level organisation charged with protecting child welfare—even before they leave Mexico, and many women live in fear of having their children taken from them. At the same time, those whose husbands are alcohol-dependent or abusive are rendered less vulnerable and have greater access to money and resources. Restrictions of employment schedules, enforced laws and societal norms provide some control for men, and protect women and children. This comes at a cost, however, as LGM women are averse to the government 'meddling in our affairs'. Through migration, they trade their historical and religious conviction of separation from the world for economic security and protective institutions.

Life Outside the Colony Isolates and Connects

Within the colony boundaries, obligation to family—including grandparents, aunts, uncles and cousins—is deep and extended. The function of the family is to contribute to the life of the colony, and the colony and the family derive their social significance from one another. When Mennonites migrate, they often leave behind parents, siblings and even children, some of whom are prevented from joining them because they lack Canadian citizenship or the resources to leave Mexico. Our interviewees spoke of the emotional pain family separation caused, particularly when kin (often the elderly) were left behind or when they could not return to attend to the sick or the dead. Yet outside the security and rigidity of the colony, women are afforded more opportunities for social interaction: e.g. access to English-language classes, where they also meet, and engage in new ways with, other LGM women. Women reported having more friends in Canada. These attempts to socialise with their cultural community, however, necessarily require ventures into 'the world' and therefore are inherently paradoxical.

Nevertheless, women experience social and geographic isolation in their new country due to language, cultural and spatial barriers. Rural geographies involve great distances and public transportation is non-existent. One woman believed that LG people's physical separation in Canada's vast rural areas contributed to their cultural and religious disintegration. They are often surrounded by people they do not know

Journal of Ethnic and Migration Studies   1511

or have difficult relationships with those who live nearby. Sometimes husbands or cultural expectations do not permit women to drive or attend immigrant service programmes. Life outside the colony isolates *and* connects.

Independence is Liberation and Burden

Within the colony, strict adherence to a traditional familial hierarchy is expected, requiring men to defer to God and fathers, women to God and husbands, and children to their parents. Overlaying this vertical order are teachings of humility and individual self-abnegation. Preserving a collective identity is difficult, however, as living in closed, geographically proximate communities is not possible in Canada. Church life is split off from everyday life; decisions cannot be made as a group. When released from the rigid rules of the colony, women and men have to make decisions for themselves with little guidance from their kin networks and religious authorities. In Canada, furthermore, men are freer to come and go. Some husbands and fathers find the burdens of poverty, vulnerability and unguided responsibility to be unbearable, and they flee—sometimes taking refuge in a bottle, sometimes to the desperate familiarity of Mexico, sometimes through suicide.

We found that LGM women seek at all costs to fulfil their primary gender role as mothers. When women lose their husbands either through premature death or alcoholism, Canada paradoxically becomes a place where female household heads can more adequately fulfil their responsibilities to ensure social reproduction. Life outside the colony allows them, among other things, to work for a wage, acquire a driver's licence, shop for the family's needs and seek medical attention. As Tina (44) explained, 'A woman has more rights here than in Mexico'. Conversely, female-headed households within the colony experience relatively greater social and economic marginalisation and are highly dependent on the benevolence of others.

Canada also offers women greater control over their reproductive health. They discussed the importance of having access to health care for themselves and their children and demonstrated little reluctance to engage in the secular world for these services, particularly for childbirth. Accessing health care in rural Canada, however, requires English language skills. Women who spoke very little Spanish—despite having spent their entire childhood in Mexico—appeared very willing to learn English, motivated in particular to avoid relating the intimacies of their bodies through interpreters. Sarah (28), when asked if she had advice for other women should they migrate to Canada, remarked: 'I advise them to go to school right away [so] that they can learn English, so it would be easier for them to go to the doctor'.

It is evident from our interviewees' narratives that the independence gained through learning English, key to navigating Canada's health-care system, is also viewed as costly. For Mennonite women, a proper religious disposition is one of yielding, acceptance and resignation. Several were unable to identify a personal preference, unwilling to offer advice, or seemingly disinterested in and unaware of their rights and entitlements. This is illustrated in the response of Aganetha (30) who, when asked whether she prefers life in Canada over life in Mexico, remarked, 'I can't see that it's worse. It's good enough. Where you are, there you are at home'. Independence and assertiveness, especially for women, are secular values that contradict the ideals of religious colony life. Learning English and navigating settlement, however, seem to generate difficult choices for women that can be divisive and destructive at the same time as they are inclusive and generative. Some women exercised their choices secretly, acquiring driver's licences or wearing 'modern' dress unbeknownst to their husbands, expressing a desire to adopt new cultural practices, mixed with a sense of obligation to family and tradition. The double-bind of transnationalism for women—of having some independence and some choice—is thus expressed in the apparently simple act of choosing clothing.

Migration Preserves and Destroys

We argue that the paradoxes of the transnational social field—each simultaneous gain and loss—are best characterised as a double-bind, wherein choice is elusive. Caught in the contest between physical and cultural/religious survival, women find themselves in the 'nothing' of in-between: between the sacred and the secular, and conflicting social fields and systems of capital. The double-bind of transnationalism is inherently gendered in nature, as the meanings of and responses to migration are different for men and women. For example, our research suggested that women are reluctant migrants, who prefer not to have to migrate in the first place but, if they must, favour settling in Canada over continuous circular migration. This does not necessarily mean that they would choose to make a home in Canada over Mexico, but rather that they prefer to be poor in Canada than poor in Mexico. The following exchange is illustrative of this sentiment:

> *If someone you knew was getting ready to come to Canada, what would you say to them?*
> Elisabeth: Oh, I would think that if they didn't have to come here then it would be better to stay there. But if they couldn't get by and anyway had to go and work out [work for someone else] then I would encourage them to come here.

Women's accounts suggest that men prefer to live in Mexico. As Sarah said: '[My husband] would gladly be over there [in Mexico], but he can see that we can't make it there, that we can make our living better here'. Men appear to have more at stake in losing ties to Mexico, where they have more control over their working lives as self-employed farmers. Further, they have more control over their family, a role supported by their community.

The gendered nature of the transnational social field is also, necessarily and essentially, religious. Preservation of religious tradition depends on women's cultural, social, religious and ethnic reproductive work—both necessary and fundamentally material. LGM women are socialised to consider their sole responsibility in life is to 'raise their children right'. Virtually every aspect of life (health care, housing, work,

Journal of Ethnic and Migration Studies   1513

language) relates to caring work, raising children in the ways of their people. In transnational spaces, confrontation with the outside world is both freeing and frightening, as women's traditional cultural and religious practices conflict with societal values and norms. In order for women to keep their children, often they must conform to 'worldly ways' (e.g. put their children in public school), thereby defying many of their beliefs and provoking rejection from their community. The risks of losing their children, either to the state or the secular world, are great in Canada. When confronted with the secular in the transnational, women's work takes on new meaning. Their work is for their very survival. Outside the colony, the home rather than the church is the centre of religious preservation and women become the 'keepers of the faith'.

The double-bind of transnationalism is seen to be not only gendered and religious in nature, but fundamentally material, as economic and social resources permit tolerance for and continuance of this in-between place—a divided self. Of our women interviewees, only one household had the material resources necessary to engage in long-term circular migration, to live as transmigrants. This degree of transnational movement, however, triggers ineligibility for Canadian public health care, the CCTB, and other social benefits ordinarily associated with citizenship. Similarly, Maria, a 39-year-old mother of six who returns to Mexico every winter to visit her extended family, demonstrates a divided self, seeming to move between the religious colony and secular Canada with the same ease and comfort with which she shifts between Low German and English or the traditional Mennonite dress to jeans and a T-shirt. It seems likely that, for these women, their relative wealth contributes to the ability to *choose*, so as not to provoke, unwillingly, a rejection of their people, tradition or self. For LGM women, engagement in multiple transnational social fields, when chosen, means something quite different to when it is forced.

Our analysis reveals that transnational women who preserve some proximity to religious colony life—geographically, socially or subjectively—experience more keenly the contradictions of the transnational social field. At the same time, women's narratives suggest a protective quality to be found in the sacred disposition, in maintaining some degree of transnational religious practice. The data evidence a link between strong connections with individuals and life in colonies in Mexico, and healthy, respectful family relationships in Canada. The strength and resources necessary to abide a divided self in the contradictory transnational social field seem to be associated not only with economic stability, but also with conjugal relationships that are characterised as partnerships, in which power and responsibility are shared despite rigidly defined gender roles. When possible, women engage in the secular only to the extent that it preserves the sacred.

Conversely, social and/or economic pressures sometimes force women to make pragmatic decisions about their engagement in the secular and their distance from the sacred. For a few women, competing value systems and beliefs are too difficult to endure over time and they gradually discard practices of the colony; to the extent possible, they adopt one life over the other. In this way, the double-bind of the transnational is resolved by choosing to reject one's roots and social identity. Justina (30) related that she migrated to Canada with her family when she was a young girl. Her parents sold their colony property shortly after. She does not return for visits and has little or no contact with family in Mexico. She has discarded traditional dress and chose to conduct her interview in English. It appears that there is little—or perhaps nothing—of value in the colony for her: no land, no family connections, no language, no traditions. In Canada, Justina unequivocally demonstrates a desire to assimilate, preferring to live in town rather than the country, expressing distaste for farm work, freely engaging with the local community, articulating strong opinions and a sense of personal entitlement, and refusing to transmit LG language and traditions to her children. She has adopted a more fundamentalist and evangelical religiosity, and holds this above extended family relations. Justina no longer engages in any form of transnational practice, adopting new religious thought and practice, unreserved secular engagement, and a non-traditional individual assertiveness.

Others, whose life experiences are marked by repeated traumas, seem stuck in the double-bind of the in-between space. Nancy (a 43-year-old mother of ten) and Anna (a 40-year-old mother of four) both exhibited outward manifestations of an attempt to preserve their cultural distinctiveness through their traditional dress, language and deferential nature. Yet, in their daily lives, neither demonstrated inclinations and practices consistent with the sacred *or* the secular. Poverty inhibits their relationships with extended family, and has destroyed the dream of the close family farming life inside the tight boundaries of the colony. Although LGM women are typically meticulous housekeepers and mothers, Nancy primarily portrayed indifference to these concerns, including her husband's alcoholism. For her, the gains of migration are minimal. The presentation of Anna, who had lost her two youngest children to child welfare services and appeared to be in an abusive relationship, suggested that she is alienated from herself, her children and the world around her. For some women who lack the necessary resources—emotionally or materially—to preserve meaningful connections with colony life, the double-bind provokes despair and a loss of self, apparent in a demeanour of apathy, defeat and hopelessness. These women remain caught in contradiction, in conflicted and dominated positions in transnational social fields.

Conclusions

At a fundamental level, these historically unusual migrations have a profoundly usual and banal quality. This particular example of forced migration is part of the movement of migrant workers from the South to the North, and back to the South. The transnational lives of LGM women are intimately linked to demands of the Canadian labour market, which make their migrations materially rewarding, as well as culturally and religiously appealing. Yet to limit our understanding of this case to yet another example of forced economic migration—or, on the other hand, a peculiar

Journal of Ethnic and Migration Studies   1515

example of religious fanaticism—is to erase the deep religious and historical meanings that are common to transnational groups and individuals all over the world.

The experiences of transnational social spaces for Mennonite women from Mexico push us toward an integrative analytical lens, toward social concepts that are dynamic and relational rather than categorical. People move within and between countries, constituting themselves as migrants whose identities and social practices are not necessarily defined by the national borders they traverse or the state citizenship they hold. Further, lives are not as readily distinguished as migrant or non-migrant, and religion cannot be separated out as a distinct social setting or social involvement. Our research suggests that migration and religion are often much more intertwined and interdependent, such that a decision to move may have profound implications for religious involvement and identity, and historical and contemporary migratory practices may have deep religious roots. For many LGM women, material need forces a non-religious migration and the greater the material need, the less they are able to engage in the transnational ethno-religious social field. Migration is a necessary move *away*. Our analysis also highlights specific ways in which formal and informal transnational expressions of religion are intensely gendered, and the processes and structures of gender sustained through religious ideology and institutions. We conclude that it is not possible to engage in the empirical study of gender separate from religion; neither can they be adequately theorised in isolation.

An integrative, relational approach to analysis forces exposure of oppressive practices and taken-for-granted assumptions. The project of secularisation—integral to global neoliberalism—relegates religion to the private realm where related beliefs and practices remain invisible and outwardly inconsequential (Kyrlezhev 2008; Morozov 2008). Migrating religious groups and individuals challenge neoliberal understandings of the world, provoking confrontation in the transnational, as religion is a way of life for many communities and peoples, permeating every aspect of daily living. In the contradictory and conflicted spaces of the transnational social field, double-binds are generated. For example, the feminisation and privatisation of religion permit the dismissal and denigration of the LGM way of life, contributing to their racialisation as less deserving and confirming their status as 'not quite white'. The standards by which entitlement, eligibility and legitimacy are determined in the delivery of social services, in the opportunities available in the labour market, and in the organisation of dominant society, are based on neoliberal ideals of secularism, individualism and competition. The operationalisation of such values—pervasive and powerful—invokes social relations and structures that are inherently gender-specific and ironically religious. When religion is minimised through its association with the falsely segregated and subordinate domestic realm, devalued through its alignment with the feminine and reduced to culture, it becomes a way of justifying practices of oppression. The resulting implications go way beyond *feeling* caught—it is being nowhere and nothing everywhere. The double-bind of transnational livelihoods is the day-to-day reality of having no choice in every act of choosing.

1516   *L. Good Gingrich & K. Preibisch*

Acknowledgements

Rural Women Making Change was funded by the Social Sciences and Humanities Research Council of Canada. We are grateful to Dr Belinda Leach for inviting us to participate, Margaret Peters and Anna Peters for their indispensible roles in our research, and Spencer Henson and two anonymous *JEMS* reviewers for their insightful comments on earlier drafts. Our greatest appreciation is to the women who had the courage to speak to us about their everyday lives.

Notes

[1]   For all Mennonites in Canada, 87 per cent of whom were rural residents in 1941, an agriculture-based livelihood was integral to their ethno-religious identity (Regehr 1996). Increasing pressure on small-scale farming in Canada over the past half-century has forced rural-to-urban migrations for the majority, and drastic and irreversible lifestyle changes for Mennonites.

[2]   A community-based researcher interviewed women one-to-one, with the exception of two cases in which husbands were also present.

[3]   The passage of assimilative school attendance acts in Manitoba and Saskatchewan induced 7,000 conservative Mennonites to migrate to Mexico and 1,800 to Paraguay. Another 1,200 headed to Paraguay and 800 to Mexico in 1948 due to rising concern that 'the mid-twentieth-century world was undermining their faith and weakening their ability to guard their inherited culture' (Loewen 2006: 169). Some stayed only a decade or two, and thriving colonies have since been established in Bolivia, Argentina and Belize (Bender *et al.* 1987; Cañás Bottos 2008, 2009).

[4]   One notable exception is various Old Order Mennonite groups of Swiss-German descent who maintain traditional closed communities primarily in Ontario and Eastern and Mid-Western United States (Good Gingrich and Lightman 2004, 2006). While similar to their Dutch-Russian Old Colony Mennonite 'cousins' in conservative religious beliefs and lifestyle, their transnational migratory history ended in the mid-nineteenth century (Epp 1974).

[5]   Return migration to Canada gathered pace in the 1970s when a Mennonite NGO discovered an obscure loophole in Canada's citizenship law. Recognising the potential for these Mennonites to provide flexible labour in Canadian agriculture, federal officials were persuaded to change their interpretation of the 1947 Citizenship law, permitting thousands of Mennonites from Mexico to claim citizenship through the 'delayed registration' provision. Without this, Mexican-born Mennonites would have little chance of qualifying under Canada's human capital model for immigration. Changes to Canadian law (2009) now narrowly restrict citizenship opportunities for LGMs.

[6]   CCTB is a monthly, tax-free cash supplement—paid to eligible low- and middle-income applicants with children under 18 years—usually issued to mothers, provided they hold status as citizens, landed immigrants or refugees.

[7]   In a 1920 letter to the Canadian government citing the motives for their intended mass migration to Latin America, a Mennonite church leader wrote that, if pressures to force their children into secular schools were to continue, 'we will be obliged to seek out a new homeland, where we and our children will be able to live by our faith' (Guenther 2005: 188).

[8]   During harvest seasons, which start and end well before and after public school summer break, it is not unusual for school-age children to be working in the fields with their parents.

References

Basch, L., Glick Schiller, N. and Szanton Blanc, C. (1994) *Nations Unbound: Transnational Projects, Postcolonial Predicaments, and Deterritorialized Nation-States*. New York: Gordon and Breach.

Bender, H.S., Friesen, M.W., Ediger, M., Hiebert, I. and Mumaw, G. (1987) *Global Anabaptist Mennonite Encyclopedia Online*, http://www.gameo.org.

Bourdieu, P. (1990) *The Logic of Practice*. Stanford, CA: Stanford University Press.

Bourdieu, P. and Wacquant, L. (1992) *An Invitation to Reflexive Sociology*. Chicago: University of Chicago Press.

Cañás Bottos, L. (2008) *Old Colony Mennonites in Argentina and Bolivia: Nation-Making, Religious Conflict and Imagination of the Future*. Leiden and Boston: Brill Academic.

Cañás Bottos, L. (2009) 'Order and dissent among Old Colony Mennonites: a regime of embedded sovereignty', in Kirsch, T.G. and Turner, B. (eds) *Permutations of Order: Religion and Law as Contested Sovereignties*. Farnham: Ashgate, 107–23.

Curran, S., Shafer, S., Donato, K. and Garip, F. (2006) 'Mapping gender and migration in sociological scholarship: is it segregation or integration?', *International Migration Review*, 40(1): 199–223.

Donato, K.M., Gabaccia, D., Holdaway, J., Manalansan, M. and Pessar, P.R. (2006) 'A glass half full? Gender in migration studies', *International Migration Review*, 40(1): 3–27.

Drbohlav, D. (2003) 'Ethnicity and international migration: focus on family and religion', *Studi Emigrazione*, 40(151): 621–37.

Ebaugh, H.R. and Chafetz, J.S. (1999) 'Agents for cultural reproduction and structural change: the ironic role of women in immigrant religious institutions', *Social Forces*, 78(2): 585–613.

Epp, F.H. (1974) *Mennonites in Canada, 1786–1920: The History of a Separate People*. Toronto: Macmillan.

Faist, T. (2000) 'Transnationalization in international migration: implications for the study of citizenship and culture', *Ethnic and Racial Studies*, 23(2): 189–222.

Gates, M. (1993) *In Default: Peasants, the Debt Crisis, and the Agricultural Challenge in Mexico*. Oxford: Westview Press.

Glick Schiller, N. (2005) 'Transnational social fields and imperialism: bringing a theory of power to transnational studies', *Anthropological Theory*, 5(4): 439–61.

Goldring, L. (1996) 'Gendered memory: constructions of reality among Mexican transnational migrants', in DuPuis, M. and Vandergeest, P. (eds) *Creating the Countryside: The Politics of Rural and Environmental Discourse*. Philadelphia: Temple University Press, 303–29.

Good Gingrich, L. and Lightman, E. (2004) 'Mediating communities and cultures: a case study of informal helpers in an Old Order Mennonite community', *Families in Society*, 85(4): 511–20.

Good Gingrich, L. and Lightman, E. (2006) 'Striving toward self-sufficiency: a qualitative study of mutual aid in an Old Order Mennonite community', *Family Relations*, 55(2): 175–89.

Guenther, T.F. (2005) '*Ältester* Martin C. Friesen (1889–1968): a man of vision for Paraguay's *Mennogemeinde*', *Journal of Mennonite Studies*, 23: 185–211.

Hondagneu-Sotelo, P. (1994) *Gendered Transitions: Mexican Experiences of Immigration*. Berkeley and Los Angeles: University of California Press.

Hondagneu-Sotelo, P. (2003) 'Gender and immigration: a retrospective and introduction', in Hondagneu-Sotelo, P. (ed.) *Gender and US Immigration: Contemporary Trends*. Berkeley: University of California Press, 3–19.

Itzigsohn, J. and Giorguli, S. (2005) 'Incorporation, transnationalism, and gender: immigrant incorporation and transnational participation as gendered processes', *International Migration Review*, 39(4): 895–920.

Janzen, W. (1998) *Build Up One Another: The Work of MCCO with the Mennonites from Mexico in Ontario 1977–1997*. Kitchener, Ontario: Mennonite Central Committee Ontario.

1518   L. *Good Gingrich & K. Preibisch*

Kyrlezhev, A. (2008) 'The postsecular age: religion and culture today', *Religion, State and Society,* 36(1): 21–31.

Levitt, P. (2001) 'Between God, ethnicity, and country: an approach to the study of transnational religion'. Paper given at the conference 'Transnational Migration: Comparative Perspectives', Princeton University, 30 June–1 July.

Levitt, P. (2003) 'Keeping feet in two worlds: transnational practices and immigrant incorporation in the United States', in Joppke, C. and Morawaska, E. (eds) *Toward Assimilation and Citizenship: Immigrants in Liberal Nation-States.* London: Palgrave Macmillan, 177–194.

Levitt, P. and Glick Schiller, N. (2004) 'Conceptualizing simultaneity: a transnational social field perspective on society', *International Migration Review,* 38(3): 1002–39.

Levitt, P., De Wind, J. and Vertovec, S. (2003) 'International perspectives on transnational migration: an introduction', *International Migration Review,* 37(3): 565–75.

Loewen, R. (2006) *Diaspora in the Countryside: Two Mennonite Communities and Mid-Twentieth-Century Rural Disjuncture.* Toronto: University of Toronto Press.

Loewen, R. (2007) 'To the ends of the earth: Low German Mennonites and old order ways in the Americas'. Paper given at the conference 'Amish in America', Elizabethtown, 7–9 June.

Morozov, A. (2008) 'Has the postsecular age begun?', *Religion, State and Society,* 36(1): 39–44.

Ong, A. (1999) *Flexible Citizenship: The Cultural Logics of Transnationality.* Durham, NC: Duke University Press.

Peake, L. and Trotz, D.A. (1999) *Gender, Ethnicity and Place: Women and Identities in Guyana.* New York: Routledge.

Preibisch, K. and Hermoso, L.M. (2006) 'Engendering labour migration: the case of foreign workers in Canadian agriculture', in Tastsoglou, E. and Dobrowolsky, A. (eds) *Women, Migration, and Citizenship: Making Local, National, and Transnational Connections.* Farnham: Ashgate, 107–30.

Regehr, T.D. (1996) *Mennonites in Canada, 1939–1970: A People Transformed.* Toronto: University of Toronto Press.

Vande Berg, T. and Kniss, F. (2008) 'Iskcon and immigrants: the rise, decline, and rise again of a new religious movement', *The Sociological Quarterly,* 49(1): 79–104.

Vertovec, S. (2002) *Religion in Migration, Diasporas and Transnationalism.* Burnaby, BC: Vancouver Centre of Excellence Working Paper No. 02-07.

Vertovec, S. (2004) 'Religion and diaspora', in Antes, P., Geertz, A.W. and Warne, R.R. (eds) *New Approaches to the Study of Religion: Textual, Comparative, Sociological, and Cognitive Approaches.* Berlin and New York: Walter de Gruyter, 275–304.

Woodhead, L. (2008) 'Secular privilege, religious disadvantage', *British Journal of Sociology,* 59(1): 53–8.

[10]

Paul Christopher Johnson | MIGRATING BODIES, CIRCULATING SIGNS: BRAZILIAN CANDOMBLÉ, THE GARIFUNA OF THE CARIBBEAN, AND THE CATEGORY OF INDIGENOUS RELIGIONS

I. INTRODUCTION

There is a certain characterization of the current study of religion that begins with the problem of boundaries, both territorial and conceptual. Here is my version of it:

The pure products have gone crazy in the plasticity of flow. Our time, said Salman Rushdie, "rejoices in mongrelization and fears the absolutism of the pure. Mélange, hotchpotch, a bit of this and a bit of that."[1] If the first "global" was called a village, the new one is more like Brazilian Carnaval, where the glittering surface is not the means to an end; it is the end. The buzz is deterritorialization, pastiche, polyrhythm, the unbundling of culture from land sites, and the detachment of ethnoscapes from geoscapes.[2] Even the body, the last epistemological glue holding it all together, from Durkheim and Malinowski to Foucault and Bourdieu, appears shaky. Whether viewed according to the organic metaphor of the hybrid or the synthetic one of the cyborg, bodies have turned out to be of interchangeable parts, merely another surface. Related to all of this flux and surface, the edges of discrete religions are thrown open to trespass:

Research for this article was supported by a National Endowment for the Humanities grant.
[1] Salman Rushdie, *Imaginary Homelands* (London: Granta, 1991), p. 394.
[2] This latter follows the terms of Arjun Appadurai, *Modernity at Large: Cultural Dimensions of Globalization* (Minneapolis: University of Minnesota Press, 1996), pp. 33–37.

even syncretism essentializes too much, implying that there were once well-behaved pure breeds before the new religious mutts gnawed through their leashes. Yet syncretism, blackballed in the 1970s, is again freely exchanged as theoretical currency today—disciplined by quotation marks, of course, to show we know we're trafficking in contraband, but traded nonetheless. "Religions," moreover, are less coherent systems than series of particular performances and practices, just as "identity" is at best a string of "identifications," and many even argue that the category of "religion" has no edges at all.[3]

Granting a degree of breathless postmodern hyperbole in such a characterization, it is nevertheless clear to even the most sober observer that territory and boundaries are a central concern of our time, as gauged by quantity of ink spilled, that very discursive emphasis suggesting their problematic nature. It is no surprise that in a historical moment when large populations live in conditions of exile, diaspora, and migration, and where even those remaining "in place" are lit up in crossfire of media, financial, and other transnational flows, that defining the boundaries of territories and identities should present a challenge for social groups and for their analysts. The extreme parameters for such discussions of spatial mobility and religion are set, to my view, by two opposed terms: the "global," commonly viewed as the unconstrained circulation of bodies, signs, and capital, and the "indigenous," a group and its religion rooted in place since time immemorial. In the first part of this article, I will describe the problematic polarization of these categories, which though apparently opposed, came into usage at roughly the same time and are in important ways enmeshed.[4] The two terms have been brought closer together by clipping the wings of "the global" to note its forms and contingencies—by bringing the global down to earth, so to say. The second

[3] It was in 1962 that Wilfred Cantwell Smith proposed doing away with "religion" altogether, in *The Meaning and End of Religion* (Minneapolis: Fortress, 1991). More recently, for quite opposite reasons, Talal Asad argued the same, in *Genealogies of Religion: Discipline and Reasons of Power in Christianity and Islam* (Baltimore: Johns Hopkins University Press, 1993). Asad makes their affinity (and where it ends) clear in "Reading a Modern Classic: W. C. Smith's *The Meaning and End of Religion*," *History of Religions*, 40, no. 3 (2001): 205–22. On "identifications" in place of "identity," see Rogers Brubaker and Frederick Cooper, "Beyond Identity," *Theory and Society* 29, no. 1 (2000): 1–47; and Andreas Glaesner, *Divided in Unity: Identity, Germany, and the Berlin Police* (Chicago: University of Chicago Press, 2000), pp. 10–11.

[4] Documenting how "local" claims have been articulated through global media and how the cultural dimension has gained force during the last two decades is widely evidenced in diverse contexts. For example, Walter D. Mignolo, *Local Histories/Global Designs: Coloniality, Subaltern Knowledges, and Border Thinking* (Princeton, N.J.: Princeton University Press, 2000), p. 39; Ulf Hannerz, *Transnational Connections* (New York: Routledge, 1996), pp. 52–53; Alcita Rita Ramos, *Indigenism: Ethnic Politics in Brazil* (Madison: University of Wisconsin Press, 1998), pp. 89–146; Terence Turner, "Representing, Resisting, Rethinking: Historical Transformations of Kayapo Culture and Anthropological Consciousness,"

task in understanding the relations between the indigenous and the global, though, evaluating the social and territorial extensions of indigenous communities, has been rarely undertaken.[5]

To address the convergence of the global and the indigenous empirically, the second part of the article will present two examples of indigenous religions in the process of territorial and social extensions: Brazilian Candomblé and the ancestor religion of the Garifuna of Central America.[6] These are indigenous communities as defined here because they imagine themselves in the indigenous form—as, in their own self-understanding and presentation, oriented toward and organically related to a particular place. I juxtapose Candomblé and Garifuna ancestor religion to present two distinct types of extension. In Candomblé, the circulation of meanings about the once-secret religion in mass media and popular culture has led to the participation of new practicing bodies; it has brought a new ethnic constituency. In Garifuna religion, by contrast,

---

in *Colonial Situations*, ed. George W. Stocking (Madison: University of Wisconsin Press, 1991); Prema Kurien, "Becoming American by Becoming Hindu: Indian Americans Take Their Place at the Multicultural Table," in *Gatherings in Diaspora: Religious Communities and the New Immigration*, ed. R. Stephen Warner and Judith G. Wittner (Philadelphia: Temple University Press, 1998), pp. 43–44; Appadurai, pp. 7–8, 37–38; Daniel Mato, "Transnational Networking and the Social Production of Representations of Identities by Indigenous Peoples' Organizations of Latin America," *International Sociology*, 15, no. 2 (June 2000): 343–60; Virginia Kerns, *Women and the Ancestors: Black Carib Kinship and Ritual* (Urbana: University of Illinois Press, 1997), pp. 202–6, just to name a few.

[5] Interpreting such extensions is not equivalent to attempts to deconstruct the indigenous, a kind of move usefully summarized, and usefully opposed, by June Nash, in "Introduction," *Anthropology of Work Review* 21, no. 2 (2000): 1–7. The present article seeks the middle way that will allow us to think critically about contemporary transformations of indigenous groups and their styles of self-presentation, but at the same time not subvert politically and socially important claims as "fabricated" or, worse, "false."

[6] These religions are, to some views, on the edge of the category. Some (e.g., Mignolo, p. 72) would distinguish between groups around whom the world has changed—Andean societies or the Pueblo peoples of what is now New Mexico—from those who have migrated or been exiled as a part of global flows—as is the case for both Candomblé and the Garifuna, whose origins derive, in part, from the forced migrations of the slave trade. Hence Nancie L. Gonzalez, e.g., calls the Garifuna a "transnational ethnic group" (*Sojourners of the Caribbean: Ethnogenesis and Ethnohistory of the Garifuna* [Urbana: University of Illinois Press, 1988], p. 8). In other important respects, however, they fit many of the typical characteristics of what is finally a thoroughly polythetic category: the primacy of orality and ritual performance to transmit knowledge, the ideological rootedness in specific homelands viewed as sources of power, a strong ethnic boundary based on descent, etc. In the literature, they are frequently, though by no means always, classified as "indigenous." The alternative approach to defining the category, elaborated below, makes the point moot. That "indigenousness" is less than clear (what amount of mobility renders a group no longer indigenous? what duration of continuous occupancy of a specific landsite qualifies as indigenous?) is a conundrum that motivates the approach taken here. A final note: In the context of Latin America, it is important not to confuse *indigenismo* with indigenous or indigenism. The former describes the formation of creole nationalisms beginning in the eighteenth century, nationalisms that often sought to establish their own identity precisely through the extermination of indigenous peoples.

the circulation is not of information but of bodies—of people emigrating to the United States—who bring new meanings back to the rituals performed in the homeland. In one, circulating symbols and meanings bring new bodies; in the other, circulating bodies bring new meanings to symbols at home.

The third point of this article will be to show that, despite the extensions beyond traditional social and spatial boundaries, which one might expect to result in a twilight of indigenous communities, discourses and practices asserting traditional continuity and territorial primordia appear in many cases to be in ascendancy rather than in decline. The two cases suggest ways in which the indigenous is a quite modern discursive style and strategy that at least in part responds to crises of dislocation, such that the more actual transformation and mobility encountered, the more valued the ideology of unchanging permanence and territorial stability becomes.[7] The modes of the identifying practices of indigenousness themselves, however, are imagined through global media and often expressed in their forms.

To say that indigenous communities are imagined, following a trajectory from Benedict Anderson to Arjun Appadurai, is not to differentiate them from other social forms that supposedly are not imagined.[8] All social identities and representations are mediated; the question is merely in what mode and through which filters. The term "imagined" is perhaps distinct in this sense from "invention" and "fabrication" used so forcefully by Hobsbawm and Gellner, respectively, to discuss the nation.[9] Hobsbawm's concept of "invented traditions," for instance, implies that some communities and traditions are not invented or fabricated, but are rather "real." In this sense such theories carry a "residential primordialism" they allegedly seek to subvert.[10] Declaring that communities are imagined asserts no such specious line dividing the true from the fabri-

---

[7] On the "revivalist" or "nativist" argument for the case of the Garifuna, see Margaret S. Sanford, "Revitalization Movements as Indicators of Completed Acculturation," *Comparative Studies in Society and History* 16 (1974): 504–18; and Gonzalez, pp. 10, 90. In comparative perspective, Vittorio Lanternari, "Nativistic and Socio-Religious Movements: A Reconsideration." *Comparative Studies in Society and History* 16 (1974): 483–503.

[8] Benedict Anderson, *Imagined Communities: Reflections on the Origins and Spread of Nationalism* (New York and London: Verso, 1991). For Anderson, "communities are to be distinguished, not by their falsity/genuineness, but by the style in which they are imagined" (p. 6). Appadurai, p. 31, stresses the social practice, work, and agency of imagination.

[9] Eric J. Hobsbawm, "Introduction: Inventing Traditions," in *The Invention of Tradition*, ed. Eric J. Hobsbawm and Terence Ranger (London: Cambridge University Press, 1983), pp. 1–14, esp. pp. 8–10, and *Nations and Nationalism since 1780* (London and New York: Cambridge University Press, 1992); Ernest Gellner, *Nations and Nationalism* (New York: Cornell University Press, 1983).

[10] Geneviève Zubrzycki, "'Residual Primordialism': A Critical Commentary on Hobsbawm, Gellner and a Few Others" (University of Chicago, Department of Sociology, unpublished manuscript, 2001).

cated. Ritual performances linking a group to a land base construct an imagined community, and the nationwide viewing of *Seinfeld* constructs an imagined community as well. The two are by no means equivalent; my point is simply that neither one nor the other is real, authentic, or natural in comparison to the other, which is merely "fabricated."

Because we can investigate the ways in which the indigenous is a style of imagined community does not mean we can or should seek to deconstruct indigenousness in its meaning of a historically enduring relation between an ethnic group and a land base. Historiographically, it is crucial to draw broad distinctions between the highly rationalized societies (in the instrumental sense) that led to the European ages of exploration and industrialization and those peoples and lands that were colonized under the application of that instrumental reason and the implementation of it in the economic world-system.[11] Moreover, I share the view that modernity and its epistemologies were derived from and were an accomplice to colonial conquest and intrusion. But that is all the more reason to investigate and interpret the insidious fact that even rebels against the world-system, however diverse their ideological motives, must stage their rebellions in strangely familiar forms—in print, on television, on the Web, in style. We need, in other words, to also evaluate issues such as the standardization of the immense variety of indigenisms into predictable forms, not to mention the identity politics wherein indigenous communities hotly debate who is "really" in the group and who is not—issues only accessible by considering the indigenous not only as a historical relation to land but as also a style of imagined community. This is no more than to say that the human relation to land is always material but also always cultural and that those dimensions are finally inseparable: the land and a group's relation to it are symbolically and cognitively mediated by words, rituals, artistic productions, and so forth. This view departs from Anderson's "imagined communities." Where he states, "all communities larger than primordial villages of face-to-face contact (and perhaps even these) are imagined," the present article states with certainty that even those primordial villages imagine their collectivity and its relation to place.[12] Indigenousness is never "natural" and unmediated;

[11] Immanual Maurice Wallerstein, *Capitalist Aggression and the Origins of the European World-Economy in the Sixteenth Century* (New York: Academic Press, 1974). It is worth noting that Wallerstein differentiates the implementation of an economic world-system with the colonization of the Americas from its implementation and naturalization as a "geoculture," which occurs only after 1789. Immanuel Wallerstein, "The Insurmountable Contradictions of Liberalism: Human Rights and the Rights of Peoples in the Geoculture of the Modern World-System," in *Nations, Identities, Cultures,* edited by V. Y. Mudimbe (Durham, N.C.: Duke University Press, 1997), p. 183. Janet Abu-Lughod places the emergence of a world-system earlier than the colonization of the Americas, in *Before European Hegemony: The World-System A.D. 1250–1350* (New York: Oxford University Press, 1989).

[12] Anderson, p. 6.

it must be imagined and standardized (not necessarily in that order) sufficiently to generate lasting and relatively stable sociopolitical affinities
and allegiances of what are typically now called "identities." Clearly,
moreover, the ways indigenousness can become a style of imagined community are subject to change.[13]

Defining indigenous religions as the religions of those communities
that imagine themselves in indigenous style—as organically bound to a
land site—brackets the impasse between so-called romantic or essential-
ist and deconstructivist views of indigenous societies. Whether the Lakota actually emerged onto the surface of the earth from Wind Cave and
are in an essential, primordial way the people of and from the Black
Hills, versus historians' claims that they migrated into the region and
conquered it after acquiring horses around 1700, is less important for my
purposes than that their community makes itself imaginatively as of and
related to that place. When the Garifuna say they were the first people to
settle much of the coast of Honduras and Belize and forget that within
a generation after their arrival in 1797 they drove the Miskito, already
there, east to what is now Nicaragua, this historical fact is less important
in this article than how the Garifuna understand and discursively present
themselves to make community in the present.[14]

---

[13] The material and cultural relation to any land site is not natural or given, but rather
made, even in contexts of long historical occupation of a specific place. This seems obvious
but is often occluded. For example, it is impossible to ignore that the indigenous category
is, analytically speaking, remarkably similar to the category of the ethnic, differentiated
only by a stronger claim to a territorial ontology, to being autochthonous to a specific site.
Both are characterized as the positing of a homogenous group of shared descent, which has
maintained a specific, unique language and culture and which is organically related to a
specific land base (see, e.g., Anthony D. Smith, *National Identity* [Reno: University of Ne-
vada Press, 1991], pp. 19–42). The ethnic has been shown, repeatedly and convincingly,
to be socially constructed and as much a process of selective forgetting as remembering;
on forgetting as key to ethnic and national forms, see Ernst Renan's 1874 "Qu'est qu'une
nation?" in *Becoming National: A Reader*, ed. by Geoff Eley and Ronald G. Suny (New
York: Oxford University Press, 1996); Geoff Eley and Ronald G. Suny, "Introduction:
From the Moment of Social History to the Work of Cultural Representation," in Eley and
Suny, eds.; and Anderson, pp. 198–206. This deconstructive project is often viewed as politically progressive, since it subverts the idea of the ethnic nation that in the Western
imagination is indelibly linked to fascism. The claims of indigenous religions, viewed analytically, are similar: a bounded group with a unique, original set of practices, and a relation to a landscape it has occupied since time immemorial, usually in conflict with the
territorial claims of a civil state. It seems, therefore, inconsistent to critically examine
the "ethnic" but to resist doing so for the "indigenous." At least in the study of religion,
indigenous religions are not typically deconstructed, both because scholars of religion
often share the view that the monolithic ontology of modernity should be resisted as merely
one construction of "reality" and because indigenous communities are seen to be the victims of modernity, and rightly so. We should be clear, nevertheless, that the analytical inconsistency between the eagerness to critically interrogate ethnicity and the resistance to
evaluating indigenousness with the same tools is politically motivated. That is all the more
reason to maintain the inconsistency, as (armchair-variety) political engagement, but it
should be explicit.

[14] Gonzales, p. 48.

II. UNCONSTRAINED FLOWS, PRIMORDIAL STABILITY

Globalization as a master trope began to emerge between Marshall Mc-Cluhan's pioneering 1964 work on world media systems and Immanuel Wallerstein's 1974 magnum opus on global trade networks, or roughly contemporaneously with the replacement of the "primitive" by the "indigenous" around 1970—though, as in the case of the indigenous, it was only fully reified in an avalanche of scholarly output over the last decade.[15] It is noteworthy that both the global and the indigenous are spatial terms, compared with earlier temporal or sequential ones like "development" and "modernization," on one hand, and the "primitive," on the other, suggesting a return to space and place as again a master trope. First, a word on the newest redaction of space/place issues, globalization. Many now view it as a shibboleth, a magic incantation that cloaks as natural and inevitable what is historically contingent.[16] Rather than subjecting globalization to critical analysis, its mere repetition may even act as a vehicle for that which it purports to merely describe.[17] In academic production, important steps have been taken to dampen the bluster. This has taken the form of specifying the local aspects of so-called globalizations: First, by noting the kinds of concentrations of technology and cheap service labor supplies required to take part in producing inputs to—not merely receiving outputs of—the global circulation of signs; and second, by devoting attention to the "glocal," to take Roland Robertson's well-known term, to emphasize that, while each locale is usefully viewed as an intersection of flows of bodies, signs, and money, each locale appropriates those flows and makes them their own differently.[18] In place of sheer neocolonial diffusion, then, there is the local creolization of worldwide media in the new "ecumene."

[15] Marshal McLuhan, *Understanding Media: The Extensions of Man* (New York: McGraw-Hill, 1964); Wallerstein, *Capitalist Aggression*.

[16] On globalization as "shibboleth," see Zygmunt Baumann, *Globalization: The Human Consequences* (New York: Columbia University Press, 1998), p. 1. On its "naturalizing" function, see Pierre Bourdieu and Loïc Wacquant, "On the Cunning of Imperialist Reason," *Theory, Culture and Society*, 16, no. 1 (1999): 41–58; and Immanuel Wallerstein, "Globalization or the Age of Transition? A Long-Term View of the Trajectory of the World System," *International Sociology* 15, no. 2 (June 2000): 249–65. On globalization as "axiomatic," a social and cultural "accord" now constitutive of our very experience and speech, see Kenneth Surin, "On Producing the Concept of a Global Culture," in *Nations, Identities, Cultures*, edited by V. Y. Mudimbe (Durham, N.C.: Duke University Press, 1997), p. 211.

[17] Jens Bartelson, "Three Concepts of Globalization," *International Sociology*, 15, no. 2 (June 2000): 180–97, 183.

[18] On specifying the kinds of labor and service concentrations necessary to create "globalization," see, e.g., Saskia Sassen, *Globalization and Its Discontents* (New York: New Press, 1998). On the "glocal," see Roland Robertson, *Globalization* (London: Sage, 1992). Edouard Glissant usefully distinguishes "globality" from "globalization" (mondialité, mondialisation): the first refers to the fact that every locale is now an intersection of global signs and symbols; the latter refers to international designs of power (Glissant, cited in Mignolo [n. 4 above], p. 77).

What does this imply for the study of religion? First, it implies that while comparison once relied on stable, bounded, and discrete religions, comparison now can suppose only provisional constraints of religions, territories, and groups. Syncretism, acculturation, the hybrid, and the creole are no longer the riddle to be solved. It is rather zones of religious purity and stability that now seem most worthy of curiosity. Clean boundaries and traditional continuity are in our time the virtuoso's most stunning religious effect or a community's most prized achievement. Second, it entails changes in how we go about comparing. The old risk of comparison was that of the totalizing panopticon, the overly objective view that had every phenomenon neatly tucked in its bounded place for convenient theorization from the ivory tower. The new comparative problem is less like a panopticon and more like the Tower of Babel, where there can be no comparison because there is only untranslatable difference; instead of essentialism, sheer uniqueness; where William James's crab eternally fumes that he is not a crustacean but rather himself alone, and, to complicate matters further, fumes not at seaside where we had him pegged on all our maps, but from barnyard or a busy street corner in the Bronx.[19]

In this context, new methods are required. Multisite ethnography is often necessary to locate "a religion" no longer of a particular territory, but rather forged across migrations and returns of both bodies and signs. And we are challenged to shift attention from bounded religious arenas to the processes by which lines are drawn, crossed, and redrawn.

Given the impact of globalization—both the concept and the flows it describes—the category of the indigenous presents special problems. There are two reasons. The most obvious one is that it conflates specific religions within an allegedly shared territorial ontology, when it is far from clear exactly what, say, the Yoruba and the Lakota share in their spatial orientations.[20] The second is that though it rings less jarring to late-modern ears, the indigenous may have reproduced some of the primitive's worst habits.[21] Here's why.

A religion that is indigenous is the religion of indigenous peoples, those etymologically characterized as "born of" or "born into" (*indi-*, in; *gegnere*, born) a specific place. Like the preferred francophone classifier

---

[19] William James, *The Varieties of Religious Experience* (Cambridge, Mass.: Harvard University Press, 1985).

[20] David Harvey, *The Condition of Postmodernity* (Oxford: Blackwell, 1990), p. 204, argues this as pertains to spatial constructions; Johannes Fabian, *Time and the Other: How Anthropology Makes Its Object* (New York: Columbia University Press, 1983) argues this for time.

[21] The challenge to deconstruct the primitive was most forcefully presented by Charles Long, *Significations: Signs, Symbols and Images in the Interpretation of Religion* (Philadelphia: Fortress, 1986), p. 62; and by Fabian, who argues there is no substantive category of the primitive, rather only the concept of the primitive, that which we can think in terms of.

for indigenous peoples, *les autochtones* (self-sprung, *auto*; land, *kthon*), it connotes the religion of peoples that is the natural growth of a particular land, an organic, biological relation between a group and a place. In the Saussurean sense, then, it "means" the same as the primitive, since it occupies the same position in a familiar set of relations.[22] In the gendered categories of the "natural" versus the "cultural," for instance, this is a passive position, the raw material awaiting cultivation.[23] Together with its predecessor the primitive, the indigenous remains the classic

[22] Let us very briefly recount the arrival of the category indigenous religions. The initial descriptor for the problematic peoples of the New World was the "savage," from *silva*, people of the forest. It extends in use to early in the twentieth century in, e.g., the work of R. R. Marrett. By mid-century it appears in ironic, critical tone, as in Claude Lévi-Strauss's double entendre *La pensée sauvage* (Paris: Plon, 1962), and by century's end the terms are inverted, and it is the European colonizer and the academic classifier who are the savages, as in David Chidester's 1996 *Savage Systems: Colonialism and Comparative Religion in Southern Africa* (Charlottesville: University Press of Virginia). The primitive replaced the savage and took three trajectories: one in Durkheim's sense of the simple or elementary, another in E. B. Tylor's sense of evolutionary priority, and a third beginning with Lèvi-Bruhl's 1910 *Les fonctions mentales dans les sociétés inférieurs* (Paris: Librairies Félix Alcan et Guillaumin Réunies), which shared much with Durkheim—the primitive as elementary," "collective representations," etc.—but departed from Durkheim on the primitive as a kind of cognitive process and ontology based in "participatory thought." Interestingly, by the time of Lévy-Bruhl's 1935 foreword to *Primitives and the Supernatural*, "primitive" was already under implied critique by appearing under the regime of quotation marks (trans. Lilian A. Clare [New York: Haskell House, 1973]). Later, in his posthumously published *Carnets*, Lévy-Bruhl had moderated his earlier position to view "participation" and "cause-effect" thought as two ontologies more or less present in all humans. Yet the primitive appears unmarked into the 1950s and even 1960s in, e.g., Paul Radin's *The World of Primitive Man* (New York: H. Schuman, 1953), or E. E. Evans-Pritchard's 1965 *Theories of Primitive Religion* (Oxford: Clarendon), and along the Durkheimian trajectory of the primitive until at least 1966 in Mary Douglas' *Purity and Danger: An Analysis of Concepts of Pollution and Taboo* (London: Routledge & Kegan Paul). Along Lévy-Bruhl's cognitive trajectory it extends further, at least to C. R. Hallpike's *The Foundations of Primitive Thought* (Oxford: Clarendon, 1979). Eliade relied upon the descriptor of "primitive" as well, sometimes with the critique of quotation marks, sometimes not (e.g., *Shamanism: Archaic Techniques of Ecstasy*, trans. Willard R. Trask [Princeton, N.J.: Princeton University Press, 1964], pp. xiii [in quotes], 11 [without notation]). He interchanged it freely with "archaic," especially apparent in *The Sacred and the Profane: The Nature of Religion*, trans. Willard R. Trask (New York: Harcourt, Brace & World, 1957). Nevertheless, he gave priority to the rival term, the archaic, both a class of societies and religions and a temporal ontology of all human beings (though mostly latent among moderns). Sam D. Gill rejected "primitive" in favor of "nonliterate," in *Beyond "the Primitive": The Religions of Nonliterate Peoples* (Englewood Cliffs, N.J.: Prentice-Hall, 1982), a term that presents a different set of problems in the contemporary moment. After these detours, we arrive at the indigenous, securely in circulation by 1970 and ready for appropriation by new secular religious studies departments in the U.S. university system. Obviously, a thorough tracing of this genealogy would itself merit the space of a full essay. Such was not my objective here.

[23] In the sense articulated in the influential article by Sherry Ortner, "Is Male to Culture as Female Is to Nature?" in her *Making Gender: The Politics and Erotics of Culture* (Boston: Beacon, 1996). The passive position within an opposition is not only homologized with gender, though; it is also construed as the "child" posture vis à vis "adults," as in the legal status of the Amerindians of Brazil. Ramos (n. 4 above), pp. 72, 98.

comparative trope in the study of religion, Bogey's Bacall for all the great lines. What would world religions be without local ones? Or the secularization of modern societies, without the cool, unchanging tradition of primitive ones? Or globalization and the religiously hybrid, without the bounded and homogenous? Or the playful textures of surfaces, without imagined depth somewhere else? On one side of these mutually defining oppositions are the deterritorialized religious fragments carried by migrating bodies and circulating media, turtles all the way down, on the other, the deep roots of a clear relation between a people, a place, and a tradition.[24]

The most important difference of the category of the indigenous from its forerunners—the primitive, the archaic, the autochthonous, and so on—was that simultaneous with its academic invocation arose its use in the discursive practice of many North, Central, and South American societies.[25] The indigenous has become a transnational title uniting disparate groups around similar political struggles.[26] This institution-building

[24] Perhaps the tension between these statements is one within postmodernism itself: on one hand, all primordialisms are to be demolished; on the other hand, since all ontologies are relative, primordial claims cannot be excluded.

[25] Stated Felipe Tsenkush, leader of the Federation of Shuar and Achuar peoples of Ecuador: "It takes a lot of work to be an indigenous leader these days. One has to send and receive a lot of faxes, attend numerous international meetings; and now, one also has to learn how to handle e-mail." Facundo Sanapi, of the Embera of Panama, said that it was important to wear traditional clothes at international meetings because, "we should present it [our proposal] as indigenous peoples in order to make the public see that those who present this document are true indigenous individuals" (Mato [n. 4 above], pp. 345–48). A similar rise of the self-conscious use of the terms of indigenous culture has been noted by Turner (n. 4 above) among the Kayapo of Brazil, and by Ramos (p. 100–14) for, among others, the Shavante. I have become accustomed to hearing both practitioners of Candomblé and leaders among the Garífuna plan how best to defend their "cultures" and "religions," terms that a half-century ago would have been incomprehensible (cf. Hannerz [n. 4 above], p. 52)— not that they are particularly comprehensible within the academy itself, a point made by Adam Kuper in his *Culture: The Anthropologists' Account* (Cambridge, Mass.: Harvard University Press, 1999).

[26] The United Nations Working Group on Indigenous Populations, the Internal Labor Organization's Convention 169 on Tribal and Indigenous Peoples (1989), the United Nations declaration of 1993 as "Year of the World's Indigenous Peoples," the IUCN Inter-Commission Task Force on Indigenous Peoples, the Charter of the Indigenous Tribal Peoples of the Tropical Forest from the 1992 Rio de Janeiro Conference on Environment and Development, or in the indigenous-style rhetoric of the 1995 Beijing Woman's Tribunal, as noted by Nash (n. 5 above), p. 5. Ramos (p. 116) notes the appeals of Brazilian Amerindians to the Universal Declaration of Human Rights (adopted by the UN in 1948). This use in international institution-building is important for land-defense issues, but complicates its use in comparison. Let me be clear: I do not think academic use is more important than political practice, quite the contrary. Yet at least within the walls of the university, it seems key to distinguish indigenous as used in political practice from its analytical uses. While it would be foolish to believe one could insulate analytical categories from those of practice, more foolish and dangerous still is to not distinguish them at all. We don't, after all, relinquish the meaning of "the nation" to nationalists, or of "religion" to its invocation in fundamentalist (or, for that matter, Supreme Court) polemics.

role of the category indigenous has fostered an internationally imagined community between groups, a putative similarity that previously may have not existed.

Indigenous is a conflicted substantive category of religions, then, because it implies stability by playing the straw man for religions in change, when in fact the religions it classifies are also in transformation and because that stability has been reified in institutional and common discursive forms. If the "global" needed to be made local to become analytically useful, the "indigenous" needs to be looked at in terms of its extensions and transformations and the ways in which the indigenous imagined community is created and maintained despite historical and empirical change. This becomes evident as soon as we know the actual people within the abstraction of an indigenous culture. Is indigenous still the right descriptor for the Dakota (Santee) man who became Catholic, migrated to Kansas City, married a Chicano girl, and opened a video store? Or the eighteenth-century Garifuna man in the Caribbean, who was of African descent, had an Arawak wife, spoke French and English, and owned slaves to produce cash crops for sale in Cuba? How about the white suburban woman outside Chicago, a self-declared shaman who studies Jívaro practices circulated in popular books written by an anthropologist—is she, at least religiously, indigenous?[27] How about the Haitian practicing African religion in Montreal, or the disfigured Jew of Mario Vargas Llosa's novel *El Hablador* who became the Machiguenga's best storyteller?[28] We tend to avoid such figures as too syncretic, disturbing hybrids off the area-studies and world religions categorical map. But what if their condition turns out to be the rule rather than the exception? We need categories that help us describe not just indigenous versus other kinds of people and religions, but the sense in which, and processes by which, peoples "indigenize" new territories and historical conditions to make them their own.

III. INDIGENOUS RELIGIONS BECOME MOBILE, OR MOBILE RELIGIONS INDIGENIZING? CANDOMBLÉ OF BRAZIL AND THE GARIFUNA OF HONDURAS

To start a constructive project, I will move the use of indigenous for my purposes from a classifier of kinds of religions to its use as an ideal type in the Weberian sense.[29] As an abstract tool, I define the indigenous

---

[27] On this particular question, see Paul C. Johnson, "Shamanism from Ecuador to Oak Park: A Case-Study in Ritual Appropriation," *Religion*, no. 2 (1995): 163–78.

[28] Mario Vargas Llosa, *The Storyteller* (El hablador), trans. Helen Lane (New York: Farrar, Straus, Giroux, 1989).

[29] The pertinent passage, from Max Weber's "Objectivity and the Social Sciences," in *The Methodology of the Social Sciences*, ed. Edward Shils (New York: Free Press, 1949),

community as one that is imagined: (1) as practiced by a discrete, bounded social group that clearly marks insiders from outsiders by genealogical descent; (2) as practiced on a discrete, bounded land site since beyond the Western historical record; and (3) to consist of traditional beliefs and practices, uniquely that group's, which are not invented, borrowed, or syncretic. This ideal-typical indigenous community fuses, in a pure, logical sense, a people, a place, and a set of beliefs and practices within clear limits. But let me repeat: There is no such purity in the world, nor has there ever been. In history, there is always mixing, always migration, always exchange; the question is only one of degree. The ideal-typical imagined indigenous community will serve as a lighthouse in reference to which we can interpret the distance of empirical religions that imagine themselves in the indigenous style from the construct.

The further key methodological and theoretical shift I want to propose is from the terms of stasis to those of process, such that I will compare not indigenous versus other kinds of religions, but rather indigenizing versus extending discourses and practices. Both are present among all religious groups, but are balanced and mobilized differently by each. Indigenizing discourses and practices have as their objective the configuration, at least imaginatively or discursively, of a pure group performing traditional practices on its original homeland. When outsider signs, symbols, and practices are relied upon, they are quickly indigenized—given a culturally specific form that makes the outside symbol "ours," even traditional. Extending discourses and practices take as their objective the lowering of social boundaries, the circulation of religious knowledge and symbols into wider availability, and the overt assimilation of new forms acknowledged to be from outside. They endorse the extension of the meaning of beliefs or practices beyond territorial limits and previous

---

p. 92, is the following: "An ideal-type is formed by the one-sided *accentuation* of one or more points of view and by the synthesis of a great many diffuse, discrete, more or less present and occasionally absent *concrete individual* phenomena, which are arranged according to those one-sidedly emphasized viewpoints into a unified *analytical* construct. . . . In its conceptual purity, this mental construct . . . cannot be found empirically anywhere in reality. It is a *utopia*." And elsewhere in the same essay, "Historical research faces the task of determining in each individual case, the extent to which the ideal construct approximates to or diverges from reality" (p. 90). And, "Whether the empirical-historical course of development was actually identical with the constructed one can be investigated only by using this construct as a heuristic device for the comparison of the ideal type and the 'facts'" (p. 101). And elsewhere, "[This] kind of terminology and classification . . . has in no sense the aim to be exhaustive or to confine the whole of historical reality in a rigid scheme. Its usefulness is derived from the fact that in a given case it is possible to distinguish what aspects of a given organized group can legitimately be identified as falling under or approximating one or another of these categories (Max Weber, *Economy and Society*, ed. Guenther Roth and Claus Wittich [Berkeley: University of California Press, 1978], p. 263).

social boundaries, such that what was once a local truth is now presented as a more broadly applicable, even a universal one. For example, when on some Native American reservations on the Plains, casinos are called "new buffalo," this is an indigenizing discursive move, a symbolic transfer of what was "outside" to "inside" and "ours." When priests of Candomblé (*pais*, or *mães de santo*) appear on Brazilian national television advising how anyone regardless of African descent, can practice the religion of the African gods (*orixás*) in the privacy of their own home, with or without initiation and a community of practice, this is an example of an extending move. What was "ours" is now proffered to all; protective boundaries are lowered, and the religion that was ethnically specific is presented as universally available.

CANDOMBLÉ

Among the popular spirit possession religions of Brazil, Candomblé most closely identifies itself in relation to a specific territory and genealogy. In its most prominent manifestations, this is traced to one of the city-states of the Yoruba, Dahomean, or Kongolese peoples of West and West-Central Africa, forcibly brought to Brazil during the Portuguese slave trade over four centuries. Candomblé reconstructs a link to Africa through the reverence of deities (*orixás*) in order to generate power, or *axé*, for human use in luck, fertility, wealth, prestige, and health—power in its most this-worldly forms. *Orixás* are linked to specific natural sites like rivers (Oxum), the sea (Iemanjá), thunder (Xangô), or doors and crossroads (Exú). In myths and incarnated dance performances, when the *orixás* possess their devotees, they also present complex models of human attributes.[30] The practice of Candomblé locates the self within the classifying grids formed by these divine models, and within initiatory hierarchies of the houses (*terreiros*) where it is practiced: One is and acts only in relation to the archetypes presented by one's *orixás*; one is and acts only in relation to the social structure and ritual calendar of the house where he or she was ritually "made."[31]

If *orixás* are the first key element for understanding location in Candomblé, the second is *axé*, which can imply transformative capacity,

[30] For example, the thunder-god Xangô is just, but also a philanderer; the creator of humans, Oxalá of the sky and pure whiteness, is wise, but also aged and fragile; Oxum of rivers is beautiful, but suffers a parvenu's greed and a nouveau riche love of vulgar display; the iron-god who clears the paths, Ogum, is brave but also impetuous and bullheaded.

[31] For example, Vivaldo da Costa Lima, "Organização do grupo de candomblé: Estratificação, senioridade e hierarquia," in *Bandeira de alairá: Outros escritos sobre a religião dos orixás*, ed. Carlos Eurênio Marcondes de Moura (São Paulo: Livraria Nobel S.A., 1982); Roger Bastide, *The African Religions of Brazil: Towards a Sociology of the Interpenetration of Civilizations*, trans. Helen Sebba (Baltimore: Johns Hopkins Press, 1978).

charisma, fecundity, success, or physical force like electricity. *Axé* is metaphysical muscle to change human destiny. As a quality of a house or a drum, however, it connotes not transformation but tradition, lineage, and legitimate foundations. *Axé* depends on correct ritual performance for its condensation and distribution. Producing *axé* in the traditional sense, "traditional" since the formation of Candomblé in the early 1800s, is a series of practices to contain, enclose and bind the elusive *axé* into loci—altars, vases, heads—from which its force can be received and re-distributed. The techniques and tools of condensing and containing *axé* are what are known as the foundational secrets (*fundmentos*) of the reli-gion. One gains access to this secret knowledge, or, more properly, to the places and practice of secrecy, by performing progressive initiations into increasingly important functions (*cargos*) in the house. Gaining practical knowledge of rituals, and access to the techniques and tools of calling, holding, and distributing *axé,* is the "traditional" path of advance.

That "traditional" way is only one path of Candomblé, however. Until the 1960s a religion predominantly of Africans and their descendants in the city of Salvador da Bahia, and Rio de Janeiro, it now has a large fol-lowing in São Paulo, adherents in Argentina and Uruguay, and priest-esses in Miami and New York. By now, most people in the coastal cities of Brazil know someone involved with the religion and can name and describe their *orixás* even if they do not cultivate them, just as you probably know your astrological sign and its associated tendencies.[32] And among the initiated, there is now a fifty-one percent chance that per-son will be "white," a stunning ethnic transformation since the 1960s.[33] A religion that what was once relatively bounded by descent group, re-gion, and the secrecy of the knowledge of *axé* gained only through long apprenticeship, is now public. New practitioners may be Brazilians (or others) of any background, and may acquire the knowledge to open a temple through books, television, video, and the internet.

The three walls of the religion—a people, a place, a protected set of practices—have become permeable. Yet, surprisingly, the discourse of Candomblé has not followed the changes in social constituency or in initiation practices. To the contrary, the indigenizing terms of "founda-tional secrets," "authenticity," and the "purely African" have, if any-thing, gained in force and the stridency of their assertion as competitive

---

[32] As in popular esoteric literature such as Monica Buonfiglio, *Orixás!* (São Paulo: Oficina Cultural Esotérica, 1995).

[33] Antônio Pierucci and Reginaldo Prandi, "Religious Diversity in Brazil: Numbers and Perspectives in a Sociological Evaluation," *International Sociology* 14, no. 4 (December 2000): 629–40; Peginaldo Prandi, *Os candomblés de São Paulo: A velha magia na metró-pole nova* (São Paulo: Hucitec & Edusp,1991). It is important to note that race classifica-tions do not work in Brazil according to the "blood purity" model of the U.S., manifested especially in Jim Crow laws.

measures of relative legitimacy, status, and success in attracting a clientele and an initiatic family.[34]

BRAZILIAN CANDOMBLÉ AND THE INDIGENOUS RELIGION

Let us now consider Candomblé in its relative distance from the analytic category of the indigenous community. The once-secret religion is now widely disseminated in public, even at times implicated in Brazil's national representations. As to a marked ethnic boundary, "African-ness" continues to be an important identifier, but it is subsumed within religious affiliation. To be initiated into Candomblé is to be "made African." "African-ness" is an existential posture and a liturgical structure and genealogy for religious practice, not an ethnic group or claim to common descent from a specific homeland.

Yet even as the ethnic disjunction has increased, there are also countermoves that seek to reindigenize the religion as African. Reputations of "deep, foundational secrets" gauged by their "real" African-ness are circulated, but now as discourse rather than in ritual practice. They are passed not through the slow initiations in the *terreiro*, but in rapid-fire exchanges of street gossip and internet hits. Moreover, the wealthiest leaders may jet to West Africa to find and retrieve the "real" African secrets, a strategy by which they elide and may even supercede the traditional hierarchy of claimed knowledge in Brazil.[35] The claim to control the knowledge of what the Yoruba do now competes for prestige with the claim to control what Africans brought to Brazil in the past. In a sense, this contest of authority based on controlling secrets is one between territory (contemporary knowledge from Africa) and time (the Afro-Brazilian knowledge from the past). Evaluating Candomblés distance from the indigenous category at different moments allows us to interpret historical changes and spatial mobility within the religion. A century ago slaves' descendants ripped from Africa had only partly indigenized their lives in the New World by ritually reconstructing "Africa" in Candomblé houses, incarnating the gods from home. In the present moment, Candomblé's distance from the analytic indigenous category is in that its practicing population is diverse and its practices publicly available. We see change in the religion by plotting its movement from one kind of disjunction from the category, an extension in space, to another disjunction from the category, the extension of social boundary when it became public.

[34] Paul Christopher Johnson, *Secrets, Gossip and Gods: The Transformation of Brazilian Candomblé* (New York: Oxford University Press, 2002).

[35] Meanwhile, in another indigenizing act, a few wealthy priests and priestesses travel to Nigeria to rediscover the "pure" African tradition perceived as too syncretically polluted in Brazil. Ironically, it is by some reports white practitioners who seem most invested in the "return to Africa" move, as described by Tina Gudrun Jensen, "Discourses on Afro-Brazilian Religion: From De-Africanization to Re-Africanization," in *Latin American Religion in Motion*, ed. Christian Smith and Joshua Prokopy (New York: Routledge, 1999).

THE RELIGION OF THE GARIFUNA (BLACK CARIB)[36]

The Garifuna, formerly called the Black Carib, are descendants both of Africans and of Carib Indians who shared the island of St. Vincent in the Caribbean. The African presence on St. Vincent derived from Carib raids on Puerto Rico, from survivors of slaver shipwrecks near the island, and from the arrival of fleeing maroons from neighboring Barbados. Even as Africans adopted the Indians' religion and language, a combination of Arawak and Carib, their descendants maintained a conscious ethnic difference and were called Black Carib by Europeans, as distinguished from the "Red Carib."[37] When the British deported the Black Carib in 1797, five thousand were taken from St. Vincent; only half arrived on the Honduran coast.

The Black Carib became the main carriers of Carib religion and language. Their subsistence on fish, yucca, and cassava was augmented by wage labor in the Spanish militia, on the British wood-cutting crews in what is now Belize or, by 1900, on the plantations of the "banana republic" of Honduras. Their traditional religion has aspects typically associated with some West African groups, like the use of drums to induce possession trance by ancestors. It also shows Carib features, like the shaman (*buyei*) who blows smoke on a patient's afflicted body to extract penetrations. And it reveals Catholic features, like the importance of baptism and images of the Virgin and the saints in homes.

A century ago, the Garifuna were relatively stable in relation to their territory. The banana industry had begun to boom, and the Standard-Fruit Company and the United Fruit Company were to provide steady jobs in the "banana republic" for four generations. Today, by contrast, most households depend on monthly contributions from relatives working in New York or on the ships of cruise lines. Many women migrate yearly to textile factory jobs, or sweat shops, in the cities.[38] With so many out-

---

[36] Columbus first misheard the word "Carib" in 1492, spoken by the Arawakan peoples in reference to the fierce man-eaters of distant islands—at least as recorded in Bartolomé de Las Casas's biography, a thirdhand account written sixty years after the fact. "Garifuna" is actually the name of the group's language. The fact that it is commonly used as the ethnic group's name bespeaks the centrality of language in defining Garifuna-ness. The current "proper" name of the ethnic group is Garinagu, a translation of the actual name of the "Carib," whose name for themselves was the Kalipuna, if a woman was speaking (in the Arawakan languages), or Kalinago if a man was speaking (in the Carib form). "Garifuna" may also be the commonly used form since it is closer to the female (Arawak) title, and since women have been the primary carriers of culture. The name has only been standardized and in currency since the 1970s, and this quite recent self-consciousness as an ethnic group, accelerated beginning in the 1980s, is noted by Gonzalez (n. 6 above), pp. xiii, 70; and Kerns (n. 4 above), p. 202.

[37] Mary Helms refers to this as the creation of "colonial tribes," in "The Cultural Ecology of a Colonial Tribe," *Ethnology* 8 (1969): 76–84.

[38] Garifuna migration to the U.S. can be schematized into stages. The first large influx was during the 1940s as Garifuna men flocked to the U.S. to fill jobs vacated by soldiers; a second wave began during the 1960s with the rise of a service-based economy and the

going migrants and incoming global signals, a village like the one where I have been working intermittently over the last three years, Corozal, faces difficult territorial and cultural transformations. All in Corozal speak Spanish, and most also Garifuna. Yet many of those born after the arrival of electricity in 1982 and with it television and radio, speak only Spanish, a cause for great concern since language is the Garifuna's primary cultural mark. Moreover, beginning in the 1980s, evangelicalism has gained a strong footing, initiating, on one hand, an increase in Garifuna language literacy and, on the other, a vitriolic attack on traditional religious ceremonies. Finally, in the last several years, the Garifuna have faced the potential privatization of communally titled lands through a constitutional amendment that would allow the sale of land to outsiders and transform Garifuna villages into Honduran mestizo villages.[39]

Even those who don't leave live in a global imaginary of broadcasts from Miami, Mexico, and Brazil. "Soaps" provide the narrative frame for much of everyday chat among women of Corozal, soccer games for men. But the global imaginary takes on flesh with the periodic return of migrants from the United States, especially from the Bronx of New York. Loaded with goods like VCRs, NBA jerseys, and Nikes, they come also bearing new signifying codes. The new codes have not only to do with consumer patterns but also with discourses of race and ethnic identification. Migrants to U.S. cities are subjected to an unfamiliar racial system, in which Garifuna identifications are subsumed by the categories of Black, or Black Hispanic, and they return from the Bronx with a different classifying consciousness from those at home. This is manifested both

---

need for labor, coupled with the reform of immigration law under the 1965 Hart-Celler Act, which expanded and diversified the immigrant population and initiated widespread Latin American and Caribbean influxes. A third stage could be said to have come with the late 1980s and 1990s economic boom, again especially in the service economy; by now, however, many Garifuna families also already had "paths" in place—relatives already in the U.S., a place to stay, and potential job networks. What is more, a mythology had grown up around the idea of migration to the U.S., such that the traditional male model of "adventuring" to find his livelihood, usually at sea, now was applied to the emigratory leap. Compare Linda Miller Matthei and David A. Smith, "Women, Households, and Transnational Migration Networks: The Garifuna and Global Economic Restructuring," in *Latin America in the World-Economy*, eds. Roberto Patricio Korzeniewicz and William C. Smith (Westport, Conn.: Greenwood, 1996), pp. 133–50; and Gonzalez. The impact is best conveyed with an example: according to a recent (2001) census in the Garifuna village of San Juan, Honduras, 1,655 inhabitants currently reside there, while 1,132 inhabitants are absent. Of those absent, 552 are laboring in larger Honduran cities like San Pedro Sula, while 485 are in the U.S. In San Juan, 79 houses are closed up and empty of any occupants whatsoever.

[39] The potential amendment is to Article 107, which prohibits the sale of coastal lands to nonnationals. The stated justification for such an amendment is to encourage foreign investment in tourist facilities and gain an important source of hard-currency revenues. Over the last five years, most Garifuna villages have acquired collective legal titles to their lands, removing much of the threat the amendment to 107 posed even a few years ago.

valued, and in discourse, where "black" movies are the preferred ones among videos circulated in the village. Ironically, these are the very terms that were strongly resisted until recently, because they confused Garifuna identity with that of other Afro-Caribbean peoples. The territorial disjunctions of migration, and the subjection of U.S. classifiers, come home to roost in the ethnic reclassification from Carib (and Amerindian) to Garifuna, "Black," and "African."

The second key change is in the frequency of "traditional" ritual performances, dramatically increased from even a half century ago. The central ritual performance the Garifuna identify as uniquely their own is called the *dügü*. The *dügü* is a multiday ritual event to summon ancestors who are causing sickness or psychic disturbance among the living and to regain their favor by plying them with food, rum, praises, and even simulated sex. The ancestors are rendered present through spirit possession. Unlike lesser rites, which can be performed in New York or Los Angeles, and with or without the whole family's presence, the *dügü* can only take place in the home village and requires the entire extended family's presence, often hundreds of people. Given the scale and demands of mounting a *dügü*, often several extended families related by marriage join together; thus a "family" ritual actually involves much of the community. The ritual unfolds in a series of subrites, the two main parts of which are the dances initiating spirit possession, and the food sacrifice for the ancestors, called the *chugu*.

Surprisingly, given that a *dügü* must be performed on the homeland, it is out-migration that led to its renaissance. There are two apparent reasons: first, the crisis of separation experienced by migrants and their families has led to greater perceived need for ritual emplacement on the land;[40] and second, the access to dollars allows for rare surpluses usable on ritual. "Tradition" in one sense, that of *dügü* performance, reconstitutes the rupture of "tradition" in another, the separation from the land. The ritual is recorded, however, as Garifuna and African, not Carib.[41] In

---

[40] For the particular case of the Garifuna, the view of accelerated "culture," including ritual performance as a distress response is proposed by Gonzalez, pp. 10, 90; its increase in recent decades has been observed by Gonzalez; as well as by Kerns, p. 165; Carol L. Jenkins, "Ritual and Resource-Flow: The Garifuna Dugu," *American Ethnologist* (10): 429–42; Milton Cohen, "The Ethnomedicine of the Garifuna (Black Caribs) of Rio Tinto, Honduras," *Anthropological Quarterly* 57 (1): 16–27; and by myself in Corozal and in San Juan, Honduras. This is not only the case for religion, but for economic relations as well. As Miller-Matthei and Smith note (p. 136), "Moreover, our findings indicate that transnational networks need not weaken over time and distance. On the contrary, social and economic pressures experienced by migrants in the United States can motivate them to strengthen their relationships with those back home."

[41] Migration and shifts in race-classifying discourse have been noted also among migrants from Puerto Rico and Haiti: Arlene Torres and Norman E. Whitten, Jr., "General Introduction: To Forge the Future in the Fires of the Past," in *Blackness in Latin America and the Caribbean: Social Dynamics and Cultural Transformations* (Bloomington: Indiana

today's *dügü*, the shaman wears clothing ordered by catalog from "African" clothiers of New York and likens his work to more well-known African systems of Yoruba and Vodou.[42] Now, moreover, the *dügü* signifies traditional fidelity with new force, cast into relief by vocal *evangélicos* who refuse to attend the so-called diabolical ceremonies. I was fortunate to take part in three *dügü* performances in Honduras in 1998 and 1999, one of which is here described.[43]

DÜGÜ

While the *dügü* is traditionally to cure a patient of pain resistant to medicine, strange dreams, or bizarre behaviors, this performance was initiated at the behest of a family in New York for reasons one family member described as "losing touch." The family consulted a shaman, who consulted his spirit-helpers (*hiruha*) at his altar, and a course of action was plotted. Announcements about the *dügü* circulated for more than a year to insure that sufficient funds were raised and that all family members, especially those in the United States, could travel to take part.

A ceremonial house (*gayunere*) was constructed in "traditional" style on the beach, as shown in figure 1. While most houses today are constructed with cindar blocks and tin roofs, the structure that will house the ritual must be in *manaca* style, of bound saplings and palm thatch. The *dügü* then formally began with the "return of the fishermen," a group sent to catch fish in the "traditional" way, in the offshore cays; their much-anticipated return from the beach appears in figure 2. They arrived at dawn, attired as stylized Garifuna ancestors (fig. 3), and were greeted

University Press, 1998), pp. 14–15; Elizabeth McAlister, "The Madonna of 115th Street Revisited: Vodou and Haitian Catholicism in the Age of Transnationalism," in *Gatherings in Diaspora: Religious Communities and the New Immigration*, ed. R. Stephen Warner and Judith G. Wittner (Philadelphia: Temple University Press, 1998), pp. 135, 147–48. For the Garifuna, Gonzalez (p. 5) notes that "African-ness" was downplayed in the 1950s, but that it has now become fashionable.

[42] Cynthia Bianchi notes the possible actual impact of Vodou, diffused from Haitians who also arrived on the coast of Honduras in the Trujillo region where the Garifuna first landed; or from earlier interactions on St. Vincent with French-speaking people of African descent, especially from Martinique ("Gubida Illness and Religious Ritual among the Garifuna of Santa Fe, Honduras: An Ethnopsychiatric Analysis" [Ph.D. diss., Ohio State University, 1988], p. 114). In this case, however, I think the identification with Vodou is because Vodou is widely disseminated and regarded as a more "established" religion of the African Diaspora. Upon asking a few questions about the relation of Garifuna practices to Vodou, it was clear that the shaman (*buyei*) knew only the title and location of Vodou and nothing of its content.

[43] Other important accounts include those of Edward Conzemius, "Ethnographic Notes on the Black Carib (Garif)," *American Anthropologist* 30 (1928): 183–205; Ruy Coelho, "The Black Carib of Honduras: A Study in Acculturation" (Ph.D. diss., Northwestern University, 1955); Douglas M. Taylor, *The Black Caribs of British Honduras* (New York: Viking Fund Publications in Anthropology, 1951); Bianchi; Jenkins; Kerns; Gonzalez; and E. Salvador Suazo B., *Irufamali: la doctrina esotérica Garifuna* (Tegucigalpa: CEDEC, 2000).

FIG. 1.—Before the ritual begins, young men construct the house of the ancestors, called *gayunere* or *dabuyaba,* in traditional style.

FIG. 2.—The beginning of the main body of the ritual is initiated by the return of the fishermen, who arrive just after dawn and are greeted with songs and drums by the assembled body.

with exuberant songs by family members attired in (often red) uniforms, given rum and laid in hammocks.[44]

Over the next two days followed a sequence of dances both to honor the ancestors and to create the conditions for their arrival in possession: first were the *amalahani,* dances to honor the ancestors. These continued for up to four hours at a time, brought to crescendo by the shaman who exhorted the large group until three persons were possessed by ancestors, shrieking, falling to the ground, and rolling wildly in the sand. Now transformed into known ancestors, they made requests, and in the two cases regarded as authentic possession, they were soothed with rum, food, and asked questions in response to which they offered individual counsel.[45]

Throughout the second and third day, the *chugu,* or food offering, was prepared. Chickens—one required from each attending nuclear family—were sacrificed, massive amounts of rum assembled, and plates prepared, especially with the most symbolically Garifuna food of all, cassava bread (*areba*).[46] On the third day, the food was piled high on a wooden table in the center of the temple, and there left for the ancestors' consumption. After the spirits had "eaten," the assembled participants took their fill, rejoicing in an abundance far exceeding that of everyday life.

At the close of that day, what remained of the spirits' food was "returned" to the sea, taken by canoe and deposited in the deeps. Finally, the shaman made sure of the ancestors' acceptance of the offerings. Pouring rum on the table, he lit it, fed the flame, and tipped the table to all sides, the strong flame proving that "all sides" of the extended family were pleased. There was great joy, embraces and whoops, and all rushed to wipe the sacred, hot rum on their bodies. As depicted in figure 4, family groups among the kin of the afflicted ran to enter the sea together, gripping a single, long cloth, in a moment of *communitas*—the reaffirmation of their bonds and the momentary transcendence of bitter conflicts.

It is that refortification of family boundaries, and territorial orientation, that returning migrants gain and that motivates their financial and organizational expenditures toward revitalizing the *dügü*. What is

[44] Red is a symbolically important color, as studied by Marilyn McKillop Wells, "Spirits See Red: The Symbolic Use of Gusueue among the Garif (Black Caribs) of Central America," *Belizean Studies* 10, no. 3 (1982): 10–16.

[45] In one case, the possession was regarded as inauthentic and merely a dramatic attempt to gain attention. In both Candomblé and among the Garifuna, it is not only scholars who evaluate possession trance with critical scrutiny, as participants have their own established codes of authenticity to measure the veracity of any particular performance.

[46] The symbolic importance of cassava and cassava bread has only increased since, in many villages of Honduras, all seedlings were washed away by Hurricane Mitch in November 1998 and since many families now raise pigs that dig up vulnerable cassava plants. As a result, cassava bread production, a central communal activity for women, is temporarily suspended in many places.

FIG. 3.—The fishermen are attired as stylized ancestors, wearing helmets woven of palm fronds. They deliver the fish to an assisting *buyei,* or shaman, who takes them to the interior of the ancestral house.

fascinating, though, is that the return is never to the imagined unity of the people, the homeland, and the ancestral practices, since the *dügü* generates not only momentary *communitas,* but in many ways creates conflict. The most notable conflict is that between evangelical family members and their kin.[47] The evangelicals refuse to attend the ritual and are accused of jeopardizing the ritual efficacy and therefore also the physical safety of everyone in their kin group. Such family rifts serve as explanations of future accidents and bad luck. Nevertheless, even in the face of such conflict, migrants return to ritually rebuild "home," which they will carry back with them to the Bronx.

[47] In Corozal the primary evangelical church is La Palabra Vivida (Living Word); in San Juan it is Baptist. In both cases the new churches were founded in the early 1980s, around the same time that electricity arrived in the two villages. The connection is not incidental because powerful sound-amplification systems with microphones and electric keyboards are absolutely central to evangelical ritualizations four nights per week. The specific denominational differences between these churches are less important than the fact that all of these churches reject Garifuna tradition and Roman Catholicism and mark themselves as "cristianos" (Christians), a title reserved exclusively for the non-Catholic converts. That usage of the term solely for evangelical converts has now been routinized among nonevangelicals as well.

Fig. 4.—After the successful burning of rum on the table, indicating the ancestors' satisfaction with the ritual, family members celebrate and seal their shared accomplishment by entering the sea, joined by a cloth that unites them.

THE GARIFUNA AND THE INDIGENOUS RELIGION

How shall we characterize changes in the Garifuna ancestor religion in relation to the indigenous category? A century ago, the Garifuna were territorially relatively stable, and in religion the dynamic syncretism of African, Amerindian, and Catholic elements had coalesced and assumed the authority of a uniquely Garifuna "tradition." At the present moment, it is in the issue of place, the identification with a specific site, that the ancestor religion shows the greatest transfomations. What is in flux is the relation to territory, due to migration to the United States, and with it the resignifying of ritual as it is indigenized in a new way, in relation to the experience in the United States and to a growing pan-African consciousness, wherein Garifuna religion is understood as related to Cuban Santeria, Brazilian Candomblé, and Haitian Vodou—a new form of imagined community. We can see a change in religion from one historical moment of disjunction from the analytic indigenous form—the religion as a recently syncretized form—to another moment of disjunction a century later—the revival and reinterpretation of the *dügü* ritual because of migration. Put in the simplest terms, the circulation of migrant bodies brought new meanings and accelerated frequency to ritual practice.

324   *Migrating Bodies*

IV. COMPARING THE RELIGIONS

Consider the two religions' forms of extension: the central extension (and disjunction) for Candomblé is in ethnic composition, in the religion going public and no longer being ethnically, but rather only liturgically, marked as African or Afro-Brazilian. The central extension (and disjunction) for Garifuna ancestor religion is in deterritorialization, through labor migrations. These two distinct extensions imply distinct processes. For Candomblé, the dissemination of information about the religion in mass media and national venues invited new participating groups. For Garifuna ancestor religion the circulation of bodies in migration led to new signifiers applied to ritual at home. In Candomblé, signs circulating outside their sites of production brought new bodies; in Garifuna religion, circulating bodies carried home new signs. Both, then, are local religions in processes of extension, but in quite distinct ways.

Extensions and disjunctions, but also indigenizations. Candomblé initiates seek to reindigenize the religion through locative discourses of secrets, of who controls them and where they reside. The Garifuna seek to reindigenize identities through increased ritual performance of the *dügü*. The two responses are comparable, in my view, to what have been called revitalization or nativist movements in that they self-consciously, ideologically construct the imagined unity of a people, place, and practice in the face of a crisis of dislocation (cf. n. 7).

Moreover, they do so by appropriating the international discourse of the indigenous, that is, in communicative modes of global circulation and in categories nurtured in the academy and popular media. In both cases, the indigenizing moves may have only limited success at creating a meaningful experience of "place," since the transformations they address are embedded in processes not likely to be reversed any time soon. But this in no way implies a twilight of the gods. Both religions have shown a resilient capacity to generate new extending and indigenizing discourses and practices to cover new terrain and make it their own. Such extensions and indigenizations will entail changes in tradition, and the purists in their factions, not to mention in ours, will not approve. That is not likely to make any difference.

V. CONCLUSION

There are problems with the category of indigenous religions as it is normally used. But thinking about why it is problematic, at least for these two boundary-religions, and how to revise it, has proved a worthwhile exercise.

Let us recapitulate the salient points. First, I tried to rethink the category of indigenous religions in such a way as to escape both the romantic and deconstructive versions, by considering the indigenous as a style of imagined community that employs identifications relating itself to a specific territory, quite apart from the actual fact of the duration of that territory's occupation. Next, I tried to show the radical extensions— primarily social in one case, primarily territorial in the other—of two indigenous religions, and the reindigenizing rejoinders. Third, I suggested that the indigenizing actions underway in both cases are responses to a perceived breach of boundaries and an attempt to redraw them. In the case of Candomblé this is in an exaggeration of the discourse of secret *fundamentos,* and in the case of the Garifuna it is in accelerated and Africanized ritual performance of the *dügü.* Finally, I suggested that such refoundings of the tradition and territory, while aimed at rebutting change, are themselves transformative, because they are imagined, mediated, and expressed in globalized modes.

For both groups, contemporary dislocations, whether of bodies or signs, have spurred religious revival and innovation, as the relation to place, and the social meaning of place, have been revised to meet new historical challenges. Having restored a degree of dynamism to the category of indigenous religions, I should like to conclude by revisiting two classic texts that have been implicit conversation partners throughout, Jonathan Z. Smith's *To Take Place* and Benedict Anderson's *Imagined Communities,* to see what can be added to them by taking the perspective of this article.[48] Smith compared three human paradigms of conceptualizing space, but demonstrated key historical transformations in only two of them: Judaism, in which space came to be structured primarily through Temple hierarchy and ritual, or Misnah; and Christianity, in which space was mapped onto the liturgical year.[49] The third comparative entry, the Tjilpa, indigenous to Australia, accomplish the opposite of the Christian transformation: instead of time absorbing space, here space absorbs time, as different striking land sites are marked as places of Ancestors, and ancestry is folded into the landscape.[50] The indigenous cases of Candomblé and the Garifuna suggest that, like Smith's Australian exemplars, territory indeed yet predominates over history as an ordering master rubric. But we cannot in any simple way juxtapose groups stressing history versus those oriented primarily to territory. For even for indigenous groups, it is an imagined territory that makes place, imagined through historical processes that I have addressed here under the broad rubric of "globalization." To the three variations of the social construction of space and place in history so brilliantly elaborated by Smith, I would add, then, two more: place as built through discourses of deep, secret

[48] Jonathan Z. Smith, *To Take Place* (Chicago: University of Chicago Press, 1987); Anderson (n. 8 above).

[49] Smith, *To Take Place,* pp. xiii, 95, and passim.

[50] Ibid., pp. 113–14.

knowledge ranked as more or less "of" a particular place quite independent of any actual relation to it; and place conceptually made through the acceleration of ritual practice and the expanded motives for ritual performance from healing to the crisis of identity itself. If the master trope for these groups is, as it is for Tjilpa, the relation to land, it is the land always viewed through history and its contingencies; viewed from a distance and often with a nostalgia and ideological intensity only possible from afar.

Benedict Anderson's model of imagined communities posits that it was the combination of distance from the "homeland" together with a new view of temporality that fostered the rise of nationalism in the Americas. The new temporality was constructed in the West by, on the one hand, the driving of a "wedge between cosmology and history"[51] as the Church's monolithic force declined and, on the other, the rise of newspapers and novels that allowed for a sense of simultaneity, shared progress, and "reading together" to emerge in the American colonies.[52] Africans carried to the Americas by the slave trade, by contrast, lost the possibility of imagining their trajectory as a single whole, or so claims Anderson for the case of Venezuela, because of the brutality and political-cultural fragmentation that resulted from that passage.[53] This seems entirely correct through the eighteenth century. By the nineteenth century, though, in parts of the Americas such as Brazil, religions such as Candomblé were formed that both presupposed and worked toward an Afro-Brazilian imagined community and shared destiny with Africa, by rendering the African gods present and feeding them in ritualizations in the Americas. True, this did not imply a temporal simultaneity with Africa—the imagined Africa of the Afro-Brazilian imagined community was usually of one two centuries prior, not of an actually shared present. Still, through a shared ritual grammar and initiatic passage an imagined Afro-Brazilian community was forged, and Anderson may be too hasty in seeing that capacity as forfeit among slaves. By now, moreover, pan-African and pan-indigenous identities are nourished by the kind of literary and scholarly print production that once forged the new creole nationalisms in the Americas. This is a dramatic transformation of individual indigenous groups into a shared, broad-based, and increasingly elaborated indigenism.

The birth of a new form of imagined community arising out of the dislocations of migration to address new social needs is surely to the good. I argued that the indigenizing moves in Candomblé and among the Garífuna can be seen as responses to a crisis of disjunction. Within the acad-

[51] Anderson, p. 36.
[52] Ibid., pp. 22–36, 61–62, 192.
[53] Ibid., p. 189n.

emy, of course, we face our own frustrating inability to establish clear, fixed boundaries, either theoretical or territorial. We should take care that the category of indigenous religions, like the primitive and archaic before it, not serve as an epistemological and comparative anchor. We should take care that the category not be used as our own crisis response, a fetish in a quixotian quest for stable, located meanings, for at least a wobbling pivot to steady shaking hands in a world where nothing rests. We should honor indigenous religions' claims to a unique relation to the land not by simply reproducing or essentializing them, but rather by critically investigating them—as we do all religious traditions—as they are mediated by language and history and as a magnificent part of the human repertoire of making place, not merely being "of" the land. Candomblé and Garifuna religions suggest that place is never made except through language and the imagination, creative forces summoned now more than ever from those religions always in motion, yet always looking back. When understood as an imagined community, as a processual term, and as an ideal type never fully manifested in history, the indigenous can yet prove an important category for the comparative study of religion, both to understand those "on the land" as well as those for whom the homeland is an idea and an image.

University of Missouri—Columbia

Part IV
Gender Relations

[11]

Journal of Refugee Studies Vol. 15, No. 2 2002

'Everywhere is Allah's Place': Islam and the Everyday Life of Somali Women in Melbourne, Australia

CELIA McMICHAEL

Key Centre for Women's Health in Society, University of Melbourne, Australia

This article explores the role of Islam in the lives of Somali women in Melbourne, Australia. It is derived from ethnographic research carried out between April 2000 and August 2001 that focused on displacement, resettlement, and the emotional well-being of Somali refugee women. As refugees, these women are dislocated from familiar life-worlds in Somalia. Yet Islam provides an enduring 'home' that is carried throughout displacement and resettlement. Islam is articulated through women's use and construction of space, daily practices, forms of interaction, and modes of thinking about their lives. Further, Islam offers a meaningful framework of practice and ideology that sustains women during the hardships of exile, displacement and resettlement and in times of emotional distress.

Introduction

Some months after Medina[1] arrived in Australia, we were sitting together drinking tea in her home and talking about her experiences of displacement and resettlement. Our conversation was interrupted as her eight children, aged between one and 11, tore through the room. In an attempt to quiet them, she sat them on a mattress and placed the Qur'an in their hands. The scribbles of the previous tenant's children marked the walls of her public housing home. These markings were partially covered with ornate Islamic texts etched onto brass plates and woven into fabric. Medina's conversation was sprinkled with references to Allah. Everyday circumstances were attributed to the will of Allah and hopes for the future were only possible if they were Allah's will. She talked of holding on to her faith when she was lonely and when she could not cope. As dusk set in and the light began to fade, she said that she could not talk any longer, as it was time to pray.

Religion has been widely conceptualized as providing a framework for apprehending and living in the world. In his influential text *The Interpretation of Cultures*, Geertz states that the importance of religion consists in:

172   *Celia McMichael*

> Its capacity to serve, for an individual or for a group, as a source of general, yet
> distinctive, conceptions of the world, the self, and the relations between
> them...Religious concepts spread beyond their specifically metaphysical
> contexts to provide a framework of general ideas in terms of which a wide
> range of experience—intellectual, emotional, moral—can be given meaningful
> form (1973: 123).

Firth (1996: 40–47, 197) writes that religious practice supplies people with
patterns for conduct in daily life and in times of crisis. However, the role of
religion in the lives of refugees during displacement, forced migration, and
resettlement is an area that has been studied very little.

This article offers an ethnographic account of Islam in the lives of Somali
refugee women in Melbourne, Australia. It focuses on the ways in which Islam
provides a 'home' as women resettle in a new country. 'Home' here does not
refer to a stable physical place where domestic life is realized (see Douglas
1991). Instead, it is conceptualized as a mobile anchor that provides stability in
the often unstable world of forced migrants and refugees. John Berger (1984)
writes that in a quintessentially migrant age, the idea of 'home' undergoes
dramatic change. A broader and more mobile conception of home is necessary,
as something 'plurilocal' (Rouse 1991: 8), something to be taken along as
individuals move through space and time. For migrants and exiles, home
comes to be found in a routine set of practices, a repetition of habitual
interactions, in styles of dress and address, in memories and myths, in stories
carried around in one's head (Berger 1984).

Forced out of their homeland and resettled in Australia, many Somali
refugee women have a vivid sense of displacement, both physical and cultural.
However, women are not uprooted from all that is familiar, nor confined to a
life in exile. Women draw upon the practices and ideologies of Islam, and in
turn Islam shapes spaces, interactions, modes of thinking, and daily activities.
In this way, Islam offers a sustaining thread in refugee women's lives and helps
them to overcome the threat of discontinuity that arises with displacement.
Islamic practice and ideology provides a plurilocal home that can be carried
through space and time. Further, Islam comes to the forefront of women's lives
during times of emotional distress. Many women experience loneliness,
sadness, anxiety and depression due to the rupturing impact of war and exile
and the exigencies of family separation and resettlement. Islam provides an
important source of solace and emotional support.

An underlying concern in this discussion is to question universal representations of Muslim people. Appadurai (1988: 36–37) notes that anthropology
tends to develop 'theoretical metonyms' that come to stand as the
quintessential aspect of a given region. Where Islam is the predominant
religion, there is a tendency for it to become a defining feature of the 'culture'
through which the lives and experiences of people are theorized and
represented (Abu-Lughod 1988). The terms 'Muslim' and 'Islam' frequently
appear within the public imagination of non-Muslim peoples as rigid,

stereotypical images, often with full prejudice as evidenced in the public discourse following the so-called 'Islamic terrorist' attacks against America on 11 September 2001. There is a view of Islam as anti-Western, anti-modern, anti-democratic, and prone to 'mob-like public outpourings' (Vertovec and Peach 1997: 8). Muslim women are represented as repressed, marginalized, excluded from public religion and Islamic rituals, and subject to the conservative forces of sexual ideology within Islamic patriarchy (Afshar 1982; Mernissi 1975). These perspectives reduce people's lives by subsuming them under the broad rubric of the Islamic world and defining them as different or 'Other'. More recent ethnographic and historical studies have entailed critical discussion of what is meant by Islam. Numerous authors argue that there is no essential Islam, and that Islamic people have different and even contradictory understandings and practices of Islam (Abu-Lughod 1988; Asad 1986; Bhatt 1997; Eickelman 1989; El-Zein and Hamid 1977; Said 1985). Fischer and Abedi (1990) describe the experience of Islamic exiles from Iran living in the United States, and their discussion reveals the diversity of opinion, style, custom and politics that runs beneath Iranian Muslim identity. As Abu-Lughod (1988) suggests, the 'Other'—such as the Islamic Other—might actually consist of many others who are not so other after all.

As previously indicated, this paper first explores the many ways in which Islam offers a 'home' for Somali refugee women during resettlement in Melbourne. Second, it discusses the ways in which Islam is an important source of emotional support during the continued trauma of resettlement. It highlights the diversity of Islamic ideologies and practices amongst Somali women by providing a wide range of women's own accounts of their religion. However, before discussing in depth the role of Islam in Somali refugee women's lives, it provides a brief sketch of Somalia's recent political history and the events leading up to the civil war that began in 1991, in order to enhance our understanding of the historical and social dimensions of Somali women's forced migration and their subsequent resettlement in Melbourne. Description of the fieldwork site and discussion of research methods follow.

Exodus and Resettlement

Somalia is situated in the northeast of Africa. It borders Kenya, Ethiopia, and Djibouti, and is one of a group of countries in the region referred to as the Horn of Africa. Somalia has a population of approximately eight to 10 million. However, the Somali people are not contained within the national borders that were drawn by the politics and ink, first of the Ottoman Empire, and later of Britain, France, Italy, and Ethiopia. Almost one-third of the Somali population now lives in adjacent Djibouti, the plateau region of Eastern Ethiopia known as Ogaden, and the Northern Frontier District (NFD) of Kenya. Many people have also resettled in countries such as Holland, Britain, Denmark, the USA, Canada, and Australia.

174   *Celia McMichael*

The forced migration of Somali people has primarily been the result of violent conflict during the civil war. Since the late 1970s, Somalia and other areas of the Horn of Africa have been in an almost perpetual state of violence and political conflict. In 1977, Somalia's leader Siad Barre launched a war to reclaim the Ogaden region in Ethiopia. Somalia was defeated, fissures within the Somali government became visible, economic and political problems emerged, and the regime became unpopular amongst the Somali people. Domestic political structures began to disintegrate in the face of 'blame and recriminations as to who lost the Ogaadeen' (Cassanelli 1993). Dissatisfied clan-based military groups launched numerous conflicts and attacks against the government. By 1986, Barre's government had lost all popular support, as increasingly brutal methods of political control emerged.

Between December 1990 and January 1991, battle between government forces and clan-backed rebel groups resulted in the collapse of Siad Barre's 21-year rule. Conflict flared up between clan-based military organizations and warlords in many areas, and civil war emerged in place of Barre's regime (Hashim 1997). Somalia has now been in a state of war for over ten years. The civil war, politically-induced famine and drought have forced many people to flee their country. Hundreds of thousands of Somali refugees remain in exile, either in refugee camps or in other locations in Africa. Most must choose between the dangers of repatriation or remaining without citizenship in countries of first asylum. Less than one per cent of Somali refugees have been accepted for resettlement in countries such as Australia (Hyndman 1999).

The Somali-speaking community is one of the fastest growing ethnic communities in Melbourne, increasing from 1,391 in 1996 to 3,226 in 2002. Melbourne has approximately 65 per cent of Australia's Somali population, the majority of whom arrived in Australia after the eruption of the civil war, 92 per cent through the Refugee and Humanitarian programmes. A high proportion of women have entered through the 'Women at Risk' refugee and humanitarian visa subclass, a category designated for women who are 'without the protection of a male relative; and in danger of victimization, harassment or serious abuse because [they] are female' (DIMA 2001; see also Manderson *et al.* 1998). The overwhelming majority of Somali people are Muslim (Metz 1993). In Australia, however, Muslims are a minority comprising only 1.13 per cent of the Australian population and 2 per cent of Melbourne's population (MRC North East 1999).

Research Methods

This article is based on qualitative research that explored displacement, resettlement, and the emotional well-being of Somali women in Melbourne. Oakley (1992: 17) suggests that qualitative methods allow exploration of the quality of experience through the study of meanings and processes. The key research methods included interviews and group discussions. In addition, I gained a richer understanding of women's lives through participant observation that included spending time with refugee women in their homes and in other social settings, and through my experiences as a resettlement caseworker. Each method informed the others to create an iterative process that could produce an ethnographic understanding of women's lives.

In April 2000, I started to work as a volunteer at the Migrant Resource Centre Northeast (MRC), which provides direct services to a large number of Somali clients. MRC is located on a busy main street in a northeastern suburb of Melbourne. It sits at the beginning of a long stretch of community service offices and shops: a local office of the Department of Immigration and Multicultural Affairs (DIMA), a Centrelink office where people seek welfare and social security payments, government funded emergency housing services, *halal* butchers, Iraqi and Turkish kebab shops, second-hand clothes and furniture stores, and the local markets. The daily thoroughfare at MRC is busy with newly arrived migrants attending the drop-in services and appointments for assistance with resettlement issues. Most of these people have emigrated in the past six years from the Former Yugoslavia, China, Iraq, and Somalia. Every week around 20 to 25 Somali people, approximately two thirds of whom are women, seek assistance with housing, health care, welfare benefits, and immigration advice.

Omidian writes that 'much fieldwork is accomplished just by being in one place over time' (Omidian 1994: 155). I began working with Malyun Ahmed, the Horn of Africa worker, and focused on resettlement issues and community development amongst Somali people. Over the first few months, Malyun taught me the basics of settlement support casework: how to assist with Office of Housing applications, refer people for material aid such as second-hand furniture, secure a No-Interest-Loan for electrical white-goods, apply for government rebates for utility service bills, nominate family for refugee visas, and use the Telephone and Interpreting Service. Soon I gained enough confidence to help people through the complex maze of social services. Through my work at MRC, I developed some understanding of Somali women's histories, learnt of the hardships and trauma that many women have suffered, and could appreciate women's resilience as well as recognize the ongoing problems that they face relating to resettlement in Australia.

Between August 2000 and July 2001, I carried out in-depth interviews with 42 Somali women, all of whom had entered Australia under the refugee and humanitarian programme. I spoke with several women on more than one occasion. The interviews elicited narratives of war, displacement, resettlement, and emotional health. They were carried out in women's homes and followed a loose thematic framework, but women directed the course and flow of conversations.

Group discussions occasionally developed as friends and family arrived: the composition of groups changing as people came and left the house, went to the kitchen to prepare food, or unrolled mats on the floor and began prayers. Writers on research methods suggest that the purpose of *focus group discussions* is to obtain general information about beliefs, attitudes, and behaviour

176   *Celia McMichael*

(Dawson *et al.* 1993; Hudelson 1994; Patton 1990) and to inform and confirm other data (Bernard 1994). The group discussions in this research did not have such explicit methodological aims, as they were informal conversations rather than tightly controlled and 'focused' conversations. Nonetheless, they provided an opportunity for differing views to emerge as women teased out divergences in their experiences.

Malyun assisted with many aspects of the interview process and her input was crucial. My rudimentary knowledge of Somali and the limited English language of many Somali women meant that I relied on Malyun to interpret for 33 of the interviews. Literature on interpreting includes various suggestions to minimize technical problems, such as assessment of interpreter skills, ensuring the interpreter understands their role is passive, and maintaining eye-contact with the interviewee in order to prevent a 'psycho-social coalition' forming between the interpreter and the interviewee (see Edwards 1998: 200–201). The aim of such approaches is to control the interpreter and render her or him invisible.

In this research, however, Malyun did not act merely as an interpreter or 'neutral mouthpiece' (see Edwards 1998). She was able to pursue sensitively issues that I might have left alone. We discussed research themes, and we talked about issues that I felt I hadn't grasped. I did not *use* an interpreter, but *worked with* an interpreter, key informant, and co-researcher. This approach enhanced the interview process, as Malyun and I were able to work together and bring different skills and perspectives to the research project.

The selection of women to participate in the study centered around Malyun's extensive network of friendships and acquaintances, the relationships I had formed with women through my work at MRC, and the willingness of people to participate in the research. To preserve confidentiality, women's names and identifying details have been changed. Despite the common *refugee* label, women's backgrounds were diverse; some had lived as nomads, others grew up in various cities in Somalia, and their levels of education were varied. Malyun was mindful of involving women who had different life-circumstances in Melbourne. For example, she included women who had no relatives in Melbourne and those who had migrated with family members, elderly and young women, and women who had been diagnosed with clinical depression as well as those who appeared resilient. However, all the women who participated in the study were Muslim.

The collection of narratives was not a tool that I used to produce an account of the *truth* of women's experience (see Scheper-Hughes 1992; Wikan 1996; Kirkman and Rosenthal 1999: 19–20). Rather, the interviews were a chance to explore how women ascribe meaning and order to their lives. Women's narratives involved selecting, omitting and ordering elements of experience. Images emerged of nostalgic memory for homeland, the civil war, fleeing Somalia, living in refugee camps and other countries of asylum, their expectations and the realities of life in Australia, and imagined futures. Women could have told their stories differently, or focused on different events or meanings. The important thing is that their stories were meaningful at the time of telling. There were also silences around specific experiences. Some women, for example, chose not to speak of the war, swiftly moving from narratives of pre-war Somalia to arrival in Australia, while others described the war as a series of events and processes entailing generalized and abstract details without emotional edge. I accepted silences within narratives out of respect for women's integrity. I also understood silence as a form of communication, in that it enabled women to construct their narratives in meaningful and acceptable ways.

Conventional anthropology has dictated that participating in a community is integral to understanding the meanings and experiences that constitute a cultural world. Abu-Lughod (1988: 22) argues that living in the social world that one is studying allows the researcher to grasp more immediately how the social world works and how members understand it. Participation in community and social activities brought richness to my understanding of women's lives. I spent many hours in rooms full of women; drinking cups of sweet milky tea and watching aspects of women's lives take place around me. I attended wedding and engagement celebrations, social gatherings, political events, picnics, and went to information sessions for Somali women organized by various service providers.

Working in social settings of displacement and resettlement, however, invites questioning of anthropological concepts of *participant* observation. A significant barrier to participant observation is that, as refugees, Somali women's life-worlds extend to spaces and experiences beyond the reach of ethnographic observation or participation. I could never share the traumas and hardships of civil war, displacement, and resettlement, be subject to racism, or live in the knowledge that I could not return to my country and life as it was before war. My *participant* observation was limited by the reality that refugees are displaced, and that a researcher from a non-refugee background can never share many aspects of their lives.

Throughout the research process, the centrality of Islam in everyday life was apparent. Conversations were peppered with reference to Allah and religious faith, and daily life was suffused and punctuated with Islamic practices. Islam shaped the course of the research on a daily level. Interviews were frequently halted so that women could pray. Prayer, five times each day, is one of the five pillars of Islam (the others being declaration of faith, giving alms, fasting, and pilgrimage to Mecca). The prayers consist of prescribed verses recited in Arabic at dawn, noon, mid-afternoon, sunset, and nightfall (MRC North East 1999). During the month of Ramadan we spent less time talking with women as they focused on religious practice and fasted between dawn and dusk.

Islam as 'Home'

For Minh-ha, 'our present age is one of exile' (Minh-ha 1994: 13–14). Many aspects of women's narratives reflect a sense of being homeless and exiled from

178　*Celia McMichael*

all that is familiar in their worlds. Recollections of Somalia were shaped by a compelling drive to present and hold onto a beautiful era. Women told stories of the good life they had, the fresh food, the beautiful weather, and the strong social networks; this was a time when everyone was happy. Representations of Somali identity and community life in Australia are strikingly different. Women lament the loss of family support and trusted social networks. They often referred to fissures and conflicts amongst Somali people in Melbourne, such as problems with gossiping and lack of trust. For many, there is an understanding that the idea of a 'Somali community' in Melbourne is a myth, and that there are strong cleavages along lines of clan membership and status. Further, women feel out of place in Melbourne, as they face an immediate reality of new environments and social networks, and the unfamiliar workings of institutions and services.

The narrative contrast between Somalia as home and Melbourne as a site of exile and disorientation is striking. This resonates with the general picture painted of refugees that focuses on vulnerability, struggle, and problems adjusting to new situations. Daniel and Knudsen, for example, describe refugees as suffering 'a crisis in culture wherein past and present remain as rigid as they are disparate, connected only by a chasm of despair' (Daniel and Knudsen 1995: 24). The metaphors employed to describe the movement of refugees refer to fluidity, as opposed to the anchoring metaphors of roots, soil, and homeland that convey settlement and stability (Malkki 1995: 16). Through this discursive form, refugees are constituted as being 'uprooted', as having lost connection with their culture and identity. Rapport and Dawson (1998: 9) write that 'exiles' and 'refugees' are expelled from the ranks of those felt deserving of combining house and home.

In this article, however, I suggest that processes of displacement and resettlement do not tear women from all that is familiar. Within the experience of exile, Islam is a way in which women recreate lives, homes, and community. Islam is a sustaining thread throughout women's lives and this helps to overcome the threat of discontinuity that arises with exile and displacement. In women's historical narratives, Islam was often central to accounts of personal and community life. As Amina said:

> A story in the Qur'an explains that if you are cooking soup then you should put in extra water so that you can share it with everybody else. As a Muslim woman, if I am cooking I don't just cook enough for my family to eat. In Somalia I used to cook a big pot of food and sometimes my kids would run out and they would miss the first lot of food, and I would have to cook for them again because the neighbours and the people that came visiting would be fed. In Ramadan we had samoosas to break the fast, and I would cook that many. Some people couldn't afford the meat and the flour. I cooked plenty for the neighbours and all the people that were fasting.

Women talked of life in pre-war Somalia as having a clear moral and social order that was defined by the framework of Islam.

Islam and Somali Women in Melbourne 179

The way it was in Somalia before the war was a good way, but now it is changed. We had a clan, but people were in the same culture, same religion, same language, we were all Somali. Life was pretty simple. The things that were good about Somalia were the religion, everyone had the same religion, and the culture we all shared, there was commonality. The food was great. There were no differences between us. The people, the weather. It was all good.

These narratives of homeland articulate nostalgic recollection of the Somali people as a community with clear religious identification. Reference to religion featured as a unifying part of their identity and society. When women's narratives turn to life in Australia, Islam is still affirmed as a central aspect of their contemporary lives and identities. Naima described how her faith has given her the strength to cope in Melbourne. She said:

If you have faith and you feel homesick or sad, you just remember that you are a human being. You remember that there is a God and that Allah has chosen that way for us. For me, when I feel homesick, I pray and I read verses of the Qur'an. I hear people who can't take life and they commit suicide. They jump over the bridges, things like that. I think those people don't have faith, they don't have faith in Allah and the things that Allah can do, and the things that Allah must do. My faith allows me to cope with my situation now. I go back to Allah and state my case and say 'Allah, help me'.

Women articulate that the Somali people have 'one religion', and many emphasize that Islam and Somali culture are inseparable as their way of life is permeated by Islamic morality and practice. In this way, Islam and Muslim identification remain constant throughout historical and contemporary life narratives.

While women themselves are resituated in Melbourne, Islam offers an anchoring home. As discussed in the introduction, the term 'home' does not refer to a traditional conceptualization of a bounded and framed physical place, or a location from which to depart and return. Rather, a home is created in the articulation of practices, routines, and ideologies. Bourdieu (1990) suggests that people come to live by the principles of an ideology through their bodies—their use of space, their practices. For Somali women, a 'home' is carried and recreated through the everyday workings of Islam; it comes to be found in the ways that space is constructed, daily practices, forms of social interaction, and modes of thinking about and understanding life-worlds.

Q: Are there any things that you would say have been good about coming to Australia?
A: Everywhere is Allah's place anyway. Every country that you go, Allah is everywhere. It is not as if we have come to a place where we are disconnected from that.

To my non-Muslim eyes, the clearest signifiers of Islam amongst Somali women initially lay in clues of practice and use of space. Bhatt (1997: 43) writes that there is an inextricable link between the production of identity, the presentation of bodies, and the transformation of the physical and social

180   *Celia McMichael*

spaces of the life-world. The expression of Islam was immediately apparent through material practices: women attend mosques, buy their meat at *halal* butchers, wear veils, and fast and feast during Ramadan; children are sent to Islamic weekend schools to learn the Qur'an; and sheikhs are called upon to recite the Qur'anic texts for good fortune and during times of crisis.

One afternoon, we arrived at a local park, a coach-load of 20 Somali women and 16 of their young children. The trip, organized by Malyun and myself at the MRC and funded through a local government council grant, aimed to give women a chance to see different parts of Melbourne and to alleviate the sense of loneliness and isolation that many women had voiced in interviews. The women spread out rugs and sat on the grass in the sun and talked while the children ran around the gardens. The women's veils ranged from dark cloth covering everything but their eyes, to brightly patterned cloth draped over their hair and bodies. Soon after midday they began to go in small groups to the public toilets to wash, and then gathered on the rugs to pray, facing towards Mecca in rows. After prayer time, lunch arrived; *halal* lamb stuffed with rice, sultanas, peas, and almonds, Turkish dips and breads, and juices. The *halal* food was bought from the restaurants and shops of longer-standing Turkish and Iraqi Islamic communities. During these few hours, Islam was made visibly apparent through the material practices of women's clothing, practice, and choice of food.

People's homes, the bland low-rise apartments and houses provided by the Department of Human Services, were transformed into Muslim spaces. Mats woven with images of Mecca were unrolled and women prayed together, veils were hurriedly readjusted if men without affinal ties entered the room, the Qur'an weighted with beautiful text lay on tables, shoes were removed at the door, and women's homes were filled with tapestries, plates and ornaments decorated with Qur'anic text and pictures of Mecca. These are some of the visible signs of Islam that are threaded into the everyday lives of many Somali women. They are not only religious practices, but are ways of inscribing Islam on new physical spaces and social landscapes following displacement. Through the inscription of Islamic faith and practice on spaces and lives, women make themselves at 'home' in Berger's sense of the word (1984).

Yet, this plethora of shared Islamic practices and the visual signifiers of 'being Muslim' can all too easily lead to a vision of a unified and authentic Islam. When depicted as a concrete and constant form, Islam operates like the concept of 'race' in that it builds an image of a different, essentialized and homogeneous social group (Abu-Lughod 1990: 9). This can create very real political and social boundaries that provide a forum for new racisms centring on immigration laws, alien-ness and policing of difference (Malkki 1995: 14). Many women, for example, talked of a sense that people regard them as passive adherents to an oppressive religion, and of staring eyes seeing their veils as the regulation of all women. Since the events of September 11, 2001, women's experiences of discrimination have been even more explicit; Muslim schools have received bomb threats and the local mosque has been defaced by racist graffiti.

Despite the apparent unity of practice, of praying in rows and words uttered together, Islam does not consist in unmediated forms that emerge from a rigid religious framework. Somali women hold diverse ideas about Islam and the appropriate expression and practice of Islamic faith. An example of the ongoing diversity in expression of Islamic faith is to be found in practices of veiling. It is a salient example because in the Western imagination, the veil remains a tangible symbol of women's oppression (Abu-Lughod 1988). Somali women might wear the full-length chador, or a veil covering their hair, forehead, shoulders and neck, or brightly coloured cloth tied around their hair, and some—particularly younger women—do not wear a veil at all. Waris, aged 38, talked about the ways in which this diversity of Islamic dress codes is disputed amongst Somali women. She said:

> The Somali community here in Melbourne is fresh from the civil war, they are made to succumb to Islamic faith and religious values predominate at the moment ... now there is a wave of fundamentalism in Australia. Maybe it is about preservation of culture because we are a minority culture here. Our traditional values are more prescriptive than they have ever been. I never remember people wearing thick veils. All of this is new for me. I started wearing a veil because of the anger and judgment of the community. I realized I was judged because I did not wear a veil.

Waris talks of wearing a veil to appease 'traditionalists' within the community. For other women the diverse use (and non-use) of veils arises from the multiplicity of personal interpretations of religious faith within the Islamic tradition, cultural pride, modesty, and resistance to Western influences.

Further diversity was to be found in women's daily Islamic practice and interpretation of the Qur'an. Some women followed the prescribed five daily prayers, while others prayed only when it was convenient. Many women chose to attend medical clinics and Western services when they were sick, yet others turned only to the Qur'an for assistance and guidance. As Amina describes:

> I don't believe that the medication would fix my sadness. My religion is the thing that keeps me going. I feel pain. The sicknesses are one of the things that Allah has brought to me, and no one else can help me with it. It is only Allah's choice to take it away. For some people the medication replaces the religion, but the religion keeps me going. I read verses of the Qur'an and put the book over my body and that keeps me going.

Interpretations of the Qur'an were also diverse. Idil, aged 63, read the Qur'an literally and it became a template for daily life. She told me:

> In the Qur'an, it says at the end of the time there will be forty years when the people must stand up before they get judged. The sun comes very close, and those of us who are not meant to go to heaven will not be able to take the heat of the sun. Everyone left standing will then be judged. The Qur'an says you can't make bad comments about things. But for us, those kinds of things have become natural. We might say 'Amina doesn't really look good, she is short'. But you can't say those things! It is a sin if you say that people are ugly. And we shouldn't

182 *Celia McMichael*

complain, but here people just say that it is cold, the weather is nasty. We are not
meant to say those things; we are not supposed to criticize the nature of Allah,
because it is Allah's creation. In one of the verses the prophet Mohammed says, 'if
you can't say anything good or worthwhile, then don't say anything at all'. For
us, those of us who don't know the verses of the Qur'an and what it actually says,
we are really in trouble. It is like someone who doesn't know the way.

Other women did not read the verses of the Qur'an literally, but used them as
guidance for how to live and behave. As a final example, some women felt that
the course of their lives is entirely the will of Allah, while others expressed the
importance of setting their own paths while living within the moral guidelines
of Islam.

Islam is negotiated and contested in the fluid and shared spaces between
people and shaped by changing situations. In short, women make sense and
make use of Islam by continually moving amongst an inventory of ideas,
practices, and modes of expression. With the above-mentioned examples in
mind, an understanding of Islam emerges that moves away from a vision of a
bounded and unified religion, to an awareness of contested meanings,
contradictions and multiple discourses. Islam, then, is not a religious
framework with one authentic Muslim way of life. The expression and
ideology of Islam alters with circumstances, individual interpretations, and
contestation between people. For Somali women, Islam involves many versions
that are created through the push and pull of ideas and practices; through self-
reflection and imagination, women elide, negotiate, embrace, and reformulate
the expectations and offerings of Islam.

Islam is nonetheless an enduring and overarching framework that shapes
how women create and perceive themselves, their lives, their surroundings and
their future. Islam can be carried and lived throughout processes of
displacement, migration and resettlement. As Hawa described, 'In a sense,
there are no boundaries in the world. Every place and every piece of earth
belongs to Allah.' Islam provides a shared frame of reference, practice, and
meaning and is a way of maintaining and recreating a 'home' in a new country.

Islam and Emotional Well-being

This section discusses the ways in which Somali women draw upon Islam to
provide emotional support, manage transitions, and frame experiences of
depression and loneliness. While Islam suffuses people's lives, it plays a
particularly important role when women are faced with anxiety, sadness,
loneliness, and depression. Time and time again, women stated that religious
faith and practice was the most important way of coping with emotional
distress in their lives:

Q: Does your religion help if you are ever worried or sad?
A: If I ever need anything, the first thing I do is pray. If I need a good friend, I
turn to Allah and I say 'Allah, I need you as a good friend'. Allah is not going to

gossip about you; Allah is not going to hate you if you return over and over, asking and asking. If anything, if you ask for something, Allah would love you for it. If I am sick, if I need a special thing, if I need a simple thing, I just pray. Allah is the only one that I seek help from, the only one I can rely on.

Unni Wikan notes that 'attention to how people actually struggle, amidst multiple constraints, to cope with distressful events may offer an insight into the rationale and conceptions they use to frame their own acts and give meaning to experience' (Wikan 1988: 453). Numerous researchers have suggested that aspects of religious faith and spirituality have a beneficial effect upon the mental health of individuals and populations, particularly in regard to subjective assessments of well-being (Chatters 2000; Ellison 1995: 1561; Fry 2000; Kaplan, Cassel and Gore 1977; Koenig, Smiley and Gonzales 1988; Levin 1996; Pardini *et al.* 2000; Schumaker 1992). Ellison, for example, argues that religious practices promote social networks and support and provide a coherent framework, religious doctrines encourage altruistic behaviour, and devotional activities allow people to relinquish psychological control and responsibility for circumstances with minimal self-blame or guilt (Ellison 1991, 1995). In the case of Somali women in Melbourne, the practice and ideology of Islam is a central framework that gives meaning to lives and helps them to cope with 'distressful events'.

Women speak of Islam as a source of social order, meaning and reassurance in daily practice and everyday life. As Haweye explained:

Our religion is very important. It is good, we love it, and it has a very important role. It protects us from a lot of things. If we have a problem we turn to Allah and ask for help. We believe that there is an afterlife and we will go to heaven. In our religion you only go to heaven if you work for it, and then you will have a good afterlife. That is what we believe in. If you have a problem or you are in trouble then you go back to the religion and that is the way that you solve your problems.

Many women said that in Somalia, Islam was central to coping with specific difficulties in life. One elderly woman talked at length about the uses of the Qur'an in pre-war Somalia; she explained that verses were read to cure people of sadness and mental illness, to ask for the return of missing people, and to protect people from lions. She said 'the Qur'an is the treatment. The first priority is the Qur'an . . . there is a strong knowledge that the Qur'an can guide you and save you'.

When women speak of the eruption of violence and the civil war and people's subsequent flight from Somalia, their narratives suggest that Islam and faith in Allah became an even more important source of strength. Women recall the war in terms of danger, fear, violence, chaos, loss of trust, and social breakdown. The immediacy and horror of the war was evoked through descriptions of people dying of starvation, dead bodies outside people's homes, witnessing murders, family separation, soldiers raping women, children going missing only to be found with their throats slit. A report by the Victorian Foundation for Survivors of Torture and Trauma (VFST 1998) states that the

184   *Celia McMichael*

trauma of war and exile can shake people's faith in religion and God. Yet, despite the horror of the war, women did not recall their experiences as unravelling their faith and belief in Allah. Islam offered its ideational foundation and practices to provide understanding and expression in response to the exigencies of the civil war and exile.

> During the civil war, people were seeing their relatives being killed in front of them and there was a lot of depression. If a woman got depressed the person would go into a state of hysteria, not function well, they couldn't sleep, wouldn't wash their hair, they wouldn't eat, they would eat very fast and nothing would fill them up. Then it would get to the stage where they wouldn't get up. What used to happen is the neighbours would acknowledge that problem, women would get together and talk to them, they would go the mosque and verses of the Qur'an would be read.

For many women, Islam offered a causal framework as a way of comprehending displacement and exile, where the adversities of exile and displacement are the will of Allah, yet simultaneously their faith gave them the strength to continue and survive.

Somali people have migrated to Australia under the refugee and humanitarian visa programme and have left behind the immediacy of war and refugee camps. In the newness of Melbourne, however, they must recreate social networks, find new resources for daily life, and come to terms with past losses and new situations. While Somali women's resilience and ability to manage transition is striking, many women speak of times of sadness, grief, loneliness, anxiety, isolation and depression. This is a response to a situation and history that includes experiences of persecution and trauma of war and violence, separation from and loss of family, fraught identity politics of clan rivalry, and the hardships of displacement, resettlement, and loss of trusted social networks.

A number of women have sought help from doctors and been prescribed anti-depressants, a handful have gone to counsellors, and many turned to friends and family for social support. However, all women mentioned or talked at length of the ways that Islam permeates their days and sustains them during times of emotional distress and through the processes of resettlement. As Fatuma explained:

> Since coming here, life has been very different. In the refugee camps there was uncertainty and fear. But now, all these things are not present. But there are other things that make life hard. There are many things that I miss. I have family, but there is no support and you can't bring those that aren't here in to this country. It is hard to manage with childcare because I don't have the help of family. The housing is tiny, and the kids drive me crazy. I have language problems. In Somalia if I couldn't find my way, my mother, my neighbours would have helped me, but here there is no help. Emotionally, sometimes I feel very happy because I am here. But sometimes I feel very sad because I don't have any support or family members around me. When I am sad, I pray to soothe my mind. I feel sad because of the war, I worried about people killing each other, death, losing your life. Sometimes now I talk to myself. I do talk to myself when I look at the children and there is

no partner. I have so many worries, that they don't have a father, and there is no one I can tell all this to except for Allah.

For many women, Islam has become even more important since the war and resettlement in Australia. Some voiced an explicit awareness that the rupturing impact of war and exile has led them to place increased importance on their religious faith. During times of emotional distress, Islam is brought to the forefront of lives. Prayer, talking to Allah, modes and moral guidelines for social relations, words uttered, and ways of apprehending life; these are some of the ways in which Islam provides explanation, meaning, solace, emotional support, and acceptance of life situations. The following examples illustrate the ways in which Islam has provided emotional support in two women's lives.

One afternoon we visited Fartun to talk with her about her experiences of displacement and resettling in Melbourne. Fartun came to Australia in 1999 with her three children and husband. She suffers from depression and has been prescribed anti-depressants. When we arrived at her home she ushered us to the front room and we began to talk. She was very quiet at first, often readjusting her veils and partially covering her face with her hands. After half an hour or so she began to talk of her depression, her sense of isolation because her extended family remain in Somalia and Kenya, and her anxiety about her sister who has been missing since the war. Fartun explained that when she feels sad she prays to Allah.

> Q: When did you last see your sister?
> A: Eight years ago. I don't know whether she is alive or not. We separated during the war. She went to the Yemen Embassy with my aunts, but I refused. I said I was going to stay in Somalia because it was my home. From then, no one knows where she is. I have searched but I can't find them ... When I am alone I talk to myself. Sometimes in the daytime I dream, and when I sleep I have nightmares that a gun has hit her and she died when she was pregnant. Sometimes, they are very real, those dreams are very real and I can see them. It happens when I am alone. Everyone else, we know where they are, but my sister is missing. She is on my thoughts all the time. I am worried about her.
> Q: What do you do when you think about these things, and you feel lonely or sad or unsupported?
> A: I'm a Muslim and I believe in prayer. I believe everything happens because it is meant to be. That is how I manage if I am sad. I pray and I go back to Allah. I pray to Allah. I try to forget about these things, these memories that are distracting me. I go back to Allah, and I give thanks that the rest have been saved, and I pray and I ask if she is alive and pray to one-day meet with her.

A month later we went to Saynab's house and spent a few hours together. Her children were sleeping and her husband working, and we sat in the lounge room drinking tea and talking. Other Somali women regard Saynab as an example of piety and Islamic commitment. Her brown veils tightly pinned around her face, she spoke of how only Allah could see what is necessary for each person. She explained that Allah allowed some people to have their family around them in Australia and then watched to see if they were grateful,

186   *Celia McMichael*

whereas other people's family were left in Somalia or killed in the war and Allah watched to see if they were patient and accepting. Saynab herself fell under the second category, and while she is lonely and misses her family, she knows that it is important not to question Allah's will. She said:

> Allah is watching me to see whether I go out there and pull my hair and say to Allah 'why not, why not'. I am not going to say 'why not'. It is the way that has been chosen for me. I talk to Allah, and I look around and see that Allah has given other people their families but Allah hasn't given them to me. So I look at what Allah has already given me, and I'm really grateful for what I've got now rather than what Allah hasn't given me yet. It would be really un-Islamic for me to cry out for things that I haven't got rather than thanking Allah for the things I have got. So, that is the reality of my situation.

After this, she rolled a rug out on the floor and prayed for several minutes before returning to continue the conversation.

For women such as Saynab and Fartun, their faith in Islam and the routine of prayer provides solace, a framework for understanding their situation, and it allows them to relinquish responsibility for circumstances. They voiced an understanding that all events and their own lived situations are the will of Allah, and that they must accept Allah's will with patience. Their Islamic faith not only provided a causal framework that helps make sense of their lives, but routine practices that assist and calm them when they experience emotional distress.

Conclusion

This article has been animated by the challenge of describing the role of Islam in the everyday lives of Somali women in Melbourne. Eickelman argues that religions remain vital and meaningful through the actions of those who subscribe to them, and maintain and shape them over historical periods and in diverse contexts (Eickelman 1989: 255). My concern has been to explore the ways in which women draw upon the ideology and practice of Islam to provide a framework of emotional and social support. 'Exiles' and 'refugees' are often regarded as homeless and displaced, clutching helplessly at a lost world and culture, with no concrete attachment to new spaces and places (Daniel and Knudsen 1995). Allusions to liminality, homelessness and a state of limbo are widespread in descriptions of the dislocation that results from exile and displacement (Amit-Talai 1998: 52). More recently, ethnographers of transnationalism, such as Olwig (1997: 35), have suggested that migrants can in fact create socio-cultural contexts of great stability and sustenance within the disruptive process of displacement and migration.

In this article I have argued that in the context of displacement and resettlement of Somali women in Melbourne, Islam is a vital source of sustenance. Islam provides continuity, a shared yet negotiated identity, and it is a 'home' built from practices that occupy, use, and make social sense of places and lives. Islam is also integral to the ways that women manage transitions and their emotional well-being. During times of sadness, depression, loneliness, and anxiety, women draw upon ideological frameworks of Islam to help them make sense of their lives, and they find solace in their faith and in prayer. Indeed, the meaning of suffering, depression, and loneliness is entwined with the language, ideology and practice of Islam.

Islam brings together memory and longing, the ideational, the affective, and the physical. It involves many versions that are created through circumstance, individual interpretation, and contestation between people, yet it provides an overarching and shared framework of expression and ideology. It is an aspect of life and at the same time, a way of forming, reflecting on, and interrelating life-worlds. When Somali women come to Australia, it is not simply as uprooted refugees who have lost all ties to their past, their identity, and their culture. Islam, in its diverse forms, is a way in which women find and maintain resilience and continuity in their lives.

1. To preserve anonymity names of interviewees have been changed.

ABU-LUGHOD, L. (1988) 'Zones of Theory in the Anthropology of the Arab World'. *Annual Review of Anthropology* **18**: 267–306.
—— (1990) 'Introduction: Emotion, Discourses and the Politics of Everyday Life', in C. Lutz and L. Abu-Lughod (eds.) *Language and the Politics of Emotion*. Cambridge: University of Cambridge Press.
AFSHAR, H. (1982) 'Khomeini's Teachings and their Implications for Iranian Women', in A. Tabari and N. Yaganeh (eds.) *The Shadow of Islam*. London: Zed Press.
AMIT-TALAI, V. (1998) 'Risky Hiatuses and the Limits of Social Imagination: Expatriacy in the Cayman Islands', in N. Rapport and A. Dawson (eds.) *Migrants of Identity: Perceptions of Home in a World of Movement*. Oxford: Berg.
APPADURAI, A. (1988) 'Putting Hierarchy in its Place'. *Cultural Anthropology* **3**: 36–49.
ASAD, T. (1986) *The Idea of an Anthropology of Islam*. Occasional Paper Series. Washington DC: Centre for Contemporary Arab Studies.
BERGER, J. (1984) *And our Faces, My Heart, Brief as Photos*. London: Writers and Readers.
BERNARD, H. R. (1994) *Research Methods in Anthropology*. London: Sage Publications.
BHATT, C. (1997) *Liberation and Purity*. London: UCL Press.
BOURDIEU, P. (1990) *The Logic of Practice*. Cambridge: Polity Press.
CASSANELLI, A. (1993) *Explaining Ethnic Conflict in Somalia*. Woodrow Wilson International Centre for Scholars.
CHATTERS, L. M. (2000) 'Religion and Health: Public Health Research and Practice'. *Annual Review of Public Health* **21**: 335–367.
DANIEL, E. V. and KNUDSEN, J. (1995) 'Introduction', in E. V. Daniel and J. Dawson (eds.) *Mistrusting Refugees*. Los Angeles: University of California Press.
DAWSON, S., MANDERSON, L. and TALLO, V. (1993) *A Manual for Focus Groups*. International Nutrition Foundation for Developing Countries.
DIMA (Department of Immigration and Multicultural Affairs) (2001) *Application for Offshore Humanitarian Visa—Refugee and Humanitarian Visa*. Commonwealth of Australia: McMillan Print.
DOUGLAS, M. (1991) 'The Idea of Home: A Kind of Space'. *Social Research* **58**(1): 287–307.
EDWARDS, R. (1998) 'A Critical Examination of the Use of Interpreters in the Qualitative Research Process'. *Journal of Ethnic and Migration Studies* **24**: 197–208.
EICKELMAN, D. F. (1989) *The Middle East*. New Jersey: Prentice Hall.
ELLISON, C. (1991) 'Religious Involvement and Subjective Well-being'. *Journal of Health and Social Behaviour* **32**: 80.
—— (1995) 'Race, Religious Involvement and Depressive Symptomatology in a South-Eastern U.S. Community'. *Social Science and Medicine* **40**: 1561–1572.
EL-ZEIN, A. and HAMID, A. (1977) 'Beyond Ideology and Theology: The Search for the Anthropology of Islam'. *Annual Review of Anthropology* **6**: 227–254.

188   *Celia McMichael*

FIRTH, R. (1996) *Religion: A Humanist Interpretation*. London: Routledge.

FISCHER, M. and **ABEDI, M.** (1990) *Debating Muslims: Cultural Dialogues on Post-modernity and Tradition*. Wisconsin: The University of Wisconsin Press.

FRY, P. (2000) 'Religious Involvement, Spirituality and Personal Meaning for Life: Existential Predictors of Psychological Well-being in Community-residing and Institutional Care Elders'. *Aging and Mental Health* **4**: 375–387.

GEERTZ, C. (1973) *The Interpretation of Cultures*. New York: Basic Books.

HASHIM, A. B. (1997) *The Fallen State: Dissonance, Dictatorship and Death in Somalia*. Maryland and Oxford: University Press of America.

HUDELSON, P. (1994) *Qualitative Research for Health Programmes*. Geneva: Division of Mental Health, World Health Organization.

HYNDMAN, J. (1999) 'A Post-Cold War Geography of Forced Migration in Kenya and Somalia'. *Professional Geographer* **51**: 104–114.

KAPLAN, B., CASSEL, J. and **GORE, S.** (1977) 'Social Support and Health'. *Medical Care* **15**: 47–58.

KIRKMAN, M. and **ROSENTHAL, D.** (1999) 'Representations of Reproductive Technology in Women's Narratives of Infertility'. *Women and Health* **29**: 17–35.

KOENIG, H., SMILEY, M. and **GONZALES, J.** (1988) *Religion, Health and Aging*. Westport CT: Greenwood Press.

LEVIN, J. S. (1996) 'How Religion Influences Morbidity and Health: Reflections on Natural History, Salutogenesis and Host Resistance'. *Social Science and Medicine* **43**: 849–864.

MALKKI, L. (1995) *Purity and Exile*. Chicago: University of Chicago Press.

MANDERSON, L., KELAHER, M., MARKOVIC, M. and **McMANUS, K.** (1998) 'A Woman without a Man is a Woman at Risk: Women at Risk in Australian Humanitarian Programmes'. *Journal of Refugee Studies* **11**(3): 267–283.

MERNISSI, F. (1975) *Beyond the Veil: Male–Female Dynamics in a Modern Muslim Society*. Massachusetts: Schenkman Publishing Company.

METZ, H. (1993) *Somalia: A Country Study*. Washington, DC: Federal Research Division.

MINH-HA, T. (1994) 'Other than Myself/My Other Self', in G. Robertson (ed.) *Travelers' Tales: Narratives of Home and Displacement*. London: Routledge.

MRC North East (1999) *Muslims of Australia*. Melbourne: MRC North East.

OAKLEY, A. (1992) *Social Support and Motherhood: The Natural History of a Research Project*. Oxford, UK: Blackwell.

OLWIG, K. F. (1997) 'Cultural Sites: Sustaining a Home in a Deterritorialised World', in K. F. Olwig and K. Hastrup (eds.) *Siting Culture: The Shifting of Anthropological Object*. London and New York: Routledge.

OMIDIAN, P. (1994) 'Life Out of Context: Recording Afghan Refugees' Stories', in L. Camino, R. Krulfeld, M. Boone, and P. DeVoe (eds.) *Reconstructing Lives, Recapturing Meaning: Refugee Identity, Gender, Culture*. Basel: Gordon and Breach Science Publishers.

PARDINI, D., PLANTE, T., SHERMAN, A. and **STUMP, J.** (2000) 'Religious Faith and Spirituality in Substance Abuse Recovery: Determining the Mental Health Benefits'. *Journal of Substance Abuse Treatment* **14**: 346–354.

PATTON, M. (1990) *Qualitative Evaluation and Research Methods*. London and New Delhi: Sage.

RAPPORT, N. and **DAWSON, A.** (1998) 'Home and Movement: A Polemic', in N. Rapport and A. Dawson (eds.) *Migrants of Identity: Perceptions of Home in a World of Movement*. Oxford: Berg.

ROUSE, R. (1991) 'Mexican Migration and the Social Space of Postmodernism'. *Diaspora* **1**.

SAID, E. (1985) *Orientalism*. Harmondsworth: Penguin.

SCHEPER-HUGHES, N. (1992) *Death Without Weeping*. Berkeley: University of California Press.

SCHUMAKER, J. (1992) *Religion and Mental Health*. New York: Oxford University Press.

VERTOVEC, S. and **PEACH, C.** (1997) 'Introduction: Islam in Europe and the Politics of Religion and Community', in S. Vertovec and C. Peach (eds.) *Islam in Europe: The politics of religion and community*. New York: St Martin's Press Inc.

VFST (1998) *Rebuilding Shattered Lives*. Melbourne: Victorian Foundation for Survivors of Torture and Trauma.

WIKAN, U. (1988) 'Bereavement and Loss in Two Muslim Communities: Egypt and Bali Compared'. *Social Science and Medicine* **27**: 451–460.

—— (1996) *Tomorrow, God Willing: Self-made Destinies in Cairo*. Chicago and London: Chicago University Press.

[12]

Journal of Borderlands Studies
Vol. XIII, No. 2, Fall 1998

Migrant Women Crossing Borders: The Role of Gender and Religion in Internal and External Mexican Migration

Alicia Re Cruz*

Abstract

This article examines the migration experience of women crossing two different borders, international-national and rural-urban. Two ethnographic examples are provided to document women's transformations through migration. The first case deals with Mexican women crossing Mexico's northern border into Texas. The second case focuses on Maya women crossing the rural border of a Maya community to urban Cancún. The core of the study is the analysis of the parallelisms between these two cases, mainly expressed in the connections between religious conversion and socioeconomic transformations resulting from these women's migration experiences. The ethnographic method allows the comparison of the two cases of female migration and facilitates the understanding of the ideological transformation, expressed through the religious conversion, interwoven with changes in their migrant socioeconomic dynamics.

Introduction

The contextual frame of this study is the current global processes of geopolitical, economic, and conceptual rearrangements. Today, physical borders have become malleable entities onto which people stamp their personal and cultural experiences, and nations carve their political, socioeconomic, and ideological features. An adequate ethnography that can deal with the current socioeconomic and cultural development of the world must situate individuals within transnational and global contexts. As such, the notion of a border as it is dealt with, conceived, and crossed, becomes pivotal in any attempt to

---

* Re Cruz is a faculty member of the Institute of Anthropology at the University of North Texas in Denton, Texas.

understand current global trends. Certainly, the border as it is perceived and constructed today, has destroyed its former definition as the culturally defining limit of the nation-state or community (Kearney 1996).

This article is an ethnographic exercise aimed at understanding the meanings that the concept of border encapsulates in the world today. It introduces Mexico through migrant actors, María and Elide, who contribute to the breakdown of the physical and ideological international/national and rural/urban borders of a country that itself was created by the delimitation of borders. The anthropological endeavor stems from the ethnographic dialogue between female Mexican migrants in Texas and female Maya migrants in Cancún, an international resort city on Mexico's Yucatán peninsula, as representatives of the Mexican borderlands. One ethnographic case impacts the other, shaping their analyses. The goal is to reach a better understanding of a very common phenomenon—uprootedness. The focus on gender role adds an intriguing dimension to the understanding of current world trends, especially in comprehending transformations caused by border crossing phenomena.

The central features of this study are the impact that the women's conversion to Protestantism has on their border crossing experiences and the connection made between female migration and religious conversion. These ethnographic sketches illustrate several significant features of women's migration experiences. An anthropological analysis of conceptual and physical Mexican borderlands follows. The goal is to provide an understanding of the female migration experience in order to explain the reasons for their religious conversion. Broader discussion on the connections between women and political and socioeconomic processes is crucial for the comprehension of the male/female roles in the migrant household. Discussion must also take place regarding the creation of networks as an accommodation mechanism to the host environment.

Migration increases the cultural diversity of the host environment. However, it is through this same process of migration that borders become blurred and broken by the cultural traditions that migrants bring with them. Once Mexicans cross the physical border into the United States, they face the foreignness of the Anglo culture. Likewise, rural Maya migrants face the challenges of interethnic relations in the unfamiliar urban setting of the resort town Cancún, with its Mexican, tourist-oriented culture. In both cases, the cultural package serves as a basis of reflection, sometimes even as a refraction, in framing their new lives "here" versus a recalled "there." The migrants' cultural identifications also individualize the experiences of border crossing and the creation of new communities. In addition to these cultural, ethnic, and class borders, the migration experience often requires women to transgress the traditional gender role. The experiences of uprootedness in María's and Elide's lives are presented here as examples, reflecting the lives of thousands of women for whom the crossing of either national/international or rural/urban borders becomes a multidimensional intersection of meanings (cultural, ethnic, socioeconomic, ideological, gender, and so forth). Religious transformation seems to articulate the different dimensions of change

Journal of Borderlands Studies, Vol. XIII, No. 2, Fall 1998   **85**

that migrant women experience when crossing borders. Although constituting different experiences of migration, both Mexicans in Texas and Mayas in Cancún seek labor opportunities in a world where the search for work is not bound by the traditional limits of gender roles, community, or nation.

Women and Borders

Female Mexican migration is beginning to be recognized as a significant factor in promoting the set of social relations that organize settlement patterns. Studies of current patterns of Mexican migration show an increase in the female/male ratio (Melville 1988; Hondaguen-Sotelo 1994; Massey and Schnabel 1983). It has been assumed that the female component of Mexican migration is male dependant; that is, that the women follow the men (Reichert and Massey 1979; 1980).

The explosion of *maquiladoras* along the northern border contributed greatly to the increase in female labor force participation. In the 1970s, women accounted for 75 to 90 percent of the *maquiladora* workers (Fernandez-Kelly 1983). The economic crises of the 1980s pushed single women, as well as married women with children, into the labor force (Benería and Roldán 1987; Escobar and González de la Rocha 1988; Chant 1991; Oliveira 1990).

As this study shows, the main axis of dialogue between the two ethnographic cases is the coexistence of cultural diversity and global integration. The diversity factor is represented by the fact that, although both are Mexican border areas, the north is colored by the Mexican "self" and the Anglo "other" as the central axis of identity. This contrasts with the southern case, colored with the rural-Indian "self" (Maya) and the urban-*dzul* "other." The globalizing factor is expressed in the commonality between the two cases in that their new geographical settings are constructed by individuals on the move. The individuals analyzed and portrayed in this study are women whose social and economic roles within the household have transformed due to their border crossing experiences. A principal way that these changes are ideologically legitimized is through religious transformation.

The Northern and Southern Mexican Borders

The northern and southern Mexican border areas have much in common. They were created in the same historical period. In 1846, the north was defined by the Guadalupe Hidalgo Treaty. At the same time, a major Maya Indian upheaval in Yucatán, known as the Caste War, forced the Mexican military to defend the *dzuloob*[1] political power in the south. Aware of the Texans' success in defining the northern border and becoming independent of Mexico, the Mayan rebels appealed to the new Texas Republic for assistance in their struggle for independence. The termination of the Caste War at the end of the nineteenth century pushed Mexico to define the borders of Guatemala and Belize (Reed 1964). Today, these two Mexican borders, which defined the emergence of Mexico as a nation-state in the nineteenth century, open the political and economic arenas to the international inferences.[2] Migration not only defines Mexico's current "unbordered" condition. It also reveals other social and cultural ironies that result from the Mexican's presence in the United States or the Maya's presence in Cancún. It is necessary to analyze these migratory processes in order to understand the complexities embedded in the notion of the Mexican nation today.

The Unbordered Mexico through Female Migration

The following is an ethnographic analysis of female Mexicans in Texas and female Mayas in Cancún in an attempt to understand the conceptual and physical borders involved in the process of border crossing, particularly as they relate to religious conversion. The Maya Yucatec case is based on fieldwork done during 1989–1990 in Cancún and Chan Kom, a Maya peasant community. This community has contributed much to promoting Yucatán as one of the most significant ethnographic laboratories of Mesoamerican studies; however, it was in a state of social upheaval. Behind this portrayal of crisis lies a social reality, characterized by intense migration toward Cancún. Such migration contributed greatly to the emergence of new social groups competing for political power. The community was divided by *los Antiguos*, defenders of the traditional, peasant order, and *los de Cancún*, those who had chosen to migrate. Religion was also intermingled in this general perception of social schism. Representatives of the peasant economy, circumscribed by the production of corn and bound to the old *caciquismo* (bossism) political style, proudly identified themselves as Catholics. They openly opposed the derivates of migration, such as the emergence of capitalist wealth, ways to promote *la Política*,[3] and the spread of Protestantism (Re Cruz 1996). Maya identity was being negotiated within this context of socioeconomic competition.

Los Antiguos ferociously defended a traditional peasant lifestyle, marked by a socially and economically defined gendered division of labor where women are mainly valued for their reproductive function. They were considered to be the reservoir of culture that would transmit it to their children. *Los Antiguos* sharply criticized women's involvement in migration. While the husband traveled back and forth from Cancún to Chan Kom, the wife and children remained at the village, maintaining the family network and ties with the extended family. Once the wife moved with the children, both the family and the village lost members. In their ideological battle against *los de Cancún*, *los Antiguos* glorified their identification as the true Mayas (as *milperos*, or corn farming peasants) by stating that *los Antiguos'* daughters stay in Chan Kom and become *rezadoras*[4] in the Catholic church. Female retention, thus, became a sign of Maya identity. Young females became tokens to reinforce the Maya identity in the struggle between traditionalists and migrants. While *Los Antiguos* denied that their daughters migrated to Cancún, the socioeconomic census from the village revealed the opposite. Women, considered a stabilizing force because of their productive, reproductive, and

Journal of Borderlands Studies, Vol. XIII, No. 2, Fall 1998 87

enculturation roles, were highly manipulated as tokens of identity, enhancing the importance of traditional roles and family ties that migration often breaks.

In this struggle to attain "the true Maya identity," religion was also manipulated for ideological purposes. According to *los Antiguos*, any type of deviation from the traditional Catholic lifestyle meant a conversion to Protestantism, a term used to encapsulate different Protestant denominations and religious systems (e.g., Evangelical, Pentecostal, Mormons, and so forth). The spread of Protestantism in the village was associated with the effects of migration. *Los Antiguos* claimed that those who decided to settle in Cancún were influenced by Protestantism. They said of the migrants, "they turn into Protestants when they go to the city." However, in the city, conversion was primarily associated with women. They believed that the female converts first and the rest of the family follows. Following the traditional role as "the family enculturator," any cultural transformation is led by the woman.

The study of Hispanic migrants in Texas began in 1992. Research initially focused on the identification of the areas where the Hispanic migrant population concentrated. Denton, a town located near Dallas in the north of Texas, is one such region. Two major areas of apartment complexes were identified as having a large percentage of Hispanic (mostly Mexican origin) tenants. "The Dream Land" was a Denton Housing Authority apartment complex built in the 1960s for low income families. At that time, most of its tenants were African-American. This apartment complex is situated across the train tracks from higher income areas of Denton, facing the county jail. Mismanagment of the apartments and lack of supervision resulted in deplorable living conditions, including the lack of running water, electricity, and gas. The peripheral location, coupled with miserable living conditions and the general perception of the area as dangerous due to high crime and violence, converted "The Dream Land" into a "ghetto." In 1988, there was a change of management and with it a change of name. "The Dream Land" became the "Phoenix." The name change metaphorically expressed a new agenda—rescuing the bird from the ashes.

The wave of Hispanic migration in the 1980s transformed the ethnic composition of the apartment complex. Today, the Hispanic community represents 67.5 percent (183 individuals) of the total population in the Phoenix apartments (86 families, 271 individuals); African Americans (77 individuals) constitute 28.5 percent; and the remaining 4 percent are Caucasian (11 individuals).

At present, most of the low income migrants, particularly large families that have recently migrated to Denton or single men living in groups, are living in apartment complexes. Most work in the informal economic sector, where they are paid by the hour or by the day. Not knowing English reduces the possibility of obtaining a job under contract. The opportunities to find employment increase when the migrant already has relatives or *compadres* (co-godparents or fictive kin) living in the area. If the family is successful in saving money, they try to leave the apartment to rent a house or buy a piece of land to install a *troila* (trailer home) bought on loan. As one individual interviewed indicated, the migrant dream is "to have a piece of land, our own house with animals—chickens, sheep—as if we were in Mexico."

The growing migrant Hispanic community in Denton is associated with the spread of Protestant churches of different denominations. There are a myriad of small churches, mostly Pentecostals, located in the Hispanic community. These areas consist mainly of mobile home camps that lack running water and electrical service. Once the family has paid for the *troila* in full, they may start saving to get these services installed. Often, the small churches in these areas are private homes that are transformed into a church for the evening. Most of the participants are women. Women are allowed to speak during the service, conduct Sunday school for children, and transfer the divine message through ecstasy and trance.

Ethnographic Portraits of Female Migrants

Experiences in Texas andYucatán are presented through the following ethnographic sketches of a Hispanic migrant woman in Texas, María, and a Maya migrant in Cancún, Elide, based on fieldwork diaries. These portraits offer contextual reading for learning about current female migrant experiences and the connection between female migration and religious conversion.

María

Far away from town, amid large cattle ranches, dirt roads, and an old gas station that only sells beer, is a large mobile home camp where María lived with her husband José. At the author's first encounter, María was sitting on the improvised wooden stairs talking to José, who stood nearby. Inside, four of their children, ages 15, 13, 8, and 5, were watching television. The 13-year-old daughter was cooking lunch: potatoes with eggs, beans, and *tortillas*. Another child, a 3-year-old girl, was in Tamaulipas with her grandmother until her next visit to the United States. Buckets of water were dispersed around the kitchen and bathroom since there was no running water in the trailer.

When María and José were first married they lived with his parents. Their dream to buy a new home compelled José to migrate to the United States. He joined an uncle and a cousin who were already settled in Denton, Texas. Three years later, María went to Denton from Tamaulipas without the knowledge of her husband because she suspected that he was planning to marry an Anglo woman in order to get a resident permit to live and work legally in the United States. Once she arrived at the bus station in Denton, she called José and said, "I am here already, come pick me up."

Initially, they lived in an apartment in the housing complex. They could only do the laundry and go shopping when José came home from work since María did not know how to drive. María begged José teach her but he was afraid of the freedom that driving would provide her. When José got a ride to work with someone else, María would practice driving the car in the parking lot. After learning to drive and passing the driver's license exam,

Journal of Borderlands Studies, Vol. XIII, No. 2, Fall 1998   **89**

María was able to work in the garment industry, ironing clothes and sewing pieces of dresses and blouses.

José was arrested several times for misdemeanors, including battery. Once, on a routine trip to the supermarket, the police picked him up and put him in jail. José was incarcerated for two months, during which time María had to survive on a job that paid a meager $4.75 per hour. Family crises involving health care issues and problems with the children in school forced María to become the prime decision-maker of the household. Through years of hard work she was able to save the income tax refund checks that she received. With this money and the advice of friends from the Church on the Rock, the Protestant religious community that María belongs to, she bought a piece of land in a small ranch town on the periphery of Denton. In the last of José's promises, he helped her buy a *troila* for $1,000. He promised to convert the trailer into an habitable unit by reconstructing the walls, ceilings, and floors that were either missing or falling apart. When José was put in jail and the family's basic economic needs were not being met, María decided to fix the trailer on her own and move from the apartment.

Elide

Elide is from Chan Kom, a Maya community on the Yucatán Peninsula. At one time she was the village seamstress. Now, she runs a neighborhood store located in one of the lower income neighborhoods of Cancún, the international tourist emporium of the Yucatán peninsula. Her home, which is attached to the store, is located in region 101, one of the last neighborhoods to be developed. Some people call these low income neighborhoods "the land of cheese streets," because of the many holes that inhibit most taxi drivers from accepting requests to go there. Lack of electricity and running water, and cardboard roofs are common in these lower income neighborhoods.

"Cancún is very dangerous; Cancún is not a life for children; there are too many cars and huge streets; and there, people are killed and robbed," were Elide's responses in 1989 when asked if she would ever join her husband, who had migrated to Cancún several years after marrying her. Through a network of cousins and uncles, he managed to find a job in construction. For the most part, his wages paid the rent and living expenses in Cancún. However, he spent most of his savings in satisfying a chronic drinking habit. Nonetheless, having the family remain in the village required the cultivation of the family farm plot to satisfy the family's demand for corn. Part of the wages of Elide's husband were expended to pay relatives to work the farm plot in Chan Kom. Thus, income from working in Cancún paid for both the high urban living expenses and the economic demands of a rural community attachment.

Eduardo, Elide's 14-year-old son was completing his secondary education in the summer of 1989. The idea of migrating to Cancún was ingrained in Chan Kom's collective conscious. Stories that migrants retell with passion about the dangers, violence, and aggression of the city ignite the adolescents' imagination and transform migration into a male rite-of-passage. Some adolescents do not even wait until finishing school to follow their father's or other relative's footsteps. As the oldest of six, Eduardo was the substitute for his absentee father and made decisions relating to the farm. He was also consulted by Elide in matters relating to the family, such as the other children's performance in school and negotiating with the *h-men* (ritual and healing specialist) for family curing rituals or other rituals related to the farm plot. Eduardo was excited about Cancún, crossing the border between the village and the city, and becoming a man. In Cancún, he could earn money to pay for the maintenance and schooling of his siblings. At the same time, Eduardo did not want to leave, stating, "I do not want to leave my mother with so much work." However, Elide replied that his father's will was to bring him to the city to work. Through his *compadres*, Elide's husband found a job in Cancún for Eduardo. He would work at a restaurant preparing drinks for the tourist clientele and live with his grandmother and a cousin who had built a small palm-thatched hut in region 102, one of the low income neighborhoods of Cancún. Elide cried when her husband came to take Eduardo. From now on she would have to deal directly with the relatives who worked their farm; she would have to give them their wages and money for the seeds, fertilizers, herbicides. Casiano, her 11-year-old son replaced Eduardo for these household duties. He helped with strenuous work at the farm plot and ran errands for Elide's seamstress business. Margarita, the 9-year-old daughter, took care of the younger children by bathing and dressing them and cooking the meals for the family.

Having a husband and a son living in the city identified Elide as a member of *los de Cancún* group in the community. Going to the corn mill to get the *tortilla* dough became a nightmare for her. If women who were members of *los Antiguos* were waiting for their dough while Elide was there, their conversation turned into corrosive depictions and commentaries on *los de Cancún*. Elide's identification as one of *los de Cancún* brought her anguish, particularly when facing her mother and brothers who were active members of *los Antiguos*. However, it opened her business to the market of *los de Cancún*. She made dresses for the growing market of village migrants and their acquaintances in Cancún.

On one of his weekend visits, Elide's husband brought an old refrigerator, which they had one year to pay for. The house soon became a refreshment store. Elide was responsible for ordering, stocking, and selling sodas to neighborhood customers. Her new responsibilities also included keeping the accounts, keeping track of refills, making available the empty bottles for pick up by the Coca-Cola truck, and assuring that the correct number of bottles were replaced as stipulated in the contract.

Casiano graduated from elementary school and left for Cancún in the summer of 1990. He began working in the vegetarian restaurant where Eduardo and his uncle already worked. Elide was left in the village pregnant and alone with her four youngest children.

When the author visited the village in the summer of 1992, Elide no longer lived there. Her son had bought a piece of land in one of the neighborhoods in Cancún and established a small grocery store, *Tienda de Abarrotes Cimé*.

Journal of Borderlands Studies, Vol. XIII, No. 2, Fall 1998   **91**

Elide ran the store. Her experience with the small refreshment business in Chan Kom helped prepare her for this effort.

Elide was reunited with her family. However, tensions within her marriage increased. There were instances when her husband came home drunk and physically abused her. She was not able to cope with him as she did in Chan Kom. Instead, Elide ran into the street and called for the police who put him in jail and released him under the condition that he would not do it again. Elide promised her husband that she would not hesitate to call the police if he abused her again.

Making the permanent move to Cancún was not easy for Elide. Although her sister's family and her mother-in-law lived in Cancún, Elide still faced the opposition of her mother and brothers who remained in the village. When Eduardo became a member of the Church of Jesus Christ of the Latter Day Saints, or the Mormons, Elide's status as one of *los de Cancún* and her detachment from traditional Catholicism were confirmed. When Elide finally convinced her mother to visit her in Cancún for Christmas in 1994, her mother suffered a heart attack and died in Elide's home. Rumors spread quickly in the village. Elide blamed herself, as did the village. Consequently, she suffered from depression. Although she attends Pentecostal services with her younger sister, she has not yet converted.

Migrant Women and the State

The 1980s and 1990s in Mexico were characterized by foreign debt, financial crises, and the state policies undertaken to solve them. These neoliberal policies had disastrous effects for millions of people throughout the world and became a major factor in uprooting many of them. To meet the demands of the modernization process, Mexico needed to cut government expenditures to face international competition and to reduce the domestic public debt. The decline of government subsidies dramatically affected the low income social sector that includes peasants, agricultural workers, and urban households outside the formal economy (Benería and Roldán 1987). When hurricane Gilbert hit the Yucatán peninsula in 1989, it destroyed Chan Kom's harvest. The Mayas' survival in Chan Kom was threatened. At least three times, the government promised to assist the population with food, but aid arrived only once. Environmental disasters, exhaustion of the land, population growth, lack of government assistance, and drastic increases in the price of fertilizers and herbicides were the main factors surrounding the increase of Chan Kom's migration to Cancún, a movement that affected 70 percent of the families in Chan Kom.[5]

The appearance of political resistance to the dominant political party of Mexico, the Partido Revolucionario Institucional (PRI), emerged within this context of economic and social deterioration. Popular discontent was expressed in the 1988 elections through support of Cuauhtémoc Cárdenas, the presidential candidate of the Partido de la Revolución Democrática (PRD). Increased female participation in the Mexican political arena is also related to this popular desire for change. Elections brought a female governor to Yucatán and a female mayor to the city of Mérida in the late 1980s. In 1992, elections to select the political officers[6] in Chan Kom included a female PAN (Partido Acción Nacional) candidate for president of the community. This woman's father was of one of the leaders of *los Antiguos*, who had cemented their political opposition to the PRI by becoming members of the PAN. The socioeconomic opposition between *los de Cancún* and *los Antiguos* became expressed politically through competition between the PRI and the PAN.

While crisis was the emblem of social character in Chan Kom from 1989 to 1990, change became the emblem at the time of a new political election in 1992. As villagers said, "Everything is changing, *comadre.*" Certainly, the changes in Mexico paralleled similar events in other countries (Cypher 1988). People from Chan Kom were aware of these shifts and explained the emergence of female political leadership in their community within the context of the global system.

The PAN candidate in Chan Kom was a brilliant young woman who had spent part of her youth working as a *promotora cultural* (cultural worker) in community development projects. Her connections in Cancún allowed her to find temporary work in the city as a secretary. *Los Antiguos* asked her to run as a candidate for municipal president. She campaigned actively in the small hamlets that were part of Chan Kom. Her message was to bring people together and maintain the ideological distance between *los Antiguos* and *los de Cancún*. As a mediator between the two competing male social divisions in Chan Kom, this female political candidate perpetuated the role that Maya women have played in the past (Re Cruz n.d.).

Maya migrant women in Cancún and Mexican migrant women in Denton activate a cultural and social brokerage as a mechanism to adapt to the new institutional and social context. As part of their enculturating role, women interact with urban institutions, school teachers, and other entities. In Denton, for example, when there is a need to contact the apartment management regarding maintenance or repair, the woman takes the initiative. Once the message is conveyed and the solution is proposed, she contacts her husband before making a decision.

This process that begins with increased female influence in decision-making when the husband migrates, continues when the entire family moves. This leads to a transformation of the social and economic roles that men and women assume. This process increases women's social representation, particularly when women are active members in the labor market, which parallels the female national and international political representation. Behind the candidacy of a Maya female for the presidency of Chan Kom (she did not win), there is a complex process of socioeconomic and political transformations focused on female/male power relationships emerging from migration.

Migration, Gender Role Dynamics, and Religious Conversion

Gender roles are important elements in the contrasting images of idealistic Chan Kom and hostile Cancún. According to the Maya cultural tradition

Journal of Borderlands Studies, Vol. XIII, No. 2, Fall 1998 93

in Chan Kom, women are identified with the ordered and safe domestic realm, while men are identified with the world outside the limits of the home. The case of Mexican migrant women in Texas is more complex. While the majority share María's earlier experience of being the spouse devoted to the domestic chores in Mexico, others were part of the labor market. In any case, migration is associated with a change in household culture and organization. Sometimes men are reluctant to change their patriarchal attitudes and behavior, as María's husband was resistant when she asked him to teach her to drive. This attitude can result in female involvement in the informal economy that can be hidden from their husbands. They may sell Avon products or clean houses while their husbands are working. With this extra money they can invest in household expenses without their husbands' knowledge.

In both Denton and Cancún, this male/female clash eventually led to marital conflicts and family breakdown. The incorporation of women into the labor market and their presence in the public arena increased their economic and social power. This explains the ability of the migrant political officers in Chan Kom to maintain political power in the community. While the president, treasurer, and secretary stay in the village to undertake their political responsibilities, their wives live in Cancún, running the family businesses and taking care of the children. This balance between home and work may imply more equality between men and women in the cases of these officers' families. However, this factor generally does not apply to all migrant families. Political officers' families are the wealthiest of the migrant group. Families that have greater economic constraints have different male/female behaviors, as Elide's case shows.

Both Mexican migrant women in the United States and Maya migrant women in Cancún pay a high price for migration—the loss of the kinship support system. Elide's case exemplifies the detachment from the family network once she migrated to Cancún, as well as the punishment that leaving the community entailed—the blame for her mother's death. However, observations indicate that women are the primary vehicles for maintaining the family's ethnic identity in both the urban and international arenas. As such, María refused to speak English because her priority is that her children speak Spanish at home. Both María and Elide bring the genderized division of labor to their migratory homes. Margarita, Elide's eldest daughter, never finished school in Chan Kom. She assists her mother at the store, takes care of the other children, and cooks for the family.

Crossing the rural/urban or the national/international borders promotes a change in household relationships and male-female power relations. More active female involvement in the labor market increases female representation in the household. Such female representation in the public domain, along with an increase of economic power within the household, must be related to the phenomenon of their religious transformations. In both cases, although the religious community is guided by the male leadership, there are female leaders who direct the choir. In Pentecostal churches, it is the women who transmit the sacred messages by falling into a trance as the divine spirit incarnates their bodies. Furthermore, women have the important responsibility of conducting the religious education of children. A large percentage of those attending the services are women. Certainly, female religious leadership in worship is more prominent within Protestantism than Catholicism, which follows a more structured service system and is always orchestrated by the priest.

When Maya women become migrants, they leave an ideological system that legitimizes male authority. This male authority is expressed in political offices, which are held by Maya men. It is also expressed in the family, in which either the husband or the father is considered the family patriarch. Likewise, the political president of the Maya community is considered the village's patriarch. And, finally, the male authority is expressed in the Catholic religion in which the vertical hierarchical institutional order headed by the male priest legitimizes the sociopolitical hierarchy in which women's roles and performances are subordinate to those undertaken by men. Thus, patriarchy dominates the family, sociopolitical, and religious arenas, as much as it incites the existence of a vertical hierarchy led by male authority.

In both Cancún and the United States, Maya and Mexican women generally become new members of the mass of wage laborers, although some, like Elide, become petty entrepreneurs. In their religious conversion, they become members of a church network. Their economic identity as proletarian and their religious identity as a sister coincides with the absence of a vertical hierarchy that, particularly for these women, provides reference points for one's identity in the patriarchal system. The church network is an expression of conceptualizing men and women at the same ideological level and it ratifies a horizontal hierarchical order since the ego's focus is on those who belong to the same generation. This is in clear ideological opposition to the vertical hierarchical order in which the female's identity is contemplated as being under her husband's or father's authority. Thus, the conversion to a new religious system provides female migrants with new ideological tools to represent their economic and social transformations within an economic rationale where both women and men are forced to work to earn their livelihood.[7]

Migrant Networks

The understanding of social networks among migrants became the focus of anthropological research in the 1970s (Lomnitz 1977). These networks are comprised of friends, relatives, and *compadres* who are already in the destination area and become the sources of information and linkages for the new migrants. The Mexican woman interviewed in this study came to Texas via *compadres* or relatives who were already settled in the area. Maya migrants use the same types of networks to find jobs, housing, and information to survive in Cancún. Elide's case illustrates the assistance network developed within the community in her husband's absence, revealing a community-based network. His relatives assisted her with the farm plot and, on occasion, represented him as the male of the household. However, Elide's case also

Journal of Borderlands Studies, Vol. XIII, No. 2, Fall 1998 95

illustrates that, with time, women become more self-sufficient and rely less on the help of these networks. They become the decision-makers of the household while their husbands are absent. In addition to the already existing networks that facilitate migrant accommodation, women develop new ones or expand those that already exist.

Among the Mexican migrant women in Denton who do not work outside of the home, but are responsible for rearing the children and household tasks, a network of female assistance is developed within the apartment complex. Those who do not have cars are dependent upon those who do to go shopping or run errands. If María needed a babysitter, her neighbor might offer. In exchange, if María's neighbor needed a ride, she might offer.

To overcome the detachment from the kinship network and as a way to cope with the new socioeconomic environment, migrant women create a fictive kinship network among neighbors, co-godparents, and friends. Membership in a Protestant church strengthens the migrant links to this network of fictive kinship. The new church groups of "sisters" and "brothers" form the migrant's fictive family.

The cultural change involved in the migratory process involves a high risk of family breakdown, particularly because the networks of assistance disintegrate as a result. The increase of female economic representation in the household may lead to competition with the husband and other marital problems, which can worsen if drinking habits exist. The Protestant emphasis on family values is a significant attraction for those who are in need of creating social ties in the new socioeconomic and cultural context since they have lost their cultural resources and social and family networks. For María, the church community has become her family and its members are her siblings.

The networks of migrant women are crucial for disseminating information about employment opportunities and institutions of the host area. They also facilitate accommodation to the new social and economic order and provide women with emotional and psychological assistance as a way to compensate for the loss of their community kinship support system.

Conclusion

Migration, or uprootedness, is a product of the world's translocal and transnational state. It is a method of analysis that was used to examine the relationship between these two ethnographic cases in order to reach an understanding of people on the move who break conceptual molds and open physical borders. Chan Kom's translocalization through migration to Cancún and Maya ethnic redefinition are intermingled processes. Similarly, Mexican migrants who create new Hispanic identities in the United States become the actors in the making of a transnational Mexico.

These ethnographic examples document a new twist in the concept of culture. Culture is no longer a place, a group of people, or a discrete unit. It is a process of transnational building and translocalization of community life. These ethnographic cases encapsulate the processes that maintain the world in a transient stage.

Traditional migration studies have focused on the roles of men. The ethnographic cases used in this study substantiate the need to understand the role of women in male/female power and authority relationships as important factors in household dynamics. The analytical focus on female migration uncovers the socioeconomic and ideological complications hidden within the migratory process, whether it be transnational (Mexico-United States), as in María's experiences, or translocal (Chan Kom-Cancún), as in Elide's case.

The ethnographic method of comparing the two cases of migration increases understanding of the ideological transformation. Both religious conversion and female migration are central factors in the organizing settlement patterns of the Mexican migration movement.

Endnotes

1. *Dzul* is a Yucatec Maya term. It means "white" referring to those of Spanish ancestry. It also may be used as a synonym of "foreigner." *Oob* is the Yucatec Maya morpheme to indicate "plural."

2. Referring to the North American Free Trade Agreement (NAFTA), the economic agreement among the United States, Mexico, and Canada, and the foreign investments of European capital and multinational corporations in Mexico, particularly channeled toward the development of international tourism (e.g., Cancún).

3. *La Política* is a term used by the Mayas of Chan Kom to refer to recent political events that have brought the leaders of the migrant group to the community. Because of this, the traditional oligarchy of wealthy peasants and cattle owners who used to monopolize the political offices, is in competition with the new economic and political power of the wealthy migrants. This competition is at the core of the social split in the community.

4. Those who pray and sing in church or in any Catholic ritual context.

5. These data are taken from the 1989–1990 Chan Kom socioeconomic census, which is analyzed in Re Cruz (1996: chapter 6).

6. In Yucatán, the municipality of Maya communities comprise a *cabecera*, the political and administrative center, and the *comisarías*, or hamlets, which depend upon the *cabecera*. The main officers of the *cabecera* are the president, secretary, and treasurer. The main authority in the *comisarías* is the *comisario*. Chan Kom is the *cabecera municipal*.

7. Here, the conversion to Protestantism is viewed in the context of rapid political and socioeconomic changes. This interpretation agrees with Earle's (1993) analysis of conversion to Protestantism in Chamula, a Tzotzil village in Chiapas, Mexico. This study discovers the intricacies of conversion in relation to drastic political and socioeconomic changes in Chamula. The author's conclusion interprets conversion to Protestantism as a way to assert domination in a capitalist and atomized future.

References

Benería, Lourdes, and Martha Roldán. 1987. *The Crossroads of Class and Gender.* Chicago: University of Chicago Press.

Journal of Borderlands Studies, Vol. XIII, No. 2, Fall 1998 **97**

Chant, Sylvia. 1991. *Women and Survival in Mexican Cities: Perspectives on Gender, Labour Markets, and Low-Income Households*. Manchester and New York: Manchester University Press.

Cypher, James. 1988. "The Crisis and the Restructuring of Capitalism in the Periphery." *Research in Political Economy* 11: 45–82.

Earle, Duncan. 1993. "Authority, Social Conflict and the Rise of Protestantism: Religious Conversion in a Maya Village." *Social Compass* 39 (3): 379–90.

Escobar Latapi, Agustín, and Mercedes González de la Rocha. 1988. "Microindustria, informalidad, y crisis en Guadalajara, 1982–1988." *Estudios Sociológicos* 6: 553–81.

Fernandez-Kelly, Maria Patricia. 1983. "Mexican Border Industrialization, Female Labor-Force Participation, and Migration." In *Men, Women and the International Division of Labor*, June Nash and Maria Patricia Fernandez-Kelly, eds. Albany: State University of New York Press.

Hondaguen-Sotelo, Pierrete. 1994. *Gendered Transitions: Mexican Experiences of Immigration*. Berkeley: University of California Press.

Kearney, Michael. 1996. *Reconceptualizing the Peasantry*. Boulder: Westview Press.

Lomnitz, Larissa. 1977. *Networks and Marginality: Life in a Mexican Shanty Town*. New York: Academic Press.

Massey, D.S., and K.M. Schnabel. 1983. "Background and Characteristics of Undocumented Hispanic Migrants to the United States." *Migration Today* 11 (1): 15–32.

Melville, Margarita B. 1988. "Mexican Women in the U.S. Wage labor Force." Pp. 1–83 in *Mexicanas at Work in the United States*, M. Melville, ed. Mexican American Studies Monograph No. 5. Houston: University of Houston.

Oliveira, Orlandina. 1990. "Empleo femenino en México en tiempos de recesión económica: tendencias recientes." In *Mujer y crisis: respuestas ante la recesión*, Neuma Aguilar, ed. Caracas: Editorial Nueva Sociedad.

Re Cruz, Alicia. 1996. *The Two Milpas of Chan Kom: Scenarios of a Maya Village Life*. Albany: State University of New York Press.

Re Cruz, Alicia. n.d. "Women in Between Modes of Production." *Sex Roles*. Forthcoming.

Reed, Nelson. 1964. *The Cast War of Yucatan*. Stanford: Stanford University Press.

Reichert, J., and D.S. Massey. 1979. "Patterns of U.S. Migration from a Mexican Sending Community: A Comparison of Legal and Illegal Migrants." *International Migration Review* 13 (4): 599–623.

Reichert, J., and D.S. Massey. 1980. "History and Trends in U.S. Bound Migration from a Mexican Town." *International Migration Review* 9 (3): 475–93.

[13]

Asia Pacific Viewpoint, Vol. 49, No. 3, December 2008
ISSN 1360-7456, pp344–353

Female transnational migration, religion and subjectivity: The case of Indonesian domestic workers

Catharina P. Williams

School of Physical, Environmental and Mathematical Sciences, The University of New South Wales at the Australian
Defence Force Academy, Canberra ACT, Australia.
Email: catharina.williams@togaware.com

Abstract: *Drawing on an analysis of in-depth interviews with returned migrant women from East Nusa Tenggara, Indonesia, this paper considers the links between migration, religious beliefs and subjectivity. Low-skilled migrant women, including domestic workers, have often been represented as marginalised. This paper argues that in the context of migration, women constantly move through trajectories of power using religion as a spiritual resource. Against the commonly patriarchal characteristics of their religion and community, the women employ cognitive strategies to face challenges in migration. In each stage of their transnational migration, the women's experiences reveal the multitude of ways in which they continue to invest in their beliefs through everyday practices, rituals and networking. These experiences highlight the women's strategies in accessing different forms of power. This study demonstrates the significance of focusing on these women's experiences, including their everyday religious practices and their shifting sense of self, as a way of broadening the conceptual basis of our understanding of female migration.*

Keywords: *Eastern Indonesia, female migration, religion, subjectivity*

Eastern Indonesian women's mobility

Every day, hundreds of Indonesian women pass through cramped ports, stations and terminals. On buses, ferries and ships, women are on the move as part of a relatively recent stream of migrants seeking work and opportunity in places away from home. Recent increases in female migration in Indonesia reflect a general rise in population mobility, which is linked to rising incomes, education and better communication and transport services (Hill, 1996). Women's mobility also positively correlates with their participation in the labour market, particularly in the fast-growing sectors of education and health services that provide sources of mass employment (Oey-Gardiner, 1997; Manning, 1998). Indonesia's integration into the global economy provides a further context for women's increased mobility. Globalisation accelerates flows of finance, goods and information as well as movements of people, including transnational migration. Since the early

1990s, contract migration has increased steadily to meet the rising demand for domestic helpers in Asian metropolitan areas such as Hong Kong, Singapore and Kuala Lumpur (Hugo, 2000). Remittances from domestic work also have increasing significance to both the government and the families of individual workers (Heyzer and Wee, 1994; Barbič and Miklavčič-Brezigar 1999), particularly in the aftermath of the financial crisis in 1998 in Indonesia. Remittances made by women working abroad help sustain the household purchasing power at home (Hugo, 2000). Following the crisis, more than one million Indonesian contract workers migrated abroad, with three quarters of them working as domestic helpers.

This paper focuses on the movement of women from one of the poorest and least developed regions in Indonesia: the province of East Nusa Tenggara. The province suffers from the combined effects of remoteness, inadequate infrastructure and limited natural resources (Corner, 1989). It is a diverse region of scattered

doi: 10.1111/j.1467-8373.2008.00382.x

islands with hilly and mountainous topography, limited arable land, poor soils, aridity and a small dispersed population that occupies pockets of fertile land pursuing subsistence lifestyles. Difficulties in transport and communication create a sense of isolation (Jones and Raharjo, 1995). The region consists of 4.7 million hectares of land supporting 4.3 million inhabitants, 90% of whom are Christians (Central Bureau of Statistics, 2005). With less than 20% of the population living in urban areas, it is one of the least urbanised and poorest provinces in Indonesia with a low annual gross regional product per capita – Rp756 000 (real 2000 price) (UNDP, 2004). In 2000, I spent six months following some of the trails of Eastern Indonesian women as they moved by sea, from the islands of Flores and Timor in East Nusa Tenggara to the urban centres of Surabaya (East Java) and Makassar (Sulawesi). In 2007, I made two follow-up visits to Central and East Flores also Kupang where I conducted interviews with some of the returned migrants. The field research conducted in 2000 focused on the popular migration destinations established by census data, and also on the places of origin of the migrants and was conducted while travelling on boats in the region.[1]

During my very first fieldwork voyage in Eastern Indonesia, I met a young woman in a boat who graciously shared 'her space' on the lower deck with me. Not only did she literally give me a space on a wooden bench to sit on, but metaphorically she also created a space for me to start an ethnography of woman travellers, by readily sharing her stories as a migrant. The main purpose of her migration was to look for opportunity. In this, her aims were similar to those of many migrants who see migration as a search for a place where happiness may be found, 'a utopian space of freedom, abundance and transparency', that would constitute a break or 'an inversion of everyday order' where new opportunities and possibilities could emerge (Curtis and Pajaczkowska, 1994).

Her story drew my attention to how contemporary Eastern Indonesian women's migration reflects the joint appeal of movement and of leaving home. *Langgar laut*, literally meaning 'crossing the ocean', also means 'crossing the threshold of home'. This threshold is both cultural and geographical, separating home and

away, and self and other. The movement of migration is more than a physical act of shifting between one geographical location or cultural experience and another. Through migration, a woman crosses from a space of familiarity to the unknown, heightening her sense of self. She is no longer confined to her gendered identity at home as a mother, sister or daughter. Moving physically in space as a transnational migrant provides women with an opportunity to imaginatively redefine themselves and adopt new subject positions as a waged worker, an urban resident and commuter, a consumer, someone with admittedly limited free time. Migration stimulates 'the self-conscious recognition' of one's position and a move beyond it (Blunt and Rose, 1994: 16).

Liberating and exciting though it may be, this shift in sense of self or subjectivity is not easy. Young women's mobility in East Nusa Tenggara is viewed differently from men's. The gender division of labour and space assigns women to home (Vatter, 1932; Tule, 2004). Therefore, travel and autonomous migration are mainly a man's entitlement. Women's mobility is usually associated with family migration; hence, a single woman who chooses to migrate is an exception. Her mobility may be viewed as a disruption, containing tensions and contradictions that require legitimation. As a head of kin and household, a man is institutionalised in *adat* (customary law) to control women's mobility by his power over decision-making. Male kinfolk assume responsibility for young women's protection and reputation (Tule, 2004). My concern in this paper is how women from relatively protected backgrounds negotiate the radical shift in subjectivity that is part of the migration process. I focus on how women use religion to achieve their goals to obtain a degree of comfort and security throughout the difficult stages of transnational migration.

Local tradition in Eastern Indonesia naturalises the notion of a woman carrying out her gendered roles and duties with love and devotion, as mother, sister, daughter and member of the clan and local community. Particularly for Lio (Flores) women, the self-sacrifice model is magnified in the legend of the Rice Maiden (*Ine Mbu*) who was prepared to die – to transform herself into rice – to feed others so they might live (Orinbao, 1992). Christianity reinforces

C.P. Williams

local tradition in serving others by 'following God's will'. As evident in the everyday ritual when they pray 'Our Father . . . , Thy will be done . . . ', local women resort to religion to legitimise their leaving home and seeking opportunity abroad. I reflect here on the stages of migration and the role that religion plays in the experience of migrating and moving into contested spaces (Tsing, 1993).

Religion, migration and women

Despite the diversity and prominence of religious beliefs and practices among migrants, most contemporary international migration theories pay attention to the political and economic reasons of the transnational flows (Massey *et al.* 1994; Hagan and Ebaugh, 2003). Hagan and Ebaugh point out that:

> By relying on economic considerations in driving the decision to migrate and social explanations for sustaining the process, theories of international migration have overlooked the cultural context of migration. More specifically, they have not addressed the role of religion in the migration process, especially the spiritual resources it provides for some immigrant populations in the decision to migrate and the psychological effects of this on migrants' commitment to endure the hardship of the migration. (1146)

Certainly, the significant role of religion in migrants' lives, particularly in their daily lives in the new place of destination, has been recognised since the 1950s in the classic writing of Handlin (1973) about America's migration experience. While he documents the importance of religion in immigrant communities at the place of destination, he does not address the equally important role of religious networks as part of the social infrastructure that supports the act of migration. More recently, the centrality of religion in the process of transnational migration has been analysed in the migration studies in the context of the USA (see Levitt, 1998a,b; Yang and Ebaugh, 2001; Hagan and Ebaugh, 2003). The analytical emphasis on religion in migration enables insights into the ways migrants access different forms of power by drawing on spiritual resources.

In a nation that is predominantly Muslim, the province of East Nusa Tenggara stands out for its predominantly Christian population. In my research, I observed the importance of religion in their daily lives. Some migrants referred to following God's will as a way of normalising their marginalised social and economic position in the community – as a woman, with low economic status and a member of a religious minority. Women told stories of how throughout the process of migration they drew strength from their religious belief as a way of coping and enduring any hardships. For them, their faith provided a support through the transformative process of migration and stepping beyond the purview of their domestic supports and constraints. The way that women's agency emerges through this process and the shifting sense of self that it entails (Gibson, 2001; Gibson-Graham, 2006) must be taken into account in increasing our conceptual understanding of female international migration.

Feminist scholars offer insights into understanding the complex influences on female migration. They look to variables such as gender, class and race as determinants of female mobility (see for example Pratt, 1992; Laws, 1997; Bondi and Domosh, 1998; Lawson, 1998; Duncan and Gregory, 1999; McDowell, 1999; Yeoh and Huang, 1999a,b). Women's mobility in these approaches is connected with a gendered space of home (Yeoh and Huang, 1999a,b). Women as a homemaker occupy a marginalised private space that lacks economic and social status. When women migrate to work, they move from one marginalised position to a different marginalised position relative to their host community and employers. A woman's marginalised position is an issue of power relations, whether and to what degree one is being included or excluded in the network of relations existing in that particular space. Feminist and post-colonial theorists problematise a simplistic take on migrant identities as marginal and analyse their ways of negotiating and inhabiting multiple subject positions (Kofman and England, 1997; McDowell, 1999; Gibson *et al.*, 2001). Migration offers a contested space for women to widen their subject positions and shift their subjectivities. As women define themselves in relation to others, when their networks expand, so do their subjectivities (Tsing, 1993; Blunt and Rose, 1994). Given the relational context of women's subject positions, Gilligan (1993) suggests that women develop a conception of morality that emphasises care and connection. In contrast, men's subject positions most likely emphasise independence and objectivity. This moral framework that shadows female relationships provides insights into how women perceive connection, responsibility with others and their relationship with God (Gilligan, 1993; Ozorak, 1996). Within this framework, women commonly pay more attention to personal relationships with a loving God and with others in the community of believers, while men are more likely to emphasise God's judgement and personal spirituality (Ozorak, 1996).

I now move on to explore the complexities of women's transnational migration and transforming subjectivities through the stories of women I interviewed on my fieldwork. I have been particularly interested in the 'creative ways in which migrants use the institution of religion and its beliefs and practices to organise the entire migration process' (Hagan and Ebaugh, 2003: 1147). Scholars of religion argue that even though many religions are characterised by patriarchal practices, women still invest in their faith because of the potential rewards of comfort, security, a sense of belonging and growth (Ozorak, 1996: 17). Most women in my study confirmed this assertion in the ways their religious faith empowered them and gave them a sense of belonging to negotiate their marginalised positions. Drawing in particular on the stories of three women, Maria, Netti and Liana, I show that religion plays a central role in each stage of the migration process, from the initial decision to migrate, to the journey and the arrival abroad.

Stages of migration

Deciding to migrate: 'Following God's will'

Maria, Netti and Liana are from communities in Central Flores that are predominantly Catholic. Bishops, priests, male community group leaders, heads of clans and fathers commonly make decisions regarding public life. An implied cultural assumption in this patriarchal society is that women do not make significant life-changing decisions, including about migration. While young men are encouraged to migrate to seek knowledge and economic opportunity, women in the region traditionally travel as part of the family, so women's autonomous mobility can still create a sense of social unease.

When I talked to local parents regarding young women migrating abroad as domestic workers, they typically indicated their disapproval or reluctance to let their daughters go. An important aspect of a father's role is guardianship of his daughter's virtue. He assumes responsibility for the consequences of his daughter's migration abroad as a single woman. Fathers in Flores give formal permission and sign the required forms initiating the process of transnational migration but often do this reluctantly as unskilled women migrants (*Tenaga Kerja Wanita/TKW*) are unfortunately associated with prostitution and abuse. From my discussions with local priests, I sense that they were not comfortable with single women migrating as domestic workers because of the possibility of becoming 'impure'. Given the social mores of the region, migration is condoned only for economic reasons, and religious beliefs are often called upon to further legitimise the decision.

Maria, Netti and Liana went to Hong Kong as contract domestic workers. All were still single and, according to the local custom, needed their male kin to give permission to migrate. Netti could not secure a job in the public service after graduating from high school. An earthquake in Ende in 1992 triggered her decision to migrate to escape her family's impoverished way of life as farmers:

> My intention to travel started when there was an earthquake in 1992, and our house was destroyed. I wanted to go and earn money. We would have liked to start building the house straight away, but we didn't have any money. . . . (Fieldwork, 2000)

The timing of the earthquake was taken as a sign from God for Netti to move on. She played the role of the 'dutiful daughter' who would go and earn money to help rebuild the family home. Netti and others were quite sure that it was God's will that they found this opportunity to

C.P. Williams

migrate at 'the right time', emphasising that 'my time' is not necessarily 'God's time', but 'God's time is always the right time'.

Krause (2004) argues that women's prayer is a complex, multidimensional phenomenon that affects their well-being, particularly when they feel that they acquire what they want. They hold beliefs about their prayers being answered and about the timing and the ways prayers are answered. 'When people pray, they have certain beliefs or expectations about the nature of the response they hope to receive' (Krause, 2004: 395). Liana's prayer was answered when an opportunity for migration abroad came up at a time when she was very disillusioned with her boyfriend. When her relationship ended, she avoided meeting people in her local community in case they questioned her about her failed marriage plan. Her accidental and rare meeting with a distant relative who had just returned from Hong Kong as a domestic worker met her need for a new direction. She needed no further encouragement to migrate abroad. For her, the timing was perfect; it was 'God's right time'. Liana referred to her migration as 'God's will', alluding to her belief and the centrality of religion in the early stage of the migration decision-making process. Others mentioned that their prayers were answered during an unemployment period, when they were able to link into domestic workers' networks and hence were provided with information to migrate. Local social networks are significant in providing information and assisting migration from the initial decision to migrate to the arrival in the place of destination (Hugo, 1999a,b, 2000).

When an opportunity to go abroad arose, these women grabbed it with both hands, giving the reason of 'following God's will'. The positive effect of this belief strengthened their resolve to go through the complicated process of transnational migration. This reasoning underlies a belief that 'God provides', which is quite a strong conviction in their everyday life as they mentioned it often. Various scholars have identified how prayers are responsible for producing beneficial effects on well-being, including with ways of dealing with stress (Krause, 2004; Kwilecki, 2004). Daughters in the region resort to prayers when faced with the first stressful period of migration – their decision to migrate. In addition to promising to help with the family

income, young women use their beliefs and faith to persuade fathers to let them go. They convince the family that God will look after them as they follow God's will to help the family.

The journey: 'I felt brave because I had my strong faith . . .'

The next step of a domestic worker's journey before leaving the country is going to Java. This in-transit period is also a time when the women are subjected to a series of physical and social examinations. These include a medical check-up, to make sure that they are physically healthy and not pregnant, and a character investigation, through criminal records held by the police, to guarantee that they have not committed any crime. They are also required to undergo an intensive training course that accustoms them to domestic tasks, such as cooking, cleaning and simple sewing. There is no fixed training period because it depends on how quickly the potential domestic worker can be placed in employment. Often the women are videoed, so that potential employers can appraise their physical appearance. Many of the women whom I interviewed were away from their family for the first time and felt exposed without the protection of their male kinfolk and they felt very anxious because they had to wait in the dormitory for between three to seven months. All of them talked about their sense of frustration while in transit.

On leaving the protected space of home, most of the women were aware of the hardship as well as the temptations of living as a domestic helper in middle-class homes in urban areas. The nature of domestic services would involve being alone with their employers without their male kin's protection. Like other migrants, the women from Ende (Flores) use religious rituals, including prayers and worship services, in order to survive the migration process (Kwilecki, 2004). Although not all coping mechanisms are fully conscious, they represent proactive decision-making and awareness in facing a challenging situation (Pargament, 1997; Kwilecki, 2004).

While in transit in Surabaya, waiting for placement overseas, Maria experienced the physical hardship of living in a crowded dormitory shelter and, worse still, sexual harassment during the job training in a middle-class home. The challenge for Maria and others in the transit period is the mere uncertainty of future employment, including relationships with future employers. In order for a woman to confront harassment, she must first perceive it. Maria understood that she was being harassed when her male employer made sexual innuendos. She felt vulnerable both when she stayed in the shelter and when she worked at the employer's home. Yet Maria managed to maintain control over the situation, to 'stay brave' (*masih berani*). In this case, Maria's faith helped her to cope:

> In Surabaya the employer I had for on-the-job training was a young unmarried man. I was only there for one day at his house when he came to me. I was asleep in my room when he tried to open the door to come in, but I had locked it. Then after two weeks he tried again. One day after coming home from work, he asked me to come to his room. He asked me to give him a body massage . . .

> I felt brave because I had my strong faith. I cried in front of him so that he would come to his senses. Perhaps he thought that I had not been aware of where that would lead to, because I was not used to a big city such as Surabaya. But I kept on praying and praying very hard, and finally he gave up and nothing happened between us . . . (Fieldnote, 2000)

The risk of sexual harassment was a real fear for all these women when they worked at their employers' homes. One reason for this group travelling together from their village was to minimise this risk. However, it was almost impossible for these women to have the same job placement with one employer. Obviously, Maria did not welcome her employer's sexual advances. Maria's moral ideals and her relationship to family, kin, community and the Church gave her a responsibility to uphold the notion of 'a good woman' or *wanita baik-baik*. (Gilligan, 1993; Ozorak, 1996). The multidimensional effects of Maria's religious beliefs are apparent when considering that, on one hand, she is actually placed under the Church's and also male kinfolk's subjection as a weak person, but, on the other hand, her belief also keeps her strong. This means that through particular practices of one's belief such as remaining in control

of her behaviour and sexuality as expected of a good single woman and a daughter, although she is under a patriarchal subjection, her belief heightens a sense of self that emits power. Paradoxically, her tears, symbolically a sign of helplessness, were strategically used to escape her employer's harassment. This episode reveals Maria's coping strategy that empowered her through her belief and expectation that God protects her. Women's faith experience and cognitive strategies are known to be used to empower themselves in challenging situations (Ozorak, 1996). Women interpret their situation in the context of their religious belief and practices as strategies of self-empowerment while struggling for everyday survival. Maria mounted her defence by being aware of her situation and found strength and power from her belief in God. She reinforced her belief through her daily routine of prayers.

The arrival: A community of faith

For most contract domestic workers, the culmination of the transnational migration involved arriving and working in the houses of their foreign employers. For Maria, Liana, Netti and the others, this was the destination of their travel where all their future economic expectations lay. Distance from home allowed this group of women the opportunity to transform themselves and to achieve the financial independence of their dreams. Their personal transformation was reflected in their physical appearance – short hair, trendy T-shirts and jeans and a pair of sneakers. Maria, Liana and Netti showed me their photos after arriving in Hong Kong. They portrayed images of carefree young women with sophisticated urban landscapes as backgrounds. Despite these physical transformations, their belief and practices of religion remained strong as shown in the following story.

Most domestic workers in my study including Maria, Liana and Netti were conscious of the constraints imposed by employers and had the expectation to work hard. They learnt this through the informal networks of friends and ex-workers even before arrival. As they were to be paid good money for their domestic services, they were ready to work hard. When Netti arrived at her employers' home, she depicted herself as being in 'top gear'. She recollected her arrival, wearing her work uniform provided by the employment agency, her hair was cut short; no lipstick, other make-up or nail polish was used. She described her first day working abroad as '*siap berjuang*', which literally means 'ready for the battle!' This metaphor reflects the state officials' perspective that migrant women are economic soldiers deployed to battle against the country's economic crisis (Chin, 1997: 366). The similarity of Netti's arrival and background, stage of life, and particularly her faith, created a bond with other domestic workers from Flores. They formed into a small community that, in some ways like other similar communities, was also characterised by a range of oppressions (Kong, 2001). In this time of transformation and under some forms of oppression, Netti spoke about how her faith kept her steady – a centring force in the midst of turbulence.

In mentioning the employers' constraints imposed upon them, Netti and her friends began to uncover their strengths. A common theme was the women's awareness of what was expected of them. They seemed confident in their ability to meet any rules imposed upon them regarding physical appearance and codes of behaviour. This opinion was widely shared by the other ex-migrants whom I talked to, reflecting a knowledge of the uneven negotiation of class, race/ethnic and gender boundaries. A number of domestic workers attributed their success in dealing with their employer to 'an awareness of knowing one's place' and 'how to conduct oneself' as strategies in relation to employers (Williams, 2005).

Arriving as minority Catholics in Hong Kong and in their employers' houses, the women negotiated their positions using their faith to empower them. In terms of their relations with the Chinese employers in Hong Kong who were not Christian, the women believed that their own faith was positively good. They alluded to this feeling while discussing their faith and felt 'right' in their Catholic belief and rituals as shown by their regular attendance at Catholic mass on Sundays. One very timid woman whom I interviewed said she did not hesitate to remind the employer of her Sunday work off because of her need to worship.[2] Mass on Sundays was celebrated by an Indonesian priest who also acted as their chaplain and spiritual

guide. The migrants' participation in the faith were emotional, social and spiritual acts as they needed to be part of the community of faith. The women agreed that they drew affirmation through the religious rituals and social activities together and described them as strengthening their bonds as 'a family'. They seemed to obtain comfort, security and a sense of belonging (Ozorak, 1996) and often referred to each other as 'sisters'. The spiritual bonds or connections include reaching out to spiritual friends and the notion that the connections are not coincidental but reflect Divine provision (Kong, 2001). The sense of connection as a family among the women and the bond of following God's will to help the family back home (particularly for the first-time migrants) were recurrent themes of the women's religious expressions in relationship with others.

Examining relationships between migration and religion is critical for understanding the ways multidimensional power and meanings of travel are attached to various scales of place (Olson and Silvey, 2006). When I asked a group of returned migrants in Flores, where all of us would meet one weekend, the leader of the group without hesitation suggested a place of pilgrimage. By this time, I had become acquainted with the returned domestic workers as I had on a number occasions met them either individually or as a small group for interviews or participated in their social activities. We arranged for a minivan to take the six of us to the place of Marian pilgrimage about one-and-half-hour journey from Ende, our base. We started early in the morning, brought our picnic lunch, candles and prayer books. We lit our candles as soon as we arrived, sang hymns and said the rosary in front of the statue of Mary. Later, we also did the ritual of the Stations of the Cross. The choice of place nor the activities that we would do there did not surprise me as, by that time, I had realised the centrality of the Catholic religion in the women's lives. The social and spiritual pilgrimage, the 'poetics' of the religious place and the sacred space became the focus of meaningful activities, apart from ordinary space (Kong, 2001). The women openly shared out loud prayers of thanksgiving for a successful journey, for their families and for some friends who were left working in Hong Kong. Their attachment to the community of faith reached across distance. This episode highlights how religious and spiritual beliefs and practices provide continuity, permeating women's lives from the decision to migrate, during the migration process and upon returning home.

Conclusion: Mobile subjectivities, religion and migration

The practice of negotiating the stages of migration (the decision to migrate, the in-transit period and at the destination) was also a journey of shifting subjectivities for the women. Maria's journey brought forth new subject positions and awareness that her race, class and gender may hold against her. Hence, when Maria cried in front of her employer, she was attentive to the multiplicities within herself and invested in as many dimensions of her roles and positions as possible to gain an advantage (Ferguson, 1993). Drawing strength from her religious belief, she also showed self-confidence in confronting the sexual approach of her male employer. Her presence in the urban space had to be negotiated with the idea of 'a good woman' who will not compromise on any sexual practice outside marriage. While her Catholic beliefs help her to remain true to her convictions, Maria was also located in relation to constantly moving trajectories of power. Ferguson (1993: 161) claims 'Mobile subjectivities are too concrete and dirty to claim innocence, too much in-process to claim closure, too interdependent to claim fixed boundaries'. Maria's ways of handling the sexual harassment show evidence of a mobile subjectivity, which produces provisional identities and opens up an unpredictable possibility (Ferguson, 1993) that generates power.

Maria, Liana and Netti's awareness of their religious belief and shifting subjectivities aided them in moving from the subject position of protected daughters with almost with no voice to that of autonomous single women working and negotiating life in metropolitan households. Liana was able to convince her father to let her migrate, arguing that God's timing was perfect. She escaped a failed relationship and achieved her goal of migration. Netti's way of coping with constraints, rules and forms of oppressions shows her drawing strength and power from religious beliefs while facing challenging

situations. Her responses to gender and class inequality reflect her using religion as 'cognitive strategies for reducing discomfort' (Ozorak, 1996). The timid migrant untypically negotiated her Sundays-off for weekly rituals. The sense that their faith was a constant and positive presence in their lives helped the women to reconcile themselves with the negative aspects of their social situations under a range of dominations. The women's subjectivity and religious belief and practices were in motion to generate a specific form of power.

The ways the women drew strength from their religious beliefs indicate a crucial force in their lives that sustained them throughout the migration process. They seemed thus able to reconcile a paradox of being placed under the Church's and also male kinfolk's subjection as a weak person, yet maintaining their beliefs as a centring force, which keep them brave (*berani*) and strong in the midst of transformation. While in transit and working abroad, the networks of relation, particularly the community of faith, enable women to keep the support of an imagined family, which in their view is bonded by God's care. The ways women use religious belief while in migration resemble cognitive strategies that can be used for reducing discomfort. Women are also able to exploit the fluidity and multiplicity of roles and identities in their changing spaces of migration, enabling shifting subjectivities. Through their religious beliefs, practices and rituals, women often have certain expectations of positive outcomes, which might be quite empowering. By considering the various effects of female migrants' religion in their transnational migration, we are also able to access the significance of relational contexts in female migration, providing insights into the motives, processes and determinants of transnational migration.

Acknowledgements

The paper greatly benefitted from the insightful comments of Katherine Gibson, Katharine McKinnon and Linda Malam. Many thanks to them. A previous version of the paper was presented to the Session: Critical Geographies and Agrarian Change in Asia-Pacific at the International Geographical Union Congress in Brisbane in 2006. Thank you to all the session

C.P. Williams

participants for their lively discussions. My gratitude to the referees for useful comments and special thanks also to Sandra Davenport for her help through the final stage.

Notes

1   This research reported here is part of a larger study on contemporary Eastern Indonesian women's travel through three routes: inter-islands, urban centres and overseas destinations (Williams, 2007).
2   However, the women's religious affiliation coincides with a particular socioeconomic profile of the majority of domestic workers from the Philippines, which may marginalise their overall position in the host society. Nevertheless, in terms of the host society's relative familiarity with Christianity, they are in a better position to receive understanding from employers of their rituals than, for example, other domestic workers from Java, who mainly were Muslim.

References

Barbič, A. and I. Miklavčič-Brezigar (1999) Domestic work abroad: A necessity and an opportunity for rural women from the Goriška borderland region of Slovenia, in J.H. Momsen (ed.), *Gender, migration and domestic service*, pp. 164–179. London: Routledge.

Blunt, A. and G. Rose (1994) Introduction: Women's colonial and postcolonial geographies, in A. Blunt and G. Rose (eds.), *Writing women and space: Colonial and postcolonial geographies*, pp. 1–25. New York: The Guildford Press.

Bondi, L. and M. Domosh (1998) On the contours of public space: A tale of three women, *Antipode* 30(3): 270–289.

Central Bureau of Statistics (2005) *Intercensal Population Surveys*. Jakarta: Biro Pusat Statistik.

Chin, C.B.N. (1997) Walls of silence and late twentieth century representations of the foreign female domestic worker: The case of Filipina and Indonesian female servants in Malaysia, *International Migration Review* 31(2): 353–385.

Corner, L. (1989) East and West Nusa Tenggara: Isolation and poverty, in H. Hill (ed.), *Unity in diversity: Regional economic development in Indonesia since 1970*, pp. 178–206. New York: Oxford University Press.

Curtis, B. and C. Pajaczkowska (1994) 'Getting there': Travel, time and narrative, in G. Robertson, M. Mash, L. Tickner, J. Bird, B. Curtis and T. Putnam (eds.), *Travellers' tales: Narratives of home and displacement*, pp. 199–215. London: Routledge.

Duncan, J. and D. Gregory (1999) Introduction, in J. Duncan and D. Gregory (eds.), *Writes of passage: Reading travel writing*, pp. 1–13. London: Routledge.

Ferguson, K.E. (1993) *The man question: Visions of subjectivity in feminist theory*. Berkeley, California: University of California Press.

Gibson, K. (2001) Regional subjection and becoming, *Environment and Planning D: Society and Space* 19(6): 639–667.

Gibson, K., L. Law and D. McKay (2001) Beyond heroes and victims: Filipina contract migrants, economic activism and class transformations, *International Feminist Journal of Politics* 3(3): 365–386.

Gibson-Graham, J.K. (2006) *A postcapitalist politics*. Minneapolis, Minnesota: University of Minnesota Press.

Gilligan, C. (1993) *In a different voice: Psychological theory and women's development*. Cambridge: Harvard University Press.

Hagan, J. and H.R. Ebaugh (2003) Calling upon the sacred: Migrants' use of religion in the migration process, *The International Migration Review* 37(4): 1145–1162.

Handlin, O. (1973) *The Uprooted*. Boston: Little, Brown and Company.

Heyzer, N. and V. Wee (1994) Domestic workers in transient overseas employment: Who benefits, who profits, in N. Heyzer, G.L.À. Nijeholt and N. Weerakoon (eds.), *The trade in domestic workers: Causes, mechanisms and consequences of international migration*, pp. 31–101. Kuala Lumpur: Malaysia, Asian and Pacific Development Centre.

Hill, H. (1996) *The Indonesian economy since 1966: Southeast Asia's emerging giant*. Melbourne: Cambridge University Press.

Hugo, G. (1999a) Managing mobilisation and migration of Southeast Asia's population, in T-C. Wong and M. Singh (eds.), *Development and challenge: Southeast Asia in the new millennium*, pp. 171–214. Singapore: Times Media Private Limited.

Hugo, G. (1999b) Undocumented international migration in Southeast Asia, in Y-F. Tseng, C. Bulbeck, L-H.N. Chiang and J-C. Hsu (eds.), *Asian migration: Pacific Rim dynamics*, pp. 15–48. Taipei: Interdisciplinary Group for Australian Studies, National Taiwan University.

Hugo, G. (2000) The crisis and international population movement in Indonesia, *Asian and Pacific Migration Journal* 9(1): 93–129.

Jones, G.W. and Y. Raharjo (eds.) (1995) *People, land and sea*. Canberra: ANU Printing Service and Demography Program, RSSS, Australian National University.

Kofman, E. and K. England (1997) Citizenship and international migration: Taking account of gender, sexuality and race, *Environment and Planning A* 29(2): 191–194.

Kong, L. (2001) Religion and technology: Refiguring place, space, identity and community, *Area* 33(4): 404–413.

Krause, N. (2004) Assessing the relationships among prayer expectancies, race and self-esteem in late life, *Journal for the Scientific Study of Religion* 43(3): 395–408.

Kwilecki, S. (2004) Religion and coping: A contribution from religious studies, *Journal for the Scientific Study of Religion* 43(3): 477–489.

Laws, G. (1997) Women's life courses, spatial mobility, and policies, in J.P. Jones III, H.J. Nast and S.M. Roberts (eds.), *Thresholds in feminist geography: Difference, methodology, representation*, pp. 47–64. Lanham, Maryland: Rowman and Littlefield Publishers.

Lawson, V.A. (1998) Hierarchical households and gendered migration in Latin America: Feminist extensions to migration research, *Progress in Human Geography* 22(1): 39–53.

Levitt, P. (1998a) Social remittances: Migration driven, local-level forms of cultural diffusion, *International Migration Review* 32(4): 926–948.

Levitt, P. (1998b) Local-level global religion: U.S.-Dominican migration, *Journal for the Scientific Study of Religion* 37(1): 74–89.

McDowell, L. (1999) *Gender, identity and place: Understanding feminist geographies*. Minneapolis, Minnesota: Polity Press.

Manning, C. (1998) *Indonesian labour in transition: An East Asian success story?* Cambridge: Cambridge University Press.

Massey, D., J. Arango, G. Hugo, A. Kouaouci, A. Pellegrino and J.E. Taylor (1994) Theories of international migration: A review and appraisal, *Population and Development* 19(3): 431–466.

Oey-Gardiner, M. (1997) Educational developments, achievements and challenges, in G.W. Jones and T.H. Hull (eds.), *Indonesia assessment. Population and human resources*, pp. 135–166. Singapore and Canberra: Institute of Southeast Asian Studies and the Research School of Pacific and Asian Studies.

Olson, E. and R. Silvey (2006) Transnational geographies: Rescaling development, migration and religion, *Environment and Planning A* 38(5): 805–808.

Orinbao, P.S. (1992) *Seni tenun suatu segi kebudayaan orang Flores*. Ledalero, Flores, Indonesia: Seminari Tinggi St Paulus.

Ozorak, E.W. (1996) The power, but not the glory: How women empower themselves through religion, *Journal for the Scientific Study of Religion* 35(1): 17–29.

Pargament, K. (1997) *The psychology of religion and coping: Theory, research, practice*, New York: The Guilford Press.

Pratt, M.L. (1992) *Imperial eyes: Travel writing and transculturation*. New York: Routledge.

Tsing, A.L. (1993) *In the realm of the diamond queen: Marginality in an out-of-the-way place*. Princeton, New Jersey: Princeton University Press.

Tule, P. (2004) *Longing for the house of God, dwelling in the house of the ancestors: Local belief and Christianity and Islam among Keo of Central Flores. Studia Instituti Anthropos*. Fribourg, Germany: Academic Press.

UNDP (2004) *Indonesia Human Development Report 2004*. Retrieved 3 October 2008, from Website: http://www.undp.or.id/pubs/ihdr2004/index.asp.

Vatter, E. (1932) *Ata Kiwan: Unbekannte Bergvölker im tropischen Holland*. Leipzig, Germany: Nusa Indah.

Williams, C.P. (2005) Knowing one's place': Gender, mobility and shifting subjectivity in Eastern Indonesia, *Global Networks* 5(4): 401–417.

Williams, C.P. (2007) *Maiden voyages: Eastern Indonesian women on the move*. Singapore: Institute of Southeast Asian Studies and KITLV Press.

Yang, F. and H.R. Ebaugh (2001) Religion and ethnicity among new immigrants: The impact of majority/minority status in home and host countries, *Journal for the Scientific Study of Religion* 40(3): 367–378.

Yeoh, B.S.A. and S. Huang (1999a) Singapore women and foreign domestic workers: Negotiating domestic work and motherhood, in J. Momsen (ed.), *Gender, migration and domestic service*, pp. 277–301. London: Routledge.

Yeoh, B.S.A. and S. Huang (1999b) Spaces at the margins: Migrant domestic workers and the development of civil society in Singapore, *Environment and Planning A* 31(7): 1149–1167.

[14]

Vol. 3, no. 1 (2013), 60-75 | URN:NBN:NL:UI:10-1-101620

Mermaids and Spirit Spouses: Rituals as Technologies of Gender in Transnational African Pentecostal Spaces

JEANNE REY*

Abstract

This article aims to approach the construction of gender in transnational spaces by focusing on the ritual practice of African Pentecostal migrants in Europe and in Africa. One dimension of African Pentecostalism is its insistence on the practice of exorcism called 'deliverance' where malevolent spirits are expelled from one's body. Within the Pentecostal demonology, several categories of spirits carry implications for how gender is constructed. This article will analyse effects of the appearance of these spirits on the construction of gender among Ghanaian and Congolese Pentecostal churches in Geneva and in Accra. It will show that variations in the appearance of spirits within rituals can be interpreted as a negotiation of gender roles in a migratory context. Shifts in Pentecostal demonology can therefore be interpreted as a response to the reconfiguration of gender roles associated with the broader gender context and work opportunities in Europe.

Key words

Pentecostalism, gender technologies, ritual, transnationalism, Geneva, Accra.

Author affiliation

Jeanne Rey holds a Doctorate in Anthropology and Sociology from the Graduate Institute of International and Development Studies in Geneva. She is a Researcher at the Department of Anthropology and Sociology at the Graduate Institute of International and Development Studies in Geneva and at the University of Teacher Education in Fribourg. Her field of research includes anthropology of religion, rituals, migration, mobility and education. In particular, she is interested in religious practices among the African diaspora and in migration and Pentecostalism.

*Correspondence: Anthropology and Sociology Department, Graduate Institute of International and Development Studies, Case postale 136, CH 1211 Genève 21, Switzerland, E-mail: jeanne.rey-pellissier@graduateinstitute.ch
Religion and Gender | ISSN: 1878-5417 | www.religionandgender.org | Igitur publishing

Rey: Mermaids and Spirit Spouses

Introduction

On a Friday night, in the multicultural urban area of *Les Pâquis* at the centre of Geneva, about one hundred migrants from several countries – mostly Africa, but also from Asia, Latin America and sometimes Europe – are gathered in the main room of the *Church for the Nations*, a Pentecostal church led by an Indian pastor who formerly worked with the United Nations. The preacher for the day is a Ghanaian pastor who had come especially from Accra. The evening prayer is attended mainly by women, most of them active members of the church. The congregation stands on both sides of the room, so that the central space remains free to perform the ritual practices. As usual, Friday night is dedicated to 'prayer and deliverance', the latter being a ritual practice whereby spirits are expelled from one's body through a 'powerful' prayer by a 'man of God'. After an hour or so of preaching, the Ghanaian pastor interrupts his talk explaining that he would like to treat a very specific problem. He introduces the topic to the international audience by pointing to its 'African' dimension: 'Let me be African!' Some people, he says, might have the impression to have sexual intercourse with an extra-marital partner. That could be the sign of a 'marriage in the spirit' with a demon. Marriages in the spirit might occur to both men and women and they are responsible for relationship problems, sterility and persisting single life. A European female listener, who seems unfamiliar with the problem explained, asks for more information. The Ghanaian pastor specifies that spirit marriages occur in dreams, not in 'reality'. After that presentation, he suggests that people concerned with that kind of problem should come to him for prayer. About ten people approach the 'man of God' who lays his hands on their heads, commanding the spirit to leave them. Most of them fall on the ground, which is perceived as a sign of a successful deliverance.

This scene was observed in one of the biggest Pentecostal church founded and attended by migrants in Geneva.[1] The scene offers an example of how ritual practices develop within transnational spaces. The non-African church attendants, who were already familiar with deliverance practices, were presented a new category of spirit that is causing troubles related to several aspects of the gendered life (like marital relationships or fertility). The spirit, however, is already well known to those who attend African Pentecostal churches as the so-called 'spirit spouse'. This figure is one of the most widely spread category of spirits in West and Central African Pentecostalism. By contrast, European Pentecostals are unfamiliar with this particular category of spirit.[2] Their introduction to a European audience raises therefore the question of the transnationalization of spirits in Pentecostal spaces.

---

[1] J. Rey, 'A la conquête des Nations (Unies): millénarisme, combat spirituel et internationalisation' in S. Fancello and A. Mary (eds.), *Chrétiens africains en Europe. Prophétismes, pentecôtismes et politique des nations*, Paris: Karthala 2010, 351–379.

[2] However, similar entities could be found in Europe in the Roman and Medieval times, which are known as *'incubus'* (male demon) and *'succubus'* (female demon). They also had sexual intercourse with their victim.

Rey: Mermaids and Spirit Spouses

Gender Construction Within Transnational Spaces

The development of transnational spaces where the nation-state no longer functions as a 'container of social, economic and political processes'.[3] opens new grounds for the study of migration processes that do not exclusively focus on the integration of immigrants. Though transnationalism cannot be considered as a new phenomenon, the expansion of travel and communication facilities offers new possibilities for the development of transnational social spaces.[4] Thus, these transnational spaces contain different social processes including the circulation of persons, information or goods, but also imaginaries, ritual practices and identification processes. Whenever people migrate, they generally carry their own ritual practices as well as the 'entities' that might be associated with them, so that 'the spirits that travel with them are as much a part of the complex processes of globalization as the migrants themselves'.[5] This is certainly the case with Pentecostalism, where spirits take part in the migration process.

One process that might be influenced by transnationalism is the construction of gender. Differing local gender configurations might coexist within transnational spaces. Thus, conflicts around gender roles might arise, whenever conflicting gender configurations meet in transnational spaces. James Clifford points to this dialectic of gender: 'On the one hand, maintaining connections with homelands, with kinship networks, and with religious and cultural traditions may renew patriarchal structures. On the other, new roles and demands, new political spaces, are opened by diaspora interactions'.[6] Migration and transnationalism can thus lead to a negotiation of gender roles[7] or to their new distribution in both the transnational and the local context.

In this article, I address the question of the role of ritual practice in the construction of gender in a migratory context. This study will focus on Pentecostalism, which is frequently associated with transnationality.[8] Pentecostal and Charismatic Churches (PCCs) in Africa often insist on taking part in a global world and developing transnational connections:

> 'What is distinctly new about PCCs is their propagation of the Prosperity Gospel and their strong global inclination. Their names, which often refer to the church's aspired 'international' or 'global' (out)reach, highlight PCCs' aim to develop and

---

[3] S. Vertovec, 'Transnationalism and Identity' in *Journal of Ethnic and Migration Studies* 27:4 (2001), 573–582: 575.

[4] L. Pries, 'Configurations of Geographic and Societal Spaces: a Sociological Proposal Between 'Methodological Nationalism' and the 'Spaces of Flows' ' in *Global Networks* 5:2 (2005), 167–190.

[5] G. Hüwelmeier and K. Krause, 'Introduction' in G. Hüwelmeier and K. Krause (eds.), *Traveling Spirits: Migrants, Markets, and Mobilities,* London and New York: Routledge 2009, 1–16: 9.

[6] J. Clifford, 'Diasporas' in *Cultural Anthropology* 9:3 (1994), 302–338: 313–314.

[7] J. Dahinden, 'Contesting Transnationalism? Lessons from the Study of Albanian Migration Networks from Former Yugoslavia' in *Global Networks* 5:2 (2005), 191–208.

[8] A. Corten and R. Marshall-Fratani, 'Introduction' in A. Corten and R. Marshall-Fratani (eds.), *Between Babel and Pentecost: Transnational Pentecostalism in Africa and Latin America*, Bloomington: Indiana University Press 2001, 1–21.

Rey: Mermaids and Spirit Spouses

maintain international branches in other African countries and the West, and to deploy notions of identity and belonging that deliberately reach beyond Africa'.[9]

In the last decades, and in particular during the last fifteen years, this claim to transnationality has found a new expression in Europe, where African migrants established branches of Pentecostal churches that often maintained connections with African denominations. These social spaces that span across borders also constitute a new place for (re-)constructing gender roles.

In the first part of this article, I will briefly describe the context of the creation of Pentecostal churches by African migrants in the Lake Geneva urban area. I will then elaborate on how rituals might be approached as a 'technology of gender'. In the next section, I will analyse Pentecostal deliverance practices and will describe the main features of some spirits who are directly involved in the construction of gender in Pentecostal African churches. Finally, I will discuss the implications of the presence of these spirits on the construction of gender and will assess how shifts in the ritual practice can be associated with a reconfiguration of gender roles in a migratory context.

African Pentecostal Migrants in the Lake Geneva Region

The flow of African migrants to Geneva and other cities in Switzerland has started in the 1960s, following the gradual independence of African states from their former colonial rulers. During the first two decades, African migration to Switzerland was mainly composed of diplomats, international civil servants and students who belonged to their countries' social and economic elite. At that time, migration was always conceived as temporary and aimed at gaining education or developing a career.[10] From 1980 onwards, several events led to major changes in African migrations: political crises and the failure of development politics together with the increase of foreign debt have led many African countries to structural adjustment programmes and economic recession. During this period, the first asylum seekers arrived to Switzerland from Zaire or Angola. Migrations from Africa increased in the following decade: wars and the further deterioration of African states have led to a growing flow of asylum seekers from Central and East Africa. More recently, migrations from West Africa has also increased including from regions where Pentecostalism tends to play a major role in the urban life, like Ghana or Nigeria.

---

[9] B. Meyer, 'Christianity in Africa: From African Independent to Pentecostal-Charismatic Churches' in *Annual Review of Anthropology* 33 (2004), 447–474: 453. While several authors stress that the growing popularity of Pentecostal and Charismatic churches in Africa is associated with this claim to open the doors of the 'global', 'modern' world, it is also attributed to the failure of the post-colonial nation state, the rise of neo-liberalism, the mediatisation of popular culture or the aspirations of young generations to overcome gerontocratic structures (for a review on these issues, see Meyer, *Ibid.*).

[10] J. Bagalwa Mapatano, *Crise de l'Etat et migrations: La diaspora congolaise-zaïroise en Suisse 1980–2005* Paris: Publibook 2007; J. Bagalwa Mapatano, 'Les réseaux diasporiques africains de Suisse entre 'intégrationnisme' et transnationalisme' in A. Manço and C. Bolzman (eds.), *Transnationalités et développement: rôles de l'interculturel*, Paris: L'Harmattan 2010, 59–70.

Rey: Mermaids and Spirit Spouses

While early attempts at founding churches were made in the 1980s, the majority of African-led Charismatic-Pentecostal churches in Switzerland were founded from the 1990s onwards. In 2009, the *Centre intercantonal d'Informations sur les Croyances* reported over sixty 'foreign evangelical churches' in the city of Geneva alone. Among these, the majority are either Charismatic or Pentecostal. They are historically linked to the broader movement of churches from the South spreading into European cities from the 1970s onwards, a phenomenon which has been increasing over the last two decades.[11] In Geneva, half of these churches were founded by Africans, mainly from the Democratic Republic of the Congo (DRC) or Ghana. Most African churches are located in the French-speaking part of the country, especially in the urban regions around Lake Geneva. This reflects the fact that migrants from Sub-Saharan Africa live mainly in urban French-speaking regions around Lake Geneva.[12] In 2009, the Federation of Protestant Churches in Switzerland estimated the number of 'new migrant churches' at about 300 for the whole country.[13] They observed that African churches generally organize into French-speaking and English-speaking churches and that the national heterogeneity of the members tends to increase with time.

Today, Congolese constitute one of the biggest populations of Sub-Saharan migrants in Switzerland.[14] From the 1960s to the mid-1980s, Congolese migrants were mainly children of civil servants under the Mobutu regime who came to study at a Swiss university before returning to their home country.[15] Those temporary migrants established neither churches nor networks based on religious affiliation. In the late 1980s and during the 1990s, as a result of economic and political changes that had led to instability in the DRC, an increasing number of migrants came to Switzerland. Many of them no longer considered their migration as temporary and most of them hoped for a better future in Europe. This situation coincides with the first wave of churches founded in Switzerland by people from Congo. Some years later, a network of African churches (the *Conférence des Eglises Africaines en Suisse*) was established – most of which were French-speaking churches led by Congolese pastors – and by the year 2000 Congolese migrants had established churches in every Swiss city.

Ghanaian migrants are about four times fewer than Congolese in Switzerland. Their migration to Switzerland is partly linked to a reorientation of migration flows to Europe from traditional destinations (like the Netherlands) due to

---

[11] See e.g. M. Bergunder and J. Haustein, *Migration und Identität: Pfingstlich-charismatische Migrationsgemeinden in Deutschland*, Frankfurt am Main: Lembeck 2006; A. Adogame, R. Gerloff and K. Hock, *Christianity in Africa and the African Diaspora*, London: Continuum 2008; S. Fancello and A. Mary, *Chrétiens africains en Europe: Prophétismes, pentecôtismes et politiques des nations*, Paris: Karthala 2010.

[12] OFS, *La population étrangère en Suisse*, Neuchâtel: Office Fédéral de la Statistique 2007; D. Efionayi-Mäder, M. Pecoraro and I. Steiner, *La population sub-saharienne en Suisse: un aperçu démographique et socio-professionnel*, Neuchatel: Forum Suisse pour l'étude des migrations et de la population, Université de Neuchâtel 2011.

[13] S. Röthlisberger and M.D. Wüthrich, *Les nouvelles Eglises de migrants en Suisse*, Berne: Editions Fédération des Eglises protestantes de Suisse FEPS 2009.

[14] Only Erithreans and Somalis are more numerous (Efionayi-Mäder et al. 2011).

[15] Bagalwa Mapatano, 2007, op. cit.

Rey: Mermaids and Spirit Spouses

increased restrictions in migration policies. Around 14,000 visas (annual permit or permanent residence) have been granted by the Swiss Embassy in Ghana between 1973 and 2003,[16] while it is estimated that only 1400 Ghanaians lived in Switzerland in 2009.[17] This gives evidence for a strong circulation among Ghanaians, whose migration to Switzerland is usually temporary. English-speaking churches were founded in Switzerland by Ghanaian pastors since the late 1990s. They attract migrants from Nigeria, Ghana but also from West African French-speaking countries, as they sometimes translate their services into French (especially in the French-speaking part of Switzerland). Some churches are also attended by (non-migrants) Swiss citizens.

Rituals as Technologies of Gender

In this article, I suggest to consider Pentecostal deliverance ritual practices as 'technologies of gender' that contribute to construct, reinforce or transform gender and gender roles. While using an ethnographic method to describe the process of gender construction, I will analyse ritual practices as 'technologies', thereby following an approach inspired by Michel Foucault's[18] 'genealogy' which aims at producing 'an analysis which can account for the constitution of the subject within a historical framework'.[19] According to Foucault, 'technologies' may include discourses, procedures and knowledge which are deeply involved in the constitution of the subject. Teresa de Laurentis developed these conceptual premises and suggested the concept of 'technologies of gender'[20] where gender becomes the product of various social technologies (like cinema, institutional discourses or epistemologies). Following this approach, ritual practices can thus be apprehended as technologies of gender as far as they convey assumptions about gender and contribute to its construction.

Ritual practices involve an embodied dimension that reinforces their performative effect on gender construction. In the case of African Pentecostal ritual practices, prayer and deliverance often imply the embodiment of spiritual entities that are valued positively (the Holy Spirit) or negatively (other spirits, also referred to as 'demons'). The latter are supposed to be expelled during ritual

---

[16] K.A. Twum-Baah, 'Volume and Characteristics of International Ghanaian Migration' in T. Manuh (ed.), *At Home in the World? International Migration and Development in Contemporary Ghana and West Africa*, Accra: Sub-Saharan Publishers 2005, 55–77.
[17] Efionayi-Mäder, et al., 2011, op. cit.
[18] M. Foucault, 'Pourquoi étudier le pouvoir: la question du sujet,' in Hubert Dreyfus and Paul Rabinow (eds.), *Michel Foucault. Un parcours philosophique*, Paris: Gallimard 1984, 297–308; M. Foucault, 'Truth and Power' in Paul Rabinow (ed.), *The Foucault Reader: An introduction to Foucault's Thought, With Major New Unpublished Material*, New York: Pantheon Books 1984, 51–75; M. Foucault, *L'herméneutique du sujet*, Paris: Gallimard 2001.
[19] Foucault, 'Truth and Power', 59.
[20] T. de Lauretis, *Technologies of Gender: Essays on Theory, Film, and Fiction*, London: Macmillan Press 1989.

Rey: Mermaids and Spirit Spouses

practices called 'deliverance'.[21] It consists of a prayer of exorcism whereby the possessed person might enter a state of trance in which the spirit manifests itself.[22] In this analysis, I will not look for possible causes of spirit possession.[23] Rather, I will focus on the effects of spirit possession and on what it does (e.g. on its performative dimension) on gender. The concept of technology of gender is thereby helpful, because it considers gender as the product of ritual practices and points to the processes of gender construction.

Pentecostalism has already been approached as a 'technology', inspired by Foucault's approach. In particular, the concept of 'technology of the self' has been applied to Pentecostal practices.[24] Foucault defined technologies of the self as technologies

> 'which permit individuals to effect by their own means or with the help of others a certain number of operations on their own bodies and souls, thoughts, conduct, and way of being, so as to transform themselves in order to attain a certain state of happiness, purity, wisdom, perfection, or immortality.'[25]

While this definition applies to some aspects of Pentecostal practices,[26] it is not always sufficient for analysing possession by spirits and deliverance practices. Indeed, these practices imply 'objectifying' (making into an object) possessed people rather than 'subjectifying' (making into a subject) them:[27] during the deliverance ritual, the possessed person is often expected to remain passive – and is sometimes explicitly asked not to pray – while the pastor is praying and

---

[21] P. Gifford, 'The Complex Provenance of Some Elements of African Pentecostal Theology' in A. Corten and R. Marshall-Fratani (eds.), *Between Babel and Pentecost: Transnational Pentecostalism in Africa and Latin America*, Bloomington and Indianapolis: Indiana University Press 2001, 62–79.

[22] This topic is also discussed by other authors in this special issue, see Duffuor and Harris and Silva and Rodrigues.

[23] Causes of spirit possession are often of central importance in approaches which consider spirit possession as an exception or as an anomaly to be explained. On this issue, see M. Lambek, 'Traveling Spirits. Unconcealment and Undisplacement' in G. Hüwelmeier and K. Krause (eds.), *Traveling Spirits: Migrants, Markets, and Mobilities*, London and New York: Routledge 2009, 17–35.

[24] R. van Dijk, 'Time and Transcultural Technologies of the Self in the Ghanaian Pentecostal Diaspora' in A. Corten and R. Marshall-Fratani (eds.), *Between Babel and Pentecost: Transnational Pentecostalism in Africa and Latin America*, Bloomington: Indiana University Press 2001, 216–234; R. Marshall, *Political Spiritualities: The Pentecostal Revolution in Nigeria*, Chicago, London: The University of Chicago Press 2009.

[25] Michel Foucault, 'Technologies of the Self' in Luther H. Martin, Huck Gutman and Patrick H. Hutton (eds.), *Technologies of the Self: A Seminar with Michel Foucault*, London: Tavistock Publications 1988, 16–49: 18.

[26] Van Dijk, 'Time and Transcultural Technologies of the Self'; Marshall, Political Spiritualities.

[27] This distinction between subjectifying and objectifying technologies appears in Foucault's work on confession and examination (cf. M. Foucault, *Histoire de la sexualité. La volonté de savoir*, Paris: Gallimard 1976; M. Foucault, *Surveiller et punir. Naissance de la prison*, Paris: Gallimard 1975; N. Fairclough, *Discourse and Social Change*, Cambridge: Polity Press 1992).

'leading the fight' against the evil spirit.[28] This passivity of the possessed person is an indicator for this objectifying process. In this case, deliverance practices do not involve the emergence of a moral subject, but rather correspond to what Foucault calls the 'dividing practices' (*'pratiques divisantes'*)[29] which divide the subject either within itself[30] or by separating it from others.[31]

Ritual deliverance practices convey strong normative aspects through the ritual practice of expelling entities that present distinctive features. Thus, characteristics of the expelled entities often point at behaviours that are considered intolerable. Once delivered, the person is not supposed to 'misbehave' again under the influence of the spirit – in which case the deliverance would be considered ineffective. Therefore, taking part in deliverance practices necessarily engages the subject in a transformative process where it is normatively shaped by the spirit expelled.

The ritual presence of spirits taking part in this transformative process carries implications for the construction and transformation of gender roles. Because Pentecostal demonology remains open and can easily integrate new categories of spirits – which is a key element in the 'plasticity' of Pentecostalism,[32] it can adapt to local gender configurations and social contexts. Thus, variations in Pentecostal demonology or in the associated ritual practices might indicate transformations of the Pentecostal construction of gender.

Spirit Spouses and Mermaids among African Migrants

The categories of spirits that I will discuss are historically part of several African cosmologies. Their integration into the Pentecostal demonology as 'evil spirits' reflects the broader historical 'translation' process of African cosmologies into Christian discourses by missionaries, in which the demonization of entities from

---

[28] Tough people might choose to ask for deliverance, as in the example above, the ritual itself rarely requires them to be active. Unlike in the Christian technique of confession which is analysed by Foucault as a *technology of the self*, in deliverance practices, the possessed person is usually asked to remain passive and the main protagonists of the ritual are the pastor and the spirit(s). The body of the possessed person might move and shake, thereby 'manifesting' the spirit(s) that inhabit the body. Thus, the subject is divided into itself (possessing spirit – possessed person) and is therby objectified, which leads us to what Foucault calls *'pratique divisante'* (cf. infra).

[29] M. Foucault, 'Pourquoi étudier le pouvoir: la question du sujet' in Hubert Dreyfus and Paul Rabinow (eds.), *M. Foucault. Un parcours philosophique,* Paris: Gallimard 1984, 297–308.

[30] By identifying the presence of a foreign entity, the spirit, within the person and by expelling it.

[31] We should notice that other practices in the process of Pentecostal conversion might include those moral aspects – whose importance also depends on the kind of Pentecostal denomination. This article will however focus on spirits and deliverance practices.

[32] J.-P. Willaime, 'Le pentecôtisme: contours et paradoxes d'un protestantisme émotionnel' in *Archives de Sciences sociales des Religions* 105 (1999), 5–28; Corten and Marshall-Fratani, 'Introduction'.

Rey: Mermaids and Spirit Spouses

African cosmologies represents a key issue.[33] This process nowadays persists in Pentecostal practices: deliverance also implies the demonization of 'African entities', as we shall see. In this context, the entities borrowed from African cosmologies remain, but they are now labelled as 'evil spirits'. Thus, deliverance practices offered by Pentecostal churches have been interpreted as a way of further living traditional spirit possession, while simultaneously condemning it as a pagan practice.[34]

In the observed Pentecostal deliverance practices, there are several ways by which spirits can be identified. The possessed person's symptoms, their body or social behaviour might indicate the kind of spirit involved. In other cases, like in the example given in the introduction, the name of the spirit is announced before the deliverance and potentially possessed people are invited to come forward to receive prayer. Though the list of existing spirits is open and can incorporate new entities,[35] some spirits appear to be more recurrent than others. Some of these frequently appearing spirits are considered responsible for gendered misbehaviours, such as in the case of the 'spirit spouse' and the 'mermaid' spirit.

Spirit spouses carry implications for how gender is constructed, especially in the field of relationships. They are supposed to negatively influence marital relationships and offer an explanation for persisting single life and recurrent conflicts in couples. Spirit spouses are said to appear in the dreams of their victims where they have sexual intercourse with them. They are known as jealous and possessive spirits who will try to prevent their victim from living a happy marriage. They are considered responsible for different problems appearing among married couple, including recurrent disputes, lack of sexual interest in one's spouse, and childlessness. They might also have 'children' with their victim, which might be visible when a woman shows pregnancy signs (like a round belly or otherwise unexplained lactation) while she does not expect a baby. Spirit spouses are also said to torment singles, preventing them from finding a spouse.

Spirit spouses are widespread in Pentecostal churches both in the Democratic Republic of the Congo[36] and in Ghana,[37] as well as in other West and Central African countries.[38] However, their existence has preceded Pentecostalism, and spiritual entities similar to spirit spouses were to be found before the

---

[33] B. Meyer, *Translating the Devil: Religion and Modernity among the Ewe in Ghana*, Edinburgh: University Press 1999.

[34] B. Meyer, 'Les églises pentecôtistes africaines, satan et la dissociation de 'la tradition', *Anthropologie et Sociétés* 22:1 (1998), 63–84.

[35] I encountered around sixty different categories of spirits during my fieldwork.

[36] J. Ndaya Tshiteku, ''Prendre le bic'. *Le combat spirituel* congolais et les transformations sociales' PhD thesis, African Studies Centre Leiden, 2008; S. Demart, 'Les territoires de la délivrance. Mises en perspectives historique et plurilocalisée du Réveil congolais (Bruxelles, Kinshasa, Paris, Toulouse)' PhD thesis, Université de Toulouse-Le-Mirail and Université catholique de Louvain-La-Neuve, 2010.

[37] B. Meyer 1999, op. cit.; P. Gifford, 2001, op. cit.

[38] S. Fancello, *Les aventuriers du pentecôtisme ghanéen. Nation, conversion et délivrance en Afrique de l'Ouest*, Paris: IRD – Karthala 2006; S. Fancello, 'D'un guérisseur à l'autre: diagnostic, délivrance et exorcisme à Bangui' in Bruno Martinelli and J. Bouju (eds.), *Sorcellerie et violence en Afrique*, Paris: Karthala 2012, 55–84.

appearance of Pentecostal churches, both in the Congo[39] and in West Africa, for instance among Baoulé (Ivory Coast), where spirit spouses (*blolo bla* or *blolo bian*) had spiritually married humans and caused similar problems.

Spirit spouses also appear in African Pentecostal transnational spaces, as I could notice in churches around the Lake Geneva region. They may be expelled during collective ritual practices, as in the Friday night prayer and deliverance session at the *Church for the Nations*. That evening, most people who received prayer were single women who were hoping to find a husband. In this case, deliverance practices can be interpreted as a technology of gender aiming at making women available for finding a partner – by expelling the jealous spirit spouses that prevent single women from meeting their future husband. This implies both that marriage is highly valued and that long-lasting single life is perceived as an abnormal status. Deliverance practices thus stress the differentiated value attributed to marriage and single life by associating singleness with evil spirits.

Spirit spouses may also be diagnosed as an answer to particular relationship issues. During an interview, a Congolese pastor reported the case of a Congolese woman who married a Swiss man. On several occasions, her husband woke up lying on the floor in the middle of the night, not understanding why he wasn't in the bed anymore. The wife regularly dreamt of having sexual intercourse with a man whose head was hidden. In the morning, she could even see his sperm on her body while taking a shower. The couple disclosed the case to the pastor who identified a spirit spouse that possessed the wife. He explained that this spirit expelled the husband from the marital bed in order to have sexual relationships with the wife. He then proposed a treatment for being delivered from the spirit spouse: three days of fasting, followed by a light meal at 6 p.m. and a long prayer. During three days, the pastor and the wife fasted and in the evening, they prayed and 'took control' over the spirit in order to expel it. Some time later, as the spirit spouse appeared to be returning, the pastor went to the couple's house and prayed there so that the spirit cannot penetrate the house again.

According to the pastor, the spirit spouse is a jealous spirit. For this reason, it was trying to keep the wife for itself by stirring troubles for the relationship. Thus, the wife had become averse to taking good care of her looks. The pastor explained that if the wife was well-dressed and nicely made up, her husband's eyes would fall on her and she would be at the centre of his attention, which the spirit spouse couldn't tolerate. But as long as she neglected herself, her husband would look away from her and feel no attraction.

In this case, deliverance practices can be interpreted as a technology of gender aiming at regulating relationships within married couples. In particular, sexuality issues and the gendered behaviour of the wife are addressed. By expelling the jealous spirit spouse, the wife is supposed to take good care of her looks and to seduce her husband again. This emphasizes the active role and obligations of the wife in the sexual life of the couple. It also carries some normative gender implications relative to body practices, like making up and dressing. Moreover, it stresses the responsibility of the wife towards the sexuality of her husband.

---

[39] S. Demart, op. cit.

Rey: Mermaids and Spirit Spouses

There is another kind of spirit which appears in Pentecostal churches both in Africa and in Europe and which carries implications for gender construction: the mermaid spirit. In another Congolese church, I listened to the testimony of a woman who married a Swiss man. She gave her testimony in front of the congregation on a Saturday afternoon. She explained that some weeks ago, the doctor diagnosed a problem in her heart. During the same period, she repeatedly had a dream in which she saw a woman intending to harm her. One day, she also had the vision of a feminine figure, which she identified as a mermaid, standing in the door of her bathroom. The woman then asked her pastor and a prophetess for help. While the prophetess confirmed that several spirits were endangering her life, the pastor advised her to pray and went to her house where he poured olive oil in various rooms in the house. The woman spent several nights praying in order to get rid of the spirit. Nonetheless, she was attacked some weeks later and nearly died. While staying at her home, she suddenly felt paralyzed and had a vision in which she was surrounded by people who had died that same moment. There was a book lying on a table on which the names of dying people were listed, but her name did not figure on the book, which meant that God did not want her to die yet. She then began to sing a song which came to her mind and was 'resurrected'. Once she got her wits back, she gazed at her face in a mirror and noticed that it was distorted and her eyelids were blown. She took the oil which she had been given by the pastor and poured it over her face, which instantly improved her appearance.

This testimony stresses the dangerous character of the 'mermaid', a spiritual entity which might even cause death. Its appearance in the door of the bathroom reveals its association with water. However, the mermaid carries other implications that are implicit for the audience of this testimony. In particular, it evokes power associated to wealth, but also seductive power of women. Mermaids appear to be both attractive and deceitful figures. While they initially cause pleasant feelings, their evil powers progressively appear and mermaids eventually turn out to be destructive spirits.

In African cosmologies, entities associated with water can be found in many places around Central and West Africa, including the Democratic Republic of the Congo and Ghana.[40] They are often known as *Mami Wata* and are represented as a feminine white body with the tail of a fish. These entities usually present a strong seductive character and are associated with the Western world and its material goods. Like other entities, they have been cast, within Pentecostal cosmology, as evil spirits.

In the Lake Geneva urban region, however, Pentecostal pastors referred to the mermaid spirit essentially in terms of the seductive power of women, and in particular in the context of prostitution. It is said that whenever a mermaid appears in a church, all men gaze at her. The presence of a mermaid is therefore seen as particularly dangerous for the church as they are perceived to be so attractive that it is almost impossible to resist their advances. Mermaid spirits often appear in the dreams of their victims through the presence of water. In fact, mermaid spirits are usually considered as belonging to the broader category

---

[40] See H.J. Drewal, *Sacred Waters: Arts for Mami Wata and Other Divinities in Africa and the Diaspora*, Bloomington and Indianapolis: Indiana University Press 2008; B. Jewsiewicki, *Mami Wata: La peinture urbaine au Congo*, Paris: Gallimard 2003.

of water spirits, among which other entities like prostitution spirits appear. One pastor told me that he once went to the prostitution area of Geneva to evangelize. On the following Sunday, some women he had met came to the church service and the pastor performed deliverance where he identified the 'spirit of prostitution', which he considers to be the same spirit as the mermaid spirit. Those spirits are considered responsible for sexual misbehaviours associated with excessive attractiveness or with prostitution. Women who are possessed by a mermaid spirit might also have problems in finding a husband, despite their attractiveness.

In the discussed cases involving mermaid spirits, deliverance practices can be interpreted as a technology of gender aiming at controlling and restraining sexuality and seduction by women, in particular when it involves financial or material compensation. By denouncing mermaids in the churches, pastors warn women against taking advantage of seductive behaviours to subvert monogamous gender order or to contest established authority in the church. Mermaids typically apply to unmarried women with multiple partners, which might also recall the practice of the *'deuxième bureau'*, as we shall see in the next section. Deliverance practices thus enhance monogamy principles and associate excessive attractiveness and sexuality outside married couples with evil spirits.

Negotiation of Gender Roles by Ritual Technologies in Transnational Spaces

I will now discuss the implications of spirits such as mermaids and spirit spouses on the construction of gender in Pentecostal transnational spaces. As I mentioned, mermaids and spirit spouses have their roots in African Pentecostalism where they echo former categories of spiritual entities (like *Mami Wata* or *blolo bla*). The increasing popularity of deliverance practices within African Pentecostalism in the 1990s has given those spirits, along with others, a prominent role in Pentecostal ritual practices. Mermaids and spirit spouses 'travelled' to Europe, carried by Pentecostal migrants, where they continued to be mentioned as a spiritual cause of misfortune or gendered disorder. But the general gender context has been changed by the migration process, and the role of spirits and rituals as technologies of gender must be considered within this new general gender context. As I will show, mermaids and spirit spouses sometimes contribute to a 'negotiation' of gender roles that question gender configurations both in Africa and in Europe.

Pentecostal discourses highly value marriage as the realization of God's plan for men and women. However, African migrants happen to be mostly unmarried. According to available statistics, more than half of the Sub-Saharan African population living in Switzerland is not married.[41] This not only reflects the fact that African migrants are often young, but also that migration trajectories tend to delay marriage. Thus, some migrants find themselves single at an age where they would probably have been married, had they not migrated. Many migrants visit church services with the hope of finding a suitable partner. Several

---

[41] Efionayi-Mäder et al., 2011, op. cit.

Rey: Mermaids and Spirit Spouses

couples I encountered have met in the context of a Pentecostal church. Attending a Pentecostal church can therefore be considered a matrimonial strategy for unmarried migrants and pastors sometimes officiate as go-between for singles in quest of a partner. In the case of persisting single life, deliverance offers a way of releasing stresses between their aspirations for marriage and their single status by casting out the responsible spirit. With this ritual practice, single people show that, although their single status impedes them from meeting the gendered ideal of masculinity or femininity in Pentecostal terms, they are determined to resolve this situation.

In the case of married African couples, rituals can also play an important role in their relationship. For one thing, the migration process may induce changes in traditional gender roles. One such reversal has to do with the opportunities offered to men and to women in terms of employment and income opportunities. While among African migrants who live in Switzerland, men are more qualified than women, they both experience a similarly high rate of unemployment. Moreover, whichever employment a qualified man may find, it seldom meets his qualifications. Therefore, the migratory setting tends to afflict men with greater downward social mobility than women. For some Pentecostal migrants, the main income source was earned by the wife, leading to frequent relationship problems that are dealt with in the context of church services.[42] Pentecostal ritual practices open a space to address the reconfiguration of gender roles due to the migration context. On the one hand, Pentecostal discourses tend to positively stress the role of women as wives, mothers as well as business-women, therefore giving legitimacy to their function as breadwinner. On the other hand, they warn women against using their income to gain authority over their husbands and stress the fact that this money must be available for their husband as well. Pentecostal discourses constantly stress the role of the wife in taking care of their husband and meeting their needs, while husbands are depicted as heads of the family.[43] These discourses convey the idea that the ideals of masculinity and femininity are not endangered by a change in the balance of income and the downward social mobility of men, while conferring legitimacy on this changing configuration of gender roles.

While questions of authority and power relations between genders are explicitly addressed in Pentecostal discourses, questions of sexuality and fertility are more often approached through deliverance practices. Mermaids and spirit spouses address the questions of sexual availability, infidelity, seduction and fertility within or outside the couple. Spirit spouses also stress the importance for women to be attractive for their husbands and to be sexually available for them. On the other hand, mermaid spirits warn women against misusing their seductive power to attract men.

---

[42] In the case of Congolese migrants, the ideal of masculinity relies on the ability of the husband to provide an income that allows his wife to 'dress up properly'. Similar tensions arise in the Democratic Republic of Congo where women have often been responsible for providing income since the 1990s. However, the ideal of masculinity has largely remained unchanged (Ndaya Tshiteku, 2008, op. cit.).

[43] In African Pentecostal settings, this might also mean taking care of their wives and meeting the need of their family. See A.S. van Klinken, 'Male Headship as Male Agency: An Alternative Understanding of a 'Patriarchal' African Pentecostal Discourse on Masculinity' in *Religion and Gender* 1:1 (2011), 104–124.

Rey: Mermaids and Spirit Spouses

Deliverance unequally applies to men and women: most of the people who are delivered in church services are women. This observation carries implications in terms of gender construction. It is important to note that although spirits theoretically attack both men and women, in practice, women constitute the overwhelming majority of people looking for deliverance in the Lake Geneva urban region.[44] By contrast, pastors who pray for deliverance are mainly men. As spirits are responsible for negatively valued behaviours, discerning their presence and casting them out involves a normative limitation of the spectrum of gendered behaviours for the possessed person. But because women are in practice more often possessed – or at least more often seeking deliverance – than men, this control over gendered behaviours through deliverance practices applies mainly to women.

So, the recourse to mermaids and spirit spouses tends to promote a gender model, where the responsibility for seduction, sexual relationships and fertility lies in the women and exonerates men from their behaviour. For instance, masculine infidelity might be attributed to the possession of a woman by a spirit, both in the case of mermaids and spirit spouses. Masculine infidelity can be attributed to the excessive attractive power of a woman possessed by a mermaid spirit to which men cannot resist. Such infidelity can also be attributed to the lack of attractiveness of a wife possessed by a spirit spouse that would lead the man to avert his gaze from her. In this case, mermaids and spirit spouses tend to formally stress monogamy principles while allowing for the maintenance of multiple relationships, especially for men, without necessarily being stigmatized for it. The responsibility for these multiple relationships is attributed to women's possession by spirits and not to men's behaviour.

Thus, Pentecostal practices meet the broader issue of masculine self-accomplishment. In some African regions, multiple relationships are important for the ideal of masculinity, and love affairs contribute to a man's status. For instance, having a *'deuxième bureau'* (second office) means to have a long-lasting relationship with an unmarried woman, which also implies supporting her financially. This practice was widespread in West and Central African regions, for instance in Zaire (under the Mobutu regime) or in Ivory Coast in the 1980s among urban civil servants and employees with a regular income.[45] Political and economic crises, however, made it increasingly difficult for a man to be able to support a *'deuxième bureau'*. Still, the association between masculine status production and multiple relationships remained.

Pentecostal ritual practices negotiate a turn in this ideal of masculinity, since faithfulness is formally promoted and the possibility of multiple sexual partners is formally rejected. In the Lake Geneva region, the practice of *'deuxième bureau'*, which found a new expression among the Congolese diaspora,[46] is sometimes mentioned and condemned in African churches. But behind this apparently clear statement, deliverance practices tend to forsake the idea of an individual

---

[44] The same observation has been reported in the West African context (Gifford 2001, op. cit.; Fancello 2006, op. cit.).

[45] B. Lacombe, 'Les unions informelles en Afrique au Sud du Sahara: l'exemple du deuxième bureau congolais' in *Genus* 43:1–2 (1987), 151–164.

[46] Julie Ndaya mentions that the *'deuxième bureau'* found a new expression among the Congolese diaspora under the name *'système des deux ba bord'* where men have relationships with two women (J. Ndaya Tshiteku, op. cit.).

Rey: Mermaids and Spirit Spouses

responsibility for one's sexual behaviour. It offers a space for the negotiation of this new ethos[47] where women are largely held responsible for the sexual behaviour of their husbands or lovers and where the inappropriate behaviour of men can also be attributed to the women through their possession by spirits.[48] Deliverance practices imply a gender causal attribution of unfaithfulness where responsibility for the sexual behaviour of men and women alike tends to be attributed to women. This case shows how deliverance technologies ritually deal with changes in gender roles and offer a space to negotiate tensions between conflicting gender models.[49]

However, in the European context, deliverance might lose part of its importance in Pentecostal practices. Several observers agree on the fact that, in Europe, Pentecostal deliverance tends to take a more euphemized form where trance becomes more marginal in deliverance practices.[50] Deliverance increasingly borrows categories from the psychological realm and forsakes some bodily practices that were central in the African context. This tendency could be linked with lower acceptance of trance practices in Europe. In the Lake Geneva urban area, I also observed that some pastors contest the presence of spirits in the European migratory context. According to these Pentecostal leaders, spirit spouses are too easily mobilized to explain marital problems. They reject these 'African' spirits which, they suggest, 'should remain in Africa'. Though this trend would deserve a deeper study, questioning the existence of spirit spouses expresses a critical stance towards deliverance as a technology of gender in a migration context. This rejection of deliverance might also imply a contestation of gender causal attribution for relationship problems.

Conclusion

In this article, I discussed the role of ritual practices in the construction of gender. I focused on deliverance practices, where spirits are expelled from a person's

---

[47] The ethos is associated to the social ideal of self-accomplishment, as suggested by Yvan Droz (Y. Droz, *Migrations kikuyus: Des pratiques sociales à l'imaginaire*, Neuchâtel: Editions de l'Institut d'ethnologie 1999), which is also gendered.

[48] This possession might in turn be attributed to a lack of prayer by the wife. This configuration of gender causal attribution of unfaithfulness can also be found in West Africa, cf. S. Fancello, 'Pouvoirs et protection des femmes dans les Églises pentecôtistes africaines' in *Revista de Estudos da Religião* 3 (2005), 78–98.

[49] In this article, I concentrate on deliverance rituals. However, other aspects of this new Pentecostal gender ethos could be mentionned, which are not limited to sexual behaviours and appear in other Pentecostal practices as well (see J.E. Soothill, *Gender, Social Change and Spiritual Power: Charismatic Christianity in Ghana*, Leiden, Boston: Brill 2007; M. Maskens, 'Cheminer avec Dieu'. *Pentecôtisme et migration à Bruxelles*, Thèse de doctorat soutenue à l'Université Libre de Bruxelles, 2010; J. Rey, *Migrations africaines et pentecôtisme en Suisse: des dispositifs rituels au commerce de l'onction*, Phd thesis in Anthropology and Sociology, Graduate Institute in International and Development Studies, Geneva, 2013).

[50] See R. van Dijk, 2001, op. cit. or A. Mary, 'Christianisme prophétique et Nations Célestes. Le combat spirituel pour la purification du monde' in S. Fancello and A. Mary (eds.), *Chrétiens africains en Europe: Pentecôtismes, prophétismes et politique des nations*, Paris: Karthala 2010, 127–153.

body. I argued that these spirits, which are held responsible for the misfortune of their victims, contribute to the construction of gender as they carry negative values against which gender models are constructed. By expelling these spirits, ritual deliverance practices aim at producing subjects that follow a Pentecostal gender model. They can therefore be considered as a 'technology of gender'.

In Pentecostal churches founded by Congolese or Ghanaian pastors in the Lake Geneva region, I identified two categories of spirit that are deeply involved in the construction of gender norms in deliverance rituals: spirit spouses and mermaid spirits. Spirit spouses regulate gendered behaviours within married couples in terms of seduction, sexual attraction and intercourse. Mermaid spirits also regulate gendered behaviours between men and women outside couples. In both cases, deliverance mainly applies to women, which suggests that women constitute the place where the problem lies and where it can be tackled. Deliverance practices tend therefore to attribute responsibility to women and exonerate men from their behaviour.

By this technology of gender, deliverance rituals address the issue of normativity and deviance in gender roles. On the one hand, deviance is attributed to spirits, which are held responsible for misfortune and for behaviours that transgress gender norms. On the other hand, naming the spirits and the undesired consequences of their presence establishes or reinforces gender norms. Pentecostal deliverance practices also contribute to edify gender norms in labelling people whose behaviours transgress those norms as 'possessed' by these spirit – which is negatively valued. Deliverance from these spirits can therefore be interpreted as a normalisation process, both in the sense of establishing gender norms and in the sense of (re-)integrating people transgressing these norms.

Deliverance as a technology of gender not only establishes norms and tackles deviance, but also opens a space for negotiating stress between conflicting gender roles. As long as deliverance is practiced, it offers a space for alternative ethos to coexist. For example, exclusive marital and multiple sexual partnerships are two possible forms of masculine ethos addressed by deliverance practices. While the former is valued and the latter condemned in Pentecostal discourses, deliverance practices still offer a space for this alternative ethos by forsaking the idea of an individual responsibility for one's sexual behaviour.

The mobilization of African categories of spirits, like spirit spouses and mermaids, underlines the importance of the transnational context and points to gender configurations in Africa. Nevertheless, the negotiation of gender in a migration context also takes the local setting into account. Migrants evaluate gender practices both in Europe and in Africa and negotiate gender relationships, gender norms and gendered behaviours through Pentecostal ritual means. Deliverance practices and Pentecostal discourses address relationship issues (e.g. in the field of sexuality or fertility) and transformations in gender configurations (due to economic changes and the confrontation with other gender models in Europe). They enhance a particular Pentecostal gendered ethos, while leaving a space for alternative gender models to coexist – in spite of their rejection – by attributing gender deviance to spirits. In this process, Pentecostal churches contribute to a redefinition of masculine and feminine ethos within transnational spaces.

Religion and Gender vol. 3, no. 1 (2013), pp. 60–75

Part V
Contexts of Reception

[15]

Ethnic and Racial Studies Vol. 33 No. 3 March 2010 pp. 376–403

Contexts of immigrant receptivity and immigrant religious outcomes: the case of Muslims in Western Europe

Phillip Connor

(*First submission August 2008; First published June 2009*)

Abstract

Among migration scholars, immigrant religiosity has become an important variable in understanding immigrant incorporation into the new society, but less studied are determinants of varying immigrant religious outcomes. Using a subsample of immigrant Muslims within the *European Social Survey* (2002, 2004, 2006), contexts of immigrant receptivity as less or more welcoming are tested on immigrant Muslim religious outcomes using multi-level modelling. Results confirm the hypothesis that less welcoming immigrant contexts are associated with higher religious outcomes among Muslim immigrants in comparison to the host region's religiosity.

Keywords: Contexts of reception; immigration; immigrant religiosity; religion; Muslims; Western Europe.

Among migration scholars, immigrant religiosity has become an important variable in understanding immigrant incorporation into the new society (Hirschman 2004; Portes and Rumbaut 2006; Massey and Higgins 2007; Alba, Roboteau and DeWind 2008). As Hirschman (2004) points out, the three 'R's of immigrant religious groups – resources, refuge, and respect – provide numerous benefits for the immigrant, including assistance in the incorporation process. Although these functional considerations are important in understanding the role of religion for immigrant incorporation, less empirical work has been devoted to understanding determinants of variation in immigrant religiosity within the adaptation process. Although religion is often viewed as the last cultural item to undergo

Routledge
Taylor & Francis Group

integration into the new society (Herberg 1960), researchers have demonstrated that the degree of immigrant religious participation does not remain constant throughout immigrant resettlement, and varies by region (Kurien 2002; Finke and Stark 2005; Connor 2007, 2008). To understand this variation, immigrant religion scholars view further analysis of immigrant contexts of reception as crucial (Cadge and Ecklund 2007), particularly those contexts outside of the United States (Ebaugh 2003).

Contexts of reception is a middle range theory capable of framing a host of immigrant outcomes (Portes and Rumbaut 2006). Additionally, sociologists of religion have used contextual factors such as religious pluralism, religious market share and secularization to explain variation in immigrant religious participation (Alanezi 2005; van Tubergen 2006; Connor 2007; van Tubergen 2007). However, can it be stated that there is an association between variation in contexts of immigrant receptivity (i.e. less versus more welcoming) and immigrant religious outcomes? And if so, how do contexts of immigrant receptivity alter the religious adaptation of immigrants to the new society? In order to effectively answer these questions, this study examines religious activity among Muslims in Western Europe. Not only is the European Muslim case of prominent importance in recent literature (Alba 2005; Kastoryano 2007; Pettersson 2007; Foner and Alba 2008), but public immigrant receptivity within Western Europe also differs greatly by region. This permits the analysis of varying contexts of receptivity for Muslim religious outcomes by region.

Unlike the United States, Europe has historically been a continent of emigration rather than immigration. However, the growing population of religiously active immigrants, of which Muslims are a paradigmatic case, has created immense pressure on European legislators and the public alike to devise appropriate strategies for immigrant incorporation. Although the recent shift of incorporation policies, particularly at the level of the European Union, represents a more multicultural stance, there still remains a popular resistance lobbying for an assimilation paradigm, making it difficult for the EU to devise a comprehensive immigrant incorporation plan agreeable to all member nation-states (Freeman 2004; Koenig 2005).

Using a subsample of Muslim immigrants within the *European Social Survey* as well as the survey's module of public immigrant attitudes, this paper examines the relationship between immigrant receptivity of the native population (i.e. less welcoming versus more welcoming) and deviation of religious outcomes (i.e. religiosity, religious service attendance, and prayer) from the host society's mean. Given the heated debate surrounding the alternative strategies for immigrant incorporation in Europe, the results of this research are of sociological interest not only to migration scholars, but also to

European policy makers as they conceptualize strategies of immigrant integration.

It can be argued that the discourse surrounding Europe's expanding reception of non-Christian migrants, particularly Muslims, is remarkably similar to America's reception of European Catholics (e.g. Irish, Italian) in the late nineteenth and early twentieth centuries. Not only was the American response racial and nativist, but there was also deliberate discourse surrounding the threat of Catholicism as deteriorating the Protestant hegemony in the United States (Higham 2002). Most of the theoretical models of immigrant integration we employ today were conceived following the influx of this non-Protestant religious group. Therefore, this paper will first elaborate on theoretical models of immigrant adaptation derived from the American experience and how religion operates within each ideal type. By doing so, the case of Muslims in Western Europe will be put in greater historical perspective.

Immigrant adaptation models and contexts of receptivity

Just prior to the sweeping changes in US immigration law in 1965, Milton Gordon (1964) produced a typology of immigrant adaptation within the new society. He identified a linear process whereby immigrants/ethnic minorities assimilate to the primary group within the host society. Gordon's ideal type of assimilation appears to conclude once all visual signs of immigrant ancestry are removed, but he does acknowledge that intrinsic cultural traits such as religious beliefs and practices may still remain. This resilience of religion is reminiscent of Warner and Srole's (1945) earlier argument that three factors – race, language, and religion – determine the level of differentiation of immigrants from their host societies. Warner and Srole demonstrate that racial distance, at least in the US, impedes the assimilation process most dramatically; however, US immigration history indicates that religious differences have also served as a clear distinction (Alba 2005), with the Irish and Italian Catholics during the late nineteenth and early twentieth centuries as a paradigmatic case (Greeley 1971).

Since Gordon's formulation, other theorists have elaborated on his typology, often leaning towards one of three incorporation alternatives: conformity, pluralism, or melting pot. Taking the weaknesses of straight-line assimilation theory into account (i.e. lack of group level consideration, majority/minority relations, primary group's intentional exclusion of immigrant group entry into society), Alba and Nee (1999) posit that a mild form of the assimilation/melting pot within American society has actually occurred and continues to operate. They cite examples of positive economic outcomes and growing spatial dispersion of immigrant groups as evidence. They also demonstrate that a

Contexts of immigrant receptivity and religious outcomes   379

dynamic and mutual system of immigrant incorporation and native adjustment is underway.

In identifying the triple melting pot of Protestants, Catholics, and Jews in the United States, Herberg (1960) finds that religious group identity is a unifying force for seemingly disparate cultures and racial backgrounds. However, Glazer and Moynihan (1963) challenged both the conformist and melting pot perspectives with their analysis of ethnic groups in New York City. Glazer and Moynihan not only demonstrated that ethnic groups were geographically isolated from each other, but also that each ethnic group operated within its own economic, educational, and religious spheres. Glazer's work combated the popularly held notion of America as a cultural melting pot, providing evidence that cultural retention of ethnic groups was the norm rather than the exception. He also simultaneously debunked the assimilation/conformist perspective by demonstrating that little conformity to a primary group actually occurs.

Each ideal type proposed in these immigrant adaptation theories – conformity, melting pot, and pluralist – contains a level of resilience for religion throughout the incorporation process. In the conformist account, persistent religious identity is an example of ethno-religious retention despite the pressures, whether latent or manifest, for the immigrant to religiously assimilate to the host society. In terms of the melting pot, a convergence of native and immigrant religious identity emerges, often along broad religious boundaries. In the pluralist account, religion is yet another dimension of difference whereby a multicultural society emerges. Regardless of the immigrant adaptation model, religious identity remains constant and can even strengthen it.

Migrants, however, do not immigrate to unsettled regions of the world; instead, they settle within a context of reception already established by a host population. Immigrant contexts of reception have been employed to understand a variety of immigrant outcomes including economic, linguistic, and modes of second-generation adaptation (Portes and Zhou 1993; Zhou 1997). More recently, the impact of immigrant contexts of reception operationalized as immigrant receptivity attitudes has been found to have an impact on immigrant naturalization (Van Hook, Brown and Bean 2006; Logan, Oh and Darrah 2007) and occupational attainment (De Jong and Steinmetz 2004).

Portes and Rumbaut (2006) posit that policies of the receiving government are one form of reception context relevant to immigrant adaptation. Their typology refers to three nodes along a continuum of immigrant receptivity, with exclusion of immigrants on one end and active encouragement on the other. Sandwiched in the middle is a passive acceptance where immigrants are essentially permitted to enter the society, yet with little assistance provided by the public purse for

380   *Phillip Connor*

their incorporation. Broadly, this typology provides the basis for a continuum of immigrant receptivity as hostile at one pole and supportive at the other. Portes and Rumbaut's continuum is similar to many other formulations of immigrant receptivity such as Bauböck's (1996) segregation–assimilation–accommodation typology and Ben Rafael's (1996) unifying versus permissive dominant culture interaction.[1]

In articulating particular nodes along this continuum of immigrant receptivity, there is certainly a parallel to the immigrant incorporation policies adopted by the state, each of which emphasizes a variety of themes including culture (Heller 1996), the state (Hollifield 2004), the market (Freeman 2004), and welfare (Faist 1996). Although tempting to identify nation-states belonging to particular nodes within an immigrant receptivity continuum, this is a defeatist exercise given the complexity of factors particular nation-states employ (e.g. citizenship, welfare programmes, socio-cultural history) in deriving their own incorporation policies (Freeman 2004). Furthermore, state incorporation policies do not always reflect actual public opinion regarding immigrant incorporation.[2] For instance, Freeman (2004) explores how the EU is attempting to lead more assimilation-styled nation-states to a multicultural position of immigrant incorporation. Therefore, actual public opinion data utilized in this study are a more representative proxy for measuring the variation of immigrant receptivity as it occurs 'on the ground'.

Muslims in Western Europe

Immigration from former colonies, refugee resettlements, and guest worker programmes have changed not only the racial makeup of Western European society, but also its religious distribution. Having been a continent of emigration more than immigration, Western Europe has only begun to experience the religious pluralism that typifies countries like the United States, Canada, and Australia.

Islam is not the only growing religious group to arrive on the European scene, but at least among the European popular media, it is the most prominent. With the Salman Rushdie, headscarf, and Danish cartoon affairs, not to mention the post-7/7/2005 world, some have described the religiosity of Muslim immigrants in relation to Europe's tradition of secularization (Kastoryano 2007) as a 'clash of civilizations' (Huntington 1993). As Zolberg and Woon (1999) describe, Muslims have become the definitive outsider all so common in the discourse surrounding politics of immigration. Muslim identity is further complicated since, unlike the United States, religion is not a bridge but instead a barrier to incorporation within Europe (Foner and Alba 2008).

By all popular accounts, religiosity among Muslim immigrants in Europe is higher than that of the native European population. Religious competition, religious enclaves, and religious reaction to secularization have all been posited to explain this heightened religiosity (van Tubergen 2006, 2007). Regardless of various initiatives to grapple with this religiously active population, it does not appear that Muslim immigrants are religiously adapting or assimilating to the limited frequency of religious practice within Europe. As previously cited, among models of immigrant adaptation, the resilience of religion is common to all adaptation accounts of conformity, melting pot, and pluralism. What is unknown is how contexts of immigrant receptivity structurally alter these adaptation outcomes, particularly among Muslims. Two opposing hypotheses are conceivable: (1) more welcoming contexts provide the cultural space for Muslims to engage in higher religiosity than the host society's population, or (2) less welcoming contexts create an 'us' versus 'them' scenario triggering a hyper-religious commitment among Muslims, much greater than the mean level of religiosity found within the host population. As we will now explore, evidence supports both hypotheses.

Much of the literature surrounding the topic of immigrant Muslim incorporation is highly theoretical, normative, yet generally optimistic for Muslim incorporation into Western European society. Most theorists advocate for a state-sponsored multiculturalism, broadly conceived (Rex 1994; Carens and Williams 1996; Modood 2001; Koenig 2005). For instance, Doomernik (1995) finds that the more accessible political structure of the Netherlands provides Muslim immigrants with greater freedom and support to establish religious organizations than the more reluctant political structure of Germany. Again reflecting on Dutch society, Pennix (1996) considers a history of pluralism to be a factor in the multicultural position the Netherlands takes in supporting religious differences within its political structure. This toleration of religious differences eases the political divisiveness between religious groups seen in other European nation-states. Using the city of Leicester in England as a case study, Vertovec (1996) finds that the Muslim leaders' civic responsibility for the Muslim population exemplifies his theoretical model of public incorporation among Muslims. From all appearances, these more welcoming contexts of reception, at least at the state level, are associated with a high level of Muslim immigrant identity. Although civic involvement does not serve as a direct proxy for higher religious outcomes (e.g. mosque attendance, prayer, etc.) than the host society, it does provide partial support to the hypothesis that a positive relationship between more welcoming contexts and higher religiosity among Muslims exists.

The counter hypothesis reasons that less welcoming contexts of receptivity create a cultural tension between the host and immigrant

382   *Phillip Connor*

societies, spurring an increased level of immigrant religiosity among Muslims and impeding the religious adaptation process. For example, Kastoryano (2007) argues that France and Germany ethnically label Muslims for their religious differences from Christianity and secular humanism, creating a clear boundary between the host and Muslim immigrant populations. This ascribed 'otherness' of Muslim communities by French and German societies has created an identifiable community of religious cleavage – an unintended consequence. Alba (2005) also recognizes this 'bright boundary' of difference surrounding the religiosity of Muslim immigrants in Germany and France. With this religious 'otherness' in the immigrant's context of reception, discriminatory differencing by the host society can further stimulate group cohesion within the immigrant community, increasing immigrant religious outcomes.

Drawing on Portes and Rumbaut's (2006) concept of forced assimilation, less welcoming contexts of reception may not only create a segregation of immigrant society, but can also result in downward assimilation for subsequent generations. Recent riots in France's *banlieues* among first- and second-generation immigrant Muslims are an example of this selective acculturation gone wrong, possibly resulting in further antagonism towards immigrants by the host society. A more antagonistic or intolerant context of reception can also create more separate ethno-religious groups in a pluralist form of adaptation; however, unlike the effect of more welcoming contexts, immigrant group identity is created through societal tension rather than state-sanctioned, cultural space.

These contrary hypotheses leave us with the following conceptual model (see Figure 1). The model assumes that immigrant Muslim religious outcomes deviate from the religious outcomes of the host population. Although it can be assumed that immigrant religious outcomes among Muslims are higher than among the European

Figure 1. *Hypotheses for immigrant Muslim religious outcomes in Western Europe*

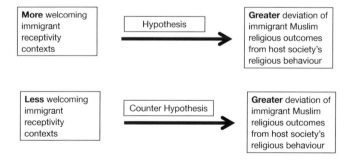

populace in general, lower deviations from the European mean can also be attributed to these counter hypotheses. For instance, more welcoming contexts usually consist of more openness to otherness, possibly encouraging the immigrant to abandon religious attachment in favour of greater association with the welcoming society. Conversely, less welcoming contexts could also be associated with considerably lower religious outcomes due to fear of economic or political repercussions such religious activities may create for the individual and their family. Although these latter formulations for the reverse direction of these hypotheses are less imaginable, they are still plausible.

Data and methods

Data

The *European Social Survey* [ESS] is a cross-sectional survey conducted bi-annually since 2002. At the time of this research project, three survey rounds (2002, 2004, 2006) were available, providing nearly 74,000 respondents among sixteen Western European countries (Jowell 2003, 2005, 2007).[3] The ESS strives to provide a balance between top-down and bottom-up approaches in administrating the survey across participating nation-states. Each country is responsible in selecting a random sample based on a population frame of residents aged 15 years and older. The survey is developed in English and translated by a central translation team into the various languages prominently used in Western Europe. To provide for congruent data among all countries, efforts are made to have a minimum response rate of 70 per cent for each country.[4]

Of importance to this research project, a subsample of Muslim immigrants is required. This subsample includes current foreign residents (i.e. born outside of their current country of residence) stating an Islamic religious affiliation. Since the majority of countries surveyed form the European Union where internal migration occurs with little governmental restriction, this subsample was further limited to Muslim migrants born outside of the Western European countries under analysis. This subsample of Muslim immigrants living in Western Europe (N = 837) originate from the following top six countries: Turkey (25 per cent), Morocco (16 per cent), Pakistan (7 per cent), Bosnia and Herzegovina (5 per cent), Iraq (5 per cent), and Algeria (4 per cent), with the remaining 37 per cent originating from other sending countries.

In determining the level of immigrant receptivity by the receiving context, immigrant Muslim respondents are coded by their residence in a given region within each country surveyed. These regions are

384   *Phillip Connor*

determined by the survey investigators for each country and range from one region to forty-one regions per country. In total, 119 regions in Western Europe were available as contexts of reception where at least one Muslim immigrant resided.[5]

These data contain a number of advantages and limitations. By best indications, this survey represents the largest cross-national survey in Europe, with a detailed, immigrant receptivity module, a geographic division of respondents, and an amply sized subsample of Muslim immigrants for analysis. Moreover, it is also a recent survey, depicting current realities in a post-9/11 world.

The most significant drawback to the ESS data is the Muslim subsample. Since these interviews were conducted in the official languages of the nation-states, there is a selection bias favouring more acculturated immigrants. Also, since immigrants are fairly transient, immigrant receptivity attitudes as measured by the region of residence for the immigrant respondent may not represent all the contexts of reception experienced by the migrant within Europe. Additionally, contexts of reception can change over time. Although the duration of stay within the immigrant's country of residence is accounted for, this does not take into consideration how the migrant's context of receptivity may have been different in earlier years of settlement compared to that measured since 2002. Ideally, longitudinal data for an immigrant cohort would resolve many of these limitations; unfortunately, no such dataset for all of Western Europe is known to exist.

Outcome variables

Three variables measuring immigrant religiosity are available in the ESS. On a scale of zero to ten with zero being not religious at all and ten being very religious, respondents were asked, 'Regardless of whether you belong to a particular religion, how religious would you say you are?' Respondents were also asked about their frequency of religious attendance and prayer, with the following seven-point, ordinal scale: every day, more than once a week, once a week, at least once a month, only on special holy days, less often, and never. Given that the sequential ordering of attendance and prayer frequency roughly doubles at each interval and it is valuable to retain a high degree of variation within the variable, we will treat this seven-point scale as a quasi-log ordering of religious behaviour; therefore, this ordinal scale is reordered with seven being the highest level of frequency. The religious outcome variables at an individual level among immigrant Muslims were subtracted from the mean level of the same religious variable for the native population corresponding to the

Muslim respondent's region of residence. To obtain a standardized deviation from this regional mean, absolute values are used.[6]

Variables of Interest

Respondents were asked a number of questions regarding their opinion of immigrants and immigrant groups. On a scale of zero to ten with zero being at the negative end of the spectrum, respondents were asked the following three questions: (1) Would you say it is generally bad or good for [country]'s economy that people from other countries come to live in [country]? (hereafter referred to as 'bad–good economy'); (2) Is [country] made a worse or a better place to live by people coming to live here from other countries? (hereafter referred to as 'worse–better country'); and (3) Would you say that [country]'s cultural life is generally undermined or enriched by people coming to live here from other countries? (hereafter referred to as 'undermine–enrich culture'). Therefore, lower levels on these scales represent less welcoming contexts of reception.

The appropriate geographic unit of analysis in which to measure contexts of receptivity is crucial. Certainly, it would be expected that religious and migration policies of the nation-state warrant a country-level analysis. However, this form of analysis would only contain sixteen countries. Moreover, receptivity measured at a country level reduces the variation compared to more local units of analysis. Given these two constraints, a smaller regional level (i.e. provinces, counties, states within countries) is justified. Nonetheless, a separate analysis at the country level is conducted and included in the appendix (see Table B). The directionality of results for the regional and country levels is identical. In calculating the contexts of receptivity at a regional level, mean levels of immigrant receptivity for each question of interest were derived from the respondents of the full survey sample by region and assigned to region of residence for each immigrant Muslim respondent.[7]

Control variables

In order to isolate the association between levels of immigrant religiosity among Muslims and their contexts of reception, a number of control variables are used in all models of analysis. Typically used demographic predictors including sex, education (number of years), employment status (dichotomous – employed full-time), monthly income, and year of birth are employed. Specific to the subsample of immigrants under investigation in this analysis, duration of time lived in the receiving country as well as country of origin is taken into account. Previous studies surrounding immigrant religiosity suggest

386   *Phillip Connor*

that familial environments are associated with higher immigrant religiosity (Saran 1985; Williams 1988; Kurien 2002); therefore spouse and children in the home are included in the models. Studies also demonstrate that religious context can impact immigrant religiosity (van Tubergen 2006; Connor 2007); therefore, the proportion Muslim in the region of residence is included in all models, effectively controlling for potential religious enclave effects.[8] Similarly, religious pluralism, measured on a scale of zero to one with values approaching one representing a highly pluralistic region, was derived from the same full survey sample by region.[9] The religious pluralism variable also controls simultaneously for the distribution of prominent religious affiliations among native Europeans, often endorsed by the state. Furthermore, the density of the foreign-born population at the regional level is taken into account. Immigrant assimilation in general, operationalized as a non-Western European language primarily spoken in the home, is controlled. To disentangle the lack of specificity of immigrant receptivity context for Muslims in particular within the variables of interest, the respondent's opinion of being religiously discriminated against is also included.[10]

Methods

Brief descriptive statistics of the immigrant Muslim subsample as well as the mapping of immigrant receptivity across Western Europe are first presented. Then, a series of graphs examining the variables of interest is provided. In assessing the relationship between contexts of receptivity and Muslim immigrant religiosity, multi-level models are employed, assuming a random intercept for each respondent. By performing this analysis, we are essentially enlarging the standard errors and consequently ensuring that results are robust. STATA's *xtreg* procedure is used in calculating random intercept estimates. Due to high correlation among the independent variables, each immigrant receptivity variable is tested separately, permitting comparison of the reduction in the intra-class correlation of the model against the null model and models with control variables.[11]

Two important concerns of internal validity are addressed throughout the data analysis. First, it is critical to note that the directional arrow of impact could be reversed, providing the hypothesis that immigrant Muslim religiosity alters immigrant receptivity at a regional level. This hypothesis is plausible, but highly unlikely given that the degree of immigrant Muslim behaviour would not be known by the average native respondent. It would be expected that any change in immigrant receptivity due to immigrant Muslim religiosity would be transmitted through media exposure or period events (i.e. governmental changes in religion or immigration policy, protests, or violent

Contexts of immigrant receptivity and religious outcomes   387

acts). However, drawing on Fetzer's work on determinants of variation in immigrant receptivity outcomes (Fetzer 1998, 2000), the reverse-causation hypothesis at a country level was performed using a number of individual-level controls, including: membership of a labour union, employment status, managerial occupation, belonging to a minority group, religious affiliation, income, gender, age, and education.[12] Unlike the ensuing results, no systematic pattern for the reverse-causation hypothesis was found to exist.

A second issue of internal validity is the historical reality that immigration to Europe is highly path-dependent on colonial and guest worker programme histories. In other words, it is possible that immigrant Muslims' region of residence is constrained to a particular path dependent upon historical circumstances. It can also be posited that immigrants without such constraints select their region of residence based on levels of immigrant receptivity. This selection concern is partially taken into account by placing all regions within Western Europe on an equal plane with multi-level modelling. Additionally, since the degree of religiosity among Muslims is not constant across the world, the migrant's country of birth is taken into account for all models.

Results

Before delving into the regression estimates for the relationship between immigrant Muslim religious outcomes and contexts of immigrant receptivity, Table 1 presents descriptive statistics of the immigrant Muslim subsample drawn from the ESS. The sample population is majority male (59 per cent), has a mean level of eleven years of education, an average age in the late thirties (born in 1967), and have mostly lived in their current country of residence for more than five years. Nearly half are employed full-time (47 per cent), and less than half have a spouse or child(ren) in the residence. In terms of time period, it is fortunate that the respondent subsample of immigrant Muslims is spread evenly across the three ESS rounds of 2002, 2004 and 2006.

Although the deviation of immigrant Muslim religious outcomes from the host society seems relatively high (2.91 for the ten-point religiosity scale and 1.61 and 2.81 for the seven-point attendance and prayer scales respectively), overall means do not acutely demonstrate the differencing of immigrant Muslim religious outcomes compared to those in their regions of residence. Figure 2 plots mean levels of immigrant Muslim religious attendance with mean levels of attendance found within the host society by region.[13] With the exception of lower bound outliers for a region in Sweden as well as Luxembourg, all means among immigrant Muslims are higher than those in their region

Table 1. *Descriptive statistics-Immigrant Muslims in Western Europe*

Variable	Description	Mean	Std. Dev	Range
Outcome Variables	*Deviation from mean religious outcomes of host region*			
Religiosity	0 =not religious; 10 =very religious	2.91	1.76	0.01/7.14
Religious Attendance	7 =every day; 6 =more than once a week; 5 =once a week;	1.61	1.21	0.02/5.17
Prayer	4 =once a month; 3 =only special holy days; 2 =less often; 1 =never	2.81	1.38	0.0/5.17
Variables of Interest				
Bad-Good Economy	Immigrants bad (0) or good (10) for country's economy	5.19	0.55	3.87/6.38
Worse-Better Country	Immigrants make country worse (0) or better (10)	5.01	0.53	3.84/6.64
Undermine-Enrich Culture	Immigrants undermine (0) or enrich (10) for country's culture	5.95	0.62	4.30/7.52
Control Variables				
ESS Round 1	ESS Wave – 2002 (reference)	0.31	–	–
ESS Round 2	ESS Wave – 2004	0.32	–	–
ESS Round 3	ESS Wave – 2006	0.37	–	–
Sex	1 =Female	0.41	0.49	0/1
Education	Years of education	11.00	4.72	0/30
Year Born	Year born	1967	12.05	1924/1991
Employment	1 =employed full time; 0 =not employed full time	0.47	0.50	0/1
Income	Household monthly income (Euros)	2092.36	1331.15	100/10000
Income Missing	1 =income missing	0.28	0.45	0/1
Live in Country <1yr	Years lived in country – less than 1 year (refererence)	0.02	–	–
Live in Country 1-5 yrs	Years lived in country – 1–5 years	0.20	–	–
Live in Country 6-10 yrs	Years lived in country – 6–10 years	0.19	–	–
Live in Country 11-20 yrs	Years lived in country – 11–20years	0.29	–	–
Live in Country >20 yrs	Years lived in country – more than 20 years	0.30	–	–
Country of Birth	Bosnia and Herzegovina (reference)	0.05	–	–

(continued overleaf)

Table 1. (*Continued*)

Variable	Description	Mean	Std. Dev	Range
Country of Birth	Algeria	0.04	–	–
Country of Birth	Iraq	0.05	–	–
Country of Birth	Morocco	0.16	–	–
Country of Birth	Pakistan	0.07	–	–
Country of Birth	Turkey	0.25	–	
Country of Birth	Other	0.37		
Language at Home	1 = Primary Language in Home non-Western European Language	0.63	0.48	0/1
Religious Discrimination	1 = Respondent feels religious discrimination for their religious group	0.14	0.35	0/1
Spouse	1 = Spouse in residence	0.41	0.39	0/1
Child(ren)	1 = Child or children in residence	0.39	0.49	0/1
Proportion Muslim	Proportion Muslim by region	0.03	0.03	0.00/0.14
Religious Pluralism	Religious Pluralism by region	0.59	0.09	0.21/0.82
Proportion Foreign Born	Proportion Foreign Born by region	0.08	0.06	0.00/0.31

Source: European Social Survey 2002–2006 ($N_i = 837$; $N_j = 119$).

390   *Phillip Connor*

Figure 2. *Immigrant Muslim religious attendance and Western European religious attendance by region*
Source: European Social Survey 2002, 2004, 2006

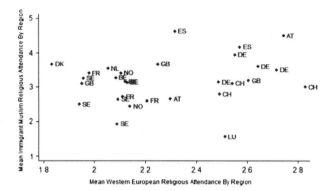

of residence. This indicates that immigrant Muslims on the aggregate have higher religious attendance than their Western European counterparts, yet also infers that the ensuing analysis in real terms is an analysis of greater deviation in religious behaviour in an upward sense.

With mean levels of immigrant receptivity by region hovering around five to six within a ten-point scale (see variables of interest in Table 1), it appears that immigrant receptivity within Western Europe stands at a certain mid-point. Yet, to get a visual sense of immigrant receptivity contexts by region, Figure 3 maps the culture variable (immigrants undermine/enrich the country's culture) using quintile cut points.[14] Regional breakdown for the 119 regions used in this analysis is displayed by country and other administrative (state, province, country, etc.) boundaries specific to particular nation-states.[15] For those regions with no shading, insufficient data are available to calculate immigrant receptivity at a regional level. With a quick glance at the map, three observations can be made. First, immigrant receptivity contexts are generally more positive in highly urban areas where immigrant presence is highest. This is demonstrated by the darker spots on the map in places like London, central Paris, and Berlin. Secondly, immigrant receptivity is lower in areas which have had little exposure to immigrant communities. Exceptions to this generalization do exist, such as northern Finland which has fewer immigrants yet favourable attitudes. Lastly, looking at nation-states as a whole, the pattern for France as one of the less welcoming countries and for Scandinavia as more welcoming fits the expected location of immigrant receptivity.

The scatter plot in Figure 4 is a comparison of immigrant receptivity as defined by the undermine/enrich culture variable on the x-axis and

Contexts of immigrant receptivity and religious outcomes   391

Figure 3. *Immigrant receptivity context by region*
Source: European Social Survey 2002–2006
Note: Regions limited to N=50 native respondents and N=>1 immigrant Muslim
respondents

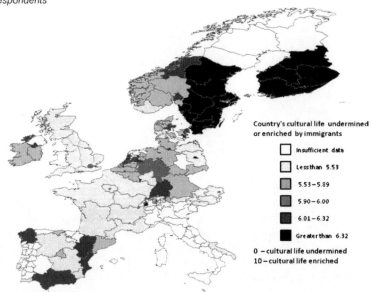

Country's cultural life undermined
or enriched by immigrants

☐   Insufficient data
☐   Less than 5.53
▨   5.53–5.89
▨   5.90–6.00
■   6.01–6.32
■   Greater than 6.32

0 – cultural life undermined
10 – cultural life enriched

the mean level of *deviation* of immigrant Muslim religious participation from the host context on the y-axis, all means by region. This
scatter plot demonstrates not only the variation in immigrant Muslim
religious outcomes across European regions, but also a potential

Figure 4. *Immigrant Muslim religious attendance deviation from regional mean
and immigrant receptivity context by region*
Source: European Social Survey 2002, 2004, 2006

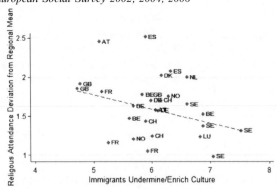

392 *Phillip Connor*

pattern. With the highest level of religious attendance deviation found in the least welcoming areas, the counter hypothesis that less welcoming contexts are associated with a greater departure in immigrant Muslim religious levels from the religious levels of the host society seems to be validated. Numerically, this general negative relationship by region (r = −0.30) further demonstrates support for the counter hypothesis. However, these descriptive statistics do not include any controls and are at an aggregate level of analysis. Multivariate, multi-level regression modelling is required.

The central analysis of importance to this paper is found in Table 2 where estimates of immigrant Muslim religious outcome deviations regressed on immigrant receptivity are presented. Complete models with control variables are presented in the appendix (Table A). The association between deviation in religiosity and contexts of immigrant receptivity as seen in Models 1, 2 and 3 is not strong since none of the receptivity context variables are statistically significant.

Moving on to religious service attendance, we do find a more significant relationship between immigrant Muslim religious outcomes and context of immigrant receptivity. Models 4, 5 and 6 (religious attendance) follow the general negative direction identified in earlier descriptive statistics. All three negative coefficients indicate that immigrant Muslims on average have a higher deviation of religious attendance in less welcoming contexts of reception. Estimates all hover near the −0.20 level ($b_{economy} = -0.201$, $b_{worse/better} = -0.158$, $b_{culture} = -0.193$). Keeping the receptivity context coefficients in perspective of the religious attendance scale (1 to 7), this means that each additional point of a more welcoming receptivity context is associated with approximately 0.20 reduction in the immigrant's deviation in religious attendance from that found in the host society. Given the actual four-point range for immigrant receptivity contexts, these results indicate that nearly a one level increase in immigrant Muslim religious attendance deviation is associated with residence in the very least welcoming compared to the most welcoming context. In real terms, an immigrant Muslim's religious attendance on the aggregate is one level higher than the host society's attendance in the least welcoming contexts compared to the most welcoming contexts. As found in the ESS, the European populace in general attends religious services only on holy days to monthly. A one level increase deviation then, in an upward direction from this European norm, would be associated with a frequency of monthly to weekly religious attendance among Muslim immigrants.

The two statistically significant effects for prayer deviation in Model 7 ($b_{economy} = -0.268$) and Model 9 ($b_{culture} = -0.138$), hovering again around −0.20, provide the same interpretation as the religious attendance deviations. However, it should be noted that prayer

Table 2. *Multivariate, multi-level regression estimates for immigrant Muslim religious outcome deviations in Western Europe – regional level*

Variables of Interest	Religiosity			Religious Attendance			Prayer		
	Model 1	Model 2	Model 3	Model 4	Model 5	Model 6	Model 7	Model 8	Model 9
	Fixed Effects								
Bad-Good Economy Worse-Better Country	−0.056	0.165		−0.201*			−0.268**	0.007	
Undermine-Enrich Culture			0.046		−0.158†	−0.193*			−0.138†
Constant	26.252*	25.059*	25.639*	23.376**	22.716**	23.007**	29.393**	26.292**	28.043**
	Random Effects								
Region standard deviation	0.412	0.417	0.414	0.119	0.139	0.156	0.000	0.209	0.072
Region standard error	0.111	0.109	0.110	0.114	0.099	0.087	0.000	0.081	0.000
	Measures of Fit								
Intra-class correlation (null)	0.098	0.098	0.098	0.050	0.050	0.050	0.044	0.044	0.044
Intra-class correlation (controls only)	0.061	0.061	0.061	0.020	0.020	0.020	0.025	0.025	0.025
Intra-class correlation (model)	0.060	0.062	0.061	0.011	0.014	0.018	0.000	0.025	0.003
Log-likelihood	−1622.820	−1622.271	−1622.817	−1312.917	−1313.863	−1312.211	−1414.043	−1416.800	−1416.348

†p <.10 *p <.05 **p <.01 ***p <.001, two-tailed.
Source: European Social Survey, 2002–2006 (N$_i$ =837; N$_j$ =119).

394   *Phillip Connor*

expectations among Muslims (five times daily) may exceed Christian prayer expectations. This would naturally inflate the higher deviation; however, the fact that there is still a difference in the variation of prayer frequency by context of receptivity is notable.

Discussion

In relating the results of this study to theories of immigrant adaptation, it appears the findings bear out that religion and religious activity remain salient for immigrant Muslims in Western Europe despite any pressures of adaptation to generally lower levels of European religiosity. More importantly, this lack of religious convergence to the European norm can be partially explained through the hypothesis that less welcoming contexts are associated with a greater departure from the mean levels of religious attendance and frequency of prayer found within the immigrant's context of settlement. In fact, these lower levels of immigrant receptivity seem to correspond to a reactive effect where religious resilience actually deepens.

Throughout the analysis, it is interesting to note that the more private elements of religion (personal level of religiosity) were not as strongly associated with immigrant receptivity as were public forms (religious attendance, prayer). Realizing that less welcoming contexts are associated with a reactive form of immigrant Muslim religious behaviour, as well as the consequential relationship that more welcoming contexts are associated with lower immigrant Muslim religious outcomes, these results are of importance not only to academics but also to policy makers and religious leaders. The results here suggest that any desired effort to limit a deepening level of immigrant Muslim religious outcomes can be at least partially mediated through the degree to which receptivity contexts of settlement view and welcome immigrants. Certainly at the individual and even neighbourhood levels, a compounding of factors will contribute to religious retention; however, these results demonstrate that, all other things being equal, less religiously active immigrant Muslims, compared to the host society's religiosity levels, are associated with more welcoming contexts of receptivity.

The current situation in Europe, at least in descriptive analysis, is not entirely different from the historical narrative in the United States when Irish and Italian Catholics were the immigrant 'other' and vibrant ethno-religious communities emerged. The major distinction between this historical narrative in the United States and current conditions with immigrant Muslims in Western Europe is the cultural objection Muslims seem to have to the secular, European society, coupled with the states' aim to prescribe and regulate immigrant adaptation rather than maintaining a more *laissez-faire* position for religious behaviour.[16]

Contexts of immigrant receptivity and religious outcomes   395

As Foner and Alba (2008) propose, whereas the historical use of religion as a bridge to immigrant incorporation in the United States is prominent, the vehicle of religion as an incorporation mechanism into European society is not, particularly when the religious group is identifiably different from the state-sanctioned religion. Drawing on the evidence within this paper, the question remains whether these two divergent paths of religious adaptation resistance among immigrant Muslims and less welcoming contexts of immigrant receptivity will only exacerbate the situation. Or, as the results in this paper suggest, will a more welcoming form of context, perhaps labelled by recent EU leadership in some spheres as being multicultural, serve to educate the European populace and simultaneously dampen immigrant hysteria, resulting in less of a collision course?

The data used in this paper are cross-sectional. Temporality, even in a repeated cross-sectional survey, is difficult to assess when determining causation. Additionally, it should be reiterated that this subsample of immigrants most likely represents more acculturated immigrants; therefore, a bias may exist whereby these immigrants are more sensitive to contextual pressures surrounding them. In order for future research to correct for these limitations, longitudinal data for a particular immigrant cohort like that found in the *New Immigrant Survey* in the United States would be ideal in assessing the direction of causation as well as any changes in immigrant Muslim religious outcomes over time. Until then, further replication using other cross-sectional European data or immigrant longitudinal data in different global regions (i.e. United States or Canada) is needed.

This study represents only a beginning to the many hypotheses surrounding immigrant religious adaptation within the new society and how various forms of contexts of reception shape immigrant religious trajectories. Additionally, this paper demonstrates how a seemingly individualized behaviour such as religiosity is contextually guided by society more generally. More specifically, contexts of immigrant receptivity as less or more welcoming should continue to be examined for a host of immigrant outcomes, regardless of how individually determined the behaviour is theorized to be. In sum, this paper agrees with Herberg (1964) and other immigration theorists (Warner and Srole 1945; Gordon 1964) that immigrant religious affiliation rarely changes. It also agrees with Portes and Rumbaut (2006) that what does change is the immigrant's context, of which varying levels of immigrant receptivity are crucial. It is this interaction between contexts of reception and immigrant religion that is the challenge for further research.

396   *Phillip Connor*

Acknowledgements

The author gratefully acknowledges the comments of Alejandro Portes, Richard Alba, Rafaela Dancygier, Robert Wuthnow, Pyong Gap Min, Gordon De Jong, and two anonymous reviewers on previous versions of this manuscript. Appreciation is expressed to the principal investigators of the European Social Survey (ESS) for making their data available for this analysis. The ESS can be accessed through the Norwegian Social Science Data Services [NSD]. By making this data freely available, it is recognized that any errors committed in this analysis are the sole responsibility of the author.

Notes

1.   There is an ever-expanding literature on contexts of immigrant receptivity and immigrant incorporation policy more generally; however, space constraints do not permit a thorough review. For a good introduction to pertinent issues, see Bauböck, Heller and Zolberg (1996), *The Challenge of Diversity: Integration and Pluralism in Societies of Immigration.*

2.   Although public policy in the United States is often reflective of public opinion (Page and Shapiro 1983), this may not be true for other liberal democracies. European states sometimes aim to educate their native populations through their policies.

3.   Participating Western European countries included in this analysis are: Austria, Belgium, Switzerland, Denmark, Germany, Spain, Finland, France, Great Britain, Ireland, Italy, Luxembourg, the Netherlands, Norway, Portugal, and Sweden.

4.   Actual response rates by country range considerably, from nearly 60 per cent among some countries to slightly over 70 per cent for others.

5.   The selection of regions for analysis was further restricted by a minimum number of fifty natives within the larger sample in determining mean levels of immigrant receptivity by region. The number of immigrant Muslim respondents by region varies from one to forty-seven with a mean count of seven.

6.   This ordinal scale was also recoded into a dichotomous variable of monthly or more frequency as well as representative annual counts of frequency. Both logistic and poisson regression models provide similar results to the OLS regression results used in this paper.

7.   Other measures of immigrant sentiment were included within the survey as well, including: allow many/few immigrants of same race/ethnic group as majority, allow many/few immigrants of different race/ethnic group as majority, and allow many/few immigrants from poorer countries outside Europe. However, factor analysis indicates that these variables do not favourably correlate with the other three selected variables. Independent variable means by region were calculated using the probability and design weights provided within the ESS.

8.   This measure of religious concentration as well as proportion foreign-born were derived by calculating proportions by region found in the full survey sample.

9.   The measure for religious pluralism is calculated using the Herfindahl Index – one minus the sum-squared proportion of each religious group. Religious groups were coded according to global religious categories (i.e. Catholic, Protestant, Eastern Orthodox, other Christian, Jewish, Muslim, Eastern religions, other non-Christian religions, and no religion).

10. Although race can influence both religious outcomes and native perceptions of immigrants, race was unavailable in the ESS.

11. Given the variety of sampling strategies employed by each participating country, ESS principal investigators recommend using population and household weights for any analysis. Unfortunately, the xtreg procedure in STATA are not friendly to weights. Additionally, the limited subsample used in this analysis defies the suitability for weights.

12.   A country level of analysis was selected since some regions only have a handful of immigrant Muslims; therefore, any testing of a reverse-causation hypothesis requiring mean levels of immigrant Muslim religiosity by region could be unrepresentative of immigrant Muslim religiosity.

13.   Means for immigrant Muslims were retained for regions with ten or more Muslim respondents.

14.   All three indicators of immigrant receptivity are highly correlated with each other and would portray little difference if mapped separately.

15.   Due to the varying level of regions by country, this map was produced by hand; therefore, division lines between regions are approximate. Any errors in these boundaries are the author's responsibility and not that of ESS principal investigators.

16.   I am indebted to Alejandro Portes for this valuable insight.

References

ALANEZI, FAWAZ 2005 'Theoretical explanations for variations in religious participation among U.S. immigrants: the impact of nativity, ethnic community, family structure, and religious markets', PhD dissertation, Department of Sociology, Southern Illinois University, Carbondale, IL

ALBA, RICHARD 2005 'Bright vs. blurred boundaries: second generation assimilation and exclusion in France, Germany, and the United States', *Ethnic and Racial Studies*, vol. 28, no. 1, pp. 20–49

ALBA, RICHARD and NEE, VICTOR 1999 'Rethinking assimilation theory for a new era of immigration', in Charles Hirschman (ed.), *The Handbook of International Migration: The American Experience*, New York: Russell Sage Foundation, pp. 137–60

ALBA, RICHARD, ROBOTEAU, ALBERT J and DEWING JOSH (eds) 2009   *Immigration and Religion in America*, New York: New York University Press

BAUBÖCK, RAINER 1996 'Social and cultural integration in a civil society', in Rainer Bauböck, Agnes Heller and Aristide R. Zolberg (eds), *The Challenge of Diversity: Integration and Pluralism in Societies of Immigration*, Aldershot: Ashgate

BAUBÖCK, RAINER, HELLER, AGNES and ZOLBERG, ARISTIDE R. (eds), *The Challenge of Diversity: Integration and Pluralism in Societies of Immigration*, Aldershot: Ashgate

BEN RAFAEL, ELIZEAR 1996 'Multiculturalism in a sociological perspective', in Rainer Bauböck, Agnes Heller and Aristide R. Zolberg (eds), *The Challenge of Diversity: Integration and Pluralism in Societies of Immigration*, Aldershot: Ashgate

CADGE, WENDY and ECKLUND, ELAINE HOWARD 2007 'Immigration and religion', *Annual Review of Sociology*, vol. 33, pp. 359–79

CARENS, JOSEPH H. and WILLIAMS, MELISSA S. 1996 'Muslim minorities in liberal democracies: the politics of misrecognition', in Rainer Bauböck, Agnes Heller and Aristide R. Zolberg (eds), *The Challenge of Diversity: Integration and Pluralism in Societies of Immigration*, Aldershot: Ashgate

CONNOR, PHILLIP 2007 'New directions for immigrant religious research', paper presented at the annual meeting for the Society for the Scientific Study of Religion, Tampa, FL

—— 2008 'Increase or decrease? The impact of the international migratory event on immigrant religious participation', *Journal for the Scientific Study of Religion*, vol. 47, no. 2, pp. 243–57

DE JONG, GORDON F. and STEINMETZ, MICHELE 2004 'Receptivity attitudes and the occupational attainment of male and female immigrant workers', *Population Research and Policy Review*, vol. 23, no. 2, pp. 91–116

DOOMERNIK, JEROEN 1995 'The institutionalization of Turkish Islam in Germany', *Ethnic and Racial Studies*, vol. 18, no. 1, pp. 46–63

398   *Phillip Connor*

EBAUGH, HELEN ROSE 2003 'Religion and the new immigrants', in Michelle Dillon (ed.), *Handbook of the Sociology of Religion*, Cambridge: Cambridge University Press

FAIST, THOMAS 1996 'Immigration, integration, and the welfare state: Germany and the USA in a comparative perspective', in Rainer Bauböck, Agnes Heller and Aristide R. Zolberg (eds), *The Challenge of Diversity: Integration and Pluralism in Societies of Immigration*, Aldershot: Ashgate

FETZER, JOEL S. 1998 'Religious minorities and support for immigrant rights in the United States, France, and Germany', *Journal for the Scientific Study of Religion*, vol. 37, no. 1, pp. 41–9

———— 2000 'Economic self-interest or cultural marginality? Anti-immigration sentiment and nativist political movements in France, Germany and the USA', *Journal of Ethnic and Migration Studies*, vol. 26, no. 1, pp. 5–23

FINKE, ROGER and STARK, RODNEY 2005 *The Churching of America, 1776–2005: Winners and Losers in our Religious Economy*, New Brunswick, NJ: Rutgers University Press

FONER, NANCY and ALBA, RICHARD 2008 'Immigrant religion in the U.S. and Western Europe: bridge or barrier to inclusion?', *International Migration Review*, vol. 42, no. 2, pp. 360–92

FREEMAN, GARY P. 2004 'Immigrant incorporation in Western democracies', *International Migration Review*, vol. 38, no. 3, pp. 945–69

GLAZER, NATHAN and MOYNIHAN, DANIEL PATRICK 1963 *Beyond the Melting Pot*, Cambridge, MA: MIT Press

GORDON, MILTON 1964 *Assimilation in American Life: The Role of Race, Religion, and National Origins*, New York: Oxford University Press

GREELEY, ANDREW M. 1971 *'Why Can't They Be Like Us? America's White Ethnic Groups'*, New York: E. P. Dutton

HELLER, AGNES 1996 'The many faces of multiculturalism', in Rainer Bauböck, Agnes Heller and Aristide R. Zolberg (eds), *The Challenge of Diversity: Integration and Pluralism in Societies of Immigration*, Aldershot: Ashgate

HERBERG, WILL 1960 *Protestant-Catholic-Jew*, Garden City, NY: Anchor Books

HIGHAM, JOHN 2002 *Strangers in the Land: Patterns of American Nativism, 1860–1925*, New Brunswick, NJ: Rutgers University Press

HIRSCHMAN, CHARLES 2004 'The role of religion in the origins and adaptation of immigrant groups in the United States', *International Migration Review*, vol. 28, no. 3, pp. 1206–34

HOLLIFIELD, JAMES 2004 'The emerging migration state', *International Migration Review*, vol. 28, no. 3, pp. 885–912

HUNTINGTON, SAMUEL 1993 'The clash of civilizations?', *Foreign Affairs*, vol. 72, no. 3, pp. 22–49

JOWELL, R. (and CENTRAL CO-ORDINATING TEAM) 2003 2005 2007 'European Social Survey 2002/2003 2004/2005 2006/2007: Technical Report', Center for Comparative Social Surveys, City University, London

KASTORYANO, RIVA 2007 'Religion and incorporation', in Alejandro Portes and Josh DeWind (eds), *Rethinking Migration*, New York: Berghahn Books

KOENIG, MATTHIAS 2005 'Incorporating Muslim migrants in Western nation states – a comparison of the United Kingdom, France, and Germany', *Journal of International Migration and Integration*, vol. 6, no. 2, pp. 219–34

KURIEN, PREMA 2002 'We are better Hindus here', in Pyong Gap Min and Kim Jung Ha Kim (eds), *Religion in Asian America: Building Faith Communities*, Walnut Creek, CA: AltaMira Press

LOGAN, JOHN R., OH, SOOKEE and DARRAH, JENNIFER 2007 'The political and community context of immigrant naturalization', paper presented at annual meetings of the Population Association of America, New York

MASSEY, DOUGLAS S. and HIGGINS, MONICA ESPINOSA 2007 'What role does religion play in the migration process? And vice versa? Evidence from the New Immigrant

Survey', paper presented at the annual meetings of the Population Association of America, New York

MODOOD, TARIQ 2001 'Their liberalism and our multiculturalism', *British Journal of Politics and International Relations*, vol. 3, no. 2, pp. 245–57

PAGE, BENJAMIN I. and SHAPIRO, ROBERT Y. 1983 'Effects of public opinion on policy', *American Political Science Review*, vol. 77, no. 1, pp. 175–90

PENNIX, RINUS 1996 'Immigration, minorities policy and multiculturalism in Dutch society since 1960', in Rainer Bauböck, Agnes Heller and Aristide R. Zolberg (eds), *The Challenge of Diversity: Integration and Pluralism in Societies of Immigration*, Aldershot: Ashgate

PETTERSSON, THORLEIF 2007 'Muslim immigrants in Western Europe: persisting value differentiation or value adaptation', in M. Moadell (ed.), *Values and Perceptions of the Islamic and Middle Eastern Publics*, New York: Palgrave Macmillan, pp. 71–104

PORTES, ALEJANDRO and RUMBAUT, RUBEN G. 2006 *Immigrant America: A Portrait*, Berkeley, CA: University of California Press

PORTES, ALEJANDRO and ZHOU, MIN 1993 'The new second generation: segmented assimilation and its variants', *Annals of the American Academy of Political and Social Science*, vol. 530, pp. 74–96

REX, JOHN 1994 'The political sociology of multiculturalism and the place of Muslims in West European societies', *Social Compass*, vol. 41, pp. 79–92

SARAN, PARMATMA 1985 *The Asian Indian Experience in the United States*, Cambridge, MA: Schenkman

VAN HOOK, JENNIFER, BROWN, SUSAN K. and BEAN, FRANK D. 2006 'For love or money? Welfare reform and immigrant naturalization', *Social Forces*, vol. 85, no. 2, pp. 643–66

VAN TUBERGEN, FRANK 2006 'Religious affiliation and attendance among immigrants in eight Western countries: individual and contextual effects', *Journal for the Scientific Study of Religion*, vol. 45, no. 1, pp. 1–22

—— 2007 'Religious affiliation and participation among immigrants in a secular society: a study of immigrants in the Netherlands', *Journal of Ethnic and Migration Studies*, vol. 33, no. 5, pp. 747–65

VERTOVEC, STEVEN 1996 'Multiculturalism, culturalism and public incorporation', *Ethnic and Racial Studies*, vol. 19, no. 1, pp. 49–69

WARNER, W. LLOYD and SROLE, LEO 1945 *The Social Systems of American Ethnic Groups*, New Haven: Yale University Press

WILLIAMS, RAYMOND BRADY 1988 *Religions of Immigrants from India and Pakistan: New Threads in the American Tapestry*, Cambridge: Cambridge University Press

ZHOU, MIN 1997 'Segmented assimilation: issues, controversies, and recent research on the new second generation', *International Migration Review*, vol. 31, no. 4, pp. 975–1008

ZOLBERG, ARISTIDE R. and WOON, LITT LONG 1999 'Why Islam is like Spanish: cultural incorporation in Europe and the United States', *Politics and Society*, vol. 27, no. 1, pp. 5–38

PHILLIP CONNOR is a Ph.D. Candidate in the Department of Sociology at Princeton University.
ADDRESS: 119 Wallace Hall, Princeton University, Princeton, NJ 08544, USA. Email: pconnor@princeton.edu

Appendix A

Table A. *Multivariate, multi-level regression estimates for immigrant Muslim religious outcome deviations in Western Europe – regional level*

Variable	Religiosity			Religious Attendance			Prayer		
	Model 1	Model 2	Model 3	Model 4	Model 5	Model 6	Model 7	Model 8	Model 9
				Fixed Effects					
Control Variables									
ESS Round 1	–	–	–	–	–	–	–	–	–
ESS Round 2	-0.160	-0.152	-0.158	0.076	0.065	0.059	-0.069	-0.047	-0.076
ESS Round 3	0.196	0.194	0.195	0.076	0.076	0.072	0.189	0.192	0.185
Sex	0.220**	0.214†	0.219†	-0.378***	-0.372***	-0.374***	0.278**	0.275**	0.281**
Education	-0.023†	-0.024†	-0.023†	-0.012	-0.010	-0.011	0.007	0.009	0.008
Year Born	-0.012*	-0.012*	-0.012*	-0.010**	-0.010*	-0.010*	-0.013*	-0.012**	-0.012**
Employment	-0.190	-0.192	-0.193	-0.123	-0.135	-0.135	-0.147	-0.171	-0.169†
Income	0.000	0.000	0.000	0.000	0.000	0.000	0.000	0.000	0.000
Income Missing	0.352*	0.353**	0.352**	0.127	0.112	0.102	0.081	0.065	0.045
Live in Country <1yr	–	–	–	–	–	–	–	–	–
Live in Country 1–5 yrs	-0.693	-0.723†	-0.714†	-0.295	-0.321	-0.282	-0.572†	-0.606†	-0.594†
Live in Country 6–10 yrs	-0.860*	-0.892*	-0.880*	-0.314	-0.322	-0.288	-0.635†	-0.669†	-0.640†
Live in Country 11–20 yrs	-0.774†	-0.816†	-0.797†	-0.341	-0.332	-0.294	-0.608†	-0.635†	-0.589†
Live in Country >20 yrs	-0.738†	-0.754†	-0.749†	-0.513†	-0.497†	-0.463	-0.619†	-0.591†	-0.580†
Country of Birth – Bosnia and Herzegovina	–	–	–	–	–	–	–	–	–
Country of Birth – Algeria	0.785†	0.833*	0.797*	0.205	0.166	0.161	0.592†	0.606†	0.559†
Country of Birth – Iraq	0.738*	0.720*	0.736*	0.168	0.203	0.198	1.073***	1.065***	1.103***
Country of Birth – Morocco	0.732*	0.781*	0.742*	0.647**	0.614**	0.629**	0.925***	0.964***	0.938***
Country of Birth – Pakistan	0.876*	0.913**	0.902*	0.711*	0.725**	0.663**	0.786**	0.831**	0.800**
Country of Birth – Turkey	0.593*	0.621*	0.601*	0.599**	0.599**	0.607**	0.583*	0.609***	0.610**
Country of Birth – Other	0.723**	0.730**	0.723**	0.345†	0.341†	0.348†	0.884***	0.903***	0.890***
Language at Home	0.269*	0.251†	0.260*	0.058	0.057	0.066	0.179†	0.164	0.169

(continued overleaf)

Table A. (*Continued*)

Variable	Religiosity			Religious Attendance			Prayer		
	Model 1	Model 2	Model 3	Model 4	Model 5	Model 6	Model 7	Model 8	Model 9
Religious Discrimination	0.333*	0.338**	0.333*	0.273*	0.266*	0.271*	0.175	0.158	0.170†
Spouse	0.033	0.035	0.032	−0.017	−0.021	−0.011	0.063	0.060	0.062
Child(ren)	0.310	0.306	0.309	−0.067	−0.065	−0.071	−0.040	−0.044	−0.046
Proportion Muslim	15.535**	16.084**	15.675**	−5.048†	−4.405	−3.445	3.637	4.227	5.171†
Religious Pluralism	−1.357	−1.129	−1.289	−0.050	−0.050	0.010	−1.163†	−0.762	−1.120†
Proportion Foreign Born	−4.852*	−5.712*	−5.245*	2.809*	2.489†	2.337†	−0.399	−1.630	−1.332
Variables of Interest									
Bad-Good Economy	−0.056			−0.201*			−0.268**		
Worse-Better Country		0.165			−0.158†			0.007	
Undermine-Enrich Culture			0.046			−0.193*			−0.138†
Constant	26.252*	25.059*	25.639*	23.376**	22.716**	23.007**	29.393**	26.292**	28.043**
Random Effects									
Region standard deviation	0.412	0.417	0.414	0.119	0.139	0.156	0.000	0.209	0.072
Region standard error	0.111	0.109	0.110	0.114	0.099	0.087	0.000	0.081	0.000
Measures of Fit									
Intra-class correlation (null)	0.098	0.098	0.098	0.050	0.050	0.050	0.044	0.044	0.044
Intra-class correlation (controls only)	0.061	0.061	0.061	0.020	0.020	0.020	0.025	0.025	0.025
Intra-class correlation (model)	0.060	0.062	0.061	0.011	0.014	0.018	0.000	0.025	0.003
Log-likelihood	−1622.820	−1622.271	−1622.817	−1312.917	−1313.863	−1312.211	−1414.043	−1416.800	−1416.348

†$p < .10$ *$p < .05$ **$p < .01$ ***$p < .001$, two-tailed.
Source: European Social Survey, 2002–2006 ($N_i = 837$; $N_j = 119$).

402   *Phillip Connor*

Table B. *Multivariate, multi-level regression estimates for immigrant Muslim religious outcome deviations in Western Europe – country level*

Variable	Religiosity			Religious Attendance			Prayer		
	Model 1	Model 2	Model 3	Model 4	Model 5	Model 6	Model 7	Model 8	Model 9
					Fixed Effects				
Control Variables									
ESS Round 1	—	—	—	—	—	—	—	—	—
ESS Round 2	-0.223†	-0.216†	-0.221†	0.086	0.080	0.079	-0.057	-0.056	-0.057
ESS Round 3	-0.165	-0.164	-0.164	-0.048	-0.050	-0.050	-0.145	-0.144	-0.142
Sex	-0.038	-0.045	-0.039	-0.155*	-0.154*	-0.154*	0.044	0.040	0.041
Education	-0.017	-0.017	-0.017	-0.010	-0.009	-0.010	-0.007	-0.008	-0.007
Year Born	-0.009†	-0.009†	-0.009	-0.008**	-0.008*	-0.008*	0.001	0.001	0.001
Employment	-0.076	-0.074	-0.074	-0.123†	-0.129†	-0.128	0.035	0.036	0.034
Income	0.000	0.000	0.000	0.000*	0.000*	0.000*	0.000	0.000	0.000
Income Missing	0.130	0.139	0.135	0.092	0.086	0.078	-0.081	-0.077	-0.071
Live in Country <1yr	—	—	—	—	—	—	—	—	—
Live in Country 1–5 yrs	-0.396	-0.404	-0.395	-0.125	-0.146	-0.123	-0.016	-0.033	-0.058
Live in Country 6–10 yrs	-0.438	-0.452	-0.440	-0.273	-0.286	-0.264	-0.033	-0.047	-0.067
Live in Country 11–20 yrs	-0.380	-0.405	-0.385	-0.212	-0.220	-0.191	-0.016	-0.035	-0.058
Live in Country >20 yrs	-0.228	-0.242	-0.234	-0.323	-0.325	-0.304	0.155	0.146	0.128
Country of Birth – Bosnia and Herzegovina	—	—	—	—	—	—	—	—	—
Country of Birth – Algeria	-0.138	-0.098	-0.134	0.387†	0.403†	0.377	0.121	0.168	0.178
Country of Birth – Iraq	-0.273	-0.285	-0.281	0.289	0.315	0.304	0.197	0.197	0.208
Country of Birth – Morocco	-0.638*	-0.604*	-0.641*	0.391*	0.400*	0.389*	-0.213	-0.177	-0.186
Country of Birth – Pakistan	-0.568*	-0.550†	-0.570*	0.276	0.287	0.253	-0.434*	-0.433*	-0.404
Country of Birth – Turkey	-0.593*	-0.572*	-0.600*	0.143	0.151	0.145	-0.471**	-0.448**	-0.452
Country of Birth – Other	-0.350	-0.344	-0.352	0.198	0.204	0.200	-0.188	-0.183	-0.187
Language at Home	-0.229*	-0.238*	-0.228*	0.022	0.019	0.029	-0.077	-0.088	-0.096
Religious Discrimination	-0.082	-0.076	-0.082	0.122	0.118	0.119	-0.120	-0.116	-0.118
Spouse	0.034	0.037	0.034	0.080	0.078	0.080	0.067	0.071	0.068
Child(ren)	0.024	0.023	0.025	-0.277*	-0.275*	-0.277*	-0.020	-0.022	-0.021

(continued overleaf)

Table B. (*Continued*)

Variable	Religiosity			Religious Attendance			Prayer		
	Model 1	Model 2	Model 3	Model 4	Model 5	Model 6	Model 7	Model 8	Model 9
Proportion Muslim	2.534	2.685	2.328	-3.828	-2.997	-3.328	3.003	3.577	3.700
Religious Pluralism	-0.050	0.083	-0.041	-0.362	-0.401	-0.251	0.037	0.064	-0.115
Proportion Foreign Born	-1.261	-1.286	-1.218	1.618	1.408	1.332	-1.607	-1.736	-1.585
Variables of Interest									
Bad-Good Economy	0.036			-0.275*			0.022		
Worse-Better Country		0.107			-0.149			0.164	
Undermine-Enrich Culture			0.023			-0.277*			0.199
Constant	20.640*	20.626*	20.754*	19.494**	18.650**	19.190**	-0.447	-1.019	-1.027
Random Effects									
Region standard deviation	0.000	0.000	0.000	0.204	0.242	0.216	0.176	0.152	0.141
Region standard error	0.000	0.000	0.000	0.065	0.069	0.061	0.075	0.073	0.068
Measures of Fit									
Intra-class correlation (null)	0.019	0.019	0.019	0.081	0.081	0.081	0.089	0.089	0.089
Intra-class correlation (controls only)	0.000	0.000	0.000	0.071	0.071	0.071	0.035	0.035	0.035
Intra-class correlation (model)	0.000	0.000	0.000	0.047	0.064	0.052	0.034	0.025	0.022
Log-likelihood	-1477.865	-1477.530	-1477.880	-1129.954	-1131.170	-1129.040	-1144.397	-1143.482	-1142.312

†p <.10 *p <.05 **p <.01 ***p <.001, two-tailed

Source: European Social Survey, 2002–2006 (N_i =837; N_j =16)

[16]

Journal of Refugee Studies Vol. 23, No. 3 © The Author 2010. Published by Oxford University Press.
All rights reserved. For Permissions, please email: journals.permissions@oxfordjournals.org
doi:10.1093/jrs/feq022   Advance Access publication 6 August 2010

Muslim Asylum-Seekers and Refugees: Negotiating Identity, Politics and Religion in the UK

ELENA FIDDIAN-QASMIYEH

Department of International Development, University of Oxford, UK

Department of Development Studies, School of Oriental and African Studies, University of London, UK
Elena.fiddian-qasmiyeh@qeh.ox.ac.uk

YOUSIF M. QASMIYEH

School of Oriental and African Studies, University of London, UK

In the current geopolitical context, religion, nationality and country of origin have increasingly become intertwined and politicized in relation to asylum, both as policy and as personal experience. Based on interviews conducted in the UK with a range of Middle Eastern Muslim asylum-seekers and refugees, this article proposes that regional and religious identity markers have grown to dictate interactions, be they real or imagined, with the host community. Throughout the article we explore the nature of changes in religious identity, identification and practice since interviewees applied for asylum in the UK. We also highlight the significance of a range of gendered factors and experiences, including childhood and growing up in the UK, effective masculinity and un/productive parenthood, in negotiating transformative political and legal realities. More broadly, our research suggests that UK-based Muslim asylum-seekers from the Middle East find themselves exposed to three intersecting vulnerabilities: firstly, their uncertain legal status; secondly, their voluntary or imposed religious identification as 'Muslims'; and lastly, their exclusion from established Muslim communities in the UK.

Keywords: Identity, Islam, Gender, Middle East, United Kingdom

Introduction

> *As you walk on the trace*
> *Of those who left before you,*
> *While the moon is faint in the sky,*
> *Say to yourself, if you can:*
> *Absence is the trace of those who disappeared.*
>
> Yousif M. Qasmiyeh

The impetus for this article derives from interviews conducted in January–March 2006 with Muslim asylum-seekers and refugees from the Middle East who were based in either Oxford or Manchester (UK) at the time of meeting. Several key issues and themes emerged throughout the research process, ranging from the planning and implementation stage to the impact of the interviews on the researchers involved, one of whom is himself a Palestinian refugee and whose participation was characterized by his role as a simultaneous insider and outsider. This article discusses a variety of ways in which our interviewees have become *spect-actors* (Boal 1992) who resist, negotiate and enact a number of discourses and counter-discourses, thereby embodying processes of individual and collective transformation. Such an expositive study is particularly necessary at a stage when religion, nationality and country of origin have increasingly become intertwined and politicized in relation to asylum, both as policy and as personal experience.

In many ways, this study complements research conducted by the Institute for Public Policy Research (Lewis 2005: 39), Information Centre about Asylum and Refugees (Finney 2005: 23), the Islamic Human Rights Commission (Islamic Human Rights Commission and Ansari 2006), Amnesty International (2006), Atfield *et al.* (2007), and the UK's Refugee Council (Rudiger 2007) on the unequal impacts of British anti-terrorism measures and the global in/security context on Muslim asylum-seekers and refugees in the UK. Based on our interviews and broader research on this area, we argue that while mis/representations of Islam have been politicized in such a fashion that they impact on all Muslims (and, indeed, all individuals perceived as such), Muslim asylum-seekers' and refugees' experiences in the UK reflect the complexities and particularities of the encounter between national and macro-politics. Broadly paralleling the abovementioned reports, we propose that Muslim asylum-seekers' and refugees' identities have been transformed in/by the public imagination, moving from an emphasis on their 'refugee-ness' and categorization as either 'bogus' or 'genuine' asylum-seekers, to a primal concern with their Muslim identity, which is equated with a threatening identity. Regional and religious identity markers have become pivotal features during interactions, be they real or imagined, with the host community and its components. This is the case both in terms of citizens' perceptions of Muslim asylum-seekers and refugees, and the ways in which these asylum-seekers and refugees themselves resist and negotiate the system as spectators and actors simultaneously, as what we call *spect-actors* in the asylum landscape.

Following the September 11 attacks and London bombings in 2001 and 2005 respectively, in addition to the controversial publication of cartoons of the Prophet Mohammed in Denmark's *Jylland's Posten* in 2005, a high level of sensitivity surrounded our attempts to contact 'Muslim asylum-seekers and refugees' to participate in a focus group in early 2006.[1] Like many individuals quoted in existing reports, prospective interviewees expressed anxieties that their opinions and religious identification could potentially

296   *Elena Fiddian-Qasmiyeh and Yousif M. Qasmiyeh*

be used by the Home Office to incarcerate or deport them in the future, as a result of being perceived to be a threat to national security. However, while refusing to meet in a group setting, all interviewees who agreed to speak with us explicitly reflected upon the current political environment, seeing the interview setting as a platform from which to discuss the location and experiences of Muslim asylum-seekers and refugees in contemporary Britain.

A discussion of religious identification thus forms the first part of the research findings presented in this article, followed by an analysis of inter-viewees' perceived visibility in particular locations, a focus on 'the house' as a realm for cultural and religious reproduction, and issues pertaining to par-enthood and parenting. Before turning to the substantive analysis offered in this article, we shall firstly provide an overview of the landscape faced by Middle Eastern Muslim asylum-seekers and refugees in the UK, and their position within British Muslim communities. We shall then provide a brief overview of the methodology upon which this study is based.

Asylum-seekers, Refugees and Muslims in the UK

A total of 23,610, 23,430, 25,670 and 24,250 applications for asylum were made in the UK in 2006, 2007, 2008 and 2009 respectively.[2] In 2006 the Home Office categorized 4,305 (18 per cent) of these applicants as being of 'Middle Eastern and North African' (MENA) origin (the first five rows of Table 1) (Bennett *et al.* 2007: 7), while in 2007 the Home Office (2008: 29)

Table 1

Numbers of Applications Made from the 'Middle East'[1], Afghanistan, Algeria and Turkey

	1997	1998	1999	2000	2001	2002	2003	2004	2005	2006	2007	2008	2009
Iran	585	745	1,320	5,610	3,420	2,630	2,875	3,455	3,150	2,375	2,210	2,270	1,835
Iraq	1,075	1,295	1,800	7,475	6,680	14,570	4,015	1,695	1,415	945	1,825	1,855	845
Libya	100	115	115	155	140	200	145	160	125	90	45	45[2]	65[2]
Syria	50	65	95	140	110	70	110	350	330	160	155	155	40
Middle East													
Other	525	565	835	1,035	915	850	825	870	715	735	825	675	500
Afghanistan	1,085	2,395	3,975	5,555	8,920	7,205	2,280	1,395	1,580	2,400	2,500	3,510	3,335
Algeria	715	1,260	1,385	1,635	1,140	1,060	550	490	255	225	260	325	225
Turkey	1,445	2,015	2,850	3,990	3,695	2,835	2,390	1,230	755	425	210	190	180

[1]Iran, Iraq, Libya, Syria and 'Other', as defined by the Home Office.
[2]As noted in the text, Libya was re-classified as an 'African' rather than 'Middle Eastern' country in 2008 and 2009.
Source: Derived from UK Home Office statistics for 2006, 2007, 2008 and 2009.

used the term 'Middle Eastern nationals' to define 5,060 (22 per cent) applicants, again the subtotal for the first five rows of the table. Such regional labels are misleading on several fronts; in part because in 2006 the stated percentage of applications originating from countries categorized as 'Middle Eastern' (as indicated in Table 1) included Iraq, Libya and Morocco, but not Afghanistan, Turkey or Algeria. Despite often being included in definitions of the Middle Eastern region (e.g. Eickelman 2001; Chatty 2010; Moghadam 1998), these three countries have systematically been categorized as 'Asian', 'European' and 'African' countries respectively by the Home Office. A further complicating factor is that from 2008 onwards, Libya has no longer been classified as a 'Middle Eastern' country by the Home Office, rather being placed alongside Algeria as an 'African' country. Having disconnected Libya and Algeria from the 'Middle East', the percentage of applicants classified by the Home Office as being of Middle Eastern origin in 2008 and 2009 has subsequently decreased to 19 per cent (4,955 applicants) and 14 per cent (3,320 applicants) respectively. However, taking Afghanistan, Algeria, Libya and Turkey consistently into consideration would lead to a larger, and more consistent, overall percentage of MENA applicants; between 29 per cent (in 2009), 31 per cent (in 2006) and 35 per cent (in 2007 and 2008) (Bennett *et al.* 2007, Home Office 2008, 2009a, 2009b, 2009c and 2009d).

Given that this article focuses in particular on Palestinian and Kurdish asylum-seekers' and refugees' experiences, a brief note is necessary with regard to their invisibility in Home Office statistics. In the data reproduced above, the category 'Middle East Other' comprises 14 additional nationalities, including 'Palestine', 'Israel', 'Egypt', 'Morocco', 'Lebanon' and 'Jordan.' Since Palestinians are based in a variety of host countries across the Middle East (primarily Jordan, Syria and Lebanon, but also Egypt and Iraq), as well as in Israel and 'the Palestinian controlled areas of the Gaza Strip and West Bank' (the phrase used by the Home Office (2006)), Palestinian applicants could be considered to be included in the statistics offered under the category 'Middle East Other', as well as being included amongst those arriving from Iraq.

The Home Office (2006) claims that although it does record applicants' language as Kurdish when relevant, it 'does not record ethnic groupings' and therefore could not, for instance, respond to a question posed under the Freedom of Information Act regarding the number of applicants of Kurdish origin who had been returned to Syria. Since Kurds 'are not recognized as a distinct nationality or ethnic group in the asylum determination process' (Griffiths 2000: 302), their absence from the statistics leads us to infer that they will have been placed under the country of their former habitual place of residence, with the majority of Kurds originating from Turkey, Iraq, Syria and Iran (*ibid.*).

Although applicants' religion is not recorded in Home Office statistics, given that the countries listed above have majority Muslim populations, it appears uncontroversial to claim that a large proportion of these Middle

298 *Elena Fiddian-Qasmiyeh and Yousif M. Qasmiyeh*

Eastern asylum-seekers are Muslim by birth and/or identify as such. According to the UK's 2001 Census, there were 1,588,890 Muslims in the country in 2001, of whom 74 per cent were from an 'Asian' ethnic background (including 43 per cent Pakistani and 16 per cent Bangladeshi), while less than 7 per cent were from 'another White background including Turkish, Cypriot, *Arab* and Eastern European' (ONS 2004, our emphasis). As such, only a minority of British Muslim citizens originate from the Middle East, meaning that Muslim Middle Eastern asylum-seekers and refugees in turn find themselves a clear minority amongst the Muslim community in the UK, and with only a limited pre-existing support system in terms of MENA-oriented masjids (mosques),[3] cultural centres, or community groups.

With reference to asylum-seekers' rights and responsibilities upon arrival in the UK, individuals applying for asylum are not normally allowed to seek work until a favourable decision on their asylum claim is reached by the British government.[4] During this period asylum-seekers may receive basic financial support, accommodation, free legal counsel and medical treatment from a range of governmental institutions including, at the time of research, the UK Border Agency, the National Asylum Support Service (NASS) (which has more recently been replaced by the Asylum Support Customer Contact Centre) and Social Services. Asylum-seekers are obliged to report on a regular basis (ranging from daily to monthly) at specified locations (including police stations and immigration/reporting centres), and to comply with a number of immigration rules. Asylum-seekers are constantly reminded that they are 'liable to be detained' if they do not strictly adhere to these regulations. Such support and obligations may continue for several years, while first hearing and subsequent appeal decisions are made.

Research Methodology

This exploratory article is based on research conducted with 14 Muslim MENA asylum-seekers, refugees and naturalized refugees in Oxford and Manchester. These two locations were selected due to the interviewers' familiarity with the general context in both cities, and existing contact with Middle Eastern asylum-seekers and refugees there. Of these interviewees, eight were Palestinians from a wide range of geo-political backgrounds: one adult male born in Ramallah (Palestinian Occupied Territories); a married couple and a married man born in different refugee camps in Lebanon; and a family (parents and two adolescent sons) from a refugee camp in Syria. Before applying for asylum, the adult Palestinians were formerly respectively employed as a hairdresser, an editor and secretary, an archaeologist, an architect and a primary-school teacher. At the time of interview, two of our research participants had been granted refugee status and subsequently British citizenship, while the remaining six Palestinians were awaiting decisions on their asylum applications or immigration status. Of the three Kurdish interviewees, two were from Iraq (where they had held ad hoc jobs) and one was from Turkey (formerly a journalist). The research sample also included one Afghan, one Yemeni (sociology graduate) and one Libyan (IT graduate), who were all asylum-seekers at the time of interview. The Palestinian adolescents and the Afghan interviewee had been studying in primary or secondary schools before arriving in the UK. Three interviewees were female (two Palestinians and one Kurd), and two were aged under eighteen (two Palestinians). Participants had lived in the UK for between four and 13 years when interviews were conducted.

Given that particular groups of asylum-seekers and refugees often form strong social networks (see Crisp 1999; Koser and Pinkerton 2002), three separate chains of contacts emerged during the research process. In Manchester, an existing Palestinian contact known to the interviewer (YMQ) led to the identification of three additional interviewees (of Yemeni, Palestinian and Libyan origins). In Oxford, one of the same interviewer's Oxford-based Palestinian contacts subsequently introduced both researchers to four Palestinian interviewees (a family), while another Palestinian known to the interviewer agreed to participate, alongside his wife. The three Kurdish refugees were contacted in Oxford through two different routes – firstly by advertising the research project to a local language centre and secondly via a researcher at the University of Oxford. The final participant, a young Afghan, consented to participate during a visit by one of the interviewers (EFQ) to an Oxford-based further education college.

Semi-structured interviews were conducted with all individual interviewees and an additional family-centred group discussion[5] was held, involving the Ramallah-born Palestinian man and the Palestinian parents and adolescents who had been born in Syria. The analysis presented below is based on these interviews alongside informal conversations held with the interviewees and observations made throughout the research period.

The Kurdish participants were interviewed by EFQ, while those based in Manchester were interviewed by YMQ. All other interviewees met with both researchers for between one and three interviews lasting a minimum of 45 and maximum of 180 minutes each. The interviews were informal in nature and the interviewer/s asked a minimum number of questions, encouraging interviewees to direct both the form and content of the discussions. All interviews started with the broad question 'Can you tell us about your experiences of living in the UK?' with the interview developing as a discussion based around the responses provided.

While the participatory and loose format of the interviews was productive with 13 participants, a greater level of intervention was required in one interview in order to overcome the interviewee's initial insecurity and anxiety. The researchers' accentuated role in this particular case, which successfully facilitated the completion of the interview and indeed the incorporation of three additional family members to the encounter, must be noted.

Three of the Palestinian interviewees felt more comfortable communicating directly in Arabic, rather than English, which affected the dynamics of the meeting accordingly. In these cases, YMQ posed a small number of questions

300   *Elena Fiddian-Qasmiyeh and Yousif M. Qasmiyeh*

in Arabic directly, and only interrupted the interviewee occasionally to translate for the second author. Given EFQ's intermediate understanding of Arabic at the time of interview, she was, as a whole, able to follow the interview, waiting for her colleague to offer a more in-depth overview of the interview upon the interviewees' departure. This collaborative approach to interviewing allowed for the interviewees to express themselves freely in their mother tongue, with minimum interruption for interpretation, and with an increased sense of dialogue between the interviewee and YMQ. Given YMQ's identity as a Palestinian refugee, it may also have been the case that the interviewees felt more comfortable communicating directly with him, rather than with a non-Muslim female researcher, and this will have influenced the course of the interviews in many ways. Indeed, there was at least one occasion when the interviewee felt able to discuss a sensitive issue in Arabic, that he stressed he would have been unable to speak about in English in an English-speaking café. It may have been the case that YMQ's background therefore offered different levels of protection and security to the interviewees that the female researcher would have been unable to grant. It is also possible, however, that interviewees will have presented themselves in a particular way due to YMQ's identity, and also due to the fact of there being two researchers rather than just one, throughout the interview.

A Note on the Researchers' Positionality

At the time of interview, the first author was a doctoral student based at the University of Oxford, and this project formed part of a pilot study designed to inform the development of her doctoral research on a refugee group based in Algeria. Her previous experience of conducting research on and with refugees and asylum-seekers from across the Middle East, Northern and Sub-Saharan Africa influenced the development of the research methodology, just as her particular interest in the gendered experiences of asylum is reflected in the analysis presented below.

As indicated at different points throughout this article, the second author of this piece was himself an asylum-seeker at the time of research. Although he had previously conducted research with refugees living in Lebanon (where he himself had been born as a refugee and was employed as a teacher at United Nations Relief and Works Agency schools) for various academic institutions and non-governmental organizations, this was the first time that YMQ conducted interviews in the UK. As a brief note concerning his role and experiences whilst working on this project, we quote from an exercise in reflexive self-analysis which YMQ completed at EFQ's request towards the end of the interviewing period:

> From the outset of this project I have felt that I have been an insider more than an outsider vis-à-vis what is happening in the 'undefined places' explored in the interviews. My legal status, as you know, also embodied a psychological barrier

at the beginning. At times I have been tempted to ask questions that are mainly associated with my situation; perhaps, subconsciously, I have tried to draw some kind of linkage, or rather an identification, between the interviewees and myself. Having the 'authority' to structure and ask questions (although most of the time these were not actually directly posed) has highlighted the indecisiveness that an asylum-seeker can have when invited to direct an interview which is intimately related to his or her own experience. I have sometimes felt under scrutiny as a co-interviewer who has failed to escape from his identity and status in the course of the interviews. It is very bizarre how I, on certain occasions, have wanted to announce my absence. I have wanted to say: I am only an asylum-seeker who desperately wants to verbalize the situation without any academic pressure. Can I be an asylum-seeker and a co-interviewer of asylum-seekers and refugees at the same time? That is a very difficult question to answer. Would I look at this from a different perspective if I had refugee status? I do not think so.

YMQ, March 2006

Both interviewers were acutely aware of the potential impact of the research project upon YMQ, given his legal status and own experiences of applying for asylum, and held regular de-briefing meetings to discuss concerns as they arose. Based on our experiences throughout this collaborative project, and the feedback obtained from our participants, this study provides an invitation for future research to invite refugees and asylum-seekers to become co-researchers rather than simply 'participants' and 'interviewees.'

Ethics

All names mentioned throughout the course of this article are pseudonyms, and in some cases personal information has been omitted to ensure interviewees' confidentiality and anonymity. All interviewees gave their consent to the anonymous use of the interview data when publishing the results of the research; in the case of the adolescents interviewed, both they themselves and their parents consented to their participation in this research project.

Limitations of the Study

The research conducted with these fourteen participants cannot be seen to be representative of all Middle Eastern Muslim asylum-seekers or refugees in the UK. Indeed, the responses provided during interviews offer insights into the commonalities and differences of these individuals' experiences according, for instance, to legal status, individual preferences and beliefs, nationality, gender, age and marital status. As such, we examine the asylum process in the UK and its impacts on those who suffer multifaceted, religious, political, legal, social and linguistic alienation. We offer these findings in the hope that further academic research may be carried out on the issues highlighted below.

302   *Elena Fiddian-Qasmiyeh and Yousif M. Qasmiyeh*

The Research Findings

Personal and Collective Identification

Bearing in mind the diversity of its interpretations and implementations, personal and collective identification in relation to Islam was a central, and often ambivalent, element arising from the interviews conducted. All of the Kurdish participants (Sidi, Farhana and Salem) responded to the authors' interest in speaking with Muslim asylum-seekers/refugees specifically, and yet even before her first interview took place, Farhana sent one of the authors a pertinent message about her non/religious and cultural identity through her choice of interview location, inviting EFQ to have a beer in a pub in East Oxford. During our first meeting, she stressed: 'I am Muslim, by birth, but I don't identify as such', highlighting repeatedly that she does not have (m)any Muslim friends, that she consumes pork and alcohol (which are haram, or Islamically prohibited), and engages in other activities which she defined in the interview as signs of a 'bad Muslim'. While Farhana is a pseudonym, her real name carries a strong Islamic connotation, and she continued her interview by indicating that she finds it very difficult having a 'Muslim name'. She stressed that for her, her name is a 'visible signifier of a religious identity which has been fixed upon me' and yet which she does not identify with. Farhana reiterated this in her second interview, strongly indicating the extent to which her name, and all it symbolizes, is a central concern for her.

Salem, another Kurdish refugee, on the other hand, did not so unequivocally distance himself from Islam, rather describing himself as 'not religious'.[6] Further, when asked about the impact of religion on his experience of living in the UK, Salem referred to his experiences of racism, but with reference to his own religiosity, ambiguously described himself as 'neither pro nor anti'. At the same time, he proposed that religion can be a great provider of comfort and that it is therefore 'normal' that some asylum-seekers/refugees should grow more interested in religious identity and practice in times of need. By simultaneously distancing himself from religion and offering this explanation of increased religiosity in others, it is possible to suggest that Salem was in turn portraying himself as not requiring such forms of 'comfort', as somehow independent of this need and therefore as emotionally self-sufficient.

These multiple re/presentations of religious identification reflect not only the heterogeneity of the category 'Muslim', but also the multiple ways in which people define themselves and present themselves to others. Both Farhana and Salem made precise references to the notion of religious practice and identity, ranging from non-committal descriptions of themselves as 'not religious' or 'neither pro nor anti', to a more dissociative labelling of being only a Muslim 'by birth' or a 'bad Muslim'. It is possible to interpret Salem and Farhana's ambivalent relationship with Islam to be of a personal or cultural nature, based on their previous and current individual understandings of their own identities. While Farhana referred to her 'visibility' as a

Muslim due to her name (while her cultural identity is 'invisible'), her distancing from her 'birth' religion did not appear to be related to her presence in the UK, since her rejection of Islam had reportedly been a motivating factor in her claim for asylum.

As we discuss below, however, transformations in religious practice and identification may be instigated by the political and social environment in which individuals are currently located, with their real or imagined visibility leading to their hiding or modifying their approaches to Islam. Indeed, while individual descriptions of religiosity and practice may of course reflect personal feelings and preferences, they may in addition be determined not only by the identity of the listener or interviewer, but also to a large extent by the national and international realities framing the topic under consideration. In this sense, interviewees can be positioned as both research participants and *spect-actors* of the broader political landscape: in the current context, where Muslim identity/identities and practice(s) have become so driven by politics, words may be dependent on external factors as much as, if not more than, internal ones. In this respect, Salem's disengagement from religion (which we can refer to as an 'in-between affiliation') could be interpreted as a strategy utilized to resist being categorized by others according to his religious identity in such a context.

Unlike Salem and Farhana, five of the Palestinian participants elaborated upon their personal relationships with Islam with particular reference to the ways in which the asylum experience has modified their religious practice, beliefs and perceptions. In line with Salem's interpretation above, Musa reflected that the 'boredom' (*ḍajar*) which accompanies processes such as being in (immigration) detention or unable to work legally, often leads one to 'focus on yourself'; he attributed his decision to grow his beard and concentrate more on fulfilling his spiritual needs directly to his sense of 'boredom', aimlessness and stagnancy since applying for asylum in the UK.

Our interviews with Khalil and Ahmed, however, did not support the proposition that these men's intensification of practice and belief was primarily related to a need to obtain internal comfort, but was rather based on their reaction to and interaction with the social unrest and instability which followed the aforementioned events. Both Khalil and Ahmed indicated that they have experienced an 'intensification' (*taṣāʿud*) and increased awareness of religious belief and practice since applying for asylum. Like the two teenage boys interviewed,[7] they indicated that this change had been a 'conscious one'. They explained that their decision had been prompted by a desire to learn more about their own religion, in part to compensate for and defend themselves from what they defined as 'ignorant attacks' on Islam in general and on themselves and their families as Muslims more precisely.

In addition to references to racism between Muslim refugees/asylum-seekers and the British community broadly, an extra dimension of religious tension and marginalization was expressed in relation to the interaction between Muslim British citizens and Muslim refugees/asylum-seekers. This is a

304   *Elena Fiddian-Qasmiyeh and Yousif M. Qasmiyeh*

tension which has been independently documented in a report commissioned by the UK's Refugee Council and the University of Birmingham (Atfield *et al.* 2007: 48).

Hence, although Khalil invoked the notion of Muslim fraternity by saying that 'all Muslims are brothers', he subsequently stated that 'Asian Muslims' tend to pray in one place (but see Naqshbandi 2006 for divisions within the British Asian Muslim community), while 'Arab Muslim refugees' pray in another. One reason for this separation may be the language used to deliver the Friday *khuṭba* (sermon), as British Asian imams often offer their *khuṭba* in the *muṣallīn*'s (worshippers') main language (such as Urdu), in addition to English, rather than in Arabic. Similarly, Ahmed (who arrived as an asylum-seeker in the mid-1990s and is now a British citizen) sadly reflected upon the rupture (*qaṭīʿa*) which exists between the British Asian Muslim community and the more recently arrived Middle Eastern Muslim asylum-seeker/refugee community, a distance which, he claimed, is epitomized in the different masjids which are frequented by these groups. In this sense, it is interesting to note these interviewees' comments vis-à-vis the visibility of refugee identity, as identifiable according to where they pray, and the importance they assigned to the masjid in its potential as a realm for shared space and belonging.

Visibility and Space/Place

Visibility, either as a Muslim or as a Muslim refugee/asylum-seeker, or as an asylum-seeker more broadly, arose as a fundamental theme in many interviews. This included six explicit accounts of racism, Farhana's perceived visibility as a Muslim due to her name and Khalil's reference to Muslim women's visibility due to the hijab or the way they dress. The latter also identified several locations where refugees and asylum-seekers are readily identifiable as such. In a range of reports documenting the impact of the September 11 attacks and the London bombings, Muslim asylum-seekers and refugees have highlighted their sense of being particularly visible and under scrutiny whilst using public transport (the target of several attacks/attempts) and public services (Rudiger 2007). The post-office, where refugees[8]/asylum-seekers cash their allowances, has also become a conspicuous example of such a location: simultaneously a key medium connecting the holders of the asylum-seekers' Application Registration Card (ARC), this space/place forces and enforces the unveiling of ARC holders not only to the clerk behind the glass, but also to 'normal' citizen-clients in the queue. Subtly withdrawing the ARC card from a pocket or wallet, attempting to minimize disclosure, the key protagonist feels that this space/place becomes a stage where all lights are on him/her.

One of the authors of this piece describes his experiences of queuing up at the post-office, and of preparing to do so, as being categorized by both attraction and repulsion:

> You are attracted to the place because it is where you obtain your money, it is
> in essence your only means of survival since the Home Office doesn't let you
> work; they won't let you contribute or act for yourself. But you are repelled
> because it forces you to become visible to a 'public' with whom you neither
> share legal status nor even the purpose of visiting such a location.

Various levels of subjectively experienced exclusion and marginalization
therefore emerged throughout the interviews, often related to different
types of space and location (on spaces and places see Escobar 2001; Gupta
and Ferguson 2002; Low and Lawrence-Zuniga 2003). Khalil referred to 'the
house' (*bayt*) and 'the home(land)' (*mawṭin*) as a symbol and forum for social
closeness and 'belonging' (*intimāʿ*), as a place where he can feel comfortable,
relaxed and welcomed. Khalil stressed that he 'cannot find the home here',
although his search continues. In the cases of both Abu Omar and Musa,
however, while these men each have a physical house and a family within the
house, there was a tangible sense of a double-edged exclusion, of otherness,
or dislocation, within this space. Not safe outside his house, where Abu
Omar is unable to communicate in English and continues to be an
asylum-seeker after six years living in the UK, he is equally unable to communicate freely with his children inside the house, as they speak his
mother-tongue (Arabic) poorly. Musa's sense of alienation from his house
and home derived from his enforced dependence upon the British government
(via NASS or Social Services) which provided his family with accommodation
and a weekly allowance whilst prohibiting him from earning a wage legally –
leading, to paraphrase Turner (1999: 2), to Musa feeling that NASS 'is a
better husband' to his wife, and 'a better father' to his two daughters.

'The House', Culture and Religious Reproduction

'The house' was also referred to by several interviewees as both the location
for the family, and for cultural and religious reproduction. Four of the
Palestinian parents interviewed (Ahmed, Nadia, Um Omar and Abu Omar)
stressed their roles as providers of religious knowledge and information for
their children within the house, and their desire for their children to have a
'deep' understanding of Islam, especially in today's political environment.
Unlike Farhana's decision to distance herself from Islam in part on the
basis that she believes this would give her more freedom as a woman,
Nadia, a Palestinian mother of two, indicated that she had recently experienced an emerging desire to learn more about Islam and what she calls 'the
self within religion', and to interact more with other Muslim women than
before. Part of the rationale behind Nadia's desire was her recognition that
she is her daughters' principal source of knowledge about Islam. For her, an
in-depth engagement with Islam, rather than a disengagement from Muslim
identity and practice, is a productive means of equipping her daughters with

306   *Elena Fiddian-Qasmiyeh and Yousif M. Qasmiyeh*

the relevant knowledge to enable them to make decisions concerning their own femininity and womanhood.

A notion of the significance of cultural and religious continuity featured strongly in many of the interviews with Palestinians, with Abu Omar in particular seeking reassurance from one of this article's authors (YMQ) that his children are 'doing alright now' and 'will be alright in the future.' During our interview with his sons, aged 14 and 16, the boys indicated that they do not want to return to the Palestinian refugee camps in Syria and find it difficult to communicate in Arabic. They stressed that they dislike Arabic-language television and prefer rap to Arabic music, although the eldest, who intends to be a music producer, said that he might consider using Arabic music 'as a sample' in one of his songs. Despite this self-perceived distance from Arabic cultural and linguistic features, the teenagers eloquently discussed the need for the British public to reject mainstream stereotypes about Islam, and concluded by stating that they are 'proud to be Muslim.' This is a sense that they explained as having developed both as a response to their personal experiences of racism on the one hand, and (unlike Khalil and Ahmed) their friendships and identification with other Muslims from their community, and the supportive role played by their parents, on the other.

Razak's situation, as a young man who left Afghanistan as a 14-year-old unaccompanied minor, and who currently shares a house with other male Afghan asylum-seekers and refugees, was diametrically opposed to that of Abu Omar's children. When asked whether religion played a role in the way that refugees experience living in the UK, Razak awkwardly admitted that he is Muslim, but does not practice. He explained:

> When I lived in Afghanistan, my mother used to tell me to pray. She would tell me to pray and I would. If I were at home now, with my mother, she would tell me to pray and I would. But now, here, I don't.

Immediately following this account, Razak recounted a story about his experiences one night when he had 'lots to drink', a key event which he appeared to use to represent his distance from Islamic practice. The explicit juxtaposition of his absent religious practice as connected to the absence of his mother, with his account of his night out 'drinking', is noteworthy. We can perhaps interpret this in relation to his age upon leaving Afghanistan, and his related dependence on, or desire for, external cultural and religious reference points.

Throughout his interview, Razak indicated that when he left the British foster family he had lived with as an unaccompanied minor, and had moved in with other Afghan young men, it was 'difficult to decide which culture to use.' He stressed that it took him 'about four months' to establish what form of cultural conduct was appropriate in each context, what he could/not or should/not do, when and with whom.[9] He referred to the correct usage of the handshake as a form of greeting, as the key cultural cue that he had failed to master. Implicit throughout his interview was the notion that he was 'too young' when he left Afghanistan to have a firm memory or independent understanding of 'correct' and 'incorrect' modes of behaviour, covering all aspects of social and religious life. Unlike Um Omar's teenage daughter, who recently approached her mother with questions about whether it was haram (prohibited) or halal (permitted in Islam) to hold hands or to kiss a boy, Razak demonstrated that he does not have a readily accessible mentor to help him determine what is acceptable behaviour, and that he often feels both culturally and religiously 'lost' as a result.

Razak's relationship with Islam has therefore also changed since arriving as an unaccompanied minor asylum-seeker in the UK, but very differently from the changes experienced and represented by the other refugee youth or Palestinian adults interviewed. In addition to providing preliminary insights into some connections between religion and the experience of living in the UK, several of the issues discussed above also indicate some ways in which religion, gender and family relations are connected in the asylum landscape.

Parenthood and Parenting

In his interview, Sidi presented himself as a Kurdish refugee, successful student, productive employee, and, most importantly, as a father. He explained that he has four children, and that he is greatly concerned about his eldest son (aged 19), who, much to his distress, is not interested in studying. He continued by stating 'I sacrifice my present day, my today, for my son.' Sidi's main concerns in the UK are related to his own and his son's social mobility and self-improvement, achievable, he explained, through a combination of education and 'meaningful' employment. Sidi is therefore saving the wages from his two jobs to buy his son a shop, 'so that he can be his own boss.'

An additional approach to good parenthood was outlined by Ahmed, a former Palestinian refugee (now a British citizen) who presented himself in terms of his productivity as an employee and as an active member of the community. For him, good parenting is intimately related to the transmission of Islamic knowledge, and to encouraging his daughters to engage critically with both Islam and 'their country's' (referring to the UK) cultural and religious frameworks. As with Sidi, productivity and employment, alongside a role as a 'good father', therefore arose as central features of manhood and masculinity.

In contrast with Sidi and Ahmed's well-established lives, Um Omar and Abu Omar were evidently encountering multiple difficulties as marginalized Muslim asylum-seekers, and as parents. Abu Omar, a Palestinian who has lived in the UK for six years, was so apprehensive throughout the initial phase of the interview that it appeared we would have to leave, until he suggested that we might like to meet his wife. While Abu Omar had quietly stated that 'Everything's OK, there's no racism, everything's fine', his wife immediately reversed this discourse upon her arrival in the living-room. Compared with her husband's barely audible whispers in both English and Arabic, Um Omar spoke with striking confidence in English (a language which she is still in the process of learning), emphasizing: 'Things are hard. There is racism and I am very concerned about my children. They are attacked and insulted, both at school and on the street.' As Abu Omar nodded, confirming his wife's words, Um Omar clearly described how difficult it was to raise their four children in the UK, outlining her fears regarding their linguistic, cultural and religious losses. The couple's concern for their children's future was palpable throughout the interview, forming the central feature of the discussion.

The close alignment between effective masculinity and effective fatherhood and productivity was evident in both Sidi and Ahmed's representations of their respective lives, while it might be possible to describe Abu Omar's situation as that of a 'weakened', 'displaced' and 'dislocated' man, father and worker. With reference to his productivity, Abu Omar moved to sit with the female interviewer to present her with a selection of letters from various UK-based companies, thanking him for the completion of satisfactory contracts. However, because Abu Omar was not eligible to be granted permission to work due to his immigration status, he was unable to be paid for his work. Despite this legal impediment, or perhaps precisely because of this, it appeared particularly important for him to stress his productivity, even if it was 'voluntary' or 'unpaid', both in front of other Muslim men, and in front of the female interviewer. In this sense, the act of working, rather than the act of being paid or being 'the breadwinner' was associated with 'being' per se, and of wanting to regain his position as an active participant and actor both in society and his own family. This short example indicates one way in which an individual's legal status and the period they have lived in the UK may influence their experiences of living and working in the UK and of being fathers and husbands in this reality.

Providing an additional perspective on experiences of masculinity in the UK, interactions with the opposite sex were a key feature discussed by the unmarried men in the group. Khalil, a Palestinian refugee who arrived in the UK four years ago, switched to Arabic before reflecting that although he may be able to establish a transient relationship in Britain, he is unable to become a potential boyfriend or husband due to his uncertain legal status. Indeed, his status would in essence dictate the dynamics of any relationship he might consider establishing, since, at the time of writing, asylum-seekers and refugees without indefinite leave to remain in the UK are required to request permission from the Home Office if they wish to marry.[10] In this case, the stability of any relationship is intimately related to achieving legal stability through being recognized as a refugee.

On the other hand, Razak, a young Afghan man, shyly admitted that he only has one female friend, and that he finds it difficult to speak with girls/ women, including with the female author of this piece, while Um Omar and

Abu Omar quite proudly commented upon their sons' popularity with girls. They accepted that, while in Syria they would not have 'gone out' with girls, they most probably would see girls socially 'here', and that they thought this was 'alright'.

A further element of change vis-à-vis gender relations or contact with the opposite sex was spontaneously expressed by Salem, a single male Kurdish refugee, who outlined how his ideas about gender roles and identities had changed since arriving in the UK almost a decade ago. Salem claimed that, while he had initially found it 'extra-ordinary' that women should have 'such a high position' in British society, today he would describe this situation as 'normal', and as an expression of 'equality'. This particular choice of words, alongside the unprompted discussion of this issue with the female interviewer, is worth brief reflection: are Salem's words an expression of his personal views or have they transcended his personal opinions and rather become part of the discursive space shaped by national and international politics? Given that women's rights and the position of women in Muslim societies have become essential symbols justifying military intervention under the auspices of the 'War on Terror' (Rutter 2004), we may ask to what extent we could interpret Salem's words as an act of striving to belong to his 'new' country, to indicate to the listener that he shares the same views as those held by his neighbours and colleagues. In this way, Salem is both an observer (or spectator) of his host society, and an active participant who projects a particular image of himself to the interviewer.

Asked specifically whether they thought that there was any difference between male and female refugees/asylum-seekers' experiences of living in the UK, the participants' responses were divided. On the one hand, Salem suggested that female asylum-seekers, perceived as weaker and less threatening than men, would find it easier to negotiate the system, and to ask for, and obtain, help. He also assumed that women were more readily accepted as refugees, with the decision being related to the British government's desire to send the women's country of origin a 'clear indication' regarding un/acceptable ways of treating women. While he also indicated that women have specific responsibilities (e.g. as mothers), neither he nor Khalil could think of any gender-specific difficulties experienced by female refugees. With regards to a perceived commonality of experience, both Um Omar and Razak claimed that male and female refugees/asylum-seekers experience asylum in the UK 'in the same way', claiming that there are 'no differences'.

Concerning Um Omar's description of male and female refugees' experiences as 'the same', the male interviewer suggested that in Syria Um Omar would have been particularly aware of the different status and experiences of men and women. YMQ would therefore have expected her to identify similar differences in the UK. It would have been insightful to speak with Um Omar in a female-only environment, to establish if she might have revealed an alternative response to this question under those circumstances. Given the candour with which she discussed other issues, straightforwardly

310   *Elena Fiddian-Qasmiyeh and Yousif M. Qasmiyeh*

contradicting her husband on several occasions, it is unclear how a female-only interview would have affected her representation of herself and her experiences in the UK.

Only Farhana, however, stressed that many female asylum-seekers, especially single women, find it particularly difficult to live in the UK, often being subjected to different forms of sexual and gender-based violence in detention and accommodation centres. She explained that her awareness of this situation arose from having lived with women who were raped in such circumstances, and from her role as a mediator in women's support groups. Her long-standing involvement in women's groups in her place of origin clearly impacted upon her interpretations, concerns and modes of involvement in relation to women's experiences as asylum-seekers in the UK, differentiating her approach from that of the other participants.

Concluding Remarks

Both the parents and the children (in particular Razak) interviewed as part of this study have shed a light on the ambivalence which may characterize Muslim asylum-seekers' perceptions and relationships both within and outside of their households. The absence of particular family structures and externally-provided cultural and religious reference-points surfaced as central concerns for interviewees facing a series of challenges in their immediate and broader hosting environments. As a result, this article directly contributes to studies pertaining to the experiences of Muslim asylum-seekers in the UK, and provides the basis for a comparative study focusing on family structures, and the transmission and representations of Islam in different European hosting countries.

More specifically, this brief analysis has aimed to complement research conducted by a range of institutions including Amnesty International, the Islamic Human Rights Commission and the Refugee Council, on the impacts of the contemporary global in/security context on Muslim asylum-seekers and refugees in the UK. In this environment, religion has increasingly become a tool used by the media and politicians as a common denominator underlying new policies and the trans/formation of public opinion. Simultaneously, Muslim asylum-seekers and refugees' lives, whether practising or not, are marked by physical and psychological alienation from both their country of origin (due to their request for political asylum) and the country which they hope will offer them protection (because of the impediments they face upon and following their arrival). This alienation is not only embodied in the specificities of their asylum journey, but also in the current political setting that incriminates and forcibly categorizes them as a threat to national security.

As indicated in the introduction to this paper, upon their arrival in the UK Muslim asylum-seekers from the Middle East region find themselves assigned to three overlapping minority groupings with respect to their uncertain legal status, their religious identification, and their exclusion from established Muslim communities in the UK. Our interviews thus suggest that the popular usage of the label 'Muslim' has overshadowed not only differences and tensions between Muslim asylum-seekers/refugees and more established Muslim British citizens (a finding supported by Atfield *et al.* 2007: 48), but also the complex politicization of individuals' voluntary or imposed identification as 'Muslim'. One proposal which thus emerges from our research is a need for a greater degree of engagement from the Muslim community in Britain to incorporate Muslim asylum-seekers and refugees into the social and political realm irrespective of their ethnic or national backgrounds.

Contrary to assumptions that religious practice intensifies in order to fill a 'void', we argue that publicly recognizing one's religious beliefs will ultimately be directly influenced by internal and external factors alike. In the cases explored above, interviewees' increased religious engagement could be understood as resulting from their legal and political disengagement and marginalization from their broader host-environment. Conversely, an explicit distancing from Islamic identity and practice could be perceived either as a result of personal preferences or as part of a discursive mechanism designed to address and convince a particular listener or interviewer in line with the national and international realities which frame the topic under consideration (also see Fiddian-Qasmiyeh 2009). In this, and other ways, Muslim asylum-seekers and refugees' experiences in the UK embody the complexities and particularities of the encounter between national and macro-politics.

1. In this respect, it is important to critique the notion that group participatory research may be a useful means of discussing sensitive topics, as proposed by Chambers (1992) and Mosse (1994). It is essential to differentiate between sensitive topics as relating to concepts of modesty and embarrassment, and issues which may enter the realm of the socially unacceptable/dangerous. In this research project, defining potential participants as 'Muslim refugees' appeared to be a sensitive and politicised issue which created scepticism for participating in the project in general, and even more so in a group-setting.

2. Bennett *et al.* (2007) and Home Office (2008, 2009a, 2009b, 2009c and 2009d). In comparison, 84,130 applications were made in 2002, dropping to 25,710 by 2005, and further to 23,610 a year later. Between 2002 and 2007, between 13 per cent and 17 per cent of applicants were recognized as refugees and granted asylum and 9–11 per cent were offered some other sort of protection (including on humanitarian grounds) (Bennett *et al.* 2007).

3. According to Naqshbandi, approximately 1,300 (96 per cent) of masjids in the UK are Sunni and 65 Shi'a (2 per cent). Of the former, the vast majority are 'Asian-run' masjids (Deobandi, Bareilli and Maudoodi-influenced in their majority) while 'approximately 12 are very large institutions with very substantial numbers of Arab-speaking worshippers' (2006).

4. Laws pertaining to asylum-seekers and refugees in the UK are frequently changed. At the time of writing (April 2010), an asylum-seeker whose initial application for asylum has not been processed within 12 months may apply for a work

312   *Elena Fiddian-Qasmiyeh and Yousif M. Qasmiyeh*

permit while awaiting a decision, though the granting of this is discretionary and may equally take some time. If, after this period, the individual's application is refused, they are no longer legally allowed to work in the UK unless their appeal is accepted.

5. Regarding the different dynamics in individual and group interviews, see Michell (1999), Morgan and Krueger (1993), and Stewart and Shamdasani (1990).

6. In an Islamic context, the term 'not religious' is usually interpreted as meaning that a Muslim does not practice in a stringent manner, but still considers him/ herself to be a believer.

7. The teenagers (aged 14 and 16) were introduced to us by their parents, who were both present throughout the interview. We explained the aims of the project, answered their questions, and obtained their informed consent, in addition to that of their parents. Hussein and Mustafa appeared fully relaxed in our presence, asked us several insightful questions about the project, and commented on each other's answers. Regarding some methodological and ethical issues surrounding interviewing youth in a participatory fashion, see Armstrong *et al.* (2004), Boyden (2000), Grover (2004) and Punch (2002).

8. Refugees continue to receive their allowance at the post office until they receive their Status Documents from the Home Office, at which point they are allocated a Job Seeker's Allowance unless they are already employed.

9. The notion of culture as a tool therefore arose in two of our interviews: the teenage boys respectively referred to Arabic music as a 'sample' to be used in a rap song, and of finding it 'difficult to decide what culture to use' when, where and with whom.

10. Whilst a highly controversial practice which has led to the Home Office being taken to the High Court, asylum-seekers and refugees who do not have indefinite leave to remain in the UK, *and who do not belong to the Church of England* (hence the charge that this practice is highly discriminatory), are required to apply to the Home Office for a Certificate of Approval, allowing them to have a religious or civil marriage. See the Home Office website for further information (www.home-office.gov.uk). Following a High Court ruling, as of April 2009 the Home Office no longer charges for the application for a Certificate for Approval.

AMNESTY INTERNATIONAL (2006) *United Kingdom. Human Rights: A Broken Promise.* Document no. EUR 45/004/2006.

ARMSTRONG, M., BOYDEN, J., GALAPPATTI, A. and **HART, J.** (2004) *Piloting Methods for the Evaluation of Psychosocial Programme Impact in Eastern Sri Lanka.* Final Report for USAID. March 2004.

ATFIELD, G., BRAHMBHATT, K. and **O'TOOLE, T.** (2007) *Refugees' Experiences of Integration.* Refugee Council and University of Birmingham.

BENNETT, K., HEATH, T. and **JEFFRIES, R.** (2007) *Asylum Statistics. United Kingdom 2006.* London: Home Office Statistical Bulletin.

BOAL, A. (1992) *Games for Actors and Non-Actors.* Translated by A. Jackson. London: Routledge.

BOYDEN, J. (2000) 'Conducting Research with War-Affected and Displaced Children: Ethics and Methods'. *Cultural Survival Quarterly,* Summer 2000: 70–72.

CHAMBERS, R. (1992) *Rural Appraisal: Rapid, Relaxed and Participatory.* IDS Discussion Paper 311. Brighton: Institute of Development Studies.

CHATTY, D. (2010) 'Introduction'. In Chatty, D. (ed.) *Deterritorialised Youth: Sahrawi and Afghan Refugees at the Margins of the Middle East.* Oxford: Berghahn Books, pp. 1–36.

CRISP, J. (1999) *Policy Challenges of the New Diasporas: Migrant Networks and their Impact on Asylum Flows and Regimes*, UNHCR Working Paper WPTC-99-05. Geneva: UNHCR.

EICKELMAN, D. (2001) *The Middle East and Central Asia: An Anthropological Approach* 4th edn. Englewoods Cliffs, NJ: Prentice Hall.

ESCOBAR, A. (2001) 'Culture Sits in Places: Reflections on Globalism and Subaltern Strategies of Localization'. *Political Geography* **20**(2): 139–174.

FIDDIAN-QASMIYEH, E. (2009) 'Gender, Islam and the Sahrawi Politics of Survival', Doctoral Thesis submitted to the Department of International Development, University of Oxford.

FINNEY, N. (2005) *Key Issues: Public Opinion on Asylum and Refugee Issues*, Information Centre about Asylum and Refugees (UK).

GRIFFITHS, D. J. (2000) 'Fragmentation and Consolidation: the Contrasting Cases of Somali and Kurdish Refugees in London'. *Journal of Refugee Studies* **13**(3): 281–302.

GROVER, S. (2004) 'Why Won't They Listen to Us? On Giving Power and Voice to Children Participating in Social Research'. *Childhood* **11**(1): 81–93.

GUPTA, A. and **FERGUSON, J.** (2002) 'Beyond "Culture": Space, Identity, and the Politics of Difference'. In Inda, J. Z. and Rosaldo, R. (eds) *The Anthropology of Globalization: A Reader.* Oxford: Blackwell Publishing.

HOME OFFICE (2006) 'How many people have been returned to Palestine since January 2004 and by what route were the majority of these people returned?' Information released under the Freedom of Information Act. Accessed at http://www.homeoffice.gov.uk/about-us/freedom-of-information/released-information/foi-archive-immigration/1216-returns-to-palestine?view=Binary on 20/08/2008.

HOME OFFICE (2008) *Asylum Statistics. United Kingdom 2007.* London: Home Office Statistical Bulletin.

HOME OFFICE (2009a) *Control of Immigration: quarterly statistical summary, United Kingdom. January–March 2009. First Quarter 2009*, Supplementary statistical Excel tables available online from http://rds.homeoffice.gov.uk/rds/immigration-asylum-stats.html.

HOME OFFICE (2009b) *Control of Immigration: quarterly statistical summary, United Kingdom. April–June 2009. Second Quarter 2009*, Supplementary statistical Excel tables available online from http://rds.homeoffice.gov.uk/rds/immigration-asylum-stats.html.

HOME OFFICE (2009c) *Control of Immigration: quarterly statistical summary, United Kingdom. July–September 2009. Third Quarter 2009*, Supplementary statistical Excel tables available online from http://rds.homeoffice.gov.uk/rds/immigration-asylum-stats.html.

HOME OFFICE (2009d) *Control of Immigration: quarterly statistical summary, United Kingdom. October–December 2009. Fourth Quarter 2009*, Supplementary statistical Excel tables available online from http://rds.homeoffice.gov.uk/rds/immigration-asylum-stats.html.

ISLAMIC HUMAN RIGHTS COMMISSION and **ANSARI, F.** (2006) *British Anti-Terrorism: A Modern Day Witch-hunt.* London: Islamic Human Rights Commission.

KOSER, K. and **PINKERTON, C.** (2002) *The Social Networks of Asylum Seekers and the Dissemination of Information about Countries of Asylum.* London: Home Office, Accessed at http://rds.homeoffice.gov.uk/rds/pdfs2/socialnetwork.pdf on 18 May 2010.

LEWIS, M. (2005) *Asylum: Understanding Public Attitudes.* London: Institute for Public Policy Research.

LOW, S. M. and **LAWRENCE-ZUNIGA, D.** (2003) 'Locating Culture'. In Low, S. M. and Lawrence-Zuniga, D. (eds) *The Anthropology of Space and Place: Locating Culture.* Oxford: Blackwell Publishing, pp. 1–48.

MICHELL, L. (1999) 'Combining Focus Groups and Interviews: Telling How it Is; Telling How it Feels'. In Barbour, R. S. and Kitzinger, J. (eds) *Developing Focus Group Research: Politics, Theory and Rractice.* London: Sage, pp. 36–46.

314   *Elena Fiddian-Qasmiyeh and Yousif M. Qasmiyeh*

MOGHADAM, V. M. (1998) *Women, Work, and Economic Reform in the Middle East and North Africa*. Boulder, CO/London: Lynne Rienner Publishers.

MORGAN, D. L. and **KRUEGER, R. A.** (1993) 'When to Use Focus Groups and Why'. In Morgan, D. L. (ed.) *Successful Focus Groups: Advancing the State of the Art*. London: Sage, pp. 1–19.

MOSSE, D. (1994) 'Authority, Gender and Knowledge: Theoretical Reflections on the Practice of Participatory Rural Appraisal'. *Development and Change* **25**(3): 497–526.

NAQSHBANDI, M. (2006) *Islam and Muslims in Britain: a Guide for Non-Muslims*. Available at http://www.muslimsinbritain.org/guide/guide.html.

ONS (OFFICE FOR NATIONAL STATISTICS) (2004) 'Focus on Religion: Ethnicity'. Accessed at http://www.statistics.gov.uk/CCI/nugget.asp?ID=957&Pos=&ColRank=2& Rank=224 on 20 May 2010.

PUNCH, S. (2002) 'Research with Children: The Same or Different from Research with Adults?' *Childhood* **9**(3): 321–341.

RUDIGER, A. (2007) *Prisoners of Terrorism? The Impact of Anti-terrorism Measures on Refugees and Asylum Seekers in Britain*, Refugee Council Research Report (UK).

RUTTER, J. (2004) '"Saving" Women in Algeria and Afghanistan: (neo)Colonialism, Liberation and the Veil'. *Eruditio Online* **24**, Spring 2004. Accessed at http://www.duke.edu/web/eruditio/rutter.html on 24 March 2006.

SCHUTZMANN, M. and **COHEN-CRUZ, J.** (1994) 'Introduction'. In Schutzmann, M. and Cohen-Cruz, J. (eds) *Playing Boal: Theatre, Therapy, Activism*. London: Routledge, pp. 1–17.

STEWART, D. W. and **SHAMDASANI, P. N.** (1990) *Focus Groups: Theory and Practice*. Newbury Park, CA: Sage.

TURNER, S. (1999) *Angry Young Men in Camps: Gender, Age and Class Relations among Burundian Refugees in Tanzania*, New Issues in Refugee Research Working Paper no. 9.

[17]

Immigrant Religion in the U.S. and Western Europe: Bridge or Barrier to Inclusion?

Nancy Foner
Hunter College and Graduate Center of the City University of New York

Richard Alba
The University at Albany, State University of New York

This article analyzes why immigrant religion is viewed as a problematic area in Western Europe in contrast to the United States, where it is seen as facilitating the adaptation process. The difference, it is argued, is anchored in whether or not religion can play a major role for immigrants and the second generation as a bridge to inclusion in the new society. Three factors are critical: the religious backgrounds of immigrants in Western Europe and the United States; the religiosity of the native population; and historically rooted relations and arrangements between the state and religious groups.

In the wake of the massive immigration of the past few decades, a growing social science literature has emerged to chart the experiences and impact of America's latest wave of newcomers and – across the Atlantic – of those in Europe as well. In the United States, the study of religion among the latest newcomers has generally taken a backseat to other topics in the immigration field. Issues pertaining to economic and labor market incorporation, residential patterns, education, social mobility and the trajectories of the second generation, race and ethnicity, transnational ties, and citizenship and political incorporation have received much more attention than religion.

This is, perhaps, not surprising. Many social science researchers rely on US Census data and other surveys conducted by government agencies, which are not allowed to ask questions on religion. But it is more than this. Religion has often been overlooked because it is not seen as a problematic area for immigrants in the contemporary United States. Indeed, those studies that do focus on religion among today's immigrants overwhelmingly emphasize its positive role in smoothing and facilitating the adaptation process.

The contrast with studies of immigrants in Western Europe could not be more striking. There, religion is at the top of the scholarly agenda, with the extensive literature overwhelmingly concerned with the Islamic presence.

DOI: 10.1111/j.1747-7379.2008.00128.x

Indeed, one estimate has it that there are "possibly a few thousand publications or more" on Islam and Muslims in Western Europe (Buijs and Rath, 2006:3). Moreover, unlike the US literature, social science studies of religion and immigrants in Western Europe, much like popular discourse on the subject, tend to stress the problems and conflict engendered by immigrants' religion and the difficulties that Islam poses for integration. In contrast to the view in the United States, religion is seen in Europe as the marker of a fundamental social divide.

In this article, we ask why the views of immigrant religion are so different on the two sides of the Atlantic and how they correspond with on-the-ground social realities. We argue that the difference is anchored in whether or not religion as belief system, institution, and community can play a major role for immigrants and the second generation as a bridge to inclusion in the new society. This question has a different answer in the two settings for three critical reasons. The religious backgrounds of immigrants in Western Europe and the United States are different, mostly Christian in the United States as compared to Western Europe, where a large proportion are Muslim. Western European populations, moreover, have much more trouble recognizing claims based on religion because they are more secular than the religiously involved United States. Furthermore, historically rooted relations and arrangements between the state and religious groups in Europe have led to greater difficulties in incorporating and accepting new religions than is the case in the United States.

What follows develops these ideas, first laying out the different views of immigrant religion in social science studies on the two sides of the Atlantic and then seeking to account for them. If the bulk of the article shows a far more favorable environment for immigrant religion in the United States than Western Europe, the concluding remarks consider, on the one hand, the threats in the United States to the generally positive picture and, on the other hand, government efforts at accommodating Islam in Western Europe. Much of what we say applies to Western European countries generally, but we mainly focus on four major receiving countries that represent different institutional approaches to religion: France, Germany, Britain, and the Netherlands.

IMMIGRANT RELIGION IN THE US: A PARADIGM OF THE POSITIVE ROLE OF RELIGION

What stands out in the American social science literature is the positive gloss on religion's role among today's newcomers, with studies often emphasizing how religion promotes the incorporation of newcomers into their new society and helps them, in a variety of ways, to cope and adapt. Participation in almost any sort of religion is depicted as a pathway into the mainstream, which, at least in comparison to other economically advanced societies, is itself characterized by an unusually high level of religious belief and behavior (the overall consistency of Americans' religious involvement and level of belief over the course of the twentieth century is described by Fischer and Hout, 2006: ch. 8). In addition, the literature stresses the functionality of religion in meeting the social needs of immigrants; to borrow Charles Hirschman's formula, these are first and foremost the three R's: refuge, respectability, and resources (2004:1228).

Refuge, Respectability, and Resources

For immigrants who are separated from their homeland and from many relatives, religious membership offers a refuge in the sense that it creates a sense of belonging and participation in the face of loss and the strains of adjustment (Hirschman, 2004:1228). Because religious organizations provide an all-encompassing system of belief, as well as a community where immigrants gather and form networks of mutual support with co-ethnics, they provide a psychological ballast helping to ameliorate the traumas of early settlement and frequent encounter with discrimination. Churches and temples offer opportunities for fellowship and friendship, often in a familiar cultural environment, and are a source of solace and shelter from the stresses, setbacks, and difficulties of coming to terms with life in a new country (Ebaugh and Chafetz, 2000:74; Min, 2001; Portes and Rumbaut, 2006:301, 329).

It is frequently noted that religious groups provide an alternative source of respectability for newcomers, something that is particularly important for those who feel they are denied social recognition in the United States or have even suffered downward occupational mobility as a result of migration. Being a good Christian, Muslim, or Buddhist brings respect within the religious (and often wider ethnic) community. Within religious groups, there are typically opportunities for leadership and service that bring prestige.

Sociologists put particular emphasis on the resources that come with religious affiliation and membership. As Hirschman notes, almost all studies of contemporary immigrant churches and temples in the United States describe the multiple services they provide to newcomers, from information about jobs, housing, and business opportunities to classes in English and seminars on various practical topics. Thus, the financial manager of a Buddhist temple catering to the Lao community in Louisiana, who is also a foreman at a firm, refers temple members for jobs; another member of the temple community provides assistance for housing through her position as a loan officer in a local bank (Hirschman, 2004:1225). Pyong Gap Min refers to Korean Christian churches as the most important social service agencies in the New York Korean community. Among the services they offer are immigration orientation, job referral, business information, Korean language and after-school programs for children, educational counseling, "filial" trips for elders, and even marriage counseling (2001:186; *see also* Foley and Hoge, 2007 on immigrant religious communities in the Washington, DC area and Zhou and Bankston, 1998 on Buddhist temples and Catholic churches among Vietnamese in New Orleans).

Constructing Identity

Many studies also stress that religious congregations reinforce and at times reshape immigrants' ethnic identity – and this is treated as a positive development. Religion has been analyzed as a socially acceptable form through which U.S. immigrants can articulate, reformulate, and transmit their ethnic culture and identities. Indeed, a common argument since Herberg's famous synthesis in the mid-1950s is that because immigrants learn that Americans are more accepting of religious than ethnic diversity, they use religion as a socially tolerated means to construct their own culture and identity (Herberg, 1960; Karpathakis, 2001:390).

Much has been written about the way immigrants use religious institutions to reproduce and reassert important aspects of their home-country cultures – for example, incorporating ethnic practices in religious ceremonies. In their churches and temples, immigrants "can worship in their own languages, enjoy the rituals, music, and festivals of their native lands, share stories from their homeland, and pass on their religious and cultural heritage to the next generation" (Ebaugh and Chafetz, 2000:141). To be sure, there are many "reinventions of tradition" in the American setting as religious practices and beliefs inevitably undergo changes. Yet as immigrants worship with co-ethnics in settings with many tangible reminders and expressions of home-country cultures, so a sense of ethnic identity is nurtured and strengthened.

The intertwining of religion and ethnic identity often assists incorporation into American society. According to a recent study of immigrant religious communities in the Washington, DC area, those that emphasized ethnic identity – sponsoring events to celebrate their own ethnic or national heritage, for example, or holding classes in the home language – were more likely to participate in local affairs and social service or community development projects in the United States (Foley and Hoge, 2007:188–189). The authors argue that religious leaders' appeals to ethnic identity to promote action on behalf of the larger ethnic community – on behalf of homeland causes or in defense of immigrant rights in the US – "paradoxically . . . integrate immigrants more deeply into American civic and political culture even as they preserve and reinforce their sense of difference" (Foley and Hoge, 2007:214).

This intertwining is also valuable to immigrants because it can provide an ethnic socialization for their children, the second generation, who celebrate home-country holidays in religious congregations, for example, and develop networks of ethnic peers there. Ethnic language classes in many churches – in the New York area more than a hundred Korean-language schools are run by Korean churches that teach Korean language, history, and culture (Min, 2001:187) – may also play a role.

Upward Mobility and Civic Skills

There are two additional positive aspects of religion for immigrants and their children that appear in the US social science literature. For one thing, religious organizations can facilitate the upward mobility of the second generation. Partly this is a matter of formal educational training that takes place in immigrant churches, such as English-language or SAT classes found in some congregations. Many congregations also sponsor classes that inculcate homeland cultural traditions and language skills. From a mobility perspective, as David Lopez (forthcoming) has argued, they encourage and reinforce habits of study. Moreover, they do so in a setting that is controlled within the ethnic community – rather than provided by benevolent outsiders – thereby reinforcing a sense of identity and cultural pride and perhaps also adding to their effectiveness.

Min Zhou and Carl Bankston (1998) stress that involvement in ethnic religious congregations helps young people move ahead in another way. In their study of Vietnamese immigrants in New Orleans, they argue that church attendance and participation in church-sponsored activities protected young people from neighborhood gangs and "immoral" influences of American culture; it strengthened their integration into the ethnic community and reinforced parental aspirations for educational achievement.

And then there is the role of immigrant religious groups as a training ground for entry into the wider society: building civic skills and encouraging active civic involvement. Indeed, according to Diana Eck, religion provides many immigrants with "one of their first training grounds in participatory democracy" as they become involved in boards of directors, elections, member-ship lists, and accountability in temple associations and Islamic societies, ranging from the American Buddhist Congress, to the American Muslim Council, to the Federation of Zoroastrians in North America. Religious communities, she maintains, are

> precisely the places where new immigrants gain their feet and practice the arts of in-ternal democracy. Long before they stand for election to the school board, they will stand for election in the governing body of the Hindu temple. Long before they enter the fray of local and state politics, they argue fiercely about their internal Sikh, Hindu, and Muslim politics. (Eck, 2001:336)

Foley and Hoge (2007) elaborate on the civic-skill-building aspects in their Washington, DC study which, tellingly, they subtitle "How Faith Communities Form Our Newest Citizens." Among the ways that the immi-grant churches, mosques, and temples in their study provided training and motivation for civic engagement were through opportunities to develop and hone skills in public speaking, plan events, organize and conduct meetings, and engage in coalition-building. The religious groups often sponsored citizenship classes and programs to register people to vote and organized efforts to lobby elected officials. And many mosques and churches encouraged volun-teer services to the larger community, beyond their own religious group, from volunteering at senior citizen centers to serving food in soup kitchens.

Becoming American through Religion

A bottom-line conclusion in the social science literature is that religion helps to turn immigrants into Americans and gives them and their children a sense of belonging or membership in the United States. Many scholars stress that religion provides a way for immigrants to become accepted in the United States – or, to put it another way, religious institutions are places where immigrants can formulate claims for inclusion in American society (Portes and Rumbaut, 2006:300; Alba, Roboteau and DeWind, forthcoming). This argument dates back to what are now regarded as classic historical studies of immigrant religious life, primary among them Will Herberg's *Protestant, Catholic, Jew.* Herberg asserted that it was "largely in and through . . . religion that he [the immigrant], or rather his children and grandchildren, found an identifiable place in American life" (1960:27–28).

Herberg was writing about the assimilation into the American main-stream of Jews and Catholics from eastern and southern Europe in the years after World War II; this was a period when Catholicism and Judaism were becoming American religions and, at the same time, America was becoming a "Judeo-Christian" nation (Casanova and Zolberg, 2002). Today, at the beginning of the twenty-first century, in the midst of a massive immigration which is bringing new diversity to America's religious landscape, Herberg's themes are still seen as having relevance. For example, in Charles Hirschman's reflections on religion's role among contemporary immigrants, he explicitly draws on Herberg's thesis, arguing that a significant share of today's immigrants "become American" through participating in religious and community activities of churches and temples (2004:1207; *see also* Portes and Rumbaut, 2006).

To be sure, one way this Americanization happens is by conversion to Christianity because of its charter status in American society. For instance, the proportion of Christians among Asian immigrants to the United States is generally much higher than is the case in their countries of origin. To some extent, this may be the result of selective immigration by those who were already Christian in the homeland. But there can be little doubt that, for other immigrants, the move to America involves conversion to Christianity. This phenomenon in exemplified by the Taiwanese. Whereas in Taiwan some 2 percent of the population is Christian, this is true for a quarter to a third of the Taiwanese population in the United States. Carolyn Chen (2006) argues that among the evangelical Christians she studied in California, Christianity mediated their acculturation to American society by repackaging some Taiwanese values in Christian trappings; at the same time, it facilitated and reinforced assimilation to middle-class American family practices such as recognizing children's autonomy and more "democratic" parent-child relationships.

Nevertheless, it is obvious that many immigrants retain their non-Christian religious attachments, and consequently that the religious diversity of the United States is growing rapidly as a result of immigration. Yet as far as anyone can tell, the immigrant religions that are relatively new to the United States, such as Buddhism and Sikhism, have many of the same integrative effects as the Christian denominations do. In their case, asserting a religious identity is seen as an acceptable way to be different and American at the same time (Levitt, 2007). The main title of Prema Kurien's much-cited article "Becoming American by Becoming Hindu," captures this "Americanizing" impact of immigrants' engagement in religion. Kurien argues that emphasizing Hinduism, albeit a recast and reformulated Hinduism, has helped Indian immigrants fit into American society and claim "a position for themselves at the American multicultural table" (1998:37).

A related theme in the literature is the "Americanization" of religious institutions and practices that immigrants bring with them to the United

States. Frequently mentioned is the trend toward developing congregational forms, that is, local religious communities comprised of people who come together voluntarily along the lines of a reformed Protestant congregation and in which, among other things, governance is in the hands of the local body and religious leaders are selected by the local organization (Warner and Wittner, 1998; Ebaugh and Chafetz, 2000; Fischer and Hout, 2006; for a critique of the "congregational" argument *see* Foley and Hoge, 2007). In line with a change to congregationalism, to give one example, a Buddhist monk may assume a more specialized and professional role closer to that of a minister. In addition, many studies point to the way immigrant religious groups adopt American forms and practices – for instance, using the English language, holding weekly services, or having a sermon as the focal point of the service (Hirschman, 2004:1215–1216; *see also* George, 1998; Hepner, 1998). Partly this may happen because immigrants (or their religious leaders) are consciously attempting to become more "American." Also the sheer exigencies and constraints of everyday life, including immigrants' work schedules and the availability of buildings for meetings, are frequently at work.

Whether the integrative role of religion for contemporary immigrant groups represents a long-standing American pattern or is the fruit of the resolution of religious conflicts during preceding eras of immigration is a legitimate question. Certainly, the mainstream of American society had a decidedly Christian, even Protestant, character for much of the country's history. Anti-Catholicism and anti-Semitism are threaded through the fabric of that history, and Catholics felt forced to establish their own school system in the middle of the nineteenth century in order to protect their children from the overtly Protestant teaching in the state-supported, or public, school system. The full acceptance of Catholicism and Judaism as American religions was not accomplished until the middle of the twentieth century – around the time that Herberg wrote his famous synthesis. Yet, what was not in doubt was the ability of these previously minority religions to form their own institutions, without much interference from the outside society. That Catholics could erect a separate school system, and eventually a panoply of organizations to channel their social and professional lives within a religiously circumscribed subsociety, was not in question. Nor was Catholicism in this respect at a disadvantage compared to Protestant churches, for, aside from temporary holdovers from the established churches of the thirteen colonies, no denomination enjoyed state support. In this sense, we will argue below, there is a distinctively US pattern implicated in the contemporary bridging role of immigrant religion. At the same time, the newer immigrant religions do benefit from an acceptance that is the result of the much more difficult integration of Catholicism and Judaism into the mainstream, which resolved uncertainties over the place of non-post-Reformation Christian religions in the society.

IMMIGRANTS AND RELIGION IN WESTERN EUROPE: A SOCIAL PROBLEM

In Western Europe, religion is generally viewed as the problem, not the solution, for immigrant minorities. The focus of scholarly commentaries on immigrant religion is almost exclusively on Islam. Far from being seen as integrating immigrants and facilitating successful adaptation to European society, Islam is analyzed as a barrier or a challenge to integration and a source of conflict with mainstream institutions and practices. An article entitled "Becoming French (or German, Dutch, or British) by Being Muslim" would be unthinkable. So would a mass-marketed book by an academic, like Diana Eck's *A New Religious America* (2001), that heralds immigrant religion as a public training ground for democracy.

Scholarly writings play out against a backdrop in which the image of Islam in "the dominant European imaginary," as David Theo Goldberg has recently written, is "one of fanaticism, fundamentalism, female suppression, subjugation, and repression" (2006:345–346). Or as Leo Lucassen puts it in his aptly titled book *The Immigrant Threat* (2005:4), discussions about Muslims' alleged failure to integrate have dominated the public debate in Western Europe since the 1990s, and a prevalent view is that the culture of Islam and that of the West are irreconcilable.

Popular attitudes toward Islam have helped to shape the social science literature. Many social scientists have documented actual practices and beliefs among Muslim immigrants and their children, often as a way to counter negative stereotypes and prejudices about these practices and beliefs; others have attempted to explain the animosities and conflicts that have developed; and still others have offered, on the bases of their analyses, policy recommendations for improving relations and reducing strains or, in some cases, preserving what are felt to be basic universal, European, or national values that are seen to be in danger (*e.g.*, Kaltenbach and Tribalat, 2002). Even analyses of the Europeanization of Islam and of positive signs of Muslim integration and accommodation are often placed in the context of prevailing popular views that deny, ignore, or downplay these developments (*e.g.*, Klausen, 2005; Lucassen, 2005; Laurence and Vaisse, 2006). In summing up the state of research on the institutionalization of Islam in Europe, Buijs and Rath (2006:28) note that

"Muslims are often associated with premodern attitudes and practices and this has, to some extent, influenced the research agenda. A lot of attention is dedicated to such themes as gender relations (including headscarves), freedom of speech (including the Rushdie affair, Muslim radicalism and so forth) and the compatibility of Islam and modernity." The titles of just a few recent scholarly books or special journal issues on Islam in Europe give a flavor of the emphasis: *The Islamic Challenge, Mosque Conflicts in European Cities, When Islam and Democracy Meet,* and *Why the French Don't Like Headscarves: Islam, the State, and Public Space.*

A Threat to Values and Integration

At one end of the spectrum are social scientists – a minority, to be sure – who suggest or explicitly argue that Islam is impeding the integration of immigrant minorities and threatening the liberal values of European states (*e.g.,* Kaltenbach and Tribalat, 2002). Their writings are part of a larger public, and politicized, debate on how much tolerance should be allowed in modern European societies for many Muslim practices and beliefs. In the Netherlands, sociologist and journalist Paul Scheffer has argued, in the context of his critique of multiculturalism, that Dutch democracy should not tolerate Muslims' lack of acceptance of the separation of church and state or their denial of the right of the Dutch to criticize religion, including Islam (Scheffer, 2000). Much of the criticism of Muslim practices focuses on those involving the subordination of women that are associated with Muslim immigrants (even if the practices are not always directly related to Islamic law). In Germany, sociologist Necla Kelek documents and condemns the practice of Turkish-Muslim men importing young Turkish girls to Germany as brides. In *The Foreign Bride* (*Die fremde Braut,* 2005), she describes domestic violence and "honor killings" carried out by brothers against women who have besmirched the family's honor; she has campaigned for legislation to raise the age at which brides can be brought to Germany and for tougher sentences for "honor killings." Norwegian anthropologist Unni Wikan's (2002) book-length study *A Generous Betrayal: Politics of Culture in a New Europe* argues that state agencies should uphold universal rights for children and women in the face of oppressive practices found in Muslim communities such as "forced marriages."

In France, where the controversy over the headscarf has assumed enormous symbolic and political importance, several social scientists, Alain Touraine among them, were members of the Stasi Commission that, in 2004, proposed legislation prohibiting visible religious symbols and dress in public schools. In a subsequent publication, Touraine argued that the new law was necessary to confront the rise of religious (that is, Islamic) extremism and violence (Renaut and Touraine, 2005).[1] Political scientist Patrick Weil, also a member of the Commission, explained his support as based on the need to protect Muslim girls who do not wish to wear the headscarf from social pressures from those who feel it is a moral obligation, thereby appealing to the broader French principle of secularization, or *laïcité*, which "rests on its guarantees of state protection against pressure from any religious group" (Weil, 2004).[2]

Discrimination and Prejudice

Another – and more common – theme in the social science literature is the discrimination and restrictions facing Muslims in Western Europe. Indeed, anti-Muslim sentiment has sometimes been characterized as "cultural racism," in which culture or religion are essentialized to the point that they become the functional equivalent of biological racism and groups are seen as inherently inferior on the basis of their culture or religion (*see* Foner, 2005:217–218). Scholars have written that "Muslimophobia is at the heart of contemporary British and European cultural racism" (Modood, 2005:37); of "European Muslimania" as a "third major artery in the historical articulation of racial eurology" (Goldberg, 2006:362); and of racialized perceptions of Islam and the racial dimensions of Islam (Cesari, 2004:32, 24).[3]

Quite apart from notions of cultural racism, many accounts discuss negative stereotypes of Islam, institutionalized discrimination, and the difficulties of practicing Islam in publicly visible ways. There are analyses of the bans on wearing the Islamic headscarf, for example, policies curtailing ritual slaughter, administrative barriers to building new mosques and enlarging old ones, and the reluctance of European governments to fund Islamic schools while, at the same time, supporting large numbers of Protestant, Catholic, and Jewish schools.

There is also considerable evidence of socioeconomic disadvantage and even of discrimination endured by Muslims, including those of the second generation who have grown up in European societies. To be sure, the immigrants

---

[1]Renaut, it should be noted, argues that the law sets a dangerous precedent.

[2]Laurence and Vaisse (2006:169) call Weil's reasoning – that the law is intended "to defend individual schoolgirls' religious freedom by allowing them the freedom *not* to believe" – a "logical somersault."

[3]A recent report by the European Monitoring Center on Racism and Xenophobia discusses the many manifestations of what it terms Islamophobia in Europe (EUMC, 2006).

themselves, coming chiefly from Africa, the Near East, and South Asia, typically brought low levels of human capital and entered European labor markets
on their lowest rungs. Simply on the grounds of social-class origins, the second
generation could be expected to face significant disadvantage in European
societies, and some studies of educational attainment indicate that second-
generation disadvantage is little more than this (*e.g.*, the studies in Vallet and
Caille, 1995; Heath, forthcoming). However, there are reasonable doubts whether
a statistical calibration that uses the education or occupations of immigrant
parents to locate similarly situated European native families for comparison is a
meaningful way of controlling for social-class origins: the immigrant parents
usually attained at least the average human capital in their countries of origin,
where the educational distributions are much lower than in advanced economies; comparing their children to the children of native European families with
the lowest levels of human capital in European societies thus sets the bar rather
low for second-generation achievements, especially since the worst-off European native families usually suffer a variety of social and personal problems. In
any event, other studies find patterns of inequality that indicate ways that
European educational systems steer the children of immigrants toward less-
valued educational outcomes, as indicated by the concentrations of the 1.5 and
2nd generation in the lowest track of the German system, the *Hauptschulen*
(Alba *et al.*, 1994; Kristen, 2002).

There is even more direct evidence of discrimination with respect to the
labor market. In France, Silberman *et al.* (2007) have found that the children
of immigrants from North Africa, sub-Saharan Africa, and Turkey, the groups
in which Muslims are prevalent, are more likely to be unemployed than are
their native French peers. The differences are only partly explained by different
educational attainments. Moreover, when they are employed, these children of
immigrants are more likely to be in positions below their level of educational
training. They are far more likely than native French to believe they have been
the victims of discrimination by employers, and frequently they perceive this
discrimination to be commonplace rather than exceptional, *i.e.*, happening to
them multiple times. (For an analysis of Belgium and Spain that reaches similar
conclusions, *see* Kalter and Kogan, 2006; on Germany, *see* Seibert and Solga,
2005 but *cf.* Kalter, 2006).

Conflicts

If discussions of conflicts between immigrant religions and mainstream
American institutions rarely appear in the American social science literature,

this is very different in Western Europe. There the struggle of Muslims to practice their religion and build up their institutions has triggered conflicts with long-established residents and institutions. The conflicts, usually over fitting Muslim practices into legal frameworks and various public arenas, are, as Jytte Klausen (2005:108) notes, repeated across Western Europe, with slight variation in themes and emphasis in particular countries despite significant differences in national legal and religious contexts. The conflicts have become major issues in public debates and political campaigns. In this context, it is not surprising that they have come in for study and analysis by social scientists.

Controversies over whether it is permissible to wear Muslim dress, from the headscarf (the prevailing symbol of Islam to Europeans, in David Theo Goldberg's [2006:346] view) to the more severe *jilbab* (a floor-length coat-like dress which is worn with a headscarf that covers the forehead and neck), have spawned numerous articles and commentaries and, most recently, an entire book (Bowen, 2006). There have also been discussions of the conflicts over burial in municipal cemeteries, ritual slaughter, coeducation, arranged marriages, the provision of prayer rooms at work and in educational institutions, and efforts to educate imams in Europe (*see* citations in Buijs and Rath, 2006).

Conflicts around the building of mosques have come in for attention, including a special issue of the *Journal of Ethnic and Migration Studies* on the topic (2005). Throughout Europe, the editor of the issue argues, resistance to mosques is linked to a meta-narrative about Islam, and requests for permits to construct new mosques come up against various arguments to justify refusal, including problems of noise and traffic nuisance (often over the *azan*, the electronically amplified call for prayer), incompatibility with existing zoning rules and urban planning, and nonconformity with security norms (*see* Kepel, 1991; Cesari, 2005:1019; Fetzer and Soper, 2005, Koopmans *et al.*, 2005; Buijs and Rath, 2006:26). Tensions over the establishment of state-funded Muslim schools and teaching Islam in the curricula of state schools have also been the subject for analysis. There have also been discussions of what Buijs and Rath (2006:27) call the "delicate question" of state-sponsored schools to train imams (*also* Klausen, 2005) as well as the theme of tolerance and the right of the long-established native-born to be critical of Islam.

A concern that stands out in the literature on these issues is how nation-state policies and institutional structures in different European countries have shaped the sources, form, and resolution of dilemmas and clashes that have arisen as a result of the growing Muslim presence (*e.g.*, Rath *et al.*, 2001; Fetzer and Soper, 2005; Buijs and Rath, 2006:23). Among the questions explored are why conflicts over the headscarf have led to bans in public places in some countries and not others and why debates over funding and building mosques have taken different turns in various national settings.

Islam as an Oppositional Identity

In contrast to upbeat analyses of religion and ethnic identity in the United States, which highlight the positive aspects of religious identity for integration into the dominant society, in Europe studies on this topic put more stress on how Muslim identities reflect discrimination and may also further reinforce marginalization and separation (Cesari, 2004:24–25). A Muslim identity, and a turn to Islam, are seen as providing a way to claim dignity in the face of the bitterness of exclusion, particularly for the second, European-born generation (*e.g.*, Khosrokhavar, 2005). As an in-between group – not accepted as French, Dutch, or German or as Algerians, Moroccans, or Turks – many members of the second generation come to see themselves as Muslims and identify with "things Muslim" in a search for a sense of belonging (Kramer, 2004).

The process of increased religious consciousness among members of the younger generation, often to a globalized Islam rather than the "family Islam" of their parents, has been termed "re-Islamization" (Laurence and Vaisse, 2006:90). While some scholars argue that an allegiance to Islam has had positive effects, such as helping young people stay away from crime and delinquency (*e.g.*, Didier Lapeyronnie cited in Laurence and Vaisse, 2006:93), there are also concerns about Islam's role in the second generation's "cultural isolationism" and, even more, the possibility that involvement in orthodox or fundamentalist Islam may lead to acts of violence and terrorism. In general, the study of the causes of Islamic radicalism, and its appeal to a segment of the European-born second generation, is, according to Buijs and Rath's survey, still in its infancy "though some important first steps have been made" (*see* Buijs and Rath, 2006:22).

In this sense, it appears that Islam has become an oppositional identity for some second-generation youth in European societies, a way of marking their rejection of the European mainstream, which they perceive as condemning them to positions of inferiority. In contrast to oppositional minority identities in the United States (Fordham and Ogbu, 1986; Portes and Zhou, 1993), one could say that an oppositional identity founded on Islam does not necessarily involve young people in patently self-destructive behaviors, such as disdain for academic success, drug use, and criminal activity (though it may in those rare cases where violent attacks on European citizens and institutions are planned or undertaken). Nevertheless, it also may bring about considerable frustration because of the mainstream rejection of claims based on religious identities, as exemplified by the French law against headscarves, and because of the prejudice and discrimination to which individuals who overtly embrace a Muslim identity may be exposed.

EXPLAINING THE DIFFERENCES

On one level, the reasons for the different emphases in the social science literatures on religion among immigrants in Europe and the United States are straightforward and obvious. If studies of immigrant religion in Europe stress a series of problems and conflicts and U.S. studies present an upbeat view, this is because the studies reflect, and seek to analyze and understand, actual social dynamics. The more basic question is why religion is such a problematic area in Western Europe and why in the United States it has helped – not prevented or made more difficult – immigrant integration. One reason is that in the United States, in contrast to Western Europe, the vast majority of immigrants, like most of the native-born, are Christians. Moreover, Americans are considerably more religious than Western Europeans, and their state institutions and constitutional principles provide a foundation for greater acceptance and integration of non-Christian religions. To put it another way: in Europe, Muslim immigrants confront, on the one hand, majority populations that are mainly secular and therefore suspicious of claims based on religion and its requirements and, on the other, societal institutions and national identities that remain anchored to an important extent in Christianity and do not make equal room for Islam.

Immigrant Religions: Christians vs. Muslims

It is not surprising that immigrant religion is seen in a more positive light in the United States, where most immigrants and their children, perhaps as high as 75 percent, share a religious orientation – Christianity – with the majority of long-established Americans.[4] In Western Europe, by contrast, Muslims have

---

[4]This estimate is from Casanova and Zolberg (2002). We do not have exact figures on the religion of immigrants in the United States because the U.S. Census is not allowed to gather statistics on religion. According to a recent survey by the Pew Forum on Religion and Public Life (2008), 74 percent of immigrant adults in the United States – and 79 percent of U.S.-born adults – are Christian.

become the largest religious minority as a result of postwar inflows; an estimated 12 to 14 million people, nearly all of immigrant background, they constitute a growing share of the population, with the highest proportion found in France, where they represent about 8 percent of the total population, compared to around 6 percent in the Netherlands, 4 percent in Germany, and 3 percent in Britain. In France, more than half of the 4 to 5 million Muslims are of Algerian or Moroccan origin, with sizable numbers of Tunisians, Turks, and Africans; about four-fifths of Germany's 3–3.2 million Muslims have origins in Turkey; three-quarters of the Netherlands' nearly 1 million Muslims are of Turkish and Moroccan origin; and almost three-quarters of Britain's 1.6 million Muslims are of South Asian background (Cesari, 2004:183–184; Buijs and Rath, 2006:7; Eumap, 2007).[5]

Equally significant is that in Western Europe Islam is associated with large immigrant groups whose successful incorporation is viewed by European natives as the most problematic. Western Europe's major Muslim groups are the most problematic immigrant minorities in terms of poverty, unemployment, and education rates – in France, these are Mahgrebins from Algeria and Morocco; in Germany, Turks; in the Netherlands, Turks and Moroccans; and in Britain, Bangladeshis and Pakistanis (Modood *et al.*, 1997; Kalter, 2006; Silberman *et al.*, 2007).

The contrast with the United States is remarkable. Mexicans, who are, by far, the largest immigrant group (nearly a third of all foreign-born) and the most problematic in terms of legal and socioeconomic status, are virtually all Christian, predominantly Catholic. In general, only a tiny proportion of the foreign-born and their children in the United States – no more than 5 percent – are Muslim.[6] There are hardly any Muslim Latinos (under 1 percent), and only 8 percent of adult Asian Americans are Muslim (most South Asian).[7]

---

[5]In Britain, the census included a question on religious affiliation for the first time in 2001, but the figures on France, Germany, and the Netherlands are estimates since religious affiliation is not a question on population censuses there and only place of birth and country of origin give any hint of religious allegiance (Cesari, 2004:9). The Eumap executive summary figures are based on longer background research reports on Muslims in France (Sonia Tebbakh), Germany (Nina Muhe), and the Netherlands (Froukje Demant, Marcel Maussen, and Jan Rath).

[6]This figure is based on the estimate that about two-thirds of the approximately 3 million Muslims in the United States are immigrants or descendants of immigrants (Wuthnow, 2005:57). In 2000, some 56 million U.S. residents were immigrants or the children of immigrants.

[7]These figures are from the 2001 American Religious Identification Survey (Kosmin and Keysar, 2006).

In fact, nearly three out of ten Muslims in the United States are African American (Kosmin and Keysar, 2006:265).[8]

Moreover, it is worth noting that unlike Europe, where Muslims are often stuck in neighborhoods with poor housing conditions and low-paying jobs and stand out for their high levels of unemployment (EUMC, 2006), Muslims in the United States have done rather well. This has not eliminated unease with, even antipathy to, them. Indeed, cases of discrimination and hate crimes against Muslims in the United States have risen since the terrorist attacks of September 11 and the ever present threat of new incidents. But one factor reducing or counteracting negative attitudes to Muslims is their comparatively high socioeconomic status. Muslims in the United States graduate from college at a higher rate than the national average, with a third earning an annual household income of at least $50,000 (Kosmin and Keysar, 2006:265–266). Mosque-goers appear to do even better. According to estimates, the average mosque-goer in the United States is a married man with children who has a bachelor's degree or higher and earns about $74,000 a year (Portes and Rumbaut, 2006:338).

Religious Commitment and Secularization

Whatever immigrants' particular religion, the fact is that religion generally is more accepted in the United States than Western Europe. In the US, to be religious is to be in synch with prevailing mainstream American norms, which put great emphasis on the value of religious observance (Fischer and Hout, 2006). This is not the case in Western Europe, where (with the exception of Ireland) those who are religious are members of a decided minority. A secular mind-set dominates in most Western European countries. Claims based on religion have much less acceptance and legitimacy there – and when the religion is Islam, these claims often lead to public unease, sometimes disdain and even anger, and, not surprisingly, tensions and conflicts (for a recent journalistic account of the reaction to Muslim demands and values in the Netherlands, *see* Buruma, 2006).

Figures from various surveys bring out the transatlantic contrasts in religious commitment. A 2004 Gallup poll found that 44 percent of Americans

---

[8]The total Muslim population in the United States is small, representing an estimated 1 percent of the U.S. population or about three million people (Kosmin and Keysar, 2006:262). A little under a quarter of U.S. Muslims are South Asian; Arabs constitute about 12 percent; Africans, 6 percent; Iranians, 4 percent; and Turks, 2 percent (Cesari, 2004:11).

said they attended a place of worship once a week, while the average figure in Europe, according to the European Social Survey, was only 15 percent – and actually below 15 percent in France, Germany, Britain, and the Netherlands (Ford, 2005a). The differences are striking with regard to reported beliefs. Americans are much more likely than Europeans to say that religion is very important to them – about six in ten Americans compared to around a fifth of Europeans.[9] According to the International Social Survey Programme (ISSP), 63 percent of Americans, compared to a fifth to a quarter of French, Dutch, German, and British, said they know that God really exists and have no doubts about it.[10] Whereas 58 percent of Americans in a Pew Research Center survey agreed that belief in God is a prerequisite to morality, this was true for only a third of the Germans, a quarter of the British, and 13 percent of the French (Pew Research Center, 2003).

Admittedly, Americans, as many observers note, tend to exaggerate their rates of church attendance and the seriousness of their religious beliefs, and a growing number think of themselves as secular; the proportion of Americans expressing no religious preference in the General Social Survey rose to 14 percent at the beginning of the twenty-first century, up from 7 percent in the 1970s (Masci and Smith, 2006). Yet religion's place in the national collective consciousness remains strong – and much stronger than in Europe. Indeed, as José Casanova and Aristide Zolberg (2002) observe, the very tendency of Americans to exaggerate their religiousness, in contrast to the opposite tendency of Europeans to discount and undercount their own persistent religiosity, is itself part of the different and consequential definitions of the situation in both places: "Americans think they are supposed to be religious, while

[9]According to a recent European Values Study that tracks attitudes in 32 European countries, just 21 percent of Europeans said that religion is "very important" to them; a survey by the Pew Forum on Religion and Public Life found that three times as many Americans, 59 percent, called their faith "very important" (Ford, 2005a). In the World Values Survey of the late 1990s, 53 percent of Americans considered religion very important in their lives compared with 16 percent in Britain, 14 percent in France, and 13 percent in Germany (Ford, 2005b). Interestingly, a recent poll conducted in 2006–2007 among Muslim populations in London, Paris, and Berlin showed that strong majorities of Muslims (68 percent in Paris, 85 percent in Berlin, and 88 percent in London) said that religion is an important part of their daily lives (Gallup Organization, 2007).

[10]Twenty-three percent of the British and West Germans, 26 percent of the Dutch, and 20 percent of the French said that they know that God really exists and have no doubts about it. Also according to the ISSP data, in the late 1990s 51 percent of Americans reported definitely believing in religious miracles in contrast to 23 percent of West Germans, 15 percent of the French and Dutch, and 14 percent of the British (International Social Survey Programme, 2001).

Europeans think they are supposed to be irreligious."[11] It is worth noting that the sharpest religious conflicts in the United States involve the claims of conservative native-born Christians who are seeking to impose their will and doctrines on others and whittle away the separation of church and state – the issue of the legality of abortion being an especially contentious issue along with support for stem-cell research, school vouchers, and state financial support for religious schools, among others.

The higher degree of secularization in Europe means that forms of social and cultural activity based on religious principles are frequently seen as illegitimate (Cesari, 2004:176). This is particularly the case when it comes to Islam. The public nature of Islam and the demands that it makes on the way its followers conduct their public lives, it has been argued, makes Islam – a religion associated with immigrants – a frequent source of group-rights claims (Koopmans *et al.*, 2005:155, 175). In the United States, demands made on the basis of religion are a common feature of American life – put forward by a broad range of religious groups, including, most vocally and most often, fundamentalist and evangelical (mostly native-born) Christians, who represent a growing proportion of Americans. (In 2001, nonmainline Christians, including Baptists and Pentecostals, made up around a third of the adult population (Kosmin and Keysar, 2006:36)). Indeed, asserting a religious identity in public, even bragging about it, can be viewed as an indication of Americanization or assimilation to American norms (Casanova and Zolberg, 2002). Thus, as the scholarly literature on immigrant religion emphasizes, becoming more religious is a way of becoming American – whereas it is often seen as a problem in Europe. In a telling quote, an Egyptian-born leader of a Muslim advocacy group in Chicago said, "Being an immigrant and organizing around faith is part of the American experience – it's part of our national identity. It's much harder to fit into a more . . . secular bloc like Europe" (Bennhold, 2006).

Institutionalized Identities and Arrangements

The way religion has been institutionalized differs profoundly in the United States and Western Europe – and has implications for whether immigrants' religious

---

[11]Robert Wuthnow (2005) also argues that the development of what he calls spiritual shopping – experimentation among some younger middle- and upper-middle-class Americans with religious teachings and practices outside the Christian tradition, including Zen Buddhism, Hare Krishna, and Transcendental Meditation – has led to a "path to a new understanding" of immigrants arriving with new religions.

beliefs and practices are seen to contribute or create barriers to integration and inclusion. The hand of constitutional and legal history is heavy in this respect.

In the United States, key constitutional principles were fashioned because of the religious diversity among the colonies that became states and the resulting impossibility of institutionalizing a single state church (though some of the colonies – *e.g.*, Massachusetts and Virginia – had established churches). The resulting principles of religious freedom and separation of church and state, enshrined in the Constitution's first amendment, have provided the framework for a multireligious nation and religious pluralism, which has characterized American society from the very beginning (Eck, 2001:384). The Constitution prohibits the government from establishing a state religion, guarantees the right to the free exercise of religion, and, through the fourteenth amendment's equal protection clause (which came into effect in 1870), bans government-supported religious discrimination.

This does not mean, of course, that non-Protestant immigrant religions were welcomed with open arms. Hardly. In the late nineteenth and early twentieth centuries, Protestant denominations were more or less "established" in that they dominated the public square, crowding out Catholicism and Judaism, both associated with disparaged southern and eastern European immigrants and seen by nativist observers as incompatible with mainstream institutions and culture (on this view of Catholicism, *see* McGreevey, 2003). (In this respect, one hears an echo of the contemporary European debate about Islam's place.) Even earlier in the nineteenth century, Irish Catholic immigrants were the target of deep-seated and virulent anti-Catholic nativism. As Alan Wolfe (2006:159) has argued, non-Protestant religions either separated from the dominant society to create their own institutions – Catholic schools are a major example – or, as was true for much of American Judaism, confined their religious beliefs and practices to the private realm and "thus acceded to Protestant domination in the public realm."

What is important is that Catholics and Jews were eventually incorporated into the system of American pluralism. Without the separation of church and state, we believe, the religions imported by past immigration streams could not have achieved parity with Protestant versions of Christianity. Because the state did not officially support or sponsor Protestantism, the newer religions were able over time to achieve parity and become part of the American mainstream as the descendants of the immigrants did. By the mid-twentieth century, Americans had come to think in terms of a tripartite perspective – Protestant, Catholic, and Jew – with Judaism treated as a kind of branch or denomination within the larger Judeo-Christian framework, a religion of believers who just happened to attend churches called synagogues (Wuthnow, 2005:32). And in the late twentieth and early twenty-first century, opponents of multiculturalism were referring to "our Judeo-Christian heritage" in uphold-ing the value of Western civilization (Alba, 2005:30).

Also important is that the very transformation of America into a "Judeo-Christian" nation – and Protestant, Catholic, and Jew into the three denomi-nations of the American civil religion (Casanova and Zolberg, 2002) – has meant that post-1965 immigrants enter a more religiously open society than their predecessors did a hundred or a hundred and fifty years ago.[12] To put it another way, the encounter of immigrant religions with American society today benefits from the awareness of and legal context deriving from the earlier incorporation of Jewish and Catholic immigrant groups. In the mid-1990s, President Bill Clinton proclaimed in a Rose Garden ceremony that "Islam is an American religion," and George W. Bush confirmed this by making a point of visiting a mosque in the wake of the September 11 attacks (Zolberg and Woon, 1999:30; Zolberg, 2002). This does not necessarily mean that the new religions will eventually attain the charter status now occupied by Catholicism and Judaism; the outcomes of the current encounter between non-Western religions and the American mainstream are not predictable.

Nor is the contemporary United States a paradise of religious tolerance – far from it. In a recent national survey, a substantial minority (about a third) of respondents said they would not welcome a stronger presence of Muslims, Hindus, and Buddhists in American society.[13] About four in ten said they would not be happy about a mosque being built in their neighborhood (about a third would be bothered by the idea of a Hindu temple being built in their community), and almost a quarter favored making it illegal for Muslim groups to meet, and a fifth in the case of Hindus or Buddhists (Wuthnow, 2005:219–220). Yet, at the same time, there is no doubt that Islam and other non-Western religions have a presence that is widely accepted as legitimate within a pluralist society. As Cesari maintains with regard to Islam, the protection of religious

[12]This is an example of a more general historical dynamic seen in the United States in which migrant inflows in an earlier period affect the social, political, economic, and cultural context that greets immigrants in the next wave, thereby shaping the experiences of the newer immigrants in a variety of ways (Foner, 2006).

[13]A national sample of 2,910 adults were surveyed, selected to be representative of the adult population of the United States and interviewed by telephone about a year after the September 11, 2001, attacks. Forty-two percent said they would not welcome Muslims' becoming a stronger presence in the United States, as did 33 percent for Hindus, and 32 percent for Buddhists (Wuthnow, 2005:220).

minorities by law and the philosophy that religious freedom is a "cornerstone of individual dignity" has worked in Muslims' favor: "They are able to use America's long history of judgments supporting the free expression of religion to their advantage, even when Islamic beliefs themselves are ridiculed or disparaged" (Cesari, 2004:84). Pluralism, Wuthnow (2005:73) argues, works best in the United States in protecting the civil rights of members of non-Western religions. Indeed, today, the new immigrant religions, including Islam, are enjoying the same freedoms to organize themselves and to support the beliefs and practices of their members as did the religions of earlier immigrants.

In Europe, in contrast, the ways in which Christian religions have been institutionalized make it difficult for Islam to achieve parity and are implicated in many of the problems and conflicts that have arisen. As secular as Europeans are, their societies have deeply institutionalized religious identities, which are the result of historic settlements and long-standing practices instituted after centuries of religious conflict. Continental religious traditions, as Klausen (2005:125, 129) notes, focused on resolving conflicts between state and government and powerful established churches:

> They have not historically emphasized the rights of nonconformists or worried about state neutrality in matters of faith. Constitutions typically contain equality commitments and promise of freedom of thought, but no language or requirement concerning the equal treatment of religion. . . . Europeans are unused to the social demands and public ethics associated with state neutrality and self-chosen . . . religious identities.

While secular natives in Western Europe may see religion as a minor feature of their societies, Muslims cannot help but be aware of the secondary status of their religion and the special privileges accorded to majority denominations (Alba, 2005:32). In France, where *laïcité*, the exclusion of religion from the affairs of state, is the official ideology, the state in fact owns and maintains most Christian churches and allows them to be used for regular religious services. The same 1905 law that established state possession of religious edifices built before that year also prevents the state from contributing to the construction of new ones, thus keeping the country's 4–5 million Muslims from enjoying the same privileges as Christians. Most French mosques are, as a consequence, ad hoc structures – in converted rooms in housing projects, garages, or even basements (Laurence and Vaisse, 2006:83).[14] Adding to the religious divide is

[14]According to Laurence and Vaisse (2006:83), two-thirds of Muslim prayer spaces in France are of this kind. At the time they wrote, there were just twenty mosques in France that could accommodate more than 1,000 people; fifty-four were big enough to hold between 500 and 1,000. A few French cities recently have found a way to provide some financial assistance by helping to fund cultural centers or facilities associated with mosques (Moore, 2007).

that half the country's ten or so state-designated national holidays are Catholic in origin; no Muslim holiday has equivalent recognition.

In a similar way in the Netherlands, the 1983 constitutional amendment instituting separation of church and state and the breakdown of the old system of "pillarization" – in which religious differences were institutionalized in separate state structures or "pillars," including parallel labor unions, daily and weekly newspapers, political parties, and even universities for Protestants and Catholics – have had the effect of privileging mainstream religions while leaving stumbling blocks in the way of Islam.[15] Between 1961 and 1975, the Dutch government offered significant subsidies for the construction of churches, with the result that there was a church for every thirty families. Although attempts were made in 1970–1981 to create a Muslim "pillar" parallel to the Catholic and Protestant "pillars," with public funding for Muslim TV and radio stations, for example, only one mosque was built with government money before 1983. The Dutch government privatized the clergy's salaries and pensions in a large buyout in 1981, in preparation for the 1983 constitutional changes, after which the government ceased paying for the construction of houses of worship (Klausen, 2005:145). The shift to state neutrality was, notes Jan Rath, "like drawing up the bridge in front of the newcomers" (quoted in Klausen, 2005:146).

Government support for religious schools has created other inequalities in Western Europe between established religions and Islam. In Britain and France the state provides financial support for religious schools as long as they teach the national secular curriculum. Inevitably, these arrangements, while seemingly fair to all religions, favor the most established ones. In Britain (where senior Anglican bishops sit in the House of Lords by right as part of the established state church) the government funds nearly 7,000 Church of England and Catholic schools but, as of 2007, only seven Islamic schools in a nation of 1.6 million Muslims. In the Netherlands, the majority of children go to state-supported religious schools, nearly all Protestant and Catholic, while the country's nearly one million Muslims in 2005 had only about thirty-five of their own publicly funded primary schools. In France, about 20 percent of French students go to religious schools (mostly Catholic) that receive the bulk of their budgets

---

[15]Under the Dutch system of pillarization, established in the latter part of the nineteenth century, Catholics and Protestants had their own organizations in all spheres of public life, including hospitals, schools, and even sports clubs. Laws and regulations were developed in which state funds and resources were distributed among the different pillars (Vermeulen and Penninx, 2000:28). The system of pillarization began to break down in the 1960s in response to increasing social and geographical mobility and increasing secularization in Dutch society.

from the government, but the first publicly subsidized Muslim school, the Lycée
Averroès, was not founded until 2003 (Sciolino, 2003; Klausen, 2005:144).

In Germany, the state, according to the 1949 constitution, must be
neutral in matters of religion, but this does not preclude linkages between church
and state. The long-dominant Catholics and Protestants, as well as Jews, but
not Islam, the third-largest faith, are entitled to federally collected church taxes
and the right to run state-subsidized religious social services and hospitals
(Klausen, 2005). Further, the established religions are taught in public schools
by regular teachers (*i.e.*, civil servants) during hours set aside for religious
instruction. Islam, however, has so far failed to be accorded the same status
(except in Berlin and Lower Saxony), and instruction in it is not universally
available; when it is, it occurs usually in some nonregular form such as an
experimental basis or in supplementary classes taught in Turkish by instructors
provided by the Turkish consulate (Engin, 2001).

The different ways that religion has been institutionalized in the United
States and Western Europe have implications for the claims of immigrant religious groups – and conflicts that may result. In the United States, immigrants
with allegiance to minority religions have generally sought inclusion in the
mainstream through public acceptance and recognition of their group. Although
an important historical exception was the unsuccessful struggle by Catholics
for public funds for parochial schools, many minority religious groups – perhaps,
most notably, Jewish organizations – have fought for a strict adherence to
separation of church and state and keeping religion out of the public sphere
(including public schools), as a way to prevent discrimination and obtain parity
with dominant religions. In Europe, equal treatment for minority religions
would require a radical structural change by removing the state from institutionalized arrangements with longer-established religions or, as Muslims have
sought, achieving at least some support from the state that longer-established
religions already have, including state support for their own religious schools.

At least so far, the kind of interlacing of the state and Christianity that
we have described in Western Europe has no parallel in the United States,
although challenges there to church-state separation have the potential to
threaten the integrative functions of immigrant religion – one of the points we
consider below in our concluding comments.

CONCLUSION

Our argument has been that a combination of factors – religious similarity
between natives and immigrants, historically rooted institutional structures,

and the religiosity of the native population – explain why the United States is more welcoming to immigrant religion than is Western Europe and, as a consequence, why the social science literature on religion among immigrants in the United States emphasizes its integrative role while in Europe conflict and exclusion come to the fore.

Yet to leave matters there would be to overlook some of the complexities and emerging trends on both sides of the Atlantic that ought to be taken into account. If studies of U.S. immigrants view religion as turning them into Americans and helping them to adjust to their new home, we also need to bear in mind that there are profound inequalities that create nonreligious barriers to inclusion – inequalities that have been documented and analyzed by a voluminous social science literature. Europe may be marked by an anti-Muslim cultural racism, but the United States is plagued by deeply rooted biological racism, which stigmatizes and disadvantages recent immigrants, who are over-whelmingly Asian, Latino, and Black and thus outside the pale of whiteness (Foner and Fredrickson, 2004; Foner, 2005). Unauthorized immigration status is the basis for another significant inequality that marginalizes and creates great difficulties for the growing number of undocumented immigrants, an estimated 11–12 million in 2006 (Passel, 2006; *see also* Massey *et al.*, 2003; Ngai, 2004).

Moreover, when it comes to religion, there are some disquieting signs that its integrative role among U.S. immigrants may be at some risk given increasing challenges to the long-standing separation between church and state. In the last decade or so, religious organizations in the United States have become eligible for an increasing stream of federal grants and contracts; the courts have started to permit tax-free financing at unabashedly religious universities and high schools (as long as the money is used for secular projects like dormitories and dining halls); and a broader tapestry of regulatory and tax exemptions has become available to religious groups for activities ranging from day-care centers and funeral homes to broadcasting networks that they sponsor (Henriques, 2006). Although the exemptions from federal, state, and local laws and taxes have applied not only to churches and synagogues but also to mosques and Hindu temples, Christian churches have been the greatest beneficiaries given the dominance of Christianity in the United States. Problems could emerge down the line if the growing inroads into church-state separation lead to favoring the Protestant-Catholic-Jewish trinity and discriminating against other religious groups.

As for the situation in Western Europe, it is also well to bear in mind developments that temper, at least somewhat, the gloomy picture we have described for the integration of Islam there. European governments realize that they must find ways to fund and support the development of an independent Islam and offer some accommodations for Muslim religious practices (Kastoryano, 1996; Fetzer and Soper, 2005:2; Klausen, 2005:2). Britain is particularly liberal on this score. To be sure, Britain has an established Anglican church; the state has not extended all the antidiscrimination protections that exist for gender, race, and ethnicity to religion (although in 2003 it banned religious discrimination in employment); and the government has refused to extend the blasphemy laws, used in the past to protect Christian values against offensive attacks on matters regarded as sacred, to all religious communities (Fetzer and Soper, 2005:37, 59; Modood, 2005:162–164). Still, on the whole, as Vertovec (1998) argues, the accommodation to many specific tenets and practices of religious minorities, including Islam, has been considerable and progressive in Britain. As early as the 1980s, Muslims' claims for the toleration of religious symbols and autonomous organizational spheres, including building and registering mosques, establishing sections of cemeteries for Muslims, permission for ritual slaughter, and exemption from religious instruction and school worship, were granted in Britain (Koenig, 2005:227). Whereas mosque building has been the subject of bitter controversy elsewhere in Europe, in Britain, as Fetzer and Soper (2005:48) note, for the most part getting permission to build a mosque or Islamic center "is no more difficult than securing permission for any other similar building."[16]

The Netherlands has also accommodated many Muslim religious demands despite a growing, and vocal, discontent with the pace of integration among many natives and the Dutch government's shift to a tougher "integration policy" for Muslim minorities. The slaying of the maverick filmmaker Theo van Gogh by a second-generation radical Muslim of Moroccan origin, among other developments, has been accompanied by a "fierce criticism of Islam and, what many people believe to be, the Muslim way of life" (Rath, 2005:31; *see also* Buruma, 2006). Moreover, Muslims had the bad fortune to arrive as the system of pillarization was on the decline, so there was no question of a Muslim pillar, comparable to the Protestant and Catholic pillars of the past, in terms of institutional arrangements. Yet the legacy of the pillarized system, it has been argued, has led to the accommodation of, and receptivity to, Muslim group claims. (This accommodation, Rath [2005:32] argues, has not

---

[16]One exception is the recent controversy over proposals for a megamosque for 12,000 worshippers in London's East End near the main park for the 2012 Olympic Games (Moore, 2007).

always occurred without a struggle. Muslims, he contends, have "in the long run achieved most of what they wanted," but obstacles have usually been put in the way of various Muslim institutional claims "from one quarter or other," and "in most cases recognition has only been achieved after long pleading.") A recent study ranked the Netherlands in 2002 with a perfect score of 1 in allowances for Islamic ritual practices outside of public institutions, the three indicators being allowance of ritual slaughter of animals according to Islamic rite, allowance of Islamic call to prayer in public, and provisions for Muslim burials (Koopmans *et al.*, 2005:55–58).[17]

Major changes are also under way in France. Perhaps the most important step has been the establishment in 2003 of a French Council of the Muslim Religion (*Conseil Français du Culte Musulman*) as a liaison between the French government and the Muslim communities. The establishment of this council, which exists on both national and regional levels, finally puts Islam on the same plane as other religions in relationship to the French state, for each of the major religions is represented by a similar body; in the case of Jews, for instance, the Jewish *Consistoire Central* dates to the emancipation of Jews in the Napoleonic era. The French Council of the Muslim Religion has a mandate to negotiate with the French state over issues affecting Islamic religious practice, such as the training of imams and the regulation of ritual slaughter; and as Laurence and Vaisse (2006) observe, it represents an attempt by the French state to establish an Islam *of* France rather than simply tolerate Islam *in* France.

A final issue, relevant throughout Europe, concerns trends among Muslims themselves, particularly the local-born second and third generations. On one hand, the aggrieved sense of exclusion felt by many Muslims who have grown up in Europe has created a pool of potential recruits for fundamentalist doctrines and radical Islamist groups, a development that could reinforce and indeed increase tensions with long-established Europeans. On the other hand, some predict that as the second generation takes over in religious associations and institutions, they will generally strive for a more liberal version of Islam than their parents practiced, one that is focused on integration into Western European society and viewed more positively by the wider population (Lucassen, 2005:157–158, 207). Just how these two trends will, in fact, unfold – and interact – is, as yet, an open question.

In the end, though, and despite these caveats, we are back to where we started. Changes may be afoot in both Western Europe and the United States,

---

[17]Britain was in second place, with a summary score of 0.33 for religious rights outside of public institutions, while France and Germany each had only a score of 0 (Koopmans *et al.*, 2005:58).

but it is likely that, for some time to come, Islam will continue to be problematic in Western Europe, engendering tensions and conflict, just as immigrant religions in the United States will continue to offer an acceptable and easily accessible way for newcomers and their children to fit into American society. And, because the social science literature inevitably reflects the concerns and realities in the societies under study, we can also expect social science work on immigrant religion to continue to be characterized by the patterns we have described here, with an emphasis on its positive role in immigrant adjustment and assimilation in the United States and its links to the difficulties of incorporating Muslim immigrants and their children into Western European societies.

REFERENCES

Alba, R.
2005 "Bright vs. Blurred Boundaries: Second-Generation Assimilation and Exclusion in France, Germany and the United States." *Ethnic and Racial Studies* 28:20–49.

———, J. Handl, and W. Müller
1994 "Ethnische Ungleichheit im Deutschen Bildungssystem." *Kölner Zeitschrift für Soziologie und Sozialpsychologie* 46:209–237.

———, A. Roboteau, and J. DeWind
Forthcoming "Introduction." In *Religion, Immigration and Civic Life in America*. Ed. R. Alba, A. Roboteau, and J. DeWind. New York, NY: New York University Press.

Bennhold, K.
2006 "For U.S. Muslims, It's the American Way." *International Herald Tribune*, November 7.

Bowen, J.
2006 *Why The French Don't Like Headscarves*. Princeton, NJ: Princeton University Press.

Buijs, F. J., and J. Rath
2006 *Muslims in Europe: The State of Research*. IMISCOE Working Paper. <http://www.imiscoe.org/workingpapers/documents/muslims_in_europe>

Buruma, I.
2006 *Murder in Amsterdam*. New York, NY: Penguin.

Casanova, J., and A. Zolberg
2002 "Religion and Immigrant Incorporation in New York." Paper presented at conference on Immigrant Incorporation in New York, The New School.

Cesari, J., ed.
2005 "Special Issue on Mosque Conflicts in European Cities." *Journal of Ethnic and Migration Studies* 31:1015–1179.

———
2004 *When Islam and Democracy Meet: Muslims in Europe and the United States*. New York, NY: Palgrave Macmillan.

Chen, C.
2006 "From Filial to Religious Piety: Evangelical Christianity Reconstructing Taiwanese Immigrant Families in the United States." *International Migration Review* 40:573–602.

Ebaugh, H. R., and J. S. Chafetz
2000 *Religion and the New Immigrants: Continuities and Adaptation in Immigrant Congregations.*
       Walnut Creek, CA: Altamira.

Eck, D.
2001 *A New Religious America.* New York, NY: HarperCollins.

Engin, H.
2001 "Wenn sechs Prozent aller Schüler Muslime sind: Islamischer Religionsunterricht an
       deutschen Schulen? Eine Bestandsaufnahme." *Der Bürger im Staat* 4. <http://
       www.lpb.bwue.de/aktuell/bis/4_01/islamreli6.htm>.

Eumap
2007 "Muslims in the EU: Executive Summaries." Open Society Institute. <http://
       www.eumap.org/topics/minority/reports/eumuslims>.

European Monitoring Centre on Racism and Xenophobia (EUMC)
2006 *Muslims in the European Union: Discrimination and Islamophobia.* Vienna: EUMC.

Fetzer, J. S., and J. C. Soper
2005 *Muslims and the State in Britain, France, and Germany.* Cambridge and New York, NY:
       Cambridge University Press.

Fischer, C., and M. Hout
2006 *A Century of Difference: How America Changed in the Last One Hundred Years.* New York,
       NY: Russell Sage Foundation.

Foley, M., and D. Hoge
2007 *Religion and the New Immigrants: How Faith Communities Form Our Newest Citizens.* New
       York, NY: Oxford University Press.

Foner, N.
2006 "Then *and* Now or Then *to* Now: Immigration to New York in Contemporary and
       Historical Perspective." *Journal of American Ethnic History* 25:33–47.

———
2005 *In a New Land: A Comparative View of Immigration.* New York, NY: New York University
       Press.

———, and G. Fredrickson, ed.
2004 *Not Just Black and White: Historical and Contemporary Perspectives on Immigration, Race,
       and Ethnicity in the United States.* New York, NY: Russell Sage Foundation.

Ford, P.
2005a "What Place for God in Europe?" *The Christian Science Monitor,* February 22.

———
2005b "Europe's Rising Class of Believers: Muslims." *The Christian Science Monitor,* February 24.

Fordham, S., and J. Ogbu
1986 "Black Students' School Success: Coping with the Burden of Acting White." *Urban
       Review* 18:176–206.

Gallup Organization
2007 *Special Report: Muslims in Europe.* <http://media.gallup.com/WorldPoll/PDF/
       WPSRMuslimsinEurope2050707.pdf>.

George, S.
1998 "Caroling with the Keralites: The Negotiation of Gendered Space in an Indian Immigrant
       Church." In *Gatherings in Diaspora: Religious Communities and the New Immigration.* Ed.
       R. S. Warner and J. G. Wittner. Philadelphia, PA: Temple University Press. Pp. 265–294.

Goldberg, D. T.
2006 "Racial Europeanization." *Ethnic and Racial Studies* 29:331–364.

Heath, A.
Forthcoming Special issue of *Ethnicities*.

Henriques, D.
2006 "As Exemptions Grow, Religion Outweighs Regulation." *The New York Times*, October 8.

Hepner, R.
1998 "The House That Rasta Built: Church-Building and Fundamentalism among New York Rastafarians." In *Gatherings in Diaspora: Religious Communities and the New Immigration*. Ed. R. S. Warner and J. G. Wittner. Philadelphia, PA: Temple University Press. Pp. 197–234.

Herberg, W.
1960 *Protestant, Catholic, Jew*. New York, NY: Anchor Books.

Hirschman, C.
2004 "The Role of Religion in the Origins and Adaptation of Immigrant Groups in the United States." *International Migration Review* 38:1206–1233.

International Social Survey Programme
2001 "ISSP 1998 Religion." <http://www.za.uni-koeln. De/data/en/issp/codebooks/s3190db.pdf>.

Kaltenbach, J.-H., and M. Tribalat
2002 *La République et l'islam, Entre Crainte et Aveuglement*. Paris: Gallimard.

Kalter, F.
2006 "Auf der Suche nach einer Erklärung für die Spezifischen Arbeitsmarktnachteile Jugendlicher Türkischer Herkunft." *Zeitschrift für Soziologie* 35:144–160.

———, and I. Kogan
2006 "Ethnic Inequalities at the Transition from School to Work in Belgium and Spain: Discrimination or Self-exclusion?" *Research in Social Stratification and Mobility* 24:259–274.

Karpathakis, A.
2001 "Conclusion: New York City's Religions." In *New York Glory: Religions in the City*. Ed. T. Carnes and A. Karpathakis. New York, NY: New York University Press. Pp. 388–394.

Kastoryano, R.
1996 *La France, l'Allemagne et leurs immigrés: Négocier l'identité*. Paris: Armand Colin.

Kelek, N.
2005 *Die fremde Braut: Ein Bericht aus dem Inneren des türkischen Lebens in Deutschland*. Cologne: Kiepenheuer and Witsch.

Kepel, G.
1991 *Les Banlieues d'Islam: Naissance d'une Religion en France*. Paris: Editions du Seuil.

Khosrokhavar, F.
2005 "The Muslims of Western Europe." Talk given at the University at Albany.

Klausen, J.
2005 *The Islamic Challenge: Politics and Religion in Western Europe*. Oxford and New York, NY: Oxford University Press.

Koenig, M.
2005 "Incorporating Muslim Immigrants in Western Nation States: A Comparison of the United Kingdom, France and Germany." *Journal of International Migration and Integration* 6:219–234.

Koopmins, R., P. Statham, M. Giugni, and F. Passey
2005   *Contested Citizenship: Immigration and Cultural Diversity in Europe.* Minneapolis, MN: University of Minnesota Press.

Kosmin, B. A., and A. Keysar
2006   *Religion in a Free Market: Religious and Non-Religious Americans, Who, What, Why, Where.* Ithaca, NY: Paramount Market Publishers.

Kramer, J.
2004   "Taking the Veil: How France's Public Schools Became the Battleground in a Culture War." *The New Yorker,* November 22:59–71.

Kristen, C.
2002   "Hauptschule, Realschule Oder Gymnasium? Ethnische Unterschiede am Ersten Bildungsübergang," *Kölner Zeitschrift für Soziologie und Sozialpsychologie* 54:534–552.

Kurien, P.
1998   "Becoming American by Becoming Hindu: Indian Americans Take Their Place at the Multicultural Table." In *Gatherings in Diaspora: Religious Communities and the New Immigration.* Ed. R. S. Warner and J. G. Wittner. Philadelphia, PA: Temple University Press. Pp. 37–70.

Laurence, J., and J. Vaisse
2006   *Integrating Islam: Political and Religious Challenges in Contemporary France.* Washington, DC: Brookings Institution Press.

Levitt, P.
2007   *God Needs No Passport.* New York, NY: New Press.

Lopez, D.
Forthcoming "Whither the Flock? The Catholic Church and the Success of Mexicans in the United States." In *Religion, Immigration and Civic Life in America.* Ed. R. Alba, A. Roboteau, and J. DeWind. New York, NY: New York University Press.

Lucassen, L.
2005   *The Immigrant Threat: The Integration of Old and New Migrants in Western Europe since 1850.* Urbana, IL: University of Illinois Press.

McGreevey, J.
2003   *Catholicism and American Freedom: A History.* New York, NY: W.W. Norton.

Masci, D., and G. A. Smith
2006   "God is Alive and Well in America." Pew Research Center. <http://pewresearch.org/pubs/15>.

Massey, D., J. Durand, and N. Malone
2003   *Beyond Smoke and Mirrors: Mexican Immigration in an Era of Economic Integration.* New York, NY: Russell Sage Foundation.

Min, P. G.
2001   "Koreans: An 'Institutionally Complete Community' in New York." In *New Immigrants in New York,* 2nd edn. Ed. N. Foner, New York, NY: Columbia University Press. Pp. 173–199.

Modood, T.
2005   *Multicultural Politics: Racism, Ethnicity and Muslims in Britain.* Minneapolis, MN: University of Minnesota Press.

———— *et al.*
1997   *Ethnic Minorities in Britain: Diversity and Disadvantage.* London: Policy Studies Institute.

Moore, M.
2007 "In a Europe Torn over Mosques, A City Offers Accommodation." *The Washington Post*, December 9.

Ngai, M.
2004 *Impossible Subjects: Illegal Aliens and the Making of Modern America.* Princeton, NJ: Princeton University Press.

Passel, J.
2006 "Size and Characteristics of the Unauthorized Migrant Population in the U.S." Pew Hispanic Center report. Washington, DC: Pew Hispanic Center.

Pew Forum on Religion and Public Life
2008 "U.S. Religious Landscape Survey." <http://religions.pewforum.org/reports>

Pew Research Center
2003 "Anti-Americanism: Causes and Characteristics." <http://people-press.org/commentary/display.php3?AnalysisID=77–16k>.

Portes, A., and M. Zhou
1993 "The New Second Generation: Segmented Assimilation and Its Variants." *Annals of the American Academy of Political and Social Sciences* 530:74–98.

———, and R. Rumbaut
2006 *Immigrant America,* 3rd edn. Berkeley, CA: University of California Press.

Rath, J.
2005 "Against the Current: The Establishment of Islam in the Netherlands." *Canadian Diversite* 4:31–34.

———, R. Penninx, K. Groenendijk, and A. Meyer
2001 *Europe and Its Islam: The Netherlands, Belgium and Britain React to an Emerging Religious Community.* Leiden: Brill.

Renaut, A., and A. Touraine
2005 *Un Debat Sur La Laïcité.* Paris: Stock.

Scheffer, P.
2000 "Het Multiculturele Drama." *NRC Handelsbad,* January 29.

Sciolino, E.
2003 "Muslim Lycée Opens in Secular France, Raising Eyebrows." *The New York Times,* September 9.

Seibert, H., and H. Solga
2005 "Gleiche Chancen dank einer abgeschlossenen Ausbildung? Zum Signalwert von Ausbildungsabschlüssen bei ausländischen und deutschen jungen Erwachsenen." *Zeitschrift für Soziologie* 34:364–382.

Silberman, R., R. Alba, and I. Fournier
2007 "Segmented Assimilation in France? Discrimination in the Labor Market against the Second Generation." *Ethnic and Racial Studies* 30:1–27.

Vallet, L.-A., and J.-P. Caille
1995 "Les Carrières Scolaires au Collège des Élèves Étrangers ou Issus de L'immigration." *Éducation et Formations* 40:5–14.

Vermeulen, H., and R. Penninx
2000 "Introduction." In *Immigrant Integration: The Dutch Case.* Ed. H. Vermeulen and R. Penninx. Amsterdam: Het Spinhuis. Pp. 1–35.

Vertovec, S.
1998   "Accommodating Religious Pluralism in Britain: South Asian Religions." In *Multicultural Policies and the State: A Comparison of Two European Societies.* Ed. M. Martiniello. Utrecht: European Research Center on Migration and Ethnic Relations. Pp. 163–177.

Warner, R. S., and J. G. Wittner, ed.
1998   *Gatherings in Diaspora: Religious Communities and the New Immigration.* Philadelphia, PA: Temple University Press.

Weil, P.
2004   "Lifting the Veil of Ignorance." *Progressive Politics* 3 (March):16–23.

Wikan, U.
2002   *A Generous Betrayal: Politics of Culture in a New Europe.* Chicago, IL: University of Chicago Press.

Wolfe, A.
2006   "Religious Diversity: The American Experiment That Works." In *Americanism: New Perspectives on the History of an Ideal.* Ed. M. Kazin and J. McCartin. Chapel Hill, NC: University of North Carolina Press. Pp. 153–167.

Wuthnow, R.
2005   *America and the Challenges of Religious Diversity.* Princeton, NJ: Princeton University Press.

Zhou, M., and C. Bankston
1998   *Growing Up American.* New York, NY: Russell Sage Foundation.

Zolberg, A. R.
2002   "Managing Diversity: European and American Recipes." Walter A. Eberstadt Professorship Inaugural Lecture, The New School, November 14.

————, and L. L. Woon
1999   "Why Islam Is Like Spanish: Cultural Incorporation in Europe and the United States." *Politics & Society* 27:5–38.

[18]

INTERNATIONAL MARGINATION

IOM International Organization for Migration

doi: 10.1111/imig.12073

Religion as A Context of Reception: The Case of Haitian Immigrants in Miami, Montreal and Paris

Margarita A. Mooney*

ABSTRACT

In this article, I use cross-national comparative and ethnographic methods to explore how religion influences the incorporation of Haitian immigrants into the US, Quebec and France. First, I explore the ideological, legal and institutional forces that shape religion-state differentiation in the US, Quebec and France. Using census and immigration data from each site as well as interviews with Haitian leaders and government officials in Miami, Montreal and Paris, I show that the general pattern of consensual differentiation between religion and state in the US favours the more successful symbolic and socio-economic incorporation of Haitians in Miami, whereas secular nationalism in Quebec and assertive secularism in France weaken the incorporation of Haitian immigrants in Montreal and Paris, respectively.

INTRODUCTION

Scholars have focused on numerous factors that influence immigrant incorporation, such as migrants' background characteristics as well as government and societal contexts of reception (Portes and Rumbaut, 2006). Elements of societal reception include labour markets, racial prejudice, and the structure of the co-ethnic community. In particular, cross-national research on a single immigrant group in multiple settings illustrates how immigrant incorporation reflects the varying institutional structures of immigrant-receiving societies (Reitz, 1998). In this article, I expand the concept of context of reception to include religion-state relations and ask: how has the context of reception regarding religion in Miami, Montreal and Paris influenced Haitians immigrants' symbolic and structural incorporation?

Foner and Alba (2008) point out that religion is often a bridge to migrant incorporation in the US whereas it is often a barrier to integration in Europe. I expand beyond this by focusing specifically how macro-level differences in religion-state relations influence the symbolic and structural incorporation of the same immigrant group in three contexts. The US population is 13.0 per cent foreign born, Quebec is 11.5 per cent and France is 10.6 per cent.[1] Since the 1960s, international migrants to each of these nations have mostly come from countries of the developing world, such as Asia, Latin America and the Caribbean, and Africa. With regards to religion, the three nations I study have differing histories that resulted in diverse ideological systems of religion-state differentiation that can be called 1) consensual differentiation in the US; 2) secular nationalism in Quebec; and 3) assertive secularism in France. In part because the consensual differentiation between religion and the state in the US enhances the legitimacy of religious institutions and promotes

---

* University of North Carolina.

© 2013 The Author
International Migration © 2013 IOM
International Migration Vol. 51 (3) 2013
ISSN 0020-7985

Published by John Wiley & Sons Ltd.

government cooperation with faith-based service institutions, Haitians in Miami have greater indicators of symbolic and structural incorporation than in Montreal or Paris.

THREE MODELS OF RELIGION-STATE RELATIONS

For late nineteenth and early twentieth century immigrants to the US, whether they were Protestant, Catholic, or Jewish, religious institutions provided a central meeting place where they could gather to create identity and meaning (Herberg, 1955). Immigrant community institutions mediated between newcomers and the host society through their social service programmes, and, by generating community social bonds and mediating between newcomers and the state, became indispensible to the larger goal of successful immigrant incorporation (Gordon, 1964). Successive waves of immigrants to the US produced a melting pot where immigrants maintained their distinct ethnic identity and religious affiliation yet also enjoyed a socio-economic standing comparable to non-immigrants (Handlin, 1951).

Hence, in particular for minorities and immigrants, religious institutions in the US have proven legitimate and effective channels of political mobilization and empowerment. In the American context ethnic, racial, and class diversity is often expressed through religious organizations, and Steve Warner argues that "religion is widely available to new immigrants as a legitimate institutional form" (1993: 1063). With regards to immigrant incorporation, the US open market for religion and its system of consensual differentiation between religion and state has meant that 1) immigrants are free to found new religious institutions, and 2) these organizations work with state agencies to promote a strong community life and successful incorporation into American society.

In Quebec, the architects of the 1960s Quiet Revolution and a generation of Quebecois scholars constructed a narrative in which Catholicism kept people attached to traditional ways of life and thus contributed to their oppression under the powerful Anglophones in Quebec (Van Die, 2001). Hence, despite some acceptance of cultural and religious diversity, the Quebec government and public are concerned that immigrants' religious practices, cultural identities, or linguistic preferences could erode Quebecois identity. Although many immigrants to Quebec express their ethnic or even racial identity, they also have internalized that they should keep their religious identity private and even fear negative repercussions if they discuss their religious convictions publicly (Beyer, 2013).

Because concerns about immigrant incorporation in Quebec are interpreted in relation to a historical narrative in which religion retards progress and in which the state needs to preserve Quebecois national identity, the context of reception for immigrants as regards to religion in Quebec can be called secular nationalism (Mooney, 2013). In this model, private religious belief and practice are tolerated, yet public religious expressions and faith-based service institutions are suspected of conflicting with Quebecois secular nationalism. Despite the historical influence of Catholicism in Quebecois identity and the active participation of some Catholic leaders and organizations in the political modernization and liberation achieved during the Quiet Revolution (Balthazar, 2009), Quebecois identity today is decidedly secular.

According to French republican ideology, the state alone is entrusted with forming citizens, providing social welfare, and ensuring social integration (Hargreaves, 1995; Noiriel, 1996; Feldblum, 1999). The modern French state, through the laws, practices, and ideologies associated with *laïcité* – the French version of secularism – has sought to limit the public influence of religion, primarily the majority religion, Catholicism (Liogier, 2006). These principles of republicanism and *laïcité* have been evoked in debates about how to deal with France's growing religious diversity. As much international migration to France since the 1970s has come from predominantly Muslim nations in North Africa, those in favour of restricting people from wearing certain forms of religious dress or symbols, such as the Muslim headscarf and the burqa, claim continuity with the principles of republicanism and *laïcité*, according to which the public realm should be secular (Liogier, 2006).

In contrast to the US system of an open market for religion and a generally favourable view of religion's public influence, in France "the state excludes religion from the public sphere and plays an 'assertive' role as the agent of a social engineering project that confines religion to the private domain" (Kuru, 2007: 572). The French sociologist Raphaël Liogier provides further evidence that the French *laïcité* is not a system of neutrality towards religion. Rather than neutrality, Liogier argues that the laws and administrative practices associated with French assertive secularism create an organized and hierarchical system of state intervention in religion (2006).[2] The 2004 ban on wearing conspicuous religious items (like the Muslim headscarf) in many public institutions and the similar 2010 ban on the burqa illustrate how the French logic of assertive secularism leads to intervention in religious matters in order to "confine religion to the home and to the individual's conscience" (Kuru, 2007: 581). Hence, immigrants to France, whether they are Christian, Muslim, or another religion, encounter a hostile context of reception regarding religion.

HAITIANS IN MIAMI, MONTREAL AND PARIS

How do these three contexts of reception regarding religion – consensual differentiation in the US, secular nationalism in Quebec, and assertive secularism in France – influence Haitians' incorporation? To assess Haitians' incorporation in Miami, Montreal and Paris, I examined census and survey data to provide general indications about Haitians' socio-economic status around the time I conducted fieldwork (for more details on research methods and design, see Mooney, 2009). I also interviewed 140 government officials, Haitian community association leaders, and Catholic religious leaders in Miami, Montreal and Paris. This allowed me to probe both Haitians' symbolic and structural incorporation.[3] I followed a semi-structured questionnaire in which I asked key informants to describe the major challenges to Haitians' incorporation, how their institution addressed those challenges, and how they worked with other institutions regarding Haitians' incorporation. At the three sites, I participated in religious ceremonies, sang in the choir, assisted at language classes, and attended numerous social events. In order to compare Haitians' religious institutions with other kinds of ethnic institutions, I also conducted participant observation at numerous civic and political events in each of the Haitian communities and interviewed leaders of the most important ethnic institutions of each city. I wrote detailed fieldnotes and transcribed recorded interviews. My analysis thus triangulates macro- and meso-level data from government sources and interviews with government officials with an ethnographic view of Haitians' religious institutions and related social service institutions to examine how contexts of reception regarding religion influence Haitians' incorporation in Miami, Montreal and Paris.

Miami and the Toussaint Center

Beginning in the 1970s, thousands of Haitians began to migrate to Miami annually, and by 2000, Miami had become the largest city of the Haitian diaspora (Jackson, 2011). In the late 1970s, the Archdiocese of Miami assigned a young priest, Father Thomas G. Wenski, to pastor the rapidly growing Haitian community.[4] Given the racial prejudice faced by many Haitians in Miami and their low socio-economic status, Wenski's goal was both to create a strong Haitian Catholic community to foster respect and legitimacy for Haitians and to build a social service center to promote their socio-economic incorporation.

Wenski convinced officials from the Archdiocese of Miami to grant 10 acres of land to build a Haitian Catholic parish, Notre Dame d'Haïti (Our Lady of Haiti), and a service center, the Pierre

Toussaint Center.[5] With the help of Haitian clergy and experienced Haitian lay leaders, Wenski built up the religious services at Notre Dame. To launch the Toussaint Center, Wenski employed many Catholic lay leaders who had worked in social programmes in Haiti and he launched a literacy programme and English language classes. Other local Catholic agencies, such as Catholic Charities and the Jesuit Refugee Corps, helped the Toussaint Center establish a day care centre, a job placement programme, and legal services. Over time, all of these programs successfully competed for government and private funding, such as from Head Start and the United Way, to expand their reach.

Although the Toussaint Center was his most visible work to outsiders, Wenski also worked vigorously to rebuild strong communities of worship, both at Notre Dame and at smaller Haitian Catholic missions in South Florida. Wenski saw Haitians' symbolic and socio-economic incorporation as closely inter-twined, and hence he insisted that religious services and rituals such as the Eucharist were indispensible to strengthening family ties and building community bonds. Because Haitians often express class divisions through language choice, Wenski used only Haitian Creole rather than French in the religious and social services he organized. In this way, he clearly identified Notre Dame with darker-skinned and generally lower-educated Creole-speaking Haitians. Not unlike other immigrants groups to the US, Haitians' vibrant Catholic community at Notre Dame generated a greater sense of respect and legitimacy for Haitians in Miami, as evidenced by the frequent visits from journalists and politicians, among others, to these institutions.

Although Wenski and his collaborators knew that Haitians' religious piety was fundamental to the strength needed to overcome the many hurdles to their socio-economic incorporation, they also worked tirelessly to attract government resources and private funding to help Haitians in Miami find opportunities for work, language training, and continuing education. Because many Haitians who had arrived in Miami were undocumented or awaiting decisions on asylum claims, and because of racial prejudice and language difficulties, many of the poorest Haitians were afraid of directly approaching government institutions that were frequently highly bureaucratic, unfriendly towards them, and unfamiliar with Haitian culture and language. To bridge this gap, the leaders of Notre Dame and the Toussaint Center mediated between Haitian immigrants and the government in three principal ways: a) political advocacy, b) social service provision, and c) community organizing. Activities in each of these realms illustrate the general pattern of consensual differentiation between religion and state in the US, and this consensual differentiation facilitated Haitians' successful immigrant incorporation in Miami.

First, to call attention to the humanitarian plight of Haitian refugees, especially during the crises of 1980 and 1994, Catholic leaders provided crucial political advocacy for Haitians. For example, in 1980, the then-Archbishop Eugene McCarthy, Wenski, and other Catholic clergy visited Haitian refugees being held in Krome Detention Centre to celebrate religious services and to assess Haitians' conditions there. Establishing Haitians' legitimacy in Miami was often central to getting the government to agree to provide socio-economic support for Haitians. For example, Catholic clergy explained to the press and government officials that, if forced to return to Haiti, many Haitians would face political repression and economic stagnation. Although much of this political advocacy was concentrated on government officials in South Florida, Catholic clergy from Miami also travelled to Washington, DC, to work with the US Conference of Catholic Bishops Committee on Migration. Since the end of World War II, refugee and immigrant resettlement has been a top concern of the US Catholic Bishops, and their staff at the Bishops' Conference have developed ties to important law-makers in this area (Mooney, 2006). Although numerous other groups advocated for Haitian immigrants' rights, Catholic leaders undoubtedly contributed to swaying public opinion and the opinion of lawmakers, politicians and judges, thus facilitating both Haitians' symbolic and socio-economic incorporation (Stotzky, 2004).

At the same time that Catholic leaders lobbied the government to legalize Haitians' status in the US, they also mobilized church resources to offer social services to Haitian immigrants through the

Toussaint Center. Given the precarious legal status of many Haitian immigrants and the political unrest in Haiti that produced several large-scale migrations to Miami, very few social services were available to most Haitians when they first arrived in Miami. Although the Toussaint Center launched its programmes by building on the skilled experience of clergy and lay leaders and using funds and land donated from the Archdiocese of Miami, the programmes would not have been able to grow and expand without complementary funds from the local, state and federal government, which by 2002 constituted 80 per cent of the Toussaint Center's funding.

A third way that the Catholic Church mediated between Haitians and the government in Miami was through its participation in PACT (People Acting for Community Together). PACT is a community organizing group that draws its membership from religious congregations in Miami. Members of PACT's network of religious congregations, like Notre Dame, meet in small groups of 8–10 people to discuss what they deem the most pressing social or political issues they face – such as transportation, water quality, education or access to banking. Of all PACT's member congregations, Notre Dame had the greatest number of participants. Notre Dame formed the single most active congregation in PACT, a feat due to the active involvement of Notre Dame's clergy and lay leaders in PACT and to the many strong small prayer groups from Notre Dame. As the hardest part of community organizing is quite often simply getting people together to talk about their problems, Notre Dame's lay leaders encouraged the parish's many home-based prayer groups to reflect on their common concerns and participate in PACT. Faith-based community-based organizing groups such as PACT not only secure more government assistance for the disadvantaged but also legitimize the symbolic inclusion of poor communities in the democratic process (Wood, 2002).

Notre Dame and the Toussaint Center formed a crossroads among Haitians of various class backgrounds and between Haitians and the rest of Miami's residents and political representatives. This two-tiered institution, comprised of mostly lower-class, dark-skinned, Creole-speaking, and extremely pious Haitian Catholics who gather for seven weekend Masses, more than 15 prayer and service groups, weekly marathons of one thousand Hail Marys in one day and loud Charismatic Masses, became the identifiable centre of the Haitian community. The stability of Notre Dame's prayer groups and the strong bonds between their members provided a foundation for the in-depth and long-term engagement required for community-based organization. All middle- and upper-class Haitians claiming to represent Haitians in Miami, as well as Anglo and Hispanic politicians, showed their respect for these institutions by attending special services at Notre Dame and collaborating with the Toussaint Center to promote Haitians' socio-economic incorporation, lending further legitimacy to those institutions.

The impoverished conditions of Little Haiti have not improved much compared to previous decades. However, by 2000, Miami-Dade County had not only become the largest city of the Haitian diaspora, surpassing New York, it had also developed a sizeable middle class in areas like North Miami.[6] Haitians in Miami undoubtedly have the strongest institutional base of support for their incorporation. Despite their disadvantageous starting position, Haitians in Miami developed a considerable middle-class community with strong community institutions and local political representation. Even though Haitians had the lowest parental human capital and income of any national-origin group in the Children of Immigrants Longitudinal Study, they also had the highest levels of religious participation (Portes and Rumbaut, 2006). Although numerous factors influence immigrant integration, Haitians' high levels of religious participation contributed to the greater educational attainment and labour market incorporation among second-generation Haitians (Portes and Rumbaut, 2006: 323)

Interviews with government officials and religious leaders in Miami further illustrate how the receiving context legitimizes Haitians' religious identity and transfers resources to Haitians' faith-based service institutions. One government official in Miami explained why cooperating with Haitians' faith-based service institutions was crucial for their incorporation: "The church is the only place people can really trust...You see the priest if you don't have food. Hey, you're not going to the government, you're not going to the social services. It's a shame to go to those places, but it's okay to tell the church that you have a problem. They're [Haitians] not thinking of social services, they're thinking of the church." Because many Haitians' experiences of political repression in Haiti and their precarious legal status in Miami, Haitians are more likely to trust the Church than the government: Leaders of the Toussaint Center and Notre Dame aimed to first mobilize resources from within the Haitian community and then seek additional support from the state. The history of the Toussaint Center – which started off as a volunteer effort in space borrowed from the church and grew to have a budget of millions of dollars in local, state and federal funding to support Haitians' incorporation – exemplifies the consensual nature of religion-state differentiation in the US, Government officials in Miami acknowledged the importance of religion to Haitians' symbolic identity and socio-economic mobility, and religious leaders successfully advocated on Haitians' behalf to get the government to work with them to promote common goals. Research on second-generation Haitians indicates that these efforts paid off in more upward assimilation than would have been likely without the strong mobilization centred on Notre Dame and the Toussaint Center.

Montreal and the Bureau of the Haitian Christian Community

In the 1960s, thousands of Haitian professionals and intellectuals migrated annually to Montreal. Haitian professionals, such as doctors and teachers, were recruited to work in the new educational and health-care institutions created during the Quiet Revolution (Labelle and Midy, 1999). As Quebecois Catholic orders had long-standing ties with Haiti, Haitian clergy travelled to Montreal either for short visits or to escape François Duvalier's repression of Catholic pro-democracy social and political movements in Haiti. Haitian clergy who moved to Montreal worked closely with numerous Catholic social institutions that had decades of experience working in social services for the disadvantaged, including immigrants. The way in which Catholic institutions and leaders were central to the early stages of Haitian incorporation points to another, and often untold story, about the Quiet Revolution in which many Catholic leaders supported the creation of a modern welfare state.[7] For example, during one of the Bureau's legalization campaigns, Quebec's Minister of Immigration was a Jesuit priest who had many personal connections to Haitian clergy. Hence, Haitians' early experiences in Montreal indicate that even after the Quiet Revolution, Catholic leaders and organizations were often central in secular institutions serving the poor and immigrants, such as Haitians.

These Catholic agencies provided the fledging Haitian community with skilled leadership, financial resources, and experience working with Quebecois politicians and social services agencies, all of which initially supported Haitians' symbolic inclusion and their socio-economic incorporation. As in Miami, the Catholic clergy advocated for Haitians' political rights and started social programmes to facilitate the incorporation of thousands of working-class Haitians who began to arrive in Montreal starting in the 1970s. Although Quebec continued to recruit highly-skilled Francophone immigrants, including some Haitians, many of the Haitians who migrated to Montreal in the 1970s were not recruited to work but rather took advantage of relatively easy entry to Quebec to travel there and then relied on their social ties with other Haitians already in Montreal to try to find work.

For these working-class Haitians, with limited education, limited French fluency, and limited urban labour experience, incorporation into Montreal did not prove easy. To support them, a group of Haitian Catholic clergy and lay leaders, led by Father Paul Dejean, founded the Bureau of Haitian Christians in Montreal.[8] The most urgent issue was the legal status of many of these Haitians, who entered on tourist visas and then stayed permanently. Similar to the Catholic Church's political advocacy for Haitians in Miami, Father Dejean wrote letters to the Quebec government on behalf of Haitians and even met personally with government officials, claiming that, because of the poor conditions in Haiti, Haitians should qualify for humanitarian visas. In a later legalization campaign, personal connections between Haitian Catholic clergy and Quebec Catholic clergy proved crucial in supporting the claims of Haitian asylum-seekers who feared political repression if they returned to Haiti.

Haitians' religious leaders sought to improve Haitians' reception by the Quebecois government and to build a strong community to support Haitians' incorporation. Up through the mid-1980s, the Bureau fulfilled multiple functions: it served as a welcoming place for newly arriving Haitians, provided an umbrella support organization to coordinate the efforts of Haitian leaders who wanted to launch social programmes, and mediated between the Haitian community and the state in order to access government funds for its social programmes. The Bureau's initial success would not have been possible without both the volunteer work and skilled leadership from the Haitian community and institutional support from other Quebecois Catholic institutions. For example, Catholic religious orders donated funds to support the Bureau's social programmes. Catholic service agencies, like the Centre for Social Aid to Immigrants run by the Sisters of Bon Secours, helped the Bureau's leaders write their initial charter. Because of its ties to Notre Dame d'Haïti Catholic mission in Montreal, the Bureau enjoyed the trust of the working-class Haitians it served.

Despite continued Haitian migration to Montreal, over time the Bureau lost much of its ability to support Haitians' incorporation there. First, after Jean-Claude Duvalier fled Haiti in 1986, some of the Bureau's initial leaders returned to Haiti. Second, Haitians in Montreal – unlike Haitians in Miami– faced deep intra-community divisions. While nearly all Haitians in Miami faced some racial prejudice, a form of external opposition that forced cooperation across class lines, incorporation proved relatively easy for light-skilled and Francophone Haitians in Montreal. When thousands of poorer, Creole-speaking, and deeply pious Haitians arrived in Montreal, their better off compatriots had already moved into different neighbourhoods and were discouraging their children from speaking Creole. Furthermore, pious acts that are common among working-class Haitian Catholics in Montreal, such as attending a Charismatic prayer service and Mass to ask the Blessed Virgin Mary to intercede for one's family, or invoking the Holy Spirit's healing powers to save one's children from gangs or drugs, or going up the hundreds of stairs in front of St. Joseph's Oratory on one's knees as a sign of penance clashed with the de-mystified and largely cultural Catholicism adopted by middle- and upper-class Haitians in Montreal. Hence, whereas Haitians' deep religious piety generated respect for them in Miami, it provoked concerns or even disdain in Montreal.

Increasing concern about the religiosity of immigrants led to changes in government policies that affected the Bureau. Haitians were the largest immigrant group to Montreal through the 1980s and, despite some difficulties, built a strong ethnic community and forged ties with government institutions there, sometimes through the Catholic Church's mediation. By the 1990s, however, Haitians were no longer the largest immigrant-sending group to Quebec, and concern about the symbolic and socio-economic incorporation of these newer immigrants, including many non-Christians, began to generate greater public and governmental concern. By the early 2000s, public uneasiness about too much ethnic and religious diversity led the Quebec government to demand that all voluntary associations receiving state funding be multiethnic and secular, thereby excluding organizations like the Bureau from most forms of government cooperation.[9] As described in the Bouchard-Taylor report (2008), policy changes such as these resulted from a perceived crisis that accommodating immigrants' ethnic and religious identities had undermined the secular and cultural identity of Quebec. In part to reinforce Quebec's identity as a secular and inter-cultural society, government agencies asserted their preference to work with multi-ethnic and secular organizations in 2003. The Bureau's leaders, yielding to this perceived loss of legitimacy with the government due to their identity as a faith-based service organization, removed the word Christian from its name in 2002. In hopes of continuing to receive government funding, the religious sisters who run the Centre for Social Aid to Immigrants also removed any reference to Christianity from their charter.

Haitians in Montreal are most highly concentrated in the two inner-city neighbourhoods of North Montreal and Saint Michel where their unemployment rates are twice those of the rest of Montreal.

These neighbourhoods also have high poverty rates, a majority of single-parent households, and high rates of youth dropping out of school (Torczyner, 2001). Both government officials and Haitian leaders in Montreal expressed grave concerns about Haitians' poor socio-economic incorporation. Although middle class Haitians settled in suburban areas of Montreal such as Laval, many more working-class Haitians have had little mobility out of the impoverished conditions of North Montreal and Saint Michel. Relatively few institutional ties exist across class boundaries among Haitians, especially as religious practice has declined rapidly among the middle- and upper-class Haitians but not the working class.

Haitians' difficulties in Montreal derive partly from their low levels of human capital and the difficult economic environment, but in addition, many community and government leaders are concerned that the increasing prejudice against Haitians makes their structural incorporation even more difficult. For example, a report on Montreal's black communities noted that "a young black person [in Montreal] inspires fear in certain communities…The justice system is the only system in which blacks and other visible minorities are over-represented" (Torczyner, 2001: 78). Despite concerns regarding Haitians' socio-economic and symbolic incorporation, government agencies are more likely to see religion as part of the problem rather than part of the solution to social problems. Although Quebecois government officials are aware of difficulties in Haitians' incorporation, they do not look to Haitians' religious institutions or faith-based service institutions for solutions. When asked about government cooperation with Haitians' religious institutions, one government official directly contrasted the Quebecois model of religion-state differentiation with that of the US, stating, "Churches only work with the poor in the US because the state is absent. In Quebec, the state has replaced the church." Such comments reflect the dominant narrative about religion-state relations in Quebec, according to which a modern, secular state took over all social welfare functions from the Catholic Church.

Paris and Haiti Development

In 1981, Catholic lay leaders and French clergy who had lived in Haiti founded the Haitian Catholic Community of Paris.[10] Twenty years later the Haitian Catholic Community of Paris had grown to a tightly knit community of a few hundred regular members who attended Sunday Mass together and formed many prayer groups which met during the week. Like Miami and Montreal, the most influential Haitian community association in Paris, Haiti Development, was founded by active leaders of Haitian Catholic Community of Paris.

René Benjamin, one of the lay members who helped begin the Haitian Catholic Mission of Paris, founded Haiti Development in the 1960s to encourage Haitian intellectuals and students living in France to return and support development in Haiti. Numerous Haitian associations in Paris exist on paper but have few members and focus mostly on politics and development in Haiti rather than Haitians' incorporation in Paris (Glaude, 2001). Benjamin was the only Haitian intellectual in Paris who eventually dedicated his efforts to supporting the incorporation of working-class Haitians in Paris. As with the Toussaint Centre in Miami and the Bureau in Montreal, Benjamin's position as a lay leader at the Haitian Catholic mission of Paris allowed him to build trust among the Haitians he served.

Benjamin used his perfect French language skills, French educational credentials, and experience working in a French bureaucracy to mediate between working-class Haitians and the French state. Given that there are so few legal ways for Haitians to migrate to France, the most common service Haiti Development provided was assistance in requesting political asylum. As in the US and Quebec, the French government relied on Haitian organizations, primarily Haiti Development, to inform them about the political conditions in Haiti that weigh heavily in deciding asylum claims. Like Quebec, Catholic organizations continue to provide some social services in France, although the republican ideology and assertive secularism, which insist on a unified national and secular identity, often make this work invisible to many French. Benjamin used contacts with other Catholic organizations like Catholic Charities to acquire funding for programs to assist Haitians in Paris with French language training and job placement assistance. However, he only obtained government funds to help with asylum claims, leaving social services to be handled by Benjamin and a few volunteers with some funds from Catholic agencies.

The symbolic boundary between French republican identity, which is decidedly secular, and Haitians' strong religious identity, made it hard for institutions like Haiti Development to gain pubic legitimacy or acquire government funding for social programmes. This symbolic boundary also limits cross-class solidarity among Haitians in Paris. Like most highly educated Haitians in Montreal, most Haitian élites in Paris who are highly educated and fluent in French found it easy to adopt many tenets of republicanism. However, by identifying with French republicanism and accepting the privatization of religion demanded by assertive secularism, upper-class Haitians in Paris no longer identified linguistically, racially, or religiously with working-class, dark-skinned, Creole-speaking and pious Haitians. One highly educated Haitian in Paris self-critically remarked that although Catholicism was brought to Haiti by the French, inculcated in Haiti through Francophone Catholic schools, and supported in Haiti partly by French religious orders, Catholicism constituted a barrier to incorporation in France. Working-class Haitians in Paris, whose background characteristics and tenuous legal status created great disadvantages for their incorporation, hold on to their strong religious and ethnic identity to aid with their incorporation. However, Haitians' associations in Paris lack much legitimacy with the government and, despite efforts by Haitian leaders, government officials have not supported their efforts to facilitate incorporation through language classes, job training, and day care. As one Haitian leader in Paris summarized the state's lack of interaction with representatives of the Haitian community, "Because of the French logic of integration [which focuses just on the individual, not groups], the state doesn't pay any attention to our [ethnic or religious] associations. We are invisible."

Have republicanism and *laïcité* worked to incorporate Haitians in Paris? Census data illustrate that few Haitians in Paris, even those who have high school degrees and beyond, work in professional occupations. The unemployment rate of nearly 30 per cent among Haitians is double that of the native population. Although Haitians' own background characteristics, namely their low levels of human capital, limited work experience, and, for some, limited French proficiency, certainly contribute to this difficult socio-economic incorporation, racial prejudice, their geographic location in the *banlieues*, and the state's practical ignorance of Haitians' mediating institutions only exacerbate this difficult incorporation (for a detailed analysis of census data on Haitians in France, see Mooney, 2011).[11] Around 90 per cent of Haitians in Paris live in the immigrant-dominated *banlieues*, which because of their high levels of unemployment and violence have now come to symbolize for many the failure of immigrant incorporation (Body-Gendrot, 2000). Although French republicanism upholds equality for all, the mostly Creole-speaking, low-skilled and dark-skinned Haitians who settled in these *banlieues* starting in the 1970s moved into an already economically segregated and socially stigmatized place known to inhibit, rather than promote, successful immigrant incorporation.

The dominant trend among French intellectuals and government officials is to hold to an assertive secularism which essentially posits that state vigilance and control over religious institutions is necessary for social progress. Despite the promises of equality in French republicanism, many immigrants in France, including Haitians, face both symbolic and structural barriers to their incorporation, as highlighted by the 2005 riots in the largely immigrant-inhabited *banlieues*. During several weeks of rioting, first- and second-generation immigrant youth – most of them North African or Sub-Saharan African in origin – burned thousands of vehicles and defaced symbols of the French Republic such as schools and government buildings, a particularly poignant rejection of the French republican model of integration. Scholars, politicians, and the French public continue to debate the causes and solutions of this failed immigrant incorporation. Some point to structural reasons, such as the lack of good education and jobs, whereas others point to cultural reasons, arguing that immigrants are just too culturally or religiously different to be integrated into the French nation. Although Haitian youth in the Parisian *banlieues* were not reported to be among the protagonists of the riots, nearly all Haitians in Paris live in *banlieues* where they lack social networks that would help them get jobs. The social stigma of living in the these neighbourhoods *banlieues* exacerbates the already difficult structural barriers Haitians face to their incorporation.

Working-class Haitians in Paris are aware that their pious religious beliefs form a symbolic boundary separating them from secular French society and from most highly educated Haitians in Paris. Whereas Haitian parents believe that successful incorporation requires both hard work and a strong community of faith, they expressed concern that the general secular climate in French society militates against their children's faith. Without a protective barrier of faith, Haitian parents fear that their children will join the downwardly mobile sector of other immigrants in the *banlieues*. Haitians in France, who face structural constraints on their incorporation—unemployment, discrimination, etc. – as well as symbolic boundaries – racial prejudice, assertive secularism—are discouraged in discourse and practice from forming "durable" ethnic and religious communities. Hence, the practice of French republicanism and assertive secularism limited the impact of Haiti Development on Haitians' socio-economic and structural incorporation in Paris.

CONCLUSIONS

Figure 1 summarizes how religion forms part of the context of reception that influenced Haitians' incorporation in Miami, Montreal and Paris. The US open market for religion encourages minorities to organize and mobilize around religious institutions, and the system of consensual differentiation between religious and state authorities facilitates the work of immigrants' religious mediating institutions. Haitians in Miami earned greater symbolic and institutional incorporation and hence will probably experience more socio-economic mobility in Miami than in Montreal or Paris. Haitian intellectuals and professionals first migrated to Montreal and initially helped more working-class Haitians incorporate, but over time and largely due to secular nationalism in Quebec, Haitians' mediating institutions lost their legitimacy with the government and much of their funding. In debates about social issues in Quebec, religion is more often seen as a problem than as part of the solution. Although Haitians in Montreal have high levels of unemployment and low education, they have weak mediating institutions that could advocate to the state on their behalf and help support their incorporation. Due to French republicanism and assertive secularism, Haitians in Paris are largely without institutional support in a difficult socio-economic context characterized by high levels of unemployment and spatial isolation in the impoverished and stigmatized *banlieues*. The French system of religion-state differentiation can be described as assertive secularism based on a cultural narrative that holds that "religion cannot contribute positively to the common public good" (Cesari, 2007: 37–38). In contrast to the cooperation between religion and state actors in the US, French "assertive secularism is a 'comprehensive doctrine' that aims to eliminate religion from the public sphere" (Kuru, 2007: 572).

Numerous factors influence immigrants' symbolic and socio-economic incorporation, such as background characteristics, the co-ethnic community, and societal and governmental reception of immigrants (Portes and Rumbaut, 2006). Despite some differences across the three communities, many Haitians in Miami, Montreal and Paris share a low socio-economic status, difficulties in attaining legal status, and face some racial prejudice. Hence, Haitian leaders in all three cities founded religious communities and faith-based social service institutions to serve a similar population and promote the symbolic and structural incorporation of disadvantaged Haitians. Despite

FIGURE 1
RELIGION AS A CONTEXT OF RECEPTION FOR HAITIANS

I. Macro-Level: Religion-State Relations	II. Meso-Level: Haitians' Mediating Institutions	III. Micro-Level: Haitians' Incorporation Paths and Outcomes
Open Market for Religion and Consensual Differentiation between Religion and State (Miami, Florida, United States)[1]	Haitians developed strong mediating institutions which developed a cooperative approach with state agencies	Increasing class diversity and strong religious identity among Haitians due, in part, to respect and cooperation between religious mediating institutions and the state
Secular Nationalism (Montreal, Quebec, Canada)[2]	Haitians' initially strong religious mediating institutions are gradually undermined by secular culture and nationalistic concerns for Quebecois cultural survival	Hindered socioeconomic mobility and increasing oppositional identity among Haitians
Assertive Secularism (Paris, France)[3]	Haitians' mediating institutions are largely ignored due to assertive secularism and a state-centered approach to immigrant incorporation	Blocked socioeconomic mobility among Haitians and strong religious identity clashes with secular culture

Notes:

1. U.S. government allows an open market for religion and cooperates with religious mediating institutions to incorporate cultural and ethnic minorities.

2. Concern for Quebecois cultural survival sets limits on immigrants' cultural and religious practices and growing secularism reduces government cooperation with religious mediating institutions.

3. Republicanism and *laïcité* are normative models for immigrant incorporation.

similar disadvantages across all three cities, the receiving context in Miami supports Haitians' religious institutions but weakens them in Montreal and Paris. Thus, the receiving context contributes in part to Haitians' stronger symbolic and socio-economic incorporation in Miami relative to Montreal or Paris.

In Paris, Catholic leaders attempt to mediate for Haitians, but feel largely invisible to the state. Haitians in Miami expressed more confidence in their children's future than did their counterparts in Montreal or Paris, in part because the Haitian community in Miami has a strong institutional mediator through the organizations and hierarchy of the Catholic Church. Despite similar efforts to support immigrant incorporation, Catholic institutions and leaders in Montreal and Paris do not enjoy much legitimacy with their respective governments.

What are the consequences for immigrant integration more generally that stem from these different contexts of reception regarding religion? Writing about immigrants in general in the US, noted immigration scholars Alejandro Portes and Rubén Rumbaut argue that although religion does not directly determine immigrants' political and social incorporation, "because religion has proved to be one of the most resilient elements of immigrants' culture across generations, the beliefs and organized activities carried out by different foreign groups in this realm can be expected to be a trademark of their long-term incorporation into American society and, simultaneously, a key force in the guiding character of this process" (2006: 341).

The greatest contrast between cases is that of the US and France. Whereas in the US, mediating institutions organized around ethnicity and religion facilitate the incorporation process, in France, the republican model of immigrant integration expects individuals to interact directly with the state. Recent debates in France have shown that, despite some differences of opinion, great support exists for continuing the republican model of immigrant integration. However, ethnographic work among immigrants in France indicates a large gap between theory and reality. Greater recognition of immigrants' religious identities and organizations would probably improve the cultural and structural incorporation of immigrants in France. The current policies of *laïcité* are perceived by many immigrants as an assertive secularism that marginalizes their religion, often reinforcing religion as a hostile boundary between religious immigrants and the secular French.

In Quebec, the Bouchard-Taylor Commission and Report generated much controversial discussion about religion in the public sphere. Although government funds do not need to directly support religious houses of worship, government funds have in the past contributed to Catholic faith-based service institutions to support immigrant integration. Continuing or even extending that practice to other immigrant faiths would probably promote greater symbolic recognition of immigrants' religious faiths as well as improved economic conditions for immigrants in Quebec. More generally, Canadian multiculturalism policy and Quebec's inter-culturalism policy recognize that ethnic identities are important community bonds, but not religious identities. Immigrants like many Haitians question this assumption, and claims made by religious groups may lead to a new understanding of religion in the public sphere in Canada and Quebec. As it is practised, Quebec's secularism seeks to privatize religious identities and organizations while actively incorporating ethnic identities and organizations into public policies and discussions. Hence, while a less rigid form of secularism than that of France, Quebec's secularism is not neutral in practice.

Policy debates about religion-state relations and immigrant integration often lack cross-national comparative studies with data from various levels. Census data and longitudinal data provide insights on structural incorporation, but ethnographic fieldwork and interviews provide further insights on how norms regarding the public expression of religion impact immigrant integration. Although the symbolic and structural integration patterns of integration may look different for second-generation immigrants or for immigrants who are a religious minority (such as Muslims or Sikhs) the conceptual model for investigating religion-state relations and immigrant integrating outlined in this article provides a starting point from which to collect empirical data to assess how religion influences immigrants' symbolic and structural incorporation in different national and local contexts.

NOTES

1. See: http://www12.statcan.ca/census-recensement/2006/as-sa/97-557/p10-eng.cfm, (accessed 1 April 2011); and United Nations, Department of Economic and Social Affairs, Population Division (2009). Trends in International Migrant Stock: The 2008 Revision (United Nations database, POP/DB/MIG/Stock/Rev.2008).
2. To back up his claims, Liogier uses evidence from laws, interviews with government officials and intellectuals, and his own work ethnographic and survey work studying new religious movements, such as Buddhism, in France.
3. In order to be able to compare a single religious institution in all three contexts, I focused only on the Haitian Catholic missions of each city.
4. Father Wenski was named Auxiliary Bishop of Miami in 1996. He was then named Bishop of Orlando, a position he held from 2002 to 2010, when he returned to Miami to serve as Archbishop. Even though he had already been ordained a bishop by the time I first interviewed him in 2001, I refer to him as Father Wenski because that was his title while he served the Haitian community.
5. For more on the history of Notre Dame and the Toussaint Center, see also Rey and Stepick (2009).
6. For greater detail on Haitians' socio-economic incorporation in Miami, see Mooney (2009) and Stepick, Stepick, et al. (2001).
7. Louis Balhazar (2009) argues that the development of a modern state in Quebec and the institutional differentiation between church and state is referred to as the "Quiet" Revolution precisely because not all church leaders fought this change. Indeed, he shows that Catholic clergy, intellectuals and lay leaders

actively supported the creation of a modern Quebecois state by giving their political support and transferring large parts of their educational and health systems, among others things, to the state.

8. In French, *le Bureau de la communauté chrétienne des Haïtiens à Montréal*.

9. As immigration to Quebec increased and diversified, there was a strong perception that religion (in particular non-Christian religion) was conflicting with largely secular (yet still culturally Catholic) Quebec. In 2007, the Quebec government formed a commission to review practices of accommodating immigrants' religious and ethnic practices. The report that resulted from the 2007-2008 Consultation Commission on Accommodation Practices Related to Cultural Differences argued that the concerns about government accommodation of immigrants' religious and cultural practices were greatly exaggerated (Bouchard and Taylor 2008). Despite expressing concerns about immigrants' lack of socio-economic incorporation, the report makes no mention of any positive contributions of faith-based service institutions to Quebec's immigrant communities, hence rendering their work invisible.

10. In French, *la Communauté catholique Haïtienne de Paris*.

11. Because Haitians are a relatively small and relatively recent immigrant group in France, and because the French census does not identify all second-generation immigrants, my research did not uncover many statistics on second-generation Haitians in France. My assessment of the future of second-generation Haitians thus relies on data about the incorporation of first-generation Haitians as well as data on second-generation immigrants from other nationalities who live in similar conditions as Haitians.

REFERENCES

Balthazar, L.
    2009   "La nationalité québécoise et l'Église catholique", in L. A. Richard (Ed.) *La nation sans religion? Le défi des ancrages au Québec*, Presses de l'Université Laval, Québec: 131–154.

Beyer, P.
    2013   "Regional Differences and Continuities at the Intersection of Culture and Religion: A Case Study
    (Forth   of Immigrant and Second Generation Young Adults in Canada", in S. Lefebvre and L. Beaman,
    coming)   (Eds) *Religion in the Public Sphere: Interdisciplinary Perspectives across the Canadian Provinces*, University of Toronto Press, Toronto.

Body-Gendrot, S.
    2000   *The Social Control of Cities: A Comparative Perspective*, Blackwell Publishers, Oxford, UK.

Bouchard, G., and C. Taylor
    2008   "Building the Future: A Time for Reconciliation", Government of Quebec, Montreal. http://www. accommodements.qc.ca/documentation/rapports/rapport-final-integral-en.pdf (accessed 10 July 2010).

Cesari, J.
    2007   "The Muslim Presence in the United States and France: Its Consequences for Secularism", *French Politics, Culture, & Societ,y* 25(2): 34–45.

Feldblum, M.
    1999   *Reconstructing Citizenship: The Politics of Nationality, Reform and Immigration in Contemporary France*, State University of New York Press, Albany.

Foner, N., and R. Alba
    2008   "Immigrant Religion in the US and Western Europe: Bridge or Barrier to Inclusion?", *International Migration Review* 42(2): 360–292.

Glaude, S.
    2001   "Le dynamisme associatif des migrants haïtiens en France métropolitaine", *Administration Économique et Sociale. Option: Développement Social*, Université Paris, Saint-Dénis, 8: 60.

Gordon, M. M.
    1964   *Assimilation in American Life: The Role of Race, Religion, and National Origins*, Oxford University Press, New York.

Handlin, O.
    1951   *The Uprooted: The Epic Story of the Great Migrations that Made the American People*, Little Brown, Boston.

Hargreaves, A. G.
   1995   *Immigration, 'Race' and Ethnicity in Contemporary Franc*, Routledge, New York.
Herberg, W.
   1955   *Protestant, Catholic, Jew: An Essay in American Religious Sociology*. University of Chicago Press,
             Chicago.
Jackson, R., (Ed.)
   2011   *Geographies of the Haitian Diaspora*, Routledge, New York.
Kuru, A. T.
   2007   "Historical Conditions, Ideological Struggles, and State Policies Toward religion", *World Politics*,
             59(4): 568–594.
Labelle, M., and F. Midy
   1999   "Re-reading Citizenship and the Transnational Practices of Immigrants", *Journal of Ethnic and
             Migration Studies*, 25:213–232.
Liogier, R.
   2006   *Une Laïcité "Légitime": la France et ses religions d'Etat*, Entrelacs, Paris.
Mooney, M.A.
   2006   "The Catholic Bishops Conferences of the United States and France: Engaging Immigration as a
             Public Issue", *American Behavioral Scientist*, 49 (11): 1455–1470.
   2009   *Faith Makes Us Live: Surviving and Thriving in the Haitian Diaspora*, University of California
             Press, Berkeley.
   2011   "Mediating Institutions and the Adaptation of Haitian Immigrants in Paris", in R. O. Jackson (Ed.),
             Geographies of the Haitian Diaspora, Routledge, New York: 113–134
   2013   (forthcoming) "Religion and the Incorporation of Haitians in Montreal", in S. Lefebvre and L. Be-
             aman (Eds), *Religion in the Public Sphere: Interdisciplinary Perspectives Across the Canadian
             Provinces*, University of Toronto Press, Toronto.
Noiriel, G.
   1996   *The French Melting Pot: Immigration, Citizenship, and National Identity*, University of Minnesota
             Press, Minneapolis.
Portes, A., and R. G. Rumbaut
   2006   *Immigrant America: A Portrait*, University of California Press, Berkeley,
Reitz, J. G.
   1998   *Warmth of the Welcome: The Social Causes of Economic Success for Immigrants in Different
             Nations and Cities*, Westview Press, Boulder.
Rey, T., and A. Stepick
   2009   "Refugee Catholicism in Little Haiti: Notre Dame d'Haiti Catholic Church", in A. Stepick, T. Rey
             and S. Mahler (Eds), *Churches and Charity in the Immigrant City*, Rutgers University Press, New
             Brunswick: 72–91
Stepick, A., and C. D. Stepick, et al.
   2001   "Shifting Identities and Intergenerational Conflict: Growing up Haitian in Miami", in R. Rumbaut
             and A. Portes, *Ethnicities: Children of Immigrants in America*, University of California Press,
             Berkeley: 229–0266
Stotzky, I. P.
   2004   "Haitian Refugees and the Rule of Law", *Guild Practicioner* 61(3): 151–192.
Torczyner, J. L.
   2001   *The Evolution of the Black Community of Montreal: Change and Challenge*, McGill Consortium
             for Ethnicity and Strategic Social Planning, Montreal.
Van Die, M.
   2001   *Religion and Public Life in Canada: Historical and Comparative Perspectives*, University of Tor-
             onto Press, Toronto.
Warner, R. S.
   1993   "Work in Progress toward a New Paradigm for the Sociological-Study of Religion in the United-
             States", *American Journal of Sociology*, 98(5): 1044–1093.
Wood, R.
   2002   *Faith in Action: Religion, Race and Democratic Organizing in America*, Univeristy of Chicago
             Press, Chicago.

[19]

Journal of Refugee Studies Vol. 15, No. 2 2002

FIELD REPORTS

Nuer Christians in America

DIANNA J. SHANDY

Department of Anthropology, Macalester College, St Paul, Minnesota

This paper interrogates the socio-political role of Christianity in the forced migration experiences of southern Sudanese refugees living in the United States. Religion is implicated in the conflict in Sudan; faith-based organizations broker these refugees' resettlement in the United States; and engagement with US Christian Churches eases the transition to a new society. Based on ethnographic research with Sudanese refugees and American service providers, this paper probes the ways in which cultural constructions of Christians influence the incorporation of these newcomers into US congregations. In addition, the paper highlights the need for more scholarly attention to the study of Nuer Christianity as an indigenized belief system that enables this population to cope with radical change in their lives.

Introduction

This report explores the socio-political role of Christianity within the refugee resettlement process of southern Sudanese in the United States. It focuses on how cultural constructions of Christians affect the nature and quality of engagement between Nuer and American Christians. In addition, it probes the ways secular social scientists relate to belief systems and matters of faith amongst their study population and highlights the need for more scholarly attention to the study of Nuer Christianity as an indigenized belief system that helps forced migrants cope with extreme and rapid social change.

Since the early 1990s, nearly 20,000 Sudanese refugees have been resettled in the United States (USDHHS 2002). This article draws on ongoing ethnographic research begun in August 1996 with several hundred Nuer and other southern Sudanese refugees in the United States. During this period I have interviewed more than 150 adult Sudanese refugees and more than 75 non-Sudanese individuals involved with this population's resettlement about myriad aspects of their lives associated with displacement, resettlement, and social change. Pseudonyms are used to preserve individuals' anonymity.

214   *Dianna J. Shandy*

Background

One facet of the protracted conflict in Sudan is Muslim–Christian religious strife. It is impossible to disentangle the threads of religion, ethnicity, and control over resources, including oil, which feed the current civil war that has raged since 1983 (see Deng 1995; Hutchinson 1996; Johnson 1994; Jok and Hutchinson 1999). Nonetheless, the politicization of religious identity in Sudan is vital to how the crisis and the refugee flows it generates are perceived internationally.[1]

The Socio-Political Role of Christianity in the Sudanese Refugee Experience

Here, I outline four points of articulation between religion and the experiences of southern Sudanese forced migrants. First, religious identity feeds the politics of difference in Sudan and legitimates the position of those seeking refugee status in ways that fleeing hunger, destruction of the means of livelihood, and other results of civil war simply do not. In contrast to many conflict settings, the religious element of the Sudanese crisis makes those who flee fit Zolberg, Suhrke, and Aguayo's (1989: 6) description of 'classic refugees' or those who are fleeing a life-threatening danger 'with "life" referring to spiritual as well as physical existence.' Framing asylum claims in the language of religious persecution allows Nuer and other southern Sudanese to make their experience meaningful to representatives of the international refugee regime. By way of illustration, some Nuer men recounted an interview experience in a refugee camp in Kenya in which a man named Ahmed Bol Deng was advised by a US legal advisor in the camp to eliminate Ahmed from his name and his son's name if he wanted to qualify for resettlement in the United States. Ahmed was claiming persecution in Sudan on the basis of being Christian, but his and his son's name (Jal Ahmed Bol Deng) were Islamic. In this case, outward markers of religious affiliation assumed importance in securing third country resettlement. This example illustrates the significance of religion in making a refugee status determination for a single case, yet religion also plays a role in the worldwide triage of third country resettlement priorities.

Second, a Christian religious identity links southern Sudanese to a wider international community. To illustrate, in a recent US symposium on Sudan,[2] a Presbyterian pastor opened the event by noting, 'As a Christian, I feel obligated to participate in these matters.' These transnational ties are significant in their ability to leverage international support for resources directed towards Sudan and southerners' quest for political autonomy. Persecution of Christians, oil, and allegations of slavery in Sudan are all issues that generate broad-based domestic constituencies in the United States. This constellation of issues has made for strange political bedfellows. Liberal, secular social scientists find themselves standing on the same platform as members of the conservative, Christian right in American politics in advocating for the cause of southern Sudan. Increased recognition of the

Sudanese conflict has coincided with the passage of the US International Religious Freedom Act of 1998, which prioritizes the promotion of free religious belief and practice within a US foreign assistance political agenda (see Hackett, Silk, and Hoover 2000). Sudan is one of the countries targeted by this legislation.

Third, in addition to its bridge building capacity connecting the southern Sudan to a global community of Christians, constructing a common Christian identity creates an idiom of kinship that has the potential to unite disparate ethnic groups and sub-groups within and across ethnicities in Sudan. This is noteworthy given the distinctive segmentary socio-political organization among groups like the Nuer and the Dinka in this region of Africa (see Evans-Pritchard 1940; Deng 1972). This unifying potential perhaps is illustrated best by the March 1999 Nuer-Dinka Peace and Reconciliation Conference in Wunlit, Sudan, sponsored by the New Sudan Council of Churches. However, any promise offered by an overarching religious identity must be viewed cautiously. Some argue that politicization of religious identities within Christianity may be implicated in escalating tensions in intra-group (i.e. Nuer) fighting in the South (Hutchinson n.d.). In light of the limited prospects for southern unity, a common religious identity as a galvanizing agent cannot be excluded without further consideration. However, as yet it remains to be seen whether any sort of overarching Christian religious identity in southern Sudan could have significant coalescing power.

And fourth, among Sudanese refugees in the United States, Christian identity serves as a vehicle for social reconstruction. From the moment refugees are met at the airport by their sponsoring agency, religious institutions manage their integration into the host society. In the United States, many of the voluntary agencies that contract with the US government to implement its refugee resettlement programme are Christian-based, including Lutheran Social Services, Episcopal Migration Ministries, and Catholic Charities. While these programmes are obliged to and do operate along secular lines, Christian churches and congregations act as sponsors, and volunteers are often recruited within these bodies to assist in easing refugees' transition to the United States. These volunteers are vital to the resettlement experience in that they are the ones who familiarize individual refugees with the essentials of quotidian life in an environment that is vastly different from the one with which they are acquainted. For example, in addition to hosting recently arrived refugees in their homes, volunteers associated with these religious institutions have gathered clothing and household materials; helped people find low-cost housing and cars, and employment; and provided instruction in how to ride a bus, do grocery shopping, and operate a microwave.

Most recently, federal legislation passed in the United States strengthens this connection between the dissemination of social services and religious institutions (see Goodstein 2001). While refugee resettlement in the United States has long been managed by these same faith-based organizations, this recent legislation will expand the role of religious institutions in administering

216   *Dianna J. Shandy*

and providing social services. Controversy around this initiative stems from concern over whether this will lead to an abrogation of governmental responsibility to provide services, shifting this undertaking to faith-based organizations.

Cultural Constructions of Christians

Churches in the United States emerge as a key venue for the incorporation of Sudanese and other refugees into US society. Aihwa Ong (1996: 745) has noted in writing about Cambodian refugees in the United States that 'churches are vital agents in converting immigrants into acceptable citizens,' and these religious institutions exert considerable influence in shaping the adaptation process in ways that are consistent with their worldview. It must be noted, however, that these processes are not unidirectional, and refugees resist as they negotiate their way through American Christianity.

Similar to the experiences of Jewish Ethiopians in Israel (see Kaplan 1992), Sudanese encounter cultural as well as spiritual Christian norms upon arriving in the United States. For example, an American woman in Nebraska who was reflecting on the interactions between Nuer and churches there put it this way: 'They attend the First Covenant, the Presbyterian, the Zion Lutheran, and the Seventh Day Adventist churches, but the majority don't go to church. They are really godly, but they live dispersed and don't always make it to church.' When Sudanese do attend, they frequent many different churches. This is related, in part, to the fact that Sudanese tend to live spatially dispersed (see Shandy 2001). It also is related to the ways that Sudanese engage with American Christianity.

Two key features of American Christianity that Sudanese refugees appear to be tapping into are voluntarism and denominationalism. Disappointment over both regular attendance and what I call 'denominational drift' was a recurrent theme in my interviews with American church members. The denominational array of Protestant Churches present in the United States did not exist in Sudan in the 1980s and 1990s when these refugees left their country. Dee, an American who attended a Presbyterian church, noted that 'in general, churches have been able to provide space, manpower, money, and promises of help, without fully thinking through what that entails' for Sudanese refugees. She went on to observe 'Sudanese jump ship for promises of aid from somewhere else. And Americans feel burnt when this happens.' Bella, another Presbyterian woman, described this in poignant detail when she described her friendship over several years with a Nuer man and his family. The family had shown up one night unannounced at the church after a long bus journey from another state where they had been resettled initially by a voluntary agency. It was the dead of winter, and they had arrived without suitable clothes for the climate; members of Bella's church mobilized and assisted the young family with housing, clothing, transportation, and a job. One day, without alerting anyone, the family loaded their minivan with some of their belongings and left. Bella grew tearful in recounting the story, saying that she would have been saddened if they had told her that they were leaving, but she was deeply hurt by the fact that they had not said goodbye to her or any of the other church members. She later learned through church channels that the man had been offered an opportunity to serve as pastor in a Covenant Church in another state.

This movement from the Presbyterian to the Covenant Church is grounded in the, perhaps predictable, way in which Sudanese pastors who ministered to congregations in Africa frequently have found their credentials and achievements devalued in the United States. This seems particularly true in the Presbyterian Church, which was among the first to send missionaries to Sudan in the nineteenth century, particularly to Nuer areas (Pitya 1996). Many Sudanese refugees were Presbyterians or Seventh Day Adventists when they arrived in the United States. Individual Presbyterian churches, like other Christian denominations, have welcomed the southern Sudanese as persecuted Christians and offered them moral and material support. Presbyterian churches, however, have been hampered by their governance structure in allowing Sudanese to serve as official pastors. According to Sheila Sundren, a Presbyterian pastor who works with other immigrant populations, the Presbyterian Church, relative to other Christian churches, is rigidly structured; it struggles to incorporate these 'other-language' pastors and makes exacting requirements for those who have not attended a US Presbyterian-approved seminary. Sheila described this dynamic in the following manner:

> In churches where there are pastors from other countries, the English-speaking pastor is always the senior pastor. The other-language pastor is paid less. The power dynamics are always there.

Sheila characterizes Presbyterian immigrants who seek to be pastors for US congregations as falling into a category called officially 'labouring within the bounds' and perhaps more descriptively falling *'between the cracks.'* These relationships manifest themselves in power and compensation inequities. Significantly, Sudanese who were pastors in Africa lack the requisite educational background to serve as Presbyterian pastors in the United States. An African service provider involved in refugee resettlement in California explained:

> A lot [of Sudanese] came here and are Presbyterian. They felt that they were not welcomed by the church. They came with elders and deacons, but there was no place for them in the church hierarchy. Truly, when pastors and deacons were ordained in Africa, it was by American missionaries. They don't understand what happened to them during their long hours of flight on the airplane from Africa. It was a disturbing thing. In Africa, there was a pastor in the refugee camp. He was asked to go through training again in America. In San Diego, we are handling this by recognizing the Sudanese pastor as a visiting pastor.

An American service provider in Texas noted that a Sudanese man 'had to walk on water to be accepted into the seminary.' Sudanese face a conundrum in

218   *Dianna J. Shandy*

engagements with the Presbyterian Church in America: By virtue of being Christian, they were denied opportunities for education in Sudan. Due to little education, they are prevented from accessing pastoral training in the United States. Some Nuer have responded by attending other Protestant churches with a less stringent set of rules governing access to pastoral positions. These institutions provide material and emotional support, but perhaps most significantly they provide space in which Sudanese can undertake social and political organizing necessary for community building. While Sudanese do disperse for weekly church attendance, they reunite at inter-denominational holiday services.

One final area relating to religion and refugees in the United States that merits mentioning is the social processes of incorporation of Nuer newcomers into existing American Christian churches. Within congregations that have incorporated Sudanese populations, there have been mixed responses ranging from extraordinary openness to hostility. For some church members, welcoming Nuer has provided opportunities to look far beyond the confines of their local community, prompting some church members to travel to East Africa and, remarkably, even to the war zone in southern Sudan. For other church members, the Sudanese newcomers have been unwanted and burdensome intruders causing dissent within the church. In light of these extremes, this is an area that warrants further investigation.

Adherents of the Secular and the Sacred

My efforts to situate the experiences of Nuer Christians within the forced migration literature, with a few notable exceptions discussed below, revealed a lacuna in the research on refugees and matters of faith or spirituality. Therefore, one final aim of this paper is to probe the ways in which secular social scientists relate to matters of religion amongst their study populations and, in pausing to consider how this relationship influences the social construction of knowledge about this subject, to prompt dialogue on this subject.

In reflecting upon the intersection of religion and forced migration, Diana Eck's perspective is helpful: 'Studying religion means trying to understand the forces of faith that have created, undergirded, and sometimes undermined the great civilizations and cultures of the world' (2000: 3). She goes on to note the importance of understanding religions as dynamic processes—and quite literally so when considered in migration contexts.

Taking anthropology as a case in point within the social sciences, one can observe that all religions are not viewed equally. For instance, an anthropologist is more likely to assume a culturally relativistic stance when talking about magic than Mormonism. It is telling that in a recent poll of college faculty in the United States, more than three out of five anthropologists claimed no religion at all, making them the highest percentage among faculty of non-believers (Wagner 1997: 95).[3] In my own fieldwork, it was only when I reviewed my notes and began to write that I realized the extent to which my own religious views shaped my research agenda. To the extent that I addressed religion at all, I focused on the socio-political role of religion but not on the affective or spiritual dimensions. Moreover, I was always more engaged when Nuer people spoke about their 'grandparents' religion' (which sounds very much like what Evans-Pritchard (1956) describes in *Nuer Religion*) than about their own connection with Christianity. In retrospect, I was viewing Nuer appropriation of Christianity as 'a type of capitulation or surrender' (Piot 1999: 174) or culture loss, and failing to appreciate the additive and improvisational nature of processes of culture change.

In a post-colonial world, the research emphasis, particularly on Christianity, remains on religion as an encroaching ideology or tool of oppression rather than on the ways in which formerly colonized peoples have made it their own (see Peterson and Allman 1999: 3; Comaroff 1986). Hutchinson (1996) describes this degree of flexibility and improvisation among Nuer belief systems relating to expiation rituals and incest. However, she goes on to develop the argument that Christianity is ill-equipped to respond to the social and spiritual ills that indigenous Nuer religion was able to address. I am not sure that Christianity and Nuer religion, at least as played out in the diaspora, exist in an adversarial framework. Hutchinson's conceptual framework that focuses on the malleability of belief could be extended to understand the ways in which Sudanese negotiate American Christianity.

This report has interrogated religion as a socio-political category but has not treated Nuer Christianity as a belief system with certain practices—creeds, codes, and cultus—that have some relationship to American Christianity, but, being culturally based, are not identical with it. Additional research is needed to understand the ways Nuer as well as other Sudanese populations have made Christianity their own. This relates to a larger research agenda in forced migration studies as faith and belief systems, as an integral orienting framework within culture, are something that forced migrants do not leave behind in their forced migration journey. Analysis of faith and belief systems is especially pertinent to the literature on forced migration that focuses predominantly on what is lost in the experiences of upheaval and trauma that characterize refugee populations (see Shandy 2001).

A point of departure for generating further inquiry into the affective and spiritual dimensions of refugee experiences could be Wendy James' (1997) work on 'fear' amongst the Uduk. In this article, James explores a violent incident between Nuer and Uduk refugees in Ethiopia. In so doing, she considers the ethnographic description and anthropological analysis of emotion in this refugee setting. By arguing against cultural and behavioural reductionism, James engages forced migration scholars in reflection on the connection between events and experience. Similarly, ethnographies of religious and spiritual beliefs as resiliency factors in the refugee journey would provide a more balanced view of the ways refugees make sense of their experiences of displacement (see Goździak and Tuskan 2000; Trix 2000; Welaratna 1993).

220   *Dianna J. Shandy*

Conclusion

Clearly, Nuer lives in America intersect with and are constituted in relation to Christianity in multiple ways: from the politicization of religious identity in Sudan; to their religious affiliation that renders their situation noticeable to a US constituency; to the agencies brokering their US resettlement; to the community support offered to support official institutional resettlement initiatives. Religion, in both a socio-political and an affective sense, is therefore a thread woven throughout the depth and breadth of Nuer refugees' experiences.

My comments in the above section on the relationship between adherents of the secular and the sacred are intended to be exploratory in nature and stem directly from dilemmas I faced in my own fieldwork experiences. Developing an understanding of the socio-political role of religion in Sudanese refugees' journeys is one dimension of their experiences. Yet, in addition to this tangible, observable set of social events and processes is a spiritual one. My understanding of Nuer refugee experiences would have been deepened through a greater appreciation of how Nuer shaped events and experience into memory and used faith and belief in Christianity to make sense of their fragmented lives (James 1997: 116). By probing the nature of secular, anthropological inquiry in the realm of the sacred, my intent is to promote dialogue among those who study and publish, and thereby construct knowledge, about forced migrant populations.

1. The advent of Islam in Sudan is traced to the seventh century. The first contact between Christian missionaries and southern Sudanese came in the mid-nineteenth century. See Pitya (1996) for a full treatment of the subject of Christianity in Sudan.
2. The Future of Southern Sudan: A Symposium, Macalester College, Saint Paul, Minnesota, USA, 1–2 March 2002.
3. Wagner (1997: 95) reports this finding from the following source: Institute for the Study of Evangelical Religion (1991) 'Thirty Percent of College Faculty Claim No Religious Belief.' *Evangelical Studies Bulletin* 8(2): 4.

COMAROFF, J. (1985) *Body of Power, Spirit of Resistance: The Culture and History of a South African People*. Chicago: University of Chicago Press.
DENG, F. M. (1972) *The Dinka of the Sudan*. Prospect Heights, IL: Waveland Press.
—— (1995) *War of Visions*. Washington, DC: Brookings Institution Press.
ECK, D. L. (2000) 'Religion and the Global Moment', pp. 3–26 in A. Samatar (ed.) *Contending Gods: Religion and the Global moment. Macalester International Volume* 8.
EVANS-PRITCHARD, E. P. (1940) *The Nuer: A Description of the Modes of Livelihood and Political Institutions of a Nilotic People*. Oxford: Clarendon Press.
—— (1956) *Nuer Religion*. Oxford: Clarendon Press.
GOODSTEIN, L. (2001) 'States Steer Religious Charities Toward Aid', *New York Times*, 21 July.
GOŹDZIAK, E. M. and **TUSKAN, Jr., J. J.** (2000) 'Operation Provide Refuge: The Challenge of Integrating Behavioral Science and Indigenous Approaches to Human Suffering', pp. 194–222 in E. M. Goździak and D. J. Shandy (eds.) *Rethinking Refuge and Displacement. Selected Papers on Refugees and Immigrants, vol. VIII*. Fairfax, VA: American Anthropological Association.
HACKETT, R. I. J., SILK, M. and **HOOVER, D.** (eds.) (2000) *Religious Persecution as US Policy Issue*. Hartford, CT: Center for the Study of Religion in Public Life.
HUTCHINSON, S. (1996) *Nuer Dilemmas: Coping with Money, War and the State. Berkeley*: University of California Press.
—— (n.d.) 'Spiritual Fragments of an Unfinished War' (unpublished ms).

Nuer Christians in America   221

JAMES, W. (1997) 'The Names of Fear: Memory, History, and the Ethnography of Feeling among Uduk Refugees', *Journal of the Royal Anthropological Institute* (n.s.) **3**: 115–131.

JOHNSON, D. H. (1994) *Nuer Prophets: A History of Prophecy from the Upper Nile in the Nineteenth and Twentieth Centuries*. Oxford: Clarendon Press.

JOK, J. M. and HUTCHINSON, S. (1999) 'Sudan's Prolonged Second Civil War and the Militarization of Nuer and Dinka Ethnic Identities', *African Studies Review* **42**(2): 125–145.

KAPLAN, S. B. (1992) *The Beta Israel (Falasha) in Ethiopia: From Earliest Times to the 20th Century*. New York: New York University Press.

ONG, A. (1996) 'Cultural Citizenship as Subject-making', *Current Anthropology* **37**(5): 737–751.

PETERSON, D. and ALLMAN, J. (1999) 'Introduction: New Directions in the History of Missions in Africa', *Journal of Religious History* **23**(1). 1–7.

PIOT, C. (1999) *Remotely Global Village Modernity in West Africa*. Chicago: University of Chicago Press.

PITYA, P. L. (1996) 'History of Western Christian Evangelism in the Sudan, 1898–1964', PhD dissertation, Boston University.

SHANDY, D. J. (2001) 'Perils and Possibilities of Nuer Refugee Migration to the United States', PhD Dissertation, Columbia University.

TRIX, F. (2000) 'Reframing the Forced Migration and Rapid Return of Kosovar Albanians', pp. 250-275 in E. M. Goździak and D. J. Shandy (eds.) *Rethinking Refuge and Displacement. Selected Papers on Refugees and Immigrants, vol. VIII*. Fairfax, VA: American Anthropological Association.

USDHHS (US Department of Health and Human Services), Administration for Children and Families, Office of Refugee Resettlement, Department of Human Services (2002) Unpublished data set.

WAGNER, M. B. (1997) 'The Study of Religion in American Society', pp. 85–102 in S. D. Glazier (ed.) *Anthropology of Religion: A Handbook*. Westport, Connecticut: Greenwood Press.

WELARATNA, U. (1993) *Beyond the Killing Fields: Voices of Nine Cambodian Survivors in America*. Stanford: Stanford University Press.

ZOLBERG, A., SUHRKE, A. and AGUAYO, S. (1989) *Escape from Violence: Conflict and the Refugee Crisis in the Developing World*. Oxford: Oxford University Press.

Part VI
Religious Identification and Practice

[20]

Ethnic and Racial Studies Vol. 34 No. 4 April 2011 pp. 643–661

Immigrants' religious participation in the United States

Ilana Redstone Akresh

(*First submission September 2009; First published November 2010*)

Abstract

Using New Immigrant Survey 2003 data, I examine immigrants' religious participation once in the United States. This is the first large-scale study to consider this question quantitatively and to compare across origin groups; the findings are key to informing our knowledge of the religious lives of the foreign born. Results indicate that, after accounting for participation before coming to the US, time in the US exhibits a robust, positive association with an increase in religious participation, suggesting the continuing importance of religion in immigrants' adjustment, in spite of the disruptive event of migration.

Keywords: Assimilation; immigrant incorporation; religion; immigrants; immigration; transnational.

An important question that has persisted in the literature on immigrants' religious participation in the US is what happens to their religious behaviour the longer they remain in the US. Immigrants come from a wide variety of religious backgrounds and practices, diversity that further highlights the importance of understanding these patterns. Much of the existing literature examining immigrants and religion has consisted of ethnographic studies focusing on small groups. While these studies have expanded our understanding of the links between religion and assimilation (Hurh and Kim 1990; Ebaugh and Chafetz 2000; Guest, 2003; Min and Kim 2003; Cavalcanti and Schleef 2005), between religion and the formation of ethnic identities (Bankston and Zhou 1996; Warner and Wittner 1998; Kurien 1998, 2001; Yang 2000; Cha 2001), between religion and transnationalism (Menjivar 1999) and between religion and positive acculturation and upward mobility (Bankston and Zhou 1995; Cao 2005), one

644   *Ilana Redstone Akresh*

important aspect of the role of religion on which they have remained largely silent is the link between immigrants' religious habits before and after coming to the US. Largely due to previous data limitations, this is the first large study able to consider this relationship and examine participation patterns across origin groups (Cadge and Ecklund 2007).

The shift in immigrant origins in the last four decades from being primarily European in nature to Asian and Latin American has also brought new diversity in religious backgrounds. In the early twentieth century, the foreign-born population was dominated by Catholics and Protestants (Herberg 1950). Although Catholics in particular continue to dominate numerically, there are now substantial Buddhist, Hindu and Muslim populations as well (Yang and Ebaugh 2001; Hirschman 2004). Data from the 2002 and 2004 General Social Survey on all foreign-born indicate that 39.4 per cent identify as Catholic, 24.1 per cent as Protestant, 2.1 as general Christian, 3.4 as Jewish, 4.6 as Muslim, 3.7 per cent as Orthodox Christian and 14.9 per cent report no religion.[1] The religious involvement of immigrants both shapes and is shaped by existing communities, making these patterns crucial for understanding immigrants' integration into the US. The primary contribution of the current study is to the understanding of immigrants' religious behaviour in the US after factoring in home-country practices. Without this, it has been impossible to distinguish between cohort differences in religiosity and real changes in individual behaviour. A secondary contribution is to inform the still contentious secularization paradigm that suggests that individuals will become more secular with modernization.

This work takes advantage of data from the 2003 cohort of the New Immigrant Survey (NIS) to examine religious participation among US immigrants systematically. The survey instrument includes questions concerning religious preference and participation in the US, in addition to soliciting information on the frequency of attendance prior to coming to the US. We know that migration disrupts religious participation (Wuthnow and Christiano 1979) and, in most cases, it will take time to make this transition complete. The current study shows evidence of an increase in participation, for some a rebound pattern, by immigrants the longer they remain in the US. Although this paper treats religious affiliation as a static state, clearly the potential for switching exists (see, for instance, work on Korean immigrants in Alba, Raboteau and Dewind 2009; Suh 2009). That said, the data indicate that 99 per cent of the NIS sample report that their current religious tradition is the same as that in which they themselves were raised, minimizing this confounding effect.

Prior studies on religion with New Immigrant Survey (2003 and pilot data)

In this section, I describe two studies that have used data from the New Immigrant Survey-Pilot (NIS-P) study, the pilot project for the data used in the current work. The first uses data from the NIS-P to examine religious service attendance. In that study, the authors find evidence supporting a negative relationship between time in the US and religious involvement (Cadge and Ecklund 2006). In other words, their work indicates that less assimilated immigrants are more likely to attend services regularly, suggesting decreased religious participation over time. The authors also find evidence supporting the fact that Christians are more likely to attend services regularly than are non-Christians. They attribute this both to the greater availability of Christian churches in the US and to the stronger requirement of weekly attendance for Christian than for Buddhist or Hindu practices (Cadge and Ecklund 2006). However, their study is subject to data limitations stemming from the use of the smaller pilot survey. They are restricted to a substantially smaller sample size that does not allow for an examination of region of origin differences, they have only two religion-based questions available and they have no information on the respondent's religious involvement prior to coming to the US. The full survey allows the current study to address each of these limitations directly.

The second work using NIS-P data takes a descriptive look at religious preference patterns (Jasso *et al.* 2003). This study, co-authored by the four principal investigators of the New Immigrant Survey, finds a substantially different distribution of religious preferences among the foreign born than among the native born.[2] For instance, the authors find that only two-thirds of the immigrant population is Christian compared with 82 per cent of the native born and that the proportion Catholic among immigrants is 42 per cent contrasted with 22 per cent among the native born (Jasso *et al.* 2003). Overall, their study points to several salient patterns of religious preference among immigrants that await further examination with the full survey (Jasso *et al.* 2003).

Perspectives on immigrants and religion

One of the reasons the current study is needed is that there are solid theoretical reasons one might expect religious participation to increase and to decrease with time in the US. In what follows, I outline each perspective.

Why immigrants' religious participation might be expected to decline

As noted early on by Wuthnow and Christiano (1979), migration disrupts religious participation. In their work looking at internal

646   *Ilana Redstone Akresh*

migration in the United States, they find that religious participation decreases with each subsequent migratory event. With international migrants, there are at least three reasons why one might expect to see a similar decline.

1. One might expect an initial decline after arrival if there is a delay in finding an appropriate and comfortable congregation to join. This might be particularly relevant for minority religions for which there are fewer places of worship. This pattern would suggest that the decline would be temporary and be followed by a subsequent restoration of previous levels.
2. Given that many immigrants come seeking job opportunities, one might expect a decline simply due to the amount of time committed to employment.
3. If religious attendance is used to buffer the adaptation process, participation might decline as time and comfort level in the US increase.
4. A fourth rationale for a decrease is linked to the secularization paradigm. In its simplest form, proponents of the traditional secularization paradigm argue that modernization is associated with a decrease in religious participation. This is thought to be linked to the increase in scientific explanations and technological advances providing explanations for previously unexplained or poorly explained phenomena. Although the validity of the 'traditional' secularization paradigm has been fiercely debated by sociologists, it has also displayed remarkable persistence as a framework for thinking about modern religious trends (Hadden 1987; Finke 1992; Stark 2000; Berger 2001; Bruce 2001; Hervieu-Léger 2001; Woodhead, Heelas and Martin 2001). For immigrants, the theoretical association might be one that unfolds over space rather than over time. For US migrants who originate in countries that are less developed (or less 'modern') than the United States, a pattern consistent with the 'traditional' paradigm would predict a negative relationship between religious attendance and time in the US. Perhaps the most important flaw in this logic is the assumption that immigrants are, in fact, arriving from less 'developed' or less 'modern' countries. In reality, some come from the middle or upper middle echelons of the income distribution (Massey 1990; Massey, Durand and Malone 2002), further raising the questions as to the empirical nature of this relationship.

Why immigrants' religious participation might be expected to increase

In contrast to the arguments developed above, there are also several reasons for predicting that immigrants' religious participation will *increase* after moving to the US. Other work has made it clear that these expectations are arguable only when the US is the destination because of its unique history, policies towards immigration and the interest in promoting religious and other types of diversity (Williams 1998). Recent work by Connor (2009) and Mooney (2009) also suggests that the effect of migration on religious participation depends heavily on the destination country. To this end, the US is uniquely open to almost all types of religious public expression.

1. If newcomers view belonging to a congregation as a pathway to a social network, this might suggest a rapid transition to a high level of religious participation. The benefits of belonging to this network have been explored in the theoretical work of Handlin (1951) and Herberg (1950) and include its ability to soothe the trauma of migration and provide continuity in newcomers' lives. Hirschman adds to these benefits religion's role in providing information and opportunities, including the essential trading of information on employment, enrolling children in school and improving language skills through organized classes for new arrivals (Hirschman 2004). Along this line, religious participation has at least two potential roles in immigrants' lives (Foner and Alba 2008). In the first, it functions as a bridge connecting new arrivals to the community; churches, synagogues and temples serve an important role in providing information about jobs, housing and general information on survival in a new place (Barton 1975; Smith 1978; Foner and Alba 2008). In the second, it serves as a buffer against further integration into US mainstream society by limiting immigrants' exposure primarily to co-ethnics and reducing other incentives to adapt (Greeley 1972; Foner and Alba 2008). Clearly the two perspectives are not necessarily mutually exclusive. Religious participation could simultaneously offer information leading to jobs and mobility and buffer against the acquisition of host-country language and customs, particularly if the place of worship is highly concentrated with co-ethnics.

2. Other work (Portes, Escobar and Radford 2007) has shown that immigrants' links to transnational organizations strengthen as they remain in the US. If religious participation facilitates the formation and maintenance of transnational ties, one might expect a corresponding increase in attendance.

3. In contrast to the traditional secularization paradigm, advocates of a 'new' paradigm cite increasing religious participation in the United States as evidence that religion is not in decline (Lechner 1991; Warner 1993; Yamane 1997; Yang and Ebaugh 2001; Levitt 2007). In the Yang and Ebaugh (2001) study of immigrants conducted in Texas, the authors find that the religious pluralism

648   *Ilana Redstone Akresh*

associated with recent immigrants has led to a 'revitalization' of religion rather than a decline.

Data

The data used in this study come from the New Immigrant Survey (NIS) 2003 cohort. The survey was originally pilot tested with a sample drawn in 1996 (refer to http://nis.princeton.edu for full information). The sampling frame for the NIS 2003 was immigrants granted legal permanent residency (LPR) between May and November of 2003 and the response rate was 69 per cent (Jasso *et al.* forthcoming). Although there are no known biases associated with the response rate, the sampling design dictates that undocumented migrants and others without LPR status are not eligible for inclusion. Compared to US migrants who do not have LPR status, those who do might have better networks or greater facility navigating the immigration system. Although those with LPR status may differ from those without it, the direction of the resulting bias with respect to the current analysis is not immediately clear. However, one could imagine that undocumented migrants might be more likely to draw from the unofficial support offered in a religious community. Further, undocumented migrants are largely comprised of Mexicans, a group that has a high level of religiosity both in their home country and in the US. They are also overwhelmingly Catholic and the church has been a strong advocate of their rights. This suggests that the overall finding in the current study of higher religious participation in the US is understated by the data.

Interviews were conducted in the language of the respondent's choice as soon as possible after legal permanent residency was granted and individuals who were new arrivals to the US as well as those who had adjusted their visa status were included in the sample (Jasso *et al.* forthcoming). This latter point means that there is substantial variation with respect to how long the respondents have been in the US. The survey methodology for the adult sample involved four strata: spouses of US citizens, employment principals, diversity principals and other immigrants (Jasso *et al.* forthcoming).[3] This analysis uses the adult sample, which was restricted to individuals who were at least 18 years old at the time of admission. Important for the current work, rather than asking an ambiguous question about year of arrival or year of immigration, which can lead to overestimates in the case of circular migration or underestimates in the presence of a migration history prior to the event of 'immigrating', the NIS allows for a cumulative measure of all time spent in the US (Redstone and Massey 2004).

The analysis uses individuals with valid responses on all variables of interest, yielding 6,381 observations. Of the 2,192 (8,573–6,381) cases that are dropped, 40 per cent are lost due to missing information on religious attendance in the US, 22 per cent are lost due to missing labour-force information and the remainder is lost due to various other covariates. With respect to age, sex, years of education and English ability, differences between individuals with religious attendance information and those without are minimal in magnitude. The one dimension on which they differ substantially is US duration; the former have approximately 1.2 years more US experience than the latter. If newer arrivals are simply uncertain how to answer the religion questions posed in the survey, the results presented here are likely to understate the transition of increased participation as we are not accounting for a number of infrequent attendees who are also recent arrivals.

Religion questions in the NIS

The survey instrument for the NIS-2003 includes multiple questions on religion and participation which are described, along with possible responses, in Table 1. There are several important factors to note in the survey questions. First, as the reader will note in the table, the questions used to elicit information on religious participation prior to migration and since being in the US are not the same. Ideally, the wording on the two points would be identical, thus minimizing error resulting from this discrepancy. This may introduce bias if the variation in the questions results in systematically different recall error or systematic differences in how individuals respond to the two types of wording, concerns I am unable to address. Second, the wording of the questions is biased toward religions that support regular communal worship. This is not a practice among Hindus or Buddhists, many of whom may have come to the United States without ever having formally belonged to a religious community. In addition, for members of some religions, in situations when they do worship communally, they do so at whatever temple or mosque is closest in proximity.

Variables

Although the current study takes into account several factors that are expected to be associated with religious participation in the US, there are four covariates of primary importance. First is the ability to account for respondents' frequency of religious participation prior to coming to the US. This facilitates a more precise examination of whether immigrants change their religious behaviour after migration. Second is the identification of an individual's degree of US integration. The proxy measure, years of US experience, is not without controversy as

650   *Ilana Redstone Akresh*

Table 1. *NIS survey questions*

Survey question	Reponses and coding	Variable measuring
What religious tradition, if any, describes your current religion (You may mention more than one if you wish)?	Catholic, Orthodox Christian, Protestant, Muslim, Jewish, Buddhist, Hindu, No Religion, Some other religion, or can name an unlisted religion	Religious preference (independent variable)
Since becoming a permanent resident, how many times have you attended religious services?	Using the frequency reported and dividing by the elapsed time between the date of admission to permanent residency and the interview data yields estimate of frequency of US attendance (religious participation in the US)	Religious attendance since legal permanent residency (dependent variable)
Before coming to the United States to live, how often did you attend religious services in your country of last residence?	Categories ranging from never to more than once per day (religious participation in home country)	Religious attendance in home country (independent variable)
Do you have a shrine, altar, or religious icons, paintings, or statues in your home?	1 if yes	Religious items in home (independent variable)

assimilation occurs at different rates and can have different meanings across individuals. However, as one of the primary reasons for the inclusion of this variable is to provide a direct empirical test of whether immigrants increase or decrease their religious participation the longer they remain in the US, it remains the most appropriate measure in this case. Third are region of origin indicators capturing differences across traditions and home-country habits respectively. As there are clearly important differences across religious traditions, indicators for Catholic, Orthodox Christian, Muslim, Jewish, Buddhist, Hindu and no religion (Protestant is omitted) are included throughout the analysis, but a discussion of these characteristics in the multivariate setting is beyond the scope of this analysis.

Results

Table 2 presents selected characteristics for the pooled sample and by region of origin. The results in Table 2 also point to several interesting patterns with respect to religious attendance. More than half of the Western European group report never attending religious services in the US, while only 29 per cent of respondents from Mexico place themselves in this category. The same two groups constitute the highest (Mexico at 23 per cent) and lowest (Western European group at 9 per cent) concentrations of respondents indicating that they attend religious services at least once per week. With the exception of Mexico, the modal category for the remaining groups is 'never attends religious services'. In addition to immigrants from Mexico and South/Central America, Africans also have high levels of religious participation such that more than half report attending several times a year or more. Looking now to patterns prior to coming to the US, Asia demonstrates the highest percentage that reports never attending while Mexico has the lowest. This pattern for Asians is largely driven by Chinese immigrants, 85 per cent of whom never attended abroad. Here again the origin groups with the greatest frequencies attending once per week or more are Africa and Latin America. These patterns are broadly consistent with those found in Van Tubergen (2006), such that immigrants from more religious countries are more religious themselves. From these tabulations, it appears that substantial transitioning occurs in the middle categories. For instance, 9.5 per cent of Asians report attendance between several times per year and less than once per week while in their home countries and 23 per cent place themselves in this category in the US.

Finally, a comparison of aggregate pre- and post-migration patterns indicates a decrease in attendance, confirming earlier work on the disruption of migration (e.g., Wuthnow and Christiano 1979) and highlighting the need to examine this question in a multivariate analysis

Table 2. Selected sample characteristics

	Pooled sample (n=6381)	South/Central America, Caribbean (n=1429)	Mexico (n=911)	Western Europe, Australia, Canada, New Zealand (n=287)	Eastern Europe, former USSR (n=803)	Asia (1348)	Indian subcontinent, Middle East (n=924)	Africa (n=679)
Years of US experience	4.39 (5.97)	6.93 (7.09)	7.46 (7.89)	4.69 (5.03)	2.43 (3.91)	2.87 (4.42)	3.36 (4.01)	1.51 (3.39)
Religious attendance in the US								
Never	39.32	35.55	28.98	54.01	45.83	47.26	38.74	32.25
Less than several times per year	15.89	17.14	15.48	17.42	16.06	9.42	22.73	16.49
Between several times per year and less than once per week	25.47	26.80	33.04	19.16	23.41	22.63	21.10	29.16
Once per week or more	19.32	20.50	22.50	9.41	14.69	20.70	17.42	22.09
Religious attendance while in home country								
Never	18.52	11.76	7.46	27.87	20.25	36.42	16.02	9.72
Less than several times per year	17.76	14.98	11.64	36.59	28.64	14.17	24.68	8.69
Between several times per year and less than once per week	16.93	19.03	20.97	15.33	21.42	9.50	19.26	13.99
Once per week or more	46.80	54.23	59.93	20.21	29.89	39.91	40.04	67.60
Has religious items at home	0.385	0.307	0.553	0.244	0.402	0.353	0.501	0.268

Note
Standard deviations are shown in parentheses below means.

Immigrants' religious participation in the United States   653

setting. It is precisely because migration is a disruptive life event that the current study asks what happens after that disruption has passed and newcomers settle into their life in the US. These patterns are further explored in Tables 3 and 4 and in the discussion section.

Table 3 presents results from a multinomial logistic regression predicting religious attendance in the US, where the omitted category is 'never attends'.[4] The first specification (the first three columns) mimics previous work in that it does not account for the individual's religious participation prior to coming to the US. The positive and statistically significant coefficients on the indicator for years of US experience suggest that more time in the US is linked with increased religious participation, relative to never attending. Specifically, each additional year in the US increases the likelihood of attending in each frequency category by between 2 and 5 per cent (relative risk ratios available upon request). This is consistent with the 'new paradigm' discussed earlier and with the role of religion in the maintenance of transnational ties. This differs from the Cadge and Ecklund (2006) findings using the NIS-P, a distinction that merits future exploration.[5] Differences also emerge across region of origin and religious preferences. After accounting for other characteristics, immigrants from South/Central America and the Western European group are less likely than Mexicans to attend more than several times per year.

The final three columns of Table 3 contain a multinomial logit specification similar to the first, yet, in this case, religious attendance prior to coming to the US is included as an explanatory variable. Not surprisingly, this important factor has a strong, positive correlation with US religious attendance. The strong, positive relationship between years of US experience and religious frequency suggests that immigrants increase their religious participation the longer they remain in the US. In this specification, as in the previous, although the magnitude of the coefficients across the three equations is similar, they do differ from one another at the one percentage level. This suggests that there is a slightly stronger link between years in the US and the highest level of religious participation.

With respect to region of origin differences, the majority of categories maintain coefficients with magnitudes and significance levels similar to the first specification in Table 3. However, a notable difference is for immigrants from Africa. After accounting for religious practice prior to coming to the US, Africans are indistinguishable from Mexicans in their likelihood of attending with any level of frequency.

Table 4 displays only the coefficients on the years of US experience variable from MNL specifications separated by region of origin. Each individual regression includes the same covariates as in Table 3. Apparent from the disaggregated specifications is that the positive link between time in the US and religious frequency is not consistent

Table 3. Multinomial logistic regressions predicting religious attendance in the US

Omitted category is never attends	Without control for religious involvement prior to migration			With control for religious involvement prior to migration		
	Less than several times per year	Between several times per year and less than once per week	Once per week or more	Less than several times per year	Between several times per year and less than once per week	Once per week or more
Years of US experience	0.023*** (0.008)	0.025*** (0.007)	0.039*** (0.007)	0.026*** (0.008)	0.029*** (0.007)	0.044*** (0.008)
Region of origin (omitted is Mexico)						
South/Central America, Caribbean	0.105 (0.139)	-0.140 (0.119)	-0.111 (0.131)	0.063 (0.141)	-0.186 (0.123)	-0.184 (0.136)
Western Europe, Australia, Canada, New Zealand	-0.235 (0.228)	-0.631*** (0.214)	-1.299*** (0.263)	-0.086 (0.232)	-0.358 (0.222)	-0.953*** (0.272)
Eastern Europe, former USSR	-0.010 (0.180)	-0.211 (0.157)	-0.478*** (0.178)	0.032 (0.185)	-0.113 (0.163)	-0.292 (0.185)
Asia	0.023 (0.184)	0.596*** (0.153)	0.784*** (0.165)	0.190 (0.189)	0.635*** (0.162)	0.736*** (0.174)
Indian subcontinent, Middle East	0.628*** (0.226)	0.659*** (0.209)	0.744*** (0.220)	0.521** (0.231)	0.468** (0.216)	0.495** (0.229)
Africa	0.617*** (0.204)	0.738*** (0.178)	0.495*** (0.192)	0.317 (0.209)	0.274 (0.184)	-0.064 (0.201)

Table 3 (*Continued*)

Immigrants' religious participation in the United States   655

	Without control for religious involvement prior to migration			With control for religious involvement prior to migration		
	Less than several times per year	Between several times per year and less than once per week	Once per week or more	Less than several times per year	Between several times per year and less than once per week	Once per week or more
Omitted category is never attends						
Attendance in home country (omitted is never)						
Less than several times per year	—	—	—	1.459***	0.877***	0.345*
				(0.172)	(0.167)	(0.180)
Between several times per year and less than once per week	—	—	—	1.893***	1.803***	1.124***
				(0.180)	(0.166)	(0.178)
Once per week or more	—	—	—	2.092***	2.317***	2.302***
				(0.172)	(0.157)	(0.160)
Constant	−1.941***	−0.705***	−1.097***	−3.772***	−2.597***	−2.824***
	(0.303)	(0.259)	(0.278)	(0.350)	(0.306)	(0.325)
Observations	6381	6381	6381	6381	6381	6381
Pseudo R^2	0.122			0.161		

Notes

Regressions also control for age, female, years of education, number in the household under 18, employment status, hours worked per week, marital status, English proficiency and the presence of religious objects in the home.

Standard errors in parentheses.

*significant at 10%; **significant at 5%; ***significant at 1%.

Table 4. Coefficients on years in the US: variables by region of origin resulting from multinomial logistic (MNL) regressions predicting US attendance (each column is a separate MNL specification while the outcomes are labeled as rows)

Attendance in the US (omitted category is never attends)	South/Central America, Caribbean	Mexico	Western Europe, Australia, Canada, New Zealand	Eastern Europe, former USSR	Asia	Indian subcontinent, Middle East	Africa
Less than several times per year	0.017	0.022	0.020	0.075**	0.013	0.037	0.088*
	(0.013)	(0.014)	(0.040)	(0.038)	(0.030)	(0.029)	(0.046)
Between several times per year and less than once per week	0.032***	0.009	0.012	0.106***	0.034	0.042	0.052
	(0.011)	(0.012)	(0.040)	(0.036)	(0.027)	(0.031)	(0.048)
Once per week or more	0.047***	−0.017	0.048	0.170***	0.106***	0.075**	0.105**
	(0.012)	(0.014)	(0.054)	(0.039)	(0.026)	(0.033)	(0.045)
Observations	1429	911	287	803	1348	924	679
Pseudo R^2	0.103	0.091	0.287	0.236	0.324	0.185	0.181

Notes
Regressions include the same covariates shown in Table 2.
Standard errors in parentheses.
*significant at 10%; **significant at 5%; ***significant at 1%.

across groups. Evidence of increased religious participation is observed among immigrants from South/Central America and the Caribbean (approximately a 2 to 5 per cent increase for each additional year in the US) and among those from Eastern Europe and the former USSR (an 8 to 19 per cent increase for each additional year in the US, relative risk ratios available upon request). Among African and Indian origin immigrants additional time in the US increases the likelihood of weekly or higher attendance, but has no relationship with lower frequencies of attendance.[6]

Discussion

In this work, I have considered the religious lives of immigrants, informing the literature theoretically in our understanding of changes in religious participation after immigration. I have examined whether the evidence indicates a trend towards increasing or decreasing religious participation the longer immigrants remain in the US. Although these questions have been considered previously, this is the first analysis using a large data set allowing for comparison across groups.

Contrary to prior evidence, the results presented here suggest that there is a tendency towards greater religious attendance with increased time in the US and no evidence of a decline, consistent with the role of religion in the maintenance of social capital and with the 'new' paradigm of increased religious participation and religious pluralism (Warner 1993; Ebaugh and Chafetz 2000). I also find that taking into account past religious practice also explains some of the variation across origin groups, particular for African immigrants. Another possibility that has been offered is that religious participation increases with time in the US due to the loss of social status often associated with migration (Min 1992). This pattern is most pronounced for immigrants from South/Central America and from Eastern Europe.

Although the results shown here are also consistent with the possibility that it simply takes newcomers time to find a suitable place of worship in their new home, there are two reasons why this is not the most likely explanation. First, the empirical findings hold in statistical significant and in magnitude when the sample is restricted to family preference migrants (immigrants who achieve legal permanent residency through a family member who is either a permanent resident or a citizen). This is important because these individuals probably arrive with a support network already in place and would not require the same adjustment period as an individual arriving with no social contacts. Second, although an adjustment period might explain the need for time in the US to find an appropriate place of worship in the new setting (in other words, attending at all versus not attending), it does not explain changes in the intensity of attendance.

An additional interpretation of this pattern is that is it a 'contextual effect'. In other words, if the US is more religious than immigrants' origin societies, as measured by religious participation, increased participation with time in the US would also be consistent with part of a broader process of adjustment to life in the US, again reinforcing religion's role in assimilation. Evidence on this is mixed: ancillary analysis of data from the World Values Survey for 1999–2004 for five of the largest immigrant-sending countries indicates that 58.4 per cent of Filipinos, 56 per cent of Mexicans, 2.2 of Chinese, 32 per cent of Indians and 3.8 per cent of Vietnamese, compared to 45.1 per cent from the United States, report attending religious services once per week or more.

Although this study has gone further than previous work in examining, on a large scale, the religious behaviour of immigrants, several questions remain unanswered and caveats must be mentioned. Concerning the former, the current work has focused on region of origin variation with respect to the relationship between time in the US and the outcome studied. A natural next step would be to study how other covariates vary along this dimension. Regarding the latter, in order better to untangle the question of the role of religion in immigrants' lives, one would like to have detailed information on both the church-related activities in which the individual participates and on the array of activities offered by the establishment. An additional omitted factor is residential context. Residence in an ethnically concentrated neighbourhood is likely to be associated with both an individual's religious participation and the ethnic composition of their gathering place. Unfortunately, the NIS at present does not release information on residential context, restricting this avenue of analysis. Additionally, little is known about an individual's ability to estimate the ethnic composition of his gathering place accurately. Without more detailed information, one might surmise that the potential for overestimation exists if the church or place of worship holds separate services in different languages and the respondent attends only the service in his native language. Finally, as with any cross-sectional dataset, results must be interpreted with caution and causal inferences should be avoided. Fortunately, the NIS-2003 will eventually be longitudinal so that researchers may observe how individuals fare over time.

Notes

1.   The General Social Survey is administered only in English, leading to a likely underrepresentation of immigrants. Other categories include 0.9 per cent identifying as

Immigrants' religious participation in the United States 659

Other, 2.9 per cent as Buddhist, 2.8 per cent as Hindu, 0.8 per cent as Other Eastern and 0.6 per cent as Inter-Denominational.
2.   The four co-PIs for the NIS have an additional book chapter relating to religion, yet the results are similar to those described above (Jasso *et al.* 2000).
3.   'Principal' refers to 'the alien who applies for immigrant status and from whom another alien may derive lawful status under migration law or regulations (usually spouses or minor unmarried children)' (US Citizenship and Immigration Services definition).
4.   A multinomial logit is preferred as the specification violates the proportional odds assumption necessary for an ordered logit specification.
5.   One possibility for this difference is that immigrants arriving after September 11, 2001 feel greater urgency to connect with a social network and alleviate feelings of isolation and alienation. Additionally, the sample size for the NIS-pilot study is substantially smaller than for the full 2003 cohort, resulting in less statistical power in identifying significant relationships. Finally, religious participation is measured differently in the two studies, perhaps accounting for the variation in results.
6.   As important differences emerged in Table 2 regarding subgroups of Asians, I re-specified the fifth column in Table 4, for Chinese, Filipino, Korean and Vietnamese immigrants separately. With one exception, none of the four major groups exhibited a significant relationship between time in the US and religious participation. The sole exception was that Vietnamese immigrants in the US for longer are more likely to attend once per week or more.

References

ALBA, R., RABOTEAU, A. J. and DEWIND, J. 2009 *Immigration and Religion in America: Comparative and Historical Perspective*, New York: New York University Press
BANKSTON, C. and ZHOU, M. 1995 'Religious participation, ethnic identification, and adaptation of Vietnamese adolescents in an immigrant community', *The Sociological Quarterly*, vol. 36, no. 3, pp. 523–34
——— 1996 'The ethnic church, ethnic identification, and the social adjustment of Vietnamese adolescents', *Review of Religious Research*, vol. 38, pp. 18–37
BARTON, J. J. 1975 *Peasants and Strangers*, Cambridge, MA: Harvard University Press
BERGER, P. 2001 'Reflections on the sociology of religion today', *Sociology of Religion*, vol. 62, no. 4, pp. 443–54
BRUCE, S. 2001 'The curious case of the unnecessary recantation: Berger and seculariza-tion', in L. Woodhead, P. Heelas and D. Martin (eds), *Peter Berger and the Study of Religion*, New York: Routledge
CADGE, W. and ECKLUND, E. H. 2006 'Religious service attendance among immigrants: evidence from the New Immigrant Survey-Pilot', *American Behavioral Scientist*, vol. 49, no. 11, pp. 1574–96
——— 2007 'Immigration and religion', *Annual Review of Sociology*, vol. 33, pp. 359–79
CAO, N. L. 2005 'The church as a surrogate family for working class immigrant Chinese youth: an ethnography of segmented assimilation', *Sociology of Religion*, vol. 66, no. 2, pp. 183–200
CAVALCANTI, H. B. and SCHLEEF, D. 2005 'The case for secular assimilation? The Latino experience in Richmond, Virginia', *Journal for the Scientific Study of Religion*, vol. 44, no. 4, pp. 473–83
CHA, P. T. 2001 'Ethnic identity formation and participation in immigrant churches: second generation Korean American experiences', in H.-Y. Kwon, K. C. Kim and R. S. Warner (eds), *Korean Americans and Their Religions: Pilgrim and Missionaries from a Different Shore*, University Park, PA: Pennsylvania State University Press
CONNOR, P. 2009 'International migration and religious participation: the mediating impact of individual and contextual effects', *Sociological Forum*, vol. 24, no. 4, pp. 779–803

660   *Ilana Redstone Akresh*

EBAUGH, H. R. and CHAFETZ, J. S. 2000 *Religion and the New Immigrants: Continuities and Adaptations in Immigrant Congregations*, Walnut Creek, CA: AltaMira Press

FINKE, R. 1992 'An unsecular America', in S. Bruce (ed.), *Religion and Modernization*, New York: Oxford University Press

FONER, N. and ALBA, R. 2008 Immigrant religion in the U.S. and Western Europe: bridge or barrier to inclusion?, *International Migration Review*, vol. 42, no. 2, pp. 360–93

GREELEY, A. 1972 *The Denominational Society: A Sociological Approach to Religion in America*, Glenview, IL: Scott, Foresman

GUEST, K. J. 2003 *God in Chinatown: Religion and Survival in New York's Evolving Immigrant Community*, New York: New York University Press

HADDEN, J. 1987 'Toward desacralizing secularization theory', *Social Forces*, vol. 65, no. 3, pp. 587–611

HANDLIN, O. 1951 *The Uprooted*, New York: Grosset & Dunlap

HERBERG, W. 1950 *Protestant, Catholic, and Jew: An Essay in American Religious Sociology*, Chicago, IL: University of Chicago Press

HERVIEU-LÉGER, D. 2001 'The twofold limit of the notion of secularization', in L. Woodhead, P. Heelas and D. Martin (eds), *Peter Berger and the Study of Religion*, New York: Routledge

HIRSCHMAN, C. 2004 The role of religion in the origins and adaptation of immigrant groups in the United States', *International Migration Review*, vol. 38, no. 3, pp. 1206–33

HURH, W. M. and KIM, K. C. 1990 Religious participation of Korean immigrants in the United States', *Journal for the Scientific Study of Religion*, vol. 29, no. 1, pp. 19–34

JASSO, G. *et al.* 2000 'Family, schooling, religiosity, and mobility among new legal immigrants to the United States: evidence from the New Immigrant Survey Pilot Study', in L. F. Tomasi and M. G. Powers (eds), *Immigration Today: Pastoral and Research Challenges*, Staten Island, NY: Center for Migration Studies

——— 2003 'Exploring the religious preferences of recent immigrants to the United States: evidence from the New Immigrant Survey Pilot', in Y. Y. Haddad, J. I. Smith and J. L. Esposito (eds), *Religion and Immigration: Christian, Jewish, and Muslim Experiences in the United States*, Walnut Creek, CA: AltaMira Press

——— forthcoming 'The U.S. New Immigrant Survey: overview and preliminary results based on the new-immigrant cohorts of 1996 and 2003', in B. Morgan and B. Nicholson (eds), *Longitudinal Surveys and Cross-Cultural Survey Design*, UK Immigration Research and Statistics Service

KURIEN, P. A. 1998 'Becoming American by becoming Hindu: Indian Americans take their place at the multicultural table', in R. S. Warner and J. G. Wittner (eds), *Gatherings in the Diaspora: Religious Communities and the New Immigration*, Philadelphia, PA: Temple University Press

——— 2001 'Religion, ethnicity, and politics: Hindu and Muslim Indian immigrants in the United States', *Ethnic and Racial Studies*, vol. 24, no. 2, pp. 263–93

LECHNER, F. J. 1991 'The case against secularization: a rebuttal', *Social Forces*, vol. 69, no. 4, pp. 1103–119

LEVITT, P. 2007 *God Needs No Passport: Immigrants and the Changing American Religious Landscape*, New York: The New Press

MASSEY, D. S. 1990 'The social and economic origins of migration', *The Annals of the American Academy of Political and Social Science*, vol. 510, no. 1, pp. 60–72

MASSEY, D. S., DURAND, J. and MALONE, N. J. 2002 *Beyond Smoke and Mirrors: Mexican Immigration in an Era of Economic Integration*, New York: Russell Sage

MENJIVAR, C. 1999 'Religious institutions and transnationalism: a case study of Catholic and Evangelical Salvadoran immigrants', *International Journal of Politics, Culture, and Society*, vol. 12, no. 4, pp. 589–612

MIN, P. G. 1992 'The structure and social functions of Korean Immigrant churches in the United States', *International Migration Review*, vol. 26, no. 4, pp. 1370–94

Immigrants' religious participation in the United States   661

MIN, P. G. and KIM, J. H. 2003 *Religions in Asian America: Building Faith Communities*, Walnut Creek, CA: Altamira Press

MOONEY, M. A. 2009 *Faith Makes Us Live: Surviving and Thriving in the Haitian Diaspora*, Los Angeles: University of California Press

PORTES, A., ESCOBAR, C. and RADFORD, A. W. 2007 'Immigrant transnational organizations and development: a comparative study', *International Migration Review*, vol. 41, no. 1, pp. 242–81

REDSTONE, I. and MASSEY, D. S. 2004 'Coming to stay: an analysis of the U.S. Census question on year of arrival', *Demography*, vol. 41, no. 4, pp. 721–38

SMITH, T. L. 1978 'Religion and ethnicity in America', *American Historical Review*, vol. 83, no. 5, pp. 1155–85

STARK, R. 2000 'Secularization, R.I.P', in W. H. Swatos Jr. and D. V. A. Olson (eds), *The Secularization Debate*, New York: Rowman & Littlefield

SUH, S. A. 2009 'Buddhism, rhetoric, and the Korean American community: the adjustment of Korean Buddhist immigrants to the United States', in R. Alba, A. J. Raboteau and J. Dewind (eds), *Immigration and Religion in America: Comparative and Historical Perspectives*, New York: New York University Press

VAN TUBERGEN, F. 2006 'Religious affiliation and attendance among immigrants in eight Western countries: individual and contextual effects', *Journal for the Scientific Study of Religion*, vol. 45, no. 1, pp. 1–22

WARNER, R. S. 1993 'Work in progress toward a new paradigm for the sociological study of religion in the United States', *American Journal of Sociology*, vol. 98, no. 5, pp. 1044–94

WARNER, R. S. and WITTNER, J. G. 1998 *Gatherings in the Diaspora: Religious Communities and the New Immigration*, Philadelphia, PA: Temple University Press

WILLIAMS, R. B. 1998 'Americans and religions in the twenty-first century: Asian Indian and Pakistani religions in the United States', *The Annals of the American Academy of Political and Social Science*, vol. 558, pp. 178–95

WOODHEAD, L., HEELAS, P. and MARTIN, D. 2001 *Peter Berger and the Study of Religion*, New York: Routledge

WUTHNOW, R. and CHRISTIANO, K. 1979 'The effect of residential migration on church attendance in the United States', in R. Wuthnow (ed.), *The Religious Dimension: New Directions in Quantitative Research*, New York: Academic Press

YAMANE, D. 1997 'Secularization on trial: in defense of a neosecularization paradigm', *Journal for the Scientific Study of Religion*, vol. 36, no. 1, pp. 109–22

YANG, F. 2000 'The Hsi-Nan Chinese Buddhist Temple: seeking to Americanize', in H. R. Ebaugh and J. S. Chafetz (eds), *Religion and the New Immigrants: Continuities and Adaptations in Immigrant Congregations*, Walnut Creek, CA: AltaMira Press

YANG, F. and EBAUGH, H. R. 2001 'Transformations in new immigrant religions and their global implications', *American Sociological Review*, vol. 66, no. 2, pp. 269–88

ILANA REDSTONE AKRESH is an assistant professor in the Department of Sociology at the University of Illinois at Urbana-Champaign.
ADDRESS: Department of Sociology, University of Illinois at Urbana-Champaign, 605 East Springfield, 57 CAB, Champaign, IL, 61801, USA. Email: redstone@illinois.edu

[21]

From Filial Piety to Religious Piety: Evangelical Christianity Reconstructing Taiwanese Immigrant Families in the United States[1]

Carolyn Chen
Department of Sociology and Asian American Studies Program,
Northwestern University

While current scholarship suggests that immigrant religion reproduces ethnic traditions, this article suggests that religion can also challenge and transform ethnic traditions. Like other immigrants from Confucian cultures, Taiwanese immigrants find that their Confucian family traditions are difficult to maintain in the United States. The immigrant church is an important community institution that offers new models of parenting and family life. This article discusses how through the influence of evangelical Christianity, the immigrant church reconstructs Taiwanese immigrant families by (i) shifting the moral vocabulary of the family from one of filial duty to religious discipleship; (ii) democratizing relationships between parents and children; and (iii) consecrating the individuality and autonomy of children. These new models of family life both reproduce and alter Taiwanese traditions in the United States. Religion mediates and shapes immigrant cultural assimilation to the United States.

Describing her frustrations with raising children in the United States, Mrs. Kau,[2] a Taiwanese immigrant in her mid-40s, proclaims, "We just can't use our OBC (Overseas-Born Chinese) ways on our ABC (American-Born Chinese) children!" Children in the United States, she claims, have too much freedom and consequently are uncontrollable, disobedient, and disrespectful. Her Taiwanese practices of parenting that are based on Confucian notions of filial obligation are no longer effective on her Taiwanese American children. To solve her parenting problems in the United States, she turns to religion – specifically, evangelical Christianity. Evangelical Christianity has become immensely popular among many Chinese immigrants, including Taiwanese[3] (Dart, 1997;

---

[1] The author is grateful to Russell Jengg, Fenggang Yang, Jim Stockinger, and members of the Chicago Area Group for the Study of Religion (CAGSR), for their helpful comments on the article.
[2] I use pseudonyms to protect the identity of individuals and institutions in this paper.
[3] By "Chinese," I am referring to people of Chinese ancestry rather than national identity, and thus include people from Mainland China, Taiwan, Hong Kong, and others in the Chinese diaspora. "Taiwanese" specifically refers to people from Taiwan, including post-1945 Mainlanders.

© 2006 by the Center for Migration Studies of New York. All rights reserved.
DOI: 10.1111/j.1747-7379.2006.00032.x

Yang, 1999a; Ly, 2003; Chen, forthcoming). When Mrs. Kau came to the United States, she, like most Taiwanese immigrants, was nominally Buddhist and non-practicing. But like many Taiwanese immigrants, Mrs. Kau converted to Christianity and became actively involved in a local Chinese evangelical church after moving to the United States. She claims that the main reason she and her family became involved in a Chinese church was for the family: "We wanted to make sure that the kids were on the right track – so we took them to church." Indeed, within the Taiwanese community the common wisdom is that children will not go astray if they attend church.

Mrs. Kau is not alone in turning to religion to solve the intergenerational tensions that arise in immigrant families. The growing body of scholarship on religion and immigrant adaptation addresses the importance of religion to parenting, particularly in reproducing traditional values and culture to the second generation (*e.g.*, Warner and Wittner, 1998; Zhou and Bankston, 1998; Ebaugh and Chafetz, 2000). This is the case even among groups who are largely converts to Christianity, like Koreans (Min, 1998, 2003) and Chinese (Yang, 1999a, 1999b). Like Mrs. Kau, other immigrants find that religion protects the second generation from the "immoral" influences of American culture (Zhou and Bankston, 1998; Waters, 1999; Yang, 1999a, 1999b; Ebaugh and Chafetz, 2000). For example, in their study of thirteen immigrant religious congregations in Houston, Helen Ebaugh and Janet Chafetz write: "Surrounded by what they *see* as immodest clothing and demeanor, a consumer-oriented culture beamed incessantly by T.V. and popular music, lax sexual standards, family breakdown, a lack of respect for authority and the elderly, guns, gangs, and drugs, immigrants want their congregations to 'do something' to inoculate their children" (2000:124).

These works emphasize the tendency for ethnic religion to reinforce traditions among immigrants and their children against Americanization. For example, religious congregations frequently offer language and cultural classes, celebrate ethnic holidays, and sponsor cultural events. Chinese and Korean churches selectively teach traditional values that conform to the Christian tradition and enforce gender and age-based hierarchies (Chong, 1998; Yang, 1999b; Min, 2003). Monthly *bala vihar* (child development) meetings among South Indian Hindu immigrants teach children Hindu songs and philosophy while imparting Indian culture and morality (Kurien, 1998). Kelly Chong (1998) argues that second-generation Korean Americans who are more religious are also more likely to embrace traditional Korean values. Min Zhou and Carl Bankston (1998) show that among Vietnamese American youth, religious participation correlates positively with stronger ethnic identity.

These works rightly point out that religion reproduces traditions, but overlooks how religion may change, rather than preserve, inherited traditions. East Asian immigrant families transform in the process of negotiating Confucian traditions in American society (Kibria, 1993; Buriel and DeMent, 1997; Min, 1998; Zhou and Bankston, 1998). Scholars have shown that East Asian immigrants respond to the environment by developing styles of parenting that are more similar to American parents – less controlling (Chiu, 1987; Lin and Fu, 1990), and more democratic and egalitarian (Chiu, 1987). Factors such as changing economic conditions, women's participation in the labor force (Hondagneu-Sotelo, 1994; Espiritu, 2003), an unbalanced sex ratio among immigrants (Kibria, 1993), American culture (Kibria, 1993; Min, 1998), and the legal system (Min, 1998) in the United States have been cited as contributing to shifting familial relationships. Relatively little attention, however, has been given to the role of religion in creating new family patterns in the United States, while instead its capacity to preserve traditions has been more extensively discussed.

Let me return to Mrs. Kau's provocative comment, "We just can't use our OBC (Overseas-Born Chinese) ways on our ABC (American-Born Chinese) children!" By turning to religion as a solution, her statement implies that ethnic religion does something more than reproduce traditional, or "OBC," ways when it comes to parenting. In fact, traditional ways don't work on second-generation children, and making sure that kids are "on the right track," as she puts it, requires something different than reinforcing traditional ethnic values.

In this article I suggest that Chinese churches do more than reproduce ethnic traditions, and offer new models of parenting and family life to Taiwanese immigrants in the U.S. Churches occupy prominent positions in immigrant communities and shape how immigrant families adapt to and transform in American society. In particular, Chinese immigrants are influenced by mainstream American evangelical Christian models of the family through their Chinese Christian churches and networks. Where immigrant parents struggle to apply Confucian principles of parenting to their American children, evangelical Christianity offers an attractive new moral model of the family. In this article I will first discuss some of the problems that Taiwanese immigrant parents face in raising children in the U.S. and why they turn to religion for parenting solutions. Second, I discuss how religious conversion to Christianity shifts the moral vocabulary of the family from one of filial duty to religious discipleship. Third, I consider how Christianity can restructure the family by democratizing relationships between parents and children and consecrating the individuality and autonomy of the children. While the church may provide new models and strategies of parenting, I argue that these have tendencies to both reproduce and transform Taiwanese traditions in the United States.

METHODS AND SETTING

My findings are based on a larger ethnographic study of Taiwanese immigrant Christians and Buddhists in Southern California. The bulk of my data in this article is based on fifteen months of fieldwork that I conducted at a Taiwanese immigrant church in Southern California between January 1999 and March 2000. To maintain the anonymity of this institution and the persons involved, I give this church the pseudonym "Grace Evangelical Church." At Grace Church, I participated in Sunday services, Sunday School, Friday Night Fellowship meetings, church visitations, church social events, youth group activities, and children's Vacation Bible School. Although I concentrated most of my fieldwork at Grace Evangelical Church, I also observed the services and meetings of other local Chinese churches and para-church Chinese Christian organizations.

In addition to participant-observation, I conducted 25 in-depth interviews with Taiwanese immigrants who converted to Christianity. The respondents, who I recruited through snowball sampling, were members of different Chinese churches in Southern California, including Grace Church. They varied in age from the mid-thirties to the mid-fifties. One person was divorced, and the rest of the respondents were married. All but one of the respondents had children. The age of their children varied from two to twenty-three. The majority had children in the range of twelve to eighteen. I also interviewed religious leaders, both lay and clergy, at Grace Church and at other local Chinese religious congregations. Taiwanese and English were used in the interviews.

Grace Evangelical Church is located in a suburb of Southern California, an area that experienced an influx of Taiwanese immigrants in the 1980s and early 1990s, and has the largest Taiwanese community in the United States. To meet the demands of a growing immigrant population, Grace Evangelical Church was "planted" by a neighboring sister church in 1989. The sister church had been in existence in Southern California since the late 1970s. Grace Church is one of many ethnic Christian churches that were started by and are composed of Chinese immigrants, and whose culture, language, and traditions reflect their Chinese heritage. Although the majority of Taiwan identifies as Buddhist, Chinese Christian churches are far more numerous than Buddhist temples in the United States. For example, in Southern

California there are one hundred and ninety-five Chinese Protestant churches but only forty-five Buddhist and Taoist temples/organizations. And within a five-mile radius of Grace Church there are four other Chinese Protestant churches.

Grace Church is like other Chinese American churches, which tend to be denominationally independent, theologically conservative, and evangelical (Yang, 1999a). Its members belong to a larger Chinese Christian network of radio shows, television shows, bookstores, publishing houses, revival meetings, and non-profit organizations that is both local and transnational (Yang, 2002). As evangelicals, these Chinese Christians are strongly influenced by trends and ideas in the larger American evangelical subculture. Chinese Christians read popular evangelical books, including some that have been translated into Chinese, and attend mainstream evangelical meetings like the Billy Graham Crusade. Furthermore, many of the local Chinese pastors are educated at Fuller Seminary in Southern California, the flagship evangelical seminary in the United States.

Grace Church differs from other Chinese churches because the vast majority of its members are Taiwanese immigrants and their children. However, a small minority of its members are mainland Chinese and Minnan-speaking Chinese from Southeast Asia. In general, Taiwanese tend to be more educated and middle class than other Chinese immigrants. The population and experiences of Grace Church members are therefore not representative of all Chinese churches, for example, urban working-class churches, but are more similar to those of other suburban middle-class Chinese Christians.[4]

The respondents in my sample reflect the patterns of length of residency and social class of Taiwanese immigrants. Although some of the respondents migrated to the United States as early as 1965 and others as late as 1997, the majority came in the 1980s and early 1990s, while they were in their late twenties and thirties. One should keep in mind that their memories of parent-child relationships are not necessarily representative of Taiwan today, but are of a less urban and less modern Taiwan of twenty to thirty years ago.

Many of the respondents came to the United States to pursue advanced degrees and then decided to settle here. Like the majority of Taiwanese men in

---

[4]For example, my respondents had quite different experiences in Asia and in the United States from the population in Kenneth Guest's study *God in Chinatown* (2003), which examines working-class Fujianese Christians in New York City. On the other hand, my respondents' experiences were far more similar to the educated, suburban Chinese Christians in Fenggang Yang's study *Chinese Christians in America* (1999a).

the Southern California area, the men in my sample are educated and skilled professionals who are concentrated in the science, technology, and medical industries. For some, however, the process of immigration has meant professional downward mobility and they have opted to run small businesses in the ethnic community. Over half of the Taiwanese women respondents are college-educated. More than one-quarter have advanced degrees, all earned in the United States. Slightly more than half of the women work outside of the home.

THE PERILS OF RAISING CHILDREN IN THE UNITED STATES: SEX, DRUGS, AND NURSING HOMES

Commenting on the perils of raising children in the United States, Dr. Lin, a father of two junior high school children, proclaims, "Freedom built this country and freedom will destroy it." He embarks on a litany of the downfalls of American freedom – school shootings, teenage pregnancies, rampant drug use, and last but not least, nursing homes. Although Dr. Lin is fairly Americanized – he received his doctorate in engineering from a prestigious American university twelve years ago and speaks flawless English – he echoes the common sentiment among Taiwanese immigrants of raising children in a land of excessive freedom. Lacking an adequate sense of limits and boundaries, children in the United States are "wild," "unmannered," "disobedient," and "disrespectful." Parents remark that children in the United States have too much individual choice. In this environment, Taiwanese parents fear that their children might succumb to the vices of American freedoms, and among these fears, sending parents to nursing homes tops the list.

Most American parents can identify with immigrants' fears of school violence, drug abuse, and teenage pregnancies, but placing nursing homes in this list of social ills seems odd. However, to Taiwanese and other immigrants from a Confucian heritage, nursing homes, along with the social problems that plague American youth, are at root all consequences of the same cause – lack of filiality or filial piety, the sense of duty and indebtedness to one's parents. That is, children become involved in shameful activities ranging from violence to parental neglect because they are not devoted or respectful to their parents, who made great sacrifices in raising them.

To immigrants from Confucian traditions, filial piety is a central moral principle that guides human behavior. Scholars have noted how Confucian traditions of the family clash with the values of mainstream society among Korean, ethnic Chinese, and Vietnamese immigrants (Kibria, 1993; Kim, 1996; Zhou and Bankston, 1998; Yang, 1999a). The principle of filial piety is based on a conception of the self and the family that is quite different from that of most Americans. Rather than the individual self as autonomous and independent, in Confucian tradition the individual is inseparable from a set of hierarchical relationships and obligations within the family. For the sake of harmony, the individual will is subordinated to the will of the family, and, more specifically, to the will of the parents. The family is based on a clear hierarchy of members of the family, where the young are deferential to the elderly. Central to filiality is the concept of obligation and indebtedness to one's parents. Consider the following quote from the Confucian scholar Tu Wei-Ming (1998:128):

> The Confucian belief that moral self-cultivation begins with the recognition that biological bondage provides an authentic opportunity for personal realization. The duty and consciousness generated by the acknowledgement that we are beneficiaries of our parents and older siblings and that our well-being is inseparable from theirs is not one-way obedience. Rather it is a response to a debt that one can never repay and an awareness that the willingness to assume responsibility for paying that debt is morally exhilarating.

My respondents, who were children in Taiwan from the 1950s to the 1970s, confirmed the significance of filial piety, and specifically parental authority, in their own family experiences in Taiwan. They reported that even for important life decisions that extended into adulthood, such as marriage, career, and even immigration, parents made these decisions for them, or at least had a final say in these matters. The respondents both romanticized and were critical of their experiences as children in Taiwan. On the one hand, they described themselves as virtuous children who did not dare disobey their elders, in comparison to their children in the United States. For example, one respondent in his mid-forties claims, "In that kind of society we could not speak out against our parents or elders. If we said, 'I don't believe this,' we'd get into trouble. We just kept quiet." But in retrospect, some are also critical of the conformity that their upbringing produced. One respondent suggests that in her experience as a child in Taiwan, "You don't really have your own thinking."

Taiwan has certainly changed with modernization in the last two decades and my respondents' childhood experiences do not necessarily reflect those in Taiwan today. Filial piety, however, continues to be a central moral principle in Taiwanese families (Huang and Wu, 1994; Jordan, 1998; Jochim, 2003), who tend to be even more traditional than families in China (Whyte, 2004). According to a 1988 survey of Taiwanese youth, the majority of respondents agreed that "filial piety is the most important among all good deeds," and listed "follow parents' opinions" and "support parents" as the most important characteristics of filial piety (Huang, 1988).

But the concept of filiality is more than a moral code of disciplinary conduct for children, but a basis of family solidarity. This sense of duty and gratefulness toward one's parents weaves an iron web of material, emotional, and spiritual interdependence between members of the family. Studies of Chinese immigrant families show that this critically shapes children's behaviors (Li, 1985; Ng, 1998). For example, if the child fails or shows deviant behavior, the whole family loses face. Similarly, if the child is very successful, the whole family shares in this achievement. This awesome responsibility is a powerful form of constraint on children's behaviors, and is also a source of intergenerational tension among immigrant families of Confucian tradition (Zhou and Bankston, 1998).

The tension between Chinese traditions of collectivism and American traditions of individualism are a constant theme in dialogues about the family in the Chinese church. According to the American moral traditions children must be given a certain allowance of freedom to develop their moral selves (Bellah *et al.*, 1985). The goal of parenting is to raise children who can eventually become independent and self-sufficient (Tobin, Wu, and Davidson, 1989). Strong middle-class families are measured by healthy relationships among individual members where the mutual exchange of respect, communication, and affection do not cultivate co-dependency and loss of self.

But Taiwanese perceive the individual freedom that Americans celebrate as a threat to family harmony. American individualism leads Taiwanese parents to warn their children as one respondent does, "When we get old and sick, you must take care of us. I don't want the American way where you don't take care of mom and dad!" Many immigrants claim that Americans face so many family problems such as high rates of divorce, marital affairs, and runaway children because they are too individualistic. Without a moral tradition that sets collective obligations before the individual, the stability of the family falls victim to the vicissitudes of the individual wills of its members. But, to mainstream middle-class Americans, filiality is an untenable solution to American "family problems." To the extreme, the practice of filial piety will only produce dysfunctional adults who are ridden by guilt, co-dependent, and, worst of all, lacking a sense of self.

REPRODUCING CONFUCIAN TRADITIONS IN THE UNITED STATES?

While Taiwanese parents bemoan the fact that their children are not so obedient and pliable in the United States, they also know that re-creating Taiwanese children in the U.S. is neither practically feasible nor desirable, particularly among a middle-class group of immigrants such as the Taiwanese. First, like other immigrant parents, it is difficult for them to maintain the authority they once had in the home country because of their own difficulties navigating American society (Kibria, 1993). Immigrant children are forced to learn things on their own and become more independent in the United States because their parents do not possess the skills and knowledge to help them (Athey and Ahearn, 1991). One woman admits, "Sometimes I just cannot help my daughter if she has a problem because I don't understand this society." When I asked one working-class respondent what problems she encountered with parenting in the United States, she said that she has a difficult time helping her children with their schoolwork. For the most part, she claimed, "They have to figure it out themselves." The extent to which she does participate in her children's schooling is signing her name, although she admits that she usually doesn't know for what she is signing her name because she cannot read English very well.

Children of immigrants expressed the other side of having to do things on their own. For example, Bill Tang, who is currently a college student, shared how he dealt alone with a frightening experience he had had in junior high. He and his other Asian schoolmates were threatened with knives by a group of Mexican students. Even though the incident garnered a schoolwide meeting among teachers, parents, and students, Bill and his Asian friends never told their immigrant parents about it. In retrospect he claims, "We pretty much took care of ourselves." Realizing the linguistic and cultural limits of their parents, Bill and the other immigrant children did not turn to their parents for help on certain matters.

As other scholars (Sung, 1980; Kibria, 1993; Tse, 1995; Zhou and Bankston, 1998) have pointed out, not only do children of immigrants learn to take care of themselves, they also learn to take care of their parents. The tables are now turned in the United States, where immigrant parents must often depend on their children's help for English translation and various other tasks. What were once clear lines between authority and subordinate are now muddled. This confusion may be even more extreme among working-class immigrants, who depend on their children more than their educated, middle-class counterparts.

Second, even if Taiwanese parents can re-create the Confucian structures of hierarchy and status to produce obedient Taiwanese children, many parents are reluctant to do so. Many of the respondents are middle-class immigrants who work in American companies and recognize that inculcating Confucian virtues such as obedience and deference may create a harmonious home, but will not lead their children to success outside of the home. When I ask respondents what qualities they need to succeed in the United States, they reply independence, aggressiveness, and courage. When I ask what qualities they need to succeed in Taiwan, they say studiousness, hard work, and obedience. From their own experiences working amongst Americans, they realize that the qualities required for success in Taiwan are quite often incompatible with those in the United States.

For example, one woman who is an executive in an American corporation says that she has become more aggressive after moving to the U.S. When I ask her why she wasn't more aggressive in Taiwan, she answers, "If I were more aggressive, I would have just been a pest. And I'm not that kind of person." Her response suggests that although aggressiveness is an effective strategy for getting what you want in the U.S., it is ineffective and off-putting in Taiwan.

Respondents agreed that to succeed, their children needed to be aggressive and independent in the United States. In many ways, the qualities that immigrants inculcate in their children are ones that stem from an *immigrant* experience, that is, the experience of being a foreigner and a minority in the United States. Immigrants realize that because they lack the networks and cultural capital to further their children's upward mobility, their children not only need to be aggressive and competitive with other Americans, but they need to be *more* aggressive and *more* competitive than the typical American. Taiwanese immigrants, many of whom are professionals, are especially cognizant of this fact. They have learned through their own experiences in the professional workplace that, despite having comparable if not superior technical skills than their American co-workers, their job mobility is beset by the phenomenon of the glass ceiling. The combination of lacking connections, American cultural sensibilities, and being Asian works against immigrants' upward mobility.

Having experienced the same barriers that will limit their own children's success, immigrant parents now encourage their children to be independent and aggressive – not to conform to one's particular station or status in life, but to jockey for more. For example, Dr. Su, an engineer who works in a large American company, claims that, because of his own experience of racism in the workplace, he encourages his sons to develop qualities of leadership and independence. He comments:

> In America I encourage my children to be more outgoing and social and develop leadership skills. If you're shy you'll never be a leader. In Taiwan you have more relatives and protection. Here you're by yourself. Alone. Especially for us immigrants who don't have white skin. I feel like I know something about American society, so I want them to be leaders in order to survive. Based on my experience, you have to be this way or you'll fall behind.

As Min Zhou and Carl Bankston (1998) note in their study of Vietnamese American children, the concerns for social mobility and cultural preservation may often work at cross-purposes. Sometimes parents are forced to choose between cultural reproduction and upward mobility. They know that the traditional Taiwanese child is not going to succeed in a white American society and yet, the child who is too "American," meaning too independent and individualistic, can threaten family harmony and solidarity.

Taiwanese immigrant parents find themselves in a dilemma regarding the family. Surrounded by the mainstream culture of American individualism, some of the claims of the Confucian family have lost their moral legitimacy within the family. Pressured by the demands of surviving and thriving in American society, Taiwanese immigrants realize that it is neither feasible nor desirable to hold on to all of the family practices of their own parents. Yet what immigrants perceive as a morally bankrupt mainstream America does not offer any more attractive models for the family.

Where then do Taiwanese immigrants turn for models and traditions of family and parenting in the United States? How do families establish a common moral language that both generations can regard as legitimate? Where some traditions of Taiwan have lost their relevance and the traditions of mainstream America offer no desirable alternatives, Taiwanese immigrants turn to the solutions offered to the immigrant public. The immigrant church is one of the most vocal institutions in this arena.

THE CHINESE CHURCH AND FAMILY IDEOLOGIES

As with other immigrant groups in the United States, the church plays a prominent role within the Taiwanese immigrant community (Warner and Wittner, 1998; Ebaugh and Chafetz, 2000). The frequent meetings and shared faith among members cultivate a sense of moral obligation, accountability, and belonging that makes the church more influential than other organizations within the ethnic community. This fact perhaps explains why a significant number of Taiwanese convert to Christianity after migrating to the United States (Chen, forthcoming). Whereas Christians comprise a mere 2% of the population in Taiwan, Christians are approximately 25% to 32% of the Chinese population in the U.S. (Dart, 1997). Although there are no precise figures of how many Taiwanese Americans are Christian, pastors of Taiwanese churches in Southern California estimate that about 60% of their congregations are converts. Other studies of Chinese churches similarly report a high percentage of converts (Yang, 1999a; Guest, 2003).

Chinese churches' emphasis on the family, particularly their conception of the "good family," is strongly informed by the larger mainstream evangelical tradition to which they belong. Chinese evangelical leaders are influenced by concerns about the dissolution of the traditional family that have preoccupied conservative Christianity since the 1970s (Hunter, 1987; Smith, 1998; Wilcox, 2004). Many Chinese pastors have been trained in American evangelical seminaries. Chinese churches like Grace Church use Bible study guides and Sunday school materials from evangelical religious education sources. For example, in one Chinese church I visited, the congregation was collectively reading the popular evangelical best-seller *The Purpose-Driven Life*. Chinese Christian publishing houses translate and distribute mainstream evangelical literature on the family to Chinese immigrants. The well-known evangelical Christian organization Focus on the Family is a familiar and respected name in the homes of many of my respondents. It should be no surprise that immigrants might be attracted to evangelical Christian ideologies of the family, for both reject and feel threatened by trends in the American family. Where Taiwanese immigrants are searching for a solution to the problems of creating a family in the United States, the evangelical Christians have a ready answer in hand.

Like other immigrant groups (Min, 1998; Yang, 1999a), some Taiwanese immigrants who are not Christian start attending an ethnic Christian church in the United States out of a concern for their children's moral upbringing. For example, Mrs. Lee, a mother of two girls in high school, claims, "When I came to the United States, people told me that the children wouldn't go the wrong way if I brought them to church. At the time I myself had no desire to attend church but I wanted my children to go to church." Another respondent, Mr. Wong, says that after his 12-year-old daughter started coming home from school and copying the language and behavior of "American" kids, he and his wife decided to bring their children to Grace Church. One man, Mr. Liu, used to belong to a Chinese Buddhist temple, but claims that he switched to Grace Church because the temple lacked a children's moral education program for his two teenage children.

Like other immigrant groups (Yang, 1999a; Ebaugh and Chafetz, 2000), many Taiwanese regard the church as the last moral bastion in an otherwise immoral American society. Several immigrants remark how in Taiwan children gain a moral foundation through the public school system. In the United States, where Taiwanese believe that the schools offer no, or severely deficient, moral education, Christianity fills this function. For this reason, Taiwanese who are not Christians will send their children to church. For example,

Mrs. Kau, a homemaker who sent her three children to Christian schools and churches before she became a Christian, explains:

> Kids are young and naive about what's right and wrong. With too much freedom they don't have anything to follow. In Taiwan they have moral education in school. America doesn't and that's not good. That's why I believe that children should be sent to a Christian elementary school. In Taiwan they teach you how to treat people in a class about morality. It has nothing to do with religion. After I came to the United States I became exposed to the Bible and I realized that it had a lot of stories of how to be a good person. I think this is good. Thank goodness in America they have the Bible. I think it's prevented many people from going astray. In Taiwan there aren't many Christians but thank goodness they have moral education.

Promoting strong families is a ministerial priority to Grace Church and other Chinese evangelical churches. For example, the cover of the Grace Church bulletin depicts a church as a hospital healing families and individuals. Knowing that immigrants struggle with intergenerational and bicultural tensions in the family, pastors are particularly mindful of addressing these problems in their ministries to maintain membership and attract new members. At Grace Church, Sunday sermons frequently address family issues. For example, in one sermon the pastor admonished Taiwanese parents for being concerned only about their children's academic achievement and yet neglecting their spiritual development. "So what," he asked them, "if your child becomes famous and successful but neglects you in your old age?" His question suggests that cultivating Christian virtues in one's children similarly cultivates traditional Taiwanese virtues of filiality.

Many of the programs at Grace Church and other Chinese churches are devoted to the family. In addition to a summer and winter retreat, Grace Church sponsors a special "family retreat" that concentrates specifically on issues of parenting and marriage, and attracts the participation of many who do not belong to the church. Chinese churches frequently invite family professionals, such as therapists, psychologists, and pediatricians, to speak on family issues during their weekly fellowship meetings. At Grace Church, children and parents gather together to study the Bible, pray, and socialize during their weekly Family Bible Studies. Quite frequently the discussions revolve around how to incorporate biblical teachings into their family lives.

Chinese churches introduce Chinese immigrants to evangelical Christian literature and resources on the family. Grace Church's publishing house translates and distributes many mainstream American evangelical books about the family that are sold in Chinese Christian bookstores. For example, three of the five new titles that Grace Church's May newsletter introduced were related to parenting: *What My Parents Did Right; Different Children, Different Needs;* and *Parents' Guide to Sex Education.* One Chinese church has its own library, and another church has a small bookstore, where both English and Chinese-translated books, many of them family-related, are available.

Chinese churches distribute the literature of and publicize events for Christian organizations, such as Focus on the Family, but also national Chinese Christian family-centered organizations, such as Focus on the Chinese Family and Chinese Family for Christ. These para-church organizations publish newsletters, hold workshops and retreats like marriage enrichment retreats, and host family vacation camps that Chinese Christians attend. For immigrants who are involved in these tight-knit church communities, evangelical Christian ideologies and models of the family are easily accessible and widely known. For example, several respondents (mostly women) told me that church friends introduced them to a popular talk show about the family on a local Chinese Christian radio station.

The church also serves as a network where immigrants can informally disseminate information on family life. During social hours at Grace Church, parents exchange tips ranging from such topics as college applications, music lessons, teenage dating, and baggy pants. Parents with older children give advice to younger parents. And more established immigrant families serve as role models for others. Parents will frequently seek the advice of the youth pastor in dealing with a variety of issues and not only spiritual problems. The youth pastor at Grace Church told me that parents often approach him for advice on how to motivate their children to study, or how to steer their children away from "bad" friends. For example, when one respondent's daughter ran away from home, the youth pastor counseled her family regularly. Now, the mother says, things have returned to normal in her home.

For youth, the church offers a supportive environment to the 1.5 and 2nd generation who struggle with family issues. Through the institutional structures of the church, the youth group becomes a venue for the children to voice their concerns and needs to the parents. For example, at Grace Church the youth group sponsors an annual "Family Night," a banquet to express their gratitude to their parents. At one Family Night, an American-trained Chinese psychologist delivered a talk describing the struggles that Chinese immigrant parents and their children face in the United States. Dr. Wei, the psychologist, discussed how Chinese American children are overwhelmed by parental pressures to achieve academically and feel emotionally neglected by their parents' "Chinese" lack of expressiveness. These concerns, delivered at the church and through the voice of a credentialed professional, gained an authority that they otherwise would not have when articulated by children in the privacy of the home.

Although most Taiwanese come from a Buddhist heritage, they do not look to Buddhist temples for family guidance. From my fieldwork at one Chinese Buddhist temple and observations at other Chinese temples, I noticed that monastics and laypeople would occasionally discuss family issues during meetings, however, the temple offered no explicit programs, talks, or literature devoted to the topic of the family. As I mentioned earlier, part of the Chinese Christian preoccupation with the family stems from the influence of the mainstream evangelical Christian culture. Chinese Christian churches are a part of a larger culture where a model of, and the resources to support, "the Christian family" exist.

In comparison to the congregational and communal nature of Protestant churches, temples in Taiwan have traditionally been places of ritual ceremony rather than religious and moral education for the laity. This is, however, slowly changing in the United States where non-Western religions assume congregational forms and functions (Warner, 2000; Yang and Ebaugh, 2001). Chinese Buddhism does not have a long-standing tradition of children's religious education like Protestant Christianity. This is largely a Chinese American development. Most immigrant Buddhist temples struggle to offer even modest children's religious education programs because they lack English-language materials (Suh, 2005). In interviews, some Buddhist parents lamented the difficulty of passing their religious tradition down to their American-raised children. They expressed that once their children entered junior high, it was hard to convince them to come to the temple. Buddhist parents, however, did not force their children to attend the temple. In contrast, Christian parents regarded church attendance as a mandatory family activity. The absence of a known tradition of children's religious education also influenced Buddhist parents' expectations of the temple. A Chinese Buddhist nun told me that parents regard her temple's children's program as "daycare," suggesting that parents do not expect the temple to engage in serious religious teaching. Consequently, there are far fewer active youth in temples compared to churches. While there is an attempt to develop children's programs in Chinese Buddhism, they still lag behind the vast resources that Christians have.

RAISING GOOD TAIWANESE KIDS: FROM FAMILY DUTY TO CHRISTIAN DISCIPLESHIP

In this section I discuss how the immigrant church shifts the moral foundation of Taiwanese immigrant families from filial piety to religious piety while simultaneously reinforcing what are perceived as traditional Taiwanese values. Rather than the Confucian language of indebtedness and obligation, immigrant parents use the new moral language of Christian discipleship to achieve traditionally Confucian ends.

A plaque that reads "Christ is the Lord of this House" adorns the homes of many Taiwanese Christians. Symbolically, it replaces the ancestral altar in the traditional Taiwanese home, where family members ritually offer fruit, food, and incense to their ancestors, who in turn protect their living descendents. The plaque symbolizes that Christ, rather than their ancestors, is the source of their protection, and the authority to whom they owe their obedience. In the Gospels, Christ demands total loyalty when he proclaims, "He who loves father or mother more than me is not worthy of me; and he who loves son or daughter more than me is not worthy of me" (Matthew 10:39). One is first a disciple of Christ before he is a father or a son. No loyalties, even to the family, may stand before Christ's authority in each person's life.[5] Christ's lordship must pervade every aspect of the disciple's life, and most certainly his family life. By insisting on the sovereignty of Christ over the family, Christianity sets a new model for *how* to be a family – one where Christ's authority reigns supreme.

The symbolism of the plaque replacing the ancestral shrine vividly illustrates how evangelical Christianity shifts the moral foundation of Taiwanese immigrant families from filial piety to religious piety.[6] Whereas the Confucian family is based on the sense of duty and indebtedness to one's parents, the Christian family is based first and foremost on discipleship to Christ. Individuals are beholden to certain codes of behavior, not because of the obligations that fall upon them as members of the family, but because as Christians they

---

[5]Indeed Chinese have historically not converted to Christianity in large numbers because of this very tension between religion and family. Protestant Christianity prohibited Chinese Christians from participating in "idolatrous" practices of ancestral veneration.

[6]Certainly the degree to which Christianity trumps competing commitments and ideologies varies by individual. For example, regarding the difficult Protestant Christian teaching prohibiting ancestral veneration, some Taiwanese Christians absolutely refuse to participate in these acts of "idolatry," while others do, however, only when they visit their family members in Taiwan. These Taiwanese Christians struggle with reconciling their new religious commitments in the United States with their family traditions in Taiwan. They often justify their participation in ancestral veneration rituals as symbolic, cultural acts of "respect" rather than worship. Similarly, some Taiwanese Christian homes also display Chinese Buddhist figures, such as the Maitreya Buddha. Christians, however, decouple the cultural and religious meanings of these figures, and claim they are symbols of Chinese culture, rather than of Buddhism.

are disciples of Christ. As a Christian, one is an obedient daughter, a nurturing mother, or a loving father because this is what Christ commands.

In reality, however, conversion is rarely the neat substitution of one system of ethics to another. Nor does religious conversion involve the total rejection of Confucian values and traditions, but rather the selective rejection and inclusion of some elements of the past, however now reinterpreted and re-prioritized through a religious lens (Harding, 1987; Stromberg, 1993). Taiwanese parents in my sample used evangelical Christianity to reproduce some traditional Taiwanese values by morally reframing these as acts of Christian discipleship rather than using the Confucian vocabulary of family duty.

Where Taiwanese parents fear the decline of their authority in the United States, some invoke the authority of Christ to discipline their children. Many Taiwanese immigrants claim that Christian teachings are very similar to tradi-tional Taiwanese values and morals, such as respecting elders, shunning drugs and alcohol, and prohibiting divorce and premarital sex. In fact several respondents claimed that because of their Christian values of honesty and hard work, they embody the traditional Taiwanese spirit better than the "modern Taiwanese" who are materialistic and greedy. By appealing to their children's sense of Christian discipleship, Christian teachings are ways to reproduce traditional Taiwanese values. For example, in this quote, Dr. Wu discusses how God's authority replaces his own loss of control over his two middle-school-aged children in the United States:

> Because of too much liberty in the United States, they allow some behaviors here that they don't allow in Taiwan. So parents start to worry about kids going in the wrong direction. Like if they get addicted to drugs or become a punk or become sexually active. What can you do? I've already talked to a lot of parents, and some who have children who are older than mine. They say you just cannot control your child because of all the liberties and human rights here. You can make suggestions but beyond that what else can you do? For example, if they get sexually involved with someone, what can you do? Well, in Taiwan we didn't know about sex at so young an age. Believe me, it's true. But in the U.S. getting sex education is very important for kids these days. But if you are a Christian you have some way to guide them in the right direc-tion. If you have sexual relations before marriage, that's not allowed in the religion. You've already crossed the boundaries before God!

As Dr. Wu's response suggests, Christianity now replaces the moral authority that parents have over their children in a traditional Confucian society. His comment, "But if you are a Christian, you have some way to guide them in the right direction," is particularly elucidating in this regard. Both parents and children now have an objective and common source of moral reference – the

Bible. Immigrant parents claim that their American children often talk back to them. When children ask "why," immigrant parents realize that the traditional answer, "because I say so," holds little ground. With Christianity, parents now have an answer. They find legitimacy through the Bible, a source of authority that is collectively recognized among children and parents alike. Immigrant parents are able to reclaim their authority by referring to the biblical teaching to honor one's parents. In so doing immigrant parents legitimate their authority over their children as God given.

An example from a Family Bible Study meeting illustrates how parents use the Bible to legitimate their authority. On a monthly basis, church members and their families meet at each other's homes, share a potluck meal, and study the Bible together. At this particular meeting children and parents read a passage from the gospel of John where, at the request of his mother Mary, Christ turns water into wine, despite feeling that it is not yet his time to perform a miracle. Parents and children offered varying interpretations of how this passage applied to their daily lives. One child teasingly suggested that the passage advocated children drinking alcohol, to which parents responded by pointing to other biblical passages where drunkenness is condemned. After much discussion, parents and children concluded that children ought to obey their parents, for Christ obeyed his mother, despite his own disinclination.

Affirming Moral Agency

Both traditional Taiwanese and Christian approaches to parenting advocate the same end – children's obedience to parents – the *means*, that is the moral concepts by which these behaviors are framed, are very different. Parents realize that it is no longer effective to use the language of familial duty and indebtedness to their American children to impress certain codes of behavior upon them. As one respondent told me, "in the end they will do what they want." Christianity, however, frames these issues as personal choices. From the earliest ages the church teaches children that Christianity is a personal choice that one makes to commit one's life to Christ. For example, in a Sunday school class, a teacher asks third-graders whether each one would like to make a "personal decision" to "ask Jesus into your heart." In true discipleship one must have the moral freedom to choose to do right. By framing things in the language of moral agency – the choice to follow Christ – rather than the traditional language of moral obligation to the family – indebtedness to parents – parents are able to affirm the children's sense of personal freedom and simultaneously discipline them. This is not to say that children are always obedient, but at least children and parents pay allegiance to the same moral tradition and share a common moral vocabulary.

The church's children's education program plays a crucial part in instilling this sense of Christian discipleship in the children. The moral language of the immigrant home reflects the moral language of the immigrant church. Through Sunday school classes, Sunday worship, and youth group meetings the church constantly affirms the language of moral agency. For example, in a high school Sunday school class Charlie, the instructor, an Asian American student at a local evangelical seminary, challenges students to keep track of what they do in their free time. "Are you using this time to honor God?" he asks. He goes on to discuss how mainstream American culture has become increasingly immoral. He points to the language and pornographic references in television, radio, and movies, as well as the teaching of evolution as a scientific fact in public schools. "It's almost come to a point where we cannot live in this world and be Christian," he concludes. The solution is a challenge to these middle-class suburban students ensconced in our media-frenzied consumer culture: "We have to step away from the values of this culture." Consider how Charlie frames "honoring God" in one's free time:

> Your free time is that one area where you have freedom to exert your independence and develop your identity. It's in those small details of life that it's hard to be uncompromising. You're not just impulsive kids anymore. You're given a certain amount of freedom to align your life with God's will.

Here Charlie suggests that doing the right thing, *i.e.*, watching wholesome movies, not engaging in premarital sex, obeying your parents, is an act of individuality and independence from our fallen culture. Doing the moral thing is not about suppressing one's individuality and meeting social expectations, but having the freedom to resist an oppressive secular culture and do what is right, or "align your life with God's will." In so doing Christianity frames morality as a personal choice, an interpretation that is far more palatable to American children.

On another occasion in a Bible study, the students examined why particular sins, such as premarital sex and drugs, were wrong. They referred to different biblical passages to substantiate their claims. They then came up with concrete strategies to resist these temptations and sins in their daily lives. The church instills the parents' own traditional moral values, however, using the language of Christian moral agency. By training them to be good Christians, parents in turn raise them to be good Taiwanese children.

SOFTENING HIERARCHIES: BECOMING FRIENDS WITH YOUR CHILDREN

But immigrant churches do more than simply reproduce Taiwanese values by repackaging them in Christian trappings. My findings suggest that the church offers a new model of parent-child relations that challenges Confucian hierarchical styles of parenting. In comparison to traditional Taiwanese parent-child relationships, evangelical Christian teachings sacralize more egalitarian relationships. When asked if and how they have changed after converting, respondents frequently cited how they had changed as parents and softened from more authoritarian styles of parenting. For example, Dr. Wu, an engineer in his mid-forties who is the father of two teenage children, recalls that in Taiwan his father was the "king" of his family. His father's word was the sole authority and indisputable.

> My father followed the traditional way. He was like a king. The son must follow. He cannot say anything. He cannot fight back. If he says, "you must study now," as a son you cannot argue. You just go. That's the way it was in my family. If you don't follow then there will be all kinds of punishment.

In his own family in the United States, Dr. Wu continued this pattern of being "king" over his wife and two children until he and his wife converted to Christianity in 1997. He claims that when he and his wife converted, they confessed their sins before God and asked God to remove the sinful patterns that had burdened their lives. One of these sinful patterns that God removed was something that he inherited from his father – the manner of relating to his children as a king.

Taiwanese immigrants learn through their own experience that the old model of parent as absolute authority is no longer effective with their "wild" American children. Through the church Dr. Wu and other Taiwanese immigrants learn that being an authoritarian parent is "wrong" and un-Christian. On this point Dr. Wu reflects:

> In the Bible God represents two things – love and justice. I am too much justice and I don't show enough love to my kids. I just want them to be good, but I don't give them enough love. *I've done it the wrong way. The old me who just showed justice but no love is wrong and I must change.*

Dr. Wu's account illustrates how evangelical Christianity can alter immigrant styles of parenting. The emphasis on love Dr. Wu refers to reflects the expressive and therapeutic turn in evangelical Christianity in the 1970s (Hunter, 1987; Wilcox, 1998). In his research on conservative Christian childrearing,

Bradford Wilcox (2004) finds that compared to religiously unaffiliated men, conservative Christian fathers are not only more involved with and emotionally supportive of their children, but are warmer and more expressive with their children.

Studies show that relative to white Americans, Chinese parents tend to be more controlling (Chiu, 1987; Lin and Fu, 1990). Asian American evangelicals who have been influenced by therapeutic evangelicalism now recognize the "dysfunctions" of their own Confucian upbringings and seek "healing" from what they perceive as the psychological damage of their emotionally distant and controlling fathers (Jeung, 2005).

In place of the traditional hierarchical relationship between parent and child, the church promulgates a new relationship that is based on a friendship between two near-equals. For example, at a Chinese Christian event, Dr. Hsu, a Western-educated Chinese psychologist, encouraged parents to shed their authoritative demeanor. "To be a good parent you need to be on the same level with your kids. You need to become friends."

Although the idea of becoming friends with one's children is admittedly foreign to most Taiwanese immigrants, accepting this proposal is far more palatable under the aegis of a Chinese Christian church than an American secular institution. Chinese Christians look to Western psychology for advice in the arena of the family. Like Dr. Hsu, many of the experts are Chinese who are trained in Western psychology. Through religion, Western models of parenting are thus filtered to Taiwanese immigrant parents through the visage of a familiar Taiwanese face.

Friendship Strategies: Respecting Individuality and Communication

To become friends with their children, parents must recognize that children are separate and autonomous individuals who belong to God. At a Grace Church fellowship meeting Dr. Lin, a child psychologist, spoke at length about the unhealthy tendency for Chinese parents to want perfect children and therefore make excessive demands on them. To solve this problem, he offered two principles of parenting:

1) Remember that your children are gifts from God. As parents you are managers of God's gifts for 18 years of their lives. Learning how to be a good manager means learning not be a control freak.
2) Remember that kids are their own person – God's person. Learn to respect them.

Here Dr. Lin offers a new model of the self and family. Instead of prioritizing the collectivity over the individual, as in the traditional family, Dr. Lin suggests that in the Christian family, the collectivity exists for the development of the individual. Christianity consecrates, and does not repress, the individuality of each child by referring to her as "God's person." The role of Christian parents is not to lord their will over that of the child, but to respectfully develop the particular calling that God has given their child. Parents must help their children become the unique selves that God created them to be. No matter how well intentioned, parents, as managers, need to be wary that their own self-will does not interfere with God's plan for their children. As Dr. Lin warns, "Don't try to make a Mozart out of a Michael Jordan."

Immigrant parents also learn that the key to becoming friends with their children is communication. Friendship is perhaps a trickier type of relationship to negotiate than the hierarchical relationship that characterized traditional parental interactions. Whereas in traditional parent-child relations communication is unidirectional from the parent to the child, a friendship assumes a mutual relationship between two equals. A friendship requires both parties to give and take, speak and listen. Children are well trained to listen to parents, but parents don't know the language of their children. In a family retreat at Grace Church, another American-educated Chinese psychologist told the audience of immigrant parents ranging from their 30s to 50s, "You have to speak to kids in their own language. Learn the trendy words like 'cool' and 'phat.' Learn the names of popular rock stars like the Backstreet Boys and Britney Spears."

Immigrants articulate this very same emphasis on communication in their own families. "Communication skills are the key to a strong family," Mrs. Su, a mother of three, tells me. She claims, "We can't order our kids anymore, we have to communicate with them. It's not the way it used to be in Taiwan, where you can just say 'no.'"

My respondents expressed the importance of setting aside time to spend with their children. For example, at a Family Bible Study, Mr. Lin, an engineer and father of two, introduced the folk song "Cat's in the Cradle" to stress this point. In the song, songwriter Harry Chapin describes a busy father who fails to spend time with his son despite his promises. When the son grows up, the situation is reversed. The father wants to spend time with the son, but the son has no time. Mr. Lin then reported the surprising finding of a recent study – the average amount of time that a father spends alone with his children each day is only three minutes.

Respondents shared how they now try to listen to their children. Consider the experience of Mrs. Chang:

> Before, if my kids did something wrong I would yell, "Why do you do this and why do you do that?" I didn't know what they were feeling. Now I look back and think that they must have been very scared. Now I've changed my behavior because I know that I acted wrong. I discuss things with my kids and I encourage them to tell me how they really are feeling. I changed. I seldom yell now.

Parents are more likely to designate special "family times" on a daily or weekly basis. For example, respondents told me that they incorporate daily or weekly family Bible studies where family members gather to sing, read the Bible, share their experiences, and pray together. By cultivating their children's spiritual lives, parents are simultaneously cultivating family ties.

Immigrants learn through the church that strong families are no longer built on a sense of obligation and indebtedness, the pillars of the old ways of filial piety. Instead, parents and children now cultivate lasting family ties through developing communication and affection for one another. In fact, traditional styles of parenting are more of a liability than an assurance of continuing family ties in the United States. Commenting on traditional styles of parenting, Dr. Wu said, "Once your children grow up and become teenagers, then there will be a lot of trouble if you follow the old traditional way. The gap will only grow."

Mrs. Wong, a mother of two, expressed similar fears of excessively individualistic children:

> As a parent I worry. But if you don't have good communication with your child before they become mature adults then you will worry even more. They'll become teenagers and graduate and then say "bye-bye." No more parents because I don't understand you and you don't understand me. They'll just leave you!

THE COSTS OF FRIENDSHIP – RELINQUISHING PARENTAL CONTROL

Despite the solutions that the immigrant Christian church offers to Taiwanese parents, these benefits do not come without some costs. By making Christ the head of the family and attempting to become friends with their children, parents lose some of the authority that they might have in a traditional Confucian tradition. Just as the parents can use biblical teachings to justify their own disciplinary decisions, so too can children use biblical teachings as a defense of their own will against that of their parents. For example, one respondent recounts how after scolding her son for misbehaving he responded, "Mom, you didn't listen to what the pastor said at church! You didn't listen. You should just talk to me and not yell at me!" Another respondent claims that she feels ashamed if she misses church on Sunday because her daughter will reprimand her.

Some parents complain that their children can be "too Christian" by prioritizing church over their schoolwork. One high school student even printed on his namecard, "Part-Time Southern California High School Student, Full-Time Christian" to advertise that his Christian commitments supersede his academic commitments. Planning and participating in church youth activities can occupy precious time that parents would prefer be spent on academic work. Christian parents have a very difficult time justifying to their children that schoolwork comes before church. The youth pastor, Pastor Tom, claims that several parents have come to him, hoping that as the pastor he can convince their children to prioritize academics over church. Given what he truly believes, that Christ comes first, he is in a difficult position to intervene. When religious commitments compete with academics, Christian teachings not necessarily work to further parents' interests. Indeed, Christian teaching may not always create family harmony, but can lead to new and different tensions.

Taiwanese youth who feel beleaguered by excessive academic demands from their parents may strategically use Christianity to ease their parents' expectations. These educated and professional Taiwanese parents who see their children as the beneficiaries of their own academic excellence may find these teachings challenging and threatening. For example, consider the reflections of Mrs. Lin, an active deaconess in the youth ministry, on a parent-youth dialogue at Grace Church:

> I knew that there were communication problems between the children and parents, and so I organized a parent and youth dialogue. The parents sat on one side of the room, and the youth sat on the other side of the room facing each other. I had them write out questions from either side, and Pastor Tom read the questions. Of course his questions were selective, and he chose to concentrate on education issues. He kept pressing the parents – "So what if they get straight A's and go to the best school, and then what?" He kept on pressing us, and then what and then what, until the parents just didn't know what to answer. The parents responded that without education we wouldn't be here. But somehow we just didn't communicate on that issue.

With Christ as the head of the household, parents can be proven wrong. Some respondents told me how they have learned to apologize to their children when before they could not imagine doing any such thing. Parents learn that in their "friendship" with their children both parties must be willing to change and compromise. Mrs. Huang told me that her disapproval of her daughter's white boyfriend had caused a great deal of tension in their relationship. After her daughter pointed out that God created everyone equal, she reflected on this for awhile and prayed about it. She then came to the conclusion that she was wrong. She asked for her daughter's forgiveness and made the attempt to accept the young man as "who he really is."

Consider how Mrs. Lin, the deaconess who is a dentist in her mid-forties, now speaks of parenting as a collaboration between herself and her two teenage sons:

> The difference between me as a mother versus my parents is that I am able to come down to their [the children's] level and tell them that I'm not perfect. These are my limits and I need you to chip in and help out. When I was a child, we were taught in school the Confucius teaching that parents are never wrong, and therefore you don't dare challenge your parents. But here, as an immigrant family, my husband and I both have to work. I'm not at home a lot, and my influence is so limited, and yet they're so open to the world online and on TV. I was very worried, especially when my sons were in that 14–15 age range. What helped us go through that was for us to bring it up and talk about it. I was fearful, and I talked about how difficult it was for me, and I told my son at the time, "I am only one mother. Only one pair of hands. I'm pulling you on one side and the world is pulling you on the other side. Compared to the world, I'm powerless. If you choose to fall on this side, then the tug-of-war is over. And so I need your help."

Given the dominance of the surrounding American culture, Taiwanese immigrants have little choice but to accept a loss of control over their children. But rather than viewing this as a threat, Christianity redefines what it means to be a good parent. God does not want parents lording over their children. God is the head of the household, and parents are to be good managers by helping children develop their God-given talents and callings. A good family is based on relationships of mutual respect and communication rather than duty and obligation. Instead of regarding these changes as the loss of tradition or Americanization, Taiwanese American Christians welcome these transformations as a movement toward becoming a more Christian family.

DISCUSSION

My findings both confirm and challenge those of other scholars who argue that religion reproduces ethnic traditions. With the case of Taiwanese Americans, Christianity does perpetuate certain traditional values, albeit using a very different moral mechanism than Confucianism – religious piety rather than filial piety. Through the language of religious discipleship rather than familial obligation, parents are able to effectively discipline their children and teach them traditional moral values. By framing these traditional values as Christian values and by considering moral agency rather than moral indebtedness as the basis of their actions, the church melds Confucian ends with more culturally effective Christian means.

But I also show that religion can transform traditional ends by legitimating and sacralizing new patterns of family relationships. While sharing certain Confucian values, evangelical Christianity is also critical of the generational hierarchy and lack of emotion that characterize traditional Confucian parent-child relationships. Instead, evangelical Christianity sanctifies more democratic relationships between parents and children, and teaches new practices that cultivate open communication and sharing.

These transformations I observed in these families are perhaps best described as "soft" rather than "radical." Evangelical Christianity does not eradicate hierarchy, but softens it; nor does it reject filial piety, but preserves the spirit. The individual will is still subordinated in evangelical Christianity – not to the collectivity of the family, but to the authority of God.

This particular case of Taiwanese immigrant Christian families gives us one example of how to theorize further about the connections between immigration, religion, and ethnicity. The centrality of the church and the prominence of evangelical Christianity are hardly distinct to Chinese immigrants, but are notable patterns among many immigrant groups and their children in the United States, such as Koreans (Chong, 1998; Park, 2001) and Mexicans (Leon, 1998; Balmer, 2003). As such, scholars must recognize that these immigrant Christian churches are not merely bastions of ethnic preservation, but participate in a larger culture of American evangelical Christianity. For many Christian immigrants, acculturation to American society is mediated through ethnic *and* evangelical Christian influences.

Although it appears that evangelical Christianity is assimilating Taiwanese immigrants into American middle-class family practices, I argue that this is not quite the case. While embracing *certain* middle-class parenting practices, such as recognizing children's autonomy, and cultivating friendship and emotional expressiveness with their children, Taiwanese immigrants also use evangelical Christianity to critique other common practices of the American middle class – such as divorce, premarital sex, and nursing homes. Studies of second-generation Asian American evangelicals report that they appear to be more culturally evangelical than ethnic (Alumkal, 1999; Jeung, 2005). Chinese Christian immigrants and their children are culturally assimilating into an American evangelical culture, and even more precisely an *Asian American evangelical culture*, rather than an amorphous American middle class.

Class mediates how religion, and other ideological and cultural influences, alters immigrant families. In working-class immigrant families, parent-child relationships often undergo more strains than middle-class families. Generational hierarchies are radically inverted because parents are even more dependent on their children for cultural and financial resources (Kibria, 1993; Zhou and Bankston, 1998). Professional and educated immigrant parents, on the other hand, who are better able to maintain an upper hand through control of family finances, may be more open, and less threatened by evangelical Christian ideas such as parent-child friendship. Middle-class immigrants not only have more time to attend parenting workshops and read parenting books, but may be more able to "afford" new parenting practices that working-class immigrants, who are strained in "authority capital," cannot.

Finally, I've made the case that evangelical Christianity simultaneously reproduces and challenges ethnic traditions, but does this generalization apply to other religions like Buddhism, Hinduism, and Islam that, unlike Christianity, are immigrants' inherited traditions and are minority religions in the United States? To this question, I answer a qualified yes. Religions are not mere extensions of ethnicity, but rich and complex traditions of their own. Religions can act independently of ethnicity, and, under certain conditions, are capable of challenging ethnic traditions. For example, scholars show that immigrant women use Buddhism (Chen, 2005; Suh, 2005) and Islam (Kurien, 1999) to challenge traditional gender ideas in the family. These findings suggest that inherited, non-Christian religions may also shape immigrant families in non-traditional ways.

REFERENCES

Alumkal, A. W.
1999 "Preserving Patriarchy: Assimilation, Gender Norms, and Second-generation Korean American Evangelicals." *Qualitative Sociology* 22:127–140.

Athey, J. L., and F. L. Ahearn
1991 "The Mental Health of Refugee Children: An Overview." In *Refugee Children: Theory, Research and Services.* Ed. F. L. Ahearn and J. L. Athey. Baltimore: Johns Hopkins University Press. Pp. 3–19.

Balmer, R.
2003 "Crossing the Borders: Evangelicalism and Migration." In *Religion and Immigration: Christian, Jewish, and Muslim Experiences in the United States.* Ed. Y. Y. Haddad, J. I. Smith, and J. L. Esposito. Walnut Creek, CA: AltaMira Press. Pp. 56–60.

Bellah, R. N. *et al.*
1985 *Habits of the Heart: Individualism and Commitment in American Life.* New York: Harper and Row.

Buriel, R., and T. DeMent
1997 "Immigration and Sociocultural Change in Mexican, Chinese and Vietnamese American Families." In *Immigration and the Family: Research and Policy on U.S. Immigrants.* Ed. A. Booth and N. Landale. Mahwah, NJ: Lawrence Erlbaum Associates. Pp. 165–300.

Chen, C.
Forthcoming   *Getting Saved in America: Immigrants from Taiwan Converting to Evangelical Christianity and Buddhism.* Princeton: Princeton University Press.

———

2005   "A Self of One's Own: Taiwanese Immigrant Women and Religious Conversion." *Gender & Society* 19(3):336–357.

Chiu, L. H.
1987   "Child-rearing Attitudes of Chinese, Chinese-American, and Anglo-American Mothers." *International Journal of Psychology* 22:409–419.

Chong, K. H.
1998   "What it Means to be Christian: The Role of Religion in the Construction of Ethnic Identity and Boundary among Second-Generation Korean Americans." *Sociology of Religion* 39(3):259–286.

Dart, J.
1997   "Poll Studies Chinese Americans." *Los Angeles Times,* July 5.

Ebaugh, H. R., and J. S. Chafetz
2000   *Religion and the New Immigrants: Continuities and Adaptations in Immigrant Congrega-tions.* Walnut Creek, CA: AltaMira.

Espiritu, Y.
2003   "Gender and Labor in Asian Immigrant Families." In *Gender and U.S. Immigration.* Ed. P. Hondagneu-Sotelo. Berkeley: University of California Press. Pp. 81–100.

Guest, K. J.
2003   *God in Chinatown: Religion and Survival in New York's Evolving Immigrant Community.* New York: New York University Press.

Harding, S. F.
1987   "Convicted by the Holy Spirit: The Rhetoric of Fundamentalist Baptist Conversion." *American Ethnologist* 14(2):167–181.

Hondagneu-Sotelo, P.
1994   *Gendered Transitions: Mexican Experiences of Immigration.* Berkeley: University of California Press.

Huang, C., and K. Wu
1994   "Taiwan and the Confucian Aspiration: Toward the Twenty-first Century." In *Cultural Change in Postwar Taiwan.* Ed. S. Harrell and C. C. Huang. Boulder, CO: Westview Press. Pp. 69–88.

Huang, J.
1988   "The Practice of Filial Piety in Modern Life." In *Zhongguo ren de xin li (The Mentality of Chinese People).* Ed. K. S. Yang. Taipei: Guiguan Publication Company. Pp. 25–38.

Hunter, J. D.
1987   *Evangelicalism: The Coming Generation.* Chicago: University of Chicago Press.

Jeung, R.
2005   *Faithful Generations: Race and New Asian American Churches.* New Brunswick, NJ: Rutgers University Press.

Jochim, C.
2003   "Carrying Confucianism into the Modern World: The Taiwan Case." In *Religion in Modern Taiwan.* Ed. P. Clart and C. B. Jones. Honolulu: University of Hawaii Press. Pp. 48–83.

Jordan, D. K.
1998   "Filial Piety in Taiwanese Popular Thought." In *Confucianism and the Family.* Ed. W. H. Slote and G. A. DeVos. Albany: State University of New York Press. Pp. 267–283.

Kibria, N.
1993 *Family Tightrope: The Changing Lives of Vietnamese Americans.* Princeton, NJ: Princeton University Press.

Kim, G. S.
1996 "Asian North American Immigrant Parents and Youth: Parenting and Growing Up in a Cultural Gap." In *People on the Way (Asian North Americans Discovering Christ, Culture, and Community).* Ed. D. Ng. Valley Forge, PA: Judson Press.

Kurien, P.
1999 "Gendered Ethnicity: Creating a Hindu Indian Identity in the United States." *American Behavioral Scientist* 42(4):648–670.

———
1998 "Becoming American by Becoming Hindu: Indian Americans Take Their Place at the Multicultural Table." In *Gatherings in Diaspora.* Ed. R. S. Warner and J. G. Wittner. Philadelphia: Temple University Press. Pp. 37–70.

Leon, L.
1998 "Born Again in East LA: The Congregation as Border Space." In *Gatherings in Diaspora.* Ed. R. S. Warner and J. G. Wittner. Philadelphia: Temple University Press. Pp. 163–196.

Li, X.
1985 "The Effect of Family on the Mental Health of the Chinese People." In *Chinese Culture and Mental Health.* Ed W. Tseng and D. Y. H. Wu. Orlando: Academic Press. Pp. 85–93.

Lin, C. Y., and V. R. Fu
1990 "A Comparison of Child-Rearing Practices among Chinese, Immigrant Chinese, and Caucasian-American Parents." *Child Development* 61:429–433.

Ly, P.
2003 "Immigrants Help to Reenergize U.S. Christianity." *The Washington Post,* 4 February.

Min, P. G.
2003 "Immigrants' Religion and Ethnicity: A Comparison of Korean Christian and Indian Hindu Immigrants." In *Revealing the Sacred in Asian and Pacific America.* Ed. J. N. Iwamura and P. Spickard. New York: Routledge Press. Pp. 125–142.

———
1998 *Changes and Conflicts: Korean Immigrant Families in New York.* Boston: Allyn and Bacon.

Ng, F.
1998 *The Taiwanese Americans.* Westport, CT: Greenwood Press.

Park, S.
2001 "The Intersection of Religion, Race, Gender, and Ethnicity in the Identity Formation of Korean American Evangelical Women." In *Korean Americans and Their Religions,* Ed. H. Kwon, K. C. Kim, and R. S. Warner. University Park: Pennsylvania State University Press. Pp. 193–208.

Smith, C.
1998 *American Evangelicalism: Embattled and Thriving.* Chicago and London: University of Chicago Press.

Stromberg, P. G.
1993 *Language and Self-Transformation: A Study of the Christian Conversion Narrative.* New York: Cambridge University Press.

Sung, B. L.
1980 *Transplanted Chinese Children.* New York: Department of Asian Studies, The City College of New York.

Suh, S.
2005 "Mapping the Buddhist Terrain in Korean American Communities of Southern California." Paper presented at the Association for Asian American Studies Annual Conference, Los Angeles, CA. April.

Tobin, J. J., D. Y. H. Wu, and D. H. Davidson
1989 *Preschool in Three Cultures: Japan, China and the United States.* New Haven: Yale University Press.

Tse, L.
1995 "Language Brokering among Latino Adolescents: Prevalence, Attitudes, and School Performance." *Hispanic Journal of Behavioral Sciences* 17:180–193.

Tu, W. M.
1998 "Probing the 'Three Bonds' and 'Five Relationships' in Confucian Humanism." In *Confucianism and the Family.* Ed. W. H. Slote and G. A. DeVos. Albany: State University of New York Press. Pp. 121–136.

Warner, R. S.
2000 "Religion and New (Post-1965) Immigrants: Some Principles Drawn from Field Research." In *American Studies* 41(2/3):267–286.

———, and J. Wittner, eds.
1998 *Gatherings in Diaspora: Religious Communities and the New Immigration.* Philadelphia: Temple University Press.

Waters, M.
1999 Black Identities: West Indian Immigrant Dreams and American Realities. Cambridge: Harvard University Press.

Whyte, M. K.
2004 "Filial Obligations in Chinese Families: Paradoxes of Modernization." In *Filial Piety: Practice and Discourse in Contemporary East Asia.* Ed. C. Ikels. Stanford: Stanford University Press. Pp. 106–127.

Wilcox, B.
2004 *Soft Patriarchs and New Men: How Christianity Shapes Fathers and Husbands.* Chicago: University of Chicago Press.

———
1998 "Conservative Protestant Childrearing: Authoritarian or Authoritative?" *American Sociological Review* 63:796–809.

Yang, F.
2002 "Chinese Christian Transnationalism: Diverse Networks of a Houston Church." In *Religion Across Borders: Transnational Immigrant Networks.* Ed. H. R. Ebaugh and J. S. Chafetz. Walnut Creek: AltaMira Press. Pp. 129–148.

———
1999a *Chinese Christians in America: Conversion, Assimilation, and Adhesive Identities.* University Park, PA: Pennsylvania State University Press.

———
1999b "ABC and XYZ: Religious, Ethnic and Racial Identities of New Second Generation Chinese in Christian Churches." *Amerasia Journal* 25(1): 89–114.

———, and H. R. Ebaugh
2001 "Transformation in New Immigrant Religions and their Global Implications." *American Sociological Review* 2:269–288.

Zhou, M., and C. L. Bankston III.
1998 *Growing Up American: How Vietnamese Children Adapt to Life in the United States.* New York: Russell Sage Foundation.

[22]

INTERNATIONAL MIGRATION

IOM International Organization for Migration

doi: 10.1111/imig.12095

Piety in a Secular Society: Migration, Religiosity, and Islam in Britain

Valerie A. Lewis* and Ridhi Kashyap**

ABSTRACT

While in the American context religion is seen to facilitate immigrant incorporation by providing both spiritual and socioeconomic resources, in Europe high levels of religiosity are theorized as a barrier for immigrant incorporation into the secular mainstream. This is particularly salient for Islam, Europe's largest minority religion. In this study, we use the 2008–2009 England and Wales Citizenship Survey to compare levels and predictors of religiosity between Muslim and non-Muslim first-generation immigrants and their native-born counterparts. Overall, Muslims are more religious than non-Muslims. The results show that among non-Muslims, the foreign-born are significantly more religious than the native-born; among Muslims, however, nativity has no impact on religiosity, indicating the native-born are as highly religious as the foreign-born. Additionally, although education is associated with reduced religiosity among non-Muslim immigrants and native-born, for Muslims it has no significant impact. Muslims across diverse ethnic and socioeconomic backgrounds show strong religious adherence. Results suggest that pathways to secular, mainstream norms do not operate in the same manner across Muslim and non-Muslim immigrant groups.

INTRODUCTION

The large inflows of migrant populations into Europe since the 1960s have transformed an erstwhile continent of emigration into one of immigration. Europe today is home to unprecedented levels of social and cultural diversity, of which one key dimension is the increasing number of minority, non-Christian religions. Islam is the largest minority religion in Western Europe (Fetzer and Soper, 2003) and features most prominently in public discourses (Klausen, 2005; Bowen, 2007). Islam in Europe has been cast in opposition to an increasingly secular European tradition where the boundaries between being Muslim and being European are 'bright', clearly demarcating Muslims in Europe as outsiders (Alba, 2005). Thus, while literature examining the role of religion in immigrant incorporation in the United States describes religion as a bridge to incorporation into American society, religious identity is theorized as a barrier to incorporation within a highly secular Western European context (Foner and Alba, 2008).

This study addresses immigrant religiosity in Britain. In contrast with other Western European contexts, quantitative empirical examinations of Muslim religiosity in Britain remain limited. Qualitative micro-studies indicate that British Muslims are a highly religious group and that personal subjective religiosity is stronger for younger Muslims than their elders (Jacobson, 1997; Glynn, 2002; Hopkins, 2006; Dwyer et al., 2008; Kibria, 2008; Archer, 2009). These qualitative data often

---

* Dartmouth College, Hanover.

** Centre d'Estudis Demogràfics (CED), Autonomous University of Barcelona, Barcelona.

© 2013 The Authors
International Migration © 2013 IOM
International Migration Vol. 51 (3) 2013
ISSN 0020-7985

Published by John Wiley & Sons Ltd.

lack generalizability, cannot describe predictors of high religiosity among Muslims, and do not provide comparisons with non-Muslim groups. Could high levels of religiosity be common among foreign-born Britons across religious groups and not just among Muslims? Could lower education levels and high unemployment, forms of socio-economic disadvantage that characterize the Muslim population (Peach, 2006; Hussain, 2008), explain high levels of Muslim religiosity? Moreover, does nativity have a similar impact on Muslim immigrants in comparison with non-Muslim immigrants? These questions have not been adequately addressed in the literature on the British context; this article attempts to do so.

IMMIGRANT RELIGIOSITY: THEORETICAL FRAMEWORKS AND EMPIRICAL PERSPECTIVES

Britain and much of Western Europe has witnessed widespread secularization over the course of the twentieth century, indicated by generational declines in religious affiliation, belief and attendance (Voas and Crockett, 2005; Crockett and Voas, 2006; Gorski and Altinordu, 2008). Trends of secularization, however, often focus on Christianity, neglecting the case of non-Christian religions practised by ethnic minorities and migrants (Chambers, 2006). This is a crucial omission, as there are theoretical reasons to believe that levels of religiosity are likely higher among immigrants than native European populations. Synthesizing insights about religion in the migration process derived from the American context, Connor (2010: 378–380) highlights that across paradigms of immigrant incorporation, some degree of resilience of religious affiliation and practice among migrant communities is presumed. While Hirschman's (2004) account for this religious adherence is the positive aspects of resources, refuge, and respectability that immigrant religious groups provide for those navigating new lives in an unfamiliar society, others acknowledge that religious identity may be closely guarded, particularly when migrants may feel their ethnic identity threatened (Bruce, 1996). For Britain these theoretical claims are descriptively borne out through data from the European Social Survey, which indicates that religiosity (including religious attendance, prayer, and subjective religiosity) is significantly higher amongst foreign-born migrants than among the native-born (Van Tubergen, 2006: 281).

While persistent religiosity for first generation migrants is unequivocally theorized, the expected generational change in religiosity for second- or third-generation descendants is less clear and arguably more context- and group-specific. Straight-line assimilation theories suggest that exposure to secular, European life may cause the native-born to assimilate to secular ways of life. This hypothesis is partially borne out by studies of Muslims in the Netherlands, which indicate that second-generation Muslims show weaker ethnic and religious identities than foreign-born (Maaliepaard et al., 2010). In contrast, the 'reactive ethnicity' hypothesis suggests that lack of upward mobility and discrimination can encourage the use of ethnic identity, and religious identity that is closely associated with ethnicity, as an alternative form of social status (Portes and Rumbaut, 2001; Greeley, 1971). Using data from the European Social Survey, Connor (2010) finds empirical support for the hypothesis that religious identity may deepen in more hostile contexts of immigrant reception. In his analysis, less welcoming contexts of reception for immigrants were associated with stronger forms of public religiosity (prayer and attendance) as compared to mean religiosity in the host society for Muslim immigrants in Western Europe. Other European studies indicate strong stability in religiosity between first- and second-generation Muslims (Diehl and Koenig, 2009; Fleischmann and Phalet, 2012).

Existing empirical work in Britain suggests that second-generation Muslim youth disassociate ethnic and religious identities, placing greater emphasis on the religious identity in terms of importance to personal life; youth identify with the global community of Muslim believers, the *ummah*

(Jacobson, 1997; Glynn, 2002; Dwyer et al., 2008; Kibria, 2008). However, these findings come from qualitative micro-studies focused on one or two cities, do not examine variations in religiosity, and do not provide comparisons to other immigrant groups or religious youth in general. These comparisons are particularly relevant in the light of broader theories in the sociology of religion that emphasize the 'individualization' of religion against wider processes of secularization and globalization. The heightened personal, subjective religiosity among Muslim youth may be an instance of this individualization among younger generations, wherein religion becomes less imposed and inherited, and in turn more adaptable to personal choice (Davie, 2004; Heelas and Woodhead, 2005). Against this backdrop of changing forms of religiosity, particularly among younger generations, it is important to ask if similar variations of religiosity are evident across different religious groups or whether in fact, Islam operates uniquely.

Recent scholarship on Britain has tried to overcome shortcomings of the qualitative literature by using survey data that facilitate comparisons across generations and religious groups. This work suggests that Muslim youth in Britain show lower levels of religious practice than their elders, but express a stronger religious identity (Kashyap and Lewis, 2012). Using the 2003 Home Office Citizenship Survey, Scourfield et al. (2012) find that the transmission of religion across three 'generations' – religion practised by the respondent as a child, his current religious affiliation, and the religious affiliation identified by the respondent's child – is significantly stronger among Muslims than other religions. The authors also find that higher religious transmission rates among Muslims were associated with lower levels of education, being unemployed, and lower levels of income (Scourfield et al., 2012: 14–15). This finding echoes European migration and religion scholarship that indicates higher levels of education and employment are associated with reduced levels of religiosity among *all* immigrants (van Tubergen, 2006; Van Tubergen, 2006) and specifically Muslim immigrants in the Netherlands and Belgium (Smits et al., 2010; Maliepaard et al., 2010). Although Muslims in Britain are a comparatively disadvantaged group, limited work in the British context has examined to what extent Muslim religiosity can be explained by socioeconomic variables and how these socioeconomic differences explain variations in religious outcomes among immigrant groups. Nevertheless, in much public discourse, many assume that Muslim migrants are an exception as regards socio-cultural adaptation (Cesari, 2004). This claim warrants comparative assessment between Muslims and non-Muslims. By comparing Muslim immigrants with non-Muslim immigrants, we examine how religiosity and its predictors vary between these two groups as well the native population. We examine religious retention across foreign-born migrants and the native-born for both Muslim and non-Muslims to examine closely if religious transmission operates differently across religious groups.

METHODS AND DATA

We use the 2008–2009 Citizenship Survey, a national survey of England and Wales conducted by the National Centre for Social Research on behalf of the Department for Communities and Local Government of the United Kingdom. The 2008–2009 version is the fifth wave of cross sectional surveys that collects data on themes such as local communities, civic engagement, values and attitudes. The survey includes a nationally representative sample of adults in England and Wales and an oversample of ethnic minority groups using a two-stage sample design. Face-to-face interviews were conducted between April 2008 and March 2009 for a total N of 14,917. The survey was offered in eight non-English languages, and approximately three percent of interviews were carried out in a language other than English. The overall response rate for the core sample and ethnic oversamples was 56 percent. All analyses here use the survey individual weights for the combined core and oversample.

Our main outcome of interest is religiosity. The Citizenship Survey asks about a respondent's religious identication with a question, "What is your religion even if you are not currently practising?" This allows us to identify Muslims in the data. The survey includes one question about religious practice. Specifically, the survey asked, "Do you consider that you are actively practising your religion?" with response options of yes or no. We consider this measure a self-identification of religiosity, in contrast to other measures of religiosity that are often practice- or belief-based (such as frequency of church attendance or strength of belief in God). We first examine descriptively how this compares across Muslims and non-Muslims and nativity.

After examining descriptively how Muslim and non-Muslim foreign-born respondents compare with native-born counterparts on religiosity, we then seek to understand the predictors of religiosity. We use multivariate regression models to examine the impact of a variety of covariates on our religiosity outcome. The survey asks in what country the respondent was born, allowing us to identify those born outside Britain (throughout the study, we use the word immigrant to refer to foreign-born individuals who now live in the UK). Finally, the Citizenship Survey also includes a selection of covariates; we use measures of household income, work status, education, gender, marital and parental status, and ethnicity as controls in our models, following previous work that has found these variables as significant predictors of religiosity across both native and immigrant populations (Norris and Inglehart, 2004; Van Tubergen, 2006; van Tubergen and Sindrado'ttir, 2011).

We use logistic regression to model respondents reporting they actively practise their religion. We first examine how religiosity varies across Muslims and non-Muslims and between foreign-born and native-born. We then examine how ethnicity, race, and socioeconomic factors impact religiosity, and how much of any gap between groups these characteristics explain. Finally, we run separate models for each of four groups: Muslim foreign-born, Muslim native-born, non-Muslim foreign-born, and non-Muslim native-born. Our interest lies primarily in the predictors of religiosity across Muslim and non-Muslim immigrants; for a useful comparison we limit our analysis of non-Muslims to other Britons who also claim a religious affiliation, excluding those who identify with no religion. We use listwise deletion to account for missing data; in total 13 per cent of the data are removed, almost entirely due to non-response on household income.[1]

RESULTS

We first examine differences in religious practice between Muslim immigrants, Muslim native-born, non-Muslim immigrants, and non-Muslim native-born Britons. Muslims most often report actively practising their religion whether foreign-born or native-born (81% and 80% respectively), followed by non-Muslim foreign-born (59%), and then native non-Muslim Britons (31%). Model 1 in Table 1 shows this baseline – Muslims are more likely to be actively practicing, as are the foreign-born. The interaction between Muslim and foreign-born indicates that among Muslims, foreign-born status is only very slightly associated with increased religiosity (evidenced by the sum of the foreign born and foreign born x Muslim interaction coefficients); in contrast, among non-Muslims the foreign-born are considerably more religious (evidenced by the foreign born main effect).

We then consider what factors may account for these descriptive differences. Model 2 of Table 1 includes controls for ethnicity; ethnicity controls substantially reduce the Muslim coefficient and somewhat reduce the foreign-born coefficient, indicating that particular ethnic groups are driving some of the Muslim and foreign-born effects. Overall, non-whites are significantly more religious than whites. In Model 3, we control for other family background characteristics; many of these are significantly predictive of religiosity, but these do little to further explain the higher religiosity among Muslims and the foreign-born.

TABLE 1

COEFFICIENTS FROM LOGISTIC REGRESSION MODEL PREDICTING ACTIVELY PRACTISING RELIGION

	Model 1 Coef. (t-score)	Model 2 Coef. (t-score)	Model 3 Coef. (t-score)
Muslim	2.21*** (9.14)	1.09** (3.11)	1.34*** (3.45)
Foreign-born	1.16*** (13.55)	0.72*** (6.52)	0.76*** (6.77)
Muslim x Foreign-born	−1.14*** (−4.10)	−0.74* (−2.42)	−0.93** (−2.75)
Race and ethnicity			
White [reference]			
Bangladeshi		1.49*** (5.53)	1.64*** (5.73)
Pakistani		1.59*** (6.38)	1.67*** (6.23)
Indian		1.29*** (11.46)	1.42*** (12.01)
Other Asian		1.01*** (5.55)	1.15*** (5.81)
Black		1.41*** (13.42)	1.62*** (14.50)
Other race		0.70*** (6.06)	0.83*** (6.75)
Economic characteristics			
Household income			0.00 (0.01)
Working			−0.30*** (−4.04)
Education			
No qualifications [reference]			
A level (High School)			−0.76*** (−7.10)
O level (10th Grade)			−0.77*** (−7.34)
College			−0.31** (−2.76)
Unknown education			−0.77*** (−8.02)
Family background			
Female			0.62*** (10.28)
Married			0.28*** (4.41)
Children at home			−0.06 (−0.77)
Constant	−0.87*** (−28.29)	−0.90*** (−28.70)	−0.70*** (−8.87)
N	11318	11318	11318
Pseudo r-square	0.051	0.064	0.104

Note: *p < 0.05; **p < 0.01; ***p < 0.001.

We illustrate the magnitude of difference in religiosity between groups in Figure 1. On the left side of the panel, we show the descriptive data on the proportion of each group that reports actively practising their religion. On the right side, we show predicted probabilities of the outcomes; these predicted probabilities are generated from Monte Carlo simulations from the logistic regression in Model 3 of Table 1, holding all control variables at the global mean for the sample (King et al., 2000). This allows us to examine how big differences are between groups, taking into account their socioeconomic and background characteristics. Overall, the differences in religiosity between native-born Britons and foreign-born (both Muslim and non-Muslim) are somewhat reduced when taking into account the control variables. However, both Muslims and non-Muslim immigrants remain significantly more religious than their native-born peers, even after taking into account ethnicity and socioeconomic characteristics.

Finally, we examine how the predictors of religiosity vary. In particular, we run separate models regressing religiosity on our covariates for foreign-born Muslims, native-born Muslims, non-Muslim foreign-born, and non-Muslim native-born (Table 2). Each model controls for household income, work status, education, gender, marital and parental status, and ethnicity and race. The most notable finding in this model is that higher levels of education are negatively associated with

FIGURE 1
PERCENT OF EACH GROUP REPORTING ACTIVELY PRACTISING THEIR RELIGION, DESCRIPTIVE
(LEFT) AND CONTROLLED (RIGHT)

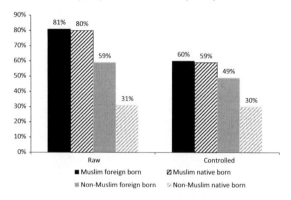

**Muslim foreign born   ☑ Muslim native born
Non-Muslim foreign born   Non-Muslim native born

**Note: control variables include household income, work status, education, race and ethnicity, gender, marital status, and parental status

actively practising one's religion among non-Muslims (both immigrants and native-born). In contrast, education is not significantly related to religiosity among Muslims. In addition, there are important race and ethnicity effects. Foreign-born ethnic minority groups (Muslim and non-Muslim) generally practise more frequently while few ethnic differences exist for native-born Muslims.

CONCLUSIONS

This work provides new evidence on how religiosity varies across Muslim and non-Muslim immigrants in Britain, and how each of these foreign-born groups compare with native-born individuals from both Muslim and non-Muslim backgrounds. Particularly in the British context, little work has examined variations in levels of religiosity across different immigrant groups, or examined predictors of religiosity across groups. Overall, we first demonstrate (as previous studies have) that the foreign-born are more religious than the native-born overall. However, both foreign-born and native-born Muslims report high levels of religiosity compared with both non-Muslim first-generation immigrants and non-Muslim native-born Britons; some of this difference can be attributed to ethnicity, although most of the difference is not explained by ethnicity or other socioeconomic and background characteristics.

Beyond simple comparisons in levels of religiosity, we also examined predictors of religiosity. The most important variation across Muslims and non-Muslims is the relationship of nativity and generation to religiosity. Among non-Muslims, first generation immigrants are more religious than native-born (second- and third-plus generation) Britons. In stark contrast, first-generation Muslim migrants are no more religious than second-generation Muslims; put another way, native-born Muslims are no less religious than those who were born outside Britain. While non-Muslim immigrant groups, in accord with assimilation theories (e.g. Gordon, 1964), appear to converge to native, secular norms as a result of being born and growing up in Britain, religious retention is much stronger among Muslims born in Britain. In addition, while education, long theorized as a secularizing force

TABLE 2

COEFFICIENTS FROM LOGISTIC REGRESSION MODELS PREDICTING ACTIVELY PRACTISING ONE'S RELIGION, STRATIFIED BY MUSLIM/NON-MUSLIM AND FOREIGN-BORN/NATIVE-BORN

	Muslim foreign-born Coef. (t-value)	Muslim Native-born Coef. (t-value)	Non-Muslim foreign-born Coef. (t-value)	Non-Muslim native-born Coef. (t-value)
Economic characteristics				
Household income	-0.01 (-1.85)	0.01 (1.92)	-0.00 (-0.20)	0.00 (0.10)
Working	-0.86*** (-3.54)	-1.27** (-2.94)	-0.39 (-1.81)	-0.28*** (-3.43)
Education				
No qualifications				
A level (High School)	-0.72 (-0.83)	2.55 (1.04)	-1.28*** (-3.57)	-0.70*** (-6.12)
O level (10th Grade)	-0.80 (-0.93)	2.33 (0.95)	-0.93* (-2.37)	-0.76*** (-6.73)
College	-0.80 (-0.95)	2.38 (0.96)	-0.68 (-1.85)	-0.21 (-1.76)
Unknown education	-0.70 (-0.87)	2.10 (0.84)	-0.40 (-1.11)	-0.88*** (-8.45)
Family background				
Female	-0.07 (-0.28)	-0.20 (-0.56)	0.45* (2.44)	0.67*** (10.16)
Married	0.48* (2.09)	0.45 (1.08)	0.11 (0.57)	0.30*** (4.20)
Children at home	-0.07 (-0.31)	0.54 (1.34)	0.10 (0.49)	-0.12 (-1.51)
Race and ethnicity				
White [reference]				
Bangladeshi	2.45*** (4.53)	0.34 (0.39)	1.50 (1.32)	3.80*** (3.37)
Pakistani	2.28*** (4.40)	0.88 (1.06)	0.98 (0.87)	1.34*** (7.63)
Indian	2.32*** (4.16)	0.66 (0.56)	1.49*** (8.29)	1.19* (2.24)
Other Asian	1.65* (2.41)	0.12 (0.10)	1.28*** (5.41)	1.35*** (10.16)
Black	2.70*** (4.91)	1.49 (1.32)	1.81*** (9.53)	0.43* (2.56)
Other race	1.16* (2.20)	-1.07 (-1.18)	1.38*** (6.49)	-0.74*** (-8.95)
Constant	0.56 (0.66)	-1.29 (-0.50)	0.37	
N	1388	467	2746	6716
Pseudo r-square	0.129	0.129	0.124	0.051

Note: *p < 0.05; **p < 0.01; ***p < 0.001.

for individuals in the sociology of religion (Weber, 1922/1964; Norris and Inglehart, 2004), predicts lower religiosity among non-Muslims, it has no statistically significant impact on religiosity among Muslims. Moreover, ethnic differences among native-born Muslims appear to be non-consequential to religious attendance, perhaps indicating a more unified Muslim rather than ethnic identity among second generation Muslims.

These findings suggest that pathways and processes of religious transmission are unique among Muslim migrants compared to other migrants. This is an important finding that echoes recent work that shows that intergenerational transmission of religion within families was strongest among Muslims compared with other faith groups in Britain (Scourfield et al., 2012). Our findings are consistent with this work, as well as other work that shows religion remains an important identity for second-generation Muslim youth (Kashyap and Lewis, 2012). Further research should examine what factors and processes are associated with higher levels of religiosity and generational religious transmission among Muslims in contrast with non-Muslims.

A moment's pause on limitations is necessary. Because we use a cross-sectional dataset, our results might not be a result of the intergenerational transmission process but rather be the result of cohort- or period-specific effects that result in the current second-generation of Muslims retaining high levels of religiosity. Despite this, data used in this study have allowed us to examine important differences between groups previously not illuminated in the literature. Another considerable limitation is that the measure of religion in the Citizenship Survey is a subjective measure not often used in other surveys, limiting the comparability of our study. Because it simply asks a respondent if he/or she is 'actively practising', it is left up to a respondent's own interpretation what 'actively practising' means. Thus, our findings may mask variation in forms of religiosity such as practice, belief, and religious salience.

Although our data do not let us empirically unpack why nativity has a differential impact on Muslims versus non-Muslims, our findings suggest that religious adherence among Muslims remains strong, despite wider secularization in the British mainstream. Previous work has argued that contexts – whether hostile immigrant receptivity contexts (Connor, 2010) or secular ones where minority religious identity is threatened (Bruce, 1996) – matter in determining immigrant religious outcomes. From a policy perspective, it is important not to view high levels of religiosity as an anomalous outcome, but as a potential indication of multiple pathways to immigrant adaptation within British society. Because the 'actively practising' Muslim community is diverse in both ethnic and socioeconomic backgrounds, institutional supports which afford equal religious opportunity (for example easing restrictions on setting up places of worship and community centres) may enable plural forms of religion catering to this diversity to take shape. In the long run, the development of local religious infrastructure, training in government settings that respect religious diversity, and legal changes that put Islam on more equal footing with the state-sanctioned Anglian Church, will nurture a British Islam in healthy public discourse and reduce public hostility against Muslims.

ACKNOWLEDGEMENTS

We thank Phillip Connor for his helpful comments on earlier drafts of this work.

NOTE

1. We created a dummy variable for missing income and tested it for significance in our models. It was not statistically significant in models including the entire sample. It was statistically significant in the separate model for foreign-born Muslims, positively predicting religious practice. However, inclusion of the missing income did not change other substantive results in our models.

REFERENCES

Alba, R.
2005 "Bright Vs. Blurred Boundaries: Second-generation Assimilation and Exclusion in France, Germany, and the United States", *Ethnic and Racial Studies* 28 (1): 20–49

Archer, L.
2009 "Race, "face", and masculinity: the identities and local geographies of Muslim boys", in P. Hopkins and R. Gale (ed.) *Muslims in Britain: Race, Place and Identities*, Edinburgh University Press, Edinburgh: 74–91

Bowen, J.R.
2007 *Why the French Don't Like Headscarves : Islam, the State, and Public Space*, Princeton University Press: Princeton, N.J.

Bruce, S.
1996 *Religion in the Modern World: From Cathedrals to Cults*, Oxford University Press, Oxford.

Cesari, J.
2004 *When Islam and Democracy Meet: Muslims in Europe and in the United States*, Palgrave Macmillan, New York.

Chambers, P.
2006 "Secularisation, Wales and Islam", *Journal of Contemporary Religion*, 21 (3): 567–584.

Connor, P.
2010 "Contexts of immigrant receptivity and immigrant religious outcomes: the case of Muslims in Western Europe", *Ethnic and Racial Studies*, 33:3: 376–403

Crockett, A. and D. Voas
2006 "Generations of decline: religious change in 20th century Britain", *Journal for the Scientific Study of Religion*, 45(4): 567–584

Davie, G.
2004 "New approaches in the sociology of religion: a western perspective", *Social Compass*, 51(1): 73–84

Diehl, C., and M. Koenig
2009 "Religiosität türkischer Migranten im Generationenverlauf: Ein Befund und einige Erklärungsversuche", *Zeitschrift für Soziologie* 38 (4): 300–319.

Dwyer, C., B. Shah, and G. Sanghera
2008 "From cricket lover to terror suspect' - challenging representations of young British Muslim men", *Gender, Place and Culture* 15(2): 117–136.

Fetzer, J. S., and J. C. Soper.
2003 "The Roots of Public Attitudes Toward State Accommodation of European Muslims' Religious Practices Before and After September 11", *Journal for the Scientific Study of Religion*, 42 (2): 247–258.

Fleischmann, F., and K. Phalet.
2012 "Integration and Religiosity Among the Turkish Second Generation in Europe: a Comparative Analysis Across Four Capital Cities", *Ethnic and Racial Studies* 35 (2): 320–341.

Foner, N., and R. Alba
2008 "Immigrant Religion in the U.S. and Western Europe: Bridge or Barrier to Inclusion?", *International Migration Review* 42 (2): 360–392.

Gordon, M.M.
1964 *Assimilation in American Life: The Role of Race, Religion, and National Origins*, Oxford University Press, New York.

Gorski, P.S. and Altinordu, A.
2008 "After secularisation?", *Annual Review of Sociology*, 34: 55–85

Glynn, S.
2002 "Bengali Muslims: the new East End radicals", *Ethnic and Racial Studies*, 25(6): 969–988.

Greeley, A.M.
1971 *Why Can't They Be Like Us? America's White Ethnic Groups*, E.P. Dutton, New York.

Heelas, P. and L. Woodhead
    2005   *The Spiritual Revolution: Why Religion Is Giving Way to Spirituality*, Blackwell Publishing,
            Oxford.
Hopkins, P.
    2006   "Youthful Muslim masculinities: gender and generational relations", *Transactions of the Institute of
            British Geographers*, 31 (3): 337–352
Hirschman, C.
    2004   "The role of religion in the origins and adaptation of immigrant groups in the United States", *International Migration Review*, 28 (3): 1206–1234
Hussain, S.
    2008   *Muslims on the Map: A National Survey of Social Trends in Britain*, Tauris Academic Studies,
            London.
Jacobson, J.
    1997   "Religion and ethnicity: dual and alternative sources of identity among young British Pakistanis",
            Ethnic and Racial Studies 20(2): 238–256
Kashyap, R. and V. A.Lewis.
    2012   "British Muslim youth and religious fundamentalism: a quantitative investigation", *Ethnic and
            Racial Studies*. DOI:10.1080/01419870.2012.672761
Kibria, N.
    2008   "The 'new Islam' and Bangladeshi Youth in Britain and the US", *Ethnic and Racial Studies* 31 (2):
            243–266.
King, G., M. Tomz, and J. Wittenberg
    2000   "Making the most of statistical analyses: improving interpretation and presentation", *American
            Journal of Political Science*, 44(2): 347–361.
Klausen, J.
    2005   *The Islamic Challenge : Politics and Religion in Western Europe*, Oxford University Press, Oxford.
Maliepaard, M., M. Lubbers, and M. Gijsbert
    2010   "Generational differences in ethnic and religious attachment and their interrelation. A study among
            Muslim minorities in the Netherlands", *Ethnic and Racial Studies*, 33:3, 451–472
Norris, P. and R. Inglehart
    2004   *Sacred and Secular. Religions and Politics Worldwide*, Cambridge University Press, Cambridge.
Peach, C.
    2006   "Muslims in the 2001 census of England and Wales: gender and economic disadvantage", *Ethnic
            and Racial Studies*, 29(4): 629–655.
Portes, A. and R.G. Rumbaut
    2001   *Legacies: The Story of the Immigrant Second Generation*, University of California Press, Berkeley.
Scourfield, J., C. Taylor, G. Moore, and S. Gilliat-Ray
    2012   "The Intergenerational Transmission of Islam in England and Wales: Evidence from the Citizenship
            Survey", *Sociology* 46 (1) (February 1): 91 –108.
Smits, F., S. Ruiter, and F. van Tubergen
    2010   "Religious practices among Islamic immigrants: Turkish and Moroccan men residing in Belgium",
            Journal of the Scientific Study of Religion, 49(2): 247–63.
Van Tubergen, F.
    2006   "Religious affiliation and attendance among immigrants in eight Western countries: individual and
            contextual effects", *Journal for the Scientific Study of Religion*, 45(1): 1–22.
Van Tubergen, F., and J. Sindrado'ttir
    2011   'The religiosity of immigrants in Europe: A cross-national study", *Journal for the Scientific Study
            of Religion*, 50(2): 272–288.
Voas, D. and A. Crockett
    2005   "Religion in Britain: Neither Believing nor Belonging.", *Sociology*, 39(1): 11–28.
Weber, Max
    1922/   *The sociology of religion*, Beacon Press, Boston, MA.
    1964

[23]

Journal of Ethnic and Migration Studies, 2013
Vol. 39, No. 3, 425–442, http://dx.doi.org/10.1080/1369183X.2013.733862

Parental Religious Transmission after Migration: The Case of Dutch Muslims

Mieke Maliepaard and Marcel Lubbers

In a secular host society where Islam is not reinforced outside the family or ethnic community, little is known of the extent to which Muslim immigrants succeed in transmitting their religion to their second-generation children. Parents are generally found to be important religious socialisation agents for children, but this has rarely been studied in a migration context. In this article we study parental religious transmission, taking into account the child's educational attainment and social contacts with Dutch friends as possible inhibitors. On the basis of data from 641 parent–child dyads, we find the expected positive relation between the parents' and the child's frequency of religious attendance and their respective attitudes toward religious homogamy and religious schools. Turkish-Dutch parents are more effective than Moroccan-Dutch in transmitting religious attendance, in line with higher levels of social cohesion in Turkish immigrant communities. Having Dutch friends and higher levels of education has little influence on the transmission of religious values from parents to children. The effective transmission of religion is a strong explanation for the continuously high religious involvement in the Turkish- and Moroccan-Dutch communities.

Keywords: Transmission; Religion; Second Generation; Muslims; Integration; The Netherlands

Introduction

In recent years, there has been a proliferation of studies on immigrant religiosity, especially among the second generation in Europe (e.g. Cesari 2003; Fleischmann and Phalet 2012; Roy 2004). In studies among majority populations, parents are found to be the main source of religious socialisation (Myers 1996). However, the role of the parents among migrant populations has rarely been studied. Since it is an exception to find children of non-religious parents turning religious, it seems that the

Mieke Maliepaard is Postdoctoral Researcher in the European Research Centre on Migration and Ethnic Relations at Utrecht University. Marcel Lubbers is Associate Professor in Sociology at Radboud University Nijmegen. Correspondence to: Dr M. Maliepaard, ERCOMER, Faculty of Social and Behavioural Sciences, Utrecht University, PO Box 80.140, 3508 TC Utrecht, The Netherlands. E-mail: m.i.maliepaard@uu.nl.

continuation of religiosity lies first and foremost in the hands of religious parents. But are religious parents also successful in transmitting their religion when they migrate to a society where their religion is not supported outside of the immediate family or community? In this study we investigate the success of the religious transmission of self-identified Muslim parents to their second-generation children who are being raised in the Netherlands, a relatively secular country. Studying this particular context is all the more interesting because of the conflicting norms regarding the role of religion in the home environment and the wider society with which migrant children are confronted, in a period—adolescence—in which they are highly susceptible to outside influences. The native-Dutch population can be characterised by low levels of religious self-identification and practice, compared to first-generation migrants from Turkey and Morocco (Gijsberts and Dagevos 2010; van Tubergen 2007). Our main research questions are:

- To what extent are first-generation migrants who identify as Muslim able to transmit their religion to their children who are being raised in the Netherlands?
- Does the social and structural integration of the children into Dutch society hamper parental religious transmission?

Although there is an extensive literature on the transmission of religion (most often church attendance), this was mostly developed on the basis of research among majority religions (Acock and Bengtson 1978; Hoge *et al.* 1982; Myers 1996). Studies of parental transmission among immigrants (e.g. de Valk and Liefbroer 2007; Nauck 2001; Phalet and Schönpflug 2001; Phinney and Vedder 1996) have rarely focused on religion. This is surprising given the fact that migrant religiosity is a salient issue in many Western European nations. Previous work on migrant religiosity has looked mostly at aggregate levels of change between generations in religious practice and attitudes (Maliepaard *et al.* 2010; Phalet *et al.* 2008). Güngör *et al.* (2011) do look at parent–child transmission, but only take into account perceived religious upbringing on religious outcomes (identification, beliefs and practices) as reported by children themselves. We use a large-scale dataset in which both parents and their adolescent children provide information on their religion, expressed as mosque attendance and attitudes towards religious intermarriage and religious schools. We know of no previous study which uses such a rich dataset to study intergenerational religious transmission among migrants. Using these data, we are able to assess the parental transmission of religion among a growing religious minority population, while taking into account the (secular) context in which the children are raised and in which this transmission takes place.

Theory and Hypotheses

International migration often entails a discontinuity in intergenerational transmission, especially from first-generation parents to their second-generation children

(Berry *et al.* 1992). The second generation is often regarded as being 'in-between' the culture and expectations of their parents and of the wider society: on the one hand, migrant parents imbue their children with cultural practices and values taken from the motherland and, on the other, children are confronted with the values of the host society through their native peers and friends as well as in school. This paper will deal with the interplay of different sources of influence. We distinguish *vertical transmission* by parents, *horizontal transmission* or the influence of friends, and *oblique transmission*—which refers to influences from authority figures other than the parents, such as schools (Berry *et al.* 1992; Cavalli-Sforza *et al.* 1982). For migrants these different forms of transmission juxtapose strong forces of culture maintenance (by transmission from parents) with forces of cultural adaptation (by transmission from Dutch friends and in educational institutions). This juxtaposition is especially relevant when the country of origin and the receiving country differ more strongly in terms of culture. Currently one of the most salient 'differences' between migrants and the native population in Western Europe seems to be religion. Islam forms a clear boundary in interethnic relations and Muslims have become the quintessential 'Other' (Alba 2005; Jensen 2008). This is also the case in the Netherlands, where Islam is truly an immigrant religion: over 90 per cent of the two largest non-Western immigrant groups (from Turkey and Morocco) are Muslim and attach much importance to their religion (Maliepaard *et al.* 2010). On the other hand, there are very few native-Dutch Muslims—less than 1 per cent of the total population (Statistics Netherlands 2007). In addition, the Netherlands (like other North-Western European countries) is a quite secular environment, with relatively low levels of religious membership and attendance—for example, only 11 per cent attend religious events weekly (Becker and de Hart 2006: 13). Migrant parental religion is thus not reinforced in the public domain, but quite the opposite; being Muslim in the Netherlands can be regarded as a stigmatised identity (Gijsberts and Dagevos 2010; Sniderman and Hagendoorn 2007). We discuss the influence of parents, friends and school in turn, taking into account the way these forms of influence may interact.

Vertical Transmission

Parents are the main agents in the socialisation of their children, transmitting attitudes and setting behavioural examples (Glass *et al.* 1986). Parents socialise their children by explicitly teaching them about culture, norms and values but, at the same time, children also internalise values and learn behaviour through observation and the imitation of parents' actions (Bandura 1986). Not all attitudes are transmitted equally strongly from parents to children; transmission can be selective and depends on the type of attitude transmitted (Pinquart and Silbereisen 2004; Rohan and Zanna 1996). According to Kohn (1983), religious beliefs—along with political orientations and lifestyles—are the most strongly transmitted by parents. This is supported by a vast body of research among majority populations which has shown that the single most important predictor of individual religiosity, especially among adolescents, is the religiosity of the parents. Reported correlations between parental and children's religion are moderately strong, most studies finding correlations between .4 and .5. This holds for religious self-identification, public religious practice such as attendance at religious ceremonies and, to a lesser extent, strength of religious commitment (Erickson 1992; Hoge and Petrillo 1978; Myers 1996; Ozorak 1989; Regnerus *et al.* 2004).

One reason why transmission is more successful in some domains than in others is salience. Issues which are more frequently discussed and thus more salient are more actively transmitted within families (Pinquart and Silbereisen 2004). For the majority of Muslims in the Netherlands, religion is a very important part of life (Verkuyten and Yildiz 2007) and Muslim minorities see transmitting religious attitudes and practices to their children as an important goal (Doomernik 1995). Among minority populations, socialisation practices serve the function of maintaining strong ethnic- or religious-group ties in the face of external pressures (Bankston and Zhou 1995; Portes and Rumbaut 2006). Religious transmission helps the ethnic community to maintain a firmer grip on later generations by setting clear rules concerning appropriate behaviour and by increasing social cohesion. We therefore expect that *parental religiosity positively affects children's religiosity (H1).*

Previous studies indicate that the success of transmission of parents to children is dependent both on the (national) context (Kelley and de Graaf 1997) and on the characteristics of the (ethno-religious) group (Phalet and Schönpflug 2001). Although in this study we focus on a single receiving context, we include two Islamic groups—the Turkish- and the Moroccan-Dutch. These groups share a migration history characterised by economic (guestworker) migration in the 1960s and 1970s, followed by family reunification. The groups also share a relatively low socio-economic status. However, the Turkish- and Moroccan-Dutch also differ in important respects. The most important difference for our study is the fact that the Turkish-Dutch community is characterised by high levels of in-group cohesion, with a strong focus on interdependence and conformity to norms, whereas the Moroccan-Dutch are much more loosely connected (Nauck *et al.* 2001; Phalet and Schönpflug 2001; Vermeulen and Penninx 2000). This is the case both at the level of the family and at that of the community. These group variations affect the way in which the community is able to influence its members, due to differences in example-setting by in-group members and the reinforcement of parental example-setting by the community. Although religion is important to both groups, we expect religious attitudes and, especially, practices to be enforced more strongly among the Turkish-Dutch. We therefore expect that *Turkish-Dutch parents will be more successful at transmitting their religion to their children than Moroccan-Dutch parents (H2).*

Horizontal Transmission

Particularly during adolescence, friends are important sources of influence in many domains. In this period, adolescents develop a tendency to re-evaluate their

Journal of Ethnic and Migration Studies 429

knowledge, ideas and beliefs in many domains (Ozorak 1989). Parents are usually the first to socialise children into a certain religion and, in later life, like-minded friends may reinforce religious commitment, whereas non-religious friends expose young people to different lifestyles, norms and values, allowing them to look more critically at their upbringing. A number of studies which have taken into account the influence of both friends and parents in studying religious expression show that friends have an effect on religious beliefs and practices independent of the parental influence (Gunnoe and Moore 2002; Hoge and Petrillo 1978; Ozorak 1989). This influence may partly be selective: it is likely that individuals choose to befriend people who reinforce their worldview and who are more similar. However, there is also evidence longitudinally of the influence of friends (Regnerus *et al.* 2004).

For adolescents from a strongly religious minority group in a secular environment, there is an especially large discrepancy between the ethno-religious group and the host population in the religious domain. Since native Dutch are hardly ever Muslim, Dutch friends are not likely to reinforce Islamic beliefs or practices, whereas this is much more likely to happen among Turkish- and Moroccan-Dutch friends. Previous studies indeed confirm that, in the Netherlands, having many native (Dutch) friends is related to lower levels of religious practice (Phalet *et al.* 2008). We expect our study to replicate this, and thus we hypothesise that *the more young Muslims engage in friendships with native Dutch, the less religious they will be (H3a).* In addition, we expect that the influence of friends will affect the success of religious transmission from parents to children. Co-ethnic friends, as members of the ethno-religious community, are likely to reinforce parental values, whereas Dutch friends are more likely to question them, hampering the parental transmission of religion. We thus expect that *the religious transmission from Muslim parents to their children will be less*

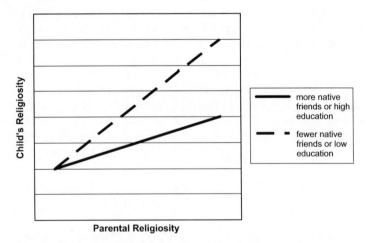

Figure 1. Graphic representation of expected interaction effects (Hypotheses 3b and 4b)

430   *M. Maliepaard & M. Lubbers*

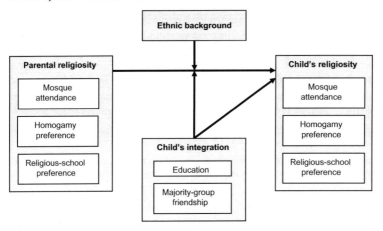

Figure 2. Hypothesised model

successful when children engage more in friendships with native Dutch (H3b)—see Figure 1 for a graphic representation of the expected interaction effect.

Oblique Transmission

Socialisation does not only occur at home; individuals are also influenced by the (institutional) social context in which they grow up. One important place in which values are transmitted, practiced and learned is the school. Schools offer formal education and also imbue children with the (dominant) culture. Although there are Islamic elementary schools (age 5–12) in many of the larger Dutch cities, they still make up only a small percentage of all schools (there are currently 44 Islamic elementary schools and one high school in the Netherlands. Most Dutch schools are either Christian or non-denominational. Since all children in the Netherlands receive compulsory education up to the age of 16, a large majority of second-generation children spend a fair amount of time in the Dutch educational system. This is even more the case for those in higher educational tracks. Education is split into lower, intermediate and higher tracks from approximately the age of 12. The higher track (six years) prepares for a longer educational route, leading to university, whereas the lower track (four years) is a vocational training, preparing for early entry into the job market.

Being in the educational system for a longer time, and attaining higher levels of education, is expected to coincide with stronger exposure to the relatively secular Dutch culture. Higher-educated people not only spend more time in the school system, but also have more native-Dutch peers in the classroom because minority students are under-represented (and over-represented at the lower educational levels; Herweijer 2008). In addition, higher education in general has been linked to a process of 'cultural broadening' (Hoge *et al.* 1994). It is argued that, going through higher education, individuals develop a more liberal and a more culturally open worldview, which is hard to equate with strict forms of religiosity (Jackman and Muha 1984; Vogt 1997). This may partly be explicit in the teaching at institutes of higher education, but may also be implicitly learned in the process of studying other matters. According to classic modernisation theory, too, higher education is related to a decrease in the importance of religion in the lives of individuals who, as they progress through the educational system, are thought to develop a more critical worldview which is not easily combined with a strongly religious one (Bruce 1999). Although this is a debated theory (see, for instance, Stark *et al.* 1996), and evidence is mixed depending on the country under study, it has found empirical support especially in Western Europe (e.g. Need and de Graaf 1996; Ruiter and van Tubergen 2009), even if effect sizes were sometimes small. In the Dutch context, higher education has repeatedly been associated with lower levels of church membership and religious participation, both among the majority population (e.g. Need and de Graaf 1996), and among religious minority populations (Phalet *et al.* 2008; van Tubergen 2007). We therefore expect that *lower-educated Muslims will be more religious than higher-educated Muslims (H4a)*. In addition, we expect that *religious transmission from Muslim parents to their children will be less successful when children are more-highly educated (H4b)*, because a Dutch education makes children more critical not only towards a general religious worldview, but also towards their parents' religious socialisation (Hoge and Petrillo 1978).

Methods

Data

We combine two waves (1998 and 2002) of the Social Positions and Use of Welfare Facilities by Ethnic Minorities surveys (SPVA). These data were gathered among the four largest minority groups in the Netherlands—those of Turkish, Moroccan, Antillean and Surinamese descent. Larger cities were over-represented in the data, since this is where most migrants live. Migrants were from 13 cities,[1] in which around 50 per cent of migrants live (SCP 2005). We selected Turkish and Moroccan respondents. In the Dutch statistics, people are considered to be Turkish or Moroccan when at least one of their parents was born in Turkey or Morocco. The Turkish- and Moroccan-Dutch groups consist of 670,000 individuals in total, or 4 per cent of the Dutch population. The second generation makes up about half of this group (Statistics Netherlands 2010). The vast majority of our respondents have parents who are both from either Turkey or Morocco, since mixed marriages are very rare among these groups (Gijsberts and Dagevos 2010). Participants were interviewed face-to-face (computer-assisted personal interviewing). Only those participants who were foreign-born and not fluent in Dutch were interviewed in their native language by bilingual interviewers. The response rate was around 50 per cent for both groups—comparable to other research among ethnic minority groups in the Netherlands.

In the SPVA study, a number of questionnaires on different topics were used, not all of which were given to all family members. In each household one of the parents (all first-generation migrants) was selected at random to fill out the questionnaire which included the religion items. The oldest child over the age of 15 (no maximum specified), still living at home and present during the interview also received this questionnaire (N = 1000 dyads). We selected those children who answered the religion questions (n = 944). After doing so, we made a further selection on a number of characteristics. Firstly, we selected only self-identified Muslim parents (thereby excluding 3 per cent of the sample) in order to assess the success of religious transmission. Secondly, we chose to exclude children who migrated to the Netherlands after the age of six (21 per cent of the sample), so that all respondents received their education in the Netherlands, and spent most of their formative period there. We think that the processes we theorised refer specifically to the experiences of the second generation being raised in the Netherlands. Finally, we excluded the 5 per cent of respondents over the age of 25. Our reason for doing so was that all respondents were living at home with their parents, and that those still living with their parents after the age of 25 were expected to be a rather specific subgroup of the population. This is supported by the fact that they make up only 5 per cent of the total. After the selection, we were left with 641 parent–child dyads.[2] The number of missing values was generally low, except on education and social contacts; the missing values were imputed by means of ICE in Stata.[3]

Measures

All respondents and their parents were asked whether they consider themselves to be religious, and if so, what religion. Only those individuals who regarded themselves as Muslim answered the following three questions on religion. The first pertains to religious practice, and asks how often the respondent attends the mosque, ranging from (1) never, to (4) weekly or more. This item is a more valid measure of religiosity for men than for women since, for women, visiting the mosque is not a prerequisite. Women thus usually report fewer visits there, while, for example, engaging more often in prayers than do men (Phalet and ter Wal 2004). Respondents and their parents were also asked for their attitude towards the preferred partner for their (hypothetical) daughter ('It is problematic when your daughter marries someone from another religion') and the preferred school for their children ('Children should attend schools that match the religion of the parents'). Both items were measured on a five-point scale ranging from 'completely agree' to 'completely disagree'. Since the three items refer to different life domains, they are analysed separately.

For respondents' education, we use an eight-point scale, ranging from no education (0), to tertiary education (7). Since many respondents are still enrolled in school, they receive the score of the level they are currently enrolled in. Some will

Journal of Ethnic and Migration Studies   433

drop out, whereas others will go on to even higher levels of education, so we might under- or over-estimate educational attainment for part of our sample. A dummy for enrolment will be included in the analyses.

Respondents' majority-group friendships are measured by combining two items. Firstly, 'Do you ever have contact with native-Dutch people in your free time?' (Yes/No), and secondly, 'In your free time, do you have more contact with native-Dutch people than with Turks/Moroccans, or more contact with Turks/Moroccans?', measured on a three-point scale. These two items were recoded into a single item with four categories: 0 = 'No social contact with native-Dutch people'; 1 = 'More contact with my own ethnic group than with Dutch people'; 2 = 'Contact with Dutch and my own ethnic group equally'; and 3 = 'More social contact with native-Dutch people than with people of my own ethnic group'. The item refers to voluntary social contact, which we understand as interactions with friends and acquaintances. We include this as a continuous variable in the model, but perform additional tests using the categorical measurement (more contact with Dutch, both equally and more/only contact with co-ethnics), in order to take into account possible non-linearity.

In addition, we include the gender, age and ethnic background of the respondents, as well as the categorical variable 'being born in the Netherlands' (vs 'having moved there before the age of six'). We also take into account whether it was the father or the mother who answered the religion questions. Descriptive statistics are shown in Table 1.

Results

The Muslim parents in our sample not only self-identify as Muslim, but are also relatively strongly religious, in line with other studies among the first generation (Phalet *et al.* 2008). They attend the mosque several times a month on average, and agree that religious homogamy is important. The scores on religious-school

Table 1. Descriptive statistics (N = 641)

	Scale	Mean (SD)
Respondent's mosque attendance	1–4	2.19 (.99)
Respondent's homogamy preference	1–5	3.46 (1.10)
Respondent's religious-school preference	1–5	2.16 (1.02)
Respondent's education	0–7	3.65 (1.37)
Respondent is enrolled in school	0/1	.67 (.47)
Respondent's majority-group friendship	0–3	1.59 (.83)
Respondent's age	15–25	17.74 (2.58)
Respondent is female	0/1	.50 (.50)
Respondent is Turkish-Dutch	0/1	.58 (.49)
Child was born in the Netherlands	0/1	.84 (.36)
Parental mosque attendance	1–4	3.22 (1.04)
Parental homogamy preference	1–5	3.86 (1.15)
Parental religious-school preference	1–5	2.71 (1.19)
Father completed questionnaire	0/1	.53 (.50)

preference are slightly lower, around the midpoint of the scale (see Table 1). In a first step, we look at the religiosity of the children on the basis of self-ascription ('I am Muslim'). Transmission of religion has failed when children of Muslim parents do not call themselves Muslim. This is the case for eight children in our data, a little over 1 per cent of the total sample. Almost 99 per cent of parents were thus successful in transmitting their religion, and apostasy is clearly an exception. The non-religious respondents are not taken into account in our further analyses, since they did not answer the questions on mosque attendance and religious attitudes. We therefore test to what extent Muslim parents are effectively transmitting their religious attitudes and practices to their Muslim children.

Comparing generations as a whole reveals that the second generation is significantly less religious than the parental generation on all three items. Also when studying individual parent–child dyads, children are a little less religious than their parents: 15 per cent of Muslim children score lower than their parents on all three measures of religiosity; only 0.5 per cent scores higher. These findings indicate a decline in religiosity over generations. Looking at parent–child dyads (Table 2), we find a moderately strong positive correlation between parents and children on all religious items. The correlation is strongest for religious-school preference ($r = .41$) and weakest for mosque attendance ($r = .27$). As one would expect, the correlation is especially high on the diagonal (same religion item asked to parents/children) and much lower ($r = .09–.18$) off the diagonal. It thus seems that parental attendance influences particularly the attendance of their children but influences to a far lesser extent their attitudes (and this also holds for the effect of parental attitudes on a child's attendance).

In multivariate models A (of Tables 3, 4 and 5), we take into account the effects of parental religiosity while also including controls. In line with the bivariate correlations, we see a strong effect of parental religiosity on all dependent variables, supporting our first hypothesis. Whether the father or the mother completed the parent questionnaire does not affect any of the dependent variables. We also do not find significant interactions of the gender of the parent who completed the questionnaire with parental religiosity (not shown). There is a small age effect on mosque attendance, indicating that the older respondents attend the mosque a little less frequently than the younger ones (the difference between the youngest and the

Table 2. Correlations (N = 641)

	Mosque attendance respondent	Homogamy preference respondent	School preference respondent
Parental mosque attendance	**.27**	.14	.18
Parental homogamy preference	.10	**.35**	.11
Parental religious-school preference	.09	.14	**.41**

Journal of Ethnic and Migration Studies 435

Table 3. Models predicting mosque attendance (N = 641)

	Model A	Model B	Model C
Constant	1.507(.174)***	2.146(.214)***	2.342(.438)***
Parental mosque attendance	.256(.036)***	.059(.053)	.052(.054)
Father completed parental questionnaire (0/1)	.015(.075)	.059(.074)	.077(.075)
Year of survey 2002 (1998 = ref)	−.009(.073)	−.011(.071)	−.008(.072)
Age (centred)	−.032(.015)*	−.038(.015)*	−.034(.015)*
Turkish-Dutch	.565(.073)***	−.508(.230)*	−.479(.230)*
Female	−.412(.071)***	−.392(.070)***	−.410(.071)***
Enrolled in school	−.160(.082)	−.160(.080)*	−.141(.086)
Born in the Netherlands	−.162(.100)	−.196(.099)*	−.200(.099)*
Parental mosque attendance * Turkish		.335(.068)***	.322(.068)***
Educational attainment			−.007(.030)
Majority-group friendship			−.097(.045)*
R²	**.202**	**.231**	**.238**

Note: *** = p <.001; ** = p <.01; * = p <.05 (2-sided tests).

oldest respondents is .3). Possibly, the younger ones join their parents when they visit the mosque, whereas the older ones are more independent in this respect. There are no (linear or quadratic) effects of the age of the children on religious attitudes. The absence of an interaction between the age of the child and the religiosity of the parents (not shown) indicates that the influence of parents does not diminish with age. Gender differences, as expected, are only found for religious attendance. In addition to gender differences in the level of religious practice and attitudes, we investigated whether the transmission of religion is gender-specific by taking into account whether the transmission from father to daughter is different from the transmission from father to son, mother to daughter and mother to son. Three-way

Table 4. Models predicting religious homogamy preference (N = 641)

	Model A	Model B	Model C
Constant	1.965(.232)***	1.873(.287)***	2.210(.315)***
Parental mosque attendance	.119(.042)**	.123(.043)**	.104(.043)*
Parental homogamy preference	.317(.036)***	.338(.053)***	.341(.053)***
Father completed parental questionnaire (0/1)	−.157(.087)	−.158(.087)	−.132(.087)
Year of survey 2002 (1998 = ref)	.095(.083)	.091(.084)	.100(.084)
Age (centred)	.002(.017)	.002(.017)	.011(.018)
Turkish-Dutch	.052(.084)	.203(.291)	.233(.291)
Female	−.154(.082)	−.155(.082)	−.174(.084)*
Enrolled in school	−.136(.094)	−.134(.094)	−.090(.102)
Born in the Netherlands	.078(.115)	.079(.115)	.070(.114)
Parental homogamy preference * Turkish		−.039(.072)	−.051(.072)
Educational attainment			−.026(.039)
Majority-group friendship			−.140(.060)*
R²	**.148**	**.148**	**.161**

Note: *** = p <.001; ** = p <.01; * = p <.05 (2-sided tests).

Table 5. Models predicting religious-school preference (N = 641)

	Model A	Model B	Model C
Constant	1.383(.191)***	1.488(.223)***	1.669(.258)***
Parental mosque attendance	.056(.038)	.056(.038)	.049(.039)
Parental religious-school preference	.325(.057)***	.290(.050)***	.291(.050)***
Father completed parental questionnaire (0/1)	.057(.077)	.063(.077)	.072(.078)
Year of survey 2002 (1998 = ref)	−.165(.075)	−.172(.075)*	−.161(.076)
Age (centred)	−.018(.015)	−.018(.015)	−.011(.016)
Turkish-Dutch	−.245(.075)**	−.401(.188)*	−.391(.187)
Female	−.094(.073)	−.091(.073)	−.091(.075)
Enrolled in school	−.160(.084)	−.166(.084)*	−.124(.091)
Born in the Netherlands	.090(.103)	.088(.103)	.082(.103)
Parental religious-school preference * Turkish		.057(.063)	.052(.063)
Educational attainment			−.033(.035)
Majority-group friendship			−.048(.054)
R^2	**.204**	**.205**	**.209**

Note: *** = p <.001; ** = p <.01; * = p <.05 (2-sided tests).

interaction results (*gender child* x *gender parent* x *religiosity parent*) indicate that this is not the case.

In multivariate models B, we test our second hypothesis regarding the ethnic differences in transmission. Results indicate that our hypothesis only holds for religious attendance: parental mosque attendance has a much stronger impact on respondent's mosque attendance for Turkish- than for Moroccan-Dutch respondents. Surprisingly, for Moroccan-Dutch respondents the main effect is no longer significant after taking up the interaction term, indicating that the transmission is very weak. Children of parents who visit the mosque more than once a week score only .24 higher (on a four-point scale) than children of parents who never visit the mosque. For Turkish-Dutch respondents the effect is about five times as strong: the difference in scores between those whose parents never attend and those who attend weekly is 1.5 on a four-point scale. Transmission of mosque attendance is thus much stronger among the Turkish-Dutch than among the Moroccan-Dutch. We do not find this ethnic differentiation for religious attitudes.

In a third step, we added majority group friendships and education (*H3a* and *H4a*). The results, presented in models C, firstly show that these indicators are not central to predicting individual religiosity: the increase in explained variance after taking up these variables is relatively small. Results indicate that respondents with more majority-group friends attend the mosque less frequently and are less positive about religious homogamy.[4] Using the categorical instead of the continuous variable does not influence the results. It does show that the significant effects are driven mainly by the group which has more Dutch than co-ethnic friends (they differ significantly from the other groups). Majority-group friendships are not related to religious-school preference. Hypothesis 3a is thus partly supported. We find no effects of education on any of the dependent variables. There is thus no support for Hypothesis 4a. Finally, we tested Hypotheses 3b and 4b, by taking up interactions of contact and education with parental religiosity (not shown). We find no significant interaction effects, with the exception of one. Higher-educated children are influenced less strongly by their parents than lower-educated children in their attitudes towards the importance of religious schools.[5] This indicates that the transmission of parental religion is generally not conditional on the child's interethnic social contacts or education.

Discussion and Conclusion

We investigated parental religious transmission from Muslim immigrants to their children who are raised in a quite secular country, the Netherlands. We find that apostasy is a very rare phenomenon among the children of Muslim parents—in our sample it was 1 per cent, which explains the high percentage (over 90 per cent) of second-generation Turkish- and Moroccan-Dutch in the population who call themselves Muslim. We have to take into account that, in the Muslim world, it is considered a big step to stop referring to oneself as Muslim. Many of the children may be only nominally Muslim, which would constitute a *de facto* failure of transmission if the parents are practising Muslims. However, we find that, in addition to their self-ascription, parents also influence the degree to which their children hold certain attitudes and the frequency with which they attend the mosque. The explained variance in our models can be attributed to a large extent to parental religiosity, indicating that this is a relevant factor for young Muslims.

We found that the attendance patterns of the Turkish-Dutch are characterised by strong intergenerational continuity, in line with research showing stronger cultural maintenance among the Turkish than among the Moroccan migrant population (Phalet and Schönpflug 2001). The transmission of religious attendance in Moroccan-Dutch families is surprisingly weak, compared to both the Turkish-Dutch and other studies of the transmission of attendance (Hoge and Petrillo 1978; Myers 1996; Ozorak 1989; Regnerus *et al.* 2004). These findings may partly have to do with the fact that the Moroccan-Dutch second generation, more so than the Turkish-Dutch, struggles with the language spoken at the mosque (Korf *et al.* 2007). The findings also point towards the importance of local-community characteristics in facilitating transmission from parents to children, especially in the transmission of practices. Whether it is the cohesion within the family or in the wider community in which the family is embedded which facilitates transmission requires a fine-grained analysis of social networks and communities. Portes and Rumbaut (2006) have shown that active religious involvement can protect young people who are at risk of downward assimilation. Young Moroccans are over-represented in Dutch crime statistics (Gijsberts and Dagevos 2010), and it is striking that it is especially this group for which the transmission of religious practice seems to have failed. At the same time, we have to be careful about applying these American findings straight to the Dutch context, and more research is necessary to substantiate this function of religion for Muslims in the Western European context.

We had expected to find a stronger 'migration component' to religious transmission among Muslim migrants, because immigrants, more than members of majority religious groups, are confronted on a daily basis with people from very different religious backgrounds, and lack the social support of their religion outside the religious group. However, on the basis of our findings we conclude that this does not hamper the degree to which parents transmit religion to their children: transmission is relatively effective, and not conditional on the children's degree of socio-structural integration. Our findings are in line with those of Myers' longitudinal study in the United States (1996), which showed that parents have a strong influence on their children's religiosity and that this influence is not hampered by developments in later life. Our findings do indicate that having Dutch friends has a modest influence on religious intermarriage attitudes and mosque attendance, in addition to parental influence. In order to rule out selection effects, we would ideally use a multi-actor design in which the religiosity of friends and of other peers is included, since peers are less likely than friends to be selected on the dependent variable. We are, however, unaware of the existence of such data among minorities. Education did not have the effect we had expected. Unlike studies among first-generation immigrants in the Netherlands (e.g. van Tubergen 2007), we found that higher-educated young Muslims are not less religious. Our finding is in line with a recent study by Fleischmann and Phalet (2012), who found no relation between education and religion for second-generation Muslims in Sweden, Belgium and the Netherlands. Taken together, these findings suggest that the cultural broadening and modernisation hypotheses do not apply to minority and majority populations in the same way, at least in the Western European context.

In this study we were able to use unique parent–child dyads among Muslim migrants. However, this brought a number of limitations. The data were gathered around ten years ago and, since then, Islam has become even more suspect and Muslims more salient as the 'other' in intergroup relations. We think that the outcomes are still valid, as they describe a process of transmission from strongly religious first-generation parents to second-generation children in a secular environment, which continues today. Possibly, with the development of more antagonistic group relations, parents have become even more conscious of their religion and their role in keeping it alive. If anything, we think that newer data would indicate stronger transmission from parents. A second shortcoming of the data is that all respondents are still living with their parents. The religiosity of the young respondents is likely to undergo some change after they leave the parental home, marry and have children (Phalet *et al.* 2008). As children become more independent, the influence of the parents may diminish. On the other hand, research among majority populations has shown that parental influence lasts well beyond adolescence (Myers 1996). The question of whether this also applies to (minority religion) immigrants necessitates further research. One might argue that we oversampled more religious children, if fewer religious children are more likely to move away at an earlier age. However, this would only hold for older respondents, since the younger ones are unlikely to leave the parental home. If the relation between parental and child's religiosity was influenced by the selectivity of the older respondents, one would have expected interaction effects of age with parental religiosity. The fact that the degree of transmission we found is highly comparable with a recent study by Güngör *et al.* (2011) among somewhat older second-generation Muslims (mean age 25) in Belgium, where retrospective data on parental mosque attendance were used, reinforces our belief that our findings are not strongly influenced by the selectivity of our respondents. Finally, we believe that, although our data are limited to the Netherlands, our findings can be generalised to other Western European countries. Although there are, of course, many differences between countries, Muslims in most of these countries have similar migration histories and social and structural positions as a disadvantaged minority religious group (Alba 2005).

This research has shown that an important cause of the strength and the stability of religious beliefs and practices among the Muslim second generation, which is well-documented, is the fact that they are raised by strongly religious parents. These parents are able to instil religious attitudes and practices in their children, despite the limited institutional support and lack of social reinforcement of this religion in their children's daily lives.

Notes

[1]   Amsterdam, Rotterdam, The Hague, Utrecht, Eindhoven, Enschede, Almere, Alphen aan den Rijn, Bergen op Zoom, Hoogezand-Sappemeer, Delft, Dordrecht and Tiel.

[2]   A small number of respondents (23 children, 11 parents) were interviewed in both 1998 and 2002. These respondents were only included once (so were removed from the 2002 data).

[3]   The higher percentage of missing data on these items (around 20 per cent) is because these questions were asked in a part of a separate questionnaire which, accidentally, not all the respondents received. This happened about equally in both 1998 and 2002 among Turkish and Moroccan respondents. We therefore assume these values are missing at random. Analyses were run on both the imputed and the non-imputed data and the outcomes are very similar. Therefore, the imputed data will be used.

[4]   In order to control for the opportunity of having majority-group friends, we included the percentage of native Dutch in the neighbourhood. However, (a) there was hardly any variance to be explained at the neighbourhood level (3 per cent), (b) the effects were non-significant and (c) they did not influence the results. We therefore left this out of the final analysis.

[5]   We also ran a test on the influence of parental education, but there are no significant direct effects on the dependent variables, nor is there mediation through child's education. Therefore the variable is not taken up in the final analyses. We also tested the models using dichotomous dependent variables ('agree' vs 'neutral/disagree' on the homogamy and religious-school preference; 'never attends the mosque' vs 'sometimes/frequently') and outcomes are highly comparable in direction and significance, indicating that our findings are robust.

References

Acock, A.C. and Bengtson, V.L. (1978) 'On the relative influence of mothers and fathers: a covariance analysis of political and religious socialization', *Journal of Marriage and the Family*, *40*(3): 519–30.

Alba, R. (2005) 'Bright vs blurred boundaries: second-generation assimilation and exclusion in France, Germany, and the United States', *Ethnic and Racial Studies*, *28*(1): 20–49.

Bandura, A. (1986) *Social Foundations of Thought and Action: A Social Cognitive Theory*. Englewood Cliffs, NJ: Prentice-Hall.

Bankston, C.L. and Zhou, M. (1995) 'Religious participation, ethnic identification, and adaptation of Vietnamese adolescents in an immigrant community', *Sociological Quarterly*, *36*(3): 523–34.

Becker, J.W. and de Hart, J. (2006) *Godsdienstige Veranderingen in Nederland: Verschuivingen in de Binding met de Kerken en de Christelijke Traditie*. The Hague: Netherlands Institute for Social Research.

Berry, J.W., Poortinga, Y.H., Segall, M.H. and Dasen, P.R. (1992) *Cross-Cultural Psychology: Research and Applications*. Cambridge: Cambridge University Press.

Bruce, S. (1999) 'Modernization, religious diversity and rational choice in Eastern Europe', *Religion, State and Society*, *27*(4): 265–75.

Cavalli-Sforza, L.L., Felman, M.W., Chen, K.H. and Dornbusch, S.M. (1982) 'Theory and observation in cultural transmission', *Science*, *218*(4567): 19–27.

Cesari, J. (2003) 'Muslim minorities in Europe: the silent revolution', in Esposito, J. and Burgat, F. (eds) *Modernizing Islam: Religion in the Public Sphere in the Middle East and in Europe*. New Brunswick: Rutgers University Press, 251–69.

de Valk, H.A.G. and Liefbroer, A.C. (2007) 'Timing preferences for women's family-life transitions: intergenerational transmission among migrants and Dutch', *Journal of Marriage and the Family*, *69*(1): 190–206.

Doomernik, J. (1995) 'The institutionalization of Turkish Islam in Germany and the Netherlands: a comparison', *Ethnic and Racial Studies*, *18*(1): 46–61.

Erickson, J.A. (1992) 'Adolescent religious development and commitment: a structural equation model of the role of family, peer group, and educational influences', *Journal for the Scientific Study of Religion*, *31*(2): 131–52.

Fleischmann, F. and Phalet, K. (2012) 'Integration and religiosity among the Turkish second generation in Europe: a comparative analysis across four capital cities', *Ethnic and Racial Studies*, *35*(2): 320–41.

Gijsberts, M. and Dagevos, J. (2010) *At Home in the Netherlands*. The Hague: Netherlands Institute for Social Research.

Glass, J., Bengtson, V.L. and Dunham, C. (1986) 'Attitude similarity in three-generation families: socialization, status inheritance, or reciprocal influence?', *American Sociological Review*, *51*(5): 685–98.

Güngör, D., Fleischmann, F. and Phalet, K. (2011) 'Religious identification, beliefs and practices among Turkish- and Moroccan-Belgian Muslims: intergenerational continuity and acculturative change', *Journal of Cross-Cultural Psychology*, *42*(8): 1356–74.

Gunnoe, M.L. and Moore, K.A. (2002) 'Predictors of religiosity among youth aged 17–22: a longitudinal study of the national survey of children', *Journal for the Scientific Study of Religion*, *41*(4): 613–22.

Herweijer, L. (2008) 'Segregatie in het basisonderwijs en voortgezet onderwijs', in SCP (ed.) *Betrekkelijke Betrokkenheid. Sociaal en Cultureel Rapport 2008*. The Hague: Netherlands Institute for Social Research, 209–36.

Hoge, D.R. and Petrillo, G.H. (1978) 'Determinants of church participation and attitudes among high school youth', *Journal for the Scientific Study of Religion*, *17*(4): 359–79.

Journal of Ethnic and Migration Studies 441

Hoge, D.R., Petrillo, G.H. and Smith, E.I. (1982) 'Transmission of religious and social values from parents to teenage children', *Journal of Marriage and the Family*, 44(3): 569–80.

Hoge, D.R., Johnson, B. and Luidens, D.A. (1994) *Vanishing Boundaries: The Religion of Mainline Protestant Baby Boomers*. Louisville, KY: John Knox Press.

Jackman, M.R. and Muha, M.J. (1984) 'Education and intergroup attitudes: moral enlightenment, superficial democratic commitment, or ideological refinement?', *American Sociological Review*, 49(6): 751–69.

Jensen, T.G. (2008) 'To be "Danish", becoming "Muslim": contestations of national identity?', *Journal of Ethnic and Migration Studies*, 34(3): 389–409.

Kelley, J. and de Graaf, N. (1997) 'National context, parental socialization and religious belief: results from 15 nations', *American Sociological Review*, 62(4): 639–59.

Kohn, M.L. (1983) 'On the transmission of values in the family: a preliminary formulation', *Research in Sociology of Education and Socialization*, 4(1): 1–12.

Korf, D.J., Nabben, T., Wouters, M. and Yeşilgöz, B. (2007) *Van Vasten tot Feesten. Leefstijl, Acceptatie en Participatie van Jonge Moslims*. Rotterdam: Ger Guijs.

Maliepaard, M., Lubbers, M. and Gijsberts, M. (2010) 'Generational differences in ethnic and religious attachment and their interrelation: a study among Muslim minorities in the Netherlands', *Ethnic and Racial Studies*, 33(3): 451–72.

Myers, S.M. (1996) 'An interactive model of religiosity inheritance: the importance of family context', *American Sociological Review*, 61(5): 858–66.

Nauck, B. (2001) 'Intercultural contact and intergenerational transmission in immigrant families', *Journal of Cross-Cultural Psychology*, 32(2): 159–73.

Nauck, B., Diefenbach, H. and Petri, K. (2001) 'Intergenerational transmission of cultural capital under the conditions of migration: on the educational achievement of children and adolescents from migrant families in Germany', *Zeitschrift fuer Paedagogik*, 44(5): 701–22.

Need, A. and de Graaf, N. (1996) '"Losing my religion": a dynamic analysis of leaving the church in the Netherlands', *European Sociological Review*, 12(1): 87–99.

Ozorak, E.W. (1989) 'Social and cognitive influences on the development of religious beliefs and commitment in adolescence', *Journal for the Scientific Study of Religion*, 28(4): 448–63.

Phalet, K. and Schönpflug, U. (2001) 'Intergenerational transmission of collectivism and achievement values in two acculturation contexts: the case of Turkish families in Germany and Turkish and Moroccan families in the Netherlands', *Journal of Cross-Cultural Psychology*, 32(2): 186–201.

Phalet, K. and ter Wal, J. (2004) *Moslim in Nederland*. The Hague: Netherlands Institute for Social Research.

Phalet, K., Gijsberts, M. and Hagendoorn, L. (2008) 'Migration and religion: testing the secularisation thesis among Turkish and Moroccan Muslims in the Netherlands 1998–2005', *Kollner Zeitschrift fur Soziologie und Sozial-Psychologie*, S48: 412–36.

Phinney, J.S. and Vedder, P. (1996) 'Family relationship values of adolescents and parents: intergenerational discrepancies and adaptation', in Berry, J.W., Phinney, J.S., Sam, D.L. and Vedder, P. (eds) *Immigrant Youth in Cultural Transition*. Mahwah, NJ: Lawrence Erlbaum, 167–84.

Pinquart, M. and Silbereisen, R.K. (2004) 'Human development in times of social change: theoretical considerations and research needs', *International Journal of Behavioral Development*, 28(4): 289–98.

Portes, A. and Rumbaut, R.G. (2006) *Immigrant America: A Portrait*. 3rd ed. Berkeley: University of California Press.

Regnerus, M.D., Smith, C. and Smith, B. (2004) 'Social context in the development of adolescent religiosity', *Applied Developmental Science*, 8(1): 27–38.

Rohan, M.J. and Zanna, M.P. (1996) 'Value transmission in families', in Seligman, C., Olson, J.M. and Zanna, M.P. (eds) *The Psychology of Values*. Mahwah, NJ: Lawrence Erlbaum, 253–76.

442   *M. Maliepaard & M. Lubbers*

Roy, O. (2004) *Globalised Islam*. London: Hurst.

Ruiter, S. and van Tubergen, F. (2009) 'Religious attendance in cross-national perspective: a multilevel analysis of sixty countries', *American Journal of Sociology*, 115(3): 863–95.

SCP (2005) *Documentation P1684 SPVA 2002*. The Hague: Netherlands Institute for Social Research.

Sniderman, P.M. and Hagendoorn, L. (2007) *When Ways of Life Collide: Multiculturalism and its Discontents in the Netherlands*. Princeton: University Presses of California, Columbia and Princeton.

Stark, R., Iannaccone, L.R. and Finke, R. (1996) 'Linkages between economics and religion: religion, science and rationality', *American Economic Review*, 86(2): 433–7.

Statistics Netherlands (2007) *Ruim 850 Duizend Islamieten in Nederland*. Http://www.cbs.nl/nl-NL/menu/themas/vrije-tijd-cultuur/publicaties/artikelen/archief/2007/2007-2278-wm.htm.

Statistics Netherlands (2010) *Bevolking: Geslacht, Leeftijd, Herkomstgroepering en Generatie, 1 Januari*. Http://statline.cbs.nl/StatWeb/publication/?DM=SLNL&PA=37325&D1=0&D2=0&D3=0&D4=0&D5=137,232&D6=l&HDR=G2,G3,G4,T&STB=G1,G5&VW=T.

van Tubergen, F. (2007) 'Religious affiliation and participation among immigrants in a secular society: a study of immigrants in the Netherlands', *Journal of Ethnic and Migration Studies*, 33(5): 747–65.

Verkuyten, M. and Yildiz, A.A. (2007) 'National (dis)identification and ethnic and religious identity: a study among Turkish-Dutch Muslims', *Personality and Social Psychology Bulletin*, 33(10): 1448–62.

Vermeulen, H. and Penninx, R. (2000) *Immigrant Integration: The Dutch Case*. Amsterdam: Het Spinhuis.

Vogt, P.W. (1997) *Tolerance and Education*. Thousand Oaks: Sage.

[24]

Sociology of Religion 2005, 66:3 263-282

Intergenerational Transmission of Religion and Culture: Korean Protestants in the U.S.

Pyong Gap Min*
Queens College and the Graduate Center of CUNY

and

Dae Young Kim
University of Maryland

This paper systematically examines the extent to which Korean Protestant immigrants in the United States have transmitted their religion and cultural traditions through religion. It is based on a survey of 1.5- and 2nd-generation Korean American adults and a survey of Korean English-language congregations in the New York-New Jersey metropolitan area. Previous studies reveal that the majority of Korean immigrants are affiliated with a Korean Protestant church and that their frequent participation in it enables them to preserve Korean cultural traditions. Results of our survey show that Korean Protestant immigrants are highly successful in transmitting their church-oriented style of Protestantism to the second generation. Approximately two-thirds of 1.5- and 2nd-generation Korean American adults who attended a Protestant church during their childhood were found to participate in a Protestant congregation regularly, with more than two-thirds of them going to a Korean congregation. Moreover, they also participate in a congregation as frequently as Korean immigrants. However, our study shows that Korean Protestant immigrants have failed to transmit their cultural traditions through religion. Korean English-language congregations for 1.5- and 2nd-generation Korean American Protestants have almost entirely eliminated Korean cultural components from worship services and other socio-cultural activities. Transmitting Korean cultural traditions through religion is difficult for Korean Protestant immigrants partly because there is a great dissociation between Korean Protestantism and Korean secular culture and partly because second-generation Korean American Protestants have embraced the white American evangelical subculture. Based on these findings, we argue that transmitting a religion does not necessarily help to transmit ethnic culture and ethnic identity unless there is a strong correlation between the two.

Many studies of earlier Judeo-Christian white immigrant groups to the United States emphasized religion as the most important cultural mechanism for ethnic preservation (Greeley 1972; Handlin 1951; Herberg 1960; Warner 1993, 1994; Warner and Srole 1945). As Herberg (1960:28-29) elaborated in his sem-

Direct correspondence to: Pyong Gap Min, Queens College and the Graduate Center of CUNY, Flushing, NY 11367, e-mail: min@troll.soc.qc.edu

264 SOCIOLOGY OF RELIGION

inal book, religion was transmitted to the third and later generations and became an important source of their ethnic identity, while language and other ethnic customs hardly survived even in the second generation. Herberg and other researchers indicated that white ethnic groups had effectively used religion as an ethnic marker largely because the United States sanctioned religious pluralism.

Post-1965, heavily Third World immigrants, by contrast, are comprised of many non-Christian—Hindu, Buddhist, Muslim and Sikh—groups, as well as Christian groups. Many studies of contemporary immigrants' religious experiences have applied the same theoretical perspective as used in the studies of earlier Judeo-Christian immigrant groups, and, similarly, have found positive effects of religion on ethnic retention (Bankston and Zhou 1995; Carnes and Yang 2004; Chen 2002; Ebaugh and Chafetz 2000; Iwamura and Spickard 2003; Min 1992; Warner and Wittner 1998; Williams 1988). These studies suggest that because of the strong emphasis on multiculturalism in contemporary America, non-Christian immigrant groups may be able to use their respective religions as ethnic identifiers more effectively than Christian immigrant groups. Several studies have argued that precisely because of their differences from mainstream Americans, Buddhist, Hindu, and other non-Christian immigrant groups are better equipped than Christian groups to employ their religion to represent their ethnic culture and ethnic identity (Chen 2002; Kurien 1998; Williams 1988; Yang and Ebaugh 2001). For example, in her comparative study of a Chinese Buddhist temple and a Chinese evangelical church, Chen (2002:233) comments: "By virtue of the association of Buddhism with the Far East and Christianity with the West, the Buddhists, rather than the Christians, are the ones to be recruited and courted as the Chinese representatives at the multicultural table."

Asian or Middle Eastern Protestant immigrants who were part of a religious minority in their country of origin will find it even easier to practise Christianity in the United States because Christians constitute the religious mainstream. However, when it comes to preserving their ethnic culture and identity through religion, they will have more difficulty because the Protestant religion is not synonymous with their home country and ethnic culture. Yet Protestant immigrants can maintain ethnic culture fairly successfully by engaging in active religious practice and participation in ethnic congregations. The greatest challenge for Protestant immigrants lies in transmitting their ethnic cultures to the second generation because second-generation Protestants are more likely to question a host of Christian religious practices that are embedded in ethnic cultural traditions.

Most Korean immigrants are affiliated with and actively participate in Korean Protestant churches (Hurh and Kim 1990; Kim and Kim 2001; Min 1992). Yet, Protestants remain "a numerical minority group" in South Korea,[1]

---

[1] We like to emphasize Protestants in South Korea as "a *numerical* minority group" because Protestants have not suffered discrimination as a minority religious group. Korea,

constituting less than 20% of the population (Korea National Statistical Office 2002:538). Moreover, because of its short history,[2] the Korean version of Protestantism has not incorporated elements of Korean folk culture, such as holidays, food, dress, music and dance, except for Confucian and shamanistic cultural traditions (Baker 1997; Kim 2000). Thus, Korean Protestants in the United States, a numerical minority religious group in the country of origin that has become part of the religious mainstream in the host society, serve as a good case for examining the intergenerational transmission of ethnic culture through religion.

Both Korean Protestant immigrants and ethnic churches have received a great deal of scholarly attention (Hurh and Kim 1990; J. Kim 1996; A. R. Kim 1996; Kwon, Kim and Warner 2001; Min 1992, 2000; Shin and Park 1988). These studies reveal that Korean Protestant immigrants attend a Korean church with exceptional frequency and that they preserve Korean cultural traditions and ethnic networks through their active participation in ethnic congregations. Several ethnographic studies of second-generation Korean English-language congregations also suggest that second-generation Korean American churches are heavily evangelical, and that their Christian identity supersedes their Korean ethnic identity (Alumkal 1999, 2001; Chai 1998, 2001; Chong 1998; Kim 2003; Park 2001). However, there is no survey study that documents the proportion of second-generation Korean adults' affiliation with and frequency of participation in a Korean congregation.[3] Also, there are no survey data that indicate how well second-generation Korean English-language congregations retain Korean cultural traditions in worship services and other socio-cultural activities.

Using two sets of survey data collected in New York, this paper examines the intergenerational transmission of religion and culture among Korean American Protestants. The first section investigates what proportion of 1.5- and second-generation Korean Americans who participated in a Korean Protestant church during their childhood have maintained their religion as adults. The second section analyzes the extent to which second-generation Korean English-language congregations retain Korean cultural traditions. This study is significant for two

---

unlike India or the Philippines, has not historically experienced a serious political, regional or social conflict *based on religious differences*.

[2] Although American missionaries brought Protestantism to Korea at the end of the nineteenth century, it was not popularized in South Korea until the 1970s. In 1962, Protestants composed only 2.8% of the population in South Korea (Park and Cho 1995:119).

[3] We define second-generation Korean Americans as those who were born in the United States with at least one parent who was born in Korea. By 1.5, we refer to those who were born in Korea and came to the United States by age 12 or younger with at least one Korean-born parent. We chose 12 because that age reflects a substantial upbringing in the United States. Unless we make distinctions between the two, the term second-generation Korean Americans includes the 1.5ers.

266 SOCIOLOGY OF RELIGION

main reasons. First, it is theoretically significant because it specifies the mechanism that facilitates the preservation of ethnic culture through religion. Second, it is substantively significant because it provides the two survey data sets, each of which measures the magnitude of second-generation Korean American Protestants' retention of their childhood religion or the extent of second-generation Korean congregations' retention of ethnic culture.

DATA SOURCES

Two major data sources serve as the basis for our argument. First, a closed-ended telephone survey with 200 23-35 year-old 1.5- and second-generation Korean Americans in the New York-New Jersey metropolitan area, conducted by the second author in 1998. This data provides information about religious affiliations and participation in a religious institution. The survey relied on a random sample of 20 prominent Korean surnames included in the 1997 public telephone directories in the New York-New Jersey metropolitan boroughs and counties[4] to target Korean households and screen for eligible 1.5- and second-generation Korean Americans. This procedure produced a total of 24,000 potential Korean households, out of which 3,500 households were randomly generated for telephone screening. Telephone contact attempts were made to 2,631 households with 20 prominent Korean surnames. More than two-thirds (1,834) of households were reached by telephone. However, two-thirds of those households (1,213) were not screened because they did not either pass the ethnicity test or refused the screener. Out of 623 households that were successfully screened, 418 Korean households were found to be ineligible for the telephone interview because there were no eligible 1.5- and second-generation Korean Americans in the household or because those present did not meet the age criteria. The second author and a graduate student successfully interviewed 202 1.5-generation and U.S-born second-generation young adults, 23-35 years old.[5] Approximately 72 of the second-generation interviewees lived with parents, 92 were on their own (alone, married, or with roommates), and 38 lived away—those second-generation interviewees were found through screened parents.[6] The questionnaire included 108 items about 1.5- and second-generation Korean Americans' socio-economic adjustment. Four questions were related to their religious experiences.

---

[4]As a rough proxy for metropolitan New York-New Jersey boroughs and counties, Korean surnames were obtained from the following area codes: New York- 718, 212, 516, 914; New Jersey- 201, 908, 973.

[5]Seventy percent of the respondents were 1.5-generation Koreans, while 30% were U.S.-born second-generation Koreans.

[6]That means the proportion of second-generation households is roughly 15% or 92/623.

Although the sample is relatively small, it is the only survey dataset available on 1.5- and second-generation Korean American adults gathered though random sampling.

Telephone interviews with the primary pastors for 35 second-generation Korean American congregations in the New York-New Jersey area, conducted by the first author between March and August 2003, comprise the other major data source for our study. The screening telephone calls revealed that out of 528 Korean immigrant churches included in the 2002 Korean Churches Directory of New York, 38 churches had established an English-language ministry for young adults (18 years old and over). The first author conducted interviews with pastors from 33 (out of 38) second-generation congregations attached to Korean immigrant churches. In addition, interviews with pastors from two (out of five) independent Korean English-language congregations in the New York-New Jersey area were conducted during the same period. The questionnaire included 45 questions, mostly open-ended. The questions were related to general information about each congregation and components of Korean ethnic culture in services and other socio-cultural activities. Korean cultural components include using the Korean language, eating Korean food, observing Korean holidays, and assessing how each pastor stresses Korean cultural components in church services. Each interview took approximately 20-55 minutes to complete.

INTERGENERATIONAL TRANSMISSION OF RELIGION

Korean religious leaders, including second-generation Korean Americans, have used the term "silent exodus" to predict or indicate the drastic drop in second-generation Korean American adults' participation in ethnic churches (Cha 1994; Chai 1998, 2001). Cha (1994) went so far as to say: "90% of postcollege Korean Americans are no longer attending church" (in Chai 2001:300). But to date, no concrete evidence has been provided that shows drastic declines in ethnic church participation among 1.5- and second-generation Korean Americans. Here, we offer generalizable survey data that indicate 1.5- and second-generation Korean Americans' affiliation with religions and their participation in ethnic churches.

As shown in Table 1, 58% of 1.5- and second-generation Korean American respondents indicated Protestantism as their childhood religion, while 19% indicated Catholicism. Only 20% indicated that they had no religious affiliation during childhood. The proportions of respondents who chose Protestantism and Catholicism as their childhood religion are similar to those of Korean immigrant respondents who chose the two Christian religions in other survey studies (Hurh and Kim 1990; Min 2000; Park, Fawcett, Arnold, and Gardner 1990). The proportional similarity comes as no surprise given that during childhood most Korean American respondents attended Korean churches accompanied by their parents.

268 SOCIOLOGY OF RELIGION

Table 1: **1.5 and Second-Generation Koreans' Choice of Previous and Current Religions and Current Affiliation with a Religious Congregation**

	Religion During Childhood	Current Religion	Affiliation with a Religious Congregation
Protestantism	118 (58%)	109 (54%)	72 (36%)
Catholicism	37 (19%)	23 (11%)	11 (5%)
Buddhism	4 (2%)	4 (2%)	1 (0.5%)
Other Religions	2 (1%)	2 (1%)	0 (0%)
No Religion Or No Affiliation	40 (20%)	64 (32%)	118 (58%)
Total	201 (100%)	202 (100%)	202 (100%)

Source: Telephone interviews with 1.5- and second-generation young adults (23-35 years old) through randomly selected households with 20 prominent Korean surnames in New York in 1998

As to their religious affiliation at the time of the interview, 54% indicated Protestantism, 11% Catholicism, while 32% chose the no-religion category. Their current religion seems to be slightly inflated because some respondents who attended a Korean church during childhood, but who were not regular participants at the time of the interview, may have chosen either Protestantism or Catholicism as their current religion. Thus, the responses to the question about their church affiliation seem to reflect their church participation more accurately than their responses to the question about their religion. These responses reveal that 36% of the respondents were affiliated with a Protestant church while only 5% were affiliated with a Catholic church. The proportion of respondents who participated in a Protestant congregation dropped from 54% during childhood to 36% at the time of the interview, while the proportion of those who participated in a Catholic church decreased from 19% to 5%. Proportionally, far more second-generation Protestants were able to retain their childhood religion than their Catholic counterparts. This finding is not surprising, given that Korean Protestant immigrant churches are more conservative and evangelical than Korean Catholic immigrant churches. Clearly, the finding that approximately two-thirds of 1.5- and second-generation Korean American Protestant (36/54=67%) adults retain their childhood religion challenges the speculation that 90% of post-college Korean Americans no longer attend church.

Among the 72 Protestant respondents who were affiliated with a church at the time of the interview, 68% (N=49) were affiliated with a Korean congregation, while the remaining respondents participated in either a white (28%) or a multiethnic (4%) congregation. Korean Protestant immigrants very highly regard the various social functions of a Korean congregation, which is why more than

Table 2:   Frequency of 1.5- and Second-Generation Koreans'
            Participation in a Religious Congregation

	Total	Protestants	Catholics
Once a year or more often	10 (12%)	5 (7%)	5 (45%)
Once a month or more often	11 (13%)	8 (11%)	1 (9%)
Once a week or more often	61 (74%)	57 (82%)	5 (45%)
Total	82(100%)	*70 (100%)	11 (100%)

Source: Telephone interviews with 1.5- and second-generation young adults (23-35 years old) through randomly selected households with 20 prominent Korean surnames in New York in 1998
*Two Protestant respondents who were affiliated with a church did not respond to the question regarding frequency of participation.

95% of them participate in a Korean congregation (Hurh and Kim 1990; Min 2000). Second-generation Korean Americans, however, are likely to attend church mainly for religious purposes and consider social purposes less important than their parents (Chai 1998:309). Thus, they may feel less compelled to attend a Korean congregation to meet their need for fellowship. Nevertheless, more than two-thirds of second-generation Korean American Protestants were found to attend a Korean congregation. Such a high proportion of second-generation Korean American Protestants participants in an ethnic congregation is possible mainly because there are sufficient English-language congregations established within Korean immigrant churches.

Survey studies show that more than 80% of Korean Protestant immigrant respondents participate in a congregation once a week or more (Hurh and Kim 1990; Min 2000). Results of the 1997-1998 Presbyterian Racial and Ethnic Panel Studies also reveal that 78% of Korean Presbyterians participate in their congregation's Sunday worship service every week, compared to 49% of Latino, 34% of African American, and 28% of Caucasian Presbyterians (Kim and Kim 2001:82). The vast majority of Korean immigrant churches have two or more meetings per week (the prayer and/or Bible study meeting) in addition to the Sunday worship service, with more than 20% of members participating in these extra meetings (Min 1992, 2000)

As Table 2 shows, 82% of 1.5- and second-generation Korean American respondents affiliated with a Protestant church participates in it at least once a week - as frequently as Korean immigrants. Compared to Latino, African American and Caucasian Christians, 1.5- and second-generation Korean American Protestants participate in a church with exceptional frequency. As will be discussed later, survey data reveal that the majority of Korean English-language congregations hold two extra meetings per week for worship service, prayer, and

270 SOCIOLOGY OF RELIGION

Bible study. These findings suggest that second-generation Korean American Protestants have inherited the Korean style of congregationalism. Given that fewer second-generation Korean Protestants participate in a Korean congregation mainly for fellowship and ethnic networks than do Korean immigrants, the level of their religiosity reflected in their frequent participation in a congregation seems to be very high.

We previously noted in Table 1 that second-generation Korean American Catholic respondents had a much lower rate of religious retention from childhood to adulthood than their Protestant counterparts. Table 2 shows that even those Catholic respondents who participated in a church did so much less frequently than those Protestant respondents. Only 45% of 1.5- and second-generation Korean American Catholics regularly participated in the Sunday worship service, compared to 82% of their Protestant counterparts. Because Korean Catholic immigrant churches are more liberal in theology than Korean Presbyterian churches, they seem to transmit a more liberal theology to the second generation, in addition to having greater difficulty transmitting their religion.

INTERGENERATIONAL TRANSMISSION OF CULTURE THROUGH RELIGION

The degree to which younger-generation Korean Protestants retain Korean cultural traditions through religion will be influenced partly by their level of participation in a Korean church. Although two-thirds of 1.5- and second-generation Korean American Protestant respondents participated in a Korean church, the vast majority of 1.5- and second-generation Korean American Protestants were likely to attend a Korean English-language congregation rather than an immigrant congregation. Previous studies indicate that second-generation Korean American English-language congregations, heavily evangelical, make a great effort to dissociate their worship and religious rituals from Korean culture and ethnic traditions (Alumkal 1999, 2001; Chai 1998, 2001; Park 2001). This suggests that participation in a Korean congregation does not necessarily enable 1.5- and second-generation Korean Americans to retain their cultural traditions.

Our survey data largely confirm results of the previous case studies regarding the near-absence of Korean cultural components in second-generation Korean Protestant congregations. However, before we examine the lack of Korean cultural content, we provide general information about the pastors and memberships of the Korean English-language congregations in New York to help to contextualize the survey data. About half of the pastors in the Korean English-language congregations were ordained pastors, while the remaining half were non-ordained evangelical pastors (*jundosa*), many of whom were enrolled in a theological seminary at the time of the interview. Two of the pastors were white Americans, one was an Asian Indian, and the rest (N=32) were Korean. Among the 32 Korean pastors, half were 1.5-generation and 31% were U.S.-born Korean Americans. The rest (19%) were Korean immigrants. The leadership of Korean immigrant churches seem to favor 1.5-generation Korean pastors over the second generation for Korean English-language congregations, because their bilingualism and biculturalism can speak to both immigrant- and second-generation members more effectively. Only four of the primary pastors were women.

Large Korean immigrant churches in New York have recently established English-language congregations for second-generation Korean Americans. Out of 35 congregations examined, only two were established before 1990. The vast majority of English-language congregations were started in the 1990s, while eight were established in 2000 or after. As more 1.5- and second-generation Korean Americans reach adulthood, the number of Korean English-language congregations within Korean immigrant churches is likely to increase. Because of financial constraints, Korean English-language congregations are still unable to become independent from Korean immigrant churches. However, as they become financially self-sufficient, they are likely to become fully independent from Korean immigrant churches.

The vast majority of Korean English-language congregations are fairly small in size, with an average membership of 65. Participants in Korean English-language congregations are usually 1.5- and second-generation Korean American young adults aged 18 to 39. In one Korean English-language congregation in an upper-middle class neighborhood in upstate New York, however, the congregation was composed of Korean children, their immigrant parents, and a small number of white participants, with ages ranging from the very young (elementary school) to the elderly. The pastor of that church said that the intergenerational congregation was integrating second-generation children with their immigrant parents for worship services to infuse Korean cultural components into the Korean English-language congregation. This integrated intergenerational worship service was possible because there were a sufficient number of Korean immigrants fluent in English. Most immigrant members who were not fluent in English generally participated in one of the two Korean-language services offered at the church. It is important to note that some second- and many 1.5-generation Korean American Protestants who are fluent in Korean participate in a Korean-language immigrant congregation rather than in an English-language congregation.[7]

All but four English-language congregations had non-Korean members, ranging from 2% to 20%. The majority of non-Korean members were Chinese, but there were some Asian Indians, Filipinos, Vietnamese, Whites, Latinos, and

---

[7]Some U.S.-born and 1.5-generation Korean Americans are married to Korean immigrants. These cross-generation Korean Protestant couples are more likely to attend a Korean immigrant church than a Korean English-language congregation.

Blacks. The White members who participated in a Korean congregation usually were married to Koreans. Emerson and Kim (2003) defined a "multiracial congregation" as one in which "less than eighty percent of the members share the same racial background." Applying this definition, none of the surveyed Korean English-language congregations in New York in our study can be considered a multiracial congregation. Four pastors in particular, however, showed great interest in developing their congregations into multiracial ones by actively recruiting non-Korean Christians. Moreover, most interviewed respondents agreed that their congregations should be open to all racial and ethnic groups; however, they would not actively recruit non-Korean members. As a 1.5-generation Korean American pastor said: "I do not intentionally target Chinese and other non-Korean members. But if non-Koreans come, we are open. If the flow of newcomers dictates the change in the ethnic composition, I will follow it." Only three pastors wanted to develop their congregations as specifically Korean ethnic congregations to meet the unique needs of Korean Americans. Given these trends, Korean English-language congregations are increasingly likely to develop into multiracial congregations in the future.

Previous research, mostly case studies, has presented second-generation Korean American Protestants and Korean English-language congregations mainly as evangelical (Alumkal 1999, 2001; Chai 1998, 2001; Kim 2003; Park 2001). The results of our survey of Korean English-language congregations in New York support their claims about the heavily evangelical orientation of Korean English-language congregations. Out of 35 congregations surveyed, 29 congregations (83%) were found to be evangelical while only six were mainline.

The specific orientation of second-generation Korean American congregations, whether mainline or evangelical, seems to be determined partly by the theological orientation of the pastor. The pastors of the six mainline congregations were trained in liberal to moderate theological seminaries (such as New York Theological Seminary, New Brunswick Theological Seminary, and Princeton Theological Seminary), while those of the other evangelical congregations were mostly trained or were being trained in conservative theological seminaries or Christian schools (such as Westminster, Gordon Conwell Seminary, and Biblical Seminary). The evangelical orientation of Korean English-language congregations has also been affected by the conservatism and evangelical orientation of Korean immigrant churches. The Korean immigrant churches within which six mainline Korean English-language congregations were established were liberal in their theological orientation, while the "mother churches" of the other evangelical congregations were generally conservative and evangelical. Conservative Korean immigrant churches are prone to hire socially and theologically conservative pastors for their Korean English-language congregations, whereas liberal churches prefer to hire liberal pastors.

Finally, Korean English-language congregations take the evangelical position partly because their members are heavily evangelical. Two pastors included in the survey commented that they had to follow the evangelical orientation to meet the spiritual needs of their members, although they personally were more comfortable with the mainline approach. A number of sources have suggested that second-generation Korean American Protestants, regardless of the region of the country, are predominantly evangelical (Busto 1996; Chai 2001:165; Kim 2003; Park 2001). They also indicate that, in addition to Korean immigrant churches, the evangelical movement in college campuses had a strong influence on the evangelization of second-generation Korean American Christians. The number of Korean American college students has gradually increased since the early 1970s when parachurch organizations, such as Campus Crusade for Christ, InterVarsity Christian Fellowship and the Navigators, began to have a significant influence on the evangelical movement on college campuses (Busto 1996). Although Korean Christian students on most East Coast college campuses have an established Korean Christian Fellowship, they have been affected by both the above-mentioned evangelical parachurch organizations and inter-college Korean Christian groups and meetings.

All English-language congregations within Korean immigrant churches were found to be financially dependent upon immigrant congregations, but independent in worship services and other socio-cultural activities. They usually held joint services with immigrant congregations two or three times a year on important religious holidays, such as Easter and Thanksgiving. But, as Chai (1998; 2001) and Park (2001) have aptly pointed out, Korean English-language congregations have developed entirely different worship styles from Korean immigrant congregations. Korean immigrant congregations sing traditional hymns accompanied by piano and organ. By contrast, Korean English-language evangelical congregations sing contemporary gospel songs projected through overhead speakers, accompanied by guitar, drum, base, and/or keyboard. Korean English-language congregations obtain worship songs and other materials produced by white American evangelical organizations, such as PASSION, Calvary Church, and the Vineyard Christian Fellowship.

Two other major differences in worship style exist between Korean immigrant and Korean English-language congregations: in the formal-informal and collective-individual continuums. Korean immigrant congregations emphasize formality and collective experience, especially for the Sunday worship service; almost all participants wear formal dress, with men wearing neckties. They try to communicate with God mainly through the medium of the pastors' sermons. By contrast, English-language congregations maintain an informal style of worship and emphasize each individual member's spiritual connections with God. Most participants, even in the Sunday worship service, are more casually dressed as they sing and clap hands to the rhythm of gospel songs. Many interviewed pastors of Korean English-language congregations responded that, for an evangelical Christian, worship is the personal encounter with and celebration of God. Therefore, spirituality and emotional engagement are far more important than formality and collectivity. Many respondents were, consequently, very critical of the tendency of Korean immigrant congregations to emphasize participation in the congregation and group activities.

Jeung's study in San Francisco (2002) revealed that pan-Asian evangelical congregations identify primarily with the broader American evangelical subculture, and as a corollary pay little attention to ethnic and Asian cultural heritage, while mainline congregations try to integrate Asian cultural resources with Christian rituals. Major findings of our survey strongly support his conclusion. The pastors were asked several questions related to ethnic cultural components in each congregation. Regarding the use of language, only one mainline English-language congregation, where parents and children held services together, was found to provide bilingual sermons, hymns, and prayers. None of the other congregations used the Korean language in any of the three components of worship services.

The pastors were also asked about the frequency of their use of one or more Korean terms or phrases in their sermons. Eleven pastors (31%) reported that they used them occasionally. Almost half of the respondents (46%) said they had never used a Korean word. The pastors were asked about the number of times they had mentioned Korea or the Korean American community in their sermons during the past year. Perhaps surprisingly, 40% reported that they had never mentioned Korea, while 20% said they had never made reference to the Korean community. These are in sharp contrast with pastors in Korean immigrant congregations, who almost always use Korea and/or the Korean immigrant community in content.

Studies of Korean immigrant churches indicate that all Korean immigrant congregations observe two major Korean cultural holidays and two national holidays (Min 1992). By contrast, only four Korean English-language congregations were found to celebrate and/or observe one or more of the four Korean holidays. In another five congregations the pastors make reference to a few Korean holidays in their sermons. The four Korean English-language congregations were able to celebrate Korean holidays largely because many members of each congregation had parents who attended immigrant congregations within the same church. When these congregations become independent from immigrant congregations, none of them is likely to celebrate or observe Korean cultural or national holidays.

The only ethnic evidence that remains in Korean English-language congregations is Korean food. Thirty-three out of the 35 congregations surveyed were found to serve snacks or full lunch after the Sunday main service. The majority (52%) of them served mostly Korean food, compared to 30% that served mostly American food. The rest served Korean and non-Korean food almost equally. If it were not for the immigrant congregations that prepared full Korean lunch for members of English-language congregations, most members of the English-language congregations would not be exposed to Korean food.[8] In the case where English-language congregations prepare their own snacks or lunch, they serve American food more often than Korean food, because, as one respondent said, "Korean food is more difficult to prepare." Because more and more Korean English-language congregations will become independent from immigrant congregations, exposure to ethnic food will diminish in the future.

As expected, the Korean English-language congregations led by immigrant pastors were found to include more ethnic components in worship services and other socio-cultural activities than those churches led by second-generation or non-Korean pastors. However, it is wrong to presume that Korean English-language congregations do not use the Korean language for services and do not practice other Korean cultural traditions because their leaders are not fluent in Korean and are not familiar with Korean customs. Not only Korean immigrant and 1.5-generation respondents, but also some second-generation respondents, were found to be fluent in Korean. In fact, they were hired partly because of their fluency in Korean. The pastors of Korean English-language congregations avoid using the Korean language for worship services and minimize Korean cultural content mainly because they and their congregations are heavily evangelical. Five of the six mainline congregations were found to put more emphasis on Korean cultural components in worship services and other socio-cultural activities and have more services together with immigrant congregations.

The pastors of Korean English-language congregations were asked the following questions: "How important do you think it is for a second-generation Korean church to preserve Korean cultural traditions? Why?" Seven of the respondents (20%) considered it very important for a second-generation Korean American congregation to preserve Korean cultural traditions; five were found to serve mainline congregations. Responding to the question of why these pastors saw it important to emphasize ethnic elements, a 57-year-old Korean immigrant pastor who was serving in a mainline congregation commented:

> I think it is important. We are all brothers and sisters under God. But we as Koreans have unique cultural traditions and a sense of affinity because we share blood. We can use our heritage and culture to strengthen our faith. I often pray for South Korea. When giving sermons I always make reference to Korean cultural holidays and Mother's Day.

About one-third of the respondents reported that it is somewhat important for second-generation Korean American congregations to preserve Korean cultural traditions. But they also emphasized that priority should be put on religious

---

[8]Because many congregations start the Sunday's worship service at 11 am or at 1/1:30 pm, their members can have full lunch prepared by their immigrant congregations before or after the service.

276 SOCIOLOGY OF RELIGION

faith rather than on Korean culture. Some of these respondents pointed to the difficulty of striking a balance between religious faith and ethnic culture. The remaining 46% expressed the view that second-generation Korean American congregations should not play a role in the preservation of Korean culture. They emphasized that priority be placed on spreading the gospel and universal Christian values and not on retaining ethnic culture. For example, a 1.5-generation Korean American pastor who serves a Korean English-language congregation within a full gospel church responded:

> When you minister a congregation, the first priority is the gospel. It is not good to empha-size a particular culture. Maintaining Korean culture is not an agenda in service. They can get it elsewhere. There is no agenda other than the gospel. Individually, I have [a] strong Korean attachment. I often watch Korean soccer games at home. But I cannot make that Korean cultural thing an agenda in my congregation.

Another 1.5-generation Korean American pastor, who is fluent in Korean, made a similar comment:

> It is important we Korean Americans maintain Korean cultural traditions. I am very eth-nic. I teach my children the Korean language and customs at home. But I try to separate the spiritual community from the family. It is the job of the family to teach Korean tra-ditions. But our spiritual community should focus on the gospel. No particular culture should be emphasized and no politics should be involved in a congregation.

As previously noted, almost all Korean English-language congregations have a small number of non-Korean members. Most respondents justified their effort to minimize Korean cultural components in their congregations by noting the presence of a few or several non-Korean members. One female pastor said that even the presence of a single non-Korean member justifies refraining from the use of the Korean language in worship services. Many respondents agreed that the inclusion of some Korean cultural components is not a problem as long as prior-ity is put on Christianity. But many respondents view Korean immigrant congre-gations as putting priority on Korean culture over Christian things. As a third-generation Korean American pastor put it: "As long as we accept Korean cultur-al components under Christianity, there is no problem. But many Korean immi-grant churches put Koreanness above Christianity." Some of the pastors were very critical of Korean immigrant churches' overemphasis on "Confucian cultur-al components" that they viewed as un-Christian. For example, a second-gener-ation pastor said:

> Definitely, I agree. They [Korean immigrant churches] put Korean culture ahead of bib-lical teachings. Korean cultural things get in the way of doing Christianity. Sexism, ageism, and overemphasis on going to good colleges are incongruent with Christian val-ues. They also prevent outreaching non-Korean members and thus the church's growth.

While most respondents are critical of Korean immigrant churches' overemphasis on Korean culture, many of them had positive views about the unique aspects of Korean Protestantism. They considered "being church-oriented" and "being fervent Christians" as two exceptional aspects of Korean Protestantism and wanted to maintain these Korean traditions of Christianity. As one respondent said: "Korean people have developed a different style of Christianity. Korean Christians are fervent, church-centered, and strongly committed to Christian life. They spend a lot of time for the church. We, younger generation Koreans, should preserve these unique elements of Korean Christianity."

Respondents were asked about the frequency of weekly congregational meetings. All English-language congregations were found to have at least one extra meeting for Bible study, prayer, discipleship, and/or social activities, in addition to the Sunday main service. Most congregations were found to have two or more extra meetings per week, usually on Wednesday, Friday and/or Saturday. Nearly half (46%) of the respondents reported that their congregations held "small group" meetings regularly for Bible study and fellowship, either at a private home, in the church, or at a restaurant. A few more respondents said their congregations would start "small group" meetings when their congregations had sufficient members. The frequency with which the congregations hold small-group meetings ranges from weekly to monthly. "Small-group meetings" for Korean English-language congregations resemble the "district service" or "cell ministry" for Korean immigrant churches (Kwon et al. 1997; Min 1992). Although not included in the questionnaire, several respondents were probed about whether the source of extra weekly meetings in their congregations can be attributed to the influence of Korean immigrant churches. They reported that both Korean immigrant and American evangelical churches had influenced Korean English-language congregations to hold two or more additional meetings per week.

Korean immigrant churches exhibit gender hierarchy and other patriarchal elements in their organization. The 2002 Korean Churches Directory of New York shows that women pastors headed only nine of 528 Korean Protestant churches. Results of the 1997-1998 Presbyterian Racial and Ethnic Panel Studies reveal that only 8% of Korean ordained elders were women (Kim and Kim 2001:84). A. R. Kim's study (1996:76) also shows that in Korean immigrant churches men control positions of power and authority while women play a predominantly nurturing role (fundraising, prayer meetings, visiting the sick etc.).

Because the majority of the respondents are critical of Korean Confucian cultural elements in Korean immigrant congregations, Korean English-language congregations are likely to be more gender-egalitarian than immigrant congregations. As expected, survey results reveal that, in terms of representation on functional committees, women seem to do better in English-language congregations. Questioned as to how well women are represented in leadership positions in their congregation, many respondents made the following comments: "women are very active," "women are more active in my congregation than in the immigrant con-

278 SOCIOLOGY OF RELIGION

gregation," "half and half," and "80% of leaders are women." However, all but four respondents stated their theological position that women should not be allowed to serve as pastors or elders. Even a woman pastor agreed that men could be more effective pastors than women.

The respondents attributed the under-representation of women in leadership positions in immigrant congregations to Korean "Confucian patriarchy." However, they pointed to "Biblical patriarchy" to justify the principle of no-woman-pastor or no-woman-elder. The following comment by a second-generation respondent most succinctly summarizes their effort to separate "Confucian patriarchy" from "Biblical patriarchy," and functional committee leaders from clergy leadership positions:

> Unlike Korean immigrant congregations, we do not endorse the position that men are better than women. Most of functional committee leaders in our congregation are women. But, according to the Bible, men and women have different roles. Most of our members accept the Biblical position that women should not serve as elders or pastors. Most women members do not feel comfortable with a woman serving as a pastor. But it does not mean that men and women have different levels of power and status. We do not accept Korean Confucian patriarchy.

Another respondent made a similar comment: "I support more male leadership in the congregation. But I do this, not because of Korean cultural traditions, but because of my Biblical theory. That is how God made men and women. They have different roles."

The above discussion helps us locate the sources of gender hierarchy and patriarchal practices in Korean immigrant congregations, as well as Korean English-language congregations. Some researchers have attributed gender hierarchy in Korean immigrant churches to Korean Confucian cultural traditions (Kim and Kim 2001; A. R. Kim 1996; Min 1992), while others have focused on the Bible as its major source (Alumkal 1999; J. H. Kim 1996). But the foregoing discussion suggests that both factors—Korean cultural traditions and evangelical Christianity—are responsible for the highly gendered organizational structure of Korean immigrant churches and other patriarchal practices there. Korean English-language congregations have moderated gender hierarchy by discarding "Confucian patriarchy," but they still maintain some level of gender hierarchy by embracing evangelical Christianity.

CONCLUSION

Korean Protestant immigrants in the United States have established Korean churches characterized by congregation-oriented evangelical Christianity and Korean Confucian ideology. By practising Korean cultural traditions through active participation in congregations, Korean Protestant immigrants have been able to preserve Korean culture. However, Korean particularistic values are increasingly colliding with Christian universalistic values (Alumkal 2001; Chai 1998). Korean Protestant immigrants, comfortable with Korean cultural traditions, are unaware of the tensions. But 1.5- and second-generation Korean American Protestants, who do not take Korean cultural traditions for granted, feel strong tensions between Korean and Christian values and perceive many "un-Christian" elements in Korean cultural practices.

Despite pessimistic speculation, our data reveal that Korean Protestant immigrants are fairly successful in transmitting their religion to their children. About two-thirds of 1.5- and second-generation Korean American Protestant adults have preserved their childhood religion, with the majority participating in Korean congregations. Moreover, following the congregation-oriented style of Korean Protestantism, they participate in Korean congregations with exceptional frequency. However, results of telephone interviews with the pastors show that Korean English-language congregations have eliminated most Korean cultural traditions from their worship services and socio-cultural activities. None of 1.5- and second-generation congregations was found to use the Korean language for sermons, praying or singing devotional songs. Only four of them were found to celebrate and/or observe one or more of the four Korean cultural and national holidays along with their parents in immigrant churches. About 40% of the respondents reported that they had not mentioned Korea in their sermons over the past year, while 20% did not make a reference to the Korean community.

To put it simply, Korean Protestant immigrants have failed to transmit Korean cultural traditions to their children through religion, although they have been fairly successful in transmitting their religion. It has been difficult for Korean Protestant immigrants to transmit Korean cultural traditions to the second generation through religion because Protestantism is not a religion indigenous to Korea. Since Protestantism has gained popularity in South Korea only over the past three decades, it has not incorporated Korean folk culture in the form of food, holidays, dress, wedding, funerals, and so on. Korean Protestant churches have incorporated some elements of Confucianism, such as age-based authority, emphasis on going to a good college, and their more sexist organization. But second-generation Korean American congregations have difficulty in accommodating these hierarchical Confucian values and customs because they, unlike elements of Korean folk culture, conflict with American individualism. Our survey and other studies (Chai 1998) reveal that both second-generation Korean pastors and lay members consider these Confucian values "very un-Christian."

The literature on Christian groups in the United States has overemphasized participation in congregations as the main channel for preserving ethnic cultural traditions. Based on our analysis, we argue that even for Christian groups, the correlation between religion and ethnic culture is more important for the intergenerational transmission of culture through religion than mere participation in congregations. Our study shows that 1.5- and second-generation Korean

280 SOCIOLOGY OF RELIGION

Protestants are in a tenuous position in terms of retaining their ethnic culture through participation in ethnic congregations because of the dissociation between Protestantism and Korean culture.

Korean English-language congregations have eliminated much of Korean cultural traditions partly because they assume a heavily evangelical orientation. Our interviews reveal that the strong evangelical orientation of Korean English-language congregations, with their emphasis on the gospel and their idea of the universal priesthood of all believers, prevents them from infusing Korean cultural components into Christian rituals. Based on his study of a Japanese American church in Canada, Mark Mullins (1987) provided the evolutionary model for the intergenerational transformation of ethnic churches from the home-language congregation for immigrants through the bilingual-bicultural congregation for the second- generation to the English-language monolingual congregation for the third and later generations. But not all Asian Christian immigrant groups are likely to follow this model. Because of their heavily evangelical orientation, most of 1.5- and second-generation Korean American congregations have already become English-language monolingual congregations.

REFERENCES

Alumkal, A. 1999. Preserving patriarchy: Assimilation, gender norms, the second-generation Korean American evangelicals. *Qualitative Sociology* 22:129-40.

———. 2001. Being Korean, being Christian: Particularism and universalism in a second-generation congregation. In *Korean Americans and their religions: Pilgrims and missionaries from a different shore*, edited by H. Y. Kwon, K. C. Kim, and R. S. Warner, 181-192. University Park, PA: Pennsylvania State University Press.

Baker, D. 1997. Christianity. In *An introduction to Korean culture*, edited by J. H. Koo and A. Nam,170-200. Elizabeth, NJ: Hollym.

Bankston III, C., and M. Zhou. 1995. The ethnic church, ethnic identification, and adaptation of Vietnamese adolescents in an immigrant community. *Sociological Quarterly* 36:523-34.

Busto, R. 1996. The gospel according to the model minority? Hazarding an interpretation of Asian American evangelical college students. *Amerasia Journal* 22 (1): 133-48.

Carnes, T, and F. Yang. 2004. *Asian American religions: The making and remaking of borders and boundaries*. New York: New York University Press.

Cha, P. 1994. Toward a vision for second generation Korean American ministry. Paper Presented at the Catalyst, Sandy Cover, Maryland.

———. 2001. Ethnic identity formation and participation in immigrant churches: Second-generation Korean American experiences. In *Korean Americans and their religions: Pilgrims and missionaries from a different shore*, edited by H. Y. Kwon, K. C. Kim, and R. S. Warner, 141-156. University Park, PA: Pennsylvania State University Press.

Chai, K. 1998. Competing for the second generation: English-language ministry at a Korean Protestant church. In *Gatherings in diaspora: Religious communities and the new immigration*, edited by R. S. Warner and J. Wittner, 295-332. Philadelphia: Temple University Press.

———. 2001. Beyond 'strictness' to distinctiveness: generational transition in Korean Protestant churches. In *Korean Americans and their religions: Pilgrims and missionaries from a different shore*, edited by H.Y. Kwon, K. C. Kim, and R. S. Warner, 157-180. University Park, PA: Pennsylvania State University Press.

Chen, C. 2002. The Religious varieties of ethnic presence: A comparison between a Taiwanese immigrant Buddhist temple and an evangelical Christian church. *Sociology of Religion* 63: 215-38.

Chong, K. 1998. What it means to be Christian: The role of religion in the construction of ethnic identity and boundary among second-generation Korean Americans. *Sociology of Religion* 59: 259-86.

Ebaugh, H. R. and J. S. Chafetz. 2000. *Religion and the new immigrants: Continuities and adaptations in immigrant congregations*. Walnut Creek, CA: Altamira Press.

Emerson, M. O. and K.C. Kim. 2003. Multiracial congregations: An analysis of their development and a typology. *Journal of the Scientific Study of Religion* 42 (2): 217-28.

Greeley, A. 1972. *The denominational society: A sociological approach to religion in America*. Glenview, IL: Scott, Foresman and Company.

Handlin, O. 1951. *The uprooted: The epic story of the great migrations that made the American People*. Boston: Little, Brown and Company.

Herberg, W. 1960. *Protestant, Catholic, and Jew: An essay in the American religious sociology*, 2nd Edition. Garden City, NY: Doubleday.

Hurh, W. M. and K. C. Kim. 1990. Religious participation of Korean immigrants in the United States. *Journal of the Scientific Study of Religion* 29 (1):19-34.

Iwamura, J. and P. Spickard. (eds.). 2003. *Revealing the sacred in Asian and Pacific America*. New York: Routledge

Jeung, R. 2002. Asian-American pan-ethnic formation and congregational culture. In *Religions in Asian America: Building faith communities*, edited by P. G. Min and J. H, Kim, 215-243. Walnut Creek, CA: Altamira Press.

Kim, A. R. 1996. *Women struggling for a new life: The role of religion in the cultural passage from Korea to America*. Albany, NY: State University of New York Press.

Kim, A. 2000. Korean religious culture and its affinity to Christianity in South Korea. *Sociology of Religion* 61 (2):117-34.

Kim, J. H. 1996. *Bridge-makers and cross-bearers: Korean-American women and the church*. Atlanta: Scholar's Press. Oxford University Press

Kim, K. C. and S. Kim. 2001. The ethnic role of Korean immigrant churches in the United States. In *Korean Americans and their religions: Pilgrims and missionaries from a different shore*, edited by H. Y. Kwon, K. C.Kim, and S. R. Warner, 71-94. University Park, PA: Pennsylvania State University Press.

Kim, R. Y. 2003. Second-Generation Korean American evangelicals: Ethnic, multiethnic, or white campus ministries. *Sociology of Religion* 65:19-34.

Korea National Statistical Office. 2002. *2002 Social indicators in Korea*. Seoul: Korea National Statistical Office.

Kurien, P. 1998. Becoming American by becoming Hindu: Indian Americans take their place at the multicultural table. In *Gatherings in diaspora: Religious communities and the new immigration*, edited by R. S. Warner and J. Wittner, 37-70. Philadelphia: Temple University Press.

Kwon, H. Y., K. C. Kim, and R. S. Warner. (eds.). 2001. *Korean Americans and their religions: Pilgrims and missionaries from a different shore*. University Park, PA: Pennsylvania State University Press.

Kwon, V. H., H. R. Ebaugh, and J. Hagan. 1997. The structure and functions of cell group ministry in Korean Christian church. *Journal of the Scientific Study of Religion*, 36 (2):247-56.

Min, P. G. 1992. The structure and social functions of Korean immigrant churches in the United States. *International Migration Review* 26:1370-94.

_____. 2000. Immigrants' religion and ethnicity: A comparison of Korean Christian and Indian Hindu immigrants. *Bulletin of the Royal Institute for Inter-Faith Studies* 2:121-40.

282 SOCIOLOGY OF RELIGION

Mullins, M. R. 1987. The life-cycle of ethnic churches in sociological perspective. *Japanese Journal of Religious Studies* 14 (4):321-34.

Park, I. H., and L. J. Cho. 1995. Confucianism and the Korean family. *Journal of Comparative Family Studies* 26 (1):117-35.

Park, I. H., J. Fawcett, F. Arnold, and R. Gardner. 1990. Koreans immigrating to the United States: A pre-departure analysis. Paper No. 114. Honolulu: Population Institute, East-West Center.

Park, S. Y. 2001. The intersection of religion, race, gender, and ethnicity. In *Korean Americans and their religions: Pilgrims and missionaries from a different shore*, edited by H. Y. Kim, K. C. Kim, and R. S. Warner, 193-209. University Park, PA: Pennsylvania State University Press.

Shin, E. H. and H. Park.1988. An analysis of causes of schisms in ethnic churches: The case of Korean-American churches. *Sociological Analysis* 49 (2):234-48.

Warner, R. S. 1993. Work in progress toward a new paradigm for the sociological study of religion in the United States. *American Journal of Sociology* 94:1044-93.

_____. 1994. The place of congregation in the American religious configuration. In *American congregations, Vol.2: New perspectives in the study of congregations*, edited by J. Wind and J. Lewis, 54-99. Chicago: University of Chicago Press.

Warner, R. S. and Wittner, J. (eds.) 1998. *Gatherings in diaspora: Religious communities and the new immigration*. Philadelphia: Temple University Press.

Warner, W. L. and L. Srole. 1945. *The social system of American ethnic groups*. New Haven, CT: Yale University Press.

Williams, R. B. 1988. *Religions of immigrants from India and Pakistan: New threads in the American tapestry*. New York: Cambridge University Press.

Yang, F. and H. R. Ebaugh. 2001. Transformations in new immigrant religions and their global implications. *American Sociological Review* 66:269-88.

[25]

Journal of Ethnic and Migration Studies
Vol. 34, No. 2, March 2008, pp. 253–269

Transnational Migrants and Transnational Spirits: An African Religion in Lisbon

Clara Saraiva

Portugal, for long a country of emigration, has in recent decades become one of immigration. One of the largest groups of newcomers is constituted by Africans from the former Portuguese colonies. This paper focuses on how religion and ritual traditions from their home country are manipulated by people from Guinea-Bissau in order to recreate their identity in the urban world of Lisbon. Based on fieldwork conducted among the Pepel of Guinea-Bissau from 1997 to the present and on ongoing research on a Pepel religious healer in Lisbon, this paper specifically dwells on the issue of transnational spirits. It explores how such entities are constructed, and the rituals around them. This entails a complex and ceaseless relation between the world of the living and the world of the dead, as well as a constant flow of goods and symbols between the physical original grounds, in Guinea-Bissau, and Lisbon: people, money, goods, practices and ideas, as well as spirits, circulate and create bridges between Europe and Africa.

Keywords: Migration; Transnationalism; Spirits; Religion; Africa; Portugal

Introduction

Focusing on the African diaspora from Guinea-Bissau in Lisbon, this paper aims to demonstrate how transnational approaches to migration, in such areas as religious practices, may prove to be a means to a better understanding of some of the adaptation processes that migration entails. To this end, I will argue that religious performances, like funerals, are both an anthropological and economic subject, since they entail remittances and a constant flow of goods from one country to the other

Clara Saraiva is Senior Researcher at the Lisbon Institute for Scientific Tropical Research (Instituto de Investigacao Cientifica Tropical) and Professor in the Department of Anthropology, Universidade Nova de Lisboa. Correspondence to: Prof. C. Saraiva, Rua Moscavide-Expo lote 4.29.01 A 5B, 1990-165, Lisbon, Portugal. E-mail: clarasaraiva@fcsh.unl.pt

ISSN 1369-183X print/ISSN 1469-9451 online/08/020253-17 © 2008 Taylor & Francis
DOI: 10.1080/13691830701823921

and back again: people, money, goods, practices and ideas circulate and create bridges between Europe and the African continent.

The paper is based on fieldwork conducted among the Pepel of Guinea-Bissau from 1997 to the present and on ongoing research on a case study of a Pepel religious healer in Lisbon.[1] I focus specifically on the issue of transnational spirits, and on the process of construction and existence of such entities. I will argue (as many authors before, see Ariés 1989; Baudry 1999; Bloch and Parry 1982; Déchaux 2001; de Coppet 1992; Hertz 1960; Metcalf and Huntington 1991; Pina-Cabral 1984; Saraiva 2004a, 2004b; Thomas 1985) that the concept of a 'good death' and the maintenance of a good relationship between the world of the living and the world of the dead are the essential conditions for ancestors to become benevolent spirits that watch over the survivors.

When Guineans migrate to Portugal, so too do their religious performances, performers, and the spirits that operate to help people in their life crises; but the links with the original setting remain and are a means of empowerment for all those who intervene—clients, religious healers and spirits. They all become transnational characters in a complex set of relations originally established between the living and the dead in Africa. Transposed to the diaspora universe, such relations incorporate transnational circumstances in which African practices become mixed with European ones, or 'translated', in order to accommodate to a different context, and give rise to a continuous flow of people, spirits and goods that move back and forth between Guinea-Bissau and Portugal.

After some historical background on Guinean migration to Lisbon, I will explain what Pepel funerary rituals entail and how their completion is essential for the creation of the ancestors' spirits that will watch over the survivors and help them in their life-crisis situations. If this is true in Africa, how does it work when the connection between these two worlds, the real and the supernatural one, becomes more complex through the process of migration and two other 'real worlds', the original setting in Guinea-Bissau and the host-country one, come into play? This raises the issue of the 'double engagement' in the formulation of the identities of both people and spiritual beings, displaced due to the diaspora movements and the creation of transnational networks based on religious and healing practices which are transposed from their original setting in Guinea-Bissau to Lisbon. Relating and articulating with Kristine Krause's proposal (see the previous paper in this special issue) of the term 'transnational therapeutic networks', and following Capone's idea of 'transnational religions' (Capone 2004), I would like to suggest the use of the term 'transnational religious networks', as an expression that portray the importance of the ties with the home grounds insofar as the re-creation of a Guinean identity in Lisbon is concerned.

Thus I argue, as Bordonaro and Pussetti have done (2006: 147), that the study of migration cannot be limited to the circulation of goods and people, but has to take into account the circulation of symbolic universes, including religion and the ritual practices that heal the states of affliction and commemorate the festive occasions.

Journal of Ethnic and Migration Studies   255

People from Guinea-Bissau in Lisbon

After being for many centuries a nation of emigration, Portugal became, in the late 1970s and during the 1980s, a destination for immigrants. This changed the face of the country, which became the locus of a multicultural and multi-ethnic society on an unprecedented scale. This was due to several circumstances. For the African populations, amongst the most important was the 1974 Portuguese revolution, which triggered the independence of the former Portuguese overseas colonies (at the time, all of the remaining Portuguese possessions were in Africa, except for Macau and Timor). The phenomenon of African immigration to Portugal forms part of the wider movements of Sub-Saharan Africans towards the richer, European countries in the northern hemisphere, which have increased significantly in the last decades, justifying discussion about the social implications of the 'new African diasporas' (Koser 2003) in the old continent.

Much of the seminal work edited by Khalid Koser on the subject mentions the exuberance around the revitalisation of the diaspora concept, and the fact that diasporas are nowadays conceived as a 'new social form characterized by special social relationships, political orientations and economic strategies', but also as a phenomenon that demands an increased awareness of its multi-locality and its condition as a 'novel mode of cultural production that interacts with globalization' (Koser 2003: 9). It is indeed important to be aware of the multiple aspects of these recent forms of social and economic production; notably some apparently hidden aspects like the practical effects of religion and therapeutical practices (Capone 2004), as well as some other performances that fall into the realm of the symbolic and are the basis for religious constructs, namely the conceptualisation of the relations between the world of the dead and of the living (with visible implications for funerals and rituals of mourning). In Portugal, although some research has been done on the recent situation of the country as a host-nation for African-origin populations (Barreto 1995; Bastos 2000; Bastos and Bastos 1999; Garcia 2000a, 2000b, 2000c; Gusmão 2004; Machado 2002; Pires 2003; Quintino 2004; Saint-Maurice 1997; Vala 1999), much remains to be done, especially as the numbers of immigrants continue to increase.

The largest concentration of Africans is in the Greater Lisbon area (including the Tagus valley and the southern district of Setúbal) and in the southern part of the country, in the Algarve. Guineans started coming to Portugal after 1974, subsequent to gaining independence, and especially from 1984 onwards, when Guinea-Bissau, following the end of Luís Cabral's regime, opened up to the outside world and adopted a more Western economic and democratic model (Machado 2002; Quintino 2004). However, in spite of several development plans and international aid the country has never emerged from a situation of severe poverty. Many Guineans migrated to Senegal and France, while Portugal rapidly became a preferential destination, mainly due to existing ties with families or friends already in the country, as well as some knowledge of the language.

In 1996, the number of people from Guinea-Bissau in Portugal, taking into account both official and illegal immigrants, was estimated at around 23,000 (Machado 2002: 86). The 1998 political crisis and armed conflict, and the subsequent worsening of social and economic conditions, increased the number of people seeking refuge. In 2005, the official data listed 25,148 Guineans, but the real figure must be much higher, since many remain undocumented and without any legal status. Portugal appears as a symbolic paradise, where one can work and send remittances back home to the families; however, many struggle, investing considerable sums, to get the much-desired visa. As a consequence, almost all families in Guinea have one or more relatives residing in Portugal, and the constant flow of people and goods back and forth is an important reality, visible in the movement of people at Lisbon airport on days of flights to and from Bissau. The airport becomes a place where people gather to meet relatives or friends and to receive goods *di tera* (from home), or to send things back, saying goodbye to those who leave, taking other 'modern' products with them.

Given the importance of the goods and materials from home, certain areas of Lisbon have been appropriated by Africans, and specifically by Guineans, as the locale for commercial exchanges. In the old, downtown part of Lisbon, a commercial centre (Mouraria) is known for its shops where one can find anything, from Indian to African food and artefacts. The same happens in a weekly street market (Feira do Relógio) and certain areas around train stations that serve the periphery of Lisbon where Guineans reside. Almost everything from Guinea-Bissau can be bought in such places—traditional cloths, artefacts, all sorts of food and medicinal products, even fresh fish and other sea products. But one of the most important sets of goods being traded has to do with the religious sphere and is constituted by all the objects, artefacts, herbs and portions of dirt from the original *tabanka* (village) necessary for these practices. Such is the case, for example, with the *mezinho*, the goat's horns used for the lucky charms that the *djambakóss* prescribes and manufactures for the patients. The downtown area of Lisbon, around the Rossio and Praça da Figueira, is also the place where everyone meets, where news circulates, and where the contractors and sub-contractors engage workers. The degree of interaction is so high that even Guineans themselves talk about this area as an extension of *tchon Pepel*, the centre of Bissau, historically the territory of the Pepel group and therefore denominated 'Pepel grounds' (*tchon Pepel*), a name it retains.[2]

Guineans in the Greater Lisbon area recreate their identity through re-elaboration of the references and codes from home and by relating them to those from the host country. They create new networks and forms of interaction, institutions, symbols and cultural practices which allow for a recreation of the past and a construction of the present. They are engaged in a permanent negotiating process, within their own community and within the encompassing Portuguese society (Quintino 2004: 26), all of which is aimed at achieving a minimal well-being in the diaspora situation.

As with any group removed from its original setting, the Guinean community in Lisbon may be regarded as an invented community, thought of as an ensemble of

Journal of Ethnic and Migration Studies   257

cultural symbols permanently reorganised and re-elaborated. Such symbols promote social cohesion, legitimate institutions, status and power relations, and act as factors of socialisation, providing the individuals with value systems, beliefs and behaviour patterns (Anderson 1991; Hobsbawm and Ranger 1983; Quintino 2004). Quintino (2004: 35) adopts the concept of 'trans-identity' as an identity forged in a permanent relation between the migrants and the host society, as well as with the original community and the desire to 'go back home one day', which is frequently uncertain or never becomes a reality, and often detonates a constant back and forth movement between the original and the host countries. The desire to go back one day counteracts the idea of paradise and is symptomatic of the *dépaisement* and feelings of non-integration that Guineans have.

Cutting across not only the different social and economic groups present in the diaspora, but also ethnic allegiance, is the *tchon* (original grounds), which Quintino (2004: 263) describes as an important territorial and ethnic reference; its symbolic construction is based on language and a common past, rooted in the social organisation of the *tabanka*, and the duties one has towards the lineage and members of the *moransa* (extended family living together in a compound). An 'ethnicity package' is thus constructed, comprising several elements that are manipulated in the highly symbolic process of relating to their origins. There is a strong associational movement of Guineans in Portugal, with over 15 legalised non-profit organisations. Many play an important role in the organisation of the rites of passage and annual festivities, constituted by overlapping of Catholic practices with animist or Muslim ones, which are also moments of reunion and intense intra-ethnic sociability (Quintino 2004: 290–7). One of the most vital functions of these associations is economic support to enable people to go back home for certain ceremonies, such as the funerary rituals.

If these elements (territory, language, skin colour, dress codes, food, music, dance) are manipulated in order to construct one's identity in relation to other Guineans and to the Portuguese, as a rule, the national origin overcomes ethnic divisions (Bordonaro and Pussetti 2006: 133), and reproduces the ethnic *mélange* and mobility that is a reality in the home country. Territory refers to the common origin in Guinean soil, expressed in Creole as *parido na Guiné* (born in Guinea) or *bibi iagu di Pidjiguiti* (someone who drunk water from the Bissau harbour). In this reference, Bissau is a central symbol, since it is the place that congregates all the different ethnic, religious and age groups. Everyone who comes to Portugal has, at some point or other, spent some time in the capital, the ultimate departure or arrival point. Nevertheless, one of the outstanding elements which aligns Guineans according to their origins is religion and the related healing and therapeutic practices.

Guinea-Bissau is a small but diversified country, with a population of approximately 1.2 million and some 23 different ethnic groups (Einarsdottir 2000). This great variety may be organised according to religious affiliation: the Islamised groups in the interior and the so-called 'animist' groups mainly around the coastal area. However, religious affiliation does not entirely follow group allegiance (Jao 1995) and

258   *C. Saraiva*

many combine traditional African religions with Christianity (both Catholic and Protestant), specially within the animist groups.

As a whole, the duality between the Islamised groups and the coastal animists holds true also in the diaspora. The case study presented in this paper, centred on the Pepel group, actually portrays the religious world of the animist groups, which include Pepel, Manjako, Bidjagós and Mancanha, and thus illustrates how religion and therapeutic practices may help to overcome distress and suffering when away from home.

Becoming a Protective Spirit

If, when in Guinea, the desire is to come to Portugal, once in Portugal the objective of many is to save enough money to go back one day, if possible in a situation that guarantees a better economic and social status. Since this may take long to achieve, certain strategies of relating to the origins, minimising the nostalgia of being away and assuring the relationship with the home grounds, are put into practice, some of them falling into the realm of the symbolic.

As elsewhere in Africa, for the Pepel religion is the pillar of the collection of norms that rule the society: there is an infinity of small spirits which are called, in Creole, *irās*, and which are scattered all over, in the houses, trees or land, and may acquire the most varied forms. The practical and everyday side of religion is the vehicle for the permanent and constant relation that the living maintain with the world of the dead. The ancestors' altars, named in Creole *testos* and *firkidjas di alma*, are placed both in the interior and exterior of the household, and, together with the different types of sanctuar, *balobas, kansarés,* are the primordial loci where the relation with the supernatural is established and where the religious specialists, *baloberos* and *djambakoses*, operate. Besides rituals performed for specific purposes, or on special occasions, the relationship with the ancestors is present in everyday life and gestures: before starting a meal, rice and drinks are poured for the ancestors (an operation called in Creole *darma,* a derivation of the Portuguese *derramar,* to pour). In the same sense, no ceremony or rite is initiated without a previous consultation of their will. The most common form of oracle to consult the schemes of the ancestors or of the *irās* is the inspection of the gonads of the rooster, which is performed after the sacrifice of the bird: if the colour is white it means that 'the path is free', that what has been done so far was done correctly and that what is planned to follow is also right.

Religious beliefs and practices are intimately related to the realm of death and the other world; hence funerals are amongst the most important ceremonies of Pepel cultural and social life. The Pepel believe that the world of the dead constitutes a replica of the world of the living, duplicating the original social structure. When someone dies their soul undertakes a voyage to the beyond, where live the deceased that have ascended to the condition of ancestors. Funerals are thus extremely important: both the first funerary ceremonies (*chur*), which entail the cleaning of the corpse and its wrapping in cloths, for days, before inhumation; and the secondary rituals (*toka chur*), signalled by the beating of the bombolom drum, the sacrifice and bleeding of animals, specific divinatory processes and wide commensality. All these rites are aimed at assuring the maintenance of a harmonic relation between the living and the dead, which is only possible if the deceased is correctly integrated in the sphere of the ancestors and, ultimately, becomes a good spirit that will watch over the living (Saraiva 1999, 2003, 2004a, 2004b).

Due to the constant and pressing relations between the two worlds, the deceased is thought of as a messenger who takes offerings for the ancestors who live in the other world, these offerings consisting basically of the cloths offered for the funeral. According to this logic, everyone attending a funeral wants to offer gifts of cloth to the dead person, not only to contribute to the success of the ceremony and for reasons of reciprocity, but also because all the households have ancestors in the other world, who would be terribly angry if they received no gifts from their descendants in this world (Saraiva 2004a, 2004b).

When the *toka chur* takes place, the sacrifice of the animals (cows, pigs, goats) is one of the most important features, together with the dancing, feasting, eating and drinking, to celebrate the entrance of an elder into the ancestral world. Hence, these two elements—cloth and cattle—are essential to understand the connection between funeral rites, the importance of the relations between the two worlds as a pillar of Pepel religion and the 'construction' of a transnational spirit. Cloth and cattle are the two main sources of wealth and prestige for the Pepel; the first is mainly feminine, the second, masculine.

Transnational Goods and Transnational Spirits: Religion in Lisbon

Looked upon in their totality, funerary rituals constitute systems of circulation of goods between the living and the dead, and contribute to the continuum between the two worlds (Saraiva 1999: 278; 2004a, 2004b): the dead do not become ancestors and protective spirits if these rites are not correctly performed.

What happens, then, with all these ritual goods and the performances they entail, once the actors move to another world, in this case a European city? If the completion of correct funerary rituals is essential for a dead person to become an ancestor, the exchange of goods between the two worlds is just as important. In Portugal, certain adaptations are made in the funeral and subsequent rituals: a funeral implies gathering and commensality but, for instance, as far as the wrapping of the corpse is concerned, some cloths are placed on the coffin, since it is not possible, according to Portuguese law, to wrap the bodies as is done in Guinea. It is estimated that one cloth in Portugal is worth 20 in Guinea. The sacrifice of animals is also restricted: the larger animals are killed in farms or houses with a garden and their meat is then brought to the place where the rituals take place, divided and consumed as usual.

Because of all these restrictions on performances with high symbolic significance, ceremonies are always considered more effective if performed in the primeval ground. This dictates that the *toka chur* should always take place in the original *tchon*, which

260   *C. Saraiva*

implies the return of the families for this specific purpose. As a result, a *defunto* (spirit of a dead person) can never reach the category of a transnational spirit unless his/her *toka chur* has been performed at home, and has conformed to the above-described sequences and ritual principles; this may therefore be considered the basis for the existence of a transnational religion.

Besides all the social performances aimed at keeping in mind the original territory and practices at home in Guinea-Bissau, the sacralisation of the new dwelling is of the utmost importance; in the case of the 'animists', the relation with the ancestors must be acknowledged through the placing of the altars for the forefathers (*testos*) and protective spirits (*irās*), as well as all the magical-religious ceremonies that go along with such emplacements, of which the *darma* (to pour beverages and food for the ancestors) is the most significant, due to its direct symbolism of the connection with the ancestors in the other world.

Only after this ceremony of the consecration of the ancestors' altars is completed can a ritual healer start his/her practice inside the house. It is in this room where the ancestors' altars are kept that the *djambakóss* (mainly female) interacts with the spirits. Due to the sacred character of this compartment, no sexual intercourse is permitted and therefore only the *djambakóss* alone, or small children, are allowed to sleep there. Normally situated in a corner of the room, the sacred grounds are protected by a red cloth, since red is the colour associated with the religious sphere. Behind this cloth are kept the *irās* (often consubstantiated in a short and bulky wooden stick) where the ancestor spirits and the spiritual forces are concentrated, and several receptacles with rum and other beverages, or with herbs and medicinal products (*mezinho*) and shells; a special gourd normally keeps water and *mezinho* to be used in the daily consultations. Attached to these *irās* are, as in the original *tabanka* grounds, the ropes that tied the animals sacrificed in the ceremonies and some strips from the cloths offered by the patients. In this room there are also specific places for the ancestors' altars, the *testos*, and no ceremony or consultation may begin without the *darma* over them.

The consultation may fall into three main categories: *djubi sorte* (consultation of the gods to know one's luck and destiny); a consultation to treat problems or sicknesses already diagnosed; or a follow-up meeting between the healer and the patient. What happens most of the time is that these three types of consultation are combined to include *djubi sorte*, some sort of treatment, and conversations between healer and patient to figure out whether more consultations or treatments should take place. A normal consultation starts with an exchange of words between the patient and the *djambakóss*, to make the client feel at ease. The payment is then put on the ground and *darma* is performed. The *djambakóss* concentrates, invokes the supernatural beings, and, in direct connection with them, throws the shells on the ground, shakes the *mezinho* to read the message given by the correct positioning of the herbs on the calabash, or simply listens to their opinion about the problems that afflict the person. These actions may be repeated several times, until the ritualist is sure how to interpret the signs and is able to announce the diagnosis to the patient.

As mentioned before, one of the performances used by the Pepel *djambakóss* is the sacrifice of a rooster (brought by the client), and the inspection of the insides of the animal. The announcement of the problems that trouble the person (or an entire family) is a crucial moment, upon which the healer prescribes the treatment.

The treatment may be simple (such as drinking a beverage given or indicated by the ritualist), or elaborate. In the latter case, the *trabadjo*—literally 'work'[3]—may then be performed by the patient, following the *djambakóss*'s instructions, or by the healer, in which case another consultation takes place The treatment often comprises libations, ceremonies at crossroads and the protection of a lucky charm, which normally has both prophylactic and healing powers. The *zimola* (donation), widely practised by the Muslims, is also employed by animists as another essential element within the domain of counter-witchcraft, acting as a warranty of the efficiency of the treatment. In the follow-up consultations the confirmation of the success of the treatment is sought, and often the same divinatory procedures that had taken place in the first session are repeated.

The Healer and the Spirit

Celeste is a Pepel woman who migrated to Portugal in the late 1980s, in the wake of her second husband. She was a widow and had four children from her first marriage; these children stayed at home in Guinea-Bissau with relatives. The three children from her second marriage were all born in Lisbon, following a pattern of families divided between Guinea-Bissau and the host country quite usual in the diaspora.

Both Celeste and her husband were employed. However, some years after her arrival she started suffering from several and continuous diseases, bad luck, and hearing voices talking to her and her husband at home. When she was diagnosed as possessed by a spirit, she returned to Biombo, in Guinea, to undergo the first set of initiation ceremonies in order to become a religious ritualist. Upon her return she quit her job in Lisbon to dedicate herself entirely to her spirits, becoming, with time, a respected and well-known *djambakóss*.

The process of becoming a fully initiated *djambakóss* entails several periods of seclusion and initiation in the original grounds. I met Celeste in Guinea-Bissau in April 2004, when she went back to Biombo to perform the second set of initiation ceremonies. She stayed there for several months in order to complete all her obligations towards the ancestral spirits and thus come to Portugal with her powers strengthened. Becoming a healer implies that the chosen person has no free will; if a spirit decides someone is to be possessed it is because he wants to work 'through' her, and the person cannot refuse such a call, at the risk of dying or having someone in her family suffer severe retaliation. This brings me to the issue of the tyranny of the spirits, which determines who is to be possessed, how, and where.

Among the spirits who possess a healer there is always a set hierarchy: some are stronger and more important than others, and their strength and importance may come from several factors, including their social and economic status while alive. The

262   *C. Saraiva*

higher the status, the stronger they may be. One other condition that can determine their status is their previous position within the realm of relations with the other world. A *djambakóss* will certainly become a powerful spirit once deceased. Another essential characteristic is that all the spirits that operate in Portugal are, by essence, transnational spirits, who come from Guinea-Bissau to possess ritual specialists and work through them to interact with Guineans in the diaspora.

Amongst the several spirits that possess Celeste, the most important and recurrent one is a male named Antonio. Celeste emphasises his condition of having been someone highly educated (in the context of Guinea-Bissau, where illiteracy prevails), who held the position of teacher (*professor*) in Bolama, the ancient capital of Guinea. The fact that he was an educated person determined his decision to become a *defunto* here in Portugal. She therefore explains that Antonio decided to possess her in Lisbon in order to popularise and spread Pepel religion and the knowledge of the *balobas* and *irãs*:

> He wants educated people, which is why he decided to come here to Portugal and not to Guinea. Antonio is a very smart and intelligent *defunto* and he knows how important these practices are and he wants them to become known and respected here in Portugal; he is also a very good person and wants to help people.

Antonio is attributed all the good qualities of a human being: he is respectable, educated and a 'good defunto': never does evil things (witchcraft), but desires only to help people. Also, he is extremely honest, and any money given to him is returned if he is not able to help. There is clearly an identification between the spirit and the healer, observable in the overlapping of the mutual discourses. The same way in which Celeste praises Antonio's honourable qualities when she talks about him, so, several times when I dialogued with Antonio himself, during times when he possessed Celeste, he also stressed her good qualities, both as a woman (hard-working, honest) and as a healer (her good relations with him and all the spirits, her will to do good, to help people and to perform all the rituals in the best possible way).

The Consultation

As I explained, people seek help from a *djambakóss* to solve all sorts of problems, such as troubles concerning health, work, family quarrels, intimate and emotional life, worries related to their children's success in school, and many problems resulting from their migrant condition, such as difficulties in obtaining official documents or work permits. At weekends it often happens that the large number of clients requires a continuous session (especially if people come from afar), in which Antonio possesses Celeste early in the morning and stays all day, as long as there are clients, normally until dawn. These consultations often incorporate the two sequences of divination and beginning of the treatment, and both the libations and the sacrifice of the animals take place.

Journal of Ethnic and Migration Studies   263

The clients arrive bringing offerings for the ancestors and the *irās*: roosters, cloths, drinks and parts of the larger, previously sacrificed animals; normally at the beginning, or half way through the session, these pieces of meat are cooked, presented as an offering to the spirit, and shared by everyone. In the middle of the living room people sit on the floor and all eat together, grabbing with their hands from the same pot, *bianda* (rice) and *máfé* (the meat or fish that accompany the rice). However, no one starts eating before the beverages and some rice are spilled on the ground, as an offering to the ancestors. Commensality, so important in any ceremony at home, helps in recreating the setting and the proper atmosphere for the follow-up rituals.

In the room where the consultations take place a cassette player continuously reproduces the sound of the ritual drums and traditional songs from Guinea. The setting is prepared with the *darmar* of beverages (all sorts of beverages are accepted, from soft drinks to schnapps, wine or beer) on the altar of the family ancestors (*testos*) and on the *irā*. Following this veneration of the ancestors, the healer, dressed in traditional *djambakóss* attire, with a predominance of white and red, specially on the cloths wrapped around her head, then sits still by the *irā* altar and awaits the coming of the spirit.

A normal consultation follows the pattern explained previously. After another set of *darma*, it begins with the presentation to the spirit of the goods brought as gifts, the beverages, cloths and the roosters for sacrifice. After payment, the client, barefoot (as in the sacred grounds in Guinea-Bissau) explains his/her problem and a dialogue is established between them and Antonio in order to clarify what the complaints are and the reasons that bring the person to ask for help. If the client can read and write, he or she is asked to write down his/her problems and secret wishes on a piece of paper, which is then sprinkled with rum and placed on the altar to remain there until the next consultation. Of the several *djambakósses* I observed, Celeste is the only one who places great importance on the writing on the paper, undoubtedly due to the specific condition of Antonio having been a professor, a fact which Celeste emphasises in every single consultation. His intellectual skills and higher social status are also the warranty of his capacities, goodness and good intentions.

Then follows, normally, the sacrifice of the rooster; the bigger ones are decapitated with the aid of a knife, the smaller ones simply with the hands. Its blood is poured over the *testos* and the *irā*. Immediately afterwards, its insides are opened and inspected. In one of the consultations I attended, the organs inspected were all white in colour, except the area corresponding to the journey that the client was about to undertake to Paris. Here, the intestines presented a dark colour, which was interpreted as a sign not to start the trip.

Upon interpretation of all these signs, the *defunto* prescribes the recipe. Commonly known in Creole as *trabadjo*, it consists of the treatment against witchcraft or maledictions. It thus congregates the forces of both good and evil, and it is crucial to clarify the use made of these forces. As a therapy system, *trabadjo* includes the *mezinho* and magical prophylactic charms, the sacrifice of animals, techniques of recuperation and recession of the sorcery and the periodic communication between the ritualist and the supernatural (Quintino 2004: 281). The *trabadjo* may include one or several actions. The performance of these actions, preferably done at a crossroads, may encompass different variations, for instance, wrapping a cloth around a piece of iron or rolling it in ashes and throwing it over one's head in order to recover from and undo the spell (Quintino 2004: 282).

In one of the cases I followed closely, the patient, a young man brought to Celeste by his brother, was bewitched by a *badjuda* (young girl) who made him fall in love with her, but did not respect him and was known to fool around with other men. Despite his knowledge of her bad conduct, he was not able to leave her, since he was *amarrado* (tied). The treatment prescribed included placing a kilogram of salt, an egg and a candle at a crossroads so as to drive away the *badjuda* he was in love with, but who, it was proven, did not love him, and was therefore not suitable to be a good future spouse or someone in whom he should invest.

Often the treatment starts right away, performed with the assistance of the spirit itself, and includes specific libations (with water and salt or water with specific plants), long talks with the patient, the making and consecration of lucky charms and other practices. Much attention is paid to the elements brought to the healer to be handled, in order to transform them into protective lucky charms. The goods used in the consultation must be, for the most part, *di tera*, from Guinea-Bissau, although adaptations are made in cases where it is impossible to have goods from home; for instance, an African herb may be substituted with a Portuguese one.

But the identification of the source of trouble often results in the conclusion that it is caused by a spirit that is interfering and causing bad things to happen, in order to remind the living of their obligations towards him; for instance, an ancestor of the same lineage whose *toka chur* has not yet been performed and who thus demands its performance in *tchon* Pepel. As a result, and as a resolution to the problems that afflict the person, many are advised to go back home and perform the rituals. The preponderance of such diagnoses brings me back to the funeral rites and their importance in mediating communication between the two worlds.

In the final part of the consultation, the cloths brought by the clients come into play, when they are offered to the *defunto*, in a ceremony crucial to the success of the treatment. The patients kneel down, holding the cloth over their heads and simulate a fight with the spirit, who tries to pull the cloth and take it from them, while they repeat 'It's mine! It's mine!'. Only at the third attempt are they supposed to let go. The meaning of this performance is that the spirit tries to take the bad things away from the person, but that he/she should hold on to it until the third time, when the spirit finally succeeds and the evil is left there, upon the *irā*, freeing the person from all badness. The cloths used may be either common European ones, such as table cloths, towels or sheets, or African, including both *panos di penti*, traditional cloths woven on the loom or *legosse,* or industrial cloths with multiple and colourful motifs. The colour and type of cloth that should be used, which influences the treatment, are indicated by the spirit.

The cloths offered are put in Antonio's *mala* (trunk). When ceremonies happen back home (whether for funerals or for initiation) and Celeste attends them, she is supposed to take the cloths indicated by Antonio, and they therefore become his contribution to such performances. If the essential condition for a deceased to become a protective spirit is the fulfilment of his/her funerary rituals, once he/she becomes a spirit he/she must also contribute to enlarge the community of spirits in the other world, and ensure this by contributing cloths for the rituals. Wrapped around a dead person's body, the cloths offered to this *defunto* in Lisbon become offerings to the lineage members in the other world: they thus return back home and back to the world of the ancestors.

Two Worlds Meet: The Living and the Dead in a Transnational Setting

Through the desire and need of Guineans to maintain contact with their spirit world, an intense communication and exchange of goods, both material and symbolic, as well as persons and ideas, is maintained between Guinea-Bissau and Portugal.

Performances, settings and material goods are transferred from Africa to Lisbon: the altars for the ancestors are recreated in apartments in Lisbon, where the ritualists operate. The *irã* altar is constructed using wood brought from the original *tchon*, and the goods that are used in the protective or healing practices are ideally supposed to come from Guinea. As much as possible, both the ritualist and the clients repeat the gestures and performances from home which are used to recreate an ethnic identity: the drums heard in the cassette player, the *darmar* of beverages offered to the *irã*, the taking off of shoes when in the grounds of the *irã*, the shared commensality, the divination using the roosters. At the same time, symbolic transactions take place: the blood of the sacrificed animals and the beverages and food poured for the ancestors are meant to reach the other world, and cross not only the spatial distance between Europe and Africa, but the division between the world of the living and the one of the dead.

Furthermore, there is an intense circulation of both persons and spirits: the healer goes back to the original grounds periodically to reinforce her powers; the clients go back to their villages to perform *toka chur* for their beloved ones. Goods also circulate with them: not only monetary, materially expressed through the money spent on the airline ticket and on the cost of the ceremonies, but also other kinds of goods. Because of their importance as primordial offerings to the ancestors, cloths are excellent mediators between the two worlds. The traditional hand-woven cloths, required by the spirit to be used in specific healing rituals, are brought from Guinea; but European cloths (such as silky sheets) are greatly appreciated and taken by Guineans who go back home for *toka chur* ceremonies. These elements are manipulated by both persons and spirits in order to adapt to a transnational setting, where one needs to accommodate the communication and circulation between the two real worlds of Africa and Europe, along with the two worlds of the living and the dead.

In concrete terms, Guineans in Lisbon organise themselves so as to be able to realise the luxury of maintaining transnational religious networks: the role of the associations is to economically help people when they need to go back home; the traffic of goods provides what is needed for the ceremonies or the good-luck charms. Participating and contributing to the *toka chur* of one's father is important to maintain one's position within the *tabanka* and *moransa*, as everyone back home expects relatives who migrated to be better-off and to contribute generously for the ceremonies; but it also essential to guarantee that one will be protected and helped by the ancestors, especially in the harsh and foreign environment of the diaspora context, where the use of the specific *mézinho* with herbs from home or the right offerings to the *irã* may make the difference in finding a good job or making sure one gets the residence permit.

As stated previously, for the Pepel, the world of the dead is a duplication of the world of the living. The *defunto* Antonio is a good example of this conceptualisation. Antonio came from Guinea, and claims to be a scholar. The fact that he was a professor in Bolama wins him prestige. He was not a poor person; as a spirit, he owns his private *mala* (literally, a trunk or suitcase, but generally meaning the collection of a person's valuable goods, such as cloths, gold and money, often kept in a trunk or box) and holds a high social and economic status. He is willing to help everyone and wants to spread the Pepel religion in Europe, where he says people are also educated and willing to learn, in order to bring them to an understanding of Pepel traditional ways as culturally valuable. With respect to the situation of Guineans resident in Portugal, he also explains that it is understandable that people seek other religions more widespread in Lisbon (referring to the Evangelical churches which attract many Africans), but that one should only frequent churches that allow one to continue with the *uso*, the traditional Pepel ways, beliefs and religious practices. In this way, the spirit enacts the 'ethnicity package' created by the Guinean community (Quintino 2004: 263): together with the emphasis on *uso*, there comes also, for instance, his use of the original languages, either Pepel or Creole, whenever he talks during the consultations. But, aware of the difficulties imposed by the diaspora situation, it also opens up to syncretism, as a strategy for people to achieve a minimum level of well-being.

The female ritualist manipulates these elements, such as Antonio's erudition and his awareness of the need to recreate Pepel traditions in a transnational setting, to construct a positive image of her religious practices and enforce her authority and prestige among her Guinean patients; but she is also fully aware that they help her to gain a larger and more diversified clientele. Although her clients are all Africans or of African origin, one of her objectives is to have Portuguese patients, an excellent way to feel more at ease and integrated. An episode illustrating such a strategy is the way in which she insists on accompanying me, as a white Portuguese visitor, to the door, making it very visible to her ground-floor Portuguese neighbour that she has Portuguese friends.

The intense relationship and dependence of the living upon the dead is also transposed to the relations established between the healers and the spirits who possess them, as a correlate of the aforementioned tyranny of the spirits. For instance, for the time being, Antonio operates only with an *irã*, which Celeste keeps in the altar in her Lisbon apartment. But she continuously repeats that she is aware that, if by chance Antonio decides to settle in a *baloba*, since such sanctuary can only exist in the original grounds, in *tchon Pepel*, she will be obliged to go back to Biombo to live. This is one of the reasons she is so grateful that Antonio has decided that he wants the *uso da tera* to be known in Portugal, allowing her to stay in Lisbon with her husband and children.

If the migrant's perception of the diaspora universe oscillates between an image of paradise and nostalgia, and a desire to go back, the world of the spirits somehow accompanies these contradictory and ambiguous relations, creating bridges that connect real and symbolic spaces, but simultaneously making people aware of their double condition, of someone who can no longer stay in Guinea, but dreams of going back one day. In a certain sense, the idea that 'diasporas always leave a trail of collective memory about another place and time and create new maps of desire and of attachment' (Appadurai and Breckenridge 1989: i, cited in Vertovec 1999: 451) holds true in this case, not only for the individuals, but also for all the desires and hopes they project onto the world of the spirits that accompanied them in the journey to a new land and cultural context.

Conclusion

We thus have a truly transnational religious system where spirits, people and goods circulate in two parallel sets of worlds: the physical, real worlds of the two contexts, the home country and the host country, and the two conceptualised universes of the living and of the ancestors. The characteristics of the elements in circulation adapt to the transnational circumstances in a more or in a less flexible way, depending on the circumstances and including the necessary adaptations, and show how religion and religious practices are examples of the idea of a processual ethnicity, more visible in the flexible frontiers of daily life, where identities are constantly re-negotiated and renewed (Barth 1969). Religion may, then, in fact, be a cultural dimension which better helps migrants re-organise sociabilities and identities that refer to the past in order to re-structure their lives in a new setting (Horowitz 1985; Quintino 2004; Wilson 1983).

Taken together, the basic elements of the religious system circulate between the two real worlds of Portugal and Guinea-Bissau and the two symbolic worlds of the living and of the dead. Antonio is a *defunto* who came from Guinea to work in Lisbon and help his fellow-countryfolk, and will eventually one day return home to settle in a *baloba*. Celeste is a ritualist who came from Guinea, where she returns periodically for ceremonies related to her capacity to communicate with the spirits, and who will also, if such will be the wish of her *defunto*, return to Biombo, to go on serving the spirit in

268   *C. Saraiva*

his *baloba*. In the meanwhile, they interact in Lisbon, in ways that bring Guinean practices and Pepel ancestors into play in a globalised urban world.

Acknowledgements

I wish to thank Ralph Grillo and Valentina Mazzucato for patiently reading and commenting on previous versions of this paper.

Notes

[1]   Fieldwork has been carried out since 1997 in the Biombo region, based on periodic stays of several months a year; the research in Lisbon started with contacts, previously acquired in Guinea-Bissau, of families and ritual specialists in the diaspora, and has included, in this case study, participation in the *djambakóss's* consultations as well as extended interviews with her, the spirit and the clients.

[2]   The Pepel were the owners of the grounds where the Portuguese founded, already in the seventeenth century, a fortress, and where the Portuguese were defeated by the Pepel in 1891; much later, in the twentieth century, Bissau became the capital of the colony, and this area, along with the connected Biombo region, remains to this date known as Pepel territory.

[3]   As Celeste Quintino (2004: 281) points out, the term *trabadjo* means both witchcraft to cause trouble to someone, and the treatment to overcome the spell.

References

Anderson, B. (1991) *Imagined Communities: Reflections on the Origin and Spread of Nationalism.* London: Verso.

Appadurai, A. and Breckenridge, C. (1989) 'On moving targets', *Public Culture*, 2(1): i–iv.

Ariés, P. (1989) *Sobre a História da Morte no Ocidente desde a Idade Média.* Lisbon: Teorema.

Barreto, A. (ed.) (1995) *Globalização e migrações.* Lisbon: Instituto de Ciências Sociais (ICS).

Barth, F. (ed.) (1969) *Ethnic Groups and Boundaries. The Social Organization of Culture Difference.* Oslo: Universitetforlaget.

Bastos, J. (2000) *Portugal Europeu. Estratégias Identitárias Inter-Nacionais dos Portugueses.* Oeiras: Celta.

Bastos, J. and Bastos, S. (1999) *Portugal Multicultural. Situação e Identificação das Minorias Etnicas.* Lisbon: Fim de Século.

Baudry, P. (1999) *La Place des Morts. Enjeux et Rites.* Paris: Armand Colin.

Bloch, M. and Parry, J. (eds) (1982) *Death and the Regeneration of Life.* Cambridge: Cambridge University Press.

Bordonaro, L. and Pussetti, C. (2006) 'Da utopia da migração à nostalgia dos migrantes: percursos migratórios entre Bubaque (Guiné-Bissau) e Lisboa', in Lima, A. and Sarró, R. (eds) *Terrenos Metropolitanos. Ensaios sobre produção etnográfica.* Lisbon: Imprensa de Ciências Sociais, 125–53.

Capone, S. (ed.) (2004) *Religions Transnationales.* Brussels: Universite libre de Bruxelles, Institut de Sociologie.

de Coppet, D. (1992) *Understanding Rituals.* London: Routledge.

Déchaux, J.H. (2001) 'Un nouvel âge du mourir: la mort en soi', *Recherches Sociologiques*, 32(2): 79–100.

Einarsdottir, J. (2000) *'We are Tired of Crying'. Child Death and Mourning among the Pepel of Guinea-Bissau.* Stockholm: Stockholm University.

Garcia, J. (2000a) *Portugal Migrante. Emigrantes e Emigrados. Dois estudos introdutórios.* Oeiras: Celta.

Garcia, J. (2000b) *Migrações e Relações Internacionais. Uma Bibliografia.* Oeiras: Celta.

Garcia, J. (2000c) *Estranhos. Juventude e Dinamicas de Exclusao Social em Lisboa.* Oeiras: Celta.

Gusmão, N. (2004) *Os Filhos de Africa em Portugal. Multiculturalismo e Educação.* Lisbon: Instituto de Ciências Sociais.

Hertz, R. (1960) *Death and the Right Hand.* Glencoe: The Free Press.

Hobsbawm, E. and Ranger, T. (eds) (1983) *The Reinvention of Tradition.* Cambridge: Cambridge University Press.

Horowitz, D. (1985) *Ethnic Groups in Conflict.* Berkeley: University of California Press.

Jao, M. (1995) 'A questão da etnicidade e a origem étnica dos Mancanhas', *Soronda. Revista de Estudos Guineenses, 20*: 19–31.

Koser, K. (ed.) (2003) *New African Diasporas.* London: Routledge.

Machado, F. (2002) *Contrastes e Continuidades. Migração, Etnicidade e Integração dos Guineenses em Portugal.* Oeiras: Celta.

Metcalf, P. and Huntington, R. (1991) *Celebrations of Death. The Anthropology of Mortuary Ritual.* Cambridge: Cambridge University Press.

Pina-Cabral, J. (1984) 'A morte na Antropologia Social', *Analise Social, 20*(2–3): 349–56.

Pires, R. (2003) *Migrações e Integração.* Oeiras: Celta.

Quintino, C. (2004) *Migrações e Etnicidade em Terrenos Portugueses. Guineenses: Estratégias de Invenção de uma Comunidade.* Lisbon: Universidade Técnica de Lisboa–Instituto Superior de Ciências Sociais e Politicas.

Saint-Maurice, A. (1997) *Identidades Reconstruídas. Cabo-Verdianos em Portugal.* Oeiras: Celta.

Saraiva, C. (1999) *Rios de Guiné do Cabo Verde. Rituais Funerarios entre Portugal e Africa. Uma Etnografia da Morte em Cabo Verde e nos Papéis da Guiné-Bissau.* Lisbon: Instituto de Investigacao Cientifica Tropical.

Saraiva, C. (2003) 'Rituais funerários entre os Papeis da Guiné-Bissau (Parte I)', *Soronda, Revista de Estudos Guineenses, 6*: 179–210.

Saraiva, C. (2004a) 'Rituais funerários entre os Papeis da Guiné-Bissau (Parte II)', *Soronda. Revista de Estudos Guineenses, 8*: 109–133.

Saraiva, C. (2004b) 'Embalming, sprinkling and wrapping bodies: death ways in America, Portugal and Guinea-Bissau', *Symposia. Journal for Studies in Ethnology and Anthropology,* 97–119.

Thomas, L.-V. (1985) *Rites de Mort. Pour la Paix des Vivants.* Paris: Fayard.

Vala, J. (ed.) (1999) *Novos racismos. Perspectivas comparativas.* Oeiras: Celta.

Vertovec, S. (1999) 'Conceiving and researching transnationalism', *Ethnic and Racial Studies, 22*(2): 447–62.

Wilson, B. (1983) 'Sympathetic detachment and disinterested involvement', *Sociological Analysis, 44*(3): 183–7.

[26]

Journal of Refugee Studies Vol. 20, No. 3 © The Author [2007]. Published by Oxford University Press.
All rights reserved. For Permissions, please email: journals.permissions@oxfordjournals.org
doi:10.1093/jrs/fem003

Living in Religious Time and Space: Iraqi Refugees in Dearborn, Michigan

MARWA SHOEB[1]
HARVEY M. WEINSTEIN[2]
JODI HALPERN[3]

[1]Joint Medical Program, University of California, Berkeley/San Francisco
marwa.shoeb@ucsf.edu
[2]Human Rights Center and School of Public Health, University of California, Berkeley
[3]Joint Medical Program and School of Public Health, University of California, Berkeley

Mental health assessments of refugees during and after conflict have relied heavily on Western psychiatric constructs and standardized scales, despite the overwhelmingly non-Western backgrounds of most survivors of contemporary wars. A strict dependence on the paradigms and language of Western psychiatry risks inappropriately prioritizing syndromes, such as post-traumatic stress disorder, which, however important, are eclipsed by the concerns of local populations for whom indigenous idioms of distress may be more salient. Working in Dearborn, Michigan, home to the largest population of Iraqi refugees in the United States, 60 Iraqi refugee life stories were collected and analysed. These narratives provided rich data regarding the centrality of faith to the constructs of Iraqi identity, home, and future in the wake of political violence and exile. For these refugees, the description of the dislocation that results from uprooting is replaced by an alternative home that transcends time and space.

Keywords: Post-traumatic Stress Disorder (PTSD), mental health assessments, Harvard Trauma Questionnaire, Iraqi refugees in US, Islam

> Oh homeland of the innocent
> Were you for us a graveyard?
> Or a homeland?
> —Iraqi poet in exile, Abd Al-Latif Ataymish (March 2004)

Rape, torture, and extrajudicial executions of family members are some of the traumas experienced by survivors of mass violence in their countries of origin; frequently these horrific experiences are followed by harrowing escapes, years of arduous existence in refugee camps, and perhaps exile. Edward Said describes exile as the 'unhealable rift forced between a human being and

442   *Marwa Shoeb, Harvey M. Weinstein and Jodi Halpern*

a native place, between the self and its true home' (2000: 357). As such, exile precipitates a 'condition of terminal loss' caused by a 'discontinuous state of being' (2000: 360).

To capture the trauma of refugees who have resettled in the West, clinicians have shifted from the traditional open-ended psychiatric interview to structured clinical interviews and shorter standardized symptom checklists for post-traumatic stress disorder (PTSD), reportedly the most prevalent diagnosis among survivors of mass violence (Wilson and Keane 2004). These measures can specify the current acuteness of a disorder, track response to treatment, and communicate assessment results efficiently. However, by transforming the local distress idioms of survivors into the universal professional language of health complaints, the scales situate trauma in individual bodies rather than social happenings, emphasizing pathology rather than such meaningful events as cultural, especially religious, dislocations. Although the PTSD diagnosis critique has received considerable discussion in the social sciences literature (de Jong and Joop 2005; Breslau 2005), it remains the most common clinical framework in thinking about the well-being of refugees in the United States and among most of the non-governmental organizations working internationally.

In collaboration with the Harvard Program in Refugee Trauma, we developed the Iraqi version of the Harvard Trauma Questionnaire (HTQ), a scale that measures trauma events and symptoms in war-affected populations.[1] Despite the fact that religion sustains many refugees in their process of uprooting, forced migration, and integration into the host country, spiritual precepts are conspicuously absent in questionnaires and, in turn, from relief work (Gozdziak 2002). Psychological treatment models rarely incorporate any spiritual dimension. Further, although refugee services in the United States include assistance with housing, employment, and healthcare, the paradigm of support focuses on deficits and not on resiliency factors. We wished to address this gap in our understanding of the contribution that religious faith can bring to refugee survival.

This absence is especially striking when meeting the needs of recent refugees from the Middle East. The movement of people from this part of the world has been associated throughout history with interrelated issues of politics, land, and war. The geopolitical and economic aspects of these displacements are well analysed in the literature of the region (Black and Robinson 1993; Castles 1993; Shami 1996). However, studies dealing with the lived experiences of Middle Eastern refugees who resettle in the West are few. Some of these reports include Aswad's (1980; Aswad and Bilgé 1996) ethnic case studies of Arabic-speaking communities in the United States and Shadid's (1991) study of the difficult integration of Muslim minorities in the Netherlands.

With the concentrated media coverage following the 2003 US-led invasion of Iraq, the Iraqi refugee community in Dearborn, Michigan, became visible. However, there has been little in-depth examination of this community despite the fact that it is the largest of its kind in North America. In this paper, we present a qualitative study of 60 Iraqi refugees resettled in Dearborn, Michigan, and illustrate how religion permeates their lives, including their core notions of identity, home, and future. We argue that a strict reliance on traditional psychiatric diagnoses and questionnaires over-looks the role faith plays in restoring self-definition to Muslim survivors. By using 'traditional psychiatric diagnoses' as a frame in this paper, we hope to influence health professionals to think far more broadly.

Context and Background

According to Weil, 'To be rooted is perhaps the most important and least recognized need of the human soul' (2001: 41). Over the past three decades, anthropologists increasingly have become engaged in ethnographic studies of forced displacement (Colson 2003). Much of their work has attempted to describe the broader psychosocial and religious matters that various refugee groups confront in their countries of resettlement. A theme that emerges frequently in such studies is the myth of return.

The myth of return is an expression of exiles' yearning to be anchored. This construct has two main functions. First, it reinforces the kinship boundaries of the community and its links with the homeland (Al-Rasheed 1994; Dahya 1973). Second, it enables the migrant to manage the pain of failing to integrate into the host society (Al-Rasheed 1994; Dahya 1973). The myth is therefore a practical solution to the dilemma of falling between the cracks of two worlds, including two sets of norms. This is especially necessary when the customs of the two worlds are in conflict. Also, when a person cannot place his or her trust either in the present or in the future, an essentialized but lost culture is summoned to compensate for the absence.

However, it is a mistake to assume that the experience of becoming a refugee is necessarily felt as losing one's culture. While some refugees will devote their exile to recreating the home they have left behind, others will commit themselves to constructing a niche in their new country of asylum (Zetter 1999). The latter accept the need for transition and place greater emphasis on the integration of past values in their present and future lives by investing, for example, in their children's education. They hope for a return but do not believe in its eventuality (Zetter 1999).

Although the above explanations are useful in conveying the different ways in which refugees react to their displacement, they fail to explain why the myth of return varies between individuals. Al-Rasheed (1994), inspired by Kunz's (1981) classification of refugees according to the nature of their identification with their country of origin, argues that the development of the myth of return depends on the refugees' relationship with their homeland prior to flight and on their degree of marginality in regard to the society they have left behind. She illustrates her point by considering two refugee groups: Iraqi Arabs and Iraqi Assyrians. The first belong to the mainstream

444   *Marwa Shoeb, Harvey M. Weinstein and Jodi Halpern*

population of Iraq, whereas the second are a Christian minority in Iraq. Al-Rasheed (1994) demonstrates that Iraqi Arab refugees, even after numerous years in exile, consider Iraq as their homeland and have every intention of returning once the desired political changes take place. In contrast, the Iraqi Assyrian refugees have severed all contacts with Iraq since their flight. Although many would like to visit Iraq, they see their exile as permanent. The same dichotomy can be found in Graham and Khosravi's (1997) description of refugees who settled in Sweden, more particularly the Armenians and Baha'is from Iran on one hand and the Iranian political refugees on the other.

Thus, exile can serve to bring together refugees' disjointed identities through their opposition to the host society's culture. The reaffirmation of refugees' identity allows them to hold fast to their past through an act of remembering and nostalgia, thereby giving constancy to their current life in exile. However, exile also has the reverse effect of preventing refugees from developing new roots, since they see full integration in the host country as letting go of the past. Consequently, the refugees find themselves 'caught between two worlds' (DeSantis 2001): the world of survival, which requires an orientation to the present, and the world of return, which results in an ambiguous orientation to almost any place of residence other than the homeland.

One of the ways refugees address the dilemma of being caught between two worlds is by turning to religion. Indeed, faith can serve as a source of emotional support, a form of social expression and political mobilization, and a vehicle for community building and group identity (De Voe 2002; Gozdziak and Shandy 2002; Welaratna 1993). Further, the role of religion in coping with trauma becomes particularly significant in the debate between Western models of trauma and indigenous approaches to human suffering, which include spiritual beliefs and practices (Gozdziak 2002). Studies have found that frequent religious involvement and greater intensity of religious experience may be associated with better health due to religion's promotion of social support, a sense of belonging, and convivial fellowship (Levin 1994). However, researchers have tended to neglect the diversity of spiritual beliefs that sustain many refugees in the processes of displacement, migration, and integration into the host society (Gozdziak and Shandy 2002).

Religion plays an especially important role in the life of Muslim refugees, who understand their faith as a way of life embracing both the external and the internal world of its believers. McMichael (2002), drawing on research with Somali refugee women living in Australia, describes the ways Islam provides an enduring home that is carried throughout displacement and resettlement. Gozdziak (2002) also illustrates how Islam offered a sustaining thread in the lives of Kosovar Albanians and helped them to overcome the threat of discontinuity that arises with displacement.

In this study, we show the importance of Islamic faith for Iraqi refugees. We argue that responses to their trauma should be explained not only in terms of a universalistic human psychology, but also through a particular Islamic lens and cultural heritage. This background serves as a source of general, yet distinctive, conceptions of the world, the self, and the relations between them and gives meaningful form to a wide range of experiences—intellectual, emotional, and moral—for both individuals and groups (Geertz 2000).

Methodology

Field Site

The study was conducted in metropolitan Detroit, Michigan, where approximately 200,000 people of Arab descent live in and around the city; it is home to the oldest, largest, and most visible population of Arabs in North America (Baker *et al.* 2004). Seventy-five per cent of residents were born outside the United States. Virtually all nationalities and ethnicities from the Middle East are represented: Lebanon/Syria (37 per cent), Iraq (35 per cent), Palestine/Jordan (12 per cent), and Yemen (9 per cent). This population is deeply religious, with 58 per cent Christian and 42 per cent Muslim. Most Christians are dispersed throughout Detroit's suburbs, while two thirds of all Muslims live in the ethnic enclave community of Dearborn, Michigan, often dubbed 'Arab Detroit'. Compared to Arabs nationwide, the Arabs of Dearborn are more likely to be young Muslim immigrants, with large families and low incomes. For example, one fourth of the population reports family incomes less than $20,000 per year. Fifteen per cent said they personally have had a bad experience after September 11 2001, because of their ethnicity. These experiences included verbal insults, workplace discrimination, special targeting by law enforcement, vandalism, and physical assault (Baker *et al.* 2004).

Since the 1991 Gulf War, metropolitan Detroit has absorbed over 3,000 Iraqis a year (Abraham and Shryock 2000). They have arrived directly from Iraq or via a third country, such as Iran, Turkey, Jordan, Syria, Lebanon, and the United Arab Emirates. Although the Iraqis seeking refuge in the United States come from a cross-section of Iraqi society, most are Southern Shi'a Muslims who fled under conditions of political duress. Thus, their lives have been disrupted in significant ways. These men and their wives tend to be poorly educated; they struggle with the English language; work in low-wage, informal sector jobs without health insurance; and reside in crowded apartments. These refugees live with feelings of remorse and reactions to trauma, not only about the conditions under which they fled their country, but also about their country's political turmoil and their own experience as a refugee. Many of these Iraqis suffer from chronic illnesses that may be a result of the deplorable conditions in Rafha, the Saudi Arabian refugee camp where the majority lived for months or years. The Turkmen and Kurdish

446   *Marwa Shoeb, Harvey M. Weinstein and Jodi Halpern*

refugees, who were mainly based in Northern Iraq, fled to refugee camps in Turkey.

The Iraqi community in metropolitan Detroit is not a cohesive unit. In addition to the divisions resulting from class, education, economic status, political convictions, and ideological beliefs, Iraqis are divided along lines of ethnicity. Three subcommunities live in the area: the Arabs, the Kurds, and the Chaldeans. Each has its own community centre, voluntary associations, and clubs. Upon arrival in Detroit, refugees are drawn toward their own ethnic group and voluntary associations.

Sample

For this study, we recruited a convenience sample of interviewees from the Arab Community Center for Economic and Social Services (ACCESS) in Dearborn. Since its creation 30 years ago, ACCESS has grown to become the nation's largest and most comprehensive provider of Arab American human services, with nearly 108,000 yearly contacts in 70 different programmes as diverse as employment and environmental projects, arts and culture, health programmes, and youth and social services activities.

We used the following inclusion criteria in this study: (a) Iraqi-born, (b) Arabic speaker, (c) adult (age 21 and above), and (d) a refugee in the United States after the 1991 Gulf War. Thirty men and 30 women from various socio-economic backgrounds, representing the ethnic and religious diversity of Iraq, participated in the study (see Table 1).

Although the majority of participants were Shi'a Arabs, all Iraqi Muslims interviewed shared many values, customs, and norms of behaviour. Further, in spite of differences in religious beliefs and rituals, there were no clear cultural boundaries between Iraqi Christians and Muslims. Finally, at the level of the refugee experience, all Iraqis suffer from the well-documented problems relating to pre-existing human rights violations, flight, displacement, and uprooting.

Ethnographic Interviews

Health professionals can refine their understanding of psychological disturbance in refugees if they recognize both the personal and the cultural dimensions to the physical, mental, and moral losses survivors are trying to absorb (Kleinman *et al.* 1997). This anthropological view shows suffering as both an intersubjective process and a collective experience shaped by background, place, and time. These two kinds of suffering are best elaborated through life stories. Given its situational constructed nature, a life story is a strategy for self-representation, an attempt to make sense of the world, and a projection for the future (Geertz 2000).

Drawing on the above anthropological framework, we conducted 60 interviews on individual life stories in Arabic. The decision to conduct the meetings in Arabic rather than Kurdish or Turkman—the other two Iraqi

Table 1

Sociodemographic Characteristics

Variable	Number (n = 60)
Sex	
Male	30
Female	30
Age, years	
18–34	17
35–54	30
55–64	7
≥65	6
Ethnicity	
Arab	42
Kurdish	6
Turkman	6
Chaldean	6
Religion	
Shi'a Muslim	48
Sunni Muslim	6
Christian	6
Place of birth in Iraq	
Arbil	3
Baghdad	10
Basra	9
Diwania	4
Kerbala	6
Kirkuk	7
Mosul	3
AnNajaf	5
Nasiriyah	4
Samawa	6
Sulaymaniyah	3
Marital status	
Married	43
Separated/Divorced	5
Widowed	9
Never Married	3
Education	
Less than primary	7
Primary	21
Secondary	9
Vocational/University	20
Imprisonment in Iraq[1]	
Yes	35
No	25

(continued)

Table 1

Continued

Variable	Number (n = 60)
Year of flight from Iraq	
1990–1995	43
1996–2001	14
2002–2003	3
Employment status[2]	
Working	24
Not working	36

[1]Only 8 women were imprisoned.
[2]Thirty out of the 36 subjects not working are women.

languages—was based on the fact that Arabic is the primary language in Iraq and is understood by the majority of citizens.

In the interviews, we encouraged participants to provide a chronological account of their experience of life in Iraq, the decision to escape, the circumstances of their flight, the escape journey and transition in refugee camps, conditions surrounding their acceptance for resettlement by the United States, their early experiences in America, and the nature of their current social participation within the Iraqi community and the wider host community. As they described each stage of their life, we asked respondents also to express their emotional reactions to what was happening in their lives at that time. This included their feelings about living in and then leaving Iraq, their hopes and expectations of eventual return, and their degree of satisfaction with life in the United States.

To reconstruct their narratives, Iraqis needed not only the words with which to tell their stories but also an audience willing to hear their words as they intended them. Research shows the importance of open-ended interviews, emotional attunement, and genuine curiosity (Langewitz *et al.* 2002; Suchman *et al.* 1997). These characteristics comprise the kind of empathy that is crucial to such interviews. Thus, the interviewer's goal is to become an empathic listener by conveying to interviewees that they are not alone and are being understood. To be empathic, listeners must strive to see the world from the other's perspective, be strong enough to hear without injury, and be ready to experience some of the terror, grief, and rage experienced by the interviewees (Halpern and Weinstein 2004; Kleinman *et al.* 1997; Langer 1991; Shay 1994).

At the choice of the participants, the interviews were held in their homes, in ACCESS, in recreation centres, or in mosques. The conversations lasted approximately one hour and were conducted over a three-week period in July 2004. All meetings were audio tape-recorded. Informed consent forms, which fully described the research, put informants at ease once they realized that the discussions were private and confidential. Further, since this community harbours deep mistrust of authorities, we offered every assurance to ensure the ultimate anonymity of the interviews. Strong support by community leaders enhanced the project's success.

We transcribed the interviews in Arabic. The Arabic transcripts constituted material for qualitative analysis using a grounded theory methodology (Miles 1984; Rubin 2005). This involved a coding procedure with three levels. The first level, the text-based category, codes words and phrases used regularly and repeatedly throughout the text. The second level, the sensitizing concept, codes culturally specific ideas and understandings implicit in the text-based categories. The third and highest level, the theoretical construct, reflects the organization of the sensitizing concepts into a theoretical framework. Each level subsumes the level below it. That is, each sensitizing concept is a cluster of text-based categories, and each theoretical construct is a cluster of sensitizing concepts. An Iraqi doctor and one of the authors (MS) coded the transcripts. As an additional check on our interpretation of the text, we presented our findings to 10 of the 60 men and women who participated in the study. The discussion occurred approximately 7 months after data collection. The subjects confirmed the accuracy of the report.

Findings

The Struggle to Define Identity

A male Muslim definition of 'refugee'. For exiles, membership and participation in their homeland is impossible. Consequently, they must redefine their social self within a new context. For Iraqi refugees in Dearborn, resettlement provided a medium through which the memory of the shared experience of uprooting was reworked to create new forms of identity based on a higher order justification.

Recognition of the enforced, and ascribed, position of 'refugee' was neither sought after nor desired by the men interviewed: 'Saddam exported our guns, not our culture.... The world viewed us as terrorists; then as victims. We are neither' (Shi'a Muslim Arab man 29 years old).

Instead, many described themselves as *Muhajirin* ('those who leave their homes in the cause of Allah'; singular, *Muhajir*), conferring a noble aura to the Iraqi plight. According to Shahrani (cited in Daniel and Knudsen 1995), who noted the same self-definition among Afghani refugees in Pakistan, the Prophet Mohammad's *hijrah*—'the migration from the Domain of Disbelief to the Domain of Faith', only to return to establish the Faith—serves as a potent paradigm shared by Muslims. Indeed, Iraqis link their struggle to take back their homeland—from Saddam and from the Americans—with the suffering of the Prophet Mohammad: 'The Prophet said that he who escapes with his faith from one land to another, even if it is only the distance of an inch, will be worthy of paradise' (Sunni Muslim Arab man, 35 years old).

450   *Marwa Shoeb, Harvey M. Weinstein and Jodi Halpern*

Thus, the identity of *Muhajir* serves as a centripetal anchor for Iraqi men, who otherwise may perceive themselves as failures living on government support in the United States. This religious notion of self empowers them by stabilizing their pre-exile identity. For the *Muhajir* leaves only to return to triumph over the enemy who has temporarily displaced him from his rightful home.

Women's quest for former selves. While men were striving for new and solid identities as religious warriors, the experience of women was quite different. Given that many women became refugees as a result of the political decisions of their husbands, exile in their case precipitated a state of liminality, a concept invoked by Al-Rasheed (1993: 92).

> I don't feel settled. Nobody prepared me for this life. When I got married, I expected my husband to look after me and support me. That is what I have been told since I was a little girl (Shi'a Muslim Arab woman, 27 years old).
>
> We live for our families and through our families. Exile (*al-ghorbah*) is a daily struggle. I feel like I'm dying every day in America (Sunni Muslim Turkman woman, 60 years old).

Al-Rasheed (1993) reported similar findings among exiled Iraqi women in London. She found that forced migration led to the breakdown of cultural expectations by threatening the notion that marriage is associated with settling down and establishing a family. And, since Iraqi women defined themselves wholly in terms of the roles they played in Iraq and for which they were evaluated and valued, they suffered more acutely from the collapse of their social world. According to Brison (2002), notions of self are created through the process of symbolic interaction. This fashioned self remains dynamic throughout people's lives, adapting as they encounter new people and situations. However, in certain extreme cases, this construct is so fundamentally challenged that individuals find themselves in a crisis of identity (Brison 2002). Indeed, even after 10 years in the United States, the restructuring of these women's assumptive worlds had not taken place. They continue to hold on to their former selves because these selves are more predictable and less damaged.

Rejection of Arab identity and creation of a unified Iraqi identity in exile. The above analysis illustrates how Iraqis negotiate on the basis of past, now lost, positions rather than present standings to secure a positive feeling of self. For Iraqi Arabs, both men and women, this identity management has also meant a rejection of their Arab character and the strengthening of their Iraqi one. In spite of a shared cultural heritage, Iraqi Arabs feel a keen sense of betrayal and mistrust vis-à-vis other Arab countries that did not come to their rescue during Saddam Hussein's reign of terror:

> I fear that there will come a day when Iraqis will reject their Arabness. There are responsibilities that come with being Arab. But, our so-called brothers—the

Egyptians, the Syrians, the Palestinians, and the Saudis—have completely abandoned us. I, for one, am ashamed of being an Arab. I just prefer to say I am Iraqi (Shi'a Muslim Arab man, 55 years old).

When the question is asked, 'Who are you?' Iraqis may reply in terms of tribal, regional, or ethnic, ties. In America, they also stress their Muslim identity (Sunni Muslim Kurdish man, 37 years old).

Thus, with uprooting, trust was violated on several fronts and yet affirmed on the national and religious levels. On the national front, Iraqis feel that their pain is communal; it is their duty to bear it. As they transmit the Iraqi language and customs to their children, they also plan to pass on the Iraqi pain as part of their national identity. On the religious stage, the sentiment of Arabness is replaced by the sentiment of Islam.

A shift toward the internal world. Iraqi men and women in Dearborn practice a more fervent form of Islam, reflecting the Islamic revivals in the Middle East (Shami 1996). For example, *hijab* or head covering is very common; it represents pride and protection from the immoral standards of the surrounding community. For many Muslims in the West, Islam is a means of being 'global and transnational but not on Western terms' (Shami 1996: 18). Thus, Islam is interpreted and reinterpreted according to the specific pressures Iraqis have encountered in America:

In Iraq, life is much simpler. What my husband and I teach at home is reinforced by the culture. But, in America, we have too much responsibility to keep the family together. America has this way of brainwashing you (Sunni Muslim Kurdish woman, 42 years old).

Religion is what pulls us together now. It is not that we carry fundamentalism with us to America. It is our experiences in this country that makes us hold on tightly to our Islamic identity (Shi'a Muslim Arab woman, 44 years old).

Thus, even if the association of home with homeland is cast into doubt during preflight events, the irony of exile is that the geographical distance from one's country of origin often brings refugees emotionally closer to it, sometimes even closer than before their escape (Habib 1996). And, to the extent that refugees are marginalized, they are likely to continue to hold onto their difference and in so doing further accentuate the host population's perception of them as a threat to social cohesion (Barnes 2001).

The Struggle to Define Home

Living between a good and a bad America. Two competing images of America loomed large in the psyche of the Iraqi refugee community in Dearborn. Iraqi Arabs in general espoused the 'Bad America' view, while Chaldeans, Turkmen, and Kurds—minority groups in Iraq—adopted the

452 *Marwa Shoeb, Harvey M. Weinstein and Jodi Halpern*

'Good America' stance. The difference between these disparate perceptions of the United States is where Iraqis imagine their home.

> My son was born here... Even though he never lived in Iraq, he is scared to set foot in the country... Why? Because he sees the traces of Iraq's torture chambers on his dad's body and feels his pain... Saddam's atrocities have even touched my child born thousands of miles away... America is the only country that opened its arms to us. Here, I can practice my religion without fear of persecution. No one is above the law. There is no glorification of the leader (Shi'a Muslim Arab woman, 39 years old).

> We don't belong in America. Americans don't want us here. I refuse to spend my life as a foreigner in a strange land. A person is only truly respected in his own country (Shi'a Muslim Arab man, 52 years old).

The Kurds, Chaldeans, and Turkmen, who concentrate primarily on the United States' internal affairs, are captivated by the country's religious freedom, cultural pluralism, and democratic processes. For these Iraqis, the opportunity to practise their faith in America, when compared to the brutality and autocracy of their own governments, remains the most thrilling aspect of life in the West. Further, these minorities regard their migration as more or less a permanent solution to a historically alienated existence in their homeland (Tripp 2000). Many of the Chaldeans interviewed had virtually no relatives left in Iraq; in Dearborn, they rely on an extended kinship network that links them with the already established Chaldean immigrants who came to Michigan in the 1950s. Individuals in these ethnic groups would like to be able to visit Iraq, but very few entertain the myth of return even after the overthrow of Saddam Hussein's regime.

In contrast, Iraqi Arabs, who focus primarily on America's foreign policy, view the United States as dominating the Muslim world and seeking to globalize its immoral culture. While many welcomed the 1991 Western attack on the Iraqi government, the majority resented the fact that it could only be done through an invasion of their homeland. However, as this conflict did not result in what most hoped for (a change of government), they now see that war as an attack on their country and its people. They find the hardships caused by the US-sponsored United Nations sanctions on Iraq and the 2003 US-led invasion of their country as further evidence of America's intentions to steal their resources and eliminate Islam. They stress that they left their country because of various political pressures rather than economic necessity. They did not come here to establish roots; the majority described their migration as temporary even in those cases where people have already spent 10 years in the United States. For many of them, America is a holding tank until they can take back their lives in Iraq. Interestingly, most Iraqi Arabs claimed that the First Gulf War American delegation, with whom they met in refugee camps, told them that they would be provided with financial assistance, adequate housing, social services, and health benefits in the

United States. They maintained that they only accepted resettlement in America because they were promised respectable lives. They found that most refugee assistance in the United States ends after eight months. Since many could not become self-supporting at that time, they felt further 'cheated' by America. According to Bukhari *et al.* (2004: 112), these latter individuals are faced with a perplexing existential dilemma. They are not part of the Western or Islamic cultural mainstream; they live on the margins of both civilizations. If they perceive themselves as Western, then they suffer from cultural alienation, and if they conceive of themselves as part of the Muslim world, then they feel exiled. Hence, as long as Iraqis in the US solely hold on to their Islamic identity, they will experience this double alienation from the West and from the Islamic nation.

Home as social cohesion. Interestingly, all groups (Arabs, Kurds, Turkmen, and Chaldeans) referred to America as *balad* (country) rather than *watan* (homeland), which is the term reserved for Iraq. This notion of a homeland was in their minds closely linked to trust and social cohesion.

> I have been in this *balad* for a long time, so I feel an obligation to America. But, my *watan* is Iraq. Iraq is very deep in my mind and in my heart (Christian Chaldean man, 51 years old).

In the United States, Iraqis feel that they need to negotiate not only in a strange culture but also even among themselves in a loose social environment wherein information about others is much harder to come by than in Iraq. According to them, in Iraq, one always knew someone who was familiar with the other party and could both supply information and exercise a kind of moral check. This especially applied to negotiating core identity ritual events, such as marriages.

> My girl is 14 years old. It's time for her to get married. I found her a suitable husband who was 24. The social workers at ACCESS told me that the police would put me in jail if I went ahead with this marriage. I would be charged with the rape of my daughter?! I don't understand. Isn't this better than all these young American girls who are pregnant with no man? (Shi'a Muslim Kurdish woman, 34 years old).

Further, Iraqi Muslims talked of life in Iraq as being defined by the framework of Islam. Many emphasized that Islam and Iraqi culture are inseparable—daily existence is infused by Islamic morality and practice and reference to religion always featured as a unifying part of their collective identity. No differentiation is made between faith and culture; customs are not relegated to local Arab identity and, therefore, are not freely shed.

Home is also a 'nodal point of social relations' (Rapport and Dawson 1998). For example, Iraqi writers and artists claim that their work requires a process of interaction with a responsive audience. In Iraq, traditional

454   *Marwa Shoeb, Harvey M. Weinstein and Jodi Halpern*

audiences, locally known as *lovers* (*usha'q*), engage in constant exchange with
the performers, from whom they receive emotions and with whom they share
their pleasure (Inati 2003). Many Iraqi writers and artists stated that they
could not draw on such an audience in the United States. All of this clearly
supports the framework of home as a space of identification (Rapport and
Dawson 1998).

Home in religious space. The above examples show that refugees are not
necessarily free to construct home according to their own will. While home
may be a negotiated sociocultural construct, it cannot be separated
completely from physical spaces (Rapport and Dawson 1998):

> With every prayer, I ask Allah to prolong my life until I visit the shrines
> in AnNajaf. I like to be surrounded by the holiness of this place. I feel
> blessed in Iraq. You can't re-create this sanctity here (Shi'a Muslim Arab man,
> 55 years old).

AnNajaf is renowned as the site of the tomb of Imam Ali, who the Shi'a
consider to be their founder. Nearby is the Wadi-us-Salam (Valley of Peace),
claimed to be the largest cemetery in the Muslim world, containing the
mausoleums of several other prophets. Many Iraqis aspire to be buried there
and to be raised from the dead with Imam Ali on Judgment Day. Over the
centuries, numerous schools, libraries, and convents were built around the
shrine to make the city the centre of Shi'a learning and theology. Thus,
although Iraqis have inscribed Islam on new physical spaces in the United
States, they do not feel that their faith has as central a role in their
contemporary lives. Islam, as all religions, therefore does have geography,
which is often the repository of religious actions, narrations, and feelings.
And, as the above quotation illustrates, certain locations have their place in
the construction of the imaginative domain of Dar ul-Islam (The House of
Islam) (Shami 1996).

The complex sense of home is conspicuous in these examples. No one
country can be said to offer everything Iraqi refugees desire, in the sense of
a home that meets all of a person's identities. There is the original homeland,
which for some people no longer represents home, but has instead become
the place of nostalgia; there is home in the sense of a place that fulfills
a person's practical needs; and there is a home whose culture and religion
best express identity.

Sense of security and threat: the aftermath of 9/11. During the interviews,
Iraqis talked about their feelings of insecurity and exclusion following the
events of 9/11:

> I didn't leave my home for weeks. I was scared. Arab stores were vandalized,
> women's hijab was pulled from their heads; men were spat on, the FBI searched

our homes. I don't feel as safe in Dearborn since these events (Shi'a Muslim Turkmen woman, 25 years old).

Many Iraqis are now concerned with the immediate task of living in an environment that at once offers freedom as well as hostility. They are saddened by the irrational and incendiary media discourse on Muslims, which frequently makes terrorism synonymous with Islam. In the face of an onslaught against their faith, Iraqis feel that they cannot defend or assert themselves in any sustained way in the public space. Hence, they see their lives as precarious in the United States and many are considering resettlement in an Arabic Islamic country, such as Syria or Jordan.

The Role of Islam in Defining One's Future[2]

Islam gives meaning to suffering. Refugees described the public and private rituals of religious worship as ways to ease anxiety, defeat loneliness, and establish a sense of being loved. Many also voiced an explicit awareness that war and displacement have led them to place increased importance on their Muslim faith. Thus, Islam offers a causal framework depicting adversities as the will of Allah:

> My suffering on this earth is a test that I must endure. I know that what has passed me by was not going to befall me and that what has befallen me was not going to pass me by. All I can do is go back to Allah and state my case and say 'Allah, help me'. The Prophet said to worship Allah as if you are seeing Him. For though I don't see him, he sees me. Being in the presence of Allah all the time brings me great comfort... If I feel homesick or sad, I recite verses from the Qur'an, I face towards Mecca and pray, and I fast (Shi'a Muslim Arab man, 61 years old).

Allah is the empathic Other, who will always listen; no one's suffering is meaningless in His eyes. To stress this point, Iraqis also cited the following two Arabic sayings: 'Complaining to anyone but Allah is humiliation' and 'Get to know Allah in prosperity and He will know you in adversity.' Hence, Iraqis communicate with God by praying five times a day. The prayers not only give them a chance to express their feelings, hopes, and needs, but also help them alleviate stress and structure their lives. In this context, faith offers both individual and group strength in times of hardship through belief in a powerful Being.

A future in the hereafter. Further, to the extent that resettled refugees view themselves within a religious framework, an additional resolution to the issue of belonging is emerging, where the meaning of one's life transcends both the country of origin and the country of resettlement:

> The Qur'an says that those who leave their homes in the cause of Allah, after suffering oppression, will be greatly rewarded in the Hereafter. Victory comes

with patience, relief with affliction, and ease with hardship. I've put my trust in Allah (Shi'a Muslim Kurdish man, 53 years old).

Muslims place much emphasis on the overriding power of God to determine all things. Not surprisingly, one of the earliest intellectual disputes in religious doctrine was over the issue of how human responsibility and free will can be reconciled with the absolute sovereignty of God in Islam, and Islam is still frequently described as fatalistic in the West. To counter that point, many Iraqis cited the following Qur'anic verse, where God says, 'Allah will not change the situation of a people until they change themselves.' Hence, the essence of suffering lies within the Muslim follower. In the same way, the exit from such a state depends on the Muslim's willingness to change him or herself in accordance with the teachings of Islam. Importantly, while some Iraqis used religious explanations and coping strategies to the exclusion of others, many more emphasized that Allah does indeed create all possibilities, but humans have the responsibility to choose their actions out of the many options before them.

This brings to the fore a central limitation of Western psychiatric instruments for assessing PTSD in grasping the experience of Iraqi refugees. The sense of agency of these refugees was truly enhanced by believing in a hereafter. For example, the majority of Iraqis had no sense of a foreshortened future—a common symptom experienced by survivors of long-lasting trauma—since they believed that God's kingdom is true home, where health and healing are promised to the faithful. The presence of this alternative world and future lifted their hopes and relieved their suffering:

> You only go to Heaven if you live according to the teachings of the Prophet. That means striving for piety, filling your heart with love, extending kindness to others, forgiving wrongdoings, accepting your lot in life, and thanking Allah for all that He has given you. I focus on these teachings in my everyday life. They give me purpose, peace, and security. My home in the Hereafter will be built with my faith and good deeds (Sunni Muslim Arabic woman, 63 years old).

Thus, a symptom of PTSD as described in the biomedical model has little meaning in a culture in which the spiritual dimension offers a future of peace and security.

Discussion and Conclusion

The crisis that precipitates refugee status is at once personal and social and therefore is a predicament that pursues refugees into their lives in the country of asylum. Therefore, to understand these refugees in terms of post-traumatic symptoms alone is to fail to grasp their daily rhythms and, in particular, the way that Iraqi refugees address the problem of meaning by living in religious time and space. Thus, in confronting the suffering of survivors of mass violence, we argue that the primary responsibility of those who work with refugees is not solely to classify their diseases. It is rather to engage intensively with the social and moral nature of their injuries. And, since the essential injuries brought about by atrocity are moral and social, so the central treatments should be moral and social. These treatments are those that restore self-definition to the survivor. Recovery is not a discrete process: it happens in people's lives and psychologies. It is grounded in the resumption of the sociocultural, spiritual, and economic activities that make the world intelligible. While there may be examples of those who have serious mental illness for whom traditional diagnoses and biomedical treatments will be most helpful, these are in the minority. For most, we argue for the larger view that recognizes and supports the unique cultural and spiritual dimensions of exile.

Western biomedicine is still grappling with a body–mind dualism that resists consensus. Consequently, the idea that one's religious background might influence health and outlook has remained 'part of the folklore of discussion on the fringes of the research community' (Levin 1994). Meitzen and his colleagues, who studied clinicians' knowledge of religious issues and their willingness to utilize such information in clinical practice, found a low level of religious awareness on the part of mental health professionals (Meitzen *et al.* 1998). They concluded, 'This level of religious knowledge would not, in many instances, suffice to comprehend the beliefs and presuppositions about life in the world which shape the inner dynamics of an authentically religious patient' (1998: 7). Sinclair (1993) further asserts that at its deepest level, PTSD is a spiritual diagnosis and that spiritual components need to be part of its treatment protocol. Finally, over the past decade, hundreds of published empirical studies have reported findings bearing on a possible salutary relationship between religion and health (Levin 1994).

In this study, we showed that religious coping was motivated by a search for meaning, intimacy, and self. In addition, religious coping was adaptively problem focused, particularly when individuals viewed God as an empathic Other. Pargament and Park (1995) proposed that as with any class of coping behaviour, religious coping can involve maladaptive processes, such as using religious explanations to the exclusion of others (attributing illness solely to sin), using only religious coping strategies (relying on prayer alone to resolve illness), and using religion to justify maladaptive behaviour (physical abuse in the name of scriptural discipline). Thus, clinicians should attend to their clients' potentially harmful religious coping behaviours while respecting religious orientation and seeking ways to support its beneficial effects.

We further argue that a better understanding of the tensions that render the constructs of identity, home, and time problematic for refugees can result in more culturally sensitive trauma instruments. However, since ethnographers interpret a field of interpersonal experience as they narrate the felt flow of the internal world, their interpretation is a creation as much as an observation (Kleinman *et al.* 1997). For ethnography to resist the transformation of human lives into stereotypes, it must not be experience-distant

458   *Marwa Shoeb, Harvey M. Weinstein and Jodi Halpern*

(Kleinman *et al.* 1997). For example, current PTSD scales only seek yes/no answers to 'sense of foreshortened future' questions, which as we have elaborated could greatly illuminate a refugee's sense of agency if pursued further to include religious time. Thus, measures developed in community refugee populations using empirical approaches combining qualitative and quantitative methods may create scales that are more valid in representing the experiences of refugees than methods where data are only obtained from the outside via expert and consensus approaches (de Jong *et al.* 2001; Flaherty *et al.* 1998; Hollifield *et al.* 2002). Only then can what is lost in biomedical renditions—the dialectical tensions found in a man or woman's world of experience—be recovered in the refugee's own words.

In the context of rehabilitation in Western countries, specific cultural practices, such as religion in our Iraqi refugee, are often deemed irrelevant by caseworkers who seek to neutralize differences to provide each person with an equal start (Daniel and Knudsen 1995). However, these cultural practices are the foundation on which a meaningful self-definition for survivors may be restored. Our experience with the Dearborn refugee population reinforces our view that it is vital for providers to understand and utilize the religious context of their clients' suffering in planning psychosocial interventions.

Researchers must consider the contextual nature of suffering, which necessarily involves issues of meaning, value, and many profoundly rooted beliefs that contribute to the way individuals see themselves and their world. Future research should place greater emphasis on these variables by ascribing more weight to alternative understandings and developing more culture-sensitive research methods. This study illustrates the importance of faith in understanding the constructs of identity, home, and future for Iraqi refugees in Michigan. Their commitment to Islam is not only lifelong, but also life-wide. For these refugees, the allusions to liminality and homelessness widespread in the descriptions of dislocation, uprooting, and exile are replaced by an alternative home that transcends time and space.

1. A report of the Iraqi version of the HTQ is in preparation.
2. With 54 of 60 respondents being Muslim, we chose to focus on Islam in our analysis. However, an examination of the transcribed interviews from the 6 Iraqi Christian refugees showed that their lives were also structured by the framework of Christianity and that their faith offered them strength in times of hardship. Although one cannot generalize from such a small sample, a question arises about whether religious coping is specific to refugees from the Middle East, where religion permeates daily life.

ABRAHAM, N. and **SHRYOCK, A.** (2000) *Arab Detroit: From Margin to Mainstream*, Detroit: Wayne State University Press.
AL-RASHEED, M. (1993) 'The Meaning of Marriage and Status in Exile: The Experience of Iraqi Women', *Journal of Refugee Studies* **6**: 89–104.

Iraqi Refugees in Dearborn   459

AL-RASHEED, M. (1994) 'The Myth of Return: Iraqi Arab and Assyrian Refugees in London', *Journal of Refugee Studies* **7**: 199–219.

ASWAD, B. and **BILGÉ, B.** (1996) *Family and Gender among American Muslims: Issues Facing Middle Eastern Immigrants and Their Descendants*, Philadelphia: Temple University Press.

ASWAD, B. C. (ed.) (1980) *Arabic Speaking Communities in American Cities*. Staten Island: Center for Migration Studies of New York, Association of Arab-American University Graduates.

BAKER, W., HOWELL, S., JAMAL, A., LIN, A. C., SHRYOCK, A., STOCKTON, R. and **TESSLER, M.** (2004) *Preliminary Findings from the Detroit Arab American Study*, Ann Arbor: University of Michigan, Institute for Social Research.

BARNES, D. (2001) 'Resettled Refugees' Attachment to their Original and Subsequent Homelands: Long-Term Vietnamese Refugees in Australia', *Journal of Refugee Studies* **14**: 394–411.

BLACK, R. and **ROBINSON, V.** (eds) (1993) *Geography and Refugees: Patterns and Processes of Change*, London: Belhaven Press.

BRESLAU, J. (2005). Response to 'Commentary: Deconstructing Critiques on the Internationalization of PTSD', *Culture, Medicine, and Psychiatry* **29**(3): 371–376.

BRISON, S. J. (2002) *Aftermath: Violence and the Remaking of a Self*, Princeton, NJ: Princeton University Press.

BUKHARI, Z. H., NYANG, N. N., AHMAD, M. and **ESPOSITO, J. L.** (eds) (2004) *Muslims' Place in the American Public Square: Hope, Fears, and Aspirations*. Walnut Creek, CA: AltaMira Press.

CASTLES, S. (1993) *The Age of Migration: International Population Movements in the Modern World*. Houndmills, Basingstoke, Hampshire: Macmillan.

COLSON, E. (2003) 'Forced Migration and the Anthropological Response', *Journal of Refugee Studies* **16**: 1–18.

DAHYA, B. (1973) 'Pakistanis in Britain: Transients or Settlers?' *Race* **13**: 241–277.

DANIEL, E. V. and **KNUDSEN, J. C.** (1995) *Mistrusting Refugees*, Berkeley: University of California Press.

DE JONG, J. T. V. M., KOMPROE, I. H., VAN OMMEREN, M., EL MASRI, M., ARAYA, M., KHALED, N., VAN DE PUT, W. and **SOMASUNDARAM, D.** (2001) 'Lifetime Events and Post-traumatic Stress Disorder in Four Postconflict Settings', *Journal of the American Medical Association* **286**: 555–562.

DE JONG, J. T. and **JOOP, T. V. M.** (2005) 'Commentary: Deconstructing Critiques on the Internationalization of PTSD', *Culture, Medicine, and Psychiatry* **29**(3): 361–370.

DESANTIS, A. D. (2001) 'Caught between Two Worlds: Bakhtin's Dialogism in the Exile Experience', *Journal of Refugee Studies* **14**: 1–19.

DE VOE, P. A. (2002) 'Symbolic Action: Religion's Role in the Changing Environment of Young Somali Women', *Journal of Refugee Studies* **15**: 234–246.

FLAHERTY, J. A., GAVIRIA, F. M., PATHAK, D., MITCHELL, T., WINTROB, R., RICHMOND, J. A. *et al.* (1998) 'Developing Instruments for Cross-Cultural Psychiatric Research', *Journal of Nervous and Mental Disease* **176**: 257–263.

GEERTZ, C. (2000) *Local Knowledge: Further Essays in Interpretive Anthropology*, 3rd Edition, New York: Basic Books.

GOZDZIAK, E. M. (2002) 'Spiritual Emergency Room: The Role of Spirituality and Religion in the Resettlement of Kosovar Albanians', *Journal of Refugee Studies* **15**: 136–152.

GOZDZIAK, E. M. and **SHANDY, D. J.** (2002) 'Editorial Introduction: Religion and Spirituality in Forced Migration', *Journal of Refugee Studies* **15**: 129–135.

GRAHAM, M. and **KHOSRAVI, S.** (1997) 'Home Is Where You Make It: Repatriation and Diaspora Culture among Iranians in Sweden', *Journal of Refugee Studies* **10**: 115–133.

HABIB, N. (1996) 'Refugee Voices: The Search for Home', *Journal of Refugee Studies* **9**: 96–102.

460   *Marwa Shoeb, Harvey M. Weinstein and Jodi Halpern*

HALPERN, J. and WEINSTEIN, H. M. (2004) 'Rehumanizing the Other: Empathy and Reconciliation', *Human Rights Quarterly* 26: 561–583.

HOLLIFIELD, M., WARNER, T. D., LIAN, N., KRAKOW, B., JENKINS, J. H., KESLER, J. *et al.* (2002) 'Measuring Trauma and Health Status in Refugees: A Critical Review', *Journal of the American Medical Association* 288: 611–621.

INATI, S. (ed.) (2003) *Iraq: Its History, People, and Politics*, Amherst, NY: Humanity Books.

KLEINMAN, A., DAS, V. and LOCK, M. (1997) *Social Suffering*, Berkeley: University of California Press.

KUNZ, E. (1981) 'Exile and Resettlement: Refugee Theory', *International Migration Review* 15: 42–51.

LANGER, L. L. (1991) *Holocaust Testimonies: The Ruins of Memory*. New Haven, CT: Yale University Press.

LANGEWITZ, W., DENZ, M., KELLER, A., KISS, A., RUTTIMANN, S. and WOSSMER, B. (2002) 'Spontaneous Talking Time at Start of Consultation in Outpatient Clinic: Cohort Study', *British Medical Journal* 325(7366): 682–683.

LEVIN, J. S. (1994) 'Religion and Health: Is There an Association, Is It Valid, and Is It Causal?', *Social Science and Medicine* 38: 1475–1482.

McMICHAEL, C. (2002) "Everywhere is Allah's Place": Islam and the Everyday Life of Somali Women in Melbourne, Australia', *Journal of Refugee Studies* 15: 171–188.

MEITZEN, M., SEIME, R. and WARD, H. (1998) 'Religious Knowledge and Its Use in Psychiatry', *Journal of Religion and Health* 37: 5–8.

MILES, M. B. (1984) *Qualitative Data Analysis: A Sourcebook of New Methods*, Beverly Hills, CA: Sage.

PARGAMENT, K. and PARK, C. (1995) 'Merely a Defense? The Variety of Religious Means and Ends', *Journal of Social Issues* 51: 13–32.

RAPPORT, N. and DAWSON, A. (1998) *Migrants of Identity: Perceptions of Home in a World of Movement*. Oxford: Berg.

RUBIN, H. J. (2005) *Qualitative Interviewing: The Art of Hearing Data*, 2nd Edition, Thousand Oaks, CA: Sage.

SAID, E. W. (2000) *Reflections on Exile and Other Essays*, Cambridge, MA: Harvard University Press.

SHADID, W. (1991) 'The Integration of Muslim Minorities in the Netherlands', *International Migration Review* 25: 355–375.

SHAMI, S. (1996) 'Transnationalism and Refugee Studies: Rethinking Forced Migration and Identity in the Middle East', *Journal of Refugee Studies* 9: 3–26.

SHAY, J. (1994) *Achilles in Vietnam: Combat Trauma and the Undoing of Character*. New York: Atheneum.

SINCLAIR, N. D. (1993) *Horrific Traumata: A Pastoral Response to the Post-traumatic Stress Disorder*, New York: Haworth Pastoral Press.

SUCHMAN, A. L., MARKAKIS, K., BECKMAN, H. B. and FRANKEL, R. (1997) 'A Model of Empathic Communication in the Medical Interview', *Journal of the American Medical Association* 277: 678–682.

TRIPP, C. (2000) *A History of Iraq*, Cambridge, UK: Cambridge University Press.

WEIL, S. (2001) *The Need for Roots: Prelude to a Declaration of Duties towards Mankind*, New York: Routledge.

WELARATNA, U. (1993) *Beyond the Killing Fields: Voices of Nine Cambodian Survivors in America*, Stanford, CA: Stanford University Press.

WILSON, J. P. and KEANE, T. M. (2004) *Assessing Psychological Trauma and PTSD*, 2nd Edition, New York: Guilford Press.

ZETTER, R. (1999) 'Reconceptualizing the Myth of Return: Continuity and Transition amongst the Greek-Cypriot Refugees of 1974', *Journal of Refugee Studies* 12: 1–22.

MS received February 2006; revised MS received July 2006

[27]

J Relig Health (2012) 51:293–309
DOI 10.1007/s10943-010-9351-x

ORIGINAL PAPER

The Immigration Experience of Iranian Baha'is in Saskatchewan: The Reconstruction of Their Existence, Faith, and Religious Experience

Miki Talebi · Michel Desjardins

Published online: 9 April 2010
© Springer Science+Business Media, LLC 2010

Abstract   For approximately 150 years, Baha'is in Iran have been persecuted on the basis of their religion. Limitations to aspects of their lives have compelled them to face "civic death" or migrate to other countries. This qualitative pilot study explored the experience of forced migration and how religion attenuates the disruption to the lives of Iranian Baha'is. Adaptive strategies that four participants utilised to re-establish continuity were examined. Participants who were satisfied with their lives developed a way to allow parallel cultural traditions (Iranian and Canadian) to co-exist; those who could not integrate found it difficult to maintain a balance between these traditions.

Keywords   Immigration experience · Iranian Baha'i · Religion · Acculturation strategies · Qualitative research

Introduction

For approximately 150 years, Baha'is in Iran have been persecuted on varying intensities, and this persecution is still alive today (Cooper 1985). Based on an agenda of religious nationalism in Iran, the Iranian government has attempted to "suffocate" the Baha'i people by limiting their livelihood in virtually every way. For instance, their marriages and divorces are not legally recognised, they are restricted from obtaining high-ranking jobs (Cooper 1985), and Baha'i students are exempt from a university education. Limitations to many aspects of their lives have compelled the Baha'is to either face "civic death" or migrate to other countries. This paper looks at the experience of migration of four people who moved to Canada around the time of the Islamic Revolution of 1979 under such restricted conditions. The paper also explores the role that religion played among them

M. Talebi (✉)
Department of Psychology, Carleton University, B550 Loeb Building, 1125 Colonel By Drive,
Ottawa, ON K1S 5B6, Canada
e-mail: mtalebi2@connect.carleton.ca

M. Desjardins
Department of Psychology, University of Saskatchewan, Saskatoon, Canada

 Springer

294 J Relig Health (2012) 51:293–309

during this stressful process and how their life in Canada is in continuity or in discontinuity with their past existence in Iran. While the immigration experience for any group of people is stressful in itself, the unique history of the Baha'i people further contextualises the significance of religion as a consistent theme in their experience, since it is at the root of their migration itself. Therefore, this paper begins by offering a short summary of the Baha'i faith and its genesis, followed by a discussion on the statistics concerning the migration and resettlement pattern of Iranian people and their adaptation to a new country. This leads into the rationale and research question, theoretical model and the findings of this exploratory investigation.

The Baha'i Faith and Its Genesis

The Baha'i faith, the most recent of the world's independent religions, was founded in Iran in the mid-nineteenth century by Bahá'u'lláh (Encyclopædia Britannica 2002; Hatcher and Martin 1984). The central tenet of the faith is that of unity (Cooper 1985; Ferraby 1957; The Baha'i Faith 2007). Proponents of the Baha'i faith believe that there is one God whereby all of the world's great religions are 'manifestations of God' and these religions are essentially a progressive revelation of one faith (Ferraby 1957; Garlington 2005). In line with the central tenet of unity, the faith also encourages diversity in unity, which refers, not to the uniformity of all people, but rather to the cooperation among the diverse citizens of the world. The faith places great emphasis on education, that there be equal status among men and women, and that there be harmony between science and religion (Ferraby 1957; Garlington 2005; Hatcher and Martin 1984).

The Bábi religion, which was founded on 23 May 1844, arose out of the teachings of a young man, known as the Báb (the 'gate'), in Shiraz, Iran (Smith 1947). Although early teachings were within the boundaries of Islam, over time Bábism shifted away from the religion and was declared independent (Cooper 1985). In 1845, Bahá'u'lláh became one of the leading advocates of the Bábi faith (The Baha'is 2005) resulting in an overwhelming majority of the Báb's followers accepting him. From that point onwards, his followers came to be known as Baha'is (Encyclopaedia Britannica 2002; Encyclopedia of Religion 1987). The dominant faith in Iran, Islam, maintains that Muhammad is the last in a succession of 12 Imáms (prophets), known as the Twelvers (Smith 1947), and *dis*believe the existence of the most recent manifestation of God, Baha'u'llah (Encyclopædia Britannica 2002). In this regard, religious Muslim nationalists saw and continue to see Baha'is as dangerous heretics and as a route through which unorthodox beliefs would tarnish Iranian morals. In 1979, under Khomeini's ascension to power, the persecution of the Baha'is became official policy and was pursued in a systematic way (Cole 2005). Under a new constitution of the Islamic Republic of Iran, drafted in 1979, only four religions were and continue to be officially recognised: Islam, Christianity, Judaism, and Zoroastrianism (Cooper 1985). In this same year, the Baha'i headquarters was invaded, and the list naming 90,000 registered Baha'is was discovered (Cole 2005). Between 1979 and 1998 over 200 Baha'is have been executed, declared missing, declared dead or killed in mob violence, and thousands jailed (Affolter 2005). With periodic acts of execution and persecution, the present situation of the Baha'i community in Iran remains precarious. For example, on 19 August 2006, a letter released by Iran's Ministry of Interior ordered officials throughout the country to tighten surveillance of Iranian Baha'is (United States Commission on International Religious Freedom 2008). More recently, six Baha'i leaders of the national coordinating group of the Baha'is in Iran were arrested without any charges in early morning raids on 14 May 2008. A seventh member had been arrested early in March on

J Relig Health (2012) 51:293–309 295

trivial grounds. Presently, these seven Baha'is, who see to the minimum needs of 300,000 Baha'is in Iran, have been accused of espionage for Israel and remain in prison in Tehran as they await a trial (Baha'i World News Service 2008).

Migration and Adaptation Patterns: The Iranian Case

Between 1979 and 1985, following the Iranian Islamic Revolution, approximately 3–4,000 Iranian Baha'is immigrated to Canada and, within the past 3–5 years, there have been approximately 2,500 Iranian Baha'is immigrate to Canada (G. Filson, Director of External Affairs for the Canadian Baha'i National Centre, personal communication, 8 December 2006). Within Saskatchewan, of 963,150 residents that were included in a census of the religions in the province, 780 were comprised of Eastern religions (which includes the Baha'i faith)—ranking one of the smallest of the religious denominations in the province and country (Statistics Canada 2001).

Although research on the immigrants of ethnic minorities is becoming more prominent in the literature, the Iranian immigrant has been claimed to be one of the least understood of all ethnic minorities in the United States, and, we would also add, in Canada (Bozorgmehr 1996; Kheirkhah 2003). Thus, it is not surprising that research on the Baha'is, an even smaller minority group, is quite limited (Garlington 2005). This is why, in order to approach the situation of the Baha'i immigrants in Saskatchewan, we have drawn mainly from literature which focuses on the immigration experiences of the Iranian population in North America.

In Kheirkhah's (2003) dissertation on the experiences of acculturation of Iranian immigrants to the United States, she interviewed seventeen people (ten men and seven women) who had left Iran surrounding the 1979 Revolution. The author found that participants tended to acculturate either by segregating their existence by maintaining two separate worlds (Iranian and American) or by integrating the two cultures. Those who acculturated by separating their two worlds, which was the preferred method, were termed "separators", and this was characterised by nostalgic reflections of life in Iran and preserving the culture by keeping the language, food, music, and arts alive in America while simultaneously adopting American ways in the public sphere. In other words, these participants were actively negotiating a niche between the boundaries of the opposing cultures. This finding illustrates that a resistance to the Western normalising ideologies of unity and assimilation can, for some people and in some contexts, serve as a successful adaptive strategy.

Indeed, a qualitative research by Hoffman (1989) that was conducted prior to Kheirkhah's (2003) dissertation seems to parallel this framework. In her study on the processes of adapting to American life, Hoffman conducted 30 interviews with Iranian professionals and uncovered two main themes: learning and self-change. Hoffman described two levels of learning: a surface level of learning which focuses on "successful social integration"; and a deep level of learning in which the "cultural nature of the self" changes (1989, p. 33). Hoffman says that the Iranian immigrants she interviewed tended to dichotomise between an inner and outer self such that the outer self underwent rapid change while preserving the integrity of the inner self. Accordingly, once again adaptation to a new society is associated to a polarisation of the self, this time according to the surface/deep dichotomy instead of the domestic/public sphere.

In terms of the Iranian Baha'i ethnic group, religious faith has been shown to be a significant coping mechanism that can facilitate the immigration as well as resettlement process. For example, Davoudi (2004) explored how immigrants' adherence to the Baha'i

Springer

296   J Relig Health (2012) 51:293–309

faith is a key factor in preserving psychological stability and mental health after their persecution. Upon comparing the severity of victims of non-religious persecution in Iran to religiously based persecution, those who were persecuted for their religious beliefs reported much lower levels of post-traumatic stress disorder (PTSD) symptoms even though they had a higher number of traumatic experiences. These results attest to the protective power that adherence to religion can have in the face of traumatic experiences (Davoudi 2004). The Baha'i participants' ability to welcome discussions associated with their persecution experience as opposed to avoiding them, which was the tendency of a majority of the non-religious participants, played a significant role in their ability to maintain their mental health.

What the author failed to acknowledge in her discussion, however, is the global context within which the coping power of religion is situated. That is, how do factors such as politics, social structure, and economics influence the dynamics of the migrants' physical, spiritual, and mental well-being in Iran compared to the new country? As we have discussed in prior sections, Iranian society is deeply seated in religion, and thus, the coping power of religion could be very different in Iran as opposed to Canada where politics, social structure, and economics are separated from religion. In other words, coping strategies that worked in the Iranian context may not necessarily work in the Canadian one.

In as much as there is some literature on persecution and the Baha'i religion, to our knowledge, no research has specifically looked at the negotiation between the immigration experience and the Baha'i religious experience. Filling this gap in the literature could serve as a formative leading point to better understand the immigration experience and adaptation of these people to a secular society like Canada. Furthermore, interviewing the immigrants after they had a chance to resettle into the host country for a number of years, offered us the opportunity to explore whether the psychological struggles related to religion in the home country persisted in Canadian society where the dynamic between the social, economic, and political forces are so different. The findings from the interviews are based on four case studies, and while this may not allow us to generalise about the role of religion in migration, they do open new avenues of research. Notably, they show that healthy adaptation to a host country does not necessitate that immigrants fully adapt to the host country, and that navigating between the home and host country can serve as a healthy acculturation strategy to keep life in balance. Exploring these navigations between opposite worlds is what we embarked on in this pilot study.

Purpose of the Study

The goal of the present pilot study was to examine the adaptation strategies of four Iranian Baha'i refugees both in Iran and in Canada—two countries where the participants had to adapt to a global world from a position of marginality. In Iran they lived at the margin of society, in conflict with its global ideological structure; in Canada, they lived at the margin of society as newcomers and in continuity and discontinuity with their past life in Iran. Thus, this study aimed to look at the paradoxes at play in these changes in continuity in the participants' lives—specifically, how one moves from one margin (in Iran) to another (in Canada) and transforms or shapes her/his religion to fit within a new environment.

Theoretical Model

The current research explores the immigration experience from a critical phenomenological perspective (Good 1994). Specifically, this research aims to reconstruct the

J Relig Health (2012) 51:293–309 297

immigrants' experience through the lens of the political, social, ideological, legal, bodily, and economic forces which are part of the different lifeworlds that they are living in. Indeed, from this perspective, each of us lives in more than one lifeworld—such as religion, poetry, science, and common sense reality (Good 1994; Geertz 2002)—and we are all deeply invested "stakeholders" in our lives within each of those lifeworlds (Kleinman 1999). Thus, it follows that a significant event, such as persecution or migration, can upset one's existence causing a disruption to some or all of his or her lifeworlds (Good 1994; Becker 1999). In the case of this research, it is not only a disruption to everyday routines and life experiences—immigrating from Iran to Canada—that is at stake, but also the restructuring of religion and its role in society and in daily life. To understand the role of religion in the migration process of Baha'i refugees, Taylor's (2004) theory of modernity was also used whereby the concept of enchantment, which points to societies where social life is shaped by religion—is seen to parallel with Iranian society, and the concept of disenchantment, which points to societies where religion is separated from various aspects of daily life—is seen to parallel with Canadian society.

After disruption, the affected lifeworlds undergo a transformation process where the individual strives to reconstruct his or her lifeworlds and to re-establish order within his or her existence. This new order can be conceptualised as four strategies, organised along two axes; the first conveys the person's position in regard to culture whereby the individual may (1) fit in with culturally normalising ideologies as a form of *cultural (re)alignment*[1] (Good 1994), or (2) resist and rise above the normalising ideologies of society, illustrating *cultural transcendence* (Becker 1999). The second axis concerns the person's social positioning, whereby the individual may (3) withdraw within a *margin* and remain in an in-between state by integrating a liminal space outside the boundaries of mainstream social relationships and social processes (Turner 1969), or (4) return to the centre of social life, including work, politics, and collective institutions and utilise a strategy of *inclusion* (Griffo 2008; Turner 1969). Throughout the participants' migration trajectory we have paid attention to these four strategies; however, it should be noted that these four strategies are by no means exclusive; rather, the dimensions have been outlined as a means to better understand and conceptualise the description of the participants' lives.

Methodology

Sample

Four participants living in Saskatoon who had emigrated from Iran to Canada shortly after the Islamic Revolution in 1979 were interviewed. Participants were recruited on the criteria that they were persecuted and consequently forced to migrate for reasons linked to their Baha'i faith. The participants consisted of two men and two women, all of whom had escaped from Iran between the years of 1981 and 1986. At the time of migration, participants' ages ranged from 18 to 32 and marital status varied.

---

[1] To clarify the difference between cultural realignment and cultural alignment, the former will be used in the context of the participants' experiences in Iran, since in this context the strategy will be utilised to *return* to normalising ideologies that they are familiar with. Whereas cultural alignment will be used in the context of the participants' experiences in Canada, since in this context the strategy will be utilised to *adapt* to normalising ideologies that are foreign to the participants.

🕮 Springer

298   J Relig Health (2012) 51:293–309

Participants were recruited using a variety of methods. The first method consisted of a gatekeeper who is a member of the Local Spiritual Assembly of the Baha'i community in Saskatoon. This recruitment strategy, however, yielded only two participants. The other two participants were recruited through personal contacts and the snowball effect. Participants were informed of the nature of the study as well as their rights to withdraw from the study at any time throughout the process and consent was obtained prior to data collection. Data was collected from January to February 2007.

Techniques

For each participant, data was collected over at least two sessions using a digital voice recorder. Interview sessions took place approximately 1 week apart. Two techniques were used to gather data. Life history interviews were conducted in an open-ended format in order to give the participants free-reign to organise, explore, and clarify the story of their immigration experience. Semi-structured interviews allowed us to pinpoint specific areas of the research question inspired by the theoretical model. Moreover, meeting the participants for a second time gave us the opportunity to target specific aspects of their experience that may have been overlooked or were unclear in the life history narrative.

Analysis

Following the principles of qualitative analysis (Rothe 2000), interview data was examined by (1) organising interviews with respect to the chronology of their immigration experience; (2) reading through each transcript to identify specific themes and re-evaluating such themes as subsequent themes arose in other transcripts; and (3) organising themes conceptually to derive at broader themes of each interview to better understand the links between the themes, segments of the narratives, and theories derived from the theoretical model. All of the analyses were conducted by the same researcher (MT) to ensure consistency in the analysis and interpretation of the data. The following reconstruction of the participants' narration of their immigration experience follows a description of the adaptation strategies along the migration/adaptation trajectory, including their time in Iran, transitory period, and time in Canada.

Results

Life in Iran

In the narrative of their time in Iran, the participants presented themselves in a way that was reflective of three adaptive strategies. Depending on the context and aspect of their lifeworld that they discussed, their stories were representative of cultural alignment, inclusion, and cultural transcendence. However, before discussing these adaptive strategies, the position within which participants were placed in Iranian society, that is, margin,[2] should be contextualised. Throughout this section of their narrative, a common theme was the stories of discrimination and exclusion that the participants experienced due to their

---

[2] Although retreat within a margin has been classified as one of the four adaptive strategies in this paper, in this context, we use margin to indicate a situation where the people are excluded from others, as opposed to the situation where they *actively* withdraw themselves from the centre of society as a strategy of adaptation.

 Springer

J Relig Health (2012) 51:293–309 299

Baha'i faith. Notably, they expressed that their view of themselves and the way they portrayed themselves to the public made them distinct from larger society. Participants spoke of how characteristics such as their level of politeness, patience, respect, and humbleness separated them from their counterparts and raised suspicion that they are indeed Baha'i. The Islamic regime imposed an extreme level of control on their daily lives. For example, participants said they were compelled to monitor how they spoke, dressed, and behaved in public in order to avoid persecution and that they struggled to maintain a balance between their belonging to the Baha'i community and their membership in Iranian society. Stuck between these two antithetical belongings, the participants utilised strategies from both axes (culture, social positioning) in order to cope with the contradiction between their faith and the religious order of global society.

The first position, cultural alignment, was represented in their deep spiritual connection to their faith, which is in keeping with the Iranian approach to religious life. For example, one of the participants mentioned that it was the social orientation of the Iranian lifestyle that made religion such a salient part of people's lives and identity. The implication here is that the participants' way to be Baha'i was profoundly Iranian; thus, there was a synchrony and sense of cultural alignment between them and the Iranian Muslims or any other ethnic minority counterpart in Iran. The idea that all Iranians, regardless of their religious affiliation, felt a deep connection between their daily life and their faith illustrates their common capacity to relate to forces higher than everyday life.

> Susie: It's a religious country. Religion is everything to every person. If you're a Jew, if you're a Christian, if you're Muslim, Baha'i, any faith, it is part of your life. You get up in the morning, you say your prayer. You come home, you know, for lunch, you say your prayer. You think about your religion in terms of your work, in terms of your marriage, your child-birth, your childrearing, everything.

In the second position, the participants underlined their alignment with Iranian social processes and structures. They made it clear that, regardless of the religious discrimination they were faced with, they always showed respect towards Muslim people and Islamic law, as prescribed by the Baha'i writings. They were thus living according to the same rules, the same laws and the same social structure as the rest of Iranian society. In brief, the participants adhered to mainstream society both in the realm of attitudes and values about religion and in the realm of social, economical and political structures.

The third social position, cultural transcendence, was reflected in the participants' choice to keep their faith and in their discourse on rising above the values of their Muslim counterparts and displaying humility towards the majority group, despite their being persecuted by them. Their ability to be trustworthy even in the face of religious persecution was something that the participants prided themselves in. They spoke of how people, Muslim and non-Muslim, entrusted them with the most important aspects of their lives. However, all of the participants suffered the consequences of religious persecution. For example, participants spoke of losing their jobs, and being dismissed from primary and post-secondary institutions. Nevertheless, taking material possessions away from them and limiting their opportunity to be equal citizens in Iran was something that the participants were willing to accept since they knew that nothing could take away their devotion to the Baha'i faith. In short, they felt that they had to shift towards the periphery of mainstream society in terms of certain ideas and values in order to preserve their integrity as a Baha'i devout.

> Yaran: This is what most Baha'is [would] answer: "They took everything from us"… "The materialistic part of it, lots of Baha'is, they lost it right. *But* they're not

300   J Relig Health (2012) 51:293–309

gonna take away my belief". Ah, so we are not gonna prostitute our opinion or idea to just simply say "we're Muslim."

However, as marginalisation towards this group reached a peak, not only did their religious world become threatened, but life itself was at stake: to preserve their integrity, the participants needed to leave the country. Lina expressed this urge to leave in the following way: "I knew they didn't want to teach my son. But before that happened, me and my husband, we decided to—if someday, the government don't teach our kids, we not gonna stay. We have to go from Iran."

To summarise, in this section, participants used three strategies in order to adapt themselves to their imposed marginality. First, participants culturally aligned to the religious orientation of Iranian society—just as these participants expressed a devotion to their Baha'i faith, almost everyone else in Iranian society was also deeply invested in a faith. Second, participants followed the laws of the country and tried to maintain their work activity. And finally, they embodied moral superiority, in contrast to their tormentors, by displaying virtues of humility towards the majority group in Iranian society, despite being persecuted by them.

Transition Between Iran and Canada: Living in a Limbo

In their narratives, the participants explained that they were not allowed to legally leave the country, and as a result, were forced to escape. Because of the extreme conditions they were faced with, the stories during their transition between Iran and Canada were reflective of them not only feeling, but being compelled to live, on the periphery of society. This exclusion from society's centre was represented in the illegal nature of their departure, their ambiguous identity and the status reversal they experienced during their transitory time. In order to escape, participants were forced to cash in their life savings, sell their personal belongings and leave with only enough food and clothing to get them across the border. They had to detach themselves from their social networks and their life-long possessions, threatening their personal and social identities. Being smuggled out of the country further contributed to their sense of being alienated from their past self; they described themselves as feeling akin to black-market commodities.

Interestingly, parallel to these feelings of alienation, one participant did report some positive experiences during their escape from Iran. Lina spoke about her experience of God's epiphany when customs officials at an airport threatened to send her and her family back to Iran.

> Lina: I was just looking outside and was just like this (*standing, rocking herself side to side*) and I'm crying. In another two hours they're going to send us to Iran… Now we lost everything, now we have to go back to Iran. If we [go] back to Iran, for sure they're going to kill my husband … And then I feel someone put his hand here, and said "don't worry". I *feel* His hand. Honest to God I feel His hand here.

At the moment that she felt the prophet's presence, Lina said that customs officials had notified her husband that they would not be deported. This religious experience reinforced her devotion to the faith and confirmed the sacred value of her and her family's exile from Iran.

The international world was well aware of political and religious sanctions the Islamic regime was imposing, including the persecution of the Baha'is, and the United Nations was granting this group asylum. As such, and according to the stories of the participants, many

J Relig Health (2012) 51:293–309   301

non-Baha'is were escaping Iran and claiming refugee status as Baha'is. Thus, not only was the participants' identity fragile due to the intense changes they were facing by leaving Iran, but also because others were fraudulently assuming the Baha'i identity. The participants reflected that the processes of having to prove their authenticity because others were taking advantage of the situation made them feel exploited, and threatened their sense of self.

Three of four participants fled to Pakistan and remained in the country for a range of time (9–18 months), until their paperwork to officially immigrate to another country was processed.[3] Surviving in this country proved to be extremely difficult. Locals mistook them as "rich Irani people" (Susie), which, from their discourse on escaping Iran, was clearly not the reality. In their stories around this time, notions of intense margin, including anonymity, absence of status, property, rank, and humility, surfaced. Seeing as this was a transient place and they had already endured cultural, religious, and social uprooting from their home country, participants were not willing to place roots in the middle country—they kept themselves withdrawn from society, keeping their minds focused on the ultimate goal of immigrating to a country where they could finally resume living their lives. Thus, in Pakistan, they lived on a day-to-day basis, anticipating that tomorrow would be the start of their new life. Interestingly, once again we encounter a specific case. Contrary to the other participants, Arun seemed to relish his stay in the transitory country. During his time in the refugees' camp, he became one of nine committee members for the Baha'i community and he spoke of the responsibilities and burdens that this position entailed with a sense of pride and self-fulfilment. Unlike the other participants, this was a comfortable phase of his life.

In sum, this phase of the participants' lives was dominated by their use of margin as a way to cope successively with persecution and uprooting. First, in terms of the strategy that the participants utilised to escape out of Iran; that is, the participants had to use methods that were not common or visible to mainstream society. And second, with respect to their living patterns in Pakistan, participants actively marginalised themselves from the centre of society as a way of maintaining a sense of continuity between their reason for leaving Iran (escaping religious persecution) and long-term goal of eventually living a better life in Canada.

During their time in the middle country, all four of the participants applied to immigrate specifically to Canada. Throughout their narratives the participants described the process to be gruelling and tiresome—where interviews and medical examinations were riddled with acts of bribery. However, and as mentioned earlier, over the course of 9–18 months, all four participants received notice that they would immigrate to Canada. The participants spoke of first flying into Ottawa to process paperwork and then either relocating to cities where they already had family or to cities assigned by immigration officers.

Life in Canada

In their narratives, the participants pointed to the many challenges or disappointments they faced after their arrival in Canada. First, they noted the contrast between the status of morality and religion in Iran and Canada. They spoke of morality and religion in Canada as being too casual, highlighting the lack of respect that people had for one another, for their elders and for their own spirituality. At special events and holy days, the difference

---

[3] In order to clarify the trajectory of the fourth participant, Lina, it should be noted that she and her family fled to Africa where they had family to stay with while they waited for their paperwork to be processed.

302   J Relig Health (2012) 51:293–309

between the behaviour that they were used to in Iran and what they experienced in Canada was very pronounced and shocking to them.

> Susie: Morality, that's the only thing I don't like about this country. It's a, it's a country of, you know, money … capitalism. Yeah, so that part I don't like. It takes over the person's morality. They don't realise, yes, you need food to eat, for your physical body; but at the same time you need to have faith, for your spirit—the food for your spirit.

From their perspective, the presence of religion seemed to be completely absent from Canadian society. Notably, they complained about the fact that within Canadian society religion is split from the state and from the public sphere. For example, they spoke of how religion and government were merged together in Iran, whereas in Canada these two bodies are separate. The contrast between religious faith in their home country and in Canada was especially salient in the narratives of the three participants who have children. Being in Canada, they spoke of having to raise their children amidst others who have different core cultural values and regretted not being able to expose their children to the rich religious ethos that was embedded in Iranian society.

Concerning their religious practice, the participants underlined the difficulty they experienced in maintaining their previous customs in Canada. Although all of the participants said that they still practise their religion, the extent of their religious practice here, as opposed to what it was in Iran, was reported to be less. The participants said that they connected to the Baha'i community by attending events for major holidays and for meetings; however, they noted a contrast between their past and present spiritual experiences. They said that maintaining a close relationship with God and remaining spiritual is more challenging in Canada. Whereas in Iran the participants said they had the support of the Baha'i community and were encouraged to be involved in religious activities, they felt that the nature of the Baha'i faith in Canada is not as strong, the community is not as close, and spirituality is not as deep (here we witness how the Baha'i faith and the way the participants observe the Baha'i faith is restructured according to the Canadian context). As Lina says, "in Canada, [it's] not like Iran, ah, people [are] Baha'i, but still, they're not that Baha'i". Instead of heavily relying on the support of the Baha'i community to nourish their spirituality, the participants spoke of engaging more in personal devotion (which is in line with the modern view of religion as a personal or private matter[4]), such as by reading Baha'i books and through prayer. In this way, and paradoxically, through their restructured faith the participants were able to preserve a sense of continuity between their past world in Iran and present world in Canada.

Second, the participants spoke of the difficulty they had in finding employment and establishing themselves within the social structure of Canadian society. In their narratives, the participants did not mention any specific professional credentials that they may have had—they simply said they were willing to take on any job they could find to get them started. For example, one participant, Yaran, spoke of his willingness to start as a dishwasher. However, as he articulated, this was much more challenging than he had anticipated. The issue of Canadian experience was continually raised as the reason that he was not a qualified recipient for this work. The participants suggested that the lack of Canadian experience was an excuse for employers to deny new immigrants an opportunity to survive and co-exist in Canada. Additionally, being visible minorities because of their hair and skin colour, they spoke of feeling judged before they could even prove their work skills. Even

---

[4] See Taylor (2004) with regard to modernity and private fate.

 Springer

J Relig Health (2012) 51:293–309 303

after years of working in particular jobs, they spoke of continually feeling looked down upon. According to them, this was not only because of their different nationality, their accent, or features that classify them as visible minorities, but because they were classified under the "immigrant" umbrella. In their discourse, they all spoke of experiencing Canadians speaking about the idea that immigrants were stealing their jobs and making it more difficult for local people to find employment.

As a result of these discriminations, the participants felt that in order to be accepted and respected in Canadian society they had to rise above cultural norms. The participants spoke of how higher expectations seemed to be placed on them compared to the average Canadian. In order to get somewhere, to succeed and survive among other Canadians, they said they needed to work much harder than their counterparts. Thus, in order to engage in the dominant society, not only were participants expected to culturally align themselves with normative standards, but also to rise above these standards to prove that they could be contributing members of society. For example, Yaran articulated that "even to do a job, like as a dishwasher, you have to show that you are three times faster, three times better, [just] to get the job, a lousy job of dishwashing".

From their perspective, only two of the participants considered that they were now successfully integrated into Canadian society. Both of these participants had immigrated to Canada when they were still young adults (18 and 19 years old) and at the time of their interviews still had intact nuclear family units, were still raising young children, and had steady jobs. All of these factors may have contributed to helping them situate their life or, at least, some important parts of it in the centre of Canadian society. However, as a result of their life circumstances, struggles to integrate dominated the other two participants' (Lina and Arun) narratives, and thus reflected their use of margin as an adaptive strategy. Lina and Arun struggled to integrate into mainstream society and to create a balance between their old existence in Iran and new existence in Canada. In their stories about life in Canada, Arun and Lina spoke of life-altering events that occurred in their lives after immigrating to Canada, namely a debilitating injury and the loss of a spouse. As a result of these events, many aspects of their life and identity, including mobility, self-esteem, their relationships with others and status in society, were altered. When discussing their inter-action with others on a daily basis, the participants spoke of feeling as though they do not belong. However, when questioned whether or not they would like to return back to Iran, both participants reiterated that they would never go back to Iran to live. For Arun, who presented this section of his narrative and his experience around a debilitating injury, he said that he could not face the notion of being an outcast in his home country. In his mind, the prospect of returning was not an option. For Lina, having been exposed to Canadian culture and lifestyle, she expressed that she could never go back to the way life was in Iran before she left. Living under scrutiny, religious discrimination, and limited freedom were no longer bearable for her.

Beginning from the religious persecution they experienced in Iran, through to their immigration and transient time between Iran and Canada, their resettlement in Canada, and the injury for Arun and loss of spouse for Lina, these two participants have been confronted with uninterrupted disruptive forces for over two decades. Reflecting on their discourse, it seems that transition has become a lasting condition for them. However, it was the final life disruptive event that these two participants experienced (loss of a spouse; debilitating injury) which most compromised their capacity to integrate into society, and situated their existence towards one of marginality. Indeed, Lina's and Arun's narratives reflect a per-manent state of withdrawal from the centre of society, where feelings of anonymity,

304 J Relig Health (2012) 51:293–309

acceptance of their suffering and simplicity to their existence have been acknowledged as their new way of life and identity following their post-migratory experience.

Listening to their narratives, it was apparent that hope, at least with regard to their inclusion into Canadian society, was not something that sustained these two participants anymore—they felt they had nothing left to look forward to. Inasmuch as their discourse reflected constant discontinuity in their social life, religion was always present in their stories across the entire immigration experience, and thus was a key marker of continuity for them. Both participants reported that they relied on their faith to guide them through each day. In this way, the Baha'i faith brought meaning to their marginalised and isolated existence. Although the construction of what it means to be Baha'i and be a member of the Baha'i community is different in Canada, the participants spoke of the private relationship (that is, the modernisation of their faith into one dominated by personal observance) that they were able to maintain with God. In this way, they expressed a purpose to the suffering they were feeling. For example, Lina acknowledged that "now, [religion is] the only thing [that] keeps me happy, because always, like Baha'u'llah helped me, he's here, he helped me all the time. In my heart I know I have him". Arun articulated the following:

> Somehow the faith is helping me to, to understand this [injury]. They say, maybe God wants this to happen to you. But I don't know why God wants to try, [with] this thing [that happened to me]. They say try to understand. Maybe this is a test. That's why the, the faith is helping me to understand.

To summarise this section, the participants utilised during this stretch of their migratory experience the four basic adaptive strategies that we have defined in our theoretical framework. Firstly, a shift in the experience of morality and religion between the home and host country was experienced. Most notably, a pronounced difference between how religion is oriented around secular life in Canada compared to Iran was felt. Participants missed the rich presence of religion in Iranian daily life and they praised (cultural transcendence) the way core religious values were respected back home. However, since they did experience difficulties in terms of connecting with members of their religious community, they have restructured their Baha'i faith in terms of the Canadian context and shaped it into a private practice (cultural alignment).

Second, while all participants struggled to integrate themselves (inclusion) into Canadian social structures, especially in the workforce, life circumstances permitted only two of them to do so. To integrate into the work market, all participants felt that they had to rise above cultural norms, which is a simultaneous expression of both cultural alignment and cultural transcendence. And finally, while all four participants experienced some form of withdrawal from the centre of society, for Lina and Arun, social circumstances imposed a particular constrain on their life outcome. Lina and Arun did not seemingly choose to marginalise themselves from society, rather their life experiences seemed to impose a particular limit to the options that may have otherwise been available to them. They turned to withdrawal within the spiritual realm (margin) as a strategy of adaptation only after life disruptive events compromised their capacity to integrate to society. In other words, they have symbolically transformed a social constraint—their exclusion from the centre of society—into a religious virtue, that is, a spiritual ascent. Thus, in a sense, enabling their tragedy to actively appropriate their situation and turn it into something meaningful and more valuable, at least from their perspective, than inclusion.

 Springer

J Relig Health (2012) 51:293–309   305

Discussion

Tactical Plurality in the Context of Migratory Trajectories

The objective of this study has been to explore the immigration experience of Iranian Baha'is. At the core of this research was the experience of their passage from an enchanted world to a disenchanted world, including the adaptive strategies that the participants utilised in order to re-establish continuity and/or order to their lives. By drawing on a theoretical model based predominantly on Good's (1994) critical phenomenology, an overall portrait of the participants' remaking strategies was constructed.

In analysing the participants' narratives, it became increasingly apparent that, throughout their migration trajectory, they engaged in multiple adaptive strategies to restore the meaning and order of their existence. At least four main strategies were utilised: cultural (re)alignment, cultural transcendence, inclusion, and withdrawal from the centre. In Iran, while participants aligned to the religious aspect of Iranian society by showing a deep investment in their religion and followed Islamic laws, they also transcended many Iranian norms, beliefs, and customs. During their transitory phase, participants mainly drew on withdrawal as a way to cope with the difficulties related to life as a refugee. And in Canada, participants drew on all four strategies in an effort to adapt to the challenges they faced in this new environment. They simultaneously rejected and endorsed the way religion and morality are defined and implemented in Canada, by accepting with regret to turn their faith into a personal matter. Participants utilised inclusion as they endeavoured to integrate into the workforce, but were met with hyper cultural alignment when higher expectations were demanded of them. Finally, after experiencing traumatic life events, two of the participants actively engaged in withdrawal from global society, but were able to reshape their marginal status into a symbolic and sacred one through their relationship with God and observance to the faith.

Regarding the most recent phase of the participants' migratory experience, we wish to emphasise that these adaptive strategies helped two participants to engage actively in Canadian life and culture while simultaneously preserving some core aspects of their religious existence and Iranian culture. For the other two participants, particular social determinants throughout their life trajectory imposed what Turner (1969) refers to as a form of permanent liminality. Having endured a lifetime of transition, they were finally able to create a permanent niche for themselves on the periphery of society, at odds with global society. This state of limbo consequently led the participants to utilise mainly a strategy of withdrawal that was associated with a limited engagement in Canadian life and culture. Throughout the stages of their immigration experience, these two participants presented themselves through a lens of despair. The following concentrates on a closer examination of the relationships between migration, plural belongings, and adaptation.

Mental Balkanization and Plural Belongings in the Context of Migration

In Paul Veyne's essay (1988) on the constitutive power of human imagination, he holds—in line with constructionist perspectives (Cassirer 1946; Crotty 1998; Geertz 1973; Good 1994)—that there is no single truth. Indeed, we experience as many truths as the number of symbolic forms that we use to understand the world: poetry, political discourse, mythology, religion, arts, common sense, science, etc. These truths, which are often contradictory, are usually internalised in a peaceful way through a process that Veyne calls "mental balkanization" (1988, p. 41). Veyne contends that, instead of rejecting whole opinions or

 Springer

306 J Relig Health (2012) 51:293–309

understandings because they are not compatible with one another, we maintain them for the kernels of truth that they contribute to our multilayered experiences of the world. This results in the cohabitation within the individual's mind of a series of parallel worlds, truths, and realities. In this sense, the concept of mental balkanization can be applied to the triple belonging—to Iran, to the Baha'i faith and to Canada—that the participants utilised in order to healthfully adapt to their host country.

With respect to the adaptive strategies that the first two participants (Susie and Yaran) utilised, their narratives were not built on only one plain of reality. Rather, they maintained a dual reality with each serving a critical role in their adaptation to the host society. While they drew on economy, democracy, human rights and freedom of choice, and most notably religious freedom, to connect to Canadian society, they simultaneously dissociated themselves from this society through the depreciation of its moral order and its secularised conception of the world and of society. Yet, at the same time, they did contradict their attachment to their original enchanted view of the world by modernising their religious practices, notably by turning it into private faith. The implication is that the multiple strategies the two participants used to reconstitute their lifeworlds—inclusion, cultural alignment, and cultural transcendence—were constructed in a way which allowed them to integrate into their new host country while keeping a strong bond, a vital mnemonic and affective connection to their old (enchanted) world. In other words, the maintenance of contradictory views of the world and identities seemed to help these participants to maintain a sense of self-continuity in the face of radical changes in their life at both personal and collective levels. Stated otherwise, they were able to fulfil their need to integrate themselves into Canadian society while keeping simultaneously a strong attachment to their cultural and spiritual roots. Reflecting on the adaptive strategies of Susie and Yaran illuminates how critical it is for some people or under certain circumstances, to be able to navigate across contradictory worlds and identities to keep life in balance.

On the other hand, the life circumstances of the other two participants (Lina and Arun) prohibited them from integrating into the social structure of Canadian society. Although all of the participants expressed experiences of a lack of possibilities and resources, it is these life circumstances, that is, Lina's loss of her spouse and Arun's debilitating injury, which separate these two participants from the other two. For example, firstly, these two participants complained that the Baha'i community in Canada fostered neither a strong sense of belonging, nor the same sense of spiritual connection to the social aspects of their faith. Furthermore, particularly for Arun, his physical disability excluded him from being able to integrate into the workforce. And third, their sense of being victims of racism or xenophobia—both participants had articulated experiences of discrimination in the workplace on account of their ethnic minority status—also contributed to their impossibility to integrate into the centre of society. As a result, these two participants sought refuge in their religion, which was the reason for their exile and which is, at least, protected from discrimination by the Canadian laws. Their retreat into the religious sphere—which means also a retreat into the domestic sphere—provided them a sanctuary to cope with the impossibility of their life in the public domain. Their ability to transform their exclusion from the centre of society into a withdrawal to a sacred space was a way for them to actively appropriate their situation and turn it into something more valuable, at least from their perspective, than inclusion. In sum, in the case of Lina and Arun we see how, when inclusion is blocked, religion can fulfil a vital adaptive function through the protective sanctuary that it can provide to the excluded.

 Springer

J Relig Health (2012) 51:293–309   307

Implications

Throughout participants' narratives, the consistent theme of their religious faith has been undeniable. For two of the participants (Susie and Yaran), their maintenance of parallel cultural traditions (Iran, Baha'i and Canada) and the interaction between them, such as in the reconstruction of the Baha'i faith, offers a new way to approach acculturation models. Traditionally, the unidirectional model of acculturation was the accepted view of acculturation (Flanner et al. 2001). This model implied the process of discarding the old culture and taking on the new culture; in other words, assimilation. More contemporary research on acculturation strategies, however, has consistently evidenced that those who endorse the integration strategy (the maintenance of one's heritage culture in concert with full participation of the host culture) fare much better in the host country (Berry 1997, 2005). In keeping with such theorising, this exploratory study shows that the participants who were satisfied with their current positions in life had developed a way for parallel cultural traditions to co-exist and even interact. Past research has shown that Iranians who have immigrated to the United States acculturated by maintaining two separate worlds (Kheirkhah 2003; Hoffman 1989). With these models, acculturation involved two levels of learning, where immigrants adapted to their host country on a surface level, but on a deeper level preserved an inner core cultural identity (Hoffman 1989); or where immigrants adapted to their host country in the public space, while preserving their Iranian culture in the domestic realm (Kheirkhah 2003). However, relegating one form of adaptation to a surface level and another form of adaptation to a deeper level does not do justice to the complex transitions and changes that the participants in our research went through—all four participants did connect deeply with issues such as democracy, human rights, freedom, commerce, and social security. These aspects of the disenchanted world were at the core of their acculturation and they had a radical impact even on their religious practices and experiences.

Conclusion and Caveats

In conclusion, the qualitative and exploratory nature of this research limits the researchers from making any concise conclusions or generalisations from the data—the findings from this research are based on the narrative constructions of only four participants. The authors wish to highlight that this was a pilot study and, as such, more research is needed to grasp how widely spread the four adaptive strategies and the plural belongings identified in the present research are used among not only Baha'i immigrants, but also among other immigrant populations who are confronted with the adaptation of their faith to the Western moral and political order. Since the core of this research centred on the adaptive strategies that the participants utilised to acculturate to Canadian lifestyle, a more comprehensive understanding of religious life in Iran, their reconstruction of their faith as well as their convergence with Baha'i religious life in Canada is necessary.

   Despite these limitations, we believe that this research has opened the path for new directions in the study of the immigration and religious experiences of Iranian Baha'i individuals who were forced out of their home country. This research has generated new concepts and themes that are useful for future research on the immigration and adaptation of future Iranian Baha'is as well as other ethnic and religious minorities. Studies have established the importance of spirituality and religiosity in the well-being of individuals (e.g., Pargament et al. 1998), yet there still remains a lack of information on the Baha'i client (Maloney 2006). Perhaps findings from the present pilot study can help illuminate

 Springer

some areas to which clinical support could be provided to Baha'is and the role that their faith plays in their ability to cope with challenging life experiences, such as immigration. To further the research in this domain, we propose that research questions and projects regarding the role of religion and of plural belongings in the adaptation of migrants be explored more systematically in the future. Furthermore, more in-depth research on the analysis of the difference between the two categories of participants that were explored here should be conducted to better understand what is involved in healthy adaptive strategies so that future immigrants who seem vulnerable to fall into the margins of their new home country can be better served. The application of these and future findings should be considered for incorporation into resettlement programme development and social policy.

References

Affolter, F. I. (2005). The specter of ideological genocide: The Baha'is of Iran. *War Crimes, Genocide, & Crimes against Humanity, 1*, 75–114.

Baha'i faith. (2002). In *The New Encyclopædia Britannica* (Vol. 1, pp. 797–798). Chicago: Encyclopædia Britannica.

Baha'i World News. (2008). *Six Bahá'í leaders arrested in Iran; pattern matches deadly sweeps of early 1980s*. Retrieved July 30, 2008, from http://news.bahai.org/.

Becker, G. (1999). *Disrupted lives: How people create meaning in a chaotic world*. California: University of California Press.

Berry, J. (1997). Immigration, acculturation, and adaptation. *Applied Psychology: An International Review, 46*, 5–34.

Berry, J. (2005). Acculturation: Living successfully in two cultures. *International Journal of Intercultural Relations, 29*, 697–712.

Bozorgmehr, M. (1996). Iranians. In D. W. Haines (Ed.), *Refugees in America in the 1990s: A reference handbook* (pp. 213–231). Westport, CT: Greenwood Press.

Cassirer, E. (1946). *Language and myth*. New York: Dover Publications.

Cole, J. I. (2005). The Baha'i minority and nationalism in contemporary Iran. In M. Shatzmiller (Ed.), *Nationalism and minority in Islamic societies* (pp. 127–163). Quebec: McGill University Press.

Cooper, R. (1985). *The Baha'is of Iran: The minority rights groups, Report No. 51*. London: Minority Rights Group.

Crotty, M. (1998). *The foundations of social research: Meaning and perspective in the research process*. Thousand Oaks, California: Sage Publications.

Davoudi, M. (2004). Spiritual dimension of adaptation to persecution and torture among Iranian Baha'i women. *Dissertation Abstracts International, 65*, DAI-B. (UMI No. 3135712).

Eliade, M. (Ed.). (1987). *The Encyclopedia of Religion* (1st ed., Vol. 2). New York: MacMillan.

Ferraby, J. (1957). *All things made new: A comprehensive outline of the Baha'i faith*. London: G. Allen and Unwin.

Flanner, W. P., Reise, S. P., & Yu, J. (2001). An empirical comparison of acculturation models. *Personality and Social Psychology Bulletin, 27*, 1035–1045.

Garlington, W. (2005). *The Baha'i faith in America*. Westport, Conn: Praeger Publishers.

Geertz, C. (1973). *The interpretation of cultures*. New York: Basic Books.

Geertz, C. (2002). Religion as a cultural system. In M. Lambeck (Ed.), *A reader in the anthropology of religion* (pp. 61–82). MA: Blackwell.

Good, B. (1994). *Medicine, rationality, and experience: An anthropological perspective*. Cambridge: Cambridge University Press.

Griffo, G. (2008). Rien sur nous sans nous. In M. Nuss (Ed.), *Handicap et sexualité. Le livre blanc* (pp. 47–57). Paris: Dunod.

Hatcher, W. S., & Martin, J. D. (1984). *The Baha'i faith: The emerging global religion*. San Francisco: Harper & Row.

Hoffman, D. (1989). Self and culture revisited: Cultural acquisition among Iranians in the United States. *Ethos, 17*, 32–49.

J Relig Health (2012) 51:293–309   309

Kheirkhah, S. (2003). Acculturation among Iranian immigrants in America: A phenomenological inquiry. *Dissertation Abstracts International, 64*, DAI-B. (UMI No. 3080419).

Kleinman, A. (1999). Experience and its moral modes: Culture, human conditions, and disorder. In G. B. Peterson (Ed.), *The Tanner lectures on human values*. Salt Lake City: University of Utah Press.

Maloney, M. (2006). Toward a Baha'i concept of mental health: Implications for clinical practice. *Counselling and Values, 50*, 119–130.

Pargament, K. I., Smith, B. W., Koenig, H. G., & Perez, L. (1998). Patterns of positive and negative religious coping with major life stressors. *Journal for the Scientific Study of Religion, 38*, 710–724.

Rothe, J. (2000). *Undertaking qualitative research: Concepts and cases in injury, health and social life*. Alberta: University of Alberta Press.

Smith, P. (1947). *The Babi and Baha'i religions: From messianic Shi'ism to a world religion*. Cambridge: Cambridge UP.

Statistics Canada. (2001). *2001 Census of Canada*. Retrieved July 29, 2009, from http://www12.statcan.ca/english/census01/products/standard/prprofile/prprofile.cfm?G=47.

Taylor, C. (2004). *Modern social imaginaries*. North Carolina: Duke University Press.

The Baha'is. (2005). *The Baha'is: A profile of the Baha'i faith and its worldwide community*. Haifa: The Office of Public Information.

The international website of The Bahá'í faith: The website of the Baha'i international community. (2007). *What is the Baha'i faith?* Retrieved November 2, 2006, from http://www.bahai.org/faq/facts.

Turner, V. W. (1969). *The ritual process: Structure and anti-structure*. Chicago: Aldine Publishing Company.

United States Commission on International Religious Freedom. (2009). *USCIRF Annual Report 2008—Iran*. May 1, 2008, available at: http://www.unhcr.org/refworld/docid/4855699864.html [accessed 27 July 2009].

Veyne, P. (1988). *Did the Greeks believe in their myths?: An essay on the constitutive imagination*. Chicago: University of Chicago Press.

[28]

Journal of Ethnic and Migration Studies
Vol. 38, No. 5, May 2012, pp. 851–868

Religion and Civic Participation among the Children of Immigrants: Insights from the Postcolonial Portuguese Context

Susana Trovão

Religious mobilisation is a central aspect of ethno-cultural diversity in European societies. Focusing on the postcolonial Portuguese context, this article investigates the religious-civic activism of two groups of immigrant offspring living in the Greater Lisbon Area. Guiding research questions are the following: How is the religious mobilisation of immigrant youth associated both with degrees of social and cultural integration and with perceived conflict in inter-ethnic relations? To what extent is religious activism mediated by historical and cultural traditions related to specific gender and inter-generational dynamics? How do experiences of living out religion affect the multi-dimensional identity constructions of immigrant youth, and how do these ongoing identity processes promote strategies for ongoing action? Comparative analysis confirms that religious identities may create varied means and projects for civic activism, not only among children of immigrants who feel positively integrated but also among those who experience inter-ethnic conflict. Situated uses of religion require, however, a tacit knowledge concerning the civic and political context, and a certain capability of networking both within and beyond communities. The findings also reveal that youths' religious mobilisation is mediated by specific gender and inter-generational dynamics. The paper calls for further work on the impact of the various forms of trans-boundary 'positional moves' upon the identity projects of immigrant emergent generations, including those sustained by long-distance emotional and imagined relations.

Keywords: Uses of Religion; Civic Participation; Immigrant Offspring; Lisbon; Postcolonial Immigration

Susana Trovão is Associate Professor of Anthropology at the Universidade Nova de Lisboa. Correspondence to: Prof. S. Trovão, Faculdade de Ciências Sociais e Humanas, Universidade Nova de Lisboa, Avenida de Berna 26-C, P 1069-061, Lisbon, Portugal. E-mail: sst@fcsh.unl.pt.

ISSN 1369-183X print/ISSN 1469-9451 online/12/050851-18 © 2012 Taylor & Francis
http://dx.doi.org/10.1080/1369183X.2012.668028

Introduction

Exploring the relationship between religious identity and civic participation among the children of immigrants is a complex challenge for those working in the Portuguese context. Immigration is a relatively recent phenomenon, characterised by sudden and diverse inflows. Portugal also has a weak welfare state and an incipiently developed civil society (Marques and Santos 2004). Moreover, in the Portuguese arena of inter-ethnic relations, strikingly little priority is given to public debates oriented towards the promotion of means of governance of cultural and religious diversity (Bastos and Bastos 2008). Additionally, the institutional opportunity structure for immigrant political engagement is quite new and attached to citizenship legal status (Albuquerque and Teixeira 2005; Horta *et al.* 2008). While debates on secularism and the public ostentation of religious signs at the European level have stimulated research on religious-political mobilisation (Bauböck *et al.* 2006), the quasi-absence of similar debates within the Portuguese public sphere means that this articulation remains a little-investigated subject.

This article uses a strategic comparison between the civic activism of two groups of immigrant offspring living in the Greater Lisbon Area—youths self-defined as Christians whose origins are in Cape Verde and São Tomé, and Muslim youths of Indo-Mozambican origin.[1] Both groups promote the belief that agency rooted in religion may create alternative means for civic participation. As the available literature often claims, the tension between religions derives from competing notions about how religion should be lived and what role it should play in society (Joppke 2009; Klausen 2006). Used here to highlight the ongoing processes of those who mobilise religion for social action, the term 'religious mobilisation' also needs to be understood as a capacity for action which is socio-historically and religiously mediated (Mahmood 2006).

Delving into the rather limited Portuguese research on civic and political immigrant participation, a multi-actor and multi-site methodological strategy was deployed to tackle the different meanings and situated uses of religious mobilisation. In my research I interviewed 36 youths whose origins are in Cape Verde and São Tomé and 15 Muslim youths of Indo-Mozambican origin. The interviewees were selected through snowball sampling, whilst ensuring various profiles in terms of age, gender (slight majority of girls), social background, family's migratory history, etc. Ages ranged from 16 to 28; however, age limits were not pre-defined, since an emic concept of 'youth' was used, including respondents' socio-cultural construction of a 'youthful' lifestyle, personal expectations of what it means to be *young*, etc. Following one of the key variables (involvement with civic participation activities), particular sites were used to approach potential interviewees. Such sites included the Youth Association of the Islamic Community of Lisbon and certain strategic neighbourhoods in the Greater Lisbon Area—Quinta do Mocho em Loures, Cova da Moura and 6 de Maio na Amadora. Pseudonyms are used in the quotes that follow.

Journal of Ethnic and Migration Studies   853

Contrasting the processes of socio-economic and inter-ethnic insertion in Portugal of the interviewees, their national and transnational identifications, the development of their civic skills, associative networks and bridging capitals, along with the Portuguese imagery concerning their communities of belonging and the existing opportunity structures for them, I seek in this paper to understand whether socio-economic integration, social contact across boundaries, and participation in and identification with the Portuguese mainstream culture are associated with religious agency. I also ask whether, conversely, experiences of discrimination and/or conflict in relation with the host Portuguese majority increase the tendency to mobilise religion for civic action.

Identity narratives are rhetorical and performative, negotiated and defined in changing and various ways that depend on local, national and global circumstances. Moreover, research from the perspective of social identity theories (Jenkins 2004; Reicher 2004) has shown that identity constructions are key factors in mobilising for action. With this in mind, I also ask how experiences of religious-civic mobilisation can affect the multi-dimensional identity constructions of immigrant youths and, further, how these ongoing identity processes may support and promote strategies for action.

Given that the patterns and meanings of the religious-civic lives under study cannot be dissociated from the relevent historical traditions, characterised by specific conceptions of the self (including responsibilities and possibilities for action) which have been developed within long-term structures of gender inequality, we take into account other dimensions and power relations at play. Additionally, a certain degree of pre-existing cooperation and social participation within family networks and communities should not be ignored. In accordance with previous research (Carter 2009; Tastsoglou 2006), I also investigate how immigrant youth's civic-religious experiences are shaped by specific gender and inter-generational dynamics.

The comparative analysis links theory and research on identity processes and inter-ethnic relations (e.g. Banton 2008; Brubaker *et al.* 2004; Wimmer 2008) with a social capital approach (Anthias 2007; Jacobs and Tillie 2004; Portes 1998), articulating them with additional research on emotional and imagined transnationalism (Baldassar 2007). Some recent contributions concerning religious mobilisation for social activism (Ebaugh and Chapetz 2000; Klausen 2006; Pedziwaitr 2007) will help us to increase the interface between religious aspects of identification processes and social agency.

Children of a Diaspora of Hope, Disillusioned by Racism

Ivone, Celeste, Irene, Esperança, Valter, António and many other children of immigrants from Cape Verde and São Tomé are part of a labour diaspora of hope mainly supported by family practices of transnationalism, while also characterised by an incipient development of collective strategies. These young people define their parents, grandparents, aunts and uncles as immigrants who came to Portugal looking

854 *S. Trovão*

for work and a degree of social mobility they believed would be within their reach. Some of their relatives counted on significant economic, social and cultural capital, and/or could rely on the support of powerful institutions (e.g. the Catholic Church or a few Evangelical churches) to facilitate their migration and settlement. Others came with far fewer resources.

The children of these immigrants do not define themselves as immigrants. Some youth were born in Cape Verde, São Tomé or in other countries but have been living in Portugal since childhood. Many were born in Portugal. The references with which they identify, their material and cultural patterns of consumption, their lifestyles, their intra- and inter-ethnic relations, and even the *crioulo* languages they speak, set them apart from the previous generation. They differ from their parents in terms of their ways of being, but their ways of belonging have much in common with the immigrant generation. In fact, these youth share with their parents and grandparents strong emotional attachments to São Tomé and Cape Verde as expressed by statements such as 'It's our land', 'The place where you feel you belong', and 'Our roots'.

While most of them have never visited their ancestral homes, they build narratives about them, based on what they 'hear' in their homes and the neighbourhoods they live in. Others, having enjoyed brief visits, seek and reinvent memories (of smells, food or family). They do so, they say, 'So I won't forget where I'm from' (António, born in Cape Verde, 18 years old), some adding 'I'm not really sure if what I feel actually exists' (Irene, born in Portugal, 22 years old). Their parents and grandparents built narratives based upon the imagined land where they would migrate in the future, while their children construct narratives based on the imagined land of their roots (which can be painfully frustrating, as many anticipate). These orientations change over the life course. Some members of the second generation are already anticipating a future outside of Portugal. Those who have stronger ties to relatives back home acknowledge that they identify with a larger diasporic community that includes people of similar ancestry around the world. They also recognise that their ways of combining being and belonging differ from their peers from other regional and national contexts.

Being born in Portugal, whether one has the Portuguese nationality or not, does not automatically translate into a feeling of belonging to Portugal for these young people of African origin. In fact, it often produces identifications and emotions which are much more ambivalent. In fact, many of these children of immigrants live in rundown neighbourhoods where life is, as they themselves say, highly problematic. Academic failure is common and school dropout rates are high. Delinquency is on the rise and the police are increasingly called in. Some neighbourhoods have such a bad reputation that local youth have difficulty finding work. Such racial discrimination engenders resentment and a rebelliousness which legitimises the delinquency which produced their 'bad reputations' in the first place. A vicious cycle of accusations and counter-accusations ensues, creating a descending spiral that, at times, has led to violent death among the police officers and youths of African origin.

Journal of Ethnic and Migration Studies   855

Within this context, we can understand why these children of immigrants feel the desire to escape from the places where they grew up, or that they so strongly identify with that small neighbourhood (that many condense in the expression, 'We are children of the neighbourhood'). This shared experience, which unites youth from many different backgrounds, leads young people to develop affinities beyond their families and specific migrant community as the same time as it creates tensions within these communities. The frequent conflicts and power plays within neighbour-hoods are just as likely to occur between groups of mixed ancestry as they are to be about between- and within-group differences. Ethnic and national differences can also take a back seat to idioms of consumption and lifestyle ('*beto*', '*dred*', '*chunga*', '*skater*', etc.) which are also used by non-immigrant Portuguese youngsters. In short, all of these affinities and idioms can stimulate or not debates about identity among young people.

These identities are incomplete, ambivalent and in constant flux. They are transnationally constituted and negotiated with respect to myriad reference points: the family's country of origin, the local neighbourhood and the wider Portuguese society. These young people also identify with other imagined communities based on global currents of ideas, information and fashion. For example, hip-hop culture is one of the deterritorialised references the most valued and deployed by these groups, both in its presentation ('style' and language) and in its cultural patterns of consumption and production.

More striking about how these young people from São Tomé and Cape Verde construct and locate their identities, however, is the mutual centrality of the homeland and the local in the processes that structure their ways of being and belonging. Inspired by the ritualised daily life of the neighbourhood (food, family, celebrations, national holidays in the country of origin), they invent, reinvent and update real and imagined family-origin cultural repertoires. From the vantage point of the neighborhood, they download transnational tools and use them in local identity-specific ways.

'We Are Not Gangs. We Are Groups of Friends Who Want to Clean Up the Neighbourhood': Transitory Modes of Youth Association

Most young people join neighbourhood associations because they want to 'organise things for the benefit of and with the help of young people in the neighbourhood' (Maria, born in Cape Verde, 21 years old, living in Lisbon since 1993). They want to take part in something that is not imposed on them by national or local authorities, things they feel are theirs, made for them and by them. Especially among young people who feel the most discriminated against, another strong motivation is the desire to 'clean up the neighbourhood' (Rui, Cape Verdean parents, born in Portugal, 21 years old) and present an alternative image to counter the prevailing one which sees them as forming gangs that are only interested in causing trouble.

Their very model of civic participation is a good example of the articulation between the local and the global. It often connects daily life and references to the neighbourhood with the manipulation and re-appropriation of homeland references or appeals to global culture. Celeste (born in São Tomé, 28 years old, living in Lisbon since 1986), for example, got involved in youth associations after listening to the lyrics of African American rappers and recognising the similarities between their experiences and her life in urban Lisbon. Through rap music, she embraced a new attitude which involved refusing 'to continue to be a victim, pointing fingers, and not doing anything to make things change' while also 'speaking of positive things, saying what can be improved and what can't'.

> Rap is also part of why I participate. Rap began not only as a way to denounce the situation of African Americans and what was happening, but also to tell something of daily life in the neighbourhood. Speaking of positive things, saying what can be improved and what can't. (. . :). They fascinated me because these were struggles we felt in our neighbourhood.

Valter (Cape Verdean parents, born in Lisbon, 21 years old) also sees his 'revolutionary rap—which, in the *crioulo* language, speaks of 'police violence', 'discrimination' and 'persecution'—as a form of civic and political participation, 'a sort of eye-opener' for 'a world that refuses to know itself, that wishes to remain hidden' and, therefore, remains undetected by authorities, courts and the Portuguese civil society.

Despite this, many interviewees stated that they thought that their involvement in organisations was only a phase in their lives, that it is a 'thing of youth', defined not only by 'bigger dreams', 'more time', 'more willingness' and 'more energy', but also 'more motivation to win and change the world'. Along the way, one becomes an autonomous adult—often used to justify the diminished commitment to civic causes they often notice in themselves and their peers.

Fieldwork carried out in their neighbourhoods does indeed bring to light a rapid ascension to adulthood through early sexual activity. Young men build their masculinity, prestige and power partly through the sexual and reproductive conquering of multiple women. Erotic and reproductive social capitals are also used by young women as a main way for negotiating social mobility and material security. However, due to the volatility of marital experiences, motherhood and the mother–children relationship become the major identity investment and source of respectability of the women-mothers, who often assume total responsibility for the subsistence and education of their children.

According to Verba and his colleagues (1996), people's level of civic engagement depends on how much time, money and civic skills they have. Many of the São Tomé and Cape Verdean youth come from families where fathers are physically and/or economically absent and mothers effectively shoulder the responsibility of supporting their children (and sometimes their daughters' children). As a result, young people often drop out of school, which prevents them from acquiring civic capital and skills;

Journal of Ethnic and Migration Studies   857

or they must struggle to put these to use while they are working. In the case of girls, these circumstances become even more complicated by early motherhood.

Even though a number of the young people eventually get high-school diplomas and become competent speakers and writers of Portuguese, social activism takes time. And time is not an abundant resource, particularly among those who have already realised that 'life on the streets is just an illusion' and that 'ending up in jail' (rap lyrics, originally in the *crioulo* language) is not an alternative.

There is one exception to this pattern, however. We found that primarily female youth who identify religiously (mostly as practising Catholics or Evangelical Christians) often follow a different path to independent adulthood and civic engagement than their non-practicing peers.

'As Jesus Did in the Primitive Church. . .'. New Meanings for Civic Participation and Citizenship

In these latter cases, they tended to become significantly more invested in civic activities, both through religious and non-religious organisations, around causes such as immigrant rights and anti-racism. They were much more likely to become involved in the government programmes, organised at the local and national level, that are set up to prevent social marginalisation and inter-ethnic conflicts. These activities often strengthen their homeland orientation by opening up opportunities to participate in international programmes. By creating bridges and synergies between different levels and sites of the transnational social fields that these youth inhabit, civic activism—inspired by religion—becomes a central reference point in identity construction.

> That which is written in the Bible, if we applied it in our associations, we would not have the problems we have, do you understand?! Because Jesus, in his teachings, and in what he wanted to show people, he spent all his time on the street, talking to people. When you meet someone in need, give them a hand, that is, change society, in a different way. And even after the death and resurrection of Jesus, in the primitive church, the first thing they did was to support widows, orphans, the needy; the rich brought their wealth to share with the poor. (. . .) (My conversion) was something good that was done to me. (. . .) The Bible is a manual, I drink from it every day, it inspires me in my daily work with people (Irene, born in São Tomé, 22 years old).

Faith tended to stimulate new ways of conceptualising citizenship that transcended its legal dimensions and was not limited strictly to 'rights and obligations'. To paraphrase some of the interviewee voices, religious citizenship demands and is sustained by different forms of social participation in civil society (Delanty 2000).

> Participation means that you give your own valid, positive and dynamic contribution to the society you live in. That's participation. Now, I think that people talk a lot more of participation in the sense of 'rights and obligations of

> citizens', but how?! I believe that participation is a concept that should be deconstructed. I call participation everything to which I can contribute, in all areas, be it in the church I attend, or my neighbourhood, or my work with the Council of Europe, with WFM (Women for Minorities), or my group of friends. (...). People think that participation means to volunteer in an organisation, or to vote ... right now, I feel Portuguese even though I'm not because I do not have nationality and can't vote, but still I'm a participative citizen, am I not? (Sonia, born in Lisbon, parents from São Tomé, 28 years old).

This participatory form of religious civic engagement is not exclusive among the Christian second generations of African origin. A similar dynamic can be found among Muslim youth of Indo-Mozambican origin.

Descendants of a Trade Diaspora, Underscored by the Independence Processes in East Africa

Nadia, Rucsana, Aziz, Ismael, Alim, Narguise, Rahim and many other young Muslims of Indo-Mozambican descent living in Portugal form part of a trade diaspora which originated in the Indian sub-continent. During the second half of the nineteenth century, the forefathers of these youths (mainly originating from Kutch, Khatiawar and Surat, in Gujarat) migrated and settled in the British colonies and protectorates of East and South Africa, and in Mozambique—a Portuguese colony. The transnational migratory culture of their forefathers resulted from the articulation of strategies and resources connected to their class background, as well as factors related to their ethnicity. They tended to organise themselves into religious and caste communities, sustain connections to specific micro-locales, and observe values and rituals that reinforced kinship which they pursued over time and across generations in several different colonial and postcolonial contexts.

After African independence, many members of these families experienced great insecurity. Beginning in the late 1960s and 1970s, many who had settled in Kenya, Uganda, Tanzania and Malawi migrated to England. Similarly, independence in Mozambique, as well the political instability and the civil war that broke out in the mid-1970s, led many Mozambican Muslim families to choose Portugal as their new migratory destination. Their intercontinental network of contacts, combined with the social, financial and human capital they brought with them, enabled them, once established in Portugal, to enjoy rapid socio-economic and cultural integration.

Young Muslims of Indo-Mozambican origin do not perceive themselves as 'children of immigrants'. Having lived most of their lives in Portugal, they do not express feelings of exclusion and social discrimination akin to those experienced by many of their peers in the United Kingdom. They refuse to conflate Portugueseness with Christianity or Catholicism and, instead, stake full claim to their right to sit at the Portuguese table.

For them, Islam constitutes a reference point that structures their identity (even though it means different things to different people). At the same time, they

Journal of Ethnic and Migration Studies　859

emphatically reject the possibility of any voluntary schism within the Portuguese cultural ecology, as well as any attempts by the native-born or immigrants alike to create impermeable categories of ethnicity, religion and race that position Islam in opposition to Portugueseness.

Parents exert a strong influence over the identity choices of their children. Because they were so committed to the successful insertion of their offspring into Portuguese society, they enrolled them in Portuguese-language state or private schools. They also strictly controlled their children's daily lives in and out of school. The transmission of religious and cultural traditions and (sometimes) their education in their parents' mother tongues (*Gujarati* or *Kutchi*) occurred within the extended family. At the same time, and since a very young age, children were encouraged to attend supplementary schooling in Islam and to participate in ethno-religious meetings and activities for youngsters organised by their own communities.

Sunni parents who had been brought up and educated in Mozambique by less traditional families devised new means for the religious education of their children. They adopted a vocabulary and discursive style similar to the predominant Catholic religious context and frequently tried to translate Muslim beliefs, ceremonies and saints into terms compatible with Catholicism. Many of our respondents considered this to be a positive aspect of their religious education. They felt that they had been given competencies that made them better able to manage inter-religious differences.

This intergenerational transmission of a positive bi-referential identity—that of 'Portuguese Muslim'—was extremely important to our respondents, as was the bi-culturalism promoted by their parents. They expressed a feeling of belonging to a 'we', which combined all that is 'best' about their original cultural and religious traditions with 'the best' that can be gleaned from their secular contact with the Portuguese cultural ecology. They feel proud to claim Portuguese Muslimness, while neither India nor Pakistan (a reference for many Sunni families since 1947) are the subject of any work of re-imagination. Moreover, unlike the case of many other Europe-born Muslims youths, Portuguese Muslims are largely uninterested in transnational forms of self-representation and belonging. They stress their Portuguese Muslimness rather than their membership in a global Muslim community.

As in the case of their European peers (Khosrokhavar 1997; Klausen 2006; Vertovec and Rogers 1998), these youth adopt different religious beliefs and want to enact their religion in different ways to their parents. They display a more individualised, thoughtful and critical stance toward their faith. They tend to make choices about 'what is or is not essential' in their religious practice, granting themselves a good deal of both internal and external freedom to compartmentalise the different aspects of their lives. They have their own ideas about religious authority and often challenge the traditional Islamic authorities. They speak an actual and symbolic language, and have learned an adopted set of practices that are not only comprehensible to their non-Muslim teachers and peers but also enable them to live their religious 'difference' acceptably in the Portuguese public space.

Because they did not experience the same level of social and religious discrimination that has characterised the second generation in other parts of Europe, they tend to reject the patterns of defence and deviance detected by Olivier Roy (2000) in several other European contexts. For instance, the Salafist option, which demands a return to an original, authentic but also global Islam, has not recruited many followers from among the Sunnis of Indian origin in Portugal. Despite the growing influence of transnational Islamic movements (such as the *Tabligh Jamaat*), initiation into such movements is not an option for the great majority. Their occasional forays into chat-rooms where many transnational perspectives on Islam (usually more literal and conservative) are articulated are not a substitute for the interpretations offered by their families and communities. In sum, extreme traditionalism and positioning themselves in cultural or religious opposition to the Portuguese society, where they feel well integrated, have not occurred.

Recently, some have joined their families in a new migratory project. Following Portugal's integration into the European Union in 1986, many community members were attracted by the opportunities for professional and educational advancement offered by the United Kingdom. Confronted by the greater diversity of Islamic identifications and practices in the UK, Portuguese Muslims in Britain clearly distinguish themselves from Indian Muslims (including those who came directly from India), seen as those who the most practise 'religion as a way of life' and 'are more careful in observing all religious laws and values'. They also differentiate themselves from the Pakistanis who they see as 'condensing their religious, national, linguistic and cultural identity into one'. Finally, they consider themselves very different from a significant percentage of East African Muslims who, despite sharing a number of cultural references (country of origin, caste, previous context of migration, etc.) tend to emphasise their Muslim identity. In the UK as in Portugal, their narratives emphasise the specificity of their identity as Portuguese Muslims.

'What Sets Us Apart is Only Our Religion. Otherwise, We Are Portuguese, Just Like You Are': The Refusal to Get Mixed Up in Politics

In contrast to their second-generation African peers, the Mozambican Indian youth define themselves as culturally Portuguese and are perceived as representative of middle-class Lisbon youth (Tiesler and Cairns 2007). Therefore, it is not surprising that their level and type of political participation are comparable to their non-Muslim Portuguese peers. A primarily two-party system, in which the political agendas of the two main protagonists are not clearly differentiated, is not particularly inspiring to young activists. This, however, may not be the only reason for their lack of interest in national politics. Again, inter-generational factors are at play.

The parents of these young people have strong, largely unpleasant political memories of their past in Mozambique. They had a quasi-magical belief 'that things would not change in Mozambique' because they wished it so. They insist upon describing the majority of Mozambican Indians as either complying with the regime, including the Salazar dictatorship, or being totally isolated from politics. They claim that their 'refusal to get mixed up in politics' stems from their greater concern for religion, family life, and the family business which has been passed down through the generations. Exceptional political activism only emerged in the student movements of the late 1960s. The rapid socio-economic and cultural integration of Indo-Mozambicans into democratic Portugal did little to challenge this a-political stance, despite the increased contact between community leaders and government institutions. Because these contacts generally centered on the development of religious organisations and infrastructure, they did not result in any larger, generic institutional 'multiculturalism'.

Like their parents, young Sunnis did not organise associations (within either schools or their respective communities) to fight for Islamic education and mother-tongue instruction in the Portuguese state-school system. They did not demand the observance of Islamic holidays or certain dietary and ritual concessions in schools and in their future workplaces, nor did they mobilise to improve the position and protect the rights of Muslim women. However, they managed to reconcile prayer times, Ramadan fasting, dietary restrictions and Muslim holidays with the public school curriculum, including physical education and classes in Catholic ethics and religion or with certain school holidays such as Christmas or Carnival. Their hard work, the flexibility of teachers and the understanding of school authorities, the 'curiosity' and 'admiration' of certain peers, and their parents' efforts to develop their bi-culturalism enabled many in this group to finish secondary school with grades above the national average and to go on to a college education.

In addition, in 1992, some of these young Muslims founded *CilJovem* (Youth Association of the Islamic Community of Lisbon), which aims to bring Muslim youths of different nationalities together through cultural, religious and recreational activities and, at the same time, to build bridges between Muslim and non-Muslim Portuguese. As members of this organisation, young people engaged in their first volunteer work, mainly oriented towards their peers as well as to a number of initiatives outside the community, such as supporting food pantries, helping at orphanages, and distributing toys to children.

Fieldwork suggests that growing up in families with strong ethno-national identities, combined with the experience of community voluntary work, increases the likelihood that the next generation will become and remain actively involved in youth groups and committees. Parents, community leaders and *Imams* encourage young people to get involved not only for religious reasons; they also clearly recognise that the next generations (like those before them, both in Mozambique and in Portugal) often socialise with non-Muslims on a daily basis. They realise that their sons and daughters juggle references, nurture affections, and construct a sense of belonging that goes well beyond their own ethno-religious community. Encouraging their children to socialise among Muslim peers, which also makes intra-community marriage more likely, is also a strategy of community maintenance and, in part, a necessary condition for the perpetuation of ethno-religious identity itself.

862 *S. Trovão*

'Becoming Public' About Things That Were (Until Recently) Considered 'Ours': A New Civic Understanding of Religious Identity

Before 11 September 2001, the members of *CilJovem* were often invisible in the Portuguese media. In order to avoid intra-community confrontation, they also adhered to the old pattern of self-silencing among the young to the benefit of the older generation. It is their parents, then, who have represented the community nationally and internationally, negotiated their interests with the Portuguese state, and been the spokespersons with the media. However, since 11 September 2001, and in particular after 11 March 2004 and 7 July 2005, *CilJovem*'s members have frequently been asked to speak about Islam-related issues in Portugal and 'they have become more engaged in Muslim activities at the international level' (Tiesler and Cairns 2007: 223).

Also at work are events on the international stage: issues such as Islamic terrorism, the invasion of Iraq and Afghanistan, and the unresolved problems of Palestine and Kashmir. These topics have also begun to emerge in interviews carried out with young Portuguese Muslims living in Portugal or in the UK, albeit only incipiently. Most people adamantly disagreed with the American and British invasion of Iraq and the Portuguese government's support of these efforts. A few, living in the UK, participated in 'Stop the War' protests or joined a range of dissident non-Muslim groups. Their attempts to understand Islamic terrorism emphasised the need to take into account recent international political history with long-term historical and cultural processes. In concomitance with their growing identification with the suffering of Muslim communities in different parts of the world, they have to face some national specificities.

> I am a Portuguese Muslim and I would find it difficult getting used to living in a Muslim country. But when I remember all the atrocities committed against Muslims, in Palestine, Bosnia, Afghanistan, Iraq ... it's very painful. It's unfair (Ismael, born in Portugal, 21 years old).

The almost total absence of significant Islamophobic movements in Portugal, in comparison to its European neighbours, has contributed to the strong belief that 'Muslims were not discriminated against in the past and they will not be in the future' (Nadia, born in Portugal, 18 years old). However, the international situation and the subsequent growth of public interest in Islam have also encouraged Portuguese Muslim youth to respond to the (repeated and predictable) questions posed by their peers, teachers and journalists (about Islamic traditions, polygamy, the *hijab*, the controversial Danish cartoons, and Islamic extremism).

> When I was younger I wasn't interested in it. But now it's necessary to speak about things that we considered ours. (...) It is helping me to understand certain issues and made me more confident to be a Muslim. Otherwise how can people understand that we share the same values? (Ruczana, born in Portugal, 27 years old).

Journal of Ethnic and Migration Studies   863

Now it's different, I am better informed about Islamic issues. My mates want to know how it is, they are always asking me. (. . .) I have to counteract some negative ideas about Muslims. But I have to explain, based on what I know and what they can understand (Aziz, born in Portugal, 23 years old).

This 'going public' on issues that until recently had been considered only the purview of the individual or the community, is opening up a new public space. It is a space in which one of the principal messages is that Muslims share most of the values that non-Muslim Portuguese embrace. They feel a sense of urgency about the importance of being able to translate Muslim 'issues' into a language which can be understood by non-Muslims. The increase in secular education at secondary and university levels, and what it allows in terms of networking, bridging capitals and mutual knowledge, gives them self-confidence about their own qualities as translators to counter stereotypical images of Islam and build bridges to their fellow citizens. It reveals a new understanding of their civic responsibilities as (Portuguese) Muslims and citizens, closely linked with a new expression of (their) Muslimness.

Uses of Religion, Civic Responsibilities and Gender Dynamics

The possibility of understanding the world as lived by non-Muslims and of translating Islam in ways that make it more understandable to the broader non-Muslim public is used by Muslim youths born in Portugal as an alternative form of social activism. The proactive attitude of some female interlocutors in processing, interpreting and translating Islamic references cannot be read as a re-inscription of traditional gender roles.

Integrated in a national context characterised by a significant evolution in terms of values and practices in gender relationships (oriented, in particular, towards the professional and sexual emancipation of women), they are the first to recognise clear asymmetries between women and men within their community. Thesse asymmetries do not accord with values of secular-liberal feminism but are accepted because they have been vital to the preservation of community 'respect' for their families. A number of them are able to transform some of their families' most conservative values into strategic arguments to promote their professional projects. However in major questions they usually accept the moral authority of their families. While justifying their acceptance in the name of love, the fear of losing parental love, and the emotional idioms of 'feeling proud of' and 'avoiding disappointing', they tend to dissociate from Islam all acts of violence and oppression of women.

Like their Muslims peers, the ways of action and meaning through which young female descendants of immigrants from Cape Verde and São Tomé reorganise their personal lives—and, more specifically, gender relations, as well as their very capacity of redefining them and re-positioning themselves within them—are historically and culturally mediated (Abu-Lughod 2004; Oyewumi 2004; Pessar and Mahler 2006). Converging with studies carried out in various African contexts (Domingues 2000; Emovon 1997; Rosander 1997), research confirms that the mother–children relation and the construction of the mother-person herself acquires a higher analytical centrality than the woman–man relation in the understanding of these youngsters' religious and civic responsibilities and practices.

Allowing them access to spaces, competencies and multiple capitals, their associative participation is generally motivated by the children's provision and upbringing (only too often without the co-responsibility or collaboration of the children's father) and/or by the will to help women-mothers in the same circumstances. Even in the case of those who hold higher social and academic capitals, whose narratives often try to combine the values of 'the old days' with progressive interests and ideals, their civic, ethical and political paths do not necessarily fit into a gender equality logic, nor do they alter long-term structures of gender inequality. Nevertheless they include some potential for change, especially when they convey to their peers that academic and professional training is crucial for their adulthood. They also express the potential for (gender) change when, as practising Catholics or Evangelists, they convey the sacred values of family and marital fidelity, even though they may accept the sexual and reproductive performances of their children's fathers (brothers, fathers, grandfathers) and forgive their infidelities.

In reality, if we distance ourselves from the topography of gender equality/ inequality—insufficient to account for the civic lives which are not necessarily captured in these terms—the female agency may be conceived from different angles and not only as a synonym of resistance, subversion or perpetuation of domination structures (Mahmood 2006). In the end, what is more meaningful is the way some of the interlocutors use religion to acquire tactics and mobility spaces and negotiate them towards but inside specific gender inequality relations.

Concluding Remarks

Both national and local issues can encourage religious mobilisation against inequalities and prejudices that receiving societies hold against immigrant communities. International circumstances also have significant influence on the development of an activist understanding of religion, as happens among Portuguese-born Muslim elites. Mobilising religion, however, requires situated strategies, with social actors possessing not only a tacit knowledge about their civic and political contexts, but also competence in handling and debating information as well as a certain capacity for networking both within and beyond communities.

As Table 1 summarises, comparative research shows that the colonial and postcolonial capitals acquired by the parental generations (be they material, social, cultural, religious, community- or association-related), influence the processes of socio-economic and inter-ethnic insertion of the emerging generations. As a result, they foster the development of their civic skills as well as the density of their social capital, both within and beyond their groups (Portes 1998). Pre-existing models of civic participation rooted in religion, which are adopted by families and communities

Journal of Ethnic and Migration Studies 865

Table 1. Comparing and contrasting the civic–religious lives of two groups of immigrant offspring

Strategic comparison	Christians from Cape Verde and São Tomé	Muslims of Indo-Mozambican origin
Postcolonial migration and integration	• Very positive • Legal status and citizenship granted instantly	• Significant degree of disappointment • Legal status and citizenship not granted instantly
Transnational connections	• Family transnationalism • Little participation in global networks • Growing bonds of emotion over distance	• Family transnationalism Emotional closeness with imagined homes
Inter-ethnic relations	• Feelings of being accepted and respected	• Feelings of discrimination and resentment
Social capital	• Density, both within and beyond ethnic community	• Scarce
Religious identification	• Structuring identity reference but not unique or exclusive	• Structuring identity reference but not unique or exclusive
Civic participation (value orientation and effects)	• Translating Islam and promoting inter-faith encounters to build bridges between Muslims and non-Muslims • Potential civic transnationalism as translators and interpreters	• Using religion to oppose inequalities and prejudice and promote skills and capital among immigrants • Potential (social) mobility and engagement in national and international networks
Identity impacts	• Renewing of Portuguese Muslimness (as hybrid, bilingual and defined by a cross-boundary sensibility)	• Emphasis on devout citizenship as an agency capable of creating inter-identity bonds • Increase of emotional transnationalism

of belonging, can offer sources for identification (Carter 2009; Pedziwaitr 2007). Without neglecting important generational changes, this paper's findings confirm, however, the need to conceptualise religious mobilisation as a capacity for action historically and culturally mediated by long-term gender dynamics.

Although both groups of youngsters pointed out that it is mainly in the current context of insertion that their civic activities can make the difference, research calls for further work on the influence of emotional transnationalism upon religious mobilisation. The children of immigrants from São Tomé and Cape Verde maintain a certain level of emotional closeness with their ancestral homes. Through a conception of devout civic participation, they often locate themselves simultaneously locally and far away. This investment in future obligations with co-nationals is a way of building and living a relationship—in a form of citizenship at a distance—with the imagined land of their roots. On the other hand, Muslims of Indo-Mozambican origin who were born in Portugal have a strong Portuguese identification. Nevertheless, the translating processes through which they actively engage to counter stereotypical images of Islam demonstrate that they are not indifferent to the international

866 *S. Trovão*

growing anti-Muslim sentiment. This reveals the role that recent international political history plays in stimulating new 'bonds of emotion across distance' (Baldassar 2007).

The lives and narratives of the interviewees place particular emphasis on the multi-dimensionality of their personal identifications and social presentations. The latter reveal meanings, strategic uses and benefits in variable and changing contexts. Religious-civic mobilisation becomes, in fact, a central reference in their self-definition as subjects and citizens. This centrality is not incompatible with a range of other selective identifications and *dis*-identifications, social alignments and *dis*-alignments (Banton 2008). Indeed, as I have shown, one important effect of the ways of living religion developed by both groups is their gradual integration within inter-ethnic and inter-faith networks and projects, and at multiple levels— local, national and international. The Muslim and Christian civic lives followed in this paper both demand and are sustained by various forms of transboundary 'positional moves' (Wimmer 2008). Perceived as a main component of active social citizenship, these 'crossings' often involve incomplete, ambivalent and reversible identity renegotiation processes. Whilst their meaning and path cannot be dissociated from long-term cultural traditions, changes—either in daily materiality or at representational and reflexive levels—draw our focus to the complexities of the articulation between referential and migratory models and between these and the global trends of contemporary identifications and practices.

Note

[1] The Portuguese Constitution forbids the counting of ethnically or religiously defined subgroups. Official numbers (2009) point to 11,484 people from São Tomé and Príncipe and 48,845 people from Cape Verde living in Portugal. We can estimate that, in the same context, currently live 9,000 to 11,000 Sunnis and 6,000 to 8,000 Ismailis of Indo-Mozambican origin. Muslims migrants also arrived from Guinea-Bissau and afterwards from Bangladesh, Pakistan, Indonesia and Senegal. Unofficial figures indicate that the number of Muslim immigrants has quadrupled in the last few decades, now reaching more than 50,000 individuals.

References

Abu-Lughod, L. (2004) 'Do muslim women really need saving? Anthropological reflections on cultural relativism on its others', *American Anthropologist*, *104*(3): 783–90.

Albuquerque, R. and Teixeira, A. (2005) *Active Civic Participation of Immigrants in Portugal. Country Report Prepared for the European Research Project.* Oldenburg: POLITIS, available online: http://www.politis-europe.uni-oldenburg.de/download/Portugal.pdf, last accessed 15 October 2009.

Anthias, F. (2007) 'Ethnic ties: social capital and the question of mobilisability', *Sociological Review*, *55*(4): 788–805.

Baldassar, L. (2007) 'Transnational families and the provision of moral and emotional support', *Identities*, *14*(4): 385–409.

Banton, M. (2008) 'The sociology of ethnic relations', *Ethnic and Racial Studies*, 31(7): 1267–85.

Bastos, S. and Bastos, J. (2008) 'Family dynamics, uses of religion and interethnic relations within the Portuguese cultural ecology', in Grillo, R. (ed.) *Immigrant Families in Multicultural Europe: Debating Cultural Difference.* Amsterdam: Amsterdam University Press, 135–63.

Bauböck, R., Kraler, A., Martiniello, M. and Perchinig, B. (2006) 'Migrants' citizenship: legal status, rights and political participation', in Penninx, R., Berger, M. and Kraal, K. (eds) *The Dynamics of International Migration and Settlement in Europe.* Amsterdam: Amsterdam University Press, 65–98.

Brubaker, R., Loveman, M. and Stamatov, P. (2004) 'Ethnicity as cognition', *Theory and Society*, 33(1): 31–64.

Carter, P. (2009) 'Predicting civic and political engagement: family socialization and age-group differences', *Sociology Today*, 7(2), available online: http://www.ncsociology.org/sociationto-day/v72/famage.htm, last accessed 19 October 2010.

Delanty, G. (2000) *Citizenship in a Global Age.* Milton Keynes: Open University Press.

Domingues, M. (2000) *Estratégias Femininas entre as Bideiras de Bissau.* Lisbon: Universidade Nova de Lisboa, unpublished PhD thesis.

Ebaugh, H.R. and Chapetz, J.S. (2000) *Religion and the New Immigrants.* Walnut Creek: Altamira Press.

Emovon, A.C. (1997) 'Women of power: a study of market women's associations in Benin City, Bendel State, Nigeria', in Kaplan, F. (ed.) *Queens, Queen Mother, Priestesses and Power: Case Studies in African Gender.* New York Academy of Sciences, 203–14.

Horta, A., Malheiros, J. and Rosa, A. (2008) 'Ethnic civic communities and political participation: the case study of Cape-Verdean associations in the region of Lisbon and in Rotterdam', in Fonseca, M. (ed.) *Cities in Movement: Migrants and Urban Change.* Lisbon: Centro de Estudos Geográficos, 165–202.

Jacobs, D. and Tillie, J. (2004) 'Introduction: social capital and the political integration of migrants', *Journal of Ethnic and Migration Studies*, 30(3): 419–27.

Jenkins, R. (2004) *Rethinking Ethnicity.* London: Sage.

Joppke, C. (2009) *The Veil: Mirror of Identity.* Cambridge: Polity Press.

Khosrokhavar, F. (1997) *L'Islam des Jeunes.* Paris: Flammarion.

Klausen, J. (2006) *The Islamic Challenge. Politics and Religion in Western Europe.* Oxford: Oxford University Press.

Mahmood, S. (2006) 'Teoria feminista, agência e sujeito liberatório: algumas reflexões sobre o revivalismo Islâmico no Egipto', *Etnográfica*, 10(1): 121–57.

Marques, M. and Santos, R. (2004) 'Top-down and bottom-up reconsidered: the dynamics of immigrant participation in local civil society', in Penninx, R., Kraal, K., Martiniello, M. and Vertovec, S. (eds) *Citizenship in European Cities. Immigrants, Local Politics and Integration Policies.* Aldershot: Ashgate, 107–26.

Oyewumi, O. (2004) 'Conceptualizing gender: Eurocentric foundations of feminist concepts and the challenge of African epistemologies', in Signe, A., Bakare-Yusuf, B., Waswa Kisiang'ani, E., Lewis, D., Oyewumi, O. and Steady, F.C. (eds) *African Gender Scholarship: Concepts, Methodologies and Paradigms.* Dakar: Codesria, 1–8.

Pedziwaitr, K. (2007) 'Religion and social citizenship amongst professional Muslim Londoners', *Kolor: Journal on Moving Communities*, 7(1): 3–22.

Pessar, P. and Mahler, S. (2006) 'Gender matters: ethnographers bring gender from the periphery towards the core of migration studies', *International Migration Review*, 40(1): 27–63.

Portes, A. (1998) 'The two meanings of social capital', *Sociological Forum*, 15(1): 1–12.

Reicher, S. (2004) 'The context of social identity', *Political Psychology*, 25(6): 921–45.

Rosander, E. (1997) *Transforming Female Identities: Women's Organizational Forms in West Africa.* Uppsala: Nordiska Afrikainstitutet.

Roy, O. (2000) 'Muslims in Europe: from ethnic identity to religious recasting', *ISIM Newsletter*, 5.

868   S. Trovão

Tastsoglou, E. (2006) *Women, Migration and Citizenship: Making Local, National and Transnational Connections*. Canada: Ashgate.

Tiesler, N. and Cairns, D. (2007) 'Representing Islam and Lisbon youth', *Lusotopie, 14*(1): 223–38.

Verba, S., Schlozman, K.L. and Brady, L.E. (1996) *Voice and Equality: Civic Voluntarism in American Politics*. Harvard: Harvard University Press.

Vertovec, S. and Rogers, A. (eds) (1998) *Muslim European Youth: Reproducing Ethnicity, Religion, Culture*. Aldershot: Ashgate.

Wimmer, A. (2008) 'Elementary strategies of ethnic boundary making', *Ethnic and Racial Studies, 31*(6): 1025–55.

[29]

African Studies, 68, 2, August 2009

The Global Portability of Pneumatic Christianity: Comparing African and Latin American Pentecostalisms

Manuel A. Vásquez
University of Florida

This article argues that Pentecostal Christianity is able to spread so quickly across the globe because it provides its adherents with the conceptual tools to deal with desire and materialism in a world of limited means and lack. It thus offers adherents an authentic belonging that is located globally as well as in the afterlife, rather than bound by geographical territory. This is particularly relevant for poor migrants – such as the African migrants in South Africa – who are faced with misfortune and lack of success. The Pentecostal imagination of what it means to be human offers them tools by which to remake their self and on which to build their hopes for a better future. It allows adherents to deal with the tension of a globalised world economy that imposes systems of exclusion and lack in third world areas.

Key words: Migrants, Pentecostal Christianity, Pneumatic Christianity, pneumatic materialism, transnationalism

A newly minted temple of the Universal Church of the Kingdom of God (UCKG) rises majestically in the midst of Soweto's bustling main market. Founded in Rio de Janeiro in 1977 by Edir Macedo, a former lottery employee, the UCKG is one of the fastest growing global neo-Pentecostal churches.[1] The 'Universal' bills its cathedral in Soweto as 'the biggest temple in South Africa'. It can comfortably hold 8,000 persons seated and has underground parking for 2,000 cars. With its soaring all-glass entrance, its massive piers, its shiny and meticulously clean floors, and its state-of-the-art illumination, sound and video systems, the temple has the feel of a hypermodern spaceship, which has landed in the heart of Africa, marking a radical break with its past and healing all its perceived moral and spiritual problems.

The UCKG's colossal, shimmering architecture is deliberately set against the beer halls that surround it. During the years of apartheid, these beer halls stood for both domination and resistance, since the white regime restricted access to essential ingredients in the production of alcoholic drinks in the township in order to guarantee the municipal government monopoly over the liquor trade and, secondarily, to control the black working class. In defiance, women in Soweto managed to produce their own brew out of the local ingredients and set their own illegal shebeens, where they often sold stronger concoctions (Crush and Ambler 1992). Today, many of these local beer halls remain, often populated by immigrants

ISSN 0002-0184 print/ISSN 1469-2872 online/09/020273–14
© 2009 Taylor & Francis Group Ltd on behalf of the University of Witwatersrand
DOI: 10.1080/00020180903109664

274 African Studies, 68:2, August 2009

from Mozambique, Zimbabwe and Angola, who find themselves at the margins of a post-apartheid South Africa. By offering lived spaces that connect cleanliness, power, progress, and spiritual salvation, that stand in sharp contrast to the low ceilings, dirt floors, and cramped and dark rooms of the surrounding beer halls, the builders of the new UCKG cathedral dramatise the neo-Pentecostal mission to win souls and take territories for Jesus Christ through an unabashed gospel of health and wealth.

Across the Atlantic Ocean, in Dallas, Texas, the Nigerian-based Redeemed Christian Church of God (RCCG), arguably the fastest growing African Pentecostal church, is busy working on Camp Redemption. It intends to build a hall with capacity for 20,000, the culmination of more than fifty years of vigorous missionary work.[2] The plan is for Camp Redemption in Dallas to resemble eventually Redemption City, a vast complex about forty-eight kilometres north of Lagos that has all the trappings of successful modernity. Redemption City has

> beautiful residential quarters with streets named from biblical registers, a primary school, a secondary school and a university. It has several guesthouses, banks, supermarkets, restaurants and a clinic. All these are in addition to typical church infrastructure, namely, four parishes of the RCCG, two auditoria (a large one measuring two by two kilometres, and a smaller one), a vast ground for open-air services, dormitories and several prayer facilities. A maintenance department ensures the smooth running of the Camp, while a security unit protects life and property. (Adeboye 2007:47)

Redemption City is also the site for the Holy Ghost Festival, a massive revival encounter that is 'now so large that it has attracted government concern because of the traffic jams that occur on the Lagos-Ibadan expressway. The average headcount of those who attend the service is about half a million, although the 1998 program, entitled "Divine Visitation", attracted nearly 6.5 million people' (Hunt 2002:191).

Like the UCKG, the RCCG is serious about the 'Great Commission', Jesus Christ's injunction to his disciples to 'go therefore and make disciples of all the nations, baptizing them in the name of the Father and the Son and the Holy Spirit' (Matt. 20:19). Also like the UCKG, the RCCG engages in open spiritual warfare and sees victory over the Devil and its minions as crucial to a successful entry into western modernity, to gaining access to prosperity and well-being beginning here on earth. However, the RCCG adds a powerful indigenous African dimension to spiritual warfare. 'A major theme of Redeemed teachings, to its Nigerian audience especially, is that becoming saved protects you from the curses, spells and sorcery that Africans, even Christian ones, commonly blame for all manner of misfortunes, from car accidents to impotence' (Rice 2009:57).

The UCKG and the RCCG are two high-profile actors in the emergence of a new Christianity. According to religion scholar Philip Jenkins (2002), Christianity is currently undergoing changes that might be as significant as those documented in Acts of the Apostles, when the religion began to spread throughout Asia

Minor and the Mediterranean world. Indeed, Christianity's centre of gravity is shifting from North to South, a shift that is the result not simply of population changes but, perhaps more importantly, of the emergence and development of vibrant indigenised types of Christianity in Africa, Latin America and Asia. These new Christianities are now key players in the global stage. The Brazilian Universal Church of the Kingdom of God, which has temples in South Africa, Angola, Mozambique, the United Kingdom, the US, Japan, and throughout Latin America, is not alone. African actors also play a leading role, a fact that is not surprising, given that between '1900 and 2000, the number of Christians in Africa grew from 10 millions to over 360 millions, from 10 per cent of the population to 46 per cent' (Jenkins 2006:9). Joining the Redeemed Christian Church of God, which is now present in fifty nations around the world (Adeboye 2007), are the Nigerian-based Kingsway International Christian Center (KICC) and Deeper Life Bible Church, and the Ghanaian-based Church of the Pentecost and the Apostolic Church (Watkin 2004). All these African churches, which have a high profile among African immigrants in global cities like London and New York, are part of what Allan Anderson (2001) calls 'New Pentecostals and Charismatic' (NPC) churches that represent the latest wave of African Initiated Churches (AICs).

Drawing from my work on Latin American and Latino Pentecostalisms and my growing interest in African Pentecostalisms, I explore what makes these indigenised Christianities better able to negotiate globalisation, to circulate globally with great ease. What is it about the Christianity performed by the UCKG and RCCG that makes it so transportable among immigrants in the African and Latin American Diasporas and through mass media, popular culture, and computer-mediated communications?

In a way, this is an old question, one posed by Max Weber (1958), when he asked us to reflect on the elective affinity – the relation of reciprocal influence – between a particular ethos, a particular religious way of being in the world which he called 'this worldly-asceticism', and the spirit of modern western capitalism. Weber is often read as an idealist, a counter-point to reductive Marxist materialism. However, Weber's notion of elective affinity in the *Protestant Ethic and the Spirit of Capitalism* can be read 'materialistically', as the confluence of a religiously inflected habitus, a set of disciplinary technologies deployed on the body directing it to produce certain kinds of practices (emphasising austerity, sobriety, thrift and hard work) and a bureaucratically-controlled, means-ends system of production (Taylorism and Fordism). This is in fact what Marxist historian EP Thompson does in his *The Making of the English Working Class* (1966). In this book, he points to the ways in which Methodism provided the discipline necessary to harness the productive power of the nascent working classes in England, while, at the same time, allowing workers to vent their frustrations with and anger at the oppressive working conditions in the safe space of highly emotional Sunday services.

276 African Studies, 68:2, August 2009

I would like to propose that what makes African and Latin American Pentecostalisms so portable today is a polymorphous 'pneumatic materialism'. I use the term pneumatic, which comes from the Greek word *pneuma*, meaning literally 'breath', the spiritual force that animates matter, to characterise forms of Christianity that make the Holy Spirit central to the experience of the sacred. Modelling itself after the early Christian community, pneumatic Christianity sees the charismata, the gifts of the Holy Spirit, such as glossolalia, divine healing, prophecy, and exorcism, as unmistakable signs of salvation.[3] Latin American and African Pentecostalisms are not only pneumatic but thoroughly materialist in the sense that they reject the European, Cartesian dichotomy between soul and body and the denigration of the latter. Drawing from indigenous traditions that link natural forces with the spirits of ancestors, these Pentecostalisms see the world in non-dualistic terms: the 'supernatural' realm of the spirits is not other-worldly; it does not stand separate from or above the natural world.[4] Rather, spirit and flesh are constitutively intertwined, as are transcendence and immanence. For these non-dualistic vernacular Christianities, individual salvation operates through a personal relation with God and manifested in this-worldly health and wealth. Conversion entails a new highly malleable 'spirit-matter' nexus, a holistic re-articulation of the self and its surroundings. This new pneumatic materialism is able to bridge in multiple contexts the tension between the seen and the unseen, among the personal, the local, and the global. It can also address the otherwise intractable condition of physical insecurity and exclusion faced by vast sectors of the world's population, particularly in Latin America and Africa. It can do so because this pneumatic materialism bears a powerful elective affinity with the current episode of globalisation.

Today's globalisation can be characterised as a 'mobility regime' marked by 'enclosed mobilities, regulated transnationalisms, and monitored rather than simple flexible sovereignties' (Cunningham 2004:332). In other words, while recent developments in communication and transportation technologies have made possible the worldwide circulation of ideas, capital, images, and people, this circulation is arguably more tightly controlled by hegemonic nation-states. In particular, the US, the European Union, and South Africa have sought to control immigration by aggressively reinforcing borders, reforming formerly generous asylum programmes, and steeping up deportations of undocumented workers. On the one hand, globalisation encourages people to migrate by undermining local ways of life and beaming cosmopolitan images of wealth and success in the metropole. On the other hand, as the tightening of immigration laws from the US to Europe to South Africa demonstrates, globalisation involves limiting the movement of people. This interplay between mobility and containment/closure allows for a new global bio-politics, the extraction of surplus from dislocated individuals, who, as 'illegal' immigrants, provide cheap and disposable labour without the right to demand any recognition and political power from their host societies.

According to Shamir 'the engine of the contemporary mobility regime is a "paradigm of suspicion" that conflates the perceived threats of crime, immigration, and terrorism (hence the notion of "integrated risk management"), and ... the technology of intervention that enables it is biosocial profiling' (2005:200). Immigrants are potentially terrorists or carriers of deadly strains of influenza. Thus, the nation-state must generate vast databanks to sort out transnational dangers lurking everywhere. The result is a 'gated globe' in which selective osmosis regulates and monitors the flows of people (Cunningham 2004). 'Thought of in spatial terms, globalization is a process constitutive of a global mobility regime that aspires to screen those substances (viruses, people, and hazardous materials) that may cross the boundaries of some designated social containers (e.g., national borders and gated communities) from those that may not' (Shamir 2005:208–9). This is why Zygmunt Bauman claims that today 'mobility has become the most powerful and most coveted stratifying factor; the stuff of which the new, increasingly world-wide, social, political, economic, and cultural hierarchies are daily built and rebuilt' (1998:9).

My argument is that Latin American and African Christianities are highly portable because their worldviews, practices, and organisational morphologies not only make sense of the contradictions of this 'gated globe' but actually thrive on these contradictions. Pneumatic materialism, with its world full of ambiguous and unpredictable spirits, agencies, and intentionalities which move about with great ease and yet are very much connected to specific territories, objects, and bodies, is both a reflection of the vulnerability of those who are affected by the new regime of closure and mobility and a means to cope effectively with the consequences of this regime in everyday life. This pneumatic materialism is the masses' own version of the 'paradigm of suspicion', where the ever-present fear of being targeted by witchcraft and/ or the evil eye requires its own spiritual risk management through their spiritual combat churches such as the UCKG and the RCCG.

Surprisingly, very little has been written on the transportability of religion that can help us flesh out the specific mechanisms through which Latin American and African pneumatic materialism operates. Nevertheless, cognitive psychologist Harvey Whitehouse offers some helpful insights. According to him, religious diversity is the result of the oscillation between these two ideal-typical modes of religiosity – 'imagistic' and 'doctrinal' – each with its own logic of transmission. The imagistic mode of religiosity involves 'religious practices [that] are very intense emotionally: they may be rarely performed and highly stimulating (for example, involving altered states of consciousness or terrible ordeals and tortures); they tend to trigger a lasting sense of revelation and produce powerful bonds between small groups of rituals' (Whitehouse 2004:63). In contrast, the doctrinal mode of religiosity is built around 'forms of religious activity [that] tend to be much less stimulating: they may be highly repetitive or "routinized," conducted in a relatively calm and sober atmosphere; such practices are often accompanied by the transmission of complex theology and doctrine and also tend to mark out large religious communities composed of people who cannot possibly all know each other (certainly not in any intimate way)' (Whitehouse 2004:63–4).

278 African Studies, 68:2, August 2009

What does this theory of modes of religiosity have to do with the global spread of Latin American and African pneumatic Christianity? According to Whitehouse, the mode of religiosity that is best suited for transmission across multiple spaces and times is the doctrinal because of its routinisation into narratives, texts, theologies, and ethics which can be presented as universal. From these universal precepts standardised ritual practices follow, which can be deployed anywhere. In contrast, the imagistic has to rely on face-to-face contact to reignite the intense but fragmentary events on which it depends (that is why Whitehouse calls the memory involved here as 'episodic' or flashbulb memory). It is then more difficult to replicate in different contexts the particularism of imagistic religion. In fact, Whitehouse goes as far as saying that 'unlike the beliefs and practices of the doctrinal mode, traditions operating in the imagistic mode do not spread widely' (2004:73).

Whitehouse's theory dovetail's nicely with Weber's account of how monotheistic world religions spread through the rise of priestly elites who were able to generate a canon out of the fragmentary teachings of the charismatic founder and to disseminate this systematised body of doctrines and practices through missionising, trade, migration, or warfare. The theory also helps us understand how some indigenous traditions are being globalised today. In a recent book exploring the Garifuna religion in St Vincent, Honduras and New York, Paul Christopher Johnson has used Whitehouse's work to highlight some transformations taking place among shamans who travel these transnational religious spaces. When asked about their New York colleagues, a Honduran shaman told Johnson (2007:99), 'They treat ritual like something you learn in school'. When Johnson went back to New York to ask shamans there what they thought of their counterparts, he heard the following: 'They know what to do, but they don't know why they do what they do'. Johnson takes this transnational conflict over religious authority and authenticity as a sign of a shift from imagistic to doctrinal religion precipitated by the need to operate across multiple Diasporic horizons. As the New York-based shamans try to establish authority in the highly pluralistic US religious fields, they try to make their practices more explicit, more rationalised, more in line with the complex theology associated with Santeria, the African-based tradition with the highest prestige. The result is the production of a more standardised, 'theologised', textualised, public, and cosmopolitan shamanism.

Despite the obvious pay off of Whitehouse's theory of modes of religiosity, it seems to run aground when it comes to the rapid spread of African and Latin American pneumatic Christianities. Like the imagistic mode of religiosity, these Christianities rely on intense episodes of elevated arousal, they often de-emphasise theology in favour of embodied and emplaced practices like glossolalia, divine healing, prophecy, and exorcism. And while texts are certainly important in these Christianities, they are not just sources of transposable universal doctrines and ethics. These texts are themselves sacred artefacts, charged with the spiritual power to transform, to purify forcibly both self and society. These texts are tools in the struggle to conquer specific worldly territories.

Whitehouse's failure to account for the great portability of pneumatic Christianities has to do with the fact that he is still caught in a modernist, representationalist mind-set that considers print media as the key vehicle for the spread of religion. However, imagistic modes of religion today, including African and Latin American Pentecost-alisms, circulate through other media. Their worldwide diffusion is rather the result of the practices of transnational networks of missionaries that rely heavily on the widespread use of electronic, image-heavy media, like TV, videos, films, and the Internet. Through this media, these religious actors render the imagistic mode of religiosity translocal, no longer only the province of small, localised communities, but rather of transnational 'communities of sentiment', to quote Arjun Appadurai, 'sodalities of worship and charisma' (1996:8), which while territorialised in London, Johannesburg or São Paulo, feel part of the larger church of the saved.

Canadian sage Marshall McLuhan wrote in *Understanding the Media* (1964) that the new technologies that are emerging are literally changing our brains, in some ways stretching our neural networks to envelop the whole world. While he might have overstated his case, he is correct in highlighting how cyber-networks are redefining the interface between embodiment and culture, between the neural and the cultural. We live in a society that is saturated with images that circulate at blinding speeds and are mixed and re-mixed endlessly, a 'society of the spec-tacle' (Debord 2006), a global society of 'permanent simulacra' (Baudrillard 1995). This society nurtures what Georg Simmel called 'a blasé attitude': the 'incapacity to react to new sensations with the appropriate energy'. For the 'blasé person' in the global metropolis of cyberspace, things appear in 'an evenly flat and gray tone; no object deserves preference over any other' (Simmel 1950:414). In the 'dessert of the real', amid the 24-7 flood of images that saturates our senses, what stands out, is remembered and thus, is more likely to be transmitted is the stark, the spectacular that sets itself apart from the profane world. And what can be more spectacular than apocalyptic and millen-arian messages, narratives of a cosmic struggle between God and the Devil that is enacted every time an exorcism takes place in a neo-Pentecostal church. In our postmodern world, where the social seems to have imploded, where signs seem to point only to other signs (Baudrillard 1995), it is imagistic religion, particularly as expressed in vivid, life-or-death encounters with travelling spirits, that is more memorable and transportable. This aesthetic of the 'spectacular', of the need to break radically with everydayness and to perform this transcendence globally, not by escaping the broken world but by embracing an exuberant pneumatic mate-rialism that brings health and wealth as visible gifts of the Holy Spirit, explains the grandiose architecture of the UCKG's cathedral in Soweto and the RCCG's ambitious plans for the farmlands it owns north of Dallas. As Adeboye (2007:48) rightly puts it, the self-sufficient and imposing nature of Redemption City 'embodies the "visions" and "dreams" of the RCCG. As the nucleus of the activities of the RCCG, the Redemption Camp is thus the theatre (physical space and institutional channel) where the "old" RCCG prophecies are expected to be fulfilled.'

The global portability of pneumatic Christianities from Africa and Latin America, thus, depends greatly on the portability of the Holy Spirit and the spirits it battles, on their fluidity and capacity to circulate through flexible transnational church and immigrant networks and to become localised through specific spirits or condensed in material objects, from bodies to money to commodities, which then become associated with dramatic, image-heavy public practices of warfare, purification, prayer and conversion, and what Jean and John Comaroff (2001) have called the 'economies of the occult'. Put in other words, the global portability of African and Latin American Christianity depends on the dialectic between the materialisation of the spirit and spiritualisation of the material at various spatio-temporal scales.

There are at least three alchemical processes driving this dialectic:

1) The nexus of spirit and matter is spatially mediated. Latin American and African Pneumatic Christianities produce 'heterotopias', spaces of livelihood that at times overlap and reinforce each other, and, at other times, stand in tension with each other. Applying and expanding Thomas Tweed's theory of the construction of sacred space in Diaspora (1998), we can say that Pentecostal and Charismatic Christianity build a supra-local space, what Henri Lefebvre called absolute space, the space of the Kingdom of God, of the ends of time, when human, depraved time will be erased. They also build a trans-local time, as the armies of God move across transnational networks to 'conquer territory', particularly in the most profane and secular places, place like London, New York, or Johannesburg, or Lagos, infested with evil spirits, in preparation for the coming of supra-local space. These churches also build local spaces of livelihood, enclaves of sacrality, where individuals, immigrants and those most vulnerable to the work of these evil spirits, can find refuge, intimacy, reciprocity and support. Finally, the churches remap the bodies of the converts, creating new spaces of the self, where the subject can reconstitute subjectivity and personal networks (families). The portability of pneumatic religion is predicated on the power to work effectively at all these spatial scales, from the most global, the cosmic, to the conversion, renewal, and salvation of the subject.

2) This whole question of the transformation of the self takes us to the second important dimension of Latin American and African pneumatic materialism. Pneumatic Christianity produces disciplined yet flexible selves, whose particular desires, needs, and capacities allow them entry into modernity but without entirely breaking with tradition. Here the work of Rijk van Dijk on Ghanaian Pentecostals is instructive. He argues that Pentecostals use deliverance and exorcism as technologies of the self to produce a totally transparent 'modern person in control of [his/her] destiny, and no longer restrained by the binding threads that have been concocted to trap the individual within tradition' (Van Dijk 2001:218). Here Pentecostalism involves 'a singular move toward individuality, a severance of kinship ties, and a rejection of all those

rituals (funerals, initiation, healing) that venerate the ancestors of the family'
(Van Dijk 2001:231). However, this freedom, which can prove extremely
helpful to an African immigrant in Europe or in America, trying to advance
socially and economically, is balanced by a strong attachment to the Pentecostal leader, who serves as the broker between the society of settlement and
Ghana. Thus, 'individuality is time and again transformed into new dividuality,
where the church-members are expected to define their identities in terms of
what is shared by the leader' (Van Dijk 2001:229). In other words, the new
self produced is not a totally uprooted, de-contextualised subject, the kind
that neo-classical economics offers as the key actors in western markets, but
an embedded one, one for whom the webs of belonging, reciprocity, and
meaning have been reconstructed from the ground up, from the bodily
habitus, to the family, to the church as the new affines.

3) Pneumatic materialism's third alchemical process has to do with the production of alternative embodied habituses. Scholars such as Peter Geschiere
   (1997) and Birgit Meyer (2002) have pointed to the close relationship
   between the introduction of new patterns of consumption to Latin America
   and Africa and the widespread presence of the Devil and, thus, the need to neu-
   tralise it through power prayers and other forms of spiritual warfare. Meyer, for
   example, makes it clear that what we are witnessing here goes beyond Marx's
   fetishism of commodities, where the objects take a life of their own, obscuring
   the praxis and labour relations that have created them in the first place. Meyer's
   informants know that the commodities they encounter are very likely to come
   from alienated labour. So, the issue here is not false consciousness. Rather the
   issue of one of purity and danger, of not knowing the exact provenance of the
   commodities, and, thus, of not knowing the spiritual forces that might have
   come to dwell in the profusion of objects. This is where the prosperity theologies or gospels of health and wealth come in: it is good to desire all these
   foreign commodities and, in fact, it is a mark of modernity to consume
   them. However, one must do so with the proper caution. These objects have
   to be purified, the potential jealousies and envies that their acquisition generates properly blocked, their abuse monitored through strategies that control
   predation (expressed in dreams and visions of zombies, headhunters, and
   other cannibalistic forces that live in our midst). No wonder why KICC's
   main motto in its website proclaims it as a church that is 'taking territories .
   . . and raising champions'.

Taken together, what is at stake in these three alchemical processes is the articulation of new forms of authority, authenticity and belonging. For many Latin
American and African immigrants in the US, Europe, or South Africa, access to
modernity's disenchanted forms of authority, authenticity, and belonging is as
elusive as obtaining legal residency and citizenship. As Hansen, Jeannerat and
Sadouni argue in their introductory essay, in South Africa, immigrants from
other parts of Africa also do not have access to traditional sources of authority,

authenticity, and belonging grounded either on kinship, the ancestors or the land or on the hermeneutics of suffering that bound together those who struggled against apartheid.

Against the nativism of black South Africans, which erupted in the violent anti-immigrant riots of May 2008, immigrants deploy the power of a universal yet indigenised Holy Spirit that casts out the spirits of the ancestors, now re-appropriated as Satan's minions, and recasts suffering in terms of the purifying blood of Jesus Christ.[5] The simultaneously deterritorialising and reterritorialising power of pneumatic materialism offers a new way for the stranger to bypass national narratives of belonging and legitimacy and to carve out alternative spaces of livelihood and to demand recognition (Glick Schiller, Çaglar and Gludbrandsen 2006). Here, identity-construction and place-making are enabled by participation in the dense networks built by the 'traveling preacher, pastor and religious specialist [who] is often seen as the bearer of extraordinary wisdom, power and insight qua his non-local origin' (Hansen, Jeannerat and Sadouni in this issue). Thus, beyond critical assistance in practical matters, such as food, job referrals, legal aid, and housing accommodations, pneumatic churches offer immigrants a new spiritual form of citizenship in the midst of a South African society 'that does not cohere'. Beyond social capital and self-help networks, what is at stake for immigrants in pneumatic Christian churches is membership in a global community of the sanctified and elect, a community that, in their perception, trumps the pathological national *Gesellschaft*, or rather, that will eventually heal and save South Africa, or the secularised societies of Europe and the US. However, this citizenship is ambivalent, because it often carries a distinctive neo-liberal inflection: a gospel of health and wealth that binds the faithful to transnational chains of commodities they do not control or understand (Glick Schiller 2005).

Pneumatic Christianity is portable because, operating from the paradigm of suspicion, it engages in effective risk management in societies that do not cohere. Pneumatic Christianity allows for the safe appropriation of all the commodities, from money to symbols, from bodies to culture, that now circulate at an unprecedented rate and have become charged with all manner of signification. Without this re-enchantment of the material world, globalisation would truly become an iron cage or it would lead to violent conflicts, as increasing segments of the population in Latin America and Africa desire more intensely to have these goods but have less and less possibility of enjoying them. Pneumatic Christianity acts then to regulate desire, simultaneously producing it, encouraging it, channelling and disciplining it.

In face of the failure of the various modernist projects of the nation-state (from socialism, to nationalism, to pan-Africanism, to neo-liberalism), the key issue in Latin America and Africa is survival in everyday life; it is chronic material and spiritual insecurity. Widespread corruption, arbitrary violence in daily life, the ever-present threat of HIV/AIDS, and the illicit use of power have left many people with no one and nothing to trust. Everything can hurt you. Bauman (2006) has referred to this condition as 'liquid fear', the all-permeating 'horror of the unmanageable'. Here, Bauman's work dovetails nicely with on-going work on witchcraft, civil society and democratisation in South Africa (Ashforth 2005; Harr 2007). '[W]hereas in the past people had traditional means at their disposal to pacify angered spirits and to persuade them to resume their natural stance to the human world, today the spirit world is often perceived to have assumed an inherently evil character in the face of which humans are rather powerless' (Harr 2007:2).

What accounts for this darkening and movement of the spirit world beyond the confines of tradition? According to Ruth Marshall-Fratani, 'the anxiety created by the continued influx of "dangerous strangers" to urban centers as a result of rural-urban migration, the extreme instrumentalisation of social relations, as well as the breakdown of many patron-client networks during the past decade have introduced a kind of urban paranoia about "evil doers" who are out to cheat, deceive, rob and kill. A kind of Hobbesian sense of "all against all" prevails; the old forms of community – ethnic, kinship, professional, hometown, neighborhood – have proven unreliable sources of support' (2001:85). Translocal Pentecostal and charismatic networks, buttressed by powerful global narratives, which are at once simple in the dualism and flexible in their capacity to interpret a multiplicity of phenomena, fill this vacuum. Their sheer imagistic power is capable of domesticating the unruly reality.

But the vitality of pneumatic materialism is not a simple reflection of social and structural pathologies. Spirits too have agency, shaping economic reality. Jean Comaroff and John Comaroff might be on to something when they write that occult economies are 'a response to a world gone awry, yet again, a world in which the only way to create real wealth seems to lie in forms of power/knowledge that transgress the conventional, the rational, the moral – thus to multiply available techniques of producing value, fair or foul' (2001:26). They continue: 'As the connections between means and ends become more opaque, more distended, more mysterious, the occult becomes an ever more appropriate, semantically saturated metaphor of our times.' Under these conditions, 'magic is everywhere, the science of the concrete, aimed at making sense of and acting upon the world – especially but not only, among those who feel themselves disempowered, emasculated, disadvantaged' (Comaroff and Comaroff 2001:27). Pneumatic Christianity also as a 'science of the concrete', an art of the material, represents a very successful set of transnational, cosmopolitan technologies to deal with disrupted (travelling) spirits, who in their wrath torment the living. This is why the UCKG's motto is *pare de sofrir!* ('stop suffering'), seeking to re-assert bodily wholeness and control and moral agency, with the by-product of health and wealth. Pneumatic Christianity is then a way to render visible and thus localised, public and relatively accountable and controllable, what has become deterritorialised and thus invisible, secret, baffling, and subject to illicit manipulation.

284 African Studies, 68:2, August 2009

We can learn important things about the contradictions and future of globalisation and its implication with religion through the comparative pneumatology, the comparative, multi-scalar study of spirits. Therefore, I close with a call to build a new, ethnographically-driven post-Hegelian global and transnational phenomenology of the spirit, one which places African and Latin American religious actors front and centre.

Notes

1. On the UKCG, see Freston (2001) and Kramer (2005).
2. The RCCG was founded in 1952 by Yoruba-speaking Josiah Akindayomi, whose parents were reputed to be devotees of Ogun, the Yoruba god of iron and war. Akindayomi emerged out of the *Aludura* ('praying people') Christian movement, which began in the 1920s in West Africa. The movement combines elements of animism, ritual healing, and charismatic Christianity. The RCCG is now led by former university math professor Enoch Adeboye. See Adeboye (2007); Gornik (2008); and Hunt (2002).
3. Contemporary Pentecostals see themselves as heirs of the early Christian community, as characterised in Acts of the Apostles. More specifically, Pentecostals trace their roots to Pentecost. Fifty days after Jesus Christ's ascension to heaven, the Apostles received the Holy Spirit, which manifested itself in a rushing wind and tongues of fire. Thereupon, the Apostle began to preach in various languages and perform miracles, including healing and exorcism of possessing spirits. From then on Christianity spread very quickly through the Mediterranean, Asia Minor, and North Africa (see Walls 2002).
4. On the connection between Pentecostalism, a movement that originated in the US in places as diverse as Azusa Street, Los Angeles, CA and Topeka, Kansas in the early 1900s, and indigenous African religions, see Olupona (2000).
5. In Latin America, the struggle over the ancestors is not so central as in Africa, except among indigenous communities in places such as southern Mexico, Guatemala, the Andes, and the Amazonian lowlands. In these places, pneumatic Christianity has alternatively clashed and cross-fertilised with shamanistic practices, often producing sharp divisions among indigenous leaders that have made collective mobilisation more difficult. Nevertheless, just as in Africa, in Latin America, pneumatic Christianity is re-articulating solidarity and collective authority, agency, and voice among subaltern groups.

References

Adeboye, Olufunke. 2007. '"Arrowhead" of Nigerian Pentecostalism: The Redeemed Christian Church of God, 1952–2005'. *Pneuma* 29:24–58.

Anderson, Allan. 2001. *African Reformation: African Initiated Christianity in the 20th Century*. Trenton, NJ: Africa World Press.

Appadurai, Arjun. 1996. *Modernity at Large: Cultural Dimensions of Globalization*. Minneapolis: University of Minnesota Press.

Ashforth, Adam. 2005. *Witchcraft, Violence, and Democracy in South Africa*. Chicago: University of Chicago Press.

Baudrillard, Jean. 1995. *Simulacra and Simulation*. Ann Arbor, MI: University of Michigan Press.

Bauman, Zygmunt. 1998. *Globalization: The Human Consequences*. New York: Columbia University Press.

Bauman, Zygmunt. 2006. *Liquid Fear*. Cambridge: Polity.

Comaroff, Jean and Comaroff, John L. 2001. 'Millennial Capitalism: First Thought on a Second Coming', in Jean Comaroff and John Comaroff (eds), *Millennial Capitalism and the Culture of Neoliberalism*. Durham, NC: Duke University Press, pp. 1–56.

Crush, Jonathan and Ambler, Charles. (eds). 1992. *Liquor and Labor in South Africa*. Athens: Ohio University Press.

Cunningham, Hilary. 2004. 'Nations Rebound?: Crossing Borders in a Gated Globe'. *Identities: Global Studies in Culture and Power* 11:329–50.

Debord, Guy. 2006. *Society of the Spectacle*. Edinburgh: AK Press.

Freston, Paul. 2001. *Evangelicals and Politics in Asia, Africa and Latin America*. Cambridge: Cambridge University Press.

Geschiere, Peter. 1997. *The Modernity of Witchcraft: Politics and the Occult in Postcolonial Africa*. Charlottesville: University of Virginia Press.

Glick Schiller, Nina. 2005. 'Transnational Social Fields and Imperialism Bringing a Theory of Power to Transnational Studies'. *Anthropological Theory* 5(4):439–61.

Glick Schiller, Nina, Çaglar, Ayse and Gludbrandsen, Thaddeus. 2006. 'Beyond the Ethnic Lens: Locality, Globality, and Born-Again Incorporation'. *American Ethnologist* 33(4):612–33.

Gornik, Mark. 2008. *'A Word Made Global: African Christianity in New York City'*, Doctoral dissertation, University of Edinburgh.

Harr, Gerrieter. 2007. *Imagining Evil: Witchcraft Beliefs and Accusations in Contemporary Africa*. Trenton, NJ: Africa World Press.

Hunt, Stephan. 2002. '"A Church for All Nations": The Redeemed Christian Church of God'. *Pneuma* 24(2):185–204.

Jenkins, Philip. 2002. *The Next Christendom: The Coming of Global Christianity*. Oxford: Oxford University Press.

Jenkins, Philip. 2006. *The New Faces of Christianity: Believing the Bible in the Global South*. Oxford: Oxford University Press.

Johnson, Paul Christopher. 2007. *Diaspora Conversions: Black Carib Religion and the Recovery of Africa*. Berkeley: University of California Press.

Kramer, Eric. 2005. 'Spectacle and Stage of Power in Brazilian Neo-Pentecostalism'. *Latin American Perspectives* 32(1):95–120.

Marshall-Fratani, Ruth. 2001. 'Mediating the Global and Local in Nigerian Pentecostal-ism', in Andre Corten and Ruth Marshall-Fratani (eds), *Between Babel and Pentecost:*

286 African Studies, 68:2, August 2009

Transnational Pentecostalism in Africa and Latin America. Bloomington, IN: Indiana University Press, pp. 80–105.

McLuhan, Marshall. 1964. *Understanding the Media: The Extensions of Man.* New York: New American Library.

Meyer, Birgit. 2002. 'Commodities and the Power of Prayer: Pentecostalist Attitudes toward Consumption in Contemporary Ghana', in Jonathan X. Inda and Renato Rosaldo (eds), *The Anthropology of Globalization: A Reader.* Oxford: Blackwell, pp. 247–69.

Olupona, Jacob (ed). 2000. *African Spirituality: Forms, Meanings and Expressions.* New York: Crossroads.

Rice, Andrew. 2009. 'The Most Profound Change in American Christianity?' *The New York Times Magazine*, 12 April:30–7, 54, 57–8.

Shamir, Ronen. 2005. 'No Borders? Notes on Globalization as a Mobility Regime'. *Sociological Theory* 23(2):197–217.

Simmel, Georg. 1950. *The Sociology of Georg Simmel.* New York: Simon and Schuster.

Thompson, E.P. 1966. *The Making of the English Working Class.* New York: Verso.

Tweed, Thomas. 1998. *Our Lady of the Exile: Diasporic Religion at a Catholic Shrine in Miami.* Oxford: Oxford University Press.

Van Dijk, Rijk. 2001. 'Time and Transcultural Technologies of the Self in the Ghanaian Pentecostal Diaspora', in Andre Corten and Ruth Marshall-Fratani (eds), *Between Babel and Pentecost: Transnational Pentecostalism in Africa and Latin America*, pp. 216–34.

Walls, Andrew. 2002. *The Cross-Cultural Process in Christian History: Studies in the Transmission and Appropriation of Faith.* Maryknoll, NY: Orbis Books.

Watkin, Daniel. 2004. 'In New York, Gospel Resounds in African Tongues'. *The New York Times* 18 April.

Weber, Max. 1958. *The Protestant Ethic and the Spirit of Capitalism.* New York: Scribner's.

Whitehouse, Harvey. 2004. *Modes of Religiosity: A Cognitive Theory of Religious Transmission.* Walnut Creek, CA: AltaMira Press.

[30]

Japanese Journal of Religious Studies 35/1: 39–59
© 2008 Nanzan Institute for Religion and Culture

Frank USARSKI

"The Last Missionary to Leave the Temple Should Turn Off the Light"

Sociological Remarks on the Decline of
Japanese "Immigrant" Buddhism in Brazil

Empirical data indicate that the so-called "Buddhism of yellow color" that
is predominantly associated with Japanese "immigrant" Buddhism, is constantly in decline in terms of "explicit" adherents. After some methodological
observations, this article gives an overview of the relevant statistical data. The
last part discusses possible reasons for these negative dynamics, referring to
causes within Buddhist institutions, the ethnic community, and at the level of
the individual.

KEYWORDS: Japanese immigration — ethnic Buddhism — preservation of tradition
— acculturation

Frank Usarski is Professor of Science of Religion at the Pontifical Catholic University, São
Paulo, Brazil.

NLIKE Western countries such as Germany, where Buddhism was introduced from the second half of the nineteenth century onwards through the efforts of a handful of occidental protagonists especially interested in Theravada Buddhism (USARSKI 1989), the history of Buddhism in Brazil was initiated with the arrival of the first Japanese (mostly of rural origin) in the port of Santos in 1908. For many decades thereafter, Japanese immigrant Buddhism, not exclusively (NAKAMAKI 2002) but predominantly in the form of Amida Buddhism, continued to be the only expression of Buddhism in the so-called largest Catholic country in the world. Moreover, at the beginning of the 1960s the traditional Soto Zen temple Busshinji, in the city of São Paulo, became the first and primary source for a small circle of non-Japanese pioneers interested in the practice of *zazen* (ROCHA 2006, 78). The same institution was for some time the spiritual home of perhaps *the* symbolic figure of the Brazilian branch of "conversion Buddhism," Cláudia Souza de Murayama, alias "Monja Coen" (USARSKI 2006). Finally, in order to evaluate the influence of Japanese immigration on Brazilian Buddhism in general, one must not forget the high proportion of Pure Land and Nichiren Buddhist temples and centers within about three hundred Buddhist entities in Brazil, while keeping in mind that the Brazilian field has become as pluralistic as that of other countries (see FIGURE 1).

Problematization

Headlines such as "Buddhism is leaving the temples,"[1] flanked by repeatedly published "news" in the Brazilian media regarding a supposed "boom" of the Brazilian sangha,[2] suggest that, after decades of relative encapsulation, traditional Japanese Buddhism has successfully gone through a process of acculturation and turned into a "trendy" religion. This optimistic image was severely challenged by an article published on 19 January 2001 by the weekly magazine *Isto é* whose title "Don't let Buddhism disappear from Brazil" did not fit at all with previous reports about the almost inevitable advance of Buddhism. According to the article, the urgent issue, at least among representatives of

---

1. A quote from the headline of the main article "Além do templo - O budismo atrai mais adeptos no Brasil e seus seguidores assumem práticas engajadas" in the weekly magazine *Isto É*, 1 October 2003.

2. To quote just four examples: "O Brasil dos Budas" (The Brazil of the Buddhas), *Isto É*, March 1997; "Onda Zen" (The Success of Zen), *Elle*, June 1998; "O Budismo conquista o Brasil" (Buddhism conquers Brazil), *Corpo & Mente*, October 2000; "A ascensão do budismo no Brasil" (The Rise of Buddhism in Brazil), *Época*, June 2003.

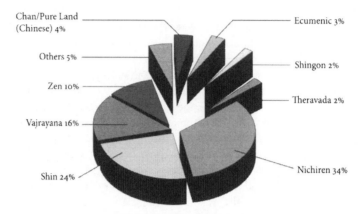

Chan/Pure Land (Chinese) 4%

Ecumenic 3%

Others 5%

Shingon 2%

Zen 10%

Theravada 2%

Vajrayana 16%

Nichiren 34%

Shin 24%

FIGURE 1. Proportions of Buddhist institutions in Brazil
(SHOJI 2004, 34)

traditional Japanese Buddhists institutions, was not how to respond to a dramatic increase of conversions or to overcrowded sessions, retreats, and workshops, but to declining communities and internal difficulties such as the lack of staff in certain local temples.

While many readers might have been taken by surprise by these "revelations," the *Isto é* report is not only in tune with similar statements from within traditional Japanese Buddhist communities, but also in line with the results of empirical research on the subject. One example for a pessimistic "emic" evaluation of the current situation of Japanese Buddhism is the statement of an official of the *Comunidade Budista Nichirenshu* of São Paulo, who, in 1995, had already emphasized that "There are many, both within and outside the Japanese community, who think that Buddhism is only for older people, and that monks fulfill their functions only in terms of funeral rites" (FEDERAÇÃO DAS SEITAS BUDISTAS DO BRASIL 1995, 42). And in 2004 a leading Jodo Shinshu minister of São Paulo added that

> When it comes to religious practice, one can easily notice that the descendents of immigrants are not very interested in what is happening in a Buddhist temple. They are more concerned with integrating themselves into Brazilian society than in maintaining the traditions of their ancestors. Therefore it is not an exaggeration to say that when the last immigrant dies, the only thing for the Buddhist missionaries to do is to close the temples and return to Japan. It would be convenient to turn off the light before leaving for the airport.
>
> (GONÇALVES 2004)

42 | *Japanese Journal of Religious Studies* 35/1 (2008)

As far as empirical research is concerned, the results of the last national censuses provided by the Brazilian Institute of Geography and Statistics (IBGE) are
especially relevant. Nonetheless, when it comes to a closer look at "immigration
Buddhism," the IBGE studies must be interpreted with caution. The most crucial
point here is the category of "color" or "race." In the census's questionnaire this
appears as a fivefold-differentiated option to be correlated with other categories,
including those subsumed under the heading "religion." As for the identification
of "immigrant Buddhists" the sub-category in the rubric "color" that spontaneously comes to mind is "yellow." However, this is obviously an ambiguous association for epistemological, methodological, and political reasons.

The main argument against an overly ingenuous interpretation of the IBGE
data is that the identification of a person's color in the census derives from the
self-declaration of an interviewee confronted with a concept that is not only
vague but also has negative connotations. This being the case, it is by no means
guaranteed that someone with an Asian background is in fact willing to agree
that he is a Brazilian of "yellow color." From an ethical-political point of view,
the discomfort with the color/race question is caused by the implicit quality
ranking of the suggested sub-categories of the item. Although it is true that the
days of the overt proclamation of the ideal of a gradual "whitening" of Brazilian
society and of racial stigmatization are over (SASAKI 2006, 100), more subtle
social mechanisms, still capable of putting members of ethnic minorities under
pressure, have prevailed. This is indicated by personal statements such as the
following: "The Japanese always encountered resistance from the Brazilian side.
Their strange customs sometimes provoked laughter [...] fear [...] or mistrust"
(AZEVEDO 1994, 47). Analysts like Maeyama, opposing the image of Brazil as an
exceptionally tolerant country, even speak of a tacit atmosphere of "cultural prejudice" that demands members "of different cultures, peoples, and ways of thinking" to "assimilate themselves into Luso-Brazilian culture which is commonly
supposed to be the only 'legitimate' Brazilian culture" (MAEYAMA 1983a, 167).

If this observation is adequate, one has to take into account the possibility
that a descendent of a Japanese immigrant family has internalized this latent
expectation of his/her "complete" assimilation into Brazil's mainstream culture
and therefore judges the option "yellow" in the IBGE questionnaire as inappropriate since it does not reflect his/her efforts to become a fully integrated
member of the Brazilian society. This is especially true for individuals born to
ethnically mixed parents. However, the rejection of the subcategory "yellow" as
a description of one's own status does not necessarily imply that the interviewee
has gotten rid of the self-concept of "Nippo-Brazilian." Rather it would signal
that in relation to the "Nippo" aspect of his/her "composed" individuality the
"Brazilian" component has gained the upper hand.

Empirical data proves the pertinence of the above considerations. Due to both
procreation and to a continuous flow of Japanese immigrants until 1973, com-

	White	Black	Yellow	Mulatto	Indigenous
1940	63.47	14.64	0.59	21.21	-
1950	61.66	10.96	0.63	26.54	-
1960	61.03	8.71	0.69	29.50	-
1980	54.23	5.92	0.56	38.85	-
1991	51.56	5.00	0.43	42.45	0.20
2000	53.74	6.21	0.45	38.45	0.43

FIGURE 2. Population of Brazil according to color or race (%)
(Instituto Brasileiro de Geografia e Estatística IBGE)

plemented by the Immigration of Chinese and Koreans from the 1950s onwards, the number of Brazilians with an Asian family background has increased constantly over the decades. As a consequence of these dynamics, it is estimated that currently more than 1.5 million Brazilians are of Asian origin, most of them (about 1.28 million) Japanese immigrants and their descendants (TSUDA 2000, 3). Figures provided by the IBGE show that, between 1980 and 2000, those of Japanese descent alone represented between 0.7 percent and 0.8 percent of the total Brazilian population (BELTRÃO, SUGAHARA AND KONTA 2006). However, the percentage of individuals predisposed to identify themselves as "yellow" did not correspond to these values (FIGURE 2).

Summing up, one has to bear in mind that correlating the variables "Buddhism" and "yellow" is heuristically limited in at least two ways. First, while Brazilian Buddhists who are not reluctant to identify themselves as "yellow" can be considered as adherents with an Asian family background, they are not necessarily Japanese descendents. Nonetheless, according to the numerical proportions between the nationalities in question (Japanese, Chinese, Korean), the numbers of Buddhists "of yellow color" do not lose their relevance in research on Japanese Buddhism in particular, as long as they are interpreted as predominant statistical tendencies within a wider context.

Second, in order to reduce the risk of distortion, one should be prepared for the possibility that a certain proportion of Brazilian Buddhists of Japanese origin appear in the statistics under a rubric other than that of Buddhists of "yellow color." With this in mind, the following section deals with the dynamics in both sub-fields of Brazilian Buddhism.

The Statistical Evolution of "Buddhism of Yellow Color" in Brazil

In 2000 only about 0.14 percent of the Brazilian population opted for the rubric "Buddhism" in the IBGE questionnaire. That is quite a modest value even if compared to the number of adherents of religious minorities such as the Adventists (0.73 percent) or Jehovah's Witnesses (0.6 percent). A comparison of the last national censuses also negates the widespread idea that Buddhism is a constantly growing religion (FIGURE 3). The opposite is true, especially when one discards a relative distinction between ethnic Buddhism and the Buddhism of converts (NUMRICH 1996) and takes into account the negative dynamics of the Buddhist field in general between 1991 (236,405 Buddhists) and 2000 (214,873 Buddhists).

This recent decline of the total number of Brazilian Buddhists not only contradicts the numerical exaggerations common in the Brazilian media, but also indicates that one should not count on the possibility that a considerable number of "Nippo-Brazilians" who had refused to continue to declare themselves "yellow" in 2000 now appear under the rubric "Non-Yellow-Buddhist."

The negative dynamics in the subfield becomes even clearer when one considers the evolution of the segment "Buddhists of yellow color" over the last three decades. Compared to the 149,633 "Buddhists of yellow color" registered in 1970, the number of self-declared Buddhists of "yellow color" had dropped to 81,345 in 2000. That is a decline of 68,288 individuals of Asian origin predisposed to identify themselves as adherents of the religion of their forefathers. Complementary data from 1950—when 152,572 Buddhists were counted prior both to the first manifestations of converts to Buddhism in Brazil and to the statistically significant Chinese and Korean immigration to the country—proves that the decline of "Buddhism of yellow color" was an ongoing process throughout the second half of the twentieth century. However, the loss between 1950 and 1970 (2,939) was relatively unimportant and not comparable with the far more dramatic decrease of 59,692 individuals that occurred between 1970 and 1991.

From the standpoint of some representatives of traditional Japanese religious institutions, the situation in the local temples is even more worrying than that expressed by the modest numbers of "Buddhists of yellow color" at the national level. In 2004, the Reverend of the Apucarana Nambei Honganji in Apucarana, in the State of Paraná, lamented: "If we asked any of the hundreds of frequent visitors who flock to the temples on the weekend if they consider themselves to be Buddhists at all, we would be alarmed. Less than one percent of the visitors declare themselves to be Buddhists."[3] Another indication that the real situation is quite different from the stereotypical rhetoric of a "boom" in Buddhism is the modest situation of the Busshinji temple in the city of São Paulo. According to a local authority, only some thirty people, most of them non-Japanese Brazilians, regularly attend the institution's meetings.[4]

3. Message posted in the discussion list buddismo@topica.com. Accessed 23 September 2004.
4. cf. http://www.ipcdigital.com/print_news.asp?descrIdioma=br&codNoticia=7538. Accessed 15 December 2007.

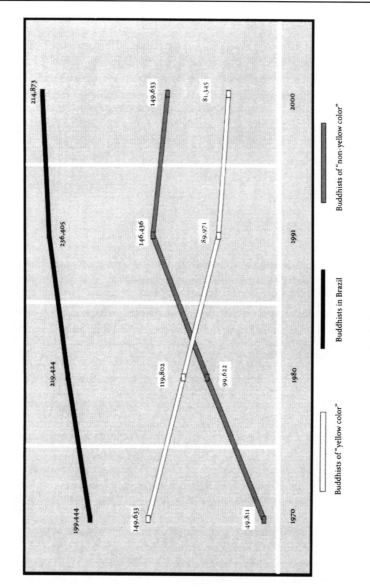

FIGURE 3. Numeric evolution of Buddhism in Brazil, 1970–2000 (IBGE)

46 | *Japanese Journal of Religious Studies* 35/1 (2008)

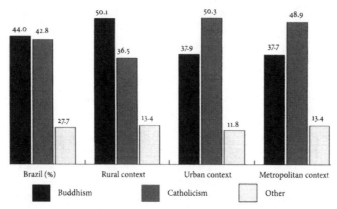

FIGURE 4. Religious preference among Japanese immigrants in percent (1958) (MAEYAMA 1973, 248)

The Decline of "Buddhism of Yellow Color"
from a Socio-Historical and Demographical Perspective

The practice of traditional Japanese religion was generally an improvised affair within families or, at best, among like-minded neighbors (USARSKI, ed. 2002). This was due to restrictions on overt religious activities followed by the Japanese government in respect for the feelings of the predominantly Catholic Brazilian population, and also because of the desire of the immigrants to prosper quickly and return to their homeland as soon as possible. Occurring only in the 1950s, a general "resurrection" of Japanese religion (MORI 1992) initially favored the rapid institutionalization of traditional Japanese Buddhist temples in those urban surroundings to which a great number of immigrants, previously concentrated in rural zones, had begun to move in search of economic opportunities. However, the consolidation of Buddhism and urban migration represented two not fully congruent dynamics. On the one hand newly founded temples offered a space for social reintegration and the preservation of transplanted cultural capital. On the other hand, the shift from demographically "dense" colonies to socio-structural and ideologically heterogeneous cities implied the weakening of the plausibility structure that had been collectively constructed according to traditional Japanese values.

This discrepancy was already evident by the end of the 1950s, the decade in which a series of Japanese Buddhist institutions were inaugurated in Brazil. According to relevant studies, when immigration began, only a minority of the Japanese who settled in Brazil were Christians (FUJII and SMITH 1959, 14). Data from 1958 draws a completely different picture. At that time, only 44.5 percent of Japanese living in Brazil still felt committed to their traditional religion, a dramatic change that was particularly significant in urban surroundings, where

50.3percent had already converted to Catholicism, while in rural areas the corresponding value was 36.5 percent (FIGURE 4).

Complementary data indicate that, in the same year, the tendency to abandon traditional Japanese religion was stronger among the younger members of the Japanese immigrant community (FIGURE 5). While more than two-thirds of the immigrants born in Japan declared themselves to be Buddhists, this percentage had dropped dramatically to 29.9 percent among the following generation born in Brazil, and to only 19 percent in the third generation (MAEYAMA 1973, 248).

The long-term consequences of the difficulties in maintaining traditional Buddhism within families of Japanese origin is mirrored by relevant data derived from the National Census conducted in 1950 and in 2000.

In 2000, despite an increase of about 15 percent in Brazil's population over the 1990s, 45.13 percent of "Buddhists of yellow color" were older than 60 while only 12.19 percent were younger than 20. The significance of these proportions becomes clear if one compares these values with corresponding figures provided by the IBGE in 1950, indicating an inverse relation to that time, when the majority (51.52 percent) of "Buddhists of yellow color" were younger than 20, while less than 5 percent were older than 60 (FIGURE 6).

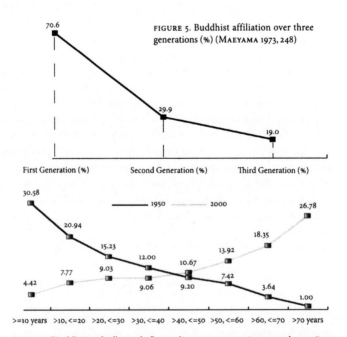

FIGURE 5. Buddhist affiliation over three generations (%) (MAEYAMA 1973, 248)

FIGURE 6. "Buddhism of yellow color" according to age groups in 1950 and 2000 (in percent).
Source: Instituto Brasileiro de Geografia e Estatística (IBGE)

48 | *Japanese Journal of Religious Studies* 35/1 (2008)

According to the theoretical assumption that a religion "must maintain a level of fertility sufficient to at least offset member mortality" in order to survive (STARK 1996, 140) this evolution poses a major challenge for a religious community incapable of attracting non-Japanese descendents.

Causes for the Decline of "Buddhism of Yellow Color" in Brazil

The following discussion of possible causes for the decline of "Buddhism of yellow color" in Brazil is organized according to three "levels" of reflection.

The first level consists of the identification of dysfunctional elements on the part of Japanese Buddhist institutions. The second level corresponds to problems of maintaining and transmitting religious heritage within the ethnic community. Aspects primarily associated with individuals are located on the third level. Needless to say, these three levels are intimately related empirically and this distinction is made for analytical purposes only.

DEFICITS AT THE LEVEL OF BUDDHIST INSTITUTIONS

Theorists favoring rational explanations suggest that religious demand generally does not develop in a "vacuum" but as a positive response to manifest supplies provided by competing local religious institutions (FINKE 1997). Seen from this angle, Buddhism in general and Japanese Buddhism in particular is not in a very comfortable position in Brazil, simply because the majority of its institutions are concentrated in the south-east and the south of the country, that is, in São Paulo, Rio de Janeiro, Paraná, and Rio Grande do Sul (FIGURE 7), that is, in those federal states that for decades have been preferred by Japanese immigrants and their descendents.

Although geographical accessibility to the physical facilities of a religion is an important prerequisite for success in a religious market, "suppliers" clearly need more than mere geographical presence in order to keep up with competitors.

In this sense, even if a local institution runs traditional Japanese Buddhism, it generally suffers from two major infrastructural limitations: first, the concentration of the temple activities in the hands of only a few individuals; and, second, the lack of a consistent strategy in general, and of linguistic competence in particular, that would be capable of attracting a wider audience, not only from outside but also from inside the ethnic Japanese context. Both aspects are addressed by a Honpa Honganji minister who, now back in Japan, looks back to his time in Brazil, and complains: "The Japanese authorities in the temple are not only incapable of transmitting the religious heritage to the young Nikkei, they are also unwilling to share their responsibility with any Brazilian. That is the reason why today only Japanese-speaking adherents frequent the temples. All this reminds me of an old people's home."[5]

5. Quote from an email message sent by Kyoya Imai on 11 September 2007.

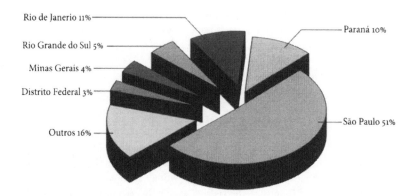

Rio de Janerio 11%

Rio Grande do Sul 5%

Minas Gerais 4%

Distrito Federal 3%

Outros 16%

Paraná 10%

São Paulo 51%

FIGURE 7. Geographic distribution of Buddhist institutions in Brazil (SHOJI 2004, 35)

The first part of the above criticism emphasizes the lack of space offered to Brazilians willing to engage themselves in temple affairs. This aspect has been academically discussed in reference to the hypothesis of the co-existence of two more or less "incompatible" congregations in traditional temples, that is, where a "parallel" group of converted Buddhists is involved. This constellation has negative effects for the future of ethnic Buddhism in Brazil, as indicated by the following words of a Brazilian Nichiren Shoshu authority: "Generally, monks from Japan come with the pretension to teach Buddhism here as a philosophy or as a Japanese ideology. But I do not think that this works. This is a land of Samba, of beaches, of Carnival. This is not Japan. The philosophy might come from there, but we have to adapt it to local conditions" (FEDERAÇÃO DAS SEITAS BUDISTAS DO BRASIL 1995, 42).

A more fundamental problem exists when, due to the lack of religious "manpower," a community is left without a resident religious authority, hence without a regular weekly schedule. One concrete example is the Honpa Honganji branch, which runs about forty-five institutions. However, only the headquarters in the city of São Paulo has religious staff, while, for example, more than twenty communities in the interior of the state[6] and three in the Federal State of Paraná[7] do not enjoy the permanent presence of a local reverend and, instead of maintaining regular temple activities, depend on the visits of a religious authority from another city in order to be properly attended.

6. In Bernardo do Campo, Álvares Machado, Adamantina, Andradina, Cafelândia, Dracena, Flórida Paulista, Guararapes, Itu, Junqueirópolis, Lucélia, Mirandópolis, Osvaldo Cruz, Pacaembu, Piedade, Pilar do Sul, Pereira Barreto, Pompéia, São José dos Campos, Tremembé, Tupi Paulista, and Votuporanga.

7. In Curitiba, Mandaguari, and Paranavaí.

50 | *Japanese Journal of Religious Studies*   35/1 (2008)

The second infrastructural deficit is the lack of a consistent strategy in general, and in particular, of linguistic competence. These can be regarded as long-term consequences of the historical circumstances under which "immigration Buddhism" was introduced to Brazil, at a time when Japanese immigrants were still convinced that their residence in their host country would be temporary. In accordance with this attitude, until the 1950s the majority of Japanese Buddhist schools refrained from adequately organizing themselves. This was counter-productive in terms not only of internal consolidation and external expansion, but also of the experiences of what it meant to systematically transplant an ethnically differentiated non-Christian religion into a predominantly Catholic, Portuguese-speaking society. If subsequent efforts were made in order to compensate for these failures, they were insufficient. This is especially true in terms of continuing linguistic restrictions, as indicated by the following statement:

> The starting point of efficient missionary work in Brazilian territory should be
> ... a clear-sighted translation of the basic religious texts of this school into Por-
> tuguese. It is essential to undertake this task with a certain urgency, because
> Japanese immigration ended some time ago. The old immigrants who under-
> stood Japanese are dead, and most of their descendants are not familiar with
> the language of their ancestors.... If, in this respect, nothing is done quickly,
> the mission could be forced to put an end to its activities at the moment the
> last Japanese immigrant to Brazil leaves this world.
>
> (GONÇALVES 1995, 9)

Problems of Maintaining Traditional Religiosity Within the Ethnic Community

The direction taken by the assimilation of an immigrant group in its new surroundings is a function of two contradictory logics: the desire to maintain the cultural heritage brought to the country of immigration; and the demand for integration according to the patterns of the host society.

During the first decades of immigration, the cultivation of traditional Japanese values in favor of the cohesion of the family and solidarity among its members was not only an expression of the immigrants' intention to stay in Brazil only as long as necessary, but also a means of strengthening the group's collective identity as a means of combating strong external anti-Japanese sentiments (STADNIKY 2001).

After World War II, this "inward" orientation was increasingly challenged as the host society offered economic opportunities in exchange for assimilation. Socio-demographic mobility in response to these opportunities contributed both to the growing flexibility of communication patterns and disfavor of the Japanese language, and to the expansion of social networks beyond the ethnic enclave. Both dynamics affected the plausibility structure that had formerly facilitated the maintenance and transmission of collective cultural heritage,

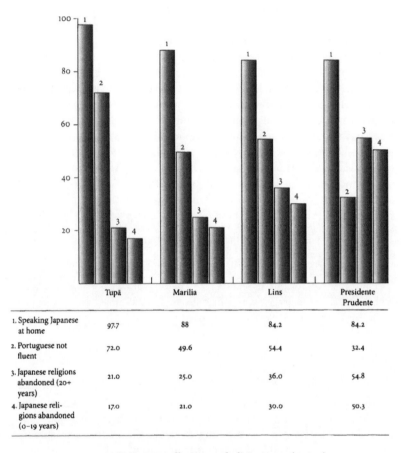

	Tupã	Marília	Lins	Presidente Prudente
1. Speaking Japanese at home	97.7	88	84.2	84.2
2. Portuguese not fluent	72.0	49.6	54.4	32.4
3. Japanese religions abandoned (20+ years)	21.0	25.0	36.0	54.8
4. Japanese religions abandoned (0–19 years)	17.0	21.0	30.0	50.3

FIGURE 8. Maintenance of language and religion in 1940 (percent)
(Instituto Brasileiro de Geografia e Estatística 1951, 48–79)

including Buddhism traditionally practiced as "the religion of the household inherited from the family ancestors" (MAEYAMA 1983b, 206).

The negative impact of the language shift has to do with the fact that language is the basic tool of expressing, preserving, and transmitting one's culture, hence an instrument of critical importance for keeping the family's religious memory alive. Seen from this angle, and remembering the paucity of religious material translated into Portuguese, one can interpret the gradual decline of the Japanese language in Brazil a result of the parent's failure of transmitting it to their children.

While this process became more obvious during the 1950s, empirical studies prove a corresponding tendency as early as the 1940s, a time of rigid political

52 | *Japanese Journal of Religious Studies*   35/1 (2008)

measures imposed by the nationalistic regime of Getúlio Vargas, including the revision of immigration laws, a compulsory assimilation program for foreigners, and the prohibition of the public use of foreign languages.

Relevant statistics can be found in an early IBGE study on demographical characteristics of four Japanese immigration "colonies" located in the state of São Paulo. As the figure below indicates, by 1940 a significant number of immigrants and their descendents had already abandoned their traditional religion, a tendency most accentuated among community members younger than twenty. However, this predisposition was less significant in the Tupã colony where some 98 percent still preferred Japanese as the principal means of communication. In opposition, the highest percentage of individuals who had abandoned Japanese religions were found in Presidente Prudente, a finding that is not only positively correlated with the relatively low percentage of colony members sticking to their original language, but also with the relatively low percentage of individuals handicapped by difficulties of speaking Portuguese fluently.

According to later studies, in 1988 less than forty-five percent of the Brazilian descendents of Japanese immigrants used Portuguese at home while thirty-three percent had no knowledge of the language of their ancestors. This tendency was most accentuated in urban surroundings, where the percentage of Portuguese speaking Nikkei was 66.25 percent while only 6 percent were still speaking elaborate Japanese (CARVALHO 2003, 39–40). This trend is in sharp contrast to the ongoing dominance of the Japanese language in traditional Japanese temples.

In addition to the religious side effects resulting from the shift from Japanese to Portuguese as the principal language of a constantly growing number of "Nippo-Brazilians," efforts to maintain cultural capital within the colonies were challenged by an increase in interethnic marriages, hence by a practice that "reflects an abandonment of a preference for one's own ethnic group" and represents "a means to challenge the traditional family system" (CARVALHO 2003, 41).

Until the 1940s, interethnic marriage was a rare option for Japanese immigrants. Less than two percent of the community members born in Japan and less than six percent of the Nikkeis were married to a partner of non-Japanese origin (LESSER 1999, 104). After World War II the situation changed gradually. Although a strong hesitation against interethnic marriage persisted on a collective level, socioeconomic factors including the family status of the potential bride or groom's heritage were often capable of overcoming the parents' resistance, even if their children saw inter-marriage as an opportunity "to 'erase' their Japanese traits" (CARVALHO 2003, 41). As a result, at the end of the 1950s and the beginning of the 1960s the rate of interethnic marriage for those of Japanese descent was 18.36 percent for males and 7.63 percent for females. According to more recent data, today interethnic marriage is more the norm rather than the exception. In 1988 more than 49.5 percent of "Nippo-Brazilians" nationwide were married to a partner of non-Japanese descent (CARVALHO 2003, 43).

The negative role of this growing trend for the maintenance of traditional cultural capital within the Japanese community is obvious. Ethnic inter-marriage, being both racially and ideologically a "mixed zone," demands mutual respect from the couple and concessions towards their respective inherited convictions and values of their partners. This is in contrast to an ethnically homogeneous family, whose generally dense plausibility structure protects them from the experience of religious contingency and offers a framework for the more or less coherent transmission of a traditional world view. The reconstruction of social reality within the newly formed family may lead to a critical reconsideration of religious matters previously supposed to be self-evident as well as "negotiations" over the correct course of the children's socialization. If the dialogue is constructive, it enriches the religious repertoire of the family. However, from the perspective of the involved individuals, the wider horizon of "acceptable" religious options may result in a reduced commitment to the particular religious community in which they have grown up. A more relaxed attitude towards one's symbolic heritage is, in the long term, even more counterproductive for the detailed and differentiated transmission of religious knowledge and spiritual practices to the following generation. One expression of this tendency, present especially within ethnically mixed families, is the statement of a leading Jodo Shinshu minister in São Paulo who claimed in a 1999 interview that for many younger "Nippo-Brazilians" the *butsudan* has lost its significance. Not fully understood in terms of its religious purpose, it is often associated with the esthetically peculiar nostalgic interior of the grandparents home, where it is supposedly maintained as an esthetically obsolete and old-fashioned collection of paraphernalia.[8]

Problems of Maintaining Traditional Japanese Religiosity at the Individual Level

In the last decades, a disproportionately high percentage of Japanese-Brazilians has successfully made use of the opportunities offered by an "emerging" country and its institutions of higher education (ADACHI 2004). In 1985, 13 percent of students and 47 percent of faculty at the University of São Paulo were of Japanese descent (CARVALHO 2003, 38). According to the last national census, about 18 percent of the Brazilian population belongs to the economically privileged stratum of society, with a monthly income five times higher than the minimum wage, which at the time was more than one thousand, nine hundred Brazilian Reais. The percentage of Brazilians of "yellow color" was more than three times higher at this income level (55.36 percent).

This and other similar data prove the following: a) "the extent to which the second- or third-generation immigrants have shifted away from the occupation and employment patterns of their parents and grandparents" (CARVALHO 2003, 45); b) the identification of younger Japanese descendents with Brazil as their

8. Quote from my interview with Shaku Riman (Mário Ricardo Gonçalves), 10 March 1999.

54 | *Japanese Journal of Religious Studies*   35/1 (2008)

permanent homeland, worthy of a long term "investment" of time and energy in the education and training necessary for an individual career that will be remunerated according to the system of gratification inherent in a capitalist, technological society; and c) their consent to modern principles and values such as individualism, rationalism, autonomy and competition.

Against this background, the question of possible causes for the decline of "Buddhism of yellow color" in Brazil at the individual level can be answered in at least two ways. Firstly, compared with the identity of first generation immigrants, the advanced processes of an individual's "acculturation" and active integration of younger descendents into their "host society" corresponds to a personality structure in which three relevant components have been reconfigured according to a new hierarchical order. These are: the self-recognition associated with secular existence as a Brazilian, ethnic origin as a Japanese, and religious commitment to Buddhism (CHANDLER 1998). While one can imagine that older immigrants saw themselves as Japanese Buddhists who came to Brazil by destiny, the younger descendents, although conscious of their Japanese heritage, are Brazilians. Religious heritage remains an issue of identity only for those who appear in the IBGE studies as explicitly "Buddhist," though in the majority of such cases, this identity is far from being an internalized "master-status."

Secondly, adherence to Buddhism is clearly not an obstacle to individual success. However, if it is true that—as it has been demonstrated for Umbanda and Pentecostalism (FRY and HOWE 1975)—the attraction of a religion depends on its capacity to address the concrete conflicts experienced by its clientele, then one can question the degree to which apparently "otherworldly" oriented Pure Land Buddhist currents (based on faith, devotion and hope in the transformative potential of a merciful transcendent being) cater to a "modern" predisposed individual. This individual's primary concern is his or her professional life "here and now," guided by principles such as rationalism, autonomy and competition (BLOOM 1998, 46) and who might be better served by a more compatible spiritual practice within the spectrum of new Japanese religions (MORI 1992, 587).

Conclusion

A detailed look at the statistical data referring to "Buddhism of yellow color" in Brazil reveals that the headline "Buddhism is leaving the temples" is perfectly adequate, but in a sense contrary to that suggested by the journalists responsible for the quoted article and, hence, to that understood by the average reader. Instead of confirming the idea that traditional Buddhism, once exclusively attending to the religious necessities of Japanese immigrant families, has began to attract a wider audience, the phrase "Buddhism is leaving the temples" alludes to a possible future when the facilities of traditional Buddhists communities are left empty of local practitioners. In various cases, such an inauspicious scene

FIGURE 9. 2007 Calendar (photo for January), distributed by the
Buddhist Community Soto Zenshu of South America

is already foreshadowed by the constant decline of visitors, as indicated by the
photo (FIGURE 9), showing a handful of practitioners seemingly "lost" in the quite
spacious assembly hall of the Zenguenji Temple in Mogi das Cruzes, São Paulo.

As various statements prove, authorities in the local temples are conscious
of this precarious situation, but they do not necessarily agree with its evaluation. Seen from a more pessimistic perspective, the currently weakened status
of traditional Buddhism will continue for quite some time, given that such a
state is considered symptomatic for a lengthy process of thorough acculturation to new conditions, as was the case for the historically complex circumstances under which Buddhism was once transplanted to Japan and China.
Seen in a more optimistic light, signs of improvement are already visible, for
example the creation of the national umbrella organization Colegiado Budista
Brasileiro and the active involvement of traditional Japanese Buddhist currents
in this organization, reflecting efforts to stimulate the engagement of younger
Japanese descendents in Buddhist communities (GONÇALVES 2005, 206–207).

It may be a relief for the leaders of traditional Japanese Buddhist authorities
in Brazil that the statistical decline of the communities of "Buddhists of yellow
color" is not restricted to Brazil, but a tendency also observable in the United
States. While this negative trend is less accentuated in ethnically-rooted North
American Zen temples (ASAI and WILLIAMS 1999), Shin Buddhist institutions

56 | *Japanese Journal of Religious Studies*   35/1 (2008)

have suffered from the same problems as their "sister" communities in Brazil (Bloom 1998; Tanaka 1999). In both countries religious activities were concentrated on the needs of the ethnic community. Here and there the Japanese language continues to play a key role in the temples, at the cost of alienating members and sympathizers who do not understand it. There is also the common problem of aging clergy and the difficulty of replacing retired ministers with younger Japanese descendents willing to sacrifice their professional ambitions and inner-worldly success for the maintenance of the religious tradition of their forefathers. In both Brazilian and North American temples, the hierarchical structure and the importance of the nuclear family as the basic religious unit are in tension with egalitarian principles and with the individualism fostered by a modern democratic society. Finally, in both countries, Japanese Buddhism is confronted with its image as a foreign religion, with the consequence that the number of converts remains insignificant.

However, while it seems that Japanese Buddhist authorities in Brazil often face the crisis too passively, North American Shin Buddhists have taken at least two initiatives to make a virtue out of necessity (Bloom 1998). The first initiative consists of "Americanization" at the national administrational level, leading to more effective ecumenical interchange and more competent participation in the political sphere. Secondly, motivated by signs of a kind of "ethnic revival," temple authorities are focusing on members of the youngest/newest generation of Japanese descendents, seeking to strengthen their commitment to their religious community, rather than dispersing resources for the propagation of their faith to a wider audience. One strategy in this context is the increase in so-called "dharma schools" associated with local temples, including the design and promotion of study-material more in tune with the current *zeitgeist*. This striving for ideological change is best illustrated by the emphasis on the egalitarian character of Buddhism and, vice versa, of the relativization of the religious importance of traditional Japanese patterns of social behavior.

Whether these measures will be adequate for the survival of Japanese Buddhist communities in the US remains a mystery. Even less certain is if they will work for Brazil. Whatever measures will be taken, the future of "Buddhism of yellow color" in Brazil will continue to be an intriguing field of study.

REFERENCES

Adachi, Nobuko
  2004   Japonês: A marker of social class or a key term in the discourse of race? *Latin American Perspectives* 136, 31/3 (May): 48–76.

ASAI, Senryō, and Duncan Ryūken WILLIAMS

1999   Japanese American Zen Temples: Cultural identity and economics. In WILLIAMS and QUEEN, eds., 20–35. Richmond: Curzon.

AZEVEDO, Suami P. de

1994   *Suzano Estrada Real: Roteiro emocionado da minha cidade.* Suzano: Empresa Jornalística e Editorial Alto de Teitê.

BELTRÃO, Kaizō Iwakami, Sonoe SUGAHARA, and Ryohei KONTA

2006   Trabalhando no Brasil: Características da população de origem japonesa segundo os censos entre 1980 e 2000. Trabalho apresentado no XV Encontro Nacional de Estudos Poulacionais, ABEP, realizado em Caxambú-MG-Brasil (18 and 22 September).

BLOOM, Alfred

1998   Shin Buddhism in America: A social perspective. In PREBISH and TANAKA, 32–47.

CARVALHO, Daniela de

2003   *Migrants and Identity in Japan and Brazil: The Nikkeijin.* London and New York: Routledge.

CHANDLER, Stuart

1998   Chinese Buddhism in America. In PREBISH and TANAKA, 14–30.

FEDERAÇÃO DAS SEITAS BUDISTAS DO BRASIL

1995   Simpósio e Conferência Brasil-Japão de Budismo. A contribuição do Budismo para a Ordem e o Progresso do Brasil. São Paulo: Federação das Seitas Budistas do Brasil.

FINKE, Roger

1997   The consequences of religious competition: Supply-side explanations for religious change. In *Rational Choice Theory and Religion: Summery and Assessment*, ed. Lawrence A. Young, 45–61. New York: London: Routledge.

FRY, Peter Henry, and Gary Nigel HOWE

1975   Duas respostas à Aflição: Umbanda e Pentecostalismo. *Debate & Crítica* 6 July: 75–94.

FUJII, Yukio, and T. Lynn SMITH

1959   *The Acculturation of the Japanese Immigrants in Brazil*, Gainesville: University of Florida Press.

GONÇALVES, Ricardo Mário

1995   Considerações sobre o trabalho de tradução de textos budistas. *Revista de Instituto Budista de Estudos Missionários* 1: 9–20.

2004   O futuro dos templos budistas no Brasil. Public speech given on the occasion of the celebration of the fiftieth anniversary of the Nambei Honganji temple in Araçatuba on 23 May.

58 | *Japanese Journal of Religious Studies* 35/1 (2008)

2005   As flores do *dharma* desabrocham sob o Cruzeiro do Sul: aspectos dos
        vários "budismos" no Brasil. REVISTA USP, 67 (September/October):
        198–207.

Instituto Brasileiro de Geografia e Estatística
1951   *Pesquisas sobre os diversos grupos de cor nas populações do Estado de São
        Paulo e do Distrito Federal.* Rio de Janeiro: Serviços Gráfico do Instituto
        de Geografia e Estatística.

Lesser, Jeffrey
1999   *Immigrants, Minorities, and Struggle for Ethnicity in Brazil.* Durham &
        London: Duke University Press.

Maeyama, Takashi
1973   Religião, parentesco e as classes médias dos japoneses no Brasil urbano. In
        Assimilação e integração dos japoneses no Brasil, Hiroshi Saito and Takashi
        Maeyama, 240–72. Petrópolis: Vozes.

1983a   Culture and value system in Brazil: A preliminary report. *Latin American
        Studies* 6: 153–68.

1983b   Japanese religions in southern Brazil: Change and syncretism. *Latin
        American Studies* 6: 181–237.

Mori, Koichi
1992   Vida religiosa dos japoneses e seus descendentes residentes no Brasil e
        religiões de origem japonesa. In *Comissão de Elaboração da História dos
        80 Anos da Imigração Japonesa no Brasil: Uma epopéia moderna. 80 anos
        da imigração japonesa no Brasil,* 559–601. São Paulo: Hucitec: Sociedade
        Brasileira de Cultura Japonesa.

Nakamaki, Hirochika
2002   A Honmon Butsuryū-shū no Brasil: Através de registros do Arcebispo
        Nissui Ibaragui. In Usarski, ed., 2002, 73–105.

Nakamura, Koryu
1995   Mensagem. In *Simpósio e Conferência Brasil-Japão de Budismo. A Con-
        tribuição do Budismo para a Ordem e o progresso do Brasil,* 48. São Paulo
        (Federação das Seitas Budistas do Brasil).

Numrich, Paul David
1996   *Old Wisdom in the New World: Americanization in Two Immigrant Thera-
        vada Buddhist Temples.* Knoxville: The University of Tennessee Press.

Prebish, Charles S., and Kenneth K. Tanaka, eds.
1998   *The Faces of Buddhism in America.* Berkeley: University of California
        Press.

Projeto Caixa Populi
1999   *Etnias.* São Paulo: Caixa Econômica Federal.

PROJETO CAIXA POPULI, SEGUNDA ETAPA

    2000   *Japoneses, judeus, chineses, coreanos, gregos, latino-americanos e europeus orientais.* São Paulo: Caixa Econômica Federal.

ROCHA, Cristina

    2006   *Zen in Brazil: The Quest for Cosmopolitan Modernity.* Honululu: University of Hawai'i Press.

SASAKI, Elisa

    2006   A imigração para o Japão. *Estudos Avançados* 20 (57): 99–117.

SHOJI, Rafael

    2004   The Nativization of East Asian Buddhism in Brazil. PhD Thesis, University of Hannover.

STADNIKY, Hilda Pívaro

    2001   Migrações para a América: A presença nipo-brasileira no Norte novo de Maringá Departamento de História da Universidade Estadual de Maringá. Paper presented at the sixteenth AHE Congress in Zaragoza.

STARK, Rodney

    1996   Why religious movements succeed or fail: A revised general model. *Journal of Contemporary Religion* 11/2: 133–46.

TANAKA, Kenneth K.

    1999   Issues of ethnicity in the Buddhist Churches of America. In WILLIAMS and QUEEN, eds., 3–19.

TSUDA, Takeyuki

    2000   The Benefits of Being Minority: The Ethnic Status of the Japanese-Brazilians in Brazil. Working Paper 21 (May), San Diego, University of California: Center for Comparative Immigration Studies.

USARSKI, Frank

    1989   Das Bekenntnis zum Buddhismus als Bildungsprivileg. Strukturmomente der "lebensweltlichen" Theravada-Rezeption in Deutschland im Zeitraum zwischen 1888 und 1924. In *Die Religion von Oberschichten*, Peter Antesand Donate Pahnke, eds., 75–86. Marburg: Diagonal.

    2006   Abraçando árvores no espírito zen: Reflexões sobre o movimento "Caminhada no Parque." *Religião & Cultura* V/9: 99–124.

USARSKI, Frank, ed.

    2002   *O Budismo no Brasil.* São Paulo: Lorosae.

WILLIAMS, Duncan Ryūken, and Christopher S. QUEEN, eds.

    1999   *American Buddhism: Methods and Findings in Recent Scholarship.* Richmond: Curzon.